THE FAT[...]

RUSSIAN REVO[...]

LOST TEXTS OF CRITICAL MARXISM

VOLUME 1

EDITED BY SEAN MATGAMNA

PHOENIX PRESS

The Fate of the Russian Revolution.
Lost Texts of Critical Marxism Volume 1.
Edited by Sean Matgamna.
Published June 1998.

Published for Phoenix Press by WL Publications Ltd,
Top Floor, 1 Warwick Court, Choumert Road, London SE15 4SE.

Articles by Max Shachtman, Hal Draper, C L R James, Al Glotzer,
Joseph Carter, Leon Trotsky, James Burnham and others.
ISBN 0-9531864-0-7

Printed by Athenaeum Press Ltd, Dukesway, Team Valley,
Gateshead, Tyne & Wear, NE11 OPZ.
Set in New Century Schoolbook.

We see before us a huge community of producers the members of which are unceasingly striving to deprive each other of the fruits of their collective labour — not by force, but on the whole in faithful compliance with legally established rules. Production is carried on for profit, not for use. Technological progress frequently results in more unemployement rather than in an easing of the burden of work for all. The profit motive leads to a huge waste of labour and to crippling the social consciousness of individuals. This crippling of individuals I consider the worst evil of capitalism. Our whole educational system suffers from this evil. There is only one way to eliminate these grave evils, namely through the establishment of a socialist economy, accompanied by an educational system which would be oriented toward social goals.

Albert Einstein

State ownership and control is not necessarily socialist — if it were then the army and the navy, the police, the judges, the gaolers, the informers and the hangmen would all be socialist functionaries, as they are all state officials — but the ownership by the state of all the lands and material for labour, combined with the co-operative control by the workers of such land and materials, would be socialist... To the cry of the middle-class reformers, 'Make this or that the property of the government', we reply — 'Yes, in proportion as the workers are ready to make the government their property'.

James Connolly

I hated thee, fallen tyrant! I did groan
To think that a most unambitious slave,
Like thou, shouldst dance and revel on the grave
Of Liberty. Thou mightst have built thy throne
Where it had stood even now: thou didst prefer
A frail and bloody pomp which Time has swept
In fragments towards Oblivion. Massacre,
For this I prayed, would on thy sleep have crept,
Treason and Slavery, Rapine, Fear and Lust,
And stifled thee, their minister. I know
Too late, since thou and France are in the dust
That Virtue owns a more eternal foe
Than Force or Fraud: old Custom, legal Crime,
And bloody Faith the foulest birth of Time.

Feelings of a republican on the fall of Bonaparte
Percy Shelley, 1816

THE FATE OF THE RUSSIAN REVOLUTION.
LOST TEXTS OF CRITICAL MARXISM

CONTENTS

ACKNOWLEDGEMENTS

I must thank the following people for help in producing this book: Mark Osborn sought and found texts, as did Ernie Haberkern, Gail Malmgreen, Paul Hampton and Mike Fenwick. Al Richardson repeatedly put himself to trouble so that I could sift through and photocopy magazines and bulletins in the Socialist Platform library; Phyllis Jacobson, Julius Jacobson, Al Glotzer, Peter Drucker, and Barry Finger were also helpful. Cathy Nugent, Cath Fletcher, Vicki Morris, Alan McArthur, Tom Rigby, David Ball, Steven Holt, Duncan Morrison and John Bloxam did typesetting, proof-reading, production and design work. Martin Thomas did a lot of everything technical. He contributed suggestions, criticism and much discussion to the attempt to trace through and untangle Trotsky's ideas about Stalinism. At the end he gave me irreplaceable help in cutting down, shaping and editing Part 2 of the introduction from a draft something more than ten times as long.
SM.

INTRODUCTION

THE RUSSIAN REVOLUTION AND MARXISM

Sean Matgamna

1. CONSTRUCTING THE SOCIALIST ORDER

"Men make their own history, but they do not make it just as they please;
they do not make it under circumstances chosen by themselves, but under
circumstances directly encountered, given and transmitted from the past".
Karl Marx, *The Eighteenth Brumaire*.

"Social life is essentially practical. All mysteries which mislead theory to
mysticism find their rational solution in human practice, and in the comprehension of this practice". **Karl Marx, *Theses on Feuerback, VIII*.**

HUMAN BEINGS MAKE their own history, but not as they themselves
will it; nor do they work in conditions which they can at will control.
People follow one intention, holding to one interpretation of their situation and its possibilities, and the result is often not at all what they
intended or would have chosen. Sometimes it is the opposite of what was
intended and would have been chosen. Other wills, other intentions, and
other interests are at work too, in unforeseen and unknown ways.
Afterwards, we do not always easily understand what has happened, or
why. Sometimes we radically misunderstand. So it was with the Bolshevik
Revolution.

Early in 1917, the workers, soldiers and peasants of Russia rose in revolt
and destroyed the autocratic Tsarist monarchy. They organised themselves in democratic councils (soviets). On 25 October 1917, according to
the Russian calendar in use at that time (7 November our style) the
Military Revolutionary Committee of the Petrograd Soviet — under the
leadership of Leon Trotsky, chair of the Petrograd Soviet — organised an
insurrection in Petrograd (St Petersburg) and overthrew the unelected
Provisional Government.

At the All-Russian Congress of Soviets which opened in Petrograd that
same day, 25 October, a clear majority supported the rising. In place of the
bourgeois Provisional Government, the Congress set up a soviet government: the rule of workers' councils. The political leadership of the soviets
was in the hands of the Russian Social-Democratic Labour Party
(Bolsheviks), at whose head stood Vladimir Ilyich Lenin and Leon Trotsky.

The Bolsheviks were Marxists. They understood the working-class conquest of state power in Russia to be the first step in an international working-class movement to build a new society, free from the exploitation of
human being by human being. "We will now proceed to construct the
socialist order", said Lenin to the Congress of Soviets on 25 October 1917.

What order? The socialist order. But in the event Lenin was not to build
"the socialist order" or even the foundations for it. The Bolsheviks would
suffer total defeat. Not socialism, but Stalinist totalitarianism would arise
in the USSR, on the grave of Bolshevism. The Bolshevik defeat, and the
unexpected forms it took, would disrupt Marxism and disorientate the left
wing of the world labour movement for the rest of the 20th century. That
was not the Bolsheviks' fault, but it was — and is — the abiding conse-

quence of their revolution. What happened to the Russian Revolution? What happened to the socialists who, holding to the Revolution's original ideas, and fighting the Stalinist counter-revolution, tried to make sense of its degeneration and defeat? What happened to the ideas and perspectives of Marxian socialism in the era of Stalinism, in the flux and friction of subsequent social and political life? What was the relationship of the "October ideas" to the Russian Stalinist society that existed from the late 1920s to the early 1990s? These questions are the subject of this book and another to follow.

II THE BOLSHEVIK PROGRAMME

"Whatever a party could offer of courage, revolutionary far-sightedness and consistency in a historic hour, Lenin, Trotsky and the other comrades have given in good measure. All the revolutionary fervour and capacity which western Social Democracy lacked were represented by the Bolsheviks. Their October uprising was not only the actual salvation of the Russian Revolution, it was also the salvation of the honour of international socialism." Rosa Luxemburg.

SOCIALISM IN 1917 had a different meaning from that it has had for most of the last 80 years. Socialism and democracy were understood to be each an essential part, one and the other, inseparable dimensions of one indivisible movement — "social democracy" — for working-class emancipation from wage slavery and from social, economic and political rule by the capitalist class. "Social democracy" aimed to replace capitalist exploitation of wage labour by a "co-operative commonwealth", in a Workers' Republic. Lenin and Trotsky defined the nature of the regime they erected on the victory of the soviet insurrection of 25 October as the dictatorship of the proletariat, of the wage-working class. They defined Britain, France, the USA, Switzerland and the other parliamentary democracies of that time as dictatorships of the bourgeoisie. They understood the dictatorship of the proletariat as they understood the dictatorship of the bourgeoisie — the rule of a class which "dictated" political and social terms of existence to the other classes.

The "dictatorship of the proletariat" was not the dictatorship of a party, or of an individual, but of a class. The soviets, not the Bolshevik party, took state power on 25 October — though without the Bolshevik Party the soviets could not have taken power and consolidated it. It was in the name of the soviets and through the soviets, which gave unimpeachable democratic legitimacy to the October insurrection, that the Bolshevik party rose to power. The "dictatorship of the proletariat" was mass democracy, dictating to the defenders of the old order. It dealt ruthlessly with the resistance of the old exploiting rulers and their supporters. All the often-quoted ferocities proclaimed and enacted by the Bolsheviks concerned the struggle to win power and hold it against armed and mass-murdering opponents; all the talk of dictatorship was about the dictatorship of a class organised democratically for mass action in the soviets, and of a party only as representative of that class. The "dictatorship of the proletariat"

— the rule of the workers — would, as the Bolsheviks understood it, define a whole epoch of history, just as had the dictatorship of the bourgeoisie. Repressive rule — even repression of the old social masters and their supporters by the majority of the people — would be a more or less short-term and transitory beginning of this epoch. Its conclusion would see the end of force and coercion in human affairs.

The Bolsheviks believed, with Marx, not only that "The emancipation of the working class is also the emancipation of all human beings without distinction of race or sex", but also, and fundamentally, that "The emancipation of the working classes must be conquered by the working classes themselves".

The rule of a class, the proletariat, which was itself in Russia a minority, had inescapably undemocratic implications if it was to be imposed against the will of the peasant majority. The new government had the support of the masses of the peasantry and would keep it, even against the peasant parties, until the end of the civil war (1918 to November 1920). The first Bolshevik-led government was (until July 1918) a coalition with the Left Socialist-Revolutionary party, which shortly after October 25 gained a majority in the Congress of Peasant Soviets. The Bolsheviks did not envisage long-term rule by a minority class in an isolated Russia.

The idea of party rule as against soviet rule, or of soviet rule being one-party rule in perpetuity, lay far in the future, at the other side of the civil war. In the form in which it is best known to us, "one-party rule" lay at the other side of Stalin's counter-revolution — the one-sided civil war of the bureaucracy to subjugate the disarmed people. That counter-revolution left intact nothing of "October" except the emptied and stolen names of the soviets, Bolshevik Party, working-class rule and Russian labour movement.

If in 1917 the Bolsheviks were dismissive and contemptuous of parliamentary ("bourgeois") democracy, as indeed they were, it was because they wanted much more than a one-dimensional political democracy. They wanted "social democracy" — the real day-to-day self-rule throughout society of the mass of the people. Democracy as both its friends and enemies had understood it up until about 1850 — rule of the majority, by the majority, in the direct material, cultural and spiritual interests of the working majority.

They said they would establish a state power "of the Paris Commune type". In Paris in 1871, 46 years earlier, the Paris City Council — "the Commune" — had seized power in the city and held it for nine weeks before the Parisian workers were defeated and massacred in their tens of thousands, or deported to tropical prison islands. They had ruled directly, without a bureaucracy or a standing army, that is, without a bureaucratic state machine raised above the people. "The Commune was formed of the municipal councillors, chosen by universal suffrage in the various wards of the town, responsible and revocable at short terms. The Commune was to be a working, not a parliamentary body, executive and legislative at the same time. From the members of the Commune downwards, the public service had to be done at workmen's wages. The whole of the educational institutions were opened to the people gratis, and at the same time cleared of all interference of Church and State". (Marx)

In Russia, after the overthrow of the Tsar in February 1917, the soviets developed a pyramid of factory, district, city and all-Russian representative gatherings. Delegates could be recalled and replaced, easily and repeatedly. This was the framework of "a state of the Paris Commune type" — a uniquely flexible and responsive system of democratic self-organisation and, increasingly, of self-rule by the Russian workers and peasants. The Soviet-Bolshevik seizure of power on 25 October had put the stamp of security on it.

When the Bolsheviks and the soviets set up the dictatorship of the proletariat in 1917, they acted in the name of democracy, and indeed of a higher and more profound form of democracy than what goes under that name in Western Europe, the USA and other places now — not of "dictatorship" understood as anybody's tyranny over the people. The "dictatorship of the proletariat", fearsome and replete with quite different meanings though it sounds to our ears after its appropriation and misuse by the Stalinist dictators, was, to its proponents in 1917, the democratic self-rule of the working people. Not until later would the terminology of Lenin and Trotsky, used by others, take on the commonplace meanings it has now. Most of the other key words in the lexicon of the Russian Revolution, of Marxism, and of the left would also by the mid-twentieth century have been given other meanings.

Nor did Lenin's conception of "the socialist order" involve the wholesale seizure by the workers' state of all economic assets, a "command economy", or a forced march for economic development to "catch up with" the advanced countries. Their ideas here were fundamentally those of Karl Marx in the Communist Manifesto. The working class, having "won the battle of democracy", would rule in its own and the working farmers' interests, using the state to regulate and control the "commanding heights" (Lenin) of the society and economy.

The Bolshevik government did not immediately intend to nationalise even large-scale industry. They favoured and helped create "workers' control" — that is, dual power between workers and owners in the factories. In 1918 the workers drove out the factory-owners and imposed on the government a decision to nationalise, that is, eliminate the capitalists.

III: THE PRECONDITIONS FOR SOCIALISM

"The working class did not expect miracles from the Commune. They have no ready-made utopias to introduce par décret du peuple. They know that in order to work out their own emancipation, and along with it that higher form to which present society is irresistibly tending by its economical agencies, they have to pass through long struggles, through a series of historical processes, transforming circumstances and men. They have no ideals to realise, but to set free the elements of the new society with which old collapsing bourgeois society is pregnant". Karl Marx.

THOUGH THE BOLSHEVIKS knew and proved in practice that the working class could take power, they did not believe that socialism could be created in backwardness and underdevelopment such as that which prevailed in the old Empire of the Tsars. The Russian economy in 1917 had not developed even the minimum preconditions for socialism. They believed, with

14

Marx, that socialism had to be built on the foundations, structures, and social potentialities that the most advanced capitalism had created. Why?

In all previous human history, ruling classes, embodying advanced culture and knowledge of social organisation and administration, had owned and administered the economy, society and the state. They had taken for themselves abundance, luxury and extravagance at the expense of the mass of the people, who were held as slaves, serfs or wage workers. To provide "surplus product" for the rulers, the subordinate classes had had their consumption rationed and restricted, their lives cramped and curtailed, their economic, social and political freedom limited to what was compatible with rule by the dominant classes in their own interests. They had been forced to work in conditions and under rules dictated to them by the master classes.

Capitalism, for the first time in history, had made possible an end to exploitative class rule by creating a society able to produce the means of life in such abundance that everybody could be guaranteed an adequate minimum. In part capitalism had even realised it. With the tremendous powers of social productivity unleashed by international capitalism, "the last form of class society", humankind had arrived at a point where it could cut the roots — low productivity of labour and scarcity — from which social division and re-division into classes, into rulers and ruled, exploiters and exploited, had sprung throughout human history. For the first time ever it had become possible for everyone to have comfort, culture and leisure, and thus for humankind to create a society free of the cannibal curse of exploitation — a classless society. The wage-working class, the proletariat, which found no class lower than itself in the social hierarchy and which did not and could not exploit any other class, could take power and begin to reorganise society on a classless basis of democratic self-rule.

Without the possibilities of producing plenty created by international capitalism, socialism would have remained a utopia — impossible. With them, socialism became a rational and realistic project for the reorganisation of human society — to realise the potential which capitalism, its creator, stifles, and thus allow humankind to move to a higher level.

"Marxism sets out from the development of technique as the fundamental spring of progress, and constructs the communist program upon the dynamic of the productive forces... Marxism is saturated with the optimism of progress... The material premise of communism should be so high a development of the economic powers of man that productive labour, having ceased to be a burden, will not require any goad, and the distribution of life's goods, existing in continual abundance, will not demand — as it does not now in any well-off family or 'decent' boardinghouse — any control except that of education, habit and social opinion. Speaking frankly, I think it would be pretty dull-witted to consider such a really modest perspective 'utopian'. Capitalism prepared the conditions and forces for a social revolution: technique, science and the proletariat."[1]

Like the modern proletariat that would create it, socialism was necessarily and inescapably the historical child of advanced capitalism. This meant that to Lenin, Trotsky, the Bolshevik party, and the Bolshevik-educated workers who made the revolution, socialism was simply not possible in

---

1. Trotsky: *Revolution Betrayed.*

15

1917 Russia. If the workers' revolution in Russia were not part of an international revolution, it would not be a socialist revolution.

The Russian working class was a comparatively small minority in a vast land inhabited by peasants scarcely two generations out of serfdom. The country was one hundred and more years behind advanced Europe. Circumstances and superb leadership had allowed the revolutionary workers to seize power; but only the spread of the revolution to advanced Europe would allow them to build socialism. The Bolsheviks would have dismissed as impossible and ridiculous the idea that the Russian workers, having seized power, would or could then begin to construct, in parallel to capitalism, and in competition with it, a closed-off society on socialist principles. They understood that in those conditions socialist principles could not for long govern society. Out of economic, social and cultural backwardness would unavoidably come a re-growth of class divisions. That, they believed, in Russian conditions, could only be the triumph of the bourgeoisie and capitalism: they were, as we shall see, radically mistaken in this.

The Bolsheviks seized state power, but they understood that there were proper limits to the use of the surgical and engineering power of the state — that is, of force — in relation to society and the people making it up. Their "reshaping reason", armed with the state power, was limited objectively by the level of the economy and social culture. It could only reorganise, modify, and set lines of development. Society could not be reduced to a *tabula rasa*, a blank slate on which anything could be written. It could not at will be recreated from the ground up. Society could not be taken by storm, like political power, but only transformed over time. The immense concentration of state power characteristic of Stalinism — and the use Stalinists made of it, from Stalin's forced collectivisation through China's Great Leap Forward to the Khmer Rouge — would have seemed to those who formed the government in October 1917 to be a throwback to Pharaoh's Egypt or pre-Spanish Inca Peru.

They would have branded the programme the Stalinist bureaucrats propounded in October 1924, building "socialism in one country", as a regression from Marxism to the utopian socialism of 70 or 80 years previously — to the socialism of Robert Owen and Etienne Cabet. Following imaginary maps of history, as far from social reality as was the chart which guided Christopher Columbus, so he thought, to the Indies, from the real geography of the Earth, Owen and Cabet had built doomed primitive-socialist colonies in the backwoods of America, thinking to prove the superiority of this "socialism" in competition with capitalism. That conception of socialism had been vanquished by Marx and Engels on the level of ideas, and bypassed by history, which had generated a tremendous development of capitalism, and of the proletariat and its labour movement within capitalism. Marx had established the all-defining nexus between capitalism, the proletariat it creates, and socialism; the development of socialist labour movements had, Marx's followers believed, shown capitalism's proletariat to be the agency of socialism. Capitalism which created the social conditions for its own replacement — an economy capable of providing abundance, and production increasingly socialised through big firms — also created its own gravedigger, the proletariat, which would break the power of the capitalist class, and take over and develop the progressive potential of the means of production created by capitalism.

By the middle of the 20th century, under the impact of Stalinism, the predominant form of "actually existing socialism" — and, extrapolated from that, the predominant idea of what socialism was — would have turned all this on its head. Socialism? State-imposed forced marches in economically backward countries for the industrial growth and development which in history and Marxist theory alike was the work of the bourgeoisie and of the bourgeois epoch. In this "socialism", an authoritarian or totalitarian state held the proletariat and the whole people in an iron grip of terror and exploitation. The model, supposedly rooted in the Russian Revolution, had nothing to do with the Bolshevik policy of 1917. It was the policy of those who drowned the Bolshevik revolution in blood, stole its identity and its symbols, and buried it in a falsely marked grave.

Before the rise of Stalin's USSR, no Marxist could have put forward such a policy as "socialism" for a backward country without inwardly hearing the voice of the founders of Marxism insisting that in such conditions, no matter what the rulers' intentions were, "all the old crap" (as Karl Marx once forcefully put it) of class society would inevitably return — in the first place, class differentiation and class exploitation. Classes cannot be abolished by decree, or merely because millions of people want their abolition. Classes cannot be abolished unless society has reached the stage where enough is produced for everyone to live comfortably, and therefore can dispense with the class structures which human history so far has found indispensible to the development of economy and culture.

If in 1917 Lenin knew all this, then what sense did his proclamation "We will now proceed to construct the socialist order" make? Lenin did not think he was making, and was not trying to make, in any purely Russian sense. He believed the Russian workers were but the advance-guard for the German and west European workers. "The absolute truth", he declared on 7 March 1918, "is that without a revolution in Germany, we shall perish". On 1 October 1918 he wrote to Trotsky and Sverdlov (the organiser of the Bolshevik Party): "We are all ready to die to help the German workers advance the revolution which has begun in Germany". Again, on 5 July 1921, he explained: "It was clear to us that without aid from the international world revolution, a victory of the proletarian revolution is impossible. Even prior to the revolution, as well as after it, we thought that the revolution would also occur either immediately or at least very soon in other backward countries and in the more highly developed capitalist countries, otherwise we would perish. Notwithstanding this conviction, we did our utmost to preserve the soviet system under any circumstances and at all costs, because we know that we are working not only for ourselves, but also for the international revolution".

Lenin believed that only in unity with the workers of the advanced countries, which were ripe for socialism, could the Russian workers begin to "construct the socialist order".

The Russian October revolution could win its proclaimed goals and survive only as part of an international working-class revolution. All its socialist and Marxist legitimacy, its right to be seen in the Marxist tradition and not in that of the utopian socialists or the Russian populists, depended on its connection with that international revolution.

IV: THE ISOLATION OF THE REVOLUTION

"United action of the leading civilised countries, at least, is one of the first conditions for the emancipation of the proletariat".   **Karl Marx and Frederick Engels,** *The Communist Manifesto.*

THE REVOLUTION WHICH the Bolsheviks had expected did erupt in Europe, beginning with Germany in November 1918. Soviets appeared all across central Europe, and even as far from Russia as rural Ireland. In 1919 Soviet regimes ruled for a few weeks in Bavaria and Hungary, before being crushed by bourgeois forces.

In Germany the workers' revolution threw out the Kaiser and set up a democratic republic. Before 1914 the creation of such a republic would have had a tremendous revolutionary democratic significance; now it was used as the platform for the bourgeois counter-revolution against the German working class. The social democratic leaders of the German workers had become "Kaiser socialists" in 1914. In 1918-19, though they failed to save the Kaiser, they saved German capitalism. Controlling the German soviets, they stifled them, slaughtering revolutionaries like Rosa Luxemburg and Karl Liebknecht. The Weimar republic enshrined the rights of bourgeois property in its constitution. It was fundamentally unstable; Hitler was 14 years in the future.

In Austria it was the same. By the end of 1919, post-war bourgeois Europe had weathered the storm unleashed in 1914. Bourgeois control was re-established. The strength of the capitalists in some countries, and the strength and loyalty of their "labour lieutenants" in others, preserved capitalism and isolated the Russian revolution. Like the lone first soldier over the parapet into the enemy fortress who finds that no-one else has got through, the Bolshevik revolution was doomed. A gap between Bolshevik intentions and expectations on one side, and uncontrollable reality on the other, opened wide under the feet of Lenin's regime, shook it out of recognisable shape, and then pulled it down.

Other wills, other intentions, other interests, other strivings, had cut across, and would ultimately nullify, the Bolsheviks' will, their hopes, their programme. Alongside Bolshevism, international socialism would go down too, and for the rest of the 20th century.

The Bolsheviks, who had will and determination in greater than common measure, did not submit passively to their fate. Though they had had great, and, as it turned out, false hopes, they had never believed that the bourgeoisie would fall like a stone tumbling into an abyss. It would have to be cut down in battle — prolonged battle, so it now seemed. They believed that the World War had radically dislocated the world economy. Capitalism had achieved no more than a temporary stability in 1920-21. The objective necessity and the possibility of a world socialist revolution remained. The difficulty, the weakness lay in the "subjective factor", in the state of the labour movements. The victorious Russian revolutionaries set out to build on the achievements of the International Socialist conferences at Zimmerwald and Kiental in 1915 and 1916, of which they had been part. A new workers' International — Lenin had called for it in 1914, when the old International collapsed at the outbreak of war — was set up in Moscow in March 1919.

V: THE CIVIL WAR REGIME

"It would be a crazy idea to think that every last thing done or left undone in an experiment with the dictatorship of the proletariat under such abnormal conditions represented the very pinnacle of perfection... nothing can be further from [Lenin's and Trotsky's] thoughts than to believe that all the things they have done or left undone under the conditions of bitter compulsion and necessity in the midst of the rushing whirlpool of events, should be recorded by the International as a shining example of socialist policy." Rosa Luxemburg.

FULL-SCALE RUSSIAN CIVIL WAR erupted in mid-1918. It would last for two and a half years. The Reds successfully contested with the counter-revolutionary "Whites" for the allegiance of the peasants in the countryside. Looking back at the revolution through the opaque, bloodily-smeared lens of the Stalinist regime, later commentators have imagined a tyrannical and bureaucratic "Stalinist" state machine inexorably working its tank-like power against the people in a drive to create a totalitarian state. Later in the century, Stalinist armies and parties calling themselves "communist" would do that, taking power as already-mighty military-bureaucratic machines, in Yugoslavia and China for example. That is not what happened in Russia! To see the civil war that way is to read backwards into past history things that did not and could not exist then; it is to mix up the pages of two different calendars, that of the workers' revolution and that of the Stalinist counter-revolution.

The party that led the revolution was working-class, unruly, argumentative, and democratic. As late as 1918 its central administration had a staff of no more than a dozen, for a party with hundreds of thousands of members. Bolshevik party centralism did not produce the authoritarian state; it was the exigencies of civil war and invasion that made the Bolsheviks develop a strong centralised party machine in the same process that produced the authoritarian state.

In October 1917, the working-class soviets firmly controlled only the cities and the major towns. In July 1918 their erstwhile partners in government, the Left SRs, took up arms against the Bolsheviks — they shot and wounded Lenin — because they could not agree to accept peace with Germany on terms dictated from strength by the Kaiser. In order to create the state that existed by 1921, at the end of the civil war, the soviets and their Bolshevik leaders had to win the leadership and support of the mass of the people, the peasantry, in a fierce, free competition of ideas, leadership and arms with their bourgeois-landlord opponents. These were led by Tsarist generals like Kolchak, Denikin, and Wrangel and supported by liberals and some of the anti-Bolshevik socialists. No fewer than 14 states intervened to subvert the workers' republic. The workers and peasants chose soviet power, and fought to consolidate it against the bourgeoisie and the landlords. If the urban soviets and the Bolshevik workers' party had not first won the competition for the minds and assent of the rural people, they would never have won the armed contest with the White armies and their foreign allies. The Bolshevik-led Soviets would have been crushed and the workers massacred, as the workers of Paris were massacred in May 1871.

In the course of the civil war much changed. This is our central concern here because from it international socialism would be radically reshaped and redefined. Not their ideas and intentions of 1917, but the exigencies of the civil war and the wars of intervention determined what the Bolsheviks did. Their democratic-socialist, soviet-socialist programme was subverted and overridden. So, ultimately, was the socialism of those who rallied to their call for a new working-class international.

Civil war wreaked great destruction, pushing Russia backwards even from the level of 1917 and what had seemed possible in 1917. The working class itself was scattered, massacred, absorbed into the machinery of state or otherwise depleted. Much of industry seized up. Self-defence imposed on the revolutionary workers the need to staff the new immense army and the state machine. Society and industry were subordinated to their struggle to survive and prevail. In the civil war the Bolsheviks felt obliged to suppress, insofar as they could, the operation of markets, and to substitute a barracks communism of backwardness, in which the produce of the peasants was simply seized in order to feed the towns and the armies. This was "war communism". A vast bureaucratic administration of society grew up. Layers of the old bureaucracy, and even of the old military bureaucrats, the officers, had to be utilised. At first they were strictly under the control of the workers' party. But soon Stalin would bring the party apparatus under the control of the state bureaucracy.

The soviets too, the organs of popular self-rule, were subverted by the civil war. Many of the Menshevik and Social-Revolutionary participants in the 1917 soviets — the bourgeois-democratic opposition to the Bolshevik-led majority in the days of the October Revolution — actively or passively supported the anti-soviet armies fighting the Bolshevik government, and therefore left the soviets or were driven out. The soviets, like so much of society, had their life and vitality drained out of them and into the work of the army and of organising a state which administered backwardness and, now, chaos and economic regression.

Very soon, the Russian workers had not a state of the Paris Commune type, free, easy-going self-administration, with minimal bureaucracy, but a heavily bureaucratised state, increasingly modelled on and intertwined with the command structures inseparable from the sort of army they felt obliged to create.

Yet the Bolshevik regime kept its popular support. It could not have survived without it. Throughout the civil war the peasants continued to support the revolutionary government — not without dissatisfaction, bitterness and episodes of militant resistance, to be sure — in the interests of winning the war against the White and foreign armies whose victory would have brought back the landowners to lord it over them once more. They supported the "Bolsheviks" who gave them the land while disliking the armed "Communists" who requisitioned their grain (the RSDLP Bolshevik Party had changed its name to "Communist Party" in 1918).

VI: THE POST-CIVIL-WAR REGIME

THUS, IN THE PROCESS of fighting to survive and prevail, the workers' state had ceased to be what it was in 1917. It was now a workers' state because it was ruled by a workers' party acting as stand-in, watchman, gatekeeper, or "locum" for the proletariat. The locum party ruled in the interests and in the name of the working class — in a backward country, where the working class was a small minority. Judged by the Bolshevik programme, the civil-war regime was already a degenerated workers' state. At the 10th congress of the Communist Party, in early 1921, Lenin himself called it a "workers' state with bureaucratic deformations". He said that in the course of championing free trade unions: the workers, he believed, would have to fight the workers' state and resist its giant pressure. 18 months later, the dying Lenin used a striking metaphor for the situation of the Bolshevik Party at the head of this state: it was, he said, like driving a car in which the wheels did not respond to the steering mechanism. Lenin did not live to analyse it, but this was because an increasingly dominant section of the party had fused with the state bureaucracy.

What were the Bolsheviks to do? They undertook now not to "construct the socialist order", but to survive in power as locum for the working class. The ruling party would defend and serve the working class and develop the backward territory over which they ruled until socialist revolution in the West would to come to their aid. The fate of the defeated Communards of 1871, the massacres of communist workers in Germany and Hungary and Finland (where maybe a quarter of the entire working class was killed), and the massacres of workers and peasants and the anti-semitic pogroms unleashed by their own opponents during the civil war — in the Ukraine, especially, a terrible slaughter of Jews was unleashed by the White armies — kept the Bolsheviks in mind of the alternative.

The idea that there could be a locum for the working class was a rational if problematic response to adverse circumstances. The "locum" would grow and develop, rationalised by the idea that wholly nationalised property, after the old rulers had been overthrown, was necessarily working class, until it dominated what passed for Communism and revolutionary socialism during the rest of the 20th century. The locum could, it would be discovered by Trotsky and others, itself have a locum.

If the Bolshevik Party of Lenin and Trotsky after the civil war could be a locum for the working class, Stalin, defending nationalised property after he had buried the Bolshevik Party, could be the locum of the locum. The idea would over the next decades stretch to encompass a wide variety of locums allegedly developing "socialism" in countries other than Russia, where no working-class revolution had occurred. The Bolsheviks never thought that Russia could be socialist on its own. Now something new and other than socialism began to develop in the workers' state — a result not of Bolshevik intentions or the socialist programme, but of backwardness, continued isolation, the exigencies of the long series of wars and the struggle against economic and cultural poverty.

In 1921, three and a half years after the October revolution, a "New Economic Policy" (NEP) put paid to war communism. Markets were restored, in which narrow self-interest and the drive for the accumulation of wealth would motivate farmers and merchants, under the ultimate control of the workers' state, which, as Lenin put it, would hold "the commanding heights" of the economy for the working class. Socialism and communism would have been better; but in Russian poverty this market was better than the primitive communism of the civil-war economy. Essentially this was a limited bourgeois counter-revolution, but regulated by the workers' state and subjected to its purposes. To control the transition from war communism and to help hold on amidst devastation and war-weariness, the government banned even those parties such as Julius Martov's Menshevik Internationalists who had never risen against the Soviet government or supported those who had. Soviet government now became in fact what it had so far not been either in fact or in theory — an institutionalised one-party monopoly. Theory would catch up. As a logical and necessary corollary of the ban on every other political party, the Tenth Congress of the Communist Party of the Soviet Union (March 1921) banned factions within the ruling party's own ranks.

This was a radical departure. In the course of 1917 and the civil war there had been many factions in the Bolshevik party. The emergency measures in 1921 were intended to be a temporary response to an extraordinarily tense and dangerous situation, not the establishment of a permanent regime in state and party, or of new norms. But in fact in this as on so much, the emergency measures — enforced Bolshevik practice, in a backward, war-torn country where the proletariat was a minority inhabiting urban atolls in an agrarian sea — came to be the norm and then the theoretical precept for Russia, and for most of those calling themselves communists in the whole world. Ideas would change to follow practice that contradicted the initial guiding ideas.

VII: PRACTICE RESHAPES THEORY

"Without... the development of the productive forces... want is generalised, and with want the struggle for necessities begins again, and that means that all the old crap must revive." Karl Marx.

THE NEW ECONOMIC POLICY would last from 1921 until Stalin created the command economy at the end of the 1920s. Under this regime occurred the struggles that would shape, reshape, and disrupt the communist movement. Despite the ban on factions, all the political struggles, the class struggles and incipient class struggles, until 1928 took place inside the ruling party which had a monopoly on politics. Layers of the ruling party — which in relation to society was already a bureaucracy, based on a much shrunken remnant of the old working class — merged with the layer of state officials carried over from the Tsarist regime and crystallised into a privileged elite. Gropingly this elite developed an awareness of its own distinct political, economic, and social interests. Slowly the new rulers began to express their interests in the language of a bureaucratically reshaped, disarranged and miscombined scholastic "Marxism". This became the ideology of a new privileged ruling class in process of formation; and the root theology of its official state religion.

22

In 1924 Stalin proclaimed the goal of the state to be the creation of "Socialism in One Country". This, he insisted, was "Marxism" and "Leninism". The old Bolshevik ideas were now "Trotskyist" heresy. "Trotskyism" would be the hood which the counter-revolution put over the head of Bolshevism as it was led to the guillotine.

On the level of ideas, the Stalinist drive was connected to and sustained by the idea of building socialism in one country. This led to a wholesale reconstruction and reinterpretation of all the ideas of world communism and of socialism in general; it lay at the root of the monstrous many-branched Stalinist tree of lies about the USSR's "socialism", and thus also about what socialism was, that would spread its poisonous branches and shoots all through the working-class movement for decades to come.

The party's political monopoly in the state became the monopoly of the ruling section of the party; the party, a prison for those who resisted the growing power of the bureaucracy, the incipient new ruling class. Before it made itself master of society, the rising bureaucracy first allied with the new bourgeoisie of traders which grew up under the NEP, and with the class of well-off, labour-hiring kulak farmers. The party-state bureaucracy raised itself above society, balancing between its working-class base and the newly-burgeoning neo-bourgeois classes. It stifled working-class initiative and used its monopoly to terrorise and control the workers in the party and in the trade unions.

VIII: LENIN AGAINST STALIN

"Stalin has accumulated immense power. I suggest that the comrades think about a way to remove Stalin from [his] post and appoint in his place another man who in all respects differs from Comrade Stalin in his superiority, that is, in being more tolerant, more loyal, more courteous and more considerate of the comrades, less capricious, etc." Lenin.

BY 1922 LENIN had become greatly alarmed. He saw that the workers were increasingly being pushed aside by the new bureaucratic elite, whose leader and personification was Stalin. The policies of the state were beginning to be shaped by that elite in its own interests and not those of the working class. From the point of view of the working class, the political system needed overhauling, cleansing, and reform. But Lenin was paralysed by a stroke in May 1922. His last Party Congress was the 11th, in 1922. Except for brief periods thereafter he was removed from the political scene, speechless for months before his death in January 1924. At the end of 1922, in a series of notes from his deathbed, Lenin indicted Great Russian chauvinism in the treatment of Georgia. He condemned the all-stifling bureaucratism that made a nullity of the Workers' and Peasants' Inspectorate in industry, and called for action against it. He ended by identifying Stalin, general secretary since the creation of the position in March 1922 — he had controlled the party apparatus for a year before that — as the most dangerous figure, the official who most embodied in himself narrowness, bureaucratism and boorish instinctive brutality. He had been against Stalin's appointment as General Secretary, saying: "This cook will make only peppery dishes." But he had not fought Zinoviev,

Stalin's sponsor, on it. Now, on the 4th January 1923, he called on the party to dismiss Stalin. But Stalin already controlled the increasingly all-powerful party machine, which was now completing its fusion with the state bureaucracy.

Trotsky launched what became the Left Opposition at the end of 1923, along the same lines as Lenin's campaign, but with ideas and proposals that were more comprehensive and more fully elaborated. For four years, first the Trotskyist opposition, and then the Joint Opposition of Trotsky and Zinoviev, fought the ever-more-powerful bureaucracy, demanding a restoration of inner-party democracy, better conditions for the working class, and a systematic drive for planned industrialisation within the system of the NEP.

Significantly, Trotsky began by protesting against a proposal that the police be used to regulate an internal affair of the party. The ban on factions decreed as a temporary transitional measure at the 10th party congress in March 1921 was two and a half years old; Trotsky's earliest co-thinkers (the "Platform of the 46") proposed to rescind it.

The Opposition fought for the material conditions that would make it possible for the workers to exercise democratic self-rule — higher standards of living, more and better industrial jobs, more leisure, so that the workers would have time and energy to devote to the affairs of the workers' state. They concerned themselves too with the health of the Communist International. Everything depended on the success or failure of the broader socialist revolution, of which the Russian revolution had been only the first part, and ultimately was only a lesser part. Without revolution in the West in the medium term, there would, they were sure, be counter-revolution in Russia that would restore the bourgeoisie. The workers' revolution would spread, or it would die.

IX: THE COUNTER-REVOLUTION

STALIN HAD AN unshakable bureaucratic control of the party. When Lenin died in January 1924, a quarter of a million people were recruited to the ruling party, a so-called "Lenin levy" of aspirants for place and office who would be a solid phalanx of support for the apparatus.

In late 1925 the party-state bureaucracy split again, when Zinoviev and Kamenev and the Leningrad organisation became alarmed at Stalin's alliance with the "right wing" around Bukharin, who openly favoured extensive concessions to the Nepmen and kulaks. In 1926 they formed a Joint Opposition with the Left, adopting the core policies of the 1923 Opposition.

The Left Opposition and the Joint Opposition feared a capitalist counter-revolution. How did they think this could occur? The NEP bourgeoisie and the bigger farmers who employed wage-labour, the kulaks, could hope for the backing of the increasingly dissatisfied middle and poor peasants. With other parties banned, the forces those parties might have represented began to find expression within the ranks of the ruling party — the neo-bourgeoisie through the right wing, led by Bukharin.

The Bukharinites were allied with the so-called "centre" faction of Stalin, which controlled the bureaucratised party and state machine. Political power was the keystone that kept everything in place. Government policy would determine the direction of development. Trotsky feared that the Bukharin wing would open the door to capitalist restoration, and that the Stalin wing would fail to resist. As against the Bukharin and Stalin and neo-bourgeois wings of the all-embracing state-party, the Trotskyists saw themselves representing the proletariat and the old ideas of 1917 Marxism.

Allied with Bukharin, and backed by all the conservative and neo-bourgeois forces in the country, Stalin defeated the Joint Opposition, as he had defeated the 1923 Trotskyist Left Opposition.

By the tenth anniversary of the Revolution, in 1927, the Stalinist bureaucracy was firmly and irremovably in power, allied to the kulaks and bourgeois forces. Stalin told the opposition in the Politburo that "only civil war will remove these cadres" — his colleagues and himself. The four-year-old split between the Bolshevik party and the congealed "party"-state bureaucracy was formalised by the expulsion — on 14 November 1927 — of the real working-class party from the ruling state-party. Its members were exiled to the wastelands of the USSR or jailed. Two years later the Stalinist state would shoot its first Oppositionists — Blumkin, Silov and Rabinovich — the precursors of millions who would die within a decade. Trotsky, the organiser of the 1917 insurrection, and of the Red Army in the Civil War, was expelled from the USSR in January 1929.

Early in 1928 a new political-economic crisis erupted. The kulaks withheld grain. The reason: the lag of industry, the gap between agriculture and industry, the paucity of industrial goods that the kulaks could buy with the price they got for their grain. There had been four years of concessions to the kulaks since a similar, milder crisis in 1923; the Bukharinite right would have continued now on the same road. Most likely that would have led on to something like the scenarios for bourgeois counter-revolution against which the Left Opposition had raised the alarm. To Trotsky it seemed as if the bourgeois counter-revolution was very close. But something startling and unexpected — and without precedent in history — now occurred.

Political power had been taken from the workers not by the neo-bourgeois forces but by Stalin and what the Left Opposition called the "centrist bureaucracy". Stalin now turned on his kulak and bourgeois and Bukharinite allies, and crushed them as social forces and social categories — and to a great extent as living people. Using immense waves of physical force, like a quarryman with dynamite — that is, using the state power at the disposal of the bureaucracy to revolutionise society from above — Stalin made his own revolution and began to shape a new socio-economic formation.

Having resisted the rational, planned industrialisation within the NEP proposed by the Opposition, Stalin now broke the framework of the NEP and embarked on an immensely destructive forced march for industrialisation and agrarian collectivisation. The trade unions were destroyed and replaced with pseudo-unions, fascist-style "labour fronts" to serve the bureaucracy and the police in controlling the workers. All of society was put under the bureaucratic whip and under severe military discipline enforced by savage terror wielded by a state with modern technological resources whose power over society was unprecedented in history.

The Opposition could not but see in Stalin's industrialisation policy something akin to their own. Unsustainable adventuristic forced march, unbalanced caricature, bureaucratic savagery, it might be — but nonetheless it was a turn away from the threatening bourgeois-peasant counter-revolution. It would be years before Trotsky ceased to believe that this "left zig-zag" would most likely be succeeded by a right zig-zag like that of 1923-28 and concessions to the kulaks — who would re-emerge from new economic differentiations within the collectivised farms.

In fact, the Bukharinite right wing, the reflection inside the apparatus of the kulaks and NEP bourgeoisie — but also of the bureaucratic leaders of the stifled trade unions — crumpled before the Stalinists. The Stalinists drummed up support among the workers for their turn, invoking (but rigidly controlling) the working-class "heaven-storming" spirit of the revolution, the civil war, and war communism. In the face of the turn, the Opposition began to fall apart.

Zinoviev and Kamenev and their followers capitulated to Stalin in late 1927. In February 1928 a wave of capitulators from the Trotskyist wing of the Opposition was led by Pyatakov and Antonov-Ovseenko; in July 1929, Radek and Preobrazhensky led a new wave; and in October 1929 there was yet another. The hard core around Trotsky and Christian Rakovsky remained; alongside them were the Democratic Centralist faction, who had gone into opposition in 1921 and concluded in the mid-20s that the working class had already lost power. Trotksy knew that it was not only what was done but how it was done and by whom, that the bureaucracy cut most heavily against the working class, stifling, persecuting, pushing aside and displacing the people who were, in Trotsky's view, the necessary protagonists of any socialist development. In world politics they had wreaked havoc with the Communist International. They were an anti-working-class force. The question of "regime" was of paramount importance. Trotsky criticised the wild and arbitrary production targets set by the bureaucracy, its bulldozing and slavedriving techniques, its suppression of all democracy and of all initiative in the working class, the substitution of blind bureaucratic edicts for informed planning, the lack of any system of feedback on the plans decreed from above, the collectivisation of agriculture before there existed the machinery to make it a step forwards.

Thus to new-born Stalinism Trotsky counterposed a rational, economically balanced and humane conception of the development of the USSR — a conception indissolubly linked in Trotsky's integrated world outlook to rule by the working class itself in the USSR, to the world revolution, and to the perspectives and politics of 1917.

The proletariat, the supposed "ruling class", was now subjected to regimentation and terror in the factories and deprived of all civil and human rights: freedom of speech, assembly, or even movement from place to place. Internal passports were introduced. From the beginning of the 1930s outright, undisguised slavery reappeared. For most of the rest of Stalin's rule, and even later, there would at any one time be eight or ten million slave labourers — people condemned on any pretext, or none. Slave labour was used, for example, to build the prestigious and "modern" Moscow underground railway system in the 1930s, under the direction of Nikita Khrushchev, who in the 1950s as the second bureaucratic Tsar would reform and humanise Stalin's system. The liberation of women which the revolution had decreed, and, despite the backward conditions, in part realised, was reversed. Hungry children of 12 were subjected to the death penalty for theft...

One of the great and most successful achievements of the revolution, its nationalities policy — self-determination and the theoretical and then sincerely believed in right to secede from the multi-national state — was also undone. The rigidly Moscow-centralised party-state machine deprived the constitutionally enshrined national rights of any meaning because it deprived the national sections of the party, the sole initiating agency, of any autonomy. By way of party and state hierarchies, the smaller nationalities were once again bolted in helpless hierarchical subordination to the Great Russian nation. The USSR was transformed from a voluntary federation of equal peoples back into a bureaucratic version of the old tsarist empire — the "prison house of nations".

Lenin and Trotsky had campaigned against Great Russian chauvinism. In his deathbed struggle against Stalin, Lenin had denounced Stalin's tendency towards Great Russian chauvinism against the Georgians (Stalin was a Georgian himself).

Now the Stalinists proclaimed anew the Tsarist doctrine: the pernicious nationalism was that of the smaller, Russia's traditionally oppressed, nations, not the nationalism of the dominant Great Russians. Soon there would be active persecution. National sub-sections of the Stalinist party were repeatedly purged to make the USSR safe for Great Russian chauvinism. For fifty or more years there would be Russification programmes, in the Ukraine in the '70s for example, and even the forcible transportation of small nations like the Crimean Tatars and the Chechens in their entirety from one end of the USSR to the other.

In the 1920s, anti-semitism was already being used by the Stalinists against the Opposition. It would gradually become a big force in USSR life until in the early 1950s Stalin was running a raging world-wide campaign against "Zionism", staging show trials in satellite countries such as Czechoslovakia, and preparing a show trial of the "Kremlin doctors", most of them Jewish, in Moscow. That might have been the starting point for rounding up and deporting the Jewish population of the USSR — or for Stalin copying Hitler on this as on other things, and slaughtering Jews. Stalin died in 1953, and his successors abandoned the scheduled trial of the Kremlin doctors.

By every possible measure of politics, culture, economy, and human relations, Stalinism was counter-revolution. Its prerequisite had been the defeat of the working class and the oppositions in the struggle between 1923 and 1927-8. Yet it was not a capitalism-restoring counter-revolution. It was a bureaucratic counter-revolution in which the state bureaucracy, led by Stalin, wiped out both the new-grown bourgeois classes and the Russian labour movement. It destroyed all the defences and the rights of the working class, and turned the peasants into slave-driven, expropriated serfs of the new bureaucratic state. Who now ruled? The bureaucracy ruled. In whose interest? Its own.

The working class cannot own industry except collectively, and therefore it can only rule itself in industry through democratic, political self-rule. In the system established after 1928, as Trotsky would put it in 1936: "The means of production belong to the state. But the state, so to speak, 'belongs' to the bureaucracy". The October Revolution had ended in defeat for the working class and, indirectly, in the creation of a strange new socio-economic formation.

"Other wills", adverse conditions, the brute necessities of the struggle, changes in the function and thinking of key people and layers, and the cumulative defeats of the working class and the Opposition, had by now changed virtually everything.

Stalin had led a section of the old Bolshevik party, a layer of politically short-sighted people, and behind them a much larger layer of the tired, the self-seeking and the relatively well-off. In the middle 1930s, almost all of the Trotskyists in Siberian exile would be slaughtered. So would almost all the leaders of the 1917 revolution. Most even of the original Stalin faction would die. The 1934 congress of what was now, after the defeat of the Trotskyists and the Bukharinites, indisputably their party, was called the Congress of Victors. By 1938 1,108 of the 1,966 delegates to that conference had been killed in Stalin's great purges.

Society was crushed beneath the power of the gigantic all-controlling Leviathan state. A large range of privileges, regulated and controlled by the state, existed for the bureaucracy, which would have its own special shops selling goods unavailable to others, in a parallel economy that was a separate consumer system for the elite.

Trotsky, summing up the experience on the eve of his assassination in 1940, said that the bureaucracy had after 1928 made itself "sole master of the surplus product". The same drive to maximise the resources in the hands of the central bureaucracy led after 1929 to "nationalisation" of everything that twitched in economic life, to a degree and with a thoroughness that in Marxist terms would have been inappropriate for a far more developed economy, or, indeed, for any existing economy. One consequence was Russia's transition from an authoritarian regime to an outright totalitarian state.

The Bolshevik party's composition and its role in society had changed, and changed again, until the party had fragmented and had ceased to be itself, and it had become impossible to identify continuity except in the forms and names — forms now filled with radically different content and names naming different things. From the worker-composed leader and defender of the workers in Lenin's time; to the worker-rooted bureaucratic state power raised above the workers to balance between the classes, until 1928-30; after 1928-30, the rigidly authoritarian "sole master of the surplus product" and of society.

But while the Revolution ended in outright defeat for the working class and for socialist hopes, those who rose to power on its defeat continued to proclaim — and Stalin may have believed it — that in their rule, working-class socialist rule was alive in the USSR and going from triumph to triumph. Thus revolutionary socialism was transmuted from the great clear cleansing truth of the October Revolution into the great lie of the twentieth century.

"SOCIALISM IN ONE COUNTRY", the organising dogma of the bureaucracy, was a radical break with genuine Marxism, with the Bolshevik conception of the Russian Revolution and with the Marxist idea of the place of socialism in the evolution of human society. On the level of ideas, it was a strange reversion to utopian socialism: a socialism that would emerge in the wilderness, on the margins of capitalism, and, by competition over decades, vanquish it.

For socialism to be built up in a backward country — leaving aside the question of whether such a regime of scarcity and backwardness could be socialism — implied decades at least of peaceful development, in which the capitalist world would leave the USSR alone. It implied the belief that there would be no socialist revolution in any other country. For the non-Russian CPs it meant, and the logic would work itself through in the 1920s, that they were not primarily revolutionary parties in their own countries, but frontier guards for the Soviet Union, foreign legions to be used as the Russian bureaucratic ruling class thought fit. Their duty was to work for Russia's advantage, irrespective of the consequences for working-class struggles in their own countries. The entire Marxist conception of the Russian Revolution and of the Communist International was thus inverted.

From the 1920s the effects of Stalinism on the non-Russian Communist Parties ensured that these parties accelerated, where they might have reversed, the degeneration of the Soviet Union. The Bolsheviks after 1920 understood that capitalism was in a fundamental state of disequilibrium and disruption and had managed only a temporary post-war stabilisation. The chance of new working-class revolutions had not gone. It was an epoch of wars and revolutions. Defeated Germany was both fundamentally unstable and "rotten ripe" for the socialist revolution aborted in 1918-19. There it would be socialism or fascism.

The bar to the international revolution was the state of the working-class movement itself, the necessary protagonist of the revolution. The Bolsheviks had set out with the Communist International in 1919 to rebuild the revolutionary movement; the degeneration of the Bolshevik revolution made the problem worse — ultimately it made it intractable for those like Leon Trotsky, who continued Bolshevik politics after the triumph of Stalinism.

Just as the bureaucratisation of the ruling party in Russia nullified the nominal autonomy of the USSR's republics, subordinating them by way of militarised hierarchical, bureaucratic control to Moscow, so the Stalinists' rise to control in the Soviet Union welded the Communist International to the ruling Kremlin bureaucracy. Russian hegemony was there from the start, rooted in the real achievements of the Bolshevik Party. It was exercised at first primarily by way of reason and debate, and by the political and moral authority of the Bolshevik leaders. The Stalinists used bribery, bureaucracy and then terror by the Russian political police outside the USSR with no scruples. They purged the International. The leaders of the French party and the Italian party, for example, backed the Opposition in the early and mid 1920s; the German party was taken through four generations of leaders before the fifth, round Thaelmann, proved docile enough for Stalin. Under the banner of "Bolshevisation" began the process of stifling the Communist International's internal life, subordinating everything to a rigid hierarchy centred in Moscow. By the late 1920s Moscow's control in the International was akin to that of a hold-up man pointing his gun — the organisational, moral and financial authority of the "International" — at the revolutionary militants of the Communist International.

The Communist International was used with undiluted cynicism as a mere collection of overseas supporters of the Soviet Union who could — with proper "Marxist", "dialectical" "explanation" — be got to do and say virtually anything. In Spain, during the civil war of 1936-9, Stalin and his Spanish party, stiffened by the Russian political police, suppressed the working-class revolution. Stalin's aim was, by doing the work of fascism, to convince the Western bourgeoisie that they did not need fascism. The CPs could do the job for them, if they should ally with the USSR to contain Hitler. Stalin would control, and where necessary kill, the "Bolshie" workers. The Stalintern could do anything.

From 1934 the Communist International preached a crusade against fascism and then, more narrowly, against German fascism. Stalin signed a pact with Hitler on 23 August 1939, and joined him in mid-September to invade and partition Poland. The Communist Parties switched round and denounced Britain and France as warmongers against peaceful Hitler. They made propaganda for Germany.

The hard-core working-class base of the Communist Parties followed the leaders of the Soviet Union, because they thought they shared a common anti-capitalism with them. There had been an enormous loss of the understanding that was basic to the politics of socialism. By now there was utter befuddlement about what their own working-class alternative to capitalism must be if it were to bring working-class liberty. Yet, even though they were tied to a ruling class worse than their own, they behaved like revolutionaries.

Future Stalinist dictators like Matyas Rakosi and Erich Honecker spent many years as prisoners of Hitler and Hungary's Admiral Horthy. The French Stalinists behaved with great courage when the signal came in 1939 to go into outright opposition. Many might have been relieved that the class-collaboration era of the Popular Front was over.

When Hitler invaded Russia in June 1941, the Communist Parties again became the best patriots of Britain and (after December 1941) the USA, newly allied with Russia. They became chauvinists and strikebreakers. In Britain, CP leader, Harry Pollitt, who had baulked momentarily at the Hitler-Stalin pact, pronounced the beginning of a new epoch in which "it is the class-conscious worker who will cross the picket line". In the USA, in 1944, the CP advocated that the striking coal miners be conscripted and forced down the pits under military discipline. Everything for the war effort!

Jews more than any other people were the victims of the convulsive crisis of mid-20th century capitalism, driven from country to country, persecuted, massacred. In this hard school, and drawing on a culture conducive to sweeping conclusions, large numbers of them, and not only workers, learned about capitalism and enrolled in what they thought was the working-class fight to overthrow it and replace it with socialism. Attitudes to Jews and to anti-semitism were a defining question for a whole age. On this question, at least, the Communist International, especially in its anti-fascist phases, seemed clean and on the side of sanity and humanity. Yet even here, Stalinism overlapped with Hitlerism. Trotsky pointed out the plain elements of anti-semitism in Stalinist policy (for example, the insistence on the original Jewish names of men known for decades as Trotsky and Kamenev and Zinoviev). Anti-semitism had been used against the Opposition in the mid-20s. In 1940 the Mexican Stalinists inveighed against the "Jewish Trotskyists". It burst out in Eastern Europe in the late 1940s as a campaign, with repression and show trials, against "Zionism" that was only thinly disguised anti-semitism.[2]

At every turn, people would leave the Communist Parties — outside Russia. If they happened to be refugees living in Russia, they would be slaughtered, as foreign communist refugees were during the Moscow Trials. The Polish Communist Party, denounced as incurably infected by Trotskyists and Luxemburgists, was dissolved in 1938 and its membership lists surreptitiously given to the Polish military dictatorship's police.

But always "the party", defined fundamentally by its allegiance to the USSR, would go on or be rebuilt, around a new policy and with new drafts of members.

In the course of the Second World War the Russian Empire, already dominating dozens of "its own" smaller nations, expanded enormously. It clawed in the East European states and half of Germany. Imperialism? No: the socialist revolution! Imperialism? That is only another name for what the big capitalist powers do.

Here too we find the turning of things on their heads and inside out, the annexation of words by their opposites, and the arbitrary confinement of words to mean only what preconceptions and ideology could tolerate allowing them to mean. "For reason in revolt now thunders..." thunders the Internationale. This was the revolt, sustained over many decades, against reason, and the destruction of both the tools of reason and the propensity to reason. The Catholic Church long ago developed a dogmatic escape clause to "explain" the accumulated absurdities of its doctrines. A doctrine like the Trinity — God is both one person and three — in fact arose out of the incoherent amalgamation by the church bureaucracy of once bitterly hostile doctrines. It makes no sense? That, says the Church, is a "mystery of religion". It makes a higher sense, above human reason. You don't need to understand. All you need do is have faith. The Stalinists used "dialectics" in exactly that way. Everything is relative, fluid, changing, historically conditioned... Stalin understands. Keep the faith! You could not get further from reason, from Marxism, from Marx's dialectics — or from the old socialism, that had set out to make war on all thrones, pontiffs and dictators.

Yet, all these attributes belonged to a movement which waved the ban-

---

2. The Communist Parties followed suit, and created a culture that is with us still, especially now, in the ranks of would-be Trotskyists, as "anti-imperialism" focused on Israel, where the Jewish population now and the Jewish national minority in the 1930s and '40s are deemed to have no rights to exist as a nation, or to defend themselves.

ner of Lenin's and Trotsky's revolution, which seemed to talk in the language of Marxism and which claimed to propound a system of ideas that codified the historical experience of the revolutionary workers' movement! For decades these people defined what socialism, Marxism and communism were. The Communist Parties were the biggest parties of the working class in France and Italy, smaller but still imposing in countries like Britain. They attracted working-class militants. They pursued the class struggle — in their own way and for their own goals — but only in ways and with means consonant with Moscow's interests; and they pursued it only until it was in Moscow's interests to betray it.

XI: COUNTER-REVOLUTION WITHIN THE FORMS OF MARXISM

THE GOVERNING IDEAS of any society are those of the ruling class, argued Karl Marx and Frederick Engels in *The German Ideology*. The unfalsified ideas of the 1917 revolution could not serve the new ruling elite. But "Marxist" forms and phrases could, filled with radically new and different social, class and historical content. "Marxism", like the collectivised property, and other forms seized by the Stalinists, was not simply overthrown but retained and altered, to serve the new bureaucratic rulers in the social struggles of the 1920s. Their state "Marxism" became for the Stalinist bureaucracy what the doctrines of the Orthodox Church had been to Tsarism, but with enormous international ramifications derived from Moscow's control of the Communist International.

Stalin's counter-revolutionary struggle against Leninism took place in the name of Lenin; his fight against communism, in the name of communism; against equality, in the name of future communist egalitarianism; against Marx, in the name of Marxism; against any form of democracy, in the name of a higher democracy. The totalitarian bureaucracy enslaved the workers and the rural population in the name of working-class freedom. The dictatorship of the proletariat was replaced by the dictatorship of the bureaucracy from "within", without a clean rupturing of forms or an open honest break with socialism. From that grew up Stalin's Dictatorship of the Lie.

This was the typically nightmarish, surreal world of Stalinism — a world of double-talk and double-speak, where "trade unions" were not trade unions, "soviets" were not soviets, "socialism" was not socialism, "Leninists" were not Leninists, "democracy" was not democracy, and where the worker-enslaving bureaucracy appropriated to itself the right to speak as the working class.

Contrast what happened in the French Revolution. The political counter-revolution against Jacobinism, started in 1794 by a section of the Jacobins, soon turned into a reaction against all Jacobins. "Terrorist", "Montagnard", "Jacobin" became terms of abuse. In the provinces the trees of liberty were chopped down and tricolour cockades trampled underfoot. Why did this not happen in the Soviet Republic? Because "the totalitarian party contained within itself all the indispensable elements of reaction, which it mobilised under the official banner of the October Revolution. The party did not tolerate any competition, not even in the struggle against its enemies. The struggle against the Trotskyists did not turn into a struggle against the Bolsheviks because the party had swallowed this struggle in its entirety, set certain limits to it, and waged it in the name of Bolshevism". Thus, in 1940, at the end of his life, Trotsky looked back over the strange and unexpected course of events that had led to the triumph of Stalinism in the USSR[3].

Something akin to this "bureaucrats' Marxism" — "Marxism" reworked and bowdlerised to express interests other than those of the socialist proletariat — had developed once before in Russia: for a while, important sections of the Russian bourgeoisie and petit bourgeoisie had expressed their interests in a dialect of Marxism.

In the 1890s, anti-Tsarist intellectuals who wanted to break with the old, heroic and self-sacrificing, gun-in-hand tradition of "Narodnik" (populist) resistance to Tsarist tyranny in the name of "the people", and of a rather ill-defined utopian socialism, had become "Marxists". They came to stress only that "anti-utopian" part of Marxism which said that capitalism was progressive and unavoidable. Thus they licensed themselves to make peace with developing Russian capitalism. These so-called "Legal Marxists" soon became liberals. The revolutionary working-class Marxists — future Mensheviks and Bolsheviks alike — agreed that capitalism was inevitable and progressive in Russia, but combatted the one-sided bourgeois Marxism. If they had not done that successfully, the militant Russian labour movement that made the revolution would not have developed.

The new-hatched state bureaucrats who took over "Marxism" and gutted it took it over from "inside", from a position of leadership of and dominance over a world-wide segment of the working class and its movement. The revolutionary Marxists of around 1900 had been able to base themselves on a rising working-class movement in their defence of an unfalsified working-class Marxism. Those who resisted Stalinised "Marxism" in the USSR had no such base.

Indeed, the responses of the Bolsheviks themselves, as they held on against all the odds in the circumstances in which isolation had trapped them, had created a powerful base for the gestation of a new bureaucratic pseudo-Marxism and a world organisation for its dissemination. This happened despite the struggle to the death of Trotsky and the Bolshevik rearguard against the Stalinist counter-revolution. The Bolsheviks had held on by way of tremendous and brutal exertions against the "other wills" operating inside and outside Russia; and, so doing, they extemporised a first draft of what the Stalinist counter-revolution, overthrowing the rule of the workers, would develop into an elaborate bureaucratically-drawn route-map of history that was as fantastic as any drawn up by the mid-19th century utopian socialist colony-builders. This they imposed on the army of revolutionary workers who had been grouped in the Communist International.

While the parties of social democracy remained tied to the bourgeoisie, except where the bourgeoisie had knocked them on the head, as in Germany, the Communist International, which had been set up to recreate independent working-class politics in opposition to social democracy,

---

3. *Stalin*, p.407.

was captured by the new anti-capitalist bureaucratic Russian ruling class. With the millions-strong Communist International and its semi-militarised parties as transmission belt, the governing ideas of the new bureaucratic ruling class in the USSR dominated the revolutionary workers in capitalist countries — the workers who still looked to the October Revolution for a lead and an example. In consequence, during the long, convulsive mid-century crisis of capitalism, the revolutionary workers' movement was removed as an independent factor from world politics. That, in a sentence, is the story of 20th century socialism from 1914, when the socialist international collapsed, to the disintegration of the USSR in the 1990s.

Inexorably, the corruption spread into every key idea of socialism and Marxism and into every model of behaviour, endeavour and precept of socialism and Marxism. Exigencies that determined so much of what was done in Russia became the source of general theories dogmatically applied to all conditions under the guiding whip of the self-serving bureaucratic rulers. Already the Bolsheviks had erred in this direction; Stalin, representing an anti-working-class new ruling class, made it a system, and, suppressing all dissent, an airtight, lightless system, designed to serve the new Russian rulers.

What Stalin did and said, and what Stalin said Lenin had done or said or would have done or said — that was Marxian socialism and "Bolshevism". All the basic shaping, morale-engendering, old left-wing ideas were twisted inside out and turned round into their opposites, as the bureaucrats took over "Marxism" and gutted it.

Specifically, what they did was take all of Marxism that was negative and critical of bourgeois society and bourgeois democracy, and cut off the positive working-class Marxist alternative to capitalism: social democracy, expanded liberties, and working-class control. In their place they put their own bureaucratic anti-working-class alternatives: bureaucratic rule and totalitarian state power, miscalled socialism. Here they followed the pattern of the reactionary or feudal socialists criticised in the *Communist Manifesto*: "incisive criticism, striking the bourgeoisie to the very heart's core... In political practice they join in all coercive measures against the working class".

The Marxist criticism of the limits and the shallowness of "bourgeois democracy" became a condemnation of it supposedly in the name of progress but in reality in the name of political regression to before the French Revolution, if not to before the Renaissance and the Reformation. Uprooted, too, were all the best old "bourgeois" notions of liberty, ideas which preceded mass democracy and were separable from it.

XII: REVOLUTION AND DEMOCRACY

"To raise the proletariat to the position of ruling class, to win the battle of democracy." Karl Marx and Frederick Engels, *The Communist Manifesto*.

IN 1917 LENIN, Trotsky and the Bolsheviks had believed that unless the revolution unleashed a great deepening and broadening of democracy, it would fail. We must pause and examine this question in some detail, for it is one of the central issues posed by the degeneration and defeat of the

Bolshevik Revolution.

Marx and Engels had written in the *Communist Manifesto* that to make the proletarian revolution was to "win the battle of democracy" and make the working class the ruling class. Everywhere, including Russia, the socialists had, under the influence of Marx and Engels, been ardent champions of parliamentary democracy and democratic liberties. Labour movements in the 19th and early 20th centuries fought to extend the suffrage and enlarge the power of parliaments — often by revolutionary means. In Belgium they organised general strikes to win the vote. Marxists had made the democratic tradition their own. It was not for any other reason that they called themselves social democrats, advocates of democracy in all, not only the political, aspects of society. Always and everywhere the socialists were for extending and unfettering democracy and for cutting down the prerogatives of capital and the power of government and bureaucracy.

The creation of new working-class forms of democracy began in St Petersburg, Russia, in 1905, when striking workers who did not have political rights elected their own local parliament - the council of workers' deputies, or "soviet". The drive for democratic self-rule overflowed existing institutions and led to the creation of new specifically working-class democratic institutions.

After October 1917, revolutionary-minded people all across the world recognised the Soviets as the working-class form of democracy. Commitment to Soviets — workers' councils, within which there would be a plurality of "soviet" parties — became a central part of the programme of revolutionary socialism.

Inevitably the Russian reality after 1921 — one-party rule and Soviets withered and curtailed — confused many communists about exactly what "soviet rule" was. The more the Stalinists turned the USSR into an unprecedentedly savage exploitative dictatorship, the more they proclaimed it to be the purest and fullest democracy — ever. Democracy? That, like socialism, is whatever exists in the USSR! The result, in a short time, was to banish concern with anything that had before 1917 been considered democracy, and to falsify the very language and conceptions of the socialist movement and the early communist movement on this fundamental question. Even before full-blown Stalinism, "communism" acquired an anti-democratic bias, rooted in the experience of the Russian civil war and its aftermath. It was "Leninism" understood as Lenin himself would not — Rosa Luxemburg was surely right on that — have wanted it understood and used.

After the full-scale Stalinist counter-revolution of the late 1920s, the one-party system was proclaimed as the true working-class democracy, universally applicable . The "party's" right to a political monopoly was written into Stalin's 1936 "democratic constitution". The very idea of socialism as democratic self-rule was thus confused, pulped and destroyed. Democratic ideals and goals that had been central to radical thought since the French Revolution or even since the English Revolutions of the 17th century had their vocabulary appropriated to endorse extreme versions of the statism and authoritarianism which the left had been fighting against for hundreds of years. Mystification, confusion, and soon an almost indecipherable corruption of language and ideas followed.

This was the fault not only of the revolutionaries, or even the Stalinists. In the hands of the right wing of the international labour movement, the old socialist commitment to perfecting the democratic institutions of capitalist society had become a commitment to defend the bourgeoisies against the revolutionary workers and their soviets, which were the realisation of all the old socialist drive for expanded democracy. In Germany the bourgeois-democratic regime set up by the 1918 revolution became the vehicle for a landlord/bourgeois/right-socialist counter-revolution against the workers. The old drive for radical social democracy was thus ground to nothingness by the upper millstone of the bourgeoisie and Stalin and the nether millstone of social democracy.

What the social democrats did with "democracy" softened up the revolutionary workers to receive the Stalinist revelation that all the old talk of democracy was nothing but bourgeois lies. Democracy became increasingly indefinable. Norms were corrupted until the existence or nonexistence of democracy became not something that could be measured by commonly-agreed standards, but a matter of assertion and counter-assertion. Here, as in so many other fields, the Stalinists took over and caricatured what the bourgeoisie did. This helped destroy the norms by which the revolutionary workers could have evaluated the Russian claims that Stalinist totalitarianism was democracy.

The association of "democracy" with the right wing all across Europe in the 1920s and 30s, and then its collapse in country after country before authoritarian right-wing regimes or fascism, helped ease revolutionary workers into acceptance of the one-party Stalinist totalitarian state as the true working-class democracy. This lie became an article of faith for two generations of revolutionary workers. Those who eventually saw it for the oxymoronic absurdity it was, tended as a rule to collapse back into acceptance of the bourgeois counterfeit of democracy.

The basic idea that socialists must continue to struggle for human liberty and freedom was expunged from the programme of "communism". "Democracy" — like "socialism" — became a cynical catch-cry, shot through with double-think about the "socialist democracy" of the society where the Stalinist bureaucrats ruled with neither socialism nor democracy.

The hazard of taking seeming for identity is strong here: the Bolsheviks and the early Communist International did impatiently denounce "bourgeois democracy", did counterpose direct action to parliament, did abuse the democratic pretensions of the reformists, did advocate general strikes and insurrectionary tactics. But, as has already been said, always and everywhere what they counterposed to "bourgeois democracy" and to constitutional methods was mass action — majority action, or action that would quickly become majority action and could not succeed if it didn't — led by Communist Parties which were free associations within which democratic norms of debate and decision-making were taken for granted. What they counterposed to parliamentarism was the soviet system, conceived of as a more radical, real, thorough-going and responsive form of democratic mass self-rule.

To confuse this with what Stalin made of it is to falsify history — indeed, it is to walk in the track of long-established Stalinist falsifications.

The Stalinists removed the positive alternative that the Bolshevik party

36

and the early Communist International opposed to the bourgeois "democracy", "narrow constitutional methods" and "parliamentarism" which they denounced — and put in its place their own totalitarian alternative. The very idea of democracy, workers' democracy or any democracy, and of liberty against the State, disappeared — except in words that in fact now denoted their very opposites.

Bolshevik "discipline", the discipline of a voluntary association of socialists, became rigid, hierarchical, semi-militarised submission of the Communist Parties to control by Moscow. A police state became the model for both their "socialism" and their "democracy". These workers' movements were not under their own control. They could not steer their own course or learn from their mistakes.

XIII: THE NEW "RELIGION OF SOCIALISM"

"Feuerbach starts out from the fact of religious self-alienation, of the duplication of the world into a religious and a secular one... That the secular basis detaches itself from itself and establishes itself as an independent realm in the clouds can only be explained by the cleavages and self-contradictions within this secular basis. The latter must, therefore, in itself be both understood in its contradiction and revolutionised in practice..." Karl Marx, *Theses on Feuerbach*.

AS "DEMOCRACY" LOST all real meaning, so too did "socialism". The model for a socialist economy became the airtight autocratically "planned" command economy of the USSR, in which even small corner shops were statified. "Socialism" came to be measured by success in industrialising a backward and underdeveloped economy, that is, in doing the work which had so far been done by capitalism in history — and doing it by slavedriving under incomparably severe totalitarian dictatorship.

A tremendous leader cult, with Stalin as Pope, Caesar and pseudo-Tribune of the People combined, developed in the USSR in the 1930s. There too Stalin and Hitler learned from each other. The intellectual life of the international "Communist" movement centred on interpreting, augmenting, justifying and implementing Papal pronouncements from on high — assertions that often flew in the face of known reality, or of the "line" of the day before — and on the "sacred books", the misappropriated books of Marxism that said many true things but could only "speak" for today as the high priests of Stalinism interpreted them. "Proof" was defined as citations from the "four great teachers", Marx, Engels, Lenin and... Stalin. This was "Marxism" degraded into a pidgin philosophy for the bureaucratic parvenus and their Caesar-Pope at the head of a new state religion.

The centrality in Stalin's "New Marxism" of the idea and practice of forcibly industrialising a backward country by autonomous state power gave it a power of attraction in underdeveloped countries for individuals and classes with no interest in socialism as conceived of in 1917. By the end of his life Trotsky would come to describe the attractions of this "Marxism" for the leaders of Stalinist parties thus: "The predominant type

... is the political careerist ... Their ideal is to attain in their own country the same position that the Kremlin oligarchy gained in the USSR"[4]. In the 1970s, for example, a sizeable section of the educated middle class and the technological elite of the armed forces in Afghanistan made up the Stalinist party there, and in the years before their failure led to the Russian invasion of December 1979 they tried to transform themselves into a new ruling elite, apeing the Russians.

The totalitarian state not only laid down standards in art and literature and music for the Communists of the whole world: by the 1940s the Russian state was even laying down the conclusions biological research should arrive at, appointing Trofim Lysenko pope, or "Stalin", in this sphere. Culture became a sub-section of the ministry of police... So did every idea capable of expression fall under police regimentation and regulation; so did the ideas that had dominated and defined socialism so far.

When the Stalinist pope pronounced that the old socialist ideas about equality had never been part of Bolshevism, but were a petty-bourgeois deviation, nobody who was under the direct control of the Stalinist police, or who wanted to remain in the Communist Parties, could dissent, or even quibble and try to qualify it. The Soviet Union — an imaginary Soviet Union — was both Vatican and heaven of the Stalinist religion... to those who did not have to live in it. The Stalinist "religion" was bureaucratically enforced and patrolled by the GPU and not only inside the USSR. The acceptance of this system indicated a self-debilitating immaturity and underdevelopment in the Communist movement.

The international Stalinist labour movement's "secular basis detached itself from itself" and became idealised not in the clouds but beyond the seas and mountains. The successive defeats — epoch-defining in the case of the victory of Hitler in Germany — to which the Stalinists led the working class enhanced the value and sharpened the need for the quasi-religious consolation offered by the myth of Stalin's "socialist fatherland", the "Sun City" beyond the mountains".

The disease of nationalism in 1914 had meant the international labour movement splitting into many inter-warring national parts; now Communist International unity, conceived in 1919 as internationalist unity for combat against capitalism, served to enforce international working-class prostration before a narrow and brutal Russian nationalism, that yet somehow was the highest form of internationalism, under the "red" Tsar who yet, somehow, was not a Tsar. The mystifications and befuddlements and a mass working-class element of culpable fantasy and unreason defined this movement of frequently heroic would-be revolutionary workers as unfit to rule even its own affairs.

All of this was a tremendous regression. All the old socialist ideas of the relationship of means to ends, of subject and object, of the proletariat as the protagonist of modern history, of what socialism was and was not, gave way to pre-bourgeois ways of thinking and organising and to relationships between people within "the movement" that were the very opposite of those appropriate to socialism and to the preparations of socialism.

Workers rooted in the modern class struggle of their own advanced capitalist countries had their ideas dictated and their strategies set by the

---

4. *Writings 1939-40*, pp350-1.

Russian ruling class; their collective performance in the class struggle shaped and reshaped to suit the needs and interests of the class-hostile bureaucratic Russian rulers. Where Marxism, even the cautious Marxism of west European socialist parties before the Russian Revolution, had rejected "saviours from on high" and seen the working class itself as its own liberator, and its own movement as the centre of the forces of liberation, now something else was central: the "workers' state", the living socialism beyond the border, the heaven over the seas and beyond the mountains, to which the world movement was subordinated. The building of socialism, somewhere else, was everything; the communist parties' alleged goals nothing.

In the mid-19th century, readers of the *Red Republican*, George Julian Harney's paper, where the *Communist Manifesto* first appeared in English (in 1850), were avid for accounts, which the paper provided, of Etienne Cabet's socialist colonies in America. That was where socialism was. Now, in a very much more developed workers' movement, devotion to a utopia far away was repeated on a gigantic, hugely-distorting scale . Socialism was again something being built somewhere else: not, except in ceremonial speeches that meant nothing in practice, the goal of the class struggle inside your own capitalism. Enormous regression!

"No saviours from on high deliver", the great socialist republican message of the Internationale, was amended in fact to mean — saviours and popes only from the liberated lands and the higher socialist civilisations far away. The parties so guided were vigorous forces on their own terrain; they drew their strength from working-class revolt; they took the will for change, the courage, the hope, the capacity for self-sacrifice and the life-enhancing idealism of generations of revolutionary working-class militants: but their guiding principle was all for the workers' fatherland — for socialism, somewhere else. Thus they destroyed generations of revolutionary militants.

"Communism" became first a rigid and rigidly-organised sect whose sole core belief was in the infallibility of Stalin and the Soviet Union — and later a spectrum of competing Brezhnevite, Maoist, Castroist, Titoite sects. Beyond faith in the leader and "the Party", any belief, alliance, loyalty or aspiration could be annulled and anathematised overnight, and new beliefs put in its place. Much of the devotional literature of "Communism" consisted of lies and fantasies about one or another Socialist Fatherland, and viscious libels against socialism and socialists, especially the unreconstructed Bolsheviks.

Thus by the middle of the second quarter of the 20th century, the most militant segments of the great working-class movement built up over three-quarters of a century in political and ideological recoil from utopian socialism reverted to a variant of it, focussed on the vast anti-capitalist utopian "colony" in the USSR — whose socialism was an edifice of lies and falsifications and whose rulers were more savage in every sense than any other ruling class. The effect on the labour movement was justly compared by Trotsky to syphilis and leprosy.

**"The worst thing that can befall a leader of an extreme party is to be compelled to take over a Government in an epoch when the movement is not yet ripe for the domination of the class which he represents and for the realisation of the measures which that domination would imply... What he can do is in contrast to all his previous actions, to all his principles, and to the present interests of his party; what he ought to do cannot be achieved".
Frederick Engels.**

THE SECOND WORST thing — in the Russian case it flowed from the first — is for a revolutionary party to have its banners, symbols and erstwhile language, appropriated by a powerful state and its dupes overseas, who proclaim plausible counterfeits of its goals as theirs, and use them to serve alien interests.

It cannot reach its own people; its place in politics is usurped and ruined; those it would help to victory, misled to defeat and catastrophe. Perhaps an epoch of history will have to pass, bringing its own slow clarifications, before it can come into its own. By then much will have changed and it will itself have mutated and have to define itself all over again. So it was with the incorruptible and unbreakable Bolsheviks, the Marxists who stood out against the bureaucratic counter-revolution and the Stalinist falsification of the ideas and perspectives of Bolshevism.

They fought the new Russian ruling class even before it was fully formed and before they had learned to recognise and define it. The surviving Bolsheviks, led by Trotsky, had to start again from almost the beginning. Now they faced adversity and complications such as the older Marxist movement had never known, in a nightmare world in which all their banners and symbols had been annexed and appropriated to be used against them .

A dozen years on from October, the international-socialist Bolsheviks were reduced to a numerically marginal force, politically expropriated, and seemingly by-passed and outmoded. The "perspectives" on which Lenin and Trotsky had oriented themselves in 1917 — the world-wide dislocation of capitalism, and the opportunities it provided, again and again, in country after country, for the working class to overthrow capitalism — were still valid, if the labour movement could take its opportunities. Yet now the Communist International, formed to push aside the social democracy and organise the working class to settle accounts with capitalism, was a force that acted against socialism with a brutality, discipline, consistency and lethal effect that pro-capitalist social democracy had matched only in Germany in 1919, if even then.

Out of the victory of 1917 had come the most debilitating of defeats. Lenin and Trotsky knew they could be defeated and possibly massacred: they did not imagine this sort of defeat, or this massacre of the ideas of Marxism and socialism.

Not only did the Bolsheviks take power, then find themselves unable to realise their programme and forced to implement, in whole or in part, another programme; but then a seeming facsimile of their programme was seized and annexed by their conquerors. "All the old crap" did reappear, but disguised as the best realisation of its very opposite. Stalinism permeated the socialist programme; it petrified it as calcifying chemicals seep into the cells of trees to turn the organic wood into another substance, stone.

The consequences for socialism can only now, after the fall of the USSR and its empire, begin to be be undone.

Against the Communist Parties, after the mid-1920s, competed tiny groups led by Trotsky, representing and embodying the ideas of the 1917 Revolution, but with few resources. The existence of state-licensed Stalinist "Marxism" made their work uniquely difficult. In addition, they would be half-buried under an enormous USSR-inspired and -financed deluge of misrepresentation, slander, and persecution, including murder. To the Stalinist counter-revolutionaries — and to the millions of revolutionary workers who followed them — these representatives of the ideas of October, and in the first place Trotsky, the organiser of the October rising, were Mensheviks, reactionaries, White Guards, and fascists. Their identity, like their banner, had been stolen by the new Russian ruling class and its agents.

The unreconstructed Jacobins and the poor people of Paris had experienced something like this when the slogans of Liberty, Equality and Fraternity, under which they had made the French Revolution, were seized by the bourgeoisie, who came to power after the Revolution had cleared the way for them and crushed the people. The bourgeoisie gave the old revolutionary slogans *their* meanings. They rendered the revolution unrecognisable and unacceptable to those who had made it. Under the self-same slogans, or the same broad ideas, an alien class had harvested the state power. The revolutionary ideas were not sharp enough and clear enough to make them undetachable from those who thought they had blazed a path that would lead to a world very different from the one that they had. Ideas are porous: reality is richer and more complex; it possesses potentialities that are not to be seen in advance.

The democrats of the 1830s and 1840s in Britain and elsewhere had seen their ideas seized and corrupted in the '50s and '60s, when democracy was tamed by the bourgeoisie, deprived of its earlier radical social dimension and turned into something other than what it had been for friends and enemies alike since the French Revolution, and earlier.

"I pondered all these things, and how men fight and lose the battle, and the thing they fought for comes about in spite of their defeat, and when it comes turns out not to be what they meant, and other men have to fight for what they meant under another name".[5]

The Bolsheviks' experience after Stalin's "Second Revolution" in 1928 had much in common with those earlier experiences.

Of course, socialists had known, and repeatedly said, that state nationalisation of industry was not socialism; that it could only serve socialist working-class goals if the workers held social and political power. These ideas had differentiated Marxism from Fabianism and middle-class reformism. In its spiralling degeneration the Russian revolution presented the problem differently. Nationalised property there was rooted in the great revolution. Though the Bolshevik Party and the revolution had been destroyed, the manner of their destruction was unexpected. The result was

5. William Morris: *A Dream of John Ball*.

unprecedented and therefore mystifying and disorienting.

Both "the Bolsheviks" and "the October Revolution" seemed to have survived. Despite the programme-rooted expectations of those who led the
revolution that there would be bourgeois counter-revolution in Russia if
the workers' revolution did not spread to the advanced countries, there had
been no bourgeois counter-revolution. The bureaucratic counter-revolution
that had taken place said it was Bolshevik, socialist, working-class.

The Stalinist counter-revolution was not only a counter-revolution within the property forms established by the workers' state, but also, as we
saw, a counter-revolution within the forms of the old governing Marxist
ideas. When it snuffed out the remnants of working-class political power,
and seized the means of production, the new ruling class seized "Marxism"
too, twisting, changing and bowdlerising the old ideas, turning the old
Marxist language into its liturgy of state and the sacerdotal language of a
bureaucratic "socialism".

When the rising collectivist ruling class, in its process of separation from
the old party, created a pseudo-Marxism that deconstructed and disman-
tled the Marxism of October, it inflicted its worst possible, because all-
embracing, defeat on Bolshevism. One consequence was to prevent the re-
emergence of a replacement for Bolshevism. The taking of power in 1917
turned out to have been a kamikaze exercise, not only for the Bolshevik
party in its physical existence, though ultimately it was that, but
kamikaze for a whole political doctrine. The Trotskyists had to rebuild
Bolshevism in a labour movement doubly poisoned — by its open enemies
and by the Stalinist imposters — against "Bolshevism". The task proved
impossible.

The "battle of ideas" is central to the outcome of class struggle. Here was
Karl Marx's idea that "the ruling ideology of an epoch is that of the ruling
class" confronting the international revolutionary movement in a new
form — as an international extension of the new USSR ruling class, assid-
uously purveying a counterfeit of the old Bolshevik ideas, and maintaining
a world-wide organisation with vast resources and no scruples or restraint
to impose its version of "Marxism". Bad slogans drove out good; opulent
counterfeits, nourished by the successes of the USSR, occupied the place of
the genuine Marxism. Possessing power and wealth — that of a ruling
class — unimaginable to the old labour movement, the bureaucracy could
define what it decreed to be Marxism, socialism, Leninism, Bolshevism.
Money, prestige, "red professors" in their version of academia, and police,
jails, and concentration camps could, and for decades did, make good the
claim. The bureaucrats' great power to set the agenda for large parts of the
labour movement could sustain it. The past was blurred, half blotted out,
and "overwritten" with the bureaucracy's myths of its own origins, purposes, and pidgin-Marxist ideologies, spread among revolutionary workers
along paths laid down to and from the USSR in the days of Bolshevism.
When parody and pastiche and scholastic kitsch "Marxism" became the
creed of the mass revolutionary labour movement, revolutionary Marxism
confronted the most murderously hostile environment it had ever had to
face — a political world in the grip of nightmare and delirium such as no
liberating movement had faced since the mysticism enshrouded primitive
revolts of the religion-bound Middle Ages.

Those in the Bolshevik party and the Communist International who resisted the rising Stalinist bureaucracy had to dispute with those who, in possession of the "conquests" of the October Revolution, were plausibly the heirs of Lenin exactly what was and was not Marxism, what was and was not Bolshevism, what was and was not the proper policy and modus operandi for the Communist Parties in capitalist countries, what was and was not the necessary socialist working-class perspective on the evolution of the USSR. They fought an immense entrenched state power which presented itself as the real — the victorious, and therefore better — embodiment of the ideals proclaimed also by the anti-Stalinists. To side with the opposition needed courage and clarity. It meant standing with a tiny persecuted minority against a vast multitude who seemed to have the successful and prosperous variant of the same ideas.

Moreover, the revolutionary socialists had the disadvantage of seeming to accept the core claims of the Stalinists. The Soviet Union was, they said, an immense gain, though they criticised the bureaucrats' methods and their rule. Its economic successes were the decisive practical proof in history so far that collectivist economy worked. So said even Trotsky.

The representative experience of the proto-Fourth International was that of Germany from September 1930, when Hitler made a spectacular electoral breakthrough, to 30 January 1933, when Hitler became Chancellor, and the few weeks after that, before the Nazi grip had taken the German labour movement by the throat, during which effective resistance was still possible. Trotsky understood Hitlerism early. He raised the alarm in good time. In pamphlets and articles he warned the German labour movement, criticised it, advocated proper anti-fascist tactics for the whole German labour movement.

Despite Trotsky's warnings, the social democracy remained the supine conservative force it had been for 20 years. The German Communist Party made violently pseudo-revolutionary statements and competed with the Nazis by mimicking their ideas (they too called for the "national liberation" of Germany) and by intermittently allying with them against the social democratic labour movement — even to collaboration with the Hitlerites in the breaking of social-democrat-led strikes. They insisted that Hitler fascism was neither the main danger nor the only "fascism".

Here the confusion about "democracy" must have been a big element in getting German Communist workers to accept the idea that Hitler's victory was not uniquely threatening to the very existence of the German labour movement, Communist and social-democratic alike. To the Communist Party, the main enemy was "social fascism", the social democracy — the old enemy, the traitors of 1918-9, "the murderers of Rosa Luxemburg and Karl Liebknecht".

The couple of hundred Trotskyists were unable to make themselves heard by those who could shape and reshape reality. They could not break through the barriers of bureaucratic organisation to influence Social-Democratic workers, or surmount the barricades of Stalinist slander to influence Communist workers.

The unquiet ghosts of old Bolshevism, still abroad in the world but no longer a force in it, they were able to see and understand but no longer able to touch reality and shape it. Revolutionary Marxist theory was divorced from the revolutionary-minded workers and thus from the possibility of practice. To the Stalinist workers, the Oppositionists were the "Trotsky fascists"; to the social democrats, the unteachable old Bolsheviks; to the working class at large, people outside their own organisations, heretics, renegades, defeatists — or agents provocateurs in the service of the enemy.

By the time Hitler came to break its back and smash its skull, German Communism was a quasi-religious mass cult, in which the Stalinist Popes and bishops — operating, like the medieval Church, by ideological terrorism supplemented by physical repression — had outlawed the propensity and capacity of the party to think, and driven unauthorised "discussion" underground. The Trotskyists? People sacrilegiously questioning the most sacred doctrines and pouring scorn and venom on the images of their leaders and teachers. Alien, petty-bourgeois, "revisionist" — subversive of the revolutionary enterprise! To disobey or disagree was to place yourself outside the great army of the revolutionary proletariat, outside the revolutionary party on which so much depended.

Trotsky was right, foreseeing events clearly and in good time to arm the workers, truthfully warning the German labour movement that it was faced with imminent destruction — and yet he was starkly cut off from any possibility of affecting events. In Germany Trotskyism was Bolshevism without masses, arguing perspectives that required masses, in conditions where the very life of the German working-class movement was at stake. This was to be the fate of Trotskyism in history. Trotskyism would be shaped and reshaped by it.

After the German CP's surrender to Hitler in 1933, Trotsky declared the Communist International dead and set out to build a new International, the "Fourth". The forces were very small. The proponents of the new International would have to do the same work as had been done for the nascent "Third" (Communist) International at the Zimmerwald and Kienthal Conferences in 1915 and 1916 after the collapse of the old International at the outbreak of war in 1914. But there were no victories like that of 1917, out of which grew the Third International. Defeat followed defeat; disaster followed disaster; massacre followed massacre at the hands of the fascists and the Stalinists. A new movement had proved necessary — but also, as Europe moved to a new world-engulfing war, impossible.

The fundamental difference between the prospects for the nascent Third International, in its day, and the still-born Fourth, lay in the existence and character of Stalinism — a rich and powerful pseudo-revolutionary force with a stable base in the USSR that allowed the Communist Parties to survive any political shift, zig-zag or glaring contradiction. This was not politics as hitherto known in the labour movement, but a variant of the state-serving politics hitherto confined to the bourgeoisie, whose parties, alternating in power, would, despite differences, commonly serve the fundamental social status quo, the rule of the bourgeoisie.

In the Stalinist parties, policy zig-zags occurred repeatedly within one entity, defined by the interests of the USSR ruling class. This would change the map of the labour movement's political world, intruding into it a bureaucratic force as powerful and unscrupulous as the state and the ruling class it served. The laws of history are stronger than the bureaucratic apparatus, Trotsky would write. In fact the Stalinist apparatus inserted a reshaping force into history — not for ever, as the once seemingly all-powerful Russian Stalinist rulers would learn in 1989-91, but for a whole epoch, and enough to derail, confuse and crush progressive forces falteringly moving forward in the class struggle. The strength of the Stalinist apparatus, against whole societies and against more easily dispersible and destructible labour movements made up of voluntary associations of workers, was something new in history. In Germany, Spain and France, Stalinism acted as one of the two giant millstones which ground into nothingness labour movements, which, had they been able to develop, might have reconstructed society on a higher socialist level.

By the time Trotsky died, on 21 August 1940, the European labour movement had been pulverised. Excepting Britain, Finland, Ireland, Switzerland and Sweden, fascism and authoritarianism ruled Europe. To the east Stalin had erected a bureaucratic throne above the grave of the Russian labour movement.

Trotskyism was an epiphenomenon of the early Communist International: a critical satellite of the mass parties of the Communist International, desperately trying to reorient them; and then a disablingly weak competitor with both the Communist International and the older social democracy. It was armed with the unfalsified ideas, goals and perspectives of 1917 Bolshevism and the early Communist International in a capitalist world rushing towards disaster and the biggest and most destructive war in history.

The contrast between what followed the collapse of the Communist International in 1933 and the aftermath of the collapse of the Second International in 1914 was decisive for the subsequent history of Europe. In 1914 and after, the Kaiser socialists and their counterparts in other countries had visibly and audibly broken with the old ideas. There was resistance — led by Karl Liebknecht, Rosa Luxemburg, Klara Zetkin, Franz Mehring, Otto Rühle and others — which swelled and grew in response to events. In 1916 the German Social Democracy split. Radicalisation grew, especially after the Russian Revolution of 1917. Revolutionaries rallied to the clean red banner of October. After the decisive collapse of the Stalinised Communist Party in 1933, nothing was clear-cut. The bureaucratic Russian state twisted and shaped everything. In 1933 and after, the Trotskyist opposition did not appear boldly and clearly as the revolutionary opposition, nor the Stalinists as renegades who had served the enemy and helped destroy the most powerful labour movement in Europe.

Decisively, the Stalinists had not gone over to the bourgeois enemy, they were demagogically very left wing and "revolutionary"; they served the anti-capitalist Russian bureaucracy. There was neither freedom to organise in the Communist Parties, nor the possibility of open discussion; nor, now, was there unadulterated Marxist education to build on. There had already been a decade of radical miseducation, of systematic falsification of the ideas of Marxism and the Russian Revolution. The very language of Marxism had been corrupted and reduced to emotion-bearing demagogic, arbitrary catch-cries.

It would be like that, with national variations, all through the 1930s, until war reshaped the world anew and for a whole epoch closed off the perspectives on which the Communist International of 1919 had organised itself.

2. BOLSHEVISM AT BAY: TROTSKY ON THE USSR

I: TROTSKY IN EXILE

IMMEDIATELY AFTER HIS expulsion from the USSR in February 1929, Trotsky, the Left Oppositionist reformer inside the USSR, was a hard-faced man of the regime to the outside world. When he wrote for the general public, his criticisms of the regime were selective, general and muted. Sharper criticism was reserved for his communist-oppositionist audience.

He split with the German Leninbund, the biggest organisation in the early international Left Opposition, because it would not support Stalin's policy of holding on to the Chinese Eastern Railway against the Chinese. (Stalin would cede it to Japan in 1935). Himself author of acute social analysis of that system (see the next section), and a critic of the lack of democracy in the USSR, one, moreover, whose comrades there were already being shot, Trotsky reacted violently, as late as 1934, against talk of general democracy in the USSR. "There is a tendency among our friends in Paris to deny the proletarian nature of the USSR, to demand that there be complete democracy in the USSR, including the legalisation of the Mensheviks, etc.... We regard this tendency as treason which must be fought implacably"[6].

By the end of the 1930s there would be a very telling inversion. Trotsky would become a strident critic of the Stalinist internal regime and Stalinist foreign policy when he addressed the general public, and write about "defence of the USSR" almost exclusively in the intra-Trotskyist literature. At the same time, after 1930, when Stalinist industrialisation seemed miraculously successful and capitalism spiralled into the great slump, many of the Social Democratic critics of Bolshevism would move towards a friendly attitude to Stalinism — friendlier, as Trotsky will note, ironically, than they ever were to Bolshevism. The leading theoretician of the Austro-Marxist school, Otto Bauer, and Mensheviks like Fyodor Dan were critical of Stalinism for its lack of democracy, but saw the USSR as representing one road to socialism, suitable for backward Russia but not for Western Europe. True to the docile philistine spirit of rationalising from hard "facts" and accommodating themselves to power, they were very impressed by the USSR's economic achievements.

The peak performance in this spiritually and intellectually athletic journey by the Social Democrats to Stalin's Moscow was the conversion of Sydney and Beatrice Webb — Lord and Lady Passfield, epitomes of the British Fabian type described by Frederick Engels as "middle-class reformers who think socialism is too good to be left to the workers" — to the conclusion that the USSR was "A New Civilisation".

As the experience of Stalinism accumulated, Trotsky virtually swapped places with most of the social-democratic critics of the USSR. By the mid-1930s, the once implacable and unrepentant defender of the Bolshevik regime against Social-Democratic and vulgar-democratic critics was scornfully castigating the Bauerites and the "Brandlerite" Right Communists, for being apologists and rationalising defence lawyers for

---

6 *Writings Supplement 1934-40*, p.538.

Stalin and Stalinism. In his root-and-branch opposition to Stalinism Trotsky after 1936 was close to Karl Kautsky. In his theoretical summaries, however, Trotsky remained tied to the idea that the Stalinist USSR was still a workers' state of some sort. What follows is an attempt to trace the evolution of Trotsky's ideas on the Stalinist USSR.

II. "A BUREAUCRATIC ECONOMY"

BY 1933 IT had become clear that Stalin's "left turn" of 1929-30 was no mere zig-zag or temporary improvisation. The regime had survived the convulsive crisis of 1932-3. It had given a new shape to USSR society. Until his death in 1940, Trotsky would continue to call the USSR a "workers' state" of sorts. Yet the basic trend of his detailed, concrete analyses of the USSR — and of most of his political conclusions — was, in my view, sharply and increasingly at odds with that summary description.

Trotsky gives his first comprehensive anatomy of Stalinist society in an article of April 1933, "The Theory of Degeneration and the Degeneration of Theory". Trotsky discusses the question of why, if, as the Stalinists say, socialism has been realised, the state is not, as in Marxist theory it should be, withering away, becoming less and less of a social force. In fact it has grown to unprecedented power and dominance. He links the state with a discussion of inflation and money: like the state, money has a necessary social function, as measure of value and means of exchange; like the state, its role will diminish with social development. It too will finally wither away.

As with two flashlights, one in each hand, playing from different angles on something obscured and darkly hidden, Trotsky examines the nature of Stalinist society from the two sides of state and economy. He lights up a picture which does not fit easily — or, indeed, fit at all — into the historical and theoretical framework that he insists on. The society he describes and anatomises is unmistakably a new form of class society, neither capitalism nor socialism, or in transition to socialism. It is what will at the end of the 30s be called bureaucratic collectivism.

"The soviets have lost the last remnants of independent significance and have ceased being soviets. The party does not exist". Insisting that "the relative independence of the trade unions is a necessary and important corrective in the system of the soviet state... the workers must defend themselves, even in a workers' state, through their trade-union organisations", Trotsky observes that "the trade unions are completely crushed... under the cover of the struggle with the right deviation".[7]

"The state not only does not wither away... but... becomes ever more openly the instrument of bureaucratic coercion... The apparatus of the trade unions themselves has become the weapon of an ever-growing pressure on the workers".

Referring to the "regime of terror against the party and the proletariat", Trotsky asks: "Where does such a terrible, monstrous, unbearable exercise of the political regime come from?". He finally answers: "The intensifica-

---

7. Tomsky, the main trade-union leader, had been a prominent Bukharinite.

tion of repression is necessary for the defence of the privileged positions of the bureaucracy".

He now draws out "an analogy between the role of money and the role of the state in the transitional epoch". Money, Trotsky says, "a direct heritage of capitalism", cannot simply be abolished. It will wither away as its functions as measure of value and means of exchange decline in a society of abundance. In the first period of working-class rule its role will grow rather than diminish: it is an essential tool of real planning and of real social knowledge. There will be an "extreme expansion" in the turnover of goods in the transition period. All branches of a growing economy "must determine their relation to each other qualitatively and quantitatively".

"Money as the means of accounting evolved by capitalism is not thrown aside but socialised. Socialist construction is unthinkable without the inclusion in the planned system of the personal interest of the producer and consumer. And this interest can actively manifest itself only when it has at its disposal a trustful and flexible weapon: a stable monetary system". That is what happens in a workers' state developing towards socialism. And in the USSR? Trotsky describes the reality of bureaucratic arbitrariness and inflation. "Money regulated by administrative prices fixed for goods loses its ability to regulate plans. In this field as in others, 'socialism' for the bureaucracy consists of freeing its will from any control: party, Soviet, trade union or money ... Economic planning frees itself from value control as bureaucratic fancy frees itself from political control. The rejection of 'objective causes' ... represents the 'theoretical' ravings of bureaucratic subjectivism ... The Soviet economy today is neither a monetary nor a planned one. It is an almost purely bureaucratic economy. To support unreliable and disproportionate tempos, a further intensification of pressure on the proletariat became imperative. Industry, freed from the material control of the producer, took on a supersocial, that is, bureaucratic, character. As a result it lost the ability to satisfy human wants even to the degree to which it had been accomplished by the less-developed capitalist industry...

"From this and from this alone... flows the necessity for the introduction of coercion into all cells of economic life (strengthening of the power of [factory] managers, laws against absentees, death penalty for spoiliation of collective-farm property by its members, war measures in sowing campaigns and harvest collections... the [internal] passport system, political departments in the villages, etc. etc.)... The dictatorship of the proletariat withers away in the form of bureaucratic inflation, that is, in the extreme swelling of coercion, persecutions, and violence. The dictatorship of the proletariat is not dissolved in a classless society, but degenerates into the omnipotence of bureaucracy over society".

By the time Trotsky writes his major study of the USSR, *The Revolution Betrayed* (1935-6), the acute monetary instability of the early 1930s has subsided. The "bureaucratic arbitrariness" — the regulation of economic and social life by the arbitrary exercise of unbridled state power more than any before known — has not. Stalinist autocracy has not. Trotsky poses the problem.

"If exploitation is "ended forever"... [as the Stalinists claim] then there remains nothing for society to do but to throw off at last the straitjacket of the state. In place of this — it is hard even to grasp this contrast with

48

the mind! — the Soviet state has acquired a totalitarian-bureaucratic character... What social cause stands behind the stubborn virility of the state and especially behind its policification? The importance of this question is obvious. In dependence upon the answer, we must either radically revise our traditional views of the socialist society in general, or as radically reject the official estimates of the Soviet Union".

The programme of the Bolsheviks was: "A strong state, but without mandarins; armed power, but without the Samurai! The party programme demands a replacement of the standing army by an armed people. The regime of proletarian dictatorship from its very beginning thus ceases to be a 'state' in the old sense of the word — a special apparatus, that is, for holding in subjection the majority of the people. The material power, together with the weapons, goes over directly and immediately into the hands of the workers' organisations such as the soviets. The state as a bureaucratic apparatus begins to die away on the first day of the proletarian dictatorship. Such is the voice of the party program... Strange: it sounds like a spectral voice from the mausoleum.".

The USSR regime has not begun to "die away" but "has grown into a hitherto unheard of apparatus of compulsion. The bureaucracy... has turned into an uncontrolled force dominating the masses. The army... has given birth to a privileged officers' caste, crowned with marshals, while the people, 'the armed bearers of the dictatorship', are now forbidden in the Soviet Union to carry even nonexplosive weapons.".

Trotsky starkly sums up the contrast between the USSR and the workers' state: "With the utmost stretch of fancy it would be difficult to imagine a contrast more striking than that which exists between the scheme of the workers' state according to Marx, Engels and Lenin, and the actual state now headed by Stalin".

"The regime became 'totalitarian' in character several years before this word arrived from Germany". "From the first days of the soviet regime the counterweight to bureaucratism was the party. If the bureaucracy managed the state, still the party controlled the bureaucracy. Keenly vigilant lest inequality transcend the limits of what was necessary, the party was always in a state of open or disguised struggle with the bureaucracy. The historic role of Stalin's faction was to destroy this duplication, subjecting the party to its own officialdom and merging the latter in the officialdom of the state. Thus was created the present totalitarian regime".

III. STATE PROPERTY AND SOCIALISM

STATE PROPERTY UNDER such a regime cannot be socialist. "The new constitution [of 1936] — wholly founded, as we shall see, upon an identification of the bureaucracy with the state, and the state with the people — says: '... the state property — that is, the possessions of the whole people.' This identification is the fundamental sophism of the official doctrine.

It is perfectly true that Marxists, beginning with Marx himself, have employed in relation to the workers' state the terms state, national and socialist property as simple synonyms. On a large historic scale, such a mode of speech involves no special inconveniences. But it becomes the source of crude mistakes, and of downright deceit, when applied to the first and still unassured stages of the development of a new society, and one moreover isolated and economically lagging behind the capitalist countries.

In order to become social, private property must as inevitably pass through the state stage as the caterpillar in order to become a butterfly must pass through the pupal stage. But the pupa is not a butterfly... State property becomes the property of 'the whole people' only to the degree that social privilege and differentiation disappear, and therewith the necessity of the state. In other words: state property is converted into socialist property in proportion as it ceases to be state property. And the contrary is true: the higher the soviet state rises above the people... the more obviously does it testify against the socialist character of this state property.".

"The transfer of the factories to the state changed the situation of the worker only juridically. In reality, he is compelled to live in want and work a definite number of hours for a definite wage... the new state resorted to the old methods of pressure upon the muscles and nerves of the worker. There grew up a corps of slave drivers. The management of industry became superbureaucratic. The workers lost all influence whatever upon the management of the factory. With piecework payment, hard conditions of material existence, lack of free movement, with terrible police repression penetrating the life of every factory, it is hard indeed for the worker to feel himself a 'free workman.' In the bureaucracy he sees the manager, in the state, the employer."

IV. CATCHING UP WITH CAPITALISM

TROTSKY RECALLS THAT in 1846 Karl Marx defined the development of the productive forces as the prerequisite of communism. "Without it want is generalised, and with want the struggle for necessities begins again, and that means that all the old crap must revive." In the USSR the "struggle for necessities" has given rise to a monstrous autocracy. A system built for forced-march industrialisation in an isolated and backward economy can be defined as socialism only by disregarding the most basic ideas of Marxism.

By socialism Marx meant: "a society which from the very beginning stands higher in its economic development than the most advanced capitalism... on a world scale communism, even in its first incipient stage, means a higher level of development that that of bourgeois society... Russia was not the strongest, but the weakest link in the chain of capitalism. The present Soviet Union does not stand above the world level of economy, but is only trying to catch up to the capitalist countries. If Marx called that society which was to be formed upon the basis of a socialisation of the productive forces of the most advanced capitalism of its epoch the lowest stage of communism, then this designation obviously does not apply to the Soviet Union, which is still today considerably poorer in technique, culture and the good things of life than the capitalist countries... The soviet regime is passing through a preparatory stage, importing, borrowing and appropriating the technical and cultural conquests of the

West... this preparatory stage is far from finished. Even under the improbable condition of a continuing complete capitalist standstill it must still occupy a whole historic period".

"Socialism, or the lowest stage of communism... assumes... more humane forms of control than those invented by the exploitative genius of capital. In the Soviet Union, however, there is now taking place a ruthlessly severe fitting in of backward human material to the technique borrowed from capitalism... state ownership of the means of production does not turn manure into gold, and does not surround with a halo of sanctity the sweatshop system...". Trotsky indicts the autocracy's use of "the classic methods of exploitation... in such naked and crude forms as would not be permitted even by reformist trade unions in bourgeois countries". In the interaction between bosses and workers — but not only there — "The relations between men... have not only not yet risen to socialism, but in many respects are still lagging behind a cultured capitalism".

And why? The programme of the Bolshevik Revolution "was based wholly upon an international perspective. 'The October revolution in Russia has realised the dictatorship of the proletariat.... The era of world proletarian communist revolution has begun.' These were the introductory lines of the program." The Bolsheviks could not then imagine or analyse "what character the Soviet state would assume, if compelled for as long as two decades to solve in isolation those economic and cultural problems which advanced capitalism had solved so long ago." That has led to "the ultra-bureaucratic character of its state"; the delay of international revolution has also "led in the capitalist countries to fascism or the pre-fascist reaction".

"In the last analysis, Soviet Bonapartism owes its birth to the belatedness of the world revolution. But in the capitalist countries the same cause gave rise to fascism... the crushing of soviet democracy by an all-powerful bureaucracy and the extermination of bourgeois democracy by fascism were produced by one and the same cause: the dilatoriness of the world proletariat in solving the problems set for it by history. Stalinism and fascism, in spite of a deep difference in social foundations, are symmetrical phenomena. In many of their features they show a deadly similarity."

V. THE NATURE OF THE STALINIST AUTOCRACY

IN "THESES" ON "The Fourth International and the Soviet Union", written in July 1936 as he finishes *The Revolution Betrayed*, Trotsky declares that the economic successes of the USSR "are already proving adequate for the emergence of a broad privileged stratum". Social antagonisms are "enormously accentuated". Inequality "is growing by leaps and bounds". "The soviet bureaucracy has acquired an actual independence from the toilers"; it is "the most privileged of all the privileged strata". For its people soviet society "presents an enormous hierarchy: from vagabond children, prostitutes, slum proletarians — to the ruling 'ten thousand' who lead the life of Western European magnates of capital".

The bureaucracy is thus, so Trotsky writes, "something more than a bureaucracy". "In its intermediary and regulating function, its concern to maintain social ranks, and its exploitation of the state apparatus for personal goals, the Soviet bureaucracy is similar to every other bureaucracy, especially the fascist. But it is also in a vast way different. In no other regime has a bureaucracy ever achieved such a degree of independence from the dominating class". By "the dominating class" Trotsky here means the working class. Why, and in what sense, Trotsky believes that it "dominates", we shall see later.

The essential point here is the contrast with the bureaucracy in capitalist society, representing the interests of "a possessing and educated class" having "innumerable means of everyday control over" the bureaucracy. The fascist bureaucracy in power intertwines with the big bourgeoisie, but "the soviet bureaucracy takes on bourgeois customs without having beside it a national bourgeoisie. In this sense we cannot deny that it is something more than a bureaucracy. It is in the full sense of the word the sole privileged and commanding stratum in the Soviet society".

"The very fact of its appropriation of political power in a country where the principal means of production are in the hands of the state, creates a new and hitherto unknown relation between the bureaucracy and the riches of the nation. The means of production belong to the state. But the state, so to speak, 'belongs' to the bureaucracy... If these as yet wholly new relations should solidify, become the norm and be legalised, whether with or without resistance from the workers, they would, in the long run, lead to a complete liquidation of the social conquests of the proletarian revolution". [emphasis added]

Here, Trotsky falls into presenting the relations between people as relations between the bureaucracy on one side and things ("the riches of the nation"), not people, on the other. And, as we shall see, Trotsky will later make great play with the qualification "so to speak" — "the state, so to speak, belongs to the bureaucracy". But the sociological picture of Stalinist society which Trotsky paints is clear and full in its outlines.

The straightforward implication is that the bureaucracy is the ruling class. It organises production in a way unique to itself. It appropriates the social surplus product on the basis of controlling the means of life. There is no other privileged elite. The entire population is at its disposal.

Many aspects of this society and this ruling class are new, mysterious and still unfolding, and its stability is not to be assumed, but the basic socio-economic relations fit the pattern of all previous class societies. Trotsky has described all this, explained the basic reasons for it, and connected it up to the whole history of class society. If the relations are not "solidified", normalised, and legalised, they do certainly exist. They are the pattern of Stalinist society as it has functioned through its industrial revolution of the last several years. In fact history will show those relations to be "solidified" enough that they survive the World War and expand and reproduce for over fifty years after 1936.

THE GREAT TERROR began in late 1934 and rose to a frenzy of unparalleled slaughter after August 1936, when Stalin organised the first of the three Moscow Trials in which almost all the surviving leaders of the 1917 revolution were forced to confess to having been "counter-revolutionaries" even while leading the October Revolution and then killed. On 1 May 1939 Trotsky wrote "The Bonapartist Philosophy of the State" (it appeared in *New International*, June 1939). Just four months before the great political dispute in the Trotskyist movement, in which he would insist on the description "workers' state", this article presents a stark picture of a distinct socio-economic formation, not of any possible sort of workers' state.

Trotsky depicts Stalinism as a system more akin to Dark Age feudalism or to the rigidifying Roman Empire of about 300 AD than to either socialism or capitalism, or anything in between.

By now Trotsky's analysis and descriptions of the USSR are in flat contradiction to his theoretical framework — it is a "degenerated workers' state" — and two distinct Trotskyisms exist in Trotsky himself. They will separate in 1939-40. Articles like this are educating those who, like Shachtman, will soon come out against Trotksy's political conclusion and then against his ossified theoretical paradigm.

"The realities of soviet life today can indeed be hardly reconciled even with the shreds of old theory. Workers are bound to the factories; peasants are bound to the collective farms. [Internal] Passports have been introduced. Freedom of movement has been completely restricted. It is a capital crime to come late to work. Punishable as treason is not only any criticism of Stalin but even the mere failure to fulfil the natural duty to get down on all fours before the 'Leader'. The frontiers are guarded by an impenetrable wall of border patrols and police dogs on a scale heretofore unknown anywhere. To all intents and purposes no one can leave and no one may enter. Foreigners [in fact, communists, and especially communist refugees from capitalist police states] who had previously managed to get into the country are being systematically exterminated.

"The... soviet constitution, 'the most democratic in the world', amounts to this, that every citizen is required at an appointed time to cast his ballot for the one and only candidate handpicked by Stalin or his agents. The press, the radio, all the organs of propaganda, agitation and national education are completely in the hands of the ruling clique... How many have been shot, thrown into jails and concentration camps, or exiled to Siberia, we do not definitely know. But undoubtedly hundreds of thousands of party members have shared the fate of millions of non-party people". Though the "official edict" is that "socialism has been realised", Stalinism has "brought the state to a pitch of wild intensity unprecedented in the history of mankind".

In this "totalitarian state", "the party, the government, the army and the diplomatic corps have been bled white and beheaded". "The growth and strengthening of the military and civil caste signifies that society is moving not towards but away from the socialist ideal". The purges and "frame-ups" "must flow from the very structure of Soviet society... Inequality always requires a safeguard; privileges always demand protection; and the encroachments of the disinherited require punishment..."

Trotsky pictures the life of the "ruling caste". In addition to publicly acknowledged salaries, "they receive secret salaries from the treasuries of the Central Committee or local committees; they have at their disposal automobiles (there even exist special plants for the production of finest automobiles for the use of 'responsible workers'), excellent apartments, summer homes, sanatoria, and hospitals. To suit their needs or their vanity all sorts of 'soviet palaces' are erected". Trotsky shows that the bureaucrats can pass on to their children, if not property in the means of production, then status and future membership in the elite: the ruling caste "almost monopolise the highest institutions of learning".

Trotsky summarises: "The Bonapartist apparatus of the state is thus an organ for defending the bureaucratic thieves and plunderers of national wealth". In his capacity as the pontiff of lies, that is, chief liar in the state, and as the chief state terrorist, Stalin is "the spokesman of privileged parasites. In the land that has gone through the proletarian revolution, it is impossible to foster inequality, create an aristocracy, and accumulate privileges save by bringing down on the masses floods of lies and ever more monstrous repressions".

Is this strange social system, in which 170 millions of people live, which is neither capitalist nor socialist, a new form of society? Indisputably, this society exists, and therefore it is a new form of society. Trotsky, confining himself to analysis and description, here says nothing of this. He does not believe it has reached stability. He stresses, as an explanation for the social convulsions, that the bureaucrats' income is in large part sanctioned neither by "the principles of socialism" nor by "the laws of the country". "Embezzlement and theft, the bureaucracy's main sources of income, do not constitute a system of exploitation in the scientific sense of the term. But from the standpoint of the interests and position of the popular masses, it is infinitely worse than any 'organic' exploitation.

The bureaucracy is not a possessing class, in the scientific sense of the term. But it contains within itself to a tenfold degree all the vices of a possessing class.

It is precisely the absence of crystallised class relations and their very impossibility on the social foundations of the October Revolution that invest the workings of the state machine with such a convulsive character. To perpetuate the systematic theft of the bureaucracy, its apparatus is compelled to resort to systematic acts of banditry. The sum total of all these things constitutes the system of Bonapartist gangsterism".

VII. GANGSTER STATE AND WORKERS' STATE?

FOR TROTSKY, AS we have seen, the Stalinist USSR, simultaneously with being a "system of Bonapartist gangsterism", was also a "degenerated workers' state". In Trotsky's mind this bizarre contradiction was possible only because the Stalinist USSR was a momentary concatenation of opposites, a freak socio-economic formation. Or so he thought. In fact he was faced with analysing and understanding and integrating into Marxist theory something entirely new in history. This new state and society were not working-class in any previously understood sense — as Trotsky himself put it, "the realities of soviet life [could] be hardly reconciled even with the shreds of old theory" — and not capitalist either. Almost to the very end — and then, in September-October 1939, he made only tentative moves to a rectification — Trotsky was like a man trying to find his way in unknown territory, using a map of another, radically different, terrain.

He saw Stalinism as in transition either to capitalism like that in, say, China, or Turkey, or to a regenerated workers' state — but not as a distinct system viable, beyond maybe a few years, in its existing form. He refused to give it a 'static' label — or identify it as a distinct socio-economic formation. He described the "system of Bonapartist gangsterism" and developed a working-class programme to fight its rulers, but on the level of theory had not, so to speak, recognised its distinct character. The rupturing of the forms of nationalised economy would lead to the first alternative, capitalism; the rupturing of the political form, bureaucratic rule, to the second, regeneration of the workers' state.

Stalinism in the Soviet Union would last six and a half decades. Trotsky's work covered its first decade and a half. It is not surprising that he left the work of analysing a new and unexpected socio-economic formation uncompleted at his death. Contrast Trotsky's situation as he analysed Stalinism with Marx's as he analysed capitalism 90 years before. When Marx began to analyse capitalist society in the 1840s, capitalism had existed in varying forms and phases and in different countries for perhaps 400 years (Marx's own dating, in *Capital*). Industrial capitalism was 70 years old. Capitalism had produced its own revolution in Holland (16th century), England (17th century), America and France (18th century). The class struggles within capitalism had a long history. Capitalism had a large body of political, social and economic theory; the working class had already created its first mass movement (Chartism, in Britain at the end of the 1830s and in the 1840s). In 1831 the silk-workers seized the city of Lyons, in France, and held it for a while.

Trotsky, however, faced a Stalinist system which came into being and developed in a short time — in all its unexpectedness, and operating by its adaptation to its own purposes of old ways and by the transmutation into their opposites of old forms, some bearing a formal resemblance to what the October Revolution had created. It had arisen within the working-class state of the October Revolution, heavily disguised and bearing its own form of nationalised economy which it established by way of conquest of the economic forms set up by the revolution. Scrupulously recording the facts of bureaucratic rule, Trotsky spent 17 years until his death wrestling with the contradictions between those facts and socialist norms and the perspectives of the October Revolution.

VIII: PROGRAMME AND ANALYSIS

TROTSKY DENOUNCED STALINISM with unequalled acuteness. He developed an adequate working-class programme of action against it. Why should the general theoretical definition — "degenerated workers' state" or otherwise — matter?

Central to the power of the Russian bureaucracy in its international political operation was its credibility as the leadership of a still-alive Russian workers' Revolution. Therefore analysis of Russia, as it evolved and mutated in the 1920s and '30s, was central to the work of marginalised Bolshevism in rebuilding a mass revolutionary international. So long as the USSR's "communist" credentials remained good with the revolutionary workers, the Trotskyists would not be a force in the labour movement. Their failure to grasp early the fact that a new class ruled — that despite appearances and despite the nationalised property, the USSR had nothing to do with working-class rule — was an immense weakness. It led to wholesale desertion from the ranks of the Russian Left Opposition in 1928-30, and it would make competition for the allegiance of revolutionary workers extraordinarily difficult for a Trotskyist movement which believed that despite everything it had a vast common ground with the Stalinists in defence of the Soviet Union. On the eve of Trotsky's death a new twist, in response to a new stage of self-assertion by the new Stalinist ruling class — the beginning of Russian imperialist expansion, at first in alliance with Hitler's Germany — would rip apart the Trotskyist movement, and set in motion a process that would change the meaning of words and symbols in a way that paralleled the changes that Stalinism had wrought in the vocabulary and perspectives of the 1917 revolution.

Revolutionary Marxism is more than a socialist programme: it is a series of broad historical perspectives based on analysis and research. On the accuracy of those analyses ultimately depends the intellectual validity of the revolutionary socialist programme. Without Marx's analysis of capitalism, in which he uncovered the mechanisms of exploitation within relations of legal equality between capitalist and worker, socialism would still be only an inchoate yearning for a better world. Stalin's "second revolution" of 1928-30 shaped the USSR for the next 60 years. Trotsky interpreted it as a continuation and development of 1917. This enormous error generated over a decade, and after Trotsky's death five decades, of theoretical disorientation and historical misunderstanding. Much of it persists, long after the collapse of the USSR. It led to an irresoluble contradiction between Trotsky's accurate and probing concrete descriptions of the USSR and his theoretical paradigm that the USSR was a degenerated workers' state.

From the 1920s to long after Trotsky's death, those who shared his view that the Stalin regime preserved the "gains" or "remains" of October found themselves ambivalent towards Stalinism. At root this was because of the nature of Stalinism itself. It was anti-capitalist: at the end of the 1920s it annihilated the pro-capitalist forces. In the 1940s and 1950s it wiped out capitalism in many countries. Stalinism's Trotskyist critics were driven into embodying two incongruous political personalities — that of the advocate and defender of the existing working class, in the USSR and outside, and that of the proponent of a broad historical perspective of anti-capitalist revolution, in which the Stalinist rulers were for now the custodians of the October Revolution, and later of other revolutions which created as much as was said to "remain" of October. The Stalinist rulers, who savagely oppressed and exploited the workers, were nonetheless, in their role of custodians or creators of nationalised property, part of the world revolution. Until the workers got rid of them, even they had to be "defended" against capitalism.

Trotsky saw the nationalised property as post-capitalist in form, less than advanced-capitalist in content, and shackled by the bureaucracy. At the heart of this contradictory system stood an ineradicable antagonism between the bureaucracy and the proletariat. Because of this contradiction, planning was vitiated. The bureaucrats ruled and planned "with all the lights out", in a system deprived of democratic self-monitoring and self-rule. The Stalinist terror functioned as a crude substitute instrument of control, dynamism and monitoring.

It was not enough to have a programme of action against the bureaucracy: the system needed to be explained, to have its real relationship to both capitalism and socialism, to the bourgeoisie and to the proletariat, and its place in historical evolution worked out and established. Nothing was what it was proclaimed to be.

The Stalinist system dressed up as the Russian workers' revolution departed most from the goals and purposes of old socialism where it seemed most to realise the methods and techniques — nationalisation for example — that socialism had advocated. Real Marxism needed to be starkly separated from the "Marxism" with which, confusingly, it seemed to share so much — the "official Marxism" of obfuscations and scholasticism purveyed by Stalinism. The Stalinist lies, and their systematic reversal of the meaning of all the terms in real Marxism, needed to be dissected and analysed. The precise points at which Stalinism parted company with unfalsified Marxism had to be clearly established; the joints at which interests alien to the working class had been grafted on to old Marxist anti-capitalist concepts located. Much of the work of Marxism was a matter of uncovering lies and falsifications and establishing on the level of plain fact the reality of the USSR, measured against Marxist theory, working-class programme and socialist purpose. The secret of how out of "common ownership" there came not socialism but this system of state tyranny had to be uncovered.

Trotsky was close to the end of his life before the problem as posed by history — the Stalinist USSR as a distinct system in its own right — was posed by him clearly: almost all his theoretical work on the Soviet Union took for granted the framework in which regression to capitalism was seen as the alternative to a new socialist revolution. He did not adequately define and characterise the social mutation that actually existed.

Faced with a new social system in the USSR Trotsky pictured it, explored its oppressions and its real meaning for working people in their day-to-day lives. He opposed to Stalin's system a working-class programme: essentially, the 1917 programme of the Bolsheviks. He put down the elements of an analysis like pin-points on a board, but did not draw the lines between the points that would make an adequate theoretical outline of the Stalinist system. In fact, in articles like "The Theory of Degeneration" and "The Bonapartist Philosophy", and in his book *The Revolution Betrayed*, he portrayed the Stalinist USSR clearly as the new system it was; but he never, until the eve of his death and then only hypothetically, defined it as such[8]. In 1936 he depicted the real relationship between the "legal" owners of state property, the workers, and its political "owners", the bureaucrats who "owned" the state. But he drew back from

8. In "The USSR in War" (September 1939) and "Again and once more..." (October 1939).

the conclusion plainly indicated by what he wrote. He was not allowed to live long enough to draw that conclusion, though he unmistakably moved towards it.

At the end of his life he still saw Stalinism in terms of other social formations — capitalism, socialism — and only tentatively, and as if through a shifting mist, as what it really was, something distinct both from capitalism and from socialism: distinct from capitalism, although the bureaucracy was exploitative; and distinct from working-class socialism, although it was anti-capitalist and, in its own bureaucratic way, collectivist.

Much of Trotsky at the end is unclear and self-contradictory. This led to a split that would define two very different "Trotskyisms" in the years after Trotsky's death. The roots of that split lay in the conflicting elements that had accumulated to the point of unmanageable contradiction in Trotsky's view of the USSR. Russia's role at the outbreak of the Second World War brought it to a head. Trotsky's heirs, after his assassination in August 1940, inherited theoretical chaos in a world undergoing changes that would shape it to the end of the twentieth century.

One reason why Trotsky at the end is "difficult" and confusing on this question is, I think, that he sometime shifts from one framework to another, and does not always make it plain — if it was always clear to him — what framework he is using. He had changed his framework for viewing the USSR substantially several times — around 1929-30; around 1933; around 1936 — and at the end was tentatively proposing yet another framework.

Trotsky had responded to each new stage, each new event, each new horror and outrage, with protests, analysis, proposals for labour movement action. He advocated revolution. But until the Stalinist status quo was disrupted by bourgeois counter-revolution or a new workers' "political" revolution — until then, the USSR remained a degenerated workers' state. Even when Trotsky believed the autocracy had become an absolute brake on the economy, it remained the supervisor of the military defence of the USSR, for its own self-interested reasons and in its own way, and in that sense it remained relatively progressive against any capitalist forces.

Time after time in the 1930s, Trotsky expected that the Stalinist system simply could not go on. The system was not — and, he thought, could not be — stable. We know now that it would survive Trotsky for half a century, and spread nationalised property in various ways, or inspire its spread, to a further one-sixth of the globe, and to vastly greater populations than the USSR's. Trotsky's position committed those who agreed with him to "defend" the USSR as it became an expansionary imperialist power and to defend the regimes it set up in Eastern Europe, first as a junior partner of Hitler (August 1939 to June 1941); then as a less junior partner of Britain and the USA (1941-45); and finally, after the fall of Hitler's Reich, as the greatest power in Europe and one of the two great powers of the world — a predatory, looting, savagely repressive, worker-enslaving, backward, ultra-reactionary empire. In fact, despite all that had changed, it was an empire strangely like the Tsarist empire, as Marx had known and loathed it, in its relationship to Europe.

Given Trotsky's baseline criteria for classifying the USSR, he was tied to that "workers' state", however degenerated, reactionary, or imperialistic it might be. To put it crudely, so long as the USSR was imperialist on the basis of nationalised property, it was not imperialist — or, anyway, not quite like reactionary capitalist imperialism. As the horrors piled up, culminating, with the Hitler-Stalin pact, in the eruption of Stalin's bureaucratic imperialism, the outlines of Trotsky's theory again and again were stretched out of shape to accommodate the dogma that this, whatever it was, remained a workers' state, and progressive so long as nationalised property was preserved. Trotsky, of course, did not think that system could last. Expecting, at point after point, the rupturing of the USSR, Trotsky was by the end disoriented — for example in his comments on the Stalinist invasion of Finland — and he must have known and felt it.

His followers, in the movement he founded to continue the work of the early Communist International, would be derailed by the survival of the Stalinist system — and its expansion as a revolutionary anti-capitalist force. If Trotsky's position on the USSR was correct, then "orthodox" neo-Trotskyism — with its ineradicable tendency to assume the role of loyal liberal critic to various Stalinist regimes — followed logically and necessarily. Who says A and B and so on to the 19th letter of the alphabet must then say the rest — or change the alphabet.

Trotsky was by the end reduced to defending his position with the argument that it would be "ridiculous" to append to the Stalinist bureaucracy and the system in which it ruled the designation of a new class society just a few years or months before its collapse.

But the system did last, and it did expand. The "orthodox" neo-Trotskyists arrived reluctantly — those who survived the ideological rocks and rapids of the strange voyage — at absurdities and ideological inversions that sometimes compounded the absurdities of Stalinism itself and, anyway, paralleled and "Trotskyised" them. They arrived at the idea of — "for now" — progressive Stalinism.

When history provided neither capitalist counter-revolution nor working-class "political" revolution, the only way out of this *reductio ad absurdum*, and the destruction by accommodation to Stalinism of the norms and parameters of socialism, was to find the original error in the calculations and to go back and learn to see the Stalinist system for what it was, a unique socio-economic formation — to reconceptualise the USSR.

IX. DISSOLVING BEING INTO BECOMING

TROTSKY'S FIRST DETAILED attempt to square the fact of the USSR as a bureaucratic tyranny with the concept of it as a workers' state was in an article of October 1933, "The Class Nature of the Soviet State". In it he codified and developed all the main ideas that would inform his polemics on this issue up to his death; though, over the next six or seven years, he would radically shift the balance and meaning of many of the terms of the theory. At the end the content of what he said would be radically different, though the terms remained the same. Through the 1930s, Trotsky stretched the meaning of the old terms again and again until by the end his theory was very difficult to understand. He maintained an increasingly fictitious continuity by a method which resembled the medieval art of palimpsestry — writing new content into an old text.

Trotsky's starting-point in the October 1933 article is the fact that, since the German Communist Party's collapse without a fight after Hitler's coming to power in January 1933, he believes that the Communist International must now be written off as a potentially revolutionary working-class force. The genuine Bolsheviks must seek to build new parties. But the same Stalinist apparatus rules both the International and the USSR. It is "equally ruinous" in the USSR and in the Communist International. "Isn't it then necessary to recognise the simultaneous collapse of the Communist International and the liquidation of the proletarian dictatorship in the USSR?".

Recall that Trotsky has written only a few months before that the USSR "is an almost purely bureaucratic economy" in which industry has "lost the ability to satisfy human wants even to the degree to which it had been accomplished by the less-developed capitalist industry...". And when in the October 1933 article Trotsky discusses the idea that Stalinism is what would be called "bureaucratic collectivism", he does not try to show any immediate factual differences between the Stalinist USSR as it is from "bureaucratic collectivism".

The view of the Social Democrat and ex-Communist Lucien Laurat that the USSR is "neither proletarian nor bourgeois" but "represents an absolutely new type of class organisation, because the bureaucracy not only rules over the proletariat politically but also exploits it economically, devouring that surplus value that hitherto fell to the lot of the bourgeoisie" is, says Trotsky, a "superficial and purely descriptive 'sociology'". He does not deny that it is an accurate description. Contemptuously, Trotsky equates the Social Democratic "compilator" Laurat with "the Russo-Polish revolutionist Makhaisky" who "with much more fire and splendour" had over 30 years previously "define[d] 'the dictatorship of the proletariat' as a scaffold for the commanding posts of an exploiting bureaucracy". Makhaisky "only 'deepened' sociologically and economically the anarchistic prejudices against state socialism". Trotsky does not here distinguish between the USSR under Stalin and the so-called "state socialism" — the regime of a profoundly democratic workers' state — which is the substance of the dispute between Marxists and anarchists. The industrial growth has produced an "economic and cultural uplift of the labouring masses" — this is in fact not true — and that "must tend to undermine the very bases of bureaucratic domination". "In the light of this fortunate historical variant, the bureaucracy turns out to be only the instrument — a bad and expensive instrument — of the socialist state".

Trotsky does not think this will happen gradually. The bureaucracy must be tamed by working-class force, and the USSR working class will assemble the necessary force only under the impulse of working-class revolution in the West.

And in the meantime, the bureaucracy retards the economic and cultural growth of the country. "The further uninhibited growth of bureaucratism must lead inevitably to the cessation of economic and cultural growth, to a terrible social crisis and the downward plunge of the entire society". But bureaucratic domination would end with this collapse. "In place of the workers' state would come not 'social bureaucratic' but capitalist relations". In this way Trotsky defines away the problem of the

USSR as it exists in the year 1933, conjuring it out of existence by logic-chopping with perspectives. Fundamentally, the USSR is a workers' state because it was one in 1917-21; it has not yet reverted to capitalism, and Trotsky is not yet ready to concede the existence in the modern era of a society outside the two main alternatives, bourgeois or workers' rule.

"Whether we take the variant of further successes for the Soviet regime or, contrariwise, the variant of its collapse, the bureaucracy in either case turns out not to be an independent class but an excrescence upon the proletariat".

The idea of the USSR as a product of development and degeneration from 1917, and as heading for either bourgeois counter-revolution or working-class regeneration, has replaced any definition of what it is. This will remain a central characteristic of Trotsky's thinking to the very end. Although in reality the USSR is already in its essentials a stable entity for a meaningful period by the scale of human life, in Trotsky's theory it is a mere moment of ever-changing historical flux. It is as if the moving film is counterposed to the "snapshots" that make it up; Trotsky replaces analysis of being by considerations of becoming and passing out of existence.

Trotsky argues with Laurat not about facts, but about the interpretation of agreed facts and of an agreed picture of the USSR. Laurat's argument about the bureaucracy's "uncontrolled appropriation of an absolutely disproportionate part of the national income" is based on "undubitable facts" but it "does not... change the social physiognomy of the bureaucracy". Decisive in Trotsky's view is the idea that "the bureaucracy derives its privileges not from any special property relations peculiar to it as a 'class', but from those property relations that have been created by the October Revolution and that are fundamentally adequate for the dictatorship of the proletariat". The bureaucracy practises "not... class exploitation, in the scientific sense of the word, but... social parasitism". The "necessity" or otherwise of the bureaucracy's role in the economy should be derived from an account of the society as it is; but Trotsky derives it from the general theory of previous societies, using that general theory against the facts of the USSR he himself has recorded.

X. "THE GATEKEEPER OF THE SOCIAL CONQUESTS"

IF FIRSTLY AND irreplaceably proletarian dictatorship means the political rule of the workers, then Trotsky's writing-off of the Communist International and his picture of the realities of the USSR must tell him that the USSR is no longer a workers' state. He arrives at the opposite answer by changing the meaning of the terms and by postulating, on the basis of the experience of the USSR, that the question of working-class politics is posed after a successful revolution altogether differently from the way it is posed in the class struggle under capitalist rule.

The Communist Parties of the West, he writes, have nothing but themselves, "no inherited capital"; by contrast, "the soviet government represents an instrument for the preservation of conquests of an already accomplished overturn... Nine-tenths of the strength of the Stalinist apparatus lies not in itself but in the social changes wrought by the victorious revolution". This explains how the Stalinist apparatus could still "preserve a part of its progressive meaning as the gatekeeper of the social conquests of the proletarian revolution". By "social conquests" he means nationalised property.

Essentially Trotsky's position now is that the workers' revolution is, so to speak, congealed in the economic forms which Trotsky sees as its product, rather as living labour is congealed in capital.

Why? Trotsky knew the arguments of the Marxist classics against identifying nationalised economy with socialism or working-class rule. For example, Antonio Labriola: "It is better to use the expression 'democratic socialisation of the means of production' than that of 'collective property' because the latter implies a certain theoretical error in that, to begin with, it substitutes for the real economic fact a juridical expression and moreover in the mind of more than one it is confused with the increase of monopolies, with the increasing statisation of public utilities and with all the other fantasmagoria of the ever-recurring State socialism, the whole effect of which is to increase the economic means of oppression in the hands of the oppressing class".[9]

Or James Connolly: "State ownership and control is not necessarily socialist — if it were then the army and the navy, the police, the judges, the gaolers, the informers and the hangmen would all be socialist functionaries, as they are all state officials — but the ownership by the state of all the lands and material for labour, combined with the co-operative control by the workers of such land and materials, would be socialist... To the cry of the middle-class reformers, 'Make this or that the property of the government', we reply — 'Yes, in proportion as the workers are ready to make the government their property'.". This was commonplace Marxism.

Or Karl Kautsky: "The economic activity of the modern state is the natural starting point of the development that leads to the Co-operative Commonwealth. It does not, however, follow that every nationalisation of an econimic function or an industry is a step towards the Co-operative Commonwealth, and that the latter could be the result of a general nationalisation of all industries without any change in the character of the state. The theory that this could be the case is that of the state Socialists. It arises from a misunderstanding of the state itself ... As an exploiter of labour, the state is superior to (i.e. worse than) any private capitalist. Besides the economic power of the capitalists, it can also bring to bear upon the exploited classes the political power which it already wields... The state will not cease to be a capitalist institution until the proletariat, the working class, has become the ruling class; not until then will it become possible to turn it into a Co-operative Commonwealth".[10]

At first, after 1928, Trotsky has seen Stalin's new command economy as a foredoomed desperate administrative attempt to flout the laws of economics and society, certain to collapse quickly. It has not collapsed. Industry has grown. At the same time, western capitalism has spiralled into slump.

Instead of identifying the creation of the totalitarian command economy

9. *In Memory of the Communist Manifesto*, 1895.
10. *Commentary of the Erfurt Programme*, 1891.

as the full social, as well as political, bureaucratic counter-revolution it was, Trotsky, extrapolating the logic of his view in 1923-8 that the neo-bourgeoisie was the main threat, and the Stalinist "centre" dangerous primarily because of its inadequate response to that threat, chooses to interpret the industrial growth of the USSR as an expression of the immanent force of the nationalised economy. He separates agency from means and begins to fetishise means, in a process that will end for Trotskyism in confusing means with ends.

Trotsky is swayed by the weight of the fact that, as he will write in *The Revolution Betrayed*, "The first concentration of the means of production in the hands of the state to occur in history was achieved by the proletariat with the method of social revolution, and not by capitalists with the method of state trustification".

This nationalised economy is a working-class conquest, allowing unique progress. If the state is preserving that nationalised economy, however badly and with whatever overhead costs, it is a workers' state. For his bottom-line argument Trotsky is reduced to vicarious boasting about Stalin's economic achievements, which he attributes to "October". But this picture depends on not giving due weight in the analysis to the part played by the "corps of slave-drivers"[11] and by the driving down of the USSR workers' share of social produce to the subsistence level of ancient serfs and slaves, and, for the enslaved many millions, below that level. It also depends on forgetting or downplaying what Trotsky himself has written: that the USSR's industrial progress is limited to catching up with the advanced capitalist countries — or, rather, reducing the distance by which it lags behind them.

XI. THE END OF CAPITALIST PROGRESS?

TROTSKY'S "OVERESTIMATION" OF the forms of nationalised property is unintelligible unless it is understood as inextricably linked with and dependent on his parallel "underestimation" of capitalism. For Trotsky in the 1930s capitalism was a collapsing system at the end of its historical span.

Marx, in contrast to previous socialists, saw socialism not just as a negation of capitalism but also as something "springing from an existing class struggle, from a historical movement going on under our very eyes"[12]. The working class, he wrote, "have no ideals to realise, but to set free the elements of the new society with which old collapsing bourgeois society itself is pregnant"[13]. In Marx's view, capitalism did progressive work, by producing the elements for socialism — advanced technology, socialised production, an educated working class, able, as a rule, to organise, even if not in full legality.

After World War 1, the communist movement believed that those elements were sufficiently developed to make socialism a short-term possi-

---

11. Trotsky: *The Revolution Betrayed*.
12. Marx: *The Communist Manifesto*.
13. Marx: *Civil War in France*.

bility: capitalism had entered a period of decay. War and crises stopped it advancing and had even begun to destroy some of its previous progressive achievements. Nevertheless, as Lenin remarked, there is no situation without a way out for the bourgeoisie. Capitalism had not reached a dead stop. If the workers failed to seize the opportunities to overthrow capitalism, then, eventually, out of blood, suffering and chaos, capitalism would revive.

Trotsky explained this as late as 1928: "Theoretically, to be sure, even a new chapter of a general capitalist progress in the most powerful, ruling and leading countries is not excluded. But for this, capitalism would first have to overcome enormous barriers of a class as well as of an inter-state character. It would have to strangle the proletarian revolution for a long time ... In the final analysis, this question will be settled in the struggle of international forces."[14]

In the 1930s, however, a blanket "negativism" in relation to capitalism became central to Trotsky's positive appreciation of nationalised economy in the USSR. In *The Transitional Programme* (1938) he would write: "The economic prerequisite for the proletarian revolution has already in general achieved the highest point of fruition that can be reached under capitalism. Mankind's productive forces stagnate... The bourgeoisie itself sees no way out".

In "The USSR in War" (September 1939) he would assert: "The disintegration of capitalism has reached extreme limits, likewise the disintegration of the old ruling class. The further existence of this system is impossible".

The classic studies of Lenin and Bukharin on imperialism had foreseen a rapid development of capitalism in the less-developed countries accompanying crises in the more advanced countries. In the long run they were right, even for the 1930s, where some Third World countries started substantial "import-substitution industrialisation"; but in 1928 the Stalinists made it their official doctrine that imperialism forced total stagnation on those less-developed countries. Trotsky never took issue with the new teaching. If in the 1930s he had seen the industrial growth of countries such as Japan and Mexico as indicating an important and substantial pattern, though limited and on the margins of world capital, that would have put Stalin's economic successes into a more balanced and nuanced perspective; but he never did.

In his last period, this vision would push Trotsky into a sort of "sectarian" anti-capitalism, and later his neo-Trotskyist followers into "unconditional" support for anything — never mind what — that was anti-capitalist.

XII. A "LOCUM" FOR THE WORKING CLASS

THE USSR MUST still be a workers' state, Trotsky argues, because it was established by means of a "political overturn" and three years of civil war. Experience shows that peaceful proletarian revolution is impossible.

---

14. Trotsky: "Strategy and Tactics in the Imperialist Epoch".

"How, in that case, is the imperceptible, 'gradual', bourgeois counter-revolution conceivable?... He who asserts that the soviet government has been gradually changed from proletarian to bourgeois is only, so to speak, running backwards the film of reformism".

Although Trotsky will continue to use this argument to the end, and it will play an immense role in the politics of neo-Trotskyism, he answers it himself in "The Workers' State, Bonapartism, and the Question of Thermidor" (1935). "The present-day domination of Stalin in no way resembles the soviet rule during the initial years of the revolution. The substitution of one regime for the other occurred not at a single stroke but through a series of measures, by means of a number of minor civil wars waged by the bureaucracy against the proletarian vanguard...".

Trotsky asks: how can the dictatorship of the bureaucracy over the proletariat be a form of the dictatorship of the proletariat? The dictatorship of the proletariat is not a pristine norm, but a historical reality, born in backward Russia and evolving in history to what it is, in which can be seen elements of continuity and of rupture. There are no *a priori* recipes for the dictatorship of the proletariat. It is rooted in its own history.

Trotsky declares that the dictatorship of a class "does not mean by a long shot that its entire mass always participates in the management of the state". He makes analogies with the rule of propertied classes — nobles ruling through monarchies, bourgeois ruling through political dictatorships, like fascism, that disenfranchise the bourgeois class. He anticipates the argument that "the bourgeoisie, as an exploiting minority, can also preserve its hegemony by means of a fascist dictatorship, the proletariat building a socialist society must manage its government itself, directly drawing ever-wider masses of the people into the task of government. In its general form this argument is undeniable". But here, he says, it means only "the present soviet dictatorship is a sick dictatorship... the bureaucracy has expropriated the proletariat politically in order to guard its social conquests with its own methods.

The anatomy of society is determined by its economic relations. So long as the forms of property that have been created by the October Revolution are not overthrown, the proletariat remains the ruling class".

In fact the issue is not, as Trotsky states it, only one of involvement of large or small numbers in government. It is fundamentally whether with the existing bureaucratic regime, and the actual place of the working class in the system, the workers can rule at all. Or, to put it another way, whether the "forms of property" actually define the economic relations, or whether new economic relations, shaped by the nature of the political power that controls the socio-economic and political relations, have been created within the formalities of nationalised property.

The Bolsheviks' idea in 1921 that they must act as a "gatekeeper", "watchman" or "locum" for the enfeebled working class, entwined with the new "norms" created when the Bolsheviks made virtue out of the exigencies of the civil war and the economic collapse in 1921, still grips and distorts Trotsky's vision even now that, on his own account: "The party does not exist" and anti-working class careerists and political turncoats rule.

He dismisses "dissertations upon 'the dictatorship of the bureaucracy over the proletariat' [which] without a much deeper analysis, that is, without a clear explanation of the social roots and the class limits of bureaucratic domination, boil down merely to high-faluting democratic phrases so extremely popular among the Mensheviks". He goes on to assert that soviet workers, though they hate the bureaucracy, fail to resort to violent mass action not simply because of repression: "The workers fear that they will clear the field for the class enemy if they overthrow the bureaucracy". So long as revolution does not come in the West, "the proletariat with clenched teeth bears ('tolerates') the bureaucracy and, in this sense, recognises it as the bearer of the proletarian dictatorship... No soviet worker would be sparing of strong words addressed to the Stalinist bureaucracy. But not a single one of them [!] would admit that the counter-revolution has already taken place. The proletariat is the spine of the soviet state.."

Here, quite fantastically, he argues from a reluctant acquiescence by the workers to Stalinism which is unknowable to him; which must seem highly spurious to us; and which anyway is not decisive. Many bourgeois-democratic regimes have been grudgingly tolerated, or even positively supported, by the majority of workers — without being workers' states. Trotsky's argument grossly and strangely minimises the power of the fierce Stalinist repression, undervalues the power of the state, and takes away the significance of the atomisation of the working class — *sans* party, *sans* soviets, *sans* unions — all of which he himself already records.

Trotsky will use this idea of the bureaucracy resting on the workers, and ideas of working-class opinion being a force in the Soviet Union, far into the 1930s, as the Stalinist system reveals its most terrible features in purges and Nazi-like mass terror. It will add an element of ideological consolation, giving a flickering aureole to his bedrock, all-else-stripped-away definition of the workers' state: nationalised property, plan, and monopoly of foreign trade, allegedly rooted in the October Revolution but in its present form the creation of Stalin's "second revolution" after 1928.

In July 1936 ("The Fourth International and the Soviet Union") he will write that "the soviet bureaucracy has acquired an actual independence from the toilers... the new constitution liquidates *de jure* the ruling position of the proletariat in the state, a position which, *de facto*, has long been liquidated"; yet in *The Revolution Betrayed*, written around the same time, he asserts that "the bureaucracy... continues to preserve state property only to the extent that it fears the proletariat".[15] As late as 1938 he will write about how "the discontent of the masses produces different currents even in the bureaucracy... the pressure of the masses produces disintegration in the ruling caste"[16]; even in 1940 he will discuss the politics of the USSR's invasion of Finland in terms of the majority of the population disapproving of the invasion but "understanding" or at least "feeling" that "behind the Finnish question... stands the problem of the existence of the USSR", which they would want to defend.

In 1933, Trotsky insists that the autocracy is a bad locum for the working class. "The bureaucracy in all its manifestations is pulling apart the moral tie-rods of soviet society". If the Marxist party were in power, "it

---

15. In part the flat meaning-of-words contradiction here is only apparent. Trotsky frequently talks of the relation of the autocracy to the nationalised property as its relation to the proletariat. The autocracy can be utterly independent from the actual living workers and simultaneously subordinated to the proletariat as a historical concept because it is tied to "proletarian" nationalised property.
16. *Writings 1937-8*, p.303

would renovate the entire political regime; it would shuffle and purge the bureaucracy and place it under the control of the masses; it would transform all of the administrative practices and inaugurate a series of capital reforms in the management of economy; but in no case would it have to undertake an overturn in the property relations, i.e., a new social revolution".

Considering the scope of the rectification, whose scale will have to be commensurate with the abuses Trotsky has repeatedly described, the question of whether the "property relations" would be the same afterwards arises. Trotsky means the forms of property: nationalised or private. The point is that the class content of nationalised property would change with the changes he proposes. But Trotsky defuses the concrete questions concerning what is by discussing what will be. He will do it again and again throughout the 1930s.

Trotsky asserts that "the further development of the bureaucratic regime can lead to the inception of a new ruling class; not organically, through degeneration, but through counter-revolution". This will be his perspective to the end of the 1930s, when he will expect the culmination of Stalin's bloody work to be the "guillotining" of Stalin by the bourgeois counter-revolution he has incubated. "Today, when there is no longer a Marxist leadership, and none forthcoming as yet", the Stalinist bureaucracy "defends the proletarian dictatorship with its own methods; but these methods are such as to facilitate the victory of the enemy tomorrow". The Stalinist bureaucratic centre is a vile and destructive locum for the working class, but a locum it is and will remain so long as it preserves nationalised property and the working class has not overthrown it.

XIII. PROPERTY FORMS AND SOCIALIST NORMS

ONE CENTRAL ARGUMENT in the 1933 article — about "norms" — is developed more vigorously in "The Workers' State, Bonapartism and the Question of Thermidor" (1935). There, Trotsky concedes: "There is no doubt that the USSR today bears very little resemblance to that type of soviet republic that Lenin depicted in 1917... The domination of the bureaucracy over the country, as well as Stalin's domination over the bureaucracy, have well-nigh attained their absolute consummation". Some say "that since the actual state that has emerged from the proletarian revolution does not correspond to ideal *a priori* norms, therefore they turn their backs on it. This is political snobbery, common to pacifist-democratic, libertarian, anarcho-syndicalist and, generally, ultra-left circles of the petty-bourgeois intelligentsia". Their mirror-images, Trotsky adds, consider criticism of the state coming out of the revolution to be "sacrilege and counter-revolution"; these are the hypocrites.

Why can only a slave to *a priori* norms, or a sniffy historical snob, baulk at accepting as a workers' state this USSR in which on Trotsky's own account the working class is in a condition close to serfdom? Trotsky himself holds to the "norms" and will base his political conclusions on them. What is he doing? As on this entire question, Trotsky combines immense lucidity in close-up and detail with dark obfuscation in the broad picture.

He is teaching to later Trotskyists a philistine spirit of accomodation to Stalinism and other malign social forms, which he himself does not have — because he has an immense background of experience and political culture, and because, as we shall see, he interprets the USSR not as a coherent system, still less in later neo-Trotskyist terms as in transition to socialism, but as a freakish combination of elements in rapid flux. The condemnation of "norms" will, alas, be a major element in what he bequeaths to followers who will have to define themselves politically in relation to a solid and expanding Stalinist system and who thus need the norms as a man drowning in a raging tide needs a life belt, and to whom he can bequeath neither his own breadth of vision and knowledge nor his skill at dialectical tightrope-walking. Trotsky thinks he is teaching historical perspective and objectivity and dialectics; he cannot conceive of the Stalinist reality that his comrades after 1940 will encounter, because he cannot conceive of Stalinism surviving for decades.

In his denunciations of "normative" thinking, Trotsky begs the central question. Is it true that this USSR concretely expresses the essence which the old abstract socialist norms sought to describe? Does it render the old-norms more real, more precise and more concrete to any degree at all, or does it shatter them and negate them and establish other norms? On Trotsky's own account, "the realities of soviet life [can] be hardly reconciled even with the shreds of old theory". The social relations — in the proper sense, that is, the relations between people — "in many respects are still lagging behind a cultured capitalism". The old socialist norms are fully rounded social norms, norms of culture, manners, morals, intellect. They embody the achievements of civilisation and the historical contribution of capitalism, and not only economics. Trotsky here reduces the essential "norm" of a workers' state to the purely economic, and within that to aridly abstract forms of property. He will show in *The Revolution Betrayed* that the concrete economic relations within those abstract forms are "a ruthlessly severe fitting in of backward human material to the technique borrowed from capitalism" and "the classic methods of exploitation... in such naked and crude forms as would not be permitted even by reformist trade unions in bourgeois countries". The only possible point of contact between Marxian socialist norms and USSR reality is the nationalised property forms. But in the Stalinist USSR those forms do not arise organically from capitalist development — as they should, if they are to play the role ascribed to them in previous Marxist theory. With the exception of the 1917-18 takeover of big industry — which the Bolsheviks were pushed into by working-class direct action when the old owners sabotaged production or simply quit — they arise from the drive of the autocracy to grab the whole of the surplus product of society.

In the 1933 article Trotsky "asks" — and the proper "answer" is clear; it can be read off from the most obvious surface facts — whether the "distortions" from the programmatic norms "have extended to the economic foundation". By "economic foundation" he means only the forms of nationalised property, considered in abstraction from the relations within them. Here Trotsky has elevated a caricature of one of the old socialist norms, nationalised property, out of the whole complex of other norms that give it its significance in Marxist theory.

The result is not a replacement of abstract and normative theorising by a more concrete approach. It is the opposite. In his polemics, Trotsky establishes a new norm — nationalised property — and argues "normatively" from that. He extrapolates the new norm from the experience of the USSR. There is here too, as on the question of the party, a dualism in Trotsky. For he holds these ideas about the USSR in parallel to the older socialist ideas about the rest of the world. The question is what it has to do with socialism. Trotsky complains that the "normative" thinkers want to turn their backs on reality and proceed according to ideal schemes in their heads. But Trotsky, too, wants to escape the reality and "begin again" — begin with the fiction that there is something of workers' rule left in the USSR, that the unspeakable tyranny is really something else deep down, in the form of its bureaucratic economy. Trotsky can only relate to the reality by way of constructing an ideal parallel of it in his head, and then defining the reality as a more-and-more distorted version of that ideal.

Though Trotsky still writes about the "roots" of the bureaucracy among the soviet workers, he has by now elaborated a baseline method of assessing the class character of the USSR that can only be called "totalitarian economism". One "factor", the nationalisation of the means of production, is valued for its "achievements", its progressive potential and its ascribed place in history, in abstraction from all that in Marxist, socialist or Bolshevik theory had so far been understood to determine the class character of a state — the political regime and the social relations erected on the nationalised means of production.

As a working-class politician, Trotsky is concerned with the real socio-economic relations in his concrete programme. He paints painfully clear and true pictures of what they are in the USSR. When he makes his theoretical summaries, however, he leaves them aside. The two parts of the picture do not match. He thinks they will match up in the flux of events, in the near future. His theory thus rests heavily on the idea that the USSR in the 1930s is not any sort of coherent system, but only a temporary concatenation of conflicting elements moving rapidly in different directions.

In the 1933 article Trotsky also erects a dual conception of working-class politics, destroying previous Marxist norms on this question. For the task of making a working-class revolution against capitalism, clear ideas and a party organised around those ideas are essential. The proletariat does not gain power, property, wealth and culture bit by bit — as the bourgeoisie did in feudal society — but remains the basic slave class, the prime source of the social surplus product, of the society it must overturn.

The proletarian revolution is not a mechanical reflex or outgrowth of even the conditions most ripe for it. That is why ideas, consciousness, programme, politics and voluntary organisation are decisive for the working-class revolution, and are at the heart of Bolshevik-Marxist politics.

This is the keynote idea of Lenin's and Trotsky's Communist International and the guide to everything Trotsky did in the 1930s to rebuild a revolutionary movement. But — so Trotsky now argues — having once taken power, the working class can lose direct political power, and yet retain social power. If the "social conquests" of the revolution survive, then the working class rules in the broad historical sense, even when the living and producing working class is in thraldom to a dictatorship of parasitic, privileged and slave-driving bureaucrats. In this argument is the seed of the later neo-Trotskyist idea that "working-class" revolutions could be made in China or Eastern Europe by brutally anti-working-class forces.

XIV. "POLITICAL REVOLUTION": FIRST APPROXIMATION

TRYING TO KEEP a balance between his recognition of the bureaucracy as a "locum" for the working class, and his condemnation of its tyranny and "parasitism", Trotsky spells out the political conclusions. "Is it possible to remove the bureaucracy 'peacefully'?... After the experience of the last few years it would be childish to suppose that the Stalin bureaucracy can be removed by means of a Party or soviet congress". The last real congress of the Bolshevik party, Trotsky writes, was the 12th at the beginning of 1923; by saying so, he seems to concede that with hindsight his present conclusions are overdue and should have been drawn soon after 1923.

No normal 'constitutional' ways to remove the ruling clique remain. The bureaucracy can be compelled to yield power into the hands of the proletarian vanguard only by force". Trotsky recalls that in 1927 Stalin had said that his "cadres" could be removed only by civil war. "Having concentrated all the levers in its hands, the bureaucracy proclaimed openly that it would not permit the proletariat to raise its head any longer".

But "the question of seizing power will arise as a practical question for [the Opposition] only when it will have consolidated around itself the majority of the working class". And the new revolution — Trotsky does not yet use the word "revolution" — will be "not an armed insurrection against the dictatorship of the proletariat but the removal of a malignant growth upon it. A real civil war could develop not between the Stalinist bureaucracy and the resurgent proletariat but between the proletariat and the active forces of the counter-revolution. In the event of an open clash between the two mass camps, there cannot even be talk of the bureaucracy playing an independent role. Its polar flanks would be flung to the different sides of the barricade". A new Bolshevik party is the essential condition for working-class victory.

This perspective, saturated with the idea of the bureaucracy as an insubstantial force, of no real substance in comparison to the "two mass camps" of bourgeois (peasant-based) counter-revolution and working-class revolution, is not very different from Trotsky's outlook when he stated his aim as reform. Then there would be crisis and a recomposition of the Bolshevik party, with the "return" of the Opposition; now, the Opposition is to be a separate party. All avenues via reform or self-recomposition of the dispersed and fragmented Bolshevik party are closed. But it still fears "spontaneity".

Struggle will decide whether a new party can be built in time to avert collapse brought on by the bureaucratic burrowing and "sapping" at the foundations of the regime. If there is a further decline of the world proletarian movement and further extension of fascist domination, "it is not possible to maintain the soviet power for any length of time by means of the internal forces alone. The fundamental condition for the only rock-bottom reform of the soviet state is the victorious spread of the world revolution". At this point, in 1933, Trotsky believes that the conditions outside the USSR are ripe for a large-scale regroupment of revolutionary forces in a Fourth International. The idea of the small forces of Trotskyism just proceeding to set up the Fourth International by themselves he sees now as absurd. He warns that no regeneration of the USSR will come from internal developments alone, without a big Fourth International being built in the West. Recalling the evidence in the Russian Stalinist press of Left Opposition activities there, Trotsky warns: "Illusions would be out of place here; the party of revolutionary internationalism will be able to free the workers from the decomposing influence of the national bureaucracy only in the event that the international proletarian vanguard will once again appear as a fighting force on the world arena". The Russian Bolshevik-Leninists cannot lead this revival. "The extremely difficult conditions under which the Russian Bolshevik-Leninists work exclude them from the possibility of playing the leading role on an international scale. More than this, the Left Opposition group in the USSR can develop into a new party only as a result of the successful formation and growth of the new International. The revolutionary centre of gravity has shifted definitively to the West, where the immediate possibilities of building parties are immeasurably greater".

XV. THE UNITED FRONT WITH STALIN

WHAT IF NO big Fourth International is built? In that case, Trotsky writes, working-class actions in the USSR — mass strikes — are likely to lead to counter-revolution rather than regeneration. "Under the conditions of the transitional epoch, the political superstructure" — even the Stalinist locum of the 1920s Bolshevik locum — "plays a decisive role. A developed and stable dictatorship of the proletariat presupposes that the party functions in the leading role as a self-acting vanguard, that the proletariat is welded together by means of trade unions, that the toilers are indissolubly bound up with the state through the system of soviets and, finally, that the workers' state is aligned through the International into a fighting unit with the world proletariat. In the meantime, the bureaucracy has strangled the party and the trade unions and the soviets and the Communist International... The strangulation of the party, the soviets and the trade unions implies the political atomisation of the proletariat...

"The first social shock, external or internal, may throw the atomised soviet society into civil war. The workers, *having lost control over the state and economy* (emphasis added), may resort to mass strikes as weapons of self-defence. The discipline of the dictatorship would be broken. Under the onslaught of the workers and because of the pressure of economic difficulties, the trusts would be forced to disrupt the planned beginnings and enter into competition with one another... The socialist state would collapse, giving place to the capitalist regime or, more correctly, to capitalist chaos". The proletariat, which can rule under Stalin, cannot take back full power without a proper Bolshevik Party...

Trotsky is cautious. Just as there was much of "revolution" in Trotsky's calls for "reform" of the USSR, so too now that he is for a new party in the USSR and advocates an early version of "political revolution" (though the name is three years in the future), there are still large elements of the old "reformism": "Today the rupture of the bureaucratic equilibrium in the USSR would almost surely serve in favour of the counter-revolutionary forces. However, given a genuine revolutionary International, the inevitable crisis of the Stalinist regime would open the possibility of revival in the USSR. This is our basic course". This vision, common to Trotsky's "reform" and to the early "political revolution" periods points up the enormity of the shift when Trotsky will call for a working class onslaught on that apparatus in conditions where its replacement is open-ended and problematic. This will be a call for full-scale revolution, the name "political revolution" notwithstanding.

"Correct evaluation of the world situation, including the class nature of the Soviet Union" is essential to the work of rebuilding the revolutionary movement. The new International, "before it will be able to reform the soviet state... must take upon itself its defence... the tragic possibility is not excluded that the first workers' state, weakened by the bureaucracy, will fall under the joint blows of its internal and external enemies. But in the event of this worst possible variant, a tremendous significance for the subsequent course of the revolutionary struggle will be borne by the question: where are those guilty for the catastrophe? Not the slightest trace of guilt must fall upon the revolutionary internationalists. In the hour of mortal danger, they must remain on the last barricade". In "the inevitable crisis of the Stalinist regime... the new International will demonstrate to the Russian workers not in words but in action that it, and it alone, stands for the defence of the workers' state... The position of the Bolshevik-Leninists inside the Soviet Union will change within twenty-four hours. The new International will offer the Stalinist bureaucracy a united front against the common foe. And if our International represents a force, the bureaucracy will be unable to evade the united front in the moment of danger. What then will remain of the many years' encrustation of lies and slander?".

Examine the flux of Trotsky's reasonings, the patterns of his polemical swordplay, and it becomes plain that he is using the method of provisional estimation, empirical calculation matched — or for now not quite matched — to theory, dancing on the rolling, bobbing logs in the flow of politics and history. He has more than one concern in his head. It is plain that he sees and understands the arguments against his theoretical conclusions, that his rebuttals and rejections are provisional and conditional, subject to further experience and the test of the political line. His first preoccupation is always with living politics, grasping links in a chain of development, seeking openings and leverage points. In 1927, in the Politburo, Trotsky had proclaimed what became known as the "Clemenceau thesis". (The patriotic French imperialist Georges Clemenceau had bitterly opposed the French Government after 1914 in order to win control and prosecute the war more effectively, which he did.) For the socialist fatherland — Yes! For the Stalinist course — No!

Right up to his death, a variant of this perspective would remain his basic practical conclusion from the "degenerated workers' state" theory. Over the years he would hugely modify the proportions of different elements in this perspective, and implicitly concede that the 1933 version, of "the many years' encrustation of lies and slander" melting away within twenty-four hours, was unreal; but the basic line would remain. One way or another — whether by palace coups, invasion, peasant uprisings, or workers' strikes — the USSR would be thrown into a crisis, facing internal counter-revolution and, probably, foreign armies. The bureaucracy would fall apart. A new leadership, formed by allying the persecuted Bolshevik-Leninists with a fraction of the apparatus, would take the lead and simultaneously repel counter-revolution and, by breaking the old bureaucratic encrustation, regenerate the soviets and the workers' state, and recompose the international communist movement. The political line of "defence of the workers' state" would be essential because otherwise the Bolshevik-Leninists will be left on the sidelines in the crisis. As the years go on, Trotsky would accumulate doubts and qualifications about this perspective, but insist that it should not be renounced unless absolutely hard evidence — he thought the coming world war would, one way or another, provide it — made that necessary; for to renounce it would mean that definitively the Marxists were back at the stage of building a new movement from scratch among the ruins of the old. Five years later, when his picture of the autocracy as having most of the features of a ruling class had become very much sharper, he would sum up the perspective in the founding programme of the Fourth International (September 1938).

"From this perspective [of a powerful section of the bureaucracy, as Trotsky saw it, desiring bourgeois restoration], impelling concreteness is imparted to the question of the 'defence of the USSR'. If tomorrow the bourgeois-fascist grouping, the [fascistic] 'faction of Butenko', so to speak, should attempt the conquest of power, the [Trotskyist] 'faction of Reiss' inevitably would align itself on the opposite side of the barricades". Butenko was a bureaucrat who had defected to fascist Italy; Reiss, a GPU officer who came out for Trotsky in 1937 and was very soon afterwards murdered, in Switzerland, by the Stalinists. "Although it [the "Reiss faction"] would find itself temporarily the ally of Stalin, it would nevertheless defend not the Bonapartist clique but the social base of the USSR... Any other course would be a betrayal... It is thus impermissible to deny in advance the possibility, in strictly defined instances, of a 'united front' with the Thermidorian section of the bureaucracy against open attack by capitalist counter-revolution." (The "Thermidorian section" here means that section of the bureaucracy with origins in the Bolshevik party of 1917, by analogy with the "Thermidorians" in the French Revolution, Jacobins who overthrew Robespierre in July 1794 and then found themselves overtaken by open big-bourgeois reaction).

Here Trotsky is trying to prefigure mentally how to "grasp the links in the chain". From it we can get a pretty firm indication that Trotsky would not have been an "orthodox" neo-Trotskyist — not a platonic revolutionary spinning "working class" fantasies around the expansion of Stalinist "revolution". But, nonetheless, the united front he proposes here is in fact one between the enslaving class and its victims. For Trotsky it is a means of reducing the enslavers to nothing; but with the survival of the bureaucracy and the eruption of Stalinist imperialist expansion in 1939-40, as we shall see, it became a way of reducing independent working-class politics to nothing.

XVI. THE "WORKERS' STATE" THEORY AND
POLITICAL REVOLUTION

IN 1936, FROM his comprehensive denunciation of the Stalinist regime in *The Revolution Betrayed*, Trotsky deduces an equally comprehensive programme. He now uses the term "political revolution". "Bureaucratic autocracy must give place to soviet democracy. A restoration of the right of criticism, and a genuine freedom of elections, are necessary conditions for the further development of the country. This assumes a revival of freedom of soviet parties, beginning with the party of Bolsheviks, and a resurrection of the trade unions. The bringing of democracy into industry means a radical revision of plans in the interests of the toilers. Free discussion of economic problems will decrease the overhead expense of bureaucratic mistakes and zig-zags. Expensive playthings — palaces of the soviets, new theatres, show-off subways — will be crowded out in favour of workers' dwellings. 'Bourgeois norms of distribution' will be confined within the limits of strict necessity, and, in step with the growth of social wealth, will give way to socialist equality. Ranks will be immediately abolished. The tinsel of decorations will go into the melting pot. The youth will receive the opportunity to breathe freely, criticise, make mistakes, and grow up. Science and art will be freed of their chains. And, finally, foreign policy will return to the traditions of revolutionary internationalism."

In substance here Trotsky is calling for full revolution. By doing so he shows, surely, that nationalised property characterises not just one social and economic system, but at least two — depending on the social-political context and on the political rulership. The revolution is "political" only in the sense that there will be continuity of nationalised property — but which nationalised property? Everything Trotsky proposes says it will not be the same nationalised property.

Moreover, Trotsky himself writes that "a bourgeois restoration would probably have to clean out fewer people than a revolutionary party", while in the July 1936 "theses" on The Fourth International and the Soviet Union he has written that "The new constitution [of 1936] seals the dictatorship of the privileged strata of soviet society over the producing masses... [it] opens up for the bureaucracy 'legal' roads for the economic counter-revolution, that is, the restoration of capitalism by means of a 'cold stroke'.". Momentarily Trotsky has abandoned an argument he makes much of both earlier and later: that the idea of a cold-stroke restoration of capitalism is "rolling the film of reformism backwards". In short, the "political revolution" he advocates is a much more deep-going affair than the "social counter-revolution" he fears. Trotsky's strength here was that on the concrete political issues he was adequate, theoretical frame and names notwithstanding. To left-wing critics (and maybe to himself) he could say: "what do you want to add, concretely?". But the programmatic adequacy also disarmed Trotsky and his comrades. It disguised the theoretical inadequacy and "for now" seemed to render it less than pressingly important. The accumulating contradictions in the realm of the general theory of the nature of the USSR would in time take their terrible political toll.

In 1935 ("The Question of Thermidor") Trotsky had written: "the inevitable collapse of Stalinist Bonapartism would immediately call into question the character of the USSR as a workers' state. A socialist economy cannot be constructed without a socialist power... the replacement of a workers' government by a bourgeois or petty-bourgeois government would inevitably lead to... [bourgeois] restoration". The notion of Stalin's regime as any sort of "socialist power" or "workers' government" had been strained enough then. Now Trotsky has recognised (in "The Fourth International and the Soviet Union", 1936) that "Control over all fields of economic and cultural life [is] in the hands of the Stalinist 'party', which is independent both of the people and of its own members and which represents a political machine of the ruling caste... The constitution liquidates *de jure* the ruling position of the proletariat in the state, a position which, *de facto*, has long been liquidated". How could this possibly be a workers' state in any sense at all?

Trotsky's answers, in *The Revolution Betrayed*, are all indirect. He argues that the bureaucracy lacks essential features of a ruling class; then, if the bureaucracy is not the ruling class, and bourgeois power has not been restored, it must follow by elimination of the other possibilities that the workers are still the ruling class. "The bureaucracy enjoys its privileges under the form of an abuse of power... It... pretends that as a special social group it does not even exist... All this makes the position of the commanding soviet stratum in the highest degree contradictory, equivocal and undignified, notwithstanding the completeness of its power and the smoke screen of flattery that conceals it". Yet Trotsky has written that the new constitution formalises the identification of the bureaucracy with the state.

"The attempt to represent the sSoviet bureaucracy as a class of 'state capitalists' will obviously not withstand criticism. The bureaucracy has neither stocks nor bonds. It is recruited, supplemented and renewed in the manner of an administrative hierarchy, independently of any special property relations of its own... The individual bureaucrat cannot transmit to his heirs his rights in the exploitation of the state apparatus". In fact, the bureaucrats can, through education, contacts, access to "party" nepotism, etc., transmit a great deal. Moreover, at any given time the parasitic autocracy as a whole, as a collective, confronts the working class as a political, social, economic, moral and intellectual force monopolising the social place of a ruling class, and excluding the working class from it. Bourgeois ideologists argue that under modern capitalism social mobility — and there is social mobility, though not quite as they say — means there is no distinct ruling class. Individuals of the proletariat can "rise". Some do; petty bourgeois can rise higher; some new people join the big bourgeoisie; and there is a downward movement too. Yet the bourgeoisie, at any given moment, exists for the working class. Even if social mobility were far greater than in fact it is, that would not negate the fundamental class relations of capitalism. Why would not the same principle apply to the Stalinist autocracy?

ALL SUCH ARGUMENTS of Trotsky's, however, are secondary to the basic idea that the bureaucracy has no "special property relations of its own". "The nationalisation of the land, the means of industrial production, transport and exchange, together with the monopoly of foreign trade, constitute the basis of the soviet social structure. Through these relations, established by the proletarian revolution, the nature of the Soviet Union as a proletarian state is for us basically defined".

Under capitalism, "in general the productive forces, upon a basis of private property and competition, have been working out their own destiny. In contrast to this, the property relations which issued from the socialist revolution are indivisibly bound up with the new state as their repository". But this is the Stalinist state, the state in which the bureaucracy is "the sole privileged and commanding stratum"! Here the nationalised property defines the class character of the state — and the state in turn gives the nationalised property its class character. This is a vicious circle; nationalised property defines the class character of the state which defines the class character of the nationalised property... Trotsky's answer to this objection, that the system originates in the October Revolution and could not have originated otherwise, cannot wipe out the social facts of bureaucratic rule; and in fact it is not true. Between October and the system he is studying came the Stalinist revolution after 1928.

Trotsky admits that: "The means of production belong to the state. But the state, so to speak, 'belongs' to the bureaucracy. If these as yet wholly new relations should solidify, become the norm and be legalised, whether with or without resistance from the workers, they would, in the long run, lead to a complete liquidation of the social conquests of the proletarian revolution". Then he pulls back: "But to speak of that now is at least premature. The proletariat has not yet said its last word. The bureaucracy has not yet created social supports for its dominion in the form of special types of property. It is compelled to defend state property as the source of its power and its income. In this aspect of its activity it still remains a weapon of proletarian dictatorship".

At the end of this passage Trotsky comes back to his starting point: the USSR is a workers' state because it retains nationalised property. But he has had to go through two stages to get there. At first, when he talks about the "wholly new relations" solidifying, he seems to have in mind the existing collectivised property — state property where the state "so to speak" belongs to the bureaucracy. He then imperceptibly slips into discussing not this continuing system but possible future destinies. In the last sentence — when Trotsky tells us that because the bureaucracy defends state property it remains "a weapon of proletarian dictatorship" — we realise that in the course of the paragraph Trotsky has slid into discussing something else. He winds up offering as reason for seeing the system as proletarian dictatorship that same nationalised property which at the beginning of the paragraph he looked at in a fresh and new way — and whose character is precisely the problem he is unravelling. The movement is circular. We wind up back where we started. Trotsky poses a problem — bureaucratic nationalised economy — then substitutes another — the danger of bourgeois restoration for it. The first problem — the fact that a nationalised economy exists and that the bureaucracy defends it — becomes the solution to the problem he has substituted for it (bourgeois restoration)! Here again, the theory depends on dissolving the USSR as it is into the flux of the process — from workers' revolution to bourgeois restoration or socialist regeneration — it is deemed to be part of.

XVIII. PROGRESSIVE TYRANNY?

IT IS NOT SURPRISING that some of Trotsky's comrades — Joseph Carter and James Burnham in the USA — conclude after *The Revolution Betrayed* that the idea that the USSR remains a workers' state makes no sense and should be formally repudiated. Yvan Craipeau in France had held that view for some time already.

On 4 November 1937 Trotsky replies to Craipeau. "This terminological radicalism does not advance things very much", he writes. If the bureaucracy is a class "in the sense of Marxist sociology", then we "have a new form of class society which is identical neither with feudal society nor with capitalist society, and which never was foreseen by Marxist theoreticians"[17].

Capitalism, writes Trotsky, is in "a blind alley" because it is no longer capable of developing the productive forces, "either in the advanced countries or in the backward countries". "The world imperialist chain was broken at its weakest link, Russia. Now we learn that in place of bourgeois society there has been established a new class society". Suppose that is so. Then clearly "the new society is progressive in comparison with capitalism". Why? With nationalised property — and, though Trotsky fades this out, with a state slave-driving, starving and working the population to death — the "new possessing 'class' has assured a development of productive forces never equalled in the history of the world". "Marxism teaches us... that the productive forces are the fundamental factor of historic progress". Capitalism surpassed feudalism because capitalism "opened up new and grandiose possibilities for the... productive forces". "The same applies to the USSR. Whatever its modes of exploitation may be, this new society is by its very character superior to capitalist society. There you have the real point of departure for Marxist analysis!"

The core of fact here — the USSR's industrial growth — is the axis around which Trotsky's analysis oscillates throughout the 1930s. Except through reasoning based on slotting the USSR into a prior historical scheme — that the economically progressive sequel to capitalism, when it falls into decay, is a workers' state — the assessment of the USSR as progressive because of its industrial growth is entirely separable from any idea of it being a workers' state. From now on Trotsky will often separate them in his polemics. The method of setting aside the question of whether the USSR is a workers' state, arguing that the USSR is in any case progressive, and identifying it as a workers' state only secondarily and by abstract deduction from the historical scheme, will come to be a central

17. *Writings 1937-8*, p.34.

feature of Trotsky's polemics. Already, in his theses, "The Fourth International and the Soviet Union", of July 1936, Trotsky has developed all his political positions without reference to the claim that the USSR was a workers' state, which is asserted only in the 18th and last of the theses. The "workers' state" idea is now just a matter of the supposed historical roots in 1917 of the USSR; the historical progressiveness of the nationalised economy; and the general Marxist scheme that says that the progressive successor to capitalism is a workers' state. Trotsky makes no substantial argument for it based on the actual, empirical relations between the Stalinist state and the real, living workers.

Now Trotsky himself will explain that: "Economic progress is not identical with socialism. America, [the] United States, had in its history more grandiose economic progress on a capitalistic basis. Socialism signifies the progressive equality and the progressive abolition of the state"[18]. Trotsky's honesty, his real understanding of social and political relations in the real USSR, make it impossible for him not to see that the USSR's "economic progress" is isolated entirely from all the social, intellectual, and political prerequisites assumed in the Marxist shorthand that says "socialism grows out of advanced capitalism" and "is created by capitalism's gravediggers, the working class". In order to replace capitalism, the proletariat must be able to organise itself and grow in culture and understanding.

Even for Trotsky's backstop argument on the progressiveness of the USSR, much depends on the idea of capitalism being at a dead end. He complains that Craipeau wishes "not to distinguish between a society which is absolutely reactionary, since it fetters and even destroys the productive forces, and a society which is relatively progressive, since it has assured a great upsurge in economy". "Relatively" embodies Trotsky's awareness of what Stalinism is — and his false picture of capitalism. Trotsky makes an utterly false and impermissible exaggeration of the decrepitude of capitalism and its effect on working-class perspectives, including the prospective end of bourgeois democracy everywhere, to "relativise" what Stalinism does to the working class. He is forced to exaggerate the hopelessness of capitalism to sustain his line on the USSR. Even Stalinism is better than dead-end capitalism. In fact, from a working-class point of view, an advanced capitalism that still allows labour movements is better than this barbaric collectivism. Its socialist potential is greater. But Trotsky is an economic fetishist by now. He makes judgements that were shared by many, even anti-socialists, in the 1930s, but which now cannot but seem bizarre .

"The nationalised and planned economy of the USSR is the greatest school for all humanity aspiring to a better future. One must be blind not to see the difference!". All this depends on the USSR being seen on split levels. On an inner, deeper level it is a "nationalised and planned economy" that exists in Trotsky's head; the empirical reality combines that deep reality with a more superficial, temporary, freakish level of reality, namely Stalinism. This is an aberration, out of kilter with the true logic and the true needs of "proper" nationalised and planned economy. There is in fact a huge gulf — so great that a revolution will be needed to cross it —

18. *Writings 1939-40*, p.23

between the actuality of Stalinist nationalised economy and the working-class nationalised-economy model from which Trotsky draws the justification, by analogy, for the real USSR.

By expounding a case for "defence of USSR" separate from the idea that it is a workers' state, Trotsky provisionally and conditionally propounds some of the bases of the later neo-Trotskyist idea of progressive Stalinism — the "deformed workers' state" created by a peasant army (China, Yugoslavia) or Russian invasion.

In the reply to Craipeau he also elaborates the first of a series of auxiliary arguments for defence. "In the war between Japan and Germany on one side, and the USSR on the other, there would be involved not a question of equality in distribution, or of proletarian democracy, or of Vyshinksy's justice, but the fate of the nationalised property and planned economy". Imperialist victory would mean "the collapse not only of the new exploiting 'class' in the USSR, but also of the new forms of production — the lowering of the whole Soviet economy to the level of a backward and semi-colonial capitalism". Trotsky puts it starkly: "Faced with the struggle between two states which are — let us admit it — both class states, but one of which represents imperialist stagnation and the other tremendous economic progress, do we not have to support the progressive state against the reactionary state? Yes or no?" Now even on Trotsky's own account the Stalinist USSR — the empirical USSR, as distinct from the USSR in Trotsky's head — has very limited possibilities of further progress even on the narrowest economic measures.

In *The Revolution Betrayed* he has written: "The progressive role of the soviet bureaucracy coincides with the period devoted to introducing into the Soviet Union the most important elements of capitalist technique. The rough work of borrowing, imitating, transplanting and grafting, was accomplished on the bases laid down by the revolution... It is possible to build gigantic factories according to a ready-made Western pattern by bureaucratic command — although, to be sure, at triple the normal cost. But the farther you go, the more the economy runs into the problem of quality... Under a nationalised economy, quality demands a democracy of producers and consumers, freedom of criticism and initiative — conditions incompatible with a totalitarian regime of fear, lies and flattery. Behind the question of quality stands a more complicated and grandiose problem which may be comprised of the concept of independent, technical and cultural creation. The ancient philosopher said that strife is the father of all things. No new values can be created where a free conflict of ideas is impossible.".

Worse, progress here is too narrowly defined. This USSR is a slave state, a state that has experienced an enormous regression on every level above that of abstract economic forms. The idea that socialist politics should be defined by choosing the side of "progress" in abstraction from class definitions and immediate class conflicts — remember, in this polemic Trotsky is still conceding for the sake of argument that the autocracy is a new exploiting class — is logically, and would be in history for the neo-Trotskyists, entirely destructive of working-class socialism. The revolutionary socialists would logically attach themselves to the progressive forms, quite apart from class rule, working-class conditions and socialism.

Socialism and the proletariat ultimately express the progressive social tendencies of capitalist economy; but in real history the really progressive real labour movement, the proletariat, fights the bourgeois, slows down accumulation, hinders adoption of labour-saving devices on capitalist terms. Despite our historic overview, we are not partisans of economic development before all else, nor inspectors general of economy. We are the warlike working-class party concerned for the class at the expense, where necessary, of "progressive" economic development. Here Trotsky lays the basis for collapsing the class viewpoint into the view of an administrator, a developmentalist or an inspector general of history and economic development.

There is another innovation, and an even worse one. From now on Trotsky's argument for defence of the USSR does not rest on its alleged working-class character or on the superiority of the "new forms of production" alone, but on the idea that defeat will reduce the USSR to a semicolony. This reflects the fragility and "immaturity" which Trotsky sees in the real USSR. Yet it is an argument entirely distinct from any idea of the USSR being a workers' state or even economically progressive. As we will see below, Trotsky will soon indicate that the USSR is itself a Great Russian empire (he will not use this term) because it oppresses many of the USSR's component peoples in the world war. Any imperial power may be dismembered after defeat. In fact, Germany will be defeated and half of it will, after barbarous plunder, be turned into a colony of the USSR. Marxists will not therefore conclude that they must defend Germany! Trotsky's defence of the USSR is of course rooted in his position that it is a workers' state, with a progressive system of production (though the two have become separable); the bringing in of the "anti-colonial argument" indicates only how shaky he now feels his position to be. But it has its implications... and they are not little ones — as we will see when, in 1939-40, Trotsky will "support" the Soviet Union expanding into the former Russian imperial provinces of Finland and Poland.[19]

XIX. POLITICS AND ECONOMICS

TROTSKY DATED THE article "Not a bourgeois and not a workers' state", a reply to the opinion of two US Trotskyists, James Burnham and Joseph Carter, exactly three weeks after his argument against Craipeau.[20] Burnham and Carter still thought the USSR progressive as against contemporary capitalism. They were for its defence against "imperialist attacks". Drawing out the logic of Trotsky's own writings — the disintegration of Trotsky's position into discrete and incongruent elements —

19. It is curious that Trotsky's argument here is the same argument used by G. Plekhanov, the "Father of Russian Marxism", for turning patriot in 1914: defeat would make Russia a German colony and destroy the progress of decades, and the progressive potential thus created.

20. Burnham responded: "Is this a 'no-class' state? Of course not. It is simply not, primarily, the instrument of either of the two major classes in contemporary society. But it is the instrument of the 'new middle class' striving to become a consolidated bourgeois class within the Soviet Union..." [James Burnham: "From Formula to Reality", in E.Haberkern and A.Lipow (eds.), *Neither Capitalism nor Socialism: Theories of Bureaucratic Collectivism*, p.17).]

they separated those questions from the "class character" of the USSR.

Plainly it was not a capitalist state; but they could see no sense in Trotsky's arguments for its working-class character. They could not, like Trotsky, draw a working-class identity from negative arguments — from what the USSR was not — and Marxist historical perspectives and Trotsky's prolonged sense of walking a tightrope across an interregnum. They represented the positive print-out from Trotsky's own position, a positive as distinct from a negative picture of the Stalinist phenomenon as Trotsky himself portrayed it, a plain, flat picture of what was. They wanted downright, categorical statements, and they offered some. Neither bourgeois, nor proletarian — what was it, then? They "admit that 'the economic structure as established by the October Revolution remains basically unchanged'", and Burnham and Carter "do not forget that the main difference between the USSR and the contemporary bourgeois state finds its expression in the powerful development of the productive forces as a result of a change in the form of ownership".

Burnham and Carter think that while the working class has ceased being the ruling class, the "economic structure [which] still remains basically unchanged" means that it is not bourgeois either. They "deny... that the bureaucracy is an independent class". Trotsky says that they conclude that the soviet state "is not an organisation of class domination"[n]. Burnham and Carter accept that the rule of the proletariat can take different forms but, they argue, a workers' state must have some form of workers' political rule. "The concept of the dictatorship of the proletariat is not primarily an economic but predominantly a political category... All forms, organs, and institutions of the class rule of the proletariat are now destroyed, which is to say that the class rule of the proletariat is destroyed".

Trotsky replies: "Of course, the dictatorship of the proletariat is not only 'predominantly' but wholly and fully a 'political category'. However, this very politics is only concentrated economics... The regime which guards the expropriated and nationalised property from the imperialists is, independent of political forms, the dictatorship of the proletariat". Even if it also "guards the expropriated property" from the workers. Trotsky takes refuge in an assertion based on the identification of nationalised property with working-class rule. He merely restates what Burnham and Carter have challenged, by asserting that though the proletariat does not rule politically, it does nonetheless rule "politically", if not through politics, because the USSR's economy is nationalised. To the question of how the proletariat can rule where clearly it rules not, Trotsky answers that the nationalised economy coming out of the October Revolution is the rule of the proletariat. In the degenerated workers' state, the formula which Trotsky quotes from Lenin — "politics is concentrated economics" — is more true the other way round: economics is congealed and concentrated bureaucratic politics. Working-class economic rule can operate only through politics, because the economic and political are fused in a way quite unlike politics and economics in a self-regulating or largely self-regulating economy. In the USSR, both politics and economics are concentrated in the hands of the autocracy and its totalitarian state.

XX. THE UKRAINE AND USSR IMPERIALISM

ON 23 AUGUST 1939 Stalin reversed his diplomatic orientation of the previous four years — which had been based on an alliance with the democratic imperialist powers, France and Britain — and signed a pact with Hitler. On 1 September Hitler seized western Poland. Britain and France stood by their treaty obligations to Poland, and declared war on Germany. On 17 September — in line with secret clauses in his pact with Hitler — Stalin invaded eastern Poland. On 30 November the USSR invaded Finland. It met fierce resistance, and had to settle (on 13 March 1940) for minor territorial gains. In April-June the German army swept through most of western Europe — Norway, Denmark, Belgium, the Netherlands, France. In June 1940 the USSR seized the Rumanian provinces of Bukovina and Bessarabia; in July, it annexed the Baltic states (Latvia, Lithuania, Estonia), which it had brought under its effective control in late 1939. These events, the beginning of the USSR's imperialist expansion, divided Trotskyism into two clearly distinct strands. Formally, Trotsky was heavily on one side; politically, as we will see, he was on both.

In the eastern part of the Polish state, seized by Stalin, Poles were a minority. According to the national composition of the population, it was more accurately described as western Ukraine and western Byelorussia. The greater portions of the Ukrainian and Byelorussian peoples lived in the USSR. There were also smaller areas of Ukrainian population in Rumania, and, after March 1939, Hungary.

Well before these events Hitler had called for a "Greater Ukraine", and early in 1939 the Nazis had allowed a conference of Ukrainian nationalists to be held in Berlin in obvious preparation for war. Trotsky responded with great urgency. The Ukrainian national question was now so explosive, he argued, that communist oppositionists in the USSR must be armed with the slogan: for the independence of the Ukraine. Otherwise the revolutionaries in the Ukraine would be disarmed and reactionaries, including Nazi invaders when they came, would be able to exploit Ukrainian national disaffection. In fact, when the Nazis eventually did invade, in June 1941, many Ukrainians did at first welcome them, though the Nazis' anti-Slav racism soon turned the people against them and drove them back to support for Stalin's state.

On 22 April 1939, Trotsky wrote "The Ukrainian Question", which was published in the *Socialist Appeal*, in New York, on 9 May. Trotsky realistically sums up how things stand for the Ukrainians outside the USSR. "Not a trace remains of the former confidence and sympathy of the Western Ukrainian masses for the Kremlin. Since the latest murderous 'purge' in the Ukraine no-one in the West wants to become part of the Kremlin satrapy which continues to bear the name of the Soviet Ukraine". Now: "The question of the fate of the Ukraine has been posed in its full scope. A clear and definite slogan is necessary that corresponds to the new situation. In my opinion there can be at the present time only one such slogan: A united, free and independent workers' and peasants' Soviet Ukraine".

Anticipating objections from the "friends" of the USSR, Trotsky replies: "The fervid worship of state boundaries is alien to us. We do not hold the position of a 'united and indivisible' whole. After all, even the [1936] constitution of the USSR acknowledges the right of its component federated peoples to self-determination, that is, to separation". To raise the slogan of Ukrainian independence in the USSR would bring immediate shooting for treason. "It is precisely this ruthless hounding of all free national thought that has led the toiling masses of the Ukraine, to an even greater degree than the masses of Great Russia, to look upon the rule of the Kremlin as monstrously oppressive... It is naturally impossible even to talk of Western Ukraine voluntarily joining the USSR as it is at present constituted. Consequently the unification of the Ukraine presupposes freeing the so-called Soviet Ukraine from the Stalinist boot".

Wouldn't this weaken the USSR militarily? The weakening is caused by the "ever-growing centrifugal tendencies generated by the Bonapartist dictatorship... In the event of war the hatred of the masses for the ruling clique can lead to the collapse of all the social conquests of October". Trotsky's new slogan is directed against Hitler — but also against Stalin. "An independent workers' and peasants' Ukraine might subsequently join the Soviet federation; but voluntarily, on conditions that it itself considers acceptable, which in turn presupposes a revolutionary regeneration of the USSR". Genuine Ukrainian independence is impossible without revolution in Western Europe. The Ukraine would join a Soviet United States of Europe. Trotsky may now even be contemplating a European working-class revolutionary war, if necessary, against Stalinism. "The proletarian revolution in Europe, in turn, would not leave one stone standing of the revolting structure of Stalinist Bonapartism".

This Trotsky, faced with real political questions, is the opposite of the Trotsky who thinks that the preservation of the forms of property is all-important. Here he advocates deliberate fomentation of a revolutionary maelstrom against both Hitler and "the rapist clique in the Kremlin". This sort of violent language, expressing all-out hostility to the Stalinist regime as to a particularly monstrous class enemy, is by now Trotsky's only public tone. It is very close to the mid-19th century tone of Karl Marx against Tsarist Russia. Trotsky's "orientation" articles on the "working-class" character of the USSR, and for its defence, are for the narrower circles of his comrades. The balance is close to being the very opposite of what it was in the early 1930s.

On 30 July Trotsky returned to the Ukrainian question, writing "Independence of the Ukraine and Sectarian Muddleheads" (published in *Socialist Appeal*, 15 and 18 September 1939) in reply to critics of his earlier article. In this polemical article against a rigid group of "Trotskyists" (those associated with Hugo Oehler) Trotsky confronts a caricature of himself on the question of defence of the USSR — the issue that will split the Fourth International within a very short time. Trotsky's critic denounces the slogan, among other reasons, because it "completely negates the position of the defence of the Soviet Union". How, asks Trotsky in reply, "can a socialist demand that a hostile Ukraine be retained within the framework of the USSR?"

Oehler does, Trotsky believes, support the political revolution against "the Bonapartist bureaucracy". But this "like every revolution, will undoubtedly present a certain danger from the standpoint of defence... Such a danger is an inescapable historical risk which cannot be evaded, for under the rule of the Bonapartist bureaucracy the USSR is doomed". "The revolutionary national uprising... *represents nothing else but a single segment of the political revolution*"[21]. This is not only full revolution but national struggle against an imperial power. And the logic of the argument for the Ukraine applies also to the USSR's other oppressed nationalities — who comprise, between them, the majority of the state's population.

What if "the separation of the Ukraine threatens to break down the plan and to lower the productive forces"? "This argument, too, is not decisive. An economic plan is not the holy of holies... [After Ukrainian independence] insofar as the plan is advantageous for the Ukraine she will herself desire and know how to reach the necessary economic agreement with the Soviet Union, just as she will be able to conclude the necessary military alliance". Here Trotsky steps outside the fetish of the planned economy, to which elsewhere all else is subordinate. He will soon split the Fourth International by championing an opposite position.

"It is impermissible to forget that the plunder and arbitrary rule of the bureaucracy constitute an important integral part of the current economic plan, and exact a heavy toll from the Ukraine... The outlived ruling caste is systematically destroying the country's economy, the army and its culture; it is annihilating the flower of the population and preparing the ground for a catastrophe. The heritage of the revolution can be saved only by an overturn" (emphasis added).

Trotsky sees the championing of self-determination as a matter of arming the Left Opposition with a full revolutionary programme... "The bolder and more resolute is the policy of the proletarian vanguard on the national question among others, all the more successful will be the revolutionary overturn, all the lower its overhead expenses".

"The barb of the slogan of an independent Ukraine is aimed directly against the Moscow bureaucracy and enables the proletarian vanguard to rally the peasant masses... the same slogan opens up for the proletarian party the opportunity of playing a leading role in the national Ukrainian movement in Poland, Rumania and Hungary. Both of these political processes will drive the revolutionary movement forward and increase the specific weight of the proletarian vanguard".

Trotsky is advocating full-scale proletarian and anti-imperialist revolution — implicitly for the majority of the peoples of the USSR where the Great Russians are the minority. The call for an independent Ukraine implied a clear-cut characterisation of Stalin's USSR, even before it started to expand, as an imperialist state. Trotsky and his comrades characterised pre-war Czechoslovakia, Yugoslavia and Poland as imperialist states because they contained minorities held against their will and variously ill-treated and discriminated against — in Czechoslovakia, for example, three million Sudeten Germans as well as Slovaks and Hungarians. "Even irrespective of its international ties, Czechoslovakia is an absolutely imperialist state"[22]. There was no logical way to exclude the USSR from the same category.

At that time, and up to the end of 1939, the US Trotskyist newspaper, the

---

21. *Writings 1939-40*, p.51, my emphasis.
22. *Writings 1938-9*, p.62

Socialist Appeal, summed up its politics as a call for "the Third Camp". Trotsky expounded it like this: "The attempt of the bourgeoisie during its internecine conflict to oblige humanity to divide up into only two camps is motivated by a desire to prohibit the proletariat from having its own independent ideas. This method is as old as bourgeois society, or more exactly, as class society in general. No one is obligated to become a Marxist; no one is obligated to swear by Lenin's name. But the whole of the politics of these two titans of revolutionary thought was directed towards this, that the fetishism of two camps would give way to a third, independent, sovereign camp of the proletariat, that camp upon which, in point of fact, the future of humanity depends"[23]. In the politics Trotsky developed on the Ukraine in the months leading up to World War 2 he applied the same approach, in essence, to conflict between the two camps of Hitler and Stalin on one side and the Allies on the other. "The question of first order is the revolutionary guarantee of the unity and independence of a workers' and peasants' Ukraine in the struggle against imperialism on the one hand, and against Moscow Bonapartism on the other".

XXI. THE PARTITION OF POLAND

TROTSKY'S RESPONSE TO the partition of Poland by Hitler and Stalin in September 1939 is in line with those politics. Ever since 1933, Trotsky and the Trotskyist press have explained from time to time that fundamentally Stalin wanted an alliance with Hitler as the best way to keep out of war; but he bitterly denounces the Hitler-Stalin pact. It is "a military alliance in the full sense of the word, for it serves the aims of aggressive imperialist war", writes Trotsky on 2 September 1939, the day after the Nazis attack Poland[24]. The German-Soviet pact "is a military alliance with a division of roles: Hitler conducts the military operations, Stalin acts as his quartermaster...". Thinking in terms of years of European war — though in fact it will be only ten months before Hitler is master of the continent — Trotsky predicts that if Hitler, with Stalin's help, wins the war, then "that will signify mortal danger for the Soviet Union". The Nazi invasion of the Soviet Union was then 22 months in the future.

Believing that Stalin's rule is too unstable for him to risk war, Trotsky does not expect the USSR invasion of eastern Poland. When it comes, he responds in high indignation. He scorns the Moscow story that its concern was to "liberate" and "unify" the Ukrainian and White Russian people. "In reality, the Soviet Ukraine, more than any part of the Soviet Union, is bound by the ferocious chains of the Moscow bureaucracy". Ukrainian aspirations for liberation and independence are legitimate and intense. "But these aspirations are directed also against the Kremlin". The Ukrainian people "will find itself 'unified', not in national liberty, but in bureaucratic enslavement... It is not a question of emancipating an oppressed people, but rather one of extending the territory where bureaucratic oppression and parasitism will be practised".

"It is true", concedes Trotsky, "that in the occupied regions the Kremlin

23. *Writings Supplement 1934-40*, p.868-9.
24. *Writings 1939-40*, p.77

is proceeding to expropriate the large proprietors. But this is not a revolution accomplished by the masses, but an administrative reform, designed to extend the regime of the USSR into the new territories. Tomorrow" — in fact, it is simultaneously — "in the 'liberated' regions, the Kremlin will pitilessly crush the workers and peasants in order to bring them into subjection to the totalitarian bureaucracy"[25].

XXII. TROTSKYISM IN 1939

BY LATE 1939, in short, the balance of Trotsky's politics has shifted heavily towards the advocacy of revolution by the workers and oppressed nationalities against the USSR autocracy; "defence of the USSR against imperialism", though not at all renounced, has become very secondary. Moreover, Trotsky sees that "defence" not as an alignment with Stalin but as a revolutionary mass slogan against the autocracy, deemed to be bound on the bourgeois road. "It is our task to call upon the working class to oppose its own strength to the pressure of the bureaucracy — for the defence of the great conquests of October"[26]. Trotsky is unsure about the theoretical definition. He does not know. That is why he oscillates between different "defencisms". He can only operate politically on what he has known, while questioning and developing and trying to hold together the possibility of revolutionary action by the Fourth International. But the exigencies of politics are wreaking havoc with "science". Trotsky's metaphysics of the nationalised economy under the Stalinist locum has separated political and international affairs from, and in the last analysis subordinated everything else to, the nationalised economy seen as the legacy of October 1917 and the polar contrast to world capitalist decline. In this conception nothing that the autocracy can do, killing millions, deporting nations, destroying labour movements, or even, after 1944-5, conquering and pillaging a large part of eastern and central Europe — nothing but denationalising the economy — can stop the USSR being a workers' state. (Nor, once Stalinism begins its vast expansion after 1944, can any crime cancel out the logical implication that Stalinism is both progressive and revolutionary.)

Trotsky has already written, in his reply to Craipeau, that the autocracy can and does do worse than any ruling class in history, and yet is still the custodian of the workers' state. "We can and must say that the Soviet bureaucracy has all the vices of a possessing class without having any of its 'virtues' (organic stability, certain moral norms, etc.)". Tied by his fetish of nationalised property to USSR "socialism" and after 1928 again and again adapting to it, Trotsky has created an immensely elastic system of ideologising around Stalinism as workers' state.

Trotsky has insisted that: "Only dialectical materialism, which teaches us to view all existence in its process of development and in the conflict of internal forces, can impart the necessary stability to thought or action". In

---

25. "The US will participate in the war", 1 October 1939; *New York Times* 4 October 1939; *Writings 1939-40* p.94.
26. "The Fourth International and the Soviet Union", July 1936.

contrast, "a superficial idealistic mode of thinking that operates with ready-made norms, mechanically fitting living processes of development to them" "easily leads one from enthusiasm to prostration". In fact, this is not a bad description of Trotsky himself, except that for the "idealistic norms" of Marxian socialism, derived from socialist extrapolation from advanced capitalism, Trotsky has, as we saw, erected a norm-fetish extrapolated from the experience of one backward country.

Trotsky's strength is that he does not let this "norm" shape his picture of the "living processes" or blur his viewpoint — that of the working class. He lets his vision split into two parallel pictures of the same world, two not-properly-integrated views of the same thing. A duality runs through it all — between the "legitimate" — norm-sustaining — nationalised economy, the one that really fits the underlying historic processes of the October Revolution and its goals and will re-emerge at the other side of a new working-class revolution, and the actually-existing autocratic nationalised economy, that is the very opposite of nationalisation that serves socialist goals.

For Trotsky's structure of a finely tuned and balanced series of conditional positions erected above his conscientious concrete analysis, his own image for Bonapartism will also do: it is a weight finely balanced on the top of a pyramid — finely balanced between his "old communist" politics and analyses on one side, and on the other the encroaching totalitarian-economist logic of his theories about the progressive nationalised economy in which the bureaucracy is locum for an enslaved working class and creates seeming economic miracles in part by driving living standards down to subsistence level and, for millions, below. Trotskyism must roll down on one side of the pyramid or the other; and, as we shall see, it starts to do so in 1939-40.

Trotsky has invoked the basic Marxist scheme of the succession so far of class societies in history to caution Craipeau and all like him and expand on the concerns that inhibit Trotsky's own thinking. Trotsky's way of keeping to it is to be unable to see the USSR as a whole ... and mentally oscillate between seeing it as bourgeois or proletarian or both. Of Craipeau Trotsky had said that he did not deal with the questions of historical perspective raised by his description of Stalinism as a class society — "if this new society is an inevitable stage between capitalism and socialism or if it is merely a historic 'accident'.".

From the point of view "of our general historical perspective as it is formulated in the *Communist Manifesto* of Marx and Engels, the sociological definition of the bureaucracy assumes capital importance". The retardation of the world revolution produced soviet degeneration. It is "the result of political and 'conjunctural' causes... Can one speak of a new... 'conjunctural' class? I really doubt that... From the point of view of the historic succession of social regimes... to give the bureaucracy the name of a possessing class is not only an abuse of terminology, but moreover a great political danger which can lead to the complete derailment of our historical perspective".

There is more than a little in this of special pleading, of an invitation to collude in a conspiracy of silence and of the incantatory, ideologically prophylactic repetition of increasingly doubtful "official truths" lest the furies escape and chaos follows. This sort of consideration — if this, then that, and we must think of the implications — is inimical to the task Trotsky is ostensibly engaged in, of thinking the problems through to the end. Trotsky's concern, let us repeat, is that of a revolutionary politician. He could truly claim to have kept the terrible chronicles of Stalinist rule and Stalinist crimes with matchless strictness, scrupulosity and objectivity. He is right to approach the question cautiously and in wishing to err rather on the side of belatedness than to rush needlessly to conclusions that will bring theoretical disarray to a movement whose morale and capacity for action at decisive moments may shape the future. Yet the art is to know when quantity passes to quality. From 1936 onwards, at least, when he comes as near as makes no difference to defining the USSR as a new form of class society and then unconvincingly retreats, Trotsky is fighting a rearguard action — and fighting it in such a way as to suggest that he knows that is what he does. His motive is honourable and understandable. Trotsky is a revolutionary politician, not an academic or backwards-focused historian. His focus and prime, proper concern is the future and the preparation of action. The cost of his theoretical tardiness for the future of his movement will be higher than he could ever have imagined.

Trotsky is teaching his followers to live on a political tightrope; he is teaching "convenience" and "implications" as a legitimate factor in political-theoretical calculations and "not yet" as a pseudo-answer to avoid an indicated but unwanted answer. Others after him will be less able to keep the balance than Trotsky is. And, on a certain level, Trotsky has revised Marxism. In the interests of a preconceived perspective and of dogmatism he is using Marxism as a narrowly conceived and defined political artefact that is as only a servant of political expediency — he has impermissibly stretched the terms and concepts so out of shape that they begin to look like the thing they supposedly encompass, the USSR.

Essentially, as we have seen, he uses the technique of palimpsestry: writing new meanings into old "texts" and concepts. The idea that the theory either solves or evades the theoretical problems posed by Stalinism is illusory: he only takes them out of rational assessment by corrupting the very language of old Marxism. Fighting Stalinism, he does, under the pressure of Stalinism, what for different reasons the Stalinist bureaucracy has done to Marxism.

By his tardiness, he has destructured his doctrine and introduced into it a disabling incoherence and many destabilising elements, including something akin to Russian patriotism (Russia will be reduced to a colony).

Trotsky believes the USSR bureaucracy cannot risk war and will collapse if war is forced on the USSR. In 1939-40 it will be the Fourth International and Trotsky who find that war throws them into chaos and political collapse.

XXIII. THE TWO SOULS OF TROTSKYISM

AT THE POLITICAL COMMITTEE of the American Trotskyist group, the SWP, on 5 September 1939, James Burnham put down a set of theses on the USSR and the war. Burnham has already, in 1937, said that the USSR is neither a fully bourgeois nor a proletarian state, and that it is reverting to capitalism. He shares Trotsky's basic framework — there are only two alternatives, capitalism or workers' power — but thinks restoration has gone very far already. He now re-raises the question and calls for a clear denunciation of the USSR as imperialist. Contrary to myth, Burnham did not argue that the USSR is "bureaucratic-collectivist". He will later write "The Managerial Revolution" with a different thesis: here he is still arguing for the perspective of capitalist restoration.

In the subsequent arguments, the only person[27] to advance the idea of bureaucratic collectivism will be Trotsky, who expounds it tentatively and defends it from the charge of "revisionism", but — for now — rejects it. Trotsky's main antagonists in the faction fight that would develop, Max Shachtman and Martin Abern, share Trotsky's basic position that the USSR is a degenerated workers' state. Shachtman has doubts and reservations — but does not propose, or indeed have, an alternative to Trotsky's formal position. Shachtman will never adopt the position of Burnham; he will adopt the position Trotsky, wearing the mask of Bruno Rizzi, puts forward. The split that develops is one in Trotsky's own camp. The dispute is not about theories of the USSR, but about political responses to the USSR's invasions of Poland and Finland, and to the beginning of the imperialist expansion of the USSR. *The essential innovators are not Shachtman and his friends. Trotsky is the innovator, on the one hand inserting new substance into the old formula of "defence of the USSR" in response to the new imperialist phase of Stalinism, and on the other provisionally sketching out a new theory of Stalinism.*

Trotsky's public comments on the invasion of Poland are such as might be a manifesto stating the views of Max Shachtman and his allies. The US Trotskyist leaders with whom he will be allied in that faction fight respond very differently: Albert Goldman initially wants to support the USSR invasion of Poland as a "lesser evil", and James P Cannon says that it is a matter of the USSR's military business rather than political right or wrong[28]. As events unfold, however, Trotsky is drawn along by the logic of "holding the line" for the theoretical system he is not yet ready to discard — and in fact into holding the line for the birth of a new, regressive "Trotskyism".

There are differences over Poland, but they are a matter of commentaries on an accomplished fact. They do not have the explosive power of differences over the four-month war in Finland that will start on 30 November. Cannon and Trotsky will say that defence of the USSR obliges them to be "Soviet partisans"; Shachtman and the opposition will oppose Stalinist conquest. They grasp that a new situation has emerged[n]. The faction fight will sharpen. Trotsky will write an article, "A Petty Bourgeois Opposition in the SWP" (15 December 1939)which pours raging scorn and contempt on the heads of Burnham, Shachtman and Abern — and on much that was "Trotskyism" in September 1939. He will savage Shachtman for advocating the "Third Camp", "oppose both sides", position he himself propounded for the Ukraine a few weeks earlier. In April 1940 the Trotskyist movement will split.

---

27. Joseph Carter had a distinct position, according to Max Shachtman, but did not put it on paper.

28. Cannon would have a *reductio ad absurdam* of this position as late as 1944, and on that basis he defended the USSR's treachery to the insurgents of Warsaw (see *The Bureaucratic Jungle*, in this volume)

IN "AGAIN AND once more on the Nature of the USSR" (18 October 1939), Trotsky replies to Albert Goldman's idea that the Stalinist occupation of eastern Poland was "a 'lesser evil'". Yes, German occupation would have been worse for the people involved. (The enslaving and exterminating genocidal Nazis in Eastern Europe have a horror all their own, and that — not nationalised property — is what Trotsky means here.) But the lesser evil was obtained "because Hitler was assured of achieving a greater evil. If somebody sets, or helps to set a house on fire and afterwards saves five out of ten of the occupants of the house in order to convert them into his own semi-slaves, that is to be sure a lesser evil than to have burned the entire ten". If Stalin, the "firebug", deserves "credit", he also deserves hanging. (In fact the population ratio was two for Hitler's slavery and one for Stalin's semi-slavery)[29].

Trotsky responds sympathetically to the alarm of some of his comrades about "unconditional defence of the USSR". In doing so he lays the basis of the policy adopted by Shachtman in the Finnish war — "conjunctural defeatism". Trotsky defines "'unconditional' defence of the USSR" to mean "that independently of the motives and causes of the war we defend the social basis of the USSR, if it is menaced by danger on the part of imperialism". He cannot, without embracing a terrible logic, interpret that to mean: we must back the USSR whenever the USSR is at war, even a war to subjugate a small neighbouring people, because imperialism may get drawn in and any military defeat will encourage the larger enemies of the USSR.

No, Trotsky says that we do not, of course, support the "Red" Army in an occupied territory — an invasion of India by the USSR in alliance with Hitler is being hypothetically discussed — any more than we support it in the USSR. "If the Red Army menaces workers' strikes or peasant protests against the bureaucracy in the USSR shall we support it? Foreign policy is the continuation of the internal. We have never promised to support all the actions of the Red Army which is an instrument in the hands of the Bonapartist bureaucracy. We have promised to defend only the USSR as a workers' state and solely those things within it which belong to a workers' state".

In fact, in war the USSR and the "Red" Army are a single entity, indivisible. But here Trotsky labels "adroit casuistry" arguments he will shortly use or imply: "If the Red Army... is beaten by the insurgent masses in India, this will weaken the USSR". He replies: "The crushing of a revolutionary movement in India, with the cooperation of the Red Army, would signify an incomparably greater danger to the social basis of the USSR *than an episodic defeat of counter-revolutionary detachments of the Red Army in India*" (emphasis added). Are not all the detachments counter-revolutionary? In any case, this is "conjunctural defeatism". When the Red Army is sent to suppress, annex and crush the Finnish nation, why are the "Red" Army detachments there not counter-revolutionary?

---

29. Of the 15 million people in the territory Stalin annexed, 6 million were Poles. Of these one and a half million were killed or deported to slave labour.

Trotsky adds: "In every case the Fourth International will know how to distinguish where and when the Red Army is acting solely as an instrument of the Bonapartist reaction and where it defends the social basis of the USSR". It is a question of judgment — of whether the Fourth International judges the "social basis" to be at stake, and other circumstances. This will be the basis of the opposition case on Finland. But when the Finnish war erupts, Trotsky's own arguments will be improvised in line with a rooted determination to stick with his theoretical, "totalitarian-economistic", basics and the "Clemenceau thesis".

In "Again and once more...", Trotsky also discusses the argument of some of his US comrades that the USSR must now be called "imperialist". In substance he gives a pretty plain "yes" to the existence of Russian imperialism, but he refuses to use the word. We must, writes Trotsky, first establish what social content is included. History has known the imperialism of ancient slave society, of feudal lords, of commercial and then industrial capital, of the Tsarist monarch, etc. The train of thought, plainly, is that history now knows the imperialism of the Stalinist bureaucracy. "The driving force behind the Moscow bureaucracy is indubitably the tendency to expand its power, its prestige, its revenues. This is the element of 'imperialism' in the widest sense of the word which was a property in the past of all monarchies, oligarchies, ruling castes, medieval estates and classes" — and now plainly of the Stalinist bureaucracy.

Having admitted this and thus opened the door to the development of a rational "Trotskyist" understanding of the enormous explosion of Russian Stalinist imperialism that the next half decade would experience, Trotsky closes it: "in... Marxist literature, imperialism is understood to mean the expansionist policy of finance capital". Trotsky keeps the facts under review with stringent honesty — as in the assimilation of Russian expansion to the many and varied experiences and types of imperialism in history — but, as on the question of class and exploitation posed by the Stalinist experience, Trotsky's essential position is: our theory does not know of this phenomenon, and our perspectives exclude it. Where the point of this discussion is what is new — what current Marxist literature, like Trotsky's, should deal with — Trotsky points to the fact that Marxist literature has not done it so far... He systematically — in the wake of and in parallel to Stalinist "dialectics" — destructures and paralyses with sophistic relativism the proper socialist and democratic response. "To employ the term 'imperialism' for the foreign policy of the Kremlin — without elucidating exactly what this signifies — means simply to identify the policy of the Bonapartist bureaucracy with the policy of monopolistic capitalism on the basis that both one and the other utilise military force for expansion".

All that is conveyed by the outrage at the impermissible abstraction involved in equating finance capital and the USSR on the basis of expansion is that these are different systems. The facts are not denied; Trotsky has put them with admirable clarity. He won't call the autocracy a class or what it does exploitation and imperialism — but he is sharp and clear about what it is they are in life and what they do — and on what a proper socialist response is, including on the national question in the USSR (Ukraine). Yet here, at the birth of expansionary Russian bureaucratic imperialism, he begins to fail to be himself.

On Finland he will fail utterly and completely to maintain his consistently Bolshevik politics. For the first time since he came out for "political revolution" in the USSR he cannot respond to a critic who wants to define the autocracy as a new exploiting class by retorting: what do you want to add to the poltical conclusions?

When Trotsky says the identification of USSR expansion and the imperialism of expansionary finance capital can sow "only confusion" and that "it is much more proper to petty bourgeois democrats than to Marxists", he puts out the eyes of his surviving comrades, of the Fourth Internationalist movement.

XXVI. THE INVASION OF FINLAND

TROTSKY'S RESPONSE FOR the general public to the invasion of Finland was "The Twin Stars: Hitler-Stalin", written on 4 December 1939[30], four days after Stalin invaded Finland on 30 November. He had not to the last moment expected the USSR to go to war against Finland, any more than he had expected Stalin's initial expansion, which he had said was impossible. He still argues that Stalin cannot wage an offensive war with any hope of victory. War will provoke revolution against Stalinism. In war, "the whole fraud of the official regime, its outrages and violence, will inevitably provoke a profound reaction on the part of the people, who have already carried out three revolutions in this century". The USSR is capable of being a reactive force only. Germany, to draw the USSR into the war, "obviously pushed Moscow against Finland". Trotsky seems to expect an easy USSR victory. "But the sovietising of the Western Ukraine and White Russia (Eastern Poland), like the present attempt to sovietise Finland — are they not acts of socialist revolution? Yes and no. More no than yes.

When the Red Army occupies a new province, the Moscow bureaucracy establishes a regime which guarantees its domination. The population has no choice but voting yes to the effected reforms in a totalitarian plebiscite. A 'revolution' of this kind is feasible only on army-occupied territory with a scattered or backward population... This 'revolution' can indeed be accepted by the Kremlin. And Hitler has no fear of it". After this article is published in *Liberty* magazine (27 January 1940) a member of the SWP minority, Dwight MacDonald, will comment that in *Liberty* Trotsky is "'in reality' a... Shachtmanite" and pro-USSR only in the Trotskyists' private discussion bulletins. In fact the "two Trotskys" phenomenon that now emerges is remarkable. It is as if the two Trotskys don't even communicate with each other very well. In his public writings, including those in the Trotskyist press, Trotsky responds as a working-class socialist to the USSR that actually exists and to what it really does; in his "internal", orienting, "esoteric" writings he deals with the USSR of his theory, with a USSR that does not exist except in Trotsky's map of history — that exists in his imagination and in his hopes.

Trotsky's first contribution to the SWP's internal debate after the inva-

---

30. *Writings 1939-40*, p.113.

sion of Finland is "The Petty Bourgeois Opposition in the SWP" (15 December 1939), a roar of anger and alarm, an attempt to beat down the opposition, which, he claims, "is leading a typical petty-bourgeois tendency". Trotsky presents James Burnham as the central leader of the opposition, and focuses on Burnham's views on dialectics, on the nature of the USSR, and on how the SWP should be organised, more than Finland. These are all issues on which Burnham has had longstanding and well-known differences with Trotsky — but on which the other leaders of the SWP opposition, Max Shachtman and Martin Abern, share Trotsky's views.

A month later Trotsky will sum up his picture of the opposition: "The relationship of forces within the bloc is completely against Shachtman. Abern has his own faction. Burnham with Shachtman's assistance can create the semblance of a faction constituting intellectuals disillusioned with Bolshevism. Shachtman has no independent programme, no independent method, no independent faction"[31].

Trotsky and Cannon fear that Burnham will dominate the opposition. But he did not dominate. After Burnham's defection from Shachtman's Workers' Party, soon after the April 1940 split, perhaps a dozen youth — no more — would join the Socialist Party. Abern would never play an independent political role in the Workers' Party. The idea of Burnham's dominance was pretty spurious in 1939-40. By 1942, when Trotsky's polemics from 1939-40 were published by the SWP as a book (*In Defence of Marxism*) and since, it had become plain, matter-of-fact libel on the Workers' Party. The spuriousness of it is displayed in an eloquent passage where Trotsky develops the idea of a parallel between dialectics and the Russian question in Burnham and Shachtman. "Burnham... possesses a method — pragmatism. Shachtman has no method. He adapts himself to Burnham". But Shachtman has a conscious method — and it is the same as Trotsky's.

If it is true that Shachtman on the USSR "gravitates" towards Burnham, an explanation for this may be sought in the difficulties and contradictions and inadequacies of the conclusions that Trotsky — and Shachtman — have, with their "dialectical" method, reached so far. The opposition asserts that their position does not depend on Burnham's thesis on the USSR; Shachtman and Abern have reasons of their own: neither of them will ever come to share Burnham's position of 1939. Trotsky's insistence that Burnham is central is a way of insisting on Trotsky's own method as he uses it and with his conclusions as the only legitimate ones — or, in other words, a refusal to admit Shachtman's and Abern's conclusions as possible from the standpoint they held in common with him. It is denial of a split in his own camp. But both on the rights of small nations against the USSR, and on "conjunctural defeatism" he has broken their ground for them. The opposition are developing the entire trend of Trotsky's thought since 1936/7 and the Workers' Party they found will continue to do it.

In "The Petty Bourgeois Opposition" when he deals with Finland, Trotsky comes out more "for" Russia than in any previous writings for many years. To punish the Stalinists "for their unquestionable crimes", Trotsky says, the opposition resolution does not mention "by so much as a

---

31. "From a Scratch to the Danger of Gangrene".

word that the Red Army in Finland expropriates large landowners and introduces workers' control while preparing for the expropriation of the capitalists". Trotsky hoped for class struggle in the interstices and maybe for the Red Army catching alight, and the revolutionary blaze spreading back to the USSR. He has explained that if, hypothetically, the Russian Army invades India: "We will teach the Indian workers to fraternise with the rank and file soldiers and denounce the repressive measures of their commanders and so on"[32]. This is Trotsky's full revolutionary attitude to the "Red" Army: we "fraternise" to disrupt it.

Yet Trotsky's disorientation here is palpable; and not only in that the entire picture he conjures up of War-Revolution is without basis in fact and contradicts the long considered and true picture he has painted only a few months back of the attitude of peoples bordering the USSR, like the Ukrainians and Finns — "no-one in the West wants to become part of the Kremlin satrapy which continues to bear the name of the Soviet Ukraine".

But even if, in December, Trotsky thinks the Red Army is introducing workers' control, how can he evaluate it as positive, as other than the Stalinist equivalent of fascist social demagogy and manipulation? Trotsky goes on: "Tomorrow the Stalinists will strangle the Finnish workers. But now they are giving — they are compelled to give — a tremendous impulse to the class struggle in its sharpest form". This "class struggle" — if it were real — would be only an auxiliary to the Russian Army, a "quisling" helpmeet of the totalitarian imperialist invaders. Anything that might "in itself" be good, like sparks of class struggle and workers' control, would "tomorrow" be stifled together with the Finnish workers. Trotsky will compare support for the USSR in Finland with support for the Republic in the Spanish civil war, but if there is a greater and a lesser evil here, an enemy using a machine gun and one dripping slow poison, then Finland is the analogue of the Spanish Republic and the Red Army of the Franco fascists.

Why, even on Trotsky's own account of things, should socialists call on the Finnish workers to be "Soviet partisans" — traitors not only to Finland but to their own labour movement? The only possible answer is that nationalised property is more important than the survival of Finland's labour movement or Finnish national rights. In Finland the dogma of defence of the USSR as part of the workers' revolution comes starkly up against defence of the Finnish labour movement — of the workers, the subjects of history in Marxist understanding. If nationalised property is, so to speak, congealed dead revolutionary activity, here it confronts a living working-class movement, whose existence the USSR threatens. The fetish of nationalised property, raised above society, politics and history, now acts as a social, political, military, historical hallucinogen. The US Trotskyist press skirmished on behalf of Stalin, making propaganda against bourgeois-democratic Finland of a shameful sort that presented it as if it were a military dictatorship identical with the regime that 20 years before massacred the Finnish Bolshevik workers.

---

32. *Writings 1939-40*, p.108.

TROTSKY WRITES AN open letter to Burnham on 7 January 1940. Civil war in Finland did not unfold, say the SWP opposition. "Your predictions did not materialise". Trotsky replies: "With the defeat and retreat of the Red Army, I reply, the civil war in Finland cannot, of course, unfold under the bayonets of Mannerheim". Carl Mannerheim commanded counter-revolutionary forces which killed thousands of communist workers in civil war in Finland in 1918-9. After twenty years in retirement, he has been recalled as Commander in Chief for the war with the USSR. Finland is a parliamentary democracy with a coalition government of Social Democrats and the Agrarian Party. But what sort of civil war can unfold under the bayonets of Stalin?

Trotsky continues: "We did not foresee the defeats of the first detachments of the Red Army", but such "a military episode... cannot determine our political line. Should Moscow... refrain from any further offensive against Finland, then the very question which today obscures the entire world situation to the eyes of the opposition would be removed from the order of the day. But there is little chance for this. On the other hand, if England, France and the United States... were to aid Finland with military force, then the Finnish question would be submerged in a war between the USSR and the imperialist countries. In this case, we must assume that even a majority of the oppositionists would remind themselves of the programme of the Fourth International". Doesn't Trotsky here admit that the actual Finnish-USSR conflict is not covered by the Fourth International programme? Or not quite? Or will be only if imperialist powers like Britain and France intervene?

Trotsky proposes a policy, determined by considerations of defending the USSR from imperialist attack - which will not in fact come by this route. Why does Trotsky not wait for this, keep separate defence of the USSR against western imperialism - as Shachtman wants - from support for USSR imperialism against Finland? Why merge defence of the USSR with half-hatched ideas of expanding bureaucratic revolution? Trotsky concedes that the notional "civil war" in Finland "is introduced on bayonets from without. It is controlled by the Moscow bureaucracy. Nevertheless", Trotsky continues, having shown it to be a very unusual, indeed an oxymoronic, sort of civil war, "it is precisely a question of civil war, of an appeal to the lowly, to the poor, a call to them to expropriate the rich, drive them out, arrest them, etc. I know of no other name for those actions except civil war".

In fact it is a call by a would-be conquering and subjugating imperialist state to the oppressed classes of invaded Finland to help them overrun the country and overthrow the old rulers whose position in society the invaders' ruling class — or as Trotsky would prefer, ruling autocracy and caste — will replace. They will not only add national oppression but a uniquely intense and all-encompassing new social oppression too. Trotsky's approach here is palimpsestry, writing new content into old terms. Workers' states that are slave states, civil wars that are invasions, appeals against the rich to the poor by worse slavemasters who want their help.

On the same level of fantasy, Trotsky constructs a policy which, he says, socialists should have followed in eastern Poland when the USSR invaded. They should "conduct a struggle against the landlords and the capitalists" (does he imagine this is somehow separate from the occupying army of the USSR?) "Do not tear yourself away from the masses" who have "naive hopes in Moscow" — "fight in their camp, try to extend and deepen their struggle, and to give it the greatest possible independence. Only in this way will you prepare the coming insurrection against Stalin".

Here, though, his picture of reality is radically false. Trotsky continues the tradition of being specific and concrete about revolutionary tasks. In principle that is correct. It does not demand calling the USSR a workers' state, being for its defence, or anything other than tact.

However, the idea that Marxists should decide what they say about the USSR's imperialism — and five thousand miles away in New York, which is where the actual dispute and Trotsky's main audience is — according not to the facts but to what they think will bring the best results implies the death of Marxism. It depends on half-truth telling, half-picture painting, opportunistically or even mimetically suspending disbelief.

The politics of fantasy here is essentially passive, manipulating ideas and images in imagination rather than grasping and changing realities. It is linked in Trotsky and neo-Trotskyism to the loss of a credible working-class agency for the immediate socialist struggle they urgently desire. Mimicry, pretence, and suspension of disbelief will be a big part of "orthodox" neo-Trotskyism and the mainstay of its relation to Stalinism. In Trotsky's scenario about revolution as an aureole around the Red Army there is more than confusion and amnesia, there is a quality of delirium. In May 1940, in a manifesto for the Fourth International, he will sum it up: the seizure of Eastern Poland, he writes, "was accompanied by the nationalisation of semi-feudal and capitalist property". Without nationalisation, he says, the new territories could not have been incorporated into the USSR. "The strangled and desecrated October Revolution served notice that it was still alive". This is King Lear at the end, drained and expiring, who thinks he sees his dead daughter Cordelia, who has been hanged, smiling at him!

Faced with new events, Trotsky has since 1927 preferred to cram and stretch old terminology and old concepts as if that can tidy up unruly reality and ward off theoretical problems. In fact it only destructures meaning and erodes and corrupts words. It was one of the historic roles of Stalinism to erode and corrupt the vocabulary, the perspectives, the goals and the models of revolutionary socialism. Here, on a different plane but accommodating to the "historical fact" of Stalinism, Trotsky is, for what he thinks are good revolutionary reasons, doing the same.

Trotsky denounces Burnham for writing about "experimental", "critical" and "scientific" — rather than "Marxist" — politics. Burnham "culled the label imperialist to describe the foreign policy of the Kremlin"; this "innovation" creates "less 'sectarian', less 'religious', less rigorous formulas, common to you and — oh happy coincidence! — bourgeois democracy". Trotsky is trying to imprison and freeze thought by freezing terminology. He asserts that: "Terminology is one of the elements of the class struggle". It can be — but not always on the real Marxist side of it.

Fixed terminology can become a substitute for thought; the living method of Marxist analysis can be and often is smothered under it like fire under ashes. Unless we reconquer the meaning of the terminology again and again, it becomes dead matter learned by rote, with unclear, imprecise and receding meanings. And this attitude to terminology would make much that neo-Trotskyism said incomprehensible to outsiders - a series of self-hypnotising mantras. The idea of insisting on a fixed and rigid terminology in, for example, journalism, is the mark and to a considerable extent the substance of a fundamentalist sect. In some neo-Trotskyist groups it would eventually lead to a uniformity of phrasing even about current events. Terminological "orthodoxy" is the enemy of thought and of effective politics if it is imposed as a rigid uniformity or cracked up as a necessary tribute of fealty to Marxism.

In this Open Letter Trotsky turns on his own politics and begins to pull them down, striking at himself. He claims that the opposition showed glaring "impotence in the face of great events" on Poland, the Baltic states and Finland. "Shachtman began by discovering a philosopher's stone: the achievement of a simultaneous insurrection against Hitler and Stalin in occupied Poland. The idea was splendid; it is only too bad that Shachtman was deprived of the opportunity of putting it into practice. The advanced workers in eastern Poland could justifiably say: 'A simultaneous insurrection against Hitler and Stalin in a country occupied by troops might perhaps be arranged very conveniently from the Bronx; but here, locally, it is more difficult. We should like to hear Burnham's and Shachtman's answer to a "concrete political question": What shall we do between now and the coming insurrection?'."

What is Trotsky saying? To "tell the truth" and point to twin tyrannies (slavery and semi-slavery, on Trotsky's own account) is not possible until we can organise insurrection, and simultaneous insurrection? What did Trotsky advocate for the Ukraine six months before? "The struggle against imperialism on the one hand, and against Moscow Bonapartism on the other". The sarcasm about simultaneous risings amounts to jeering at the weakness of the proletariat and of the Trotskyist movement. Trotsky was wont to quote Lassalle: Every great movement begins with the statement of what is. When, here, he reduces his own idea of "Third Camp" politics to the nonsense of simultaneous insurrection, Trotsky is being pushed into one of two camps — Stalin's.

XXVIII. BUREAUCRATIC REVOLUTION?

TWO WEEKS LATER, following his Open Letter to Burnham with another long polemic, Trotsky wrote "From a Scratch — to the Danger of Gangrene" (24 January 1940). Charging that "the petty-bourgeois tendency reveals its confusion in its attempt to reduce the programme of the party to the small coin of 'concrete' questions", Trotsky excises Finnish national self-determination and the right to life of the Finnish labour movement from his programme in deference to Russian nationalised property — that is, he counterposes the supposed dead residue of the Russian workers' revolution to the living workers' movement of Finland.

In contrast to the small-coin petty bourgeois, "the proletarian tendency...

97

strives to correlate all the partial questions into theoretical unity". Aye, but do they unify when you "correlate" them?

The system-building of Trotsky increasingly traps him in absurdity. This too is dialectical; because the errors in Trotsky's system are now all-devouring, his striving for wholeness and virtue is transformed dialectically into a ragged and politically vicious travesty. Fear that the whole intricate Chinese-box theoretical structure he has built on the USSR will collapse (probably) and belief in the likelihood of immediate clashes between the USSR and Britain or France in Finland (certainly) push Trotsky to "abstract" everything except nationalised property from the situation. It is nationalised-property fetishism pushed to the point of an absolute and flat contradiction with the working class — immediately, with the Finnish working class.

Invoking basic Marxist ideas on the ultimately fundamental role of economics, Trotsky complains: "Our attempt to reduce the politics of the Kremlin to nationalised economy, refracted through the interests of the bureaucracy, provokes frantic resistance from Shachtman". But what do you get if you try to see the USSR economy as crudely expressed in Stalin's foreign policy? Economic pillage, a slave hunt and confiscation of the surplus product for the autocracy. Even if nationalised property forms can give a boost to production, how does the spread from a backward society of this property form, coupled with national oppression and "semi-slavery", constitute progress? Take it as a whole — nationalised property and "semi-slavery" — and what kind of economic form superior to capitalism is this? Trotsky is, of course, impelled by the seeming hopeless collapse of capitalism and the scenario of a succession of world wars rapidly digging "the grave of civilisation". But the idea of Stalinist "bureaucratic revolution" would become the dominant operational element in neo-Trotskyism, and serve to obfuscate and disguise the class realities of the new Stalinist states of the 1940s and after, seemingly assimilating them to the October Revolution.

What Trotsky says on this in "Gangrene..." is a fantastic tissue of contradictions. Trotsky accuses Shachtman: "My remarks that the Kremlin with its bureaucratic methods" — police-state methods, totalitarian conquest — "gave an impulse to the socialist revolution" — what revolution? — "is converted by Shachtman into an assertion that in my opinion a 'bureaucratic revolution' of the proletariat is presumably possible. This is not only incorrect but disloyal. My expression was rigidly limited. It is not a question of 'bureaucratic revolution' but only a bureaucratic impulse". Impulse to what? And what is the result now, which we must defend in the annexed territories as we defend the nationalised property in the USSR?

"The popular masses in western Ukraine and Byelo Russia, in any event, felt this impulse, understood its meaning and used it to accomplish a drastic overturn in property relations". What has happened, then, was the result of a fleeting moment of workers' revolution? In backward east Poland, where there is very little industry and most of the people are peasants? The idea of deformed workers' states encapsulating a fleeting moment of real revolution would become common in neo-Trotskyism.

But what did the Red Army and the GPU do? Who had control at the end? What property relations replaced the ones overturned? Whose is the property now, after the "drastic overturn"? "This impulse in the direction of socialist revolution was possible only because the bureaucracy of the USSR straddles and has its roots in the economy of a workers' state. The revolutionary utilisation of this 'impulse' by the Ukrainian Byelo Russians [sic] was possible only through the class struggle in the occupied territories and through the power of the example of the October Revolution. Finally, the swift strangulation or semi-strangulation of this revolutionary mass movement was made possible through the isolation of this movement and the might of the Moscow bureaucracy".

Trotsky is repairing the theoretical fabric — with assertions, "deductions", and fantasies. Mocking "Shachtman's" Third Camp policy as tantamount to a "rising on two fronts organised from the Bronx", Trotsky winds up with something far more awkward, especially for those doing it not from the Bronx or Coyoacan but on the spot — organising a proletarian revolution, in a largely agrarian society, under the guns and the military-political surveillance of a totalitarian invader!

When he goes on to discuss Poland, Trotsky starts with a coherent account of the call by the puppet "People's Government" for workers' control — "nothing more than crowding out the native bourgeoisie, whose place the bureaucracy proposes to take". Exactly! "Furthermore... of greatest urgency to the Kremlin is the extraction of a new administrative apparatus from among the toiling population of the occupied areas" — that is the cooption of workers and peasants into the new ruling class as quislings. Then, once again, as with the "Third Camp", Trotsky turns to mock his own politics.

Shachtman asked Trotsky why he placed significance in the manifesto of "the idiot" Kuusinen, head of Stalin's stooge "government" for Finland. Trotsky replies: "The 'idiot' Kuusinen acting on the ukase of the Kremlin and with the support of the Red Army represents a far more serious political factor than scores of superficial wise-acres who refuse to think through the internal logic (dialectics) of events". And how many battalions does the Fourth International have?

Imagine Trotsky writing in response to such a thing six months earlier; nameless seriousness and classless politics! No: the difference in Trotsky's approach has to be that things are on the move. "The strangled and desecrated October Revolution served notice that it was still alive". This is the revolution, for now. The politics here are of two camps (back Stalin against Hitler) and two stages (Stalin-controlled bureaucratic revolution first, working-class revolution later). And Trotsky adds a further devastating twist: "The programme of the Kuusinen government, even if approached from a 'formal' point of view does not differ from the programme of the Bolsheviks in November 1917". As Trotsky, after Lenin, said to the Left Opposition "administrators" who capitulated in 1929-30, the decisive question is "who? whom?" The "1917 programme" — or shards of it, *sans* internationalism, *sans* workers' democracy — is now in the hands of an oligarchic elite.

Trotsky's great mistake in 1939-40 is that he deepens the confusion on Stalinism that has reigned since, after 1928, he interpreted the Stalinist autocracy's move against the kulaks and Nepmen as a deformed working-class response rather than the consolidation of a new exploiting class. When the autocracy moves out on to the world arena, challenging capitalists and destroying capitalist classes - not "defending" or "deepening" what the 1917 revolution had achieved, but acting plainly as an independent anti-bourgeois and simultaneously anti-working-class force — that is the point when Trotsky's theory comes into irreconcilable conflict with international working-class politics and becomes a satellite of expansionary Stalinism.

Essentially, Trotsky says "wait"; it is too early to identify the autocracy as a new exploiting class; it is absurd to imagine Stalinist conquest reaching beyond small border states. "It is fantastic to imagine that Germany could be sovietised from Moscow as was small and backward Galicia" (i.e. eastern Poland: Outline of Hitler-Stalin twin star article. 15 November 1939). James P Cannon would put this even more clearly: "Stalin could take the path of Napoleonic conquest not merely against small border states, but against the greatest imperialist powers, only on one condition: that the Soviet bureaucracy in reality represents a new triumphant class which is in harmony with its economic system..."[33].

By the time the USSR does conquer half of Germany, Cannon and his comrades will be too walled off by Trotsky's fierce polemics of this period, and by their own factional elaborations and party competition with the Shachtmanites, to rethink. A logic will unfold which relegates the proletarian socialist programme to something for the future: a quasi-private set of glosses on the horrors unfolding in the world in the "first stage" of "the revolution". The parallel with the destruction of norms after 1917 is important; the continuity, blurring, merging with what Stalin did — the Trotskyist programme relegated to the future; "centuries of deformed workers' states" — all that is there implicitly in Trotsky, seeds waiting to sprout.

XXIX. BALANCE SHEET OF THE FINNISH EVENTS

"GANGRENE..." IS TROTSKY'S last writing for the SWP faction fight, followed only by a "Balance Sheet of the Finnish Events" written (25 April 1940) after the end of the Finnish war and after the Trotskyists have split. "The attempt of the conjunctural defeatists, i.e. the adventurers in defeatism, to extricate themselves from their difficulty" — the Trotskyists' common difficulty — "by promising that in the event the Allies intervene they will change their defeatist policy to a defencist one is a contemptible evasion. It is in general not easy to determine one's policies according to a stopwatch, especially under wartime conditions". It is known now, Trotsky writes, that the Allied general staffs discussed bombing the Murmansk railway to aid Finland. Intervention "hung by a hair. From the same hair, apparently, the principled position of the 'third camp' also dangled. But... we considered that it was necessary to determine one's position in accordance with the basic class camps in the war. This is much more reliable".

Why was it not sufficient to switch if Murmansk was bombed? And in fact it wasn't bombed. Here Trotsky justifies a monolithic position, unnuanced, making no distinction between defence against imperialism and support for the USSR in a predatory war, by what might but did not hap-

33. *Struggle for a Proletarian Party*, p.104.

pen. It was a policy of eyes closed and steering with Stalin's politics and army as lode star — because Stalin is the custodian of nationalised property.

Why does Stalin represent the working-class "camp"? Trotsky restates his reasons for "defence of the USSR". "First, the defeat of the USSR would supply imperialism with new colossal resources and could prolong for many years the death agony of capitalist society. Secondly, the social foundations of the USSR, cleansed of the parasitic bureaucracy, are capable of assuring unbounded economic and cultural progress, while the capitalist foundations disclose no possibilities except further decay".

Yet, subject to conditions — a workers' revolution, essentially identical to what "cleansing" the USSR involves — the capitalist "foundations" in a wealthy country like Germany can do what Trotsky says the USSR can do, "on condition", and greatly more so. In every respect advanced capitalism is more progressive than the USSR. Trotsky implies a concession to the Stalinist utopia of "Socialism in One Country" here, by placing the USSR (after revolution) above advanced capitalism (after revolution). But if socialism must grow out of advanced capitalism, then the idea that imperialism is "the main enemy of the world working class" — and that it would be decisively worse for Germany or Britain to feed off a defeated USSR than for the USSR to feed off a defeated Germany — is nonsensical from an international socialist point of view, when the alternative is the triumph and expansion of the non-capitalist, backward USSR (which is also imperialist).

The basic question here is as old as the *Communist Manifesto*'s arguments against reactionary socialists and Lenin's argument against the petty bourgeois anti-imperialists. One descendant of these ideas will be neo-Trotskyist support for many varieties of Third World barbarism in the name of "World Revolution".

XXX. THE OTHER TROTSKY

AFTER "GANGRENE" (JANUARY 1940), Trotsky, however, continues to develop another strand of his politics in his public writings. In a press interview on 14 February 1940, he explains again what he knew and said before the invasion of Poland: "The strangling of the peoples of the USSR, particularly of the national minorities, by police methods, repelled the majority of the toiling masses of the neighbouring countries from Moscow. The invasion of the Red Army is seen by the populations not as an act of liberation but as an act of violence".

After the end of the Finnish war, he sums it up like this (13 March 1940): "Under Hitler's cover Stalin attempted to apply Hitler's methods in foreign policy... Not capable of evaluating the tradition of the long Finnish struggle for independence, Stalin expected to break the Helsinki government by mere diplomatic pressure. He was badly mistaken... So began a shameful war without a clear perspective, without moral and material preparation...". The bureaucratic revolution is there only as a flimsy speculation on what might have been. For Stalin "to reconcile the peoples of the USSR to the senseless invasion of Finland, would be possible only in one way — namely, by winning the sympathy of at least part of the Finnish peasants and workers by means of a social upheaval". Trotsky insists that: "I stand completely for the defence of the Soviet Union", but it is very strange defence.

Trotsky does not want the USSR overrun, but his "defence" is such bitter condemnation of policy and government that it must seem either hypocrisy or self-contradictory to those who do not grasp the "secret doctrine". "All this does not lead me to defend the foreign policy of the Kremlin". An open struggle against "Stalin and the oligarchy headed by him... in the view of world public opinion, is inseparably connected for me with the defence of the USSR". There is as little left of substance, as distinct from claim, in Trotsky's "defence" as there is of a real workers' state in the name of workers' state.

In a "Letter to the Workers of the USSR" (23 April 1940)[34] Trotsky gives a very different picture of the Finnish war than that of a bureaucratically-impelled socialistic revolution stalled only by the "bayonets of Mannerheim". "During the war with Finland, not only the majority of the Finnish peasants but also the majority of the Finnish workers proved to be on the side of their bourgeoisie. This is hardly surprising since they know of the unprecedented oppression to which the Stalinist bureaucracy submits the workers of nearby Leningrad and the whole of the USSR". Trotsky calls for defence of the USSR, but says this can only be promoted by overthrowing the autocracy. "The conquests of the October Revolution will serve the people only if they prove themselves capable of dealing with the Stalinist bureaucracy, as in their day they dealt with the Tsarist bureaucracy and the bourgeoisie". And who exactly will the "conquests of October" serve otherwise?

The whole idea of "defending October" is now displaced by the imperative to fight the existing bureaucratic system. All that is left is the hope that this will be done by the USSR people and not by Germany and Britain.

Trotsky's last major writing on the USSR before he was murdered (20/21 August 1940) by a Stalinist agent is "The Comintern and the GPU" (17 August 1940)[35]. Here he definitely revises the conclusion he has reached from the Spanish Civil War and his notion of the Stalinist autocracy as too inorganic to have any substantial international programme of its own.

"As organisations, the GPU [the Stalinist secret police] and the Comintern are not identical but they are indissoluble... the GPU... completely dominates the Comintern". The Comintern is the obedient tool of the Kremlin. The Comintern's "leading tier... comprises people who did not join the October Revolution but the triumphant oligarchy, the fountainhead of high political titles and material boons. The predominating type among the present 'communist' bureaucrats is the political careerist, and in consequence the polar opposite of the revolutionist. Their ideal is to attain in their own countries the same position that the Kremlin oligarchy gained in the USSR. They are not the revolutionary leaders of the proletariat but aspirants to totalitarian rule. They dream of gaining success with the aid of this same Soviet bureaucracy and its GPU. They view with

34. *Writings 1939-40*, p.165
35. *Writings 1939-40*, p.348

admiration and envy the invasion of Poland, Finland, the Baltic states, Bessarabia by the Red Army, because these invasions immediately bring about the transfer of power into the hands of the local Stalinist candidates for totalitarian rule".

The word "immediately" implies also a revision of Trotsky's previous scheme of bureaucratically-impelled workers' revolution followed by suppression. And it is accurate. It is an enormous comment on the recent dispute in the Fourth International. Trotsky plainly comes down on the side of the most "extreme" of his factional opponents.

Finally, in his unfinished book on Stalin, Trotsky radically revised his old view and the fundamental mistake from which so much confusion and self-contradiction grew and will grow long after Trotsky is no more — that Stalin's turn in 1928-30 reflected working-class pressure, and reclassified it as driven by the autocracy's drive to grab the fruits of exploitation. "The kulak, jointly with the petty industrialist, worked for the complete restoration of capitalism. Thus opened the irreconcilable struggle over the surplus product of national labour. Who will dispose of it in the nearest future — the new bourgeoisie or the Soviet bureaucracy? — that became the next issue. He who disposes of the surplus product has the power of the state at his disposal. It was this that opened the struggle between the petty-bourgeoisie, which had helped the bureaucracy to crush the resistance of the labouring masses and of their spokesman the Left Opposition, and the Thermidorian bureaucracy... for the surplus product and for power"[36].

If we take Trotsky's final assessment of the Comintern and of Stalinist expansion in 1939-40 together with this summation of the class content of the 1928-30 struggle in the USSR, they add up to an enormous step towards the idea that the bureaucracy is a new ruling class.

XXXI. TROTSKY ON BUREAUCRATIC COLLECTIVISM

IN THE SWP faction fight the minority were in revolt — like Romantics against Enlightenment rationalism or women against an insensitive "male" consensus — against a worked-out all-embracing system, which none of them could fully see through, not even Burnham and Carter, who had started to criticise Trotsky's system three years earlier. The further development of a sound theoretical basis for working-class politics could only come through backing out of the common theoretical frame which, despite all their bitter and brave indignation, yoked Trotsky and his comrades to Stalinism, the idea that the statised property of the USSR defined it as a workers' state. In two articles at the beginning of the 1939-40 dispute Trotsky tentatively suggested ideas — soon sidelined as the faction fight escalated — which pointed to the way out. Taken together with his reassessment of 1928-30 in Trotsky's unfinished biography of Stalin, it pointed to a radically different post-Trotsky "Trotskyism" than the one Trotsky's "best disciples" developed. In 1939-40 Trotsky was very near — waiting for the war to put the final stamp on events — to devel-

---

36. *Stalin*, pp.221, 236.

oping the logic of his trajectory since 1936. Unless the factional polemics represented a great shift by Trotsky towards a quite different political trajectory — and the evidence of his writings after "Gangrene..." suggests the opposite — they were only a "blip" or zig-zag.

In "The USSR in War" (25 September 1939), as we have already seen, Trotsky writes: "In order that nationalised property in the occupied areas, as well as in the USSR, become a basis for genuinely progressive, that is to say socialist development, it is necessary to overthrow the Moscow bureaucracy". Later in the faction fight, and even in the same article, he would repeat his old idea, that the nationalised property was progressive even with the bureaucracy. This sentence, however, seems to close off one of the main strands of Trotsky's thinking since 1936: that the USSR's nationalised economy is progressive as it is, and can be "genuinely progressive" without being "socialist".

We have seen how, in reply to Craipeau for example, Trotsky dealt with all the political issues in dispute on the basis of the claim that the economy was progressive, while conceding for the sake of argument Craipeau's claim that the autocracy was a new exploiting class. In "The USSR in War" Trotsky draws this strand in his thought — the idea that the USSR represents a new form of class exploitation, more progressive than capitalism — out into a theory, and discusses it head-on. In "The USSR in War" Trotsky focuses his polemic against one Bruno Rizzi — though at that point no-one in the USA had heard of Rizzi, or read his book — because he wants to discuss, not Burnham's version of Trotsky's own restorationist idea, but the more radical notion that the Stalinist autocracy is a new sort of ruling class. Evidently he thinks it is the logical and necessary conclusion that must follow if one abandons Trotsky's own position that Stalin's USSR is an untenable temporary combination of incompatible elements. Trotsky is, as it were, wearing Rizzi as a mask of convenience: creating a dialogue about what he thinks are the issues.

Let us, Trotsky writes, concede "for the moment" that the autocracy is a new class and that the USSR is "a special system of class exploitation". Then, he asks, "what new political conclusions follow for us from these definitions? The Fourth International long ago recognised the necessity of overthrowing the bureaucracy by means of a revolutionary uprising of the toilers. Nothing else is proposed or can be proposed by those who proclaim the bureaucracy to be an exploiting 'class'.". The goal is to overthrow the bureaucracy and re-establish the rule of the soviets. "Nothing different can be proposed or is proposed by the leftist critics".

For Trotsky, "inasmuch as the question of overthrowing the parasitic oligarchy still remains linked with that of preserving the nationalised (state) property, we call the future revolution political". Some "want, come what may, to call the future revolution social. Let us grant this definition. What does it alter in essence? To those tasks of the revolution which we have enumerated it adds nothing whatsoever". Grant the critics their "terminology" — not a workers' state; a ruling class; a social, not a political, revolution — and they "would not know what to do with their purely verbal victory". Therefore it would, Trotsky proclaims, "be a piece of monstrous nonsense to split with comrades who on the question of the sociological nature of the USSR have an opinion different from ours, insofar as they solidarise with us in regard to the political tasks".

Trotsky has come a long way since the first half of the decade, when he wrote that "denying the proletarian character of the USSR is incompatible with membership in the Bolshevik-Leninists" (11 November 1934)[37].

He has not even included "defence of the USSR" in the political tasks, so far. "I hope that... we shall succeed by means of simply rendering our own ideas more precise to preserve unanimity on the basis of the programme of the Fourth International... despite the attempt of some comrades to uncover differences on the question of the 'defence of the USSR'.". Scientifically and politically, as distinct from terminologically, "the question poses itself as follows: does the bureaucracy represent a temporary growth on a social organism or has this growth already been transformed into a historically indispensable organ?".

Trotsky responds to this question by sketching out a hypothetical future within which subsequent development will prove that the Stalinist autocracy has indeed "already been transformed" into a new exploiting class. The whole discussion depends on one stark assertion: "The disintegration of capitalism has reached extreme limits, likewise the disintegration of the old ruling class. The further existence of this system is impossible. The productive forces must be organised in accordance with a plan. But who will accomplish this task — the proletariat or a new ruling class of 'commissars' — politicians, administrators and technicians?" "If... it is conceded that the present war will provoke not revolution but" — the "but" is not a straight link but a sharp corner turn; what follows is a restatement that capitalism is in irrevocable decline - "but a decline of the proletariat, then" — then what? - "there remains another alternative: the further decay of monopoly capitalism, its further fusion with the state and the replacement of democracy wherever it still exists by a totalitarian regime".

Then, capitalism having played out its historic role and the proletariat being shown congenitally incapable, "it would be necessary in retrospect to establish that in its fundamental traits the present USSR was the precursor of a new exploiting regime on an international scale". "The historic alternative, carried to the end, is as follows: either the Stalin regime is an abhorrent relapse in the process of transforming bourgeois society into a socialist society, or the Stalin regime is the first stage of a new exploiting society. "If the second prognosis proves to be correct, then, of course, the bureaucracy will become a new exploiting class".

What is impossible is not the (fantastic) scenario of the Stalinist USSR showing the shape of their future to all other countries, but the idea of admitting that it is so. But in the possible-but-not-yet-to-be-admitted scenario the bureaucracy will, as part of a new world system, do exactly as it does now in the USSR. It will have exactly the same relationship with the people and the proletariat as it has now. If it will be a new exploiting class then, worldwide, it is a new exploiting class now, in the USSR! If the bureaucracy, essentially unchanged, can "become" an exploiting class, then it is that already.

37. *Writings Supplement 1934-40*, p.538.

TROTSKY, OF COURSE, is talking about the conditions in which Marxists would have to recognise "bureaucratic collectivism" as such. But the idea that it can be recognised and identified in the USSR, the only place it now exists, only if it spread into a world system, is arbitrary and plainly false.

The other alternative, that the Stalinist autocracy is only "a parasitic growth on a workers' state", Trotsky likewise tests by sketching a future that will confirm it. "If this war provokes, as we firmly believe, a proletarian revolution", then the bureaucracy will be overthrown and soviet democracy regenerated "on a far higher economic and cultural basis than 1918. In that case the question of whether the Stalinist bureaucracy was a 'class' or a growth on the workers' state will be automatically solved".

Having sketched the alternatives — the actual outcome, revival and spread of capitalism and of the working class, is not dismissed as improbable, as it might reasonably have been, but as inconceivable — Trotsky concludes that what seem to be "terminological experiments" imply "a new historic conception... in an absolute contradiction with our programme, strategy and tactics". To adopt them would be an "adventuristic jump", and "doubly criminal now" when in the world war "the perspective of socialist revolution becomes an imminent reality and when the case of the USSR will appear to everybody as a transitorial episode in the process of world socialist revolution". Trotsky writes that we have not "the slightest right" — as revolutionaries, concerned with action in the new situation — to throw the theory on which we must act, and which we cannot quickly mend or replace, into disarray.

The alternatives are exaggerated fantastically. Trotsky states that "if... the October Revolution fails during the course of the present war, or immediately thereafter, to find its continuation in any of the advanced countries", then we must revise our concept of the socialist potential of the working class. This ultimatum to history is unwarranted by the facts and could only lead to despair — or the hysterical fighting-off of incipient despair.

Later in the article, Trotsky puts it as an ultimatum to the activists: "in the process of this war and those profound shocks which it must engender, will a genuine revolutionary leadership be formed capable of leading the proletariat to the conquest of power?". The urgency comes from Trotsky's picture of capitalism and the prospects for civilisation, and part of his purpose is to stiffen and galvanise the cadres; yet it is a form of political adventurism to pose it like this.

With the defeat of his mid-30s attempts at broad revolutionary regroupment, in the later 1930s Trotsky has shifted towards expecting revolutionary benefits from the war, a drive towards revolution generated as a mechanical product of the worsening crisis of capitalism. "The harsh and tragic dialectic of our epoch is working in our favour. Brought to the extreme pitch of exasperation and indignation, the masses will find no other leadership than that offered to them by the Fourth International"[38].

---

38. "A Great Achievement", 1938.

The notion of "leadership" here, abstracted from any perspective for transforming the existing labour movement and starkly juxtaposed to an expected sudden mass upsurge of raw working-class rage, can very easily lead to the disruption of Marxist politics by the towering need to "build the party" and therefore to adopt whatever policies will speed that work, even if they make no Marxist sense. It can lead to the concept of building an elite sect, an "alternative" leadership, to do single combat with the incumbents: to the typical mix of spontaneism and sect-ism in neo-Trotskyism...

Nor does Trotsky give any reason why, if workers' revolution is delayed, the future of human society can or should be extrapolated from a mutation in a backward country. Inverting Marx, Trotsky seems to say that the backward country shows their future to the advanced ones. The perspective is a derivative form of the Stalinist idea of USSR "Socialism in One Country" showing the world's future. World revolution is neatly inverted.

What evidence from the present does Trotsky offer for the idea that the autocracy has not yet destroyed the workers' state? Only the violence of the Stalinist purges. "The historical justification for every ruling class consisted in this — that the system of exploitation it heads raised the development of the productive forces to a new level. Beyond the shadow of a doubt, the soviet regime gave a mighty impulse to economy". Therefore the autocracy which, in its own brutal way, organised this "impulse to economy", is both a ruling class and progressive? No. "The source of this impulse was the nationalisation of the means of production and the planned beginnings, and by no means the fact that the bureaucracy usurped command over the economy". As the economy rose higher, its needs grew more complex and the bureaucratic regime became "unbearable". The "constantly sharpening contradiction between them leads to uninterrupted political convulsions, to systematic annihilation of the most outstanding creative elements in all spheres of activity. Thus, before the bureaucracy could succeed in exuding from itself a 'ruling class', it came into irreconcilable contradiction with the demands of development". This shows that "the bureaucracy is not the bearer of a new system of economy peculiar to itself and impossible without itself, but is a parasitic growth on a workers' state". Trotsky's argument here depends entirely on his dual system, his split-level view of the USSR. The "deep" reality is Trotsky's ghostly version of what might have happened, rooted in October 1917; the empirical reality is that essence distorted and corrupted by what Trotsky dubs "'accidental' (i.e. temporary and extraordinary) enmeshing of historical circumstances", namely, the bureaucratic counter-revolution against October. Trotsky uses it to insist that "being" — the autocratic system which has been a fact for 12 years or more — is still only a flickering moment in a different "becoming", to dissolve being into becoming, to argue that what is and long has been is less than real because, he believes, it does not exist "stably". Always the "snapshot" is abolished in favour of projecting the moving film into the future. This is the dialectic here, and there is nothing artificial in Trotsky using it in his polemics against Burnham and Shachtman. For Trotsky it has become everything.

Method is splitting from its application to become the last auxiliary argument — and here, it is sophism.

IN A SUPPLEMENTARY article discussing reactions to "The USSR in War" ("Again and Once More...") Trotsky adds: "Some comrades evidently were surprised that I spoke in my article ("The USSR in War") of the system of 'bureaucratic collectivism' as a theoretical possibility. They discovered in this even a complete revision of Marxism. This is an apparent misunderstanding".

In later years, Cannon and others will nevertheless go on flinging this nonsense about "revisionism" at those, like Max Shachtman, who develop Trotsky's ideas. They will feel bolstered because of Trotsky's frequent use in the SWP faction fight of the charge "revisionist", aimed against elements of the opposition. In fact what Trotsky considered "revisionist" on the USSR was Burnham and Carter's theory, which he took as claiming that there was no ruling class in the USSR. He defined "bureaucratic collectivism" not as "revisionist" but as the proper Marxist alternative to the "revisionist" view if one were to abandon his "degenerated workers' state" theory — which he was not yet ready to do.

Trotsky certified "bureaucratic collectivism" as both Marxist and as the conclusion that must follow rejection of the workers' state theory if the USSR neither reverted to capitalism nor was transformed by a workers' revolution.

In the second article Trotsky sets out the idea that should have been at the heart of post-Trotsky Trotskyism when it ceased to be even residually reasonable to continue what was in Trotsky already culpably wrong, the theoretical policy of "wait". "The Marxist comprehension of historical necessity has nothing in common with fatalism. Socialism is not realisable 'by itself', but as a result of the struggle of living forces, classes and their parties".

Trotsky believes the working class will conquer. "But we have full right to ask ourselves: What character will society take if the forces of reaction conquer?" Trotsky is talking about world-wide alternatives. Yet his thought plainly applies to the USSR now. In the USSR, in the struggle of living forces, the bureaucracy has conquered and Trotsky is not remiss in describing its barbaric character. Without first, as Trotsky did in "The USSR in War", running up the ladder of grand historic generalities, apply what Trotsky says to the USSR and both the conclusion and the inner logic of Trotsky's thinking on the USSR are clear and unavoidable.

Trotsky goes on: Marxists have formulated the broad historical alternatives as socialism or barbarism. After Mussolini's victory — communism or fascism. Shachtman and the Workers' Party will develop this train of thought in the face of expanding Stalinism: socialism or Stalinist barbarism. Events, Trotsky continues, have shown that the delay of the socialist revolution engenders barbarism — "chronic unemployment, pauperisation of the petty bourgeoisie, fascism, finally wars of extermination which do not open up any new road... We have the possibility of expressing ourselves on [barbarism] more concretely than Marx. Fascism on one hand, degeneration of the soviet state on the other outline the social and political forms of a neo-barbarism. An alternative of this kind — socialism or totalitarian servitude — has not only theoretical interest, but also enor-

mous importance in agitation, because in its light the necessity for socialist revolution appears most graphically".

However much this is attached in Trotsky's article to speculations about
the future, it applies also to the present: Stalinism is barbarism. The
reductio ad absurdam of Trotsky's final position in that what Trotsky,
expecting that it will soon be overthrown, calls a political, social, and economic system in one country, or one empire, becomes outright barbarism
in the prototype of threatening world barbarism if it spreads to the world
at large and is consolidated. It spread only to a further large part mainly
of the backward parts of the world, but it was consolidated there — and it
was barbarism.

"It is self-evident that owing to the needs of the 'system' he [Hegel] very often had to resort to those forced constructions about which his pigmy opponents make such a terrible fuss even today. But... even though unconsciously, he showed us the way out of the labyrinth of systems to real positive knowledge of the world". Frederick Engels, *Ludwig Feuerbach*

THERE WERE THUS two distinct, and by the end sharply contradictory, strands in Trotsky's political legacy. The one that would dominate in "orthodox" neo-Trotskyism, however, was the strand developed around the idea of the Stalinist autocracy being a "watchman", "gatekeeper", or locum for the working class. Let me recapitulate.

The end of the civil war, in November 1920, brought stalemate. The Bolsheviks had won, but the Russian Revolution could not thrive or indefinitely survive unless it spread; the counter-revolution could not triumph unless and until it smashed the apparatus of state power sustained by the Bolsheviks; and it had failed definitively to do that. The Bolsheviks could not at will spread the revolution; but they could "hold on" until it spread: from this situation grew the policy that the Bolshevik party would act *"in loco proletariis"*, as stand-in or "watchman" (Trotsky) for the Russian working class — for the class which had been massacred by the Whites, dispersed by great dislocation of industry, or absorbed into the state bureaucracy and the Red Army, and which was only in the process of being recomposed in the NEP.

This was the situation that Lenin at the 10th Party Congress described as a "workers' state with bureaucratic deformations". From this practice and this policy came the idea that governed Trotsky's understanding of the USSR for the next two decade, namely that something other than the proletariat could act historically for the proletariat.

It started as the rational and limited idea that an association of the most determined and educated working-class activists (the Bolshevik Old Guard) could guard and develop the gains of a broader working class that had temporarily been diminished, dispersed and exhausted. It grew into the notion that the post-Civil-War Russian bureaucracy and then the totalitarian Stalinist autocracy acted as locums for the working class, and represented the working class in power so long as they still defended the nationalised economy — for this nationalised economy was the settled residue of the expropriation of the bourgeoisie in 1917.

Despite all the qualifications which Trotsky added to it, and which led him to a programme of a new full-scale workers' revolution against the Stalinist autocracy, in its fully-extended form the doctrine of the "locum" implied that the workers could rule as abstract historical subjects, in "high theory", even where as living people, in practice, they were beasts of burden exploited by a privileged autocracy.

The metaphysics of nationalised economy and the idea of the locum intertwined with and mutually conditioned and sustained each other.

From this idea, embedded in Trotsky's defence of the proposition that the Stalinist USSR remained a workers' state, neo-Trotskyists developed a series of extensions and extrapolations to embrace Titoites, Maoists, Castroites, Ho-ists, etc. etc. etc. The locums too could have locums and then again locums. Thus the post-Trotsky "Trotskyists" solved the "crisis of working class leadership" that Trotsky defined by discovering that the "socialist" revolution could be made (distortedly, unsatisfactorily, and only in a preliminary way, to be sure) without either the proletariat or a revolutionary socialist party.

In Trotsky, the idea was over the years modified and qualified by intense loathing, resentment, condemnation and hatred for the Stalinist bureaucracy and its crimes. By the end of his life, so the evidence suggests, Trotsky was close to breaking with it entirely. But he never did break with the notion that the survival of nationalised economy made the USSR still working-class and progressive or — according to Trotsky at the end — potentially progressive, even under what he himself denounced as the totalitarian rule of an autocracy with all the vices of history's ruling classes, differing from pre-Holocaust Nazism (so he wrote in *The Transitional Programme*, 1938) "only in more unbridled savagery".

That notion was, for Trotsky and Trotskyism, the shirt of Nessus, which once put on seeped poison and corrosion into the tissues of its doomed wearer. It was a garment that could not be removed a piece at a time. So long as the basic notion was upheld, no crime by the totalitarian rulers could destroy their credentials as a residually progressive locum for the proletariat and guardian of the economy and social system coming from October — no crime at all, not destruction of the labour movement, not industrial enslavement of the workers, not the murder of millions of workers and revolutionaries, not the creation of huge privileges and social inequalities while workers starved — no crime, that is, except dismantling the nationalised economy. So long as nationalised economy existed, defined and assessed as Trotsky continued to assess it, as the solid residue of the workers' expropriation of the bourgeoisie in 1917-18, there was no limit. It was all-defining.

Thus, out of the reasonable and unavoidable Bolshevik solution to the dilemma of the Russian working-class revolution at the end of the civil war had grown the root idea of a totalitarian economistic "socialism" subversive of every key notion that had defined Marxism from the *Communist Manifesto* onwards.

Trotsky thought that he was formulating provisional theorisations for a very brief historical aberration. The Stalinist regime — a "workers' state" with a regime more savagely anti-worker than any bourgeois state — could not last for long. The USSR would break down, either through bourgeois counter-revolution or through a new workers' revolution. In fact it would last 50 years after Trotsky. Ideas Trotsky juggled with as interim, short-term solutions took on a life of their own, drawing their strength from the survival and expansion of Stalinism.

Despite enormous shifts, in reality and in Trotsky's thinking, there is continuity in this idea from the end of the civil war to Trotsky's death and way beyond.

In Lenin's time, when the party was a party of working-class revolutionaries, whose selfless loyalty to socialism had been proved again and again, the idea was rational and true. In the circumstances, what else could they do? Then, the ruling group periodically purged itself of self-seekers and careerists. By 1924 Stalin's bureaucracy was harvesting careerists and promoting self-seekers, while persecuting revolutionaries. In 1927 it expelled the authentic Bolsheviks, and in December 1929, with the shooting of Jacob Blumkin, a Soviet official who had dared to visit Trotsky in Turkey, it started to kill them. After 1928 the bureaucracy destroyed the Russian labour movement and began to reduce the working class and the whole people to slavery and semi-slavery.

It could now be seen as locum for the working class only if the autocratically collectivised socio-economic system could be defined as a conquest and residue of the workers' revolution. In fact, that system, as it was shaped after 1928, was a system erected by an autocracy which seized the institutions and forms created by the working class in 1917-21 and perverted them for its own use on ground cleared by the revolution. Except for the eruption of Russian imperialism and the beginning of the expansion of this system a decade or so later nothing fundamental changed for 60 years. The distinction made in some of the texts in this book, that before 1928-30 Trotsky defined the working-class character of the regime only by the political regime and its alleged reformability, is, though valid, far too sharply drawn. Already in the mid-1920s Trotsky used the "social conquests" as central to his idea of the USSR as a workers' state; as late as the early 1930s he cited the possibility of the workers regaining power by "reform" as crucial to the "proletarian" character of the state; even in 1938, his perception of the Stalinist leadership was conditioned by the idea that it (unlike the newer elements of the bureaucracy, surrounding it) was closely tied to the nationalised economy and would be in a "united front" with the workers against the bourgeois counter-revolution he saw as an imminent danger.

In the 1920s, Trotsky had called for "reform" in the USSR. He publicly changed his position only in October 1933, adopting then a somewhat understated early variant of what he would from July 1936 call "political revolution". Yet Trotsky's own word for

111

his policy before 1933, "reform", is radically misleading. How could the exiled, jailed, hounded and murdered Opposition have expected to reform the Stalinist regime? Was this "reform" in the usual sense of peaceful and gradual change? Trotsky himself explained:

"The Democratic-Centralists ... criticize our road of reform in a very "Left" manner — a road which, I hope, we have sshown by deeds is not at all the road of Stalinist legality; but they do not show the working masses any other road. They content themselves with sectarian mutterings against us, and count meanwhile on spontaneous movements."

In fact all Trotsky's perspectives for "reform" were centred on the eruption of a radical crisis, towards which Trotsky thought all the regime's policies — positive actions and derelictions alike — were inexorably building. In this crisis, the apparatus would fragment; the scattered forces of the Bolshevik party would regroup and reorganise themselves; the Left Opposition, with its clarity, programme, far-sightedness and tempering would, overtly or implicitly, assume the leadership. Most likely this crisis would include civil war, or elements of civil war. Not between the bureaucracy and the working class, but between the regime and bourgeois counter-revolution, whose mass forces would be the peasantry. In this the Opposition would ally with the regime and support it as the Bolsheviks supported Kerensky against the attempted army coup of Kornilov in 1917 — in Lenin's phrase "as the rope supports the hanged man". They grew in strength and soon dealt with Kerensky. Reform was displacement of the Stalinist regime in the civil war against the counter-revolution.

The policy was "reform" only to the extent that it included the retention of the reformed — politically, revolutionised — apparatus. In this process the workers would reconquer power from the bureaucracy. The apparatus which, despite everything, preserved structures created in the revolution and civil war against what Trotsky saw as the urgent threat of fascistic peasant-based bourgeois counter-revolution, would be cleansed, purged, deprived of its Stalinist-bureaucratic technique of domination over the people, and subordinated to a newly reconstituted Bolshevik party.

This was "reform" in the midst of revolutionary convulsion. There was much of revolution in it. And, likewise, the idea of the bureaucratic locum underlies and interweaves with Trotsky's policy at every point, lending to it an ambivalence that is there even in his strongest condemnations of bureaucratic rule and most ardent and vehement advocacy of working-class action to overthrow the bureaucracy. He will name it, variously, bureaucratic centrist; Bonapartist; absolutist; totalitarian; a ruling caste; a new aristocracy. He accuses it of concentrating in itself all the vices of all the ruling classes of history and, though he avoids the word, of imperialism. In all of these phases, though the criticism and hatred intensify, as do the negative evaluations of the elite, there is always something left: nationalised property, mixed in Trotsky with increasingly tenuous but always present degrees of ideologising and fantasising about its connections to the working class.

Trotsky continues to see the autocracy, despite everything, as in some essential ways still a reflective, mechanical, passive agency of the workers' revolution, as if the "soul" of the dead party and the murdered working-class revolution has passed to the nationalised economy and from that to the state and the autocracy.

The working class does not hold power (or not "direct" power). The autocratic locum rules, and rules savagely, over the workers. But the social conquests of the dead and defeated working class revolution remain because the bureaucracy has a dual role.

Trotsky is forced to insist that the key idea that the working class, unlike the bourgeoisie, can only rule politically, that is democratically, is operational only on a higher stage and in other situations. The USSR is different. History, Trotsky, insists, is richer than socialist norms. Where, he asks, has a degenerated workers' state been observed before?

Trotsky is a scientist — genuinely so, but also in a self-disabling "abstracted" sense, forcing himself into the pose of a "disinterested observer". "Objectivity", caution and restraint work against drawing "hasty" conclusions about the class character of the Stalinist USSR — conclusions that in fact would have been not at all hasty. The socialist norms get progressively battered out of shape and are relegated to the background, rather as the 17th century British empirical scientists pushed God to the margin of their concerns, as the distant "first cause", while they explored material reality beyond the first cause.

The consequence was the disorientation of generations of revolutionary socialists. With neither Trotsky's political balance nor his historical perspective, the post-Trotsky Trotskyists reduced Trotsky's idea to arid totalitarian economism: a state like Mao's China, which as a political system was fascistic and as a socio-economic formation was nearer to oriental despotism than to the capitalist society which for Marxism prepares the economic, social and cultural pre-requisite for the emergence of socialism, was defined by nationalised economy as working-class and in transition to socialism.

Trotsky describes the autocracy accurately as having all the vices of a ruling class, and yet continues to reject the idea that it is a ruling class because of the fatal combination of the two ideas: totalitarian economism and the locum. So long as the view that there could be a locum was held, and so long as nationalised property defined the USSR as working-class, Trotsky's was an impregnable ideological system. So long as the Stalinist autocracy's post-1928 bureaucratic revolution remained shrouded in myth and was not properly separated out from the working-class October Revolution the "defence of the nationalised economy" could be logically extended into defence of a full-blown Stalinist empire.

If nationalised property defines a totalitarian socio-political system as a workers' state — and if you do not recognise or become inhibited by *reductio ad absurdum* — then the extension of the system has infinite possibilities. The ideology can and did develop in parallel with the development of the Russian empire and the spread of Stalinism. In principle, you can recognise the "progressive" aspects of new workers' states formed by peasant armies such as Mao's or Pol Pot's, or by Stalin's conquering army; and simultaneously advocate self-determination for the component parts of the Russian Empire, and 'political' revolution against the bureaucratic locum.

One pre-requisite of this ideological system is a fetish of the economic form of nationalised property. Another is a pre-Marxian form of nihilistic negation of capitalism or "sectarianism towards capitalism" — substituting a fixed stance of desiring what is anti-capitalist, regardless of what it may represent positively, for the Marxian notion of a socialism built on the progressive achievements of capitalism.

This system puts the definition of "workers' states" essentially outside all political judgement. If the fetish — nationalised property — exists, or is coming into existence in China or Cuba, then the regime is by definition a working-class "locum", no matter what atrocities it commits against living workers. The ideology is a closed system defined entirely by its own inner points of reference. Large areas of political judgement are pre-empted and killed off. Within such a system, unconditional defence of the USSR, conceived of by Trotsky as a policy to maximise the chances of working-class regeneration of the USSR and forestall its full collapse into the fascistic capitalist barbarism which was engulfing much of the world in the 1930s, becomes socialist *hara-kiri* in the service of the "progressive" system and vicarious Russian imperialism.

Trotsky should have drawn the indicated Marxist conclusions when the bureaucracy crushed both bourgeois and proletarians and made itself "sole master of the surplus product". That was the point at which the idea of the Bolshevik Party acting as locum turned into support for a collectivised class of exploiters ruling over the working class. The Bolshevik Party was genuinely the locum for the working class. The Stalinist "locum" for this locum was a new, exploiting, counter-revolutionary ruling class.

While holding to the idea of the Stalinist locum that remained at least residually progressive as custodian of nationalised property, Trotsky did not think that it could go on indefinitely and evolve into socialism. This is of fundamental importance. Trotsky finally put a term to it and indicated empirical tests for reassessing the USSR. In September-October 1939 he put a question mark over the whole idea and indicated that if the Stalinist USSR should survive the convulsions of world war, then it must be reassessed even if it retained nationalised property. Had he been allowed to hold these tests, the experience of the next few years after August 1940 would, on Trotsky's published reasoning, have compelled him to break with the idea that the bureaucracy was a locum for working-class rule, and the USSR still a workers' state.

Trotsky's disciples would continue to see the autocracy — and other bureaucracies modelled on Stalin's — as locums until 1991. This idea led to very strange things.

The Trotskyists, unlike the ignorant honest CP members or fellow travellers, knew the main facts. From Trotsky's idea that the "what" of a working-class essence contained in the socio-economic formation, supposedly defined by the nationalised-economy residue from 1917-21, could develop autonomously from the "who" of the working class, flowed the possibility of mentally "lifting out" the idea of working-class revolution above the actuality of the working class.

With these ideological spectacles, the neo-Trotskyists could see working-class revolutions being made by "locums" which reduced the working class itself to semi-slavery. Stalin's Russia could spread revolution by its "Red" Armies (World War 2). "Workers'" revolutions could be made by peasant armies. This vision contained the seeds of religion. For a while in the early 1950s, the Fourth International was dominated by an idea closer to medieval millenarianism — the idea of social transformation through the miracle-working second coming of Christ — than to a Marxist view of socialism being made by the agency of the working class and through the opportunities created by the contradictions and achievements of capitalism.

The neo-Trotskyists looked to a "War-Revolution" in which a hidden logic of history, operating from above and beyond all particular human agency, would transform a Third World War between the USSR and the USA into socialist revolution. The little literary apparatus that called itself the leadership of the Fourth International could work literary wonders, make fantastic compounds and combinations in their heads, and project fantasies on to the activities of the Stalinist movements, as they did for decades, only because the notion of the locum had become central to neo-Trotskyism.

Considering the pressures on them, the true heroism of the post-Trotsky Trotskyists is seen in their stubborn resistance to the logic of the theories which they accepted, of the "locum" and of "totalitarian economism", and their presentation in however battered a form of a Marxist critique of Stalinism, together with a programme for transforming the Stalinist societies. Sometimes,as we shall see, they were bent out of shape under the pressure, but they remained — or returned to — what they fundamentally were. By doing so they kept alive a revolutionary socialist movement which today can renew itself by rediscovering and building on the other thread in Trotsky's ideas on the USSR, the thread represented by the concrete and detailed analyses in The *Degeneration of Theory*, *The Revolution Betrayed* and *The Bonapartist Philosophy*, by the indications for reconceptualisation given in "The USSR in War", and by Trotsky's increasingly militant advocacy of workers' revolution against the Stalinist autocracy and an independent proletarian "Third Camp" against both capitalism and Stalinism.

3. THE NEO-TROTSKYISTS AND STALINIST EXPANSION

I. PROVISIONAL FORMULA ERECTED INTO WORLD-HISTORIC INTERPRETATION

"The leadership oriented itself without any synthesised understanding of our epoch and its inner tendencies, only by groping (Stalin) and by supplementing the fragmentary conclusions thus obtained with scholastic schema renovated for each occasion (Bukharin). The political line as a whole, therefore, represents a chain of zig-zags. The ideological line is a kaleidoscope of schemas tending to push to absurdity every segment of the Stalinist zigzags. The Sixth Congress would act correctly if it decided to elect a special commission in order to compile all the theories created by Bukharin and intended by him to serve as a basis, say, for all the stages of the Anglo-Russian Committee; these theories would have to be compiled chronologically and arranged systematically so as to draw a fever chart of the ideas contained in them. It would be a most instructive strategical diagram. The same also holds for the Chinese revolution, the economic development of the USSR, and all other less important questions. Blind empiricism multiplied by scholasticism". Leon Trotsky, *The Third International After Lenin.*

TROTSKY REJECTED THE idea that the Russian system at the end of the 1930s was even minimally solid and coherent: it lacked "crystallised class relations". Only because of this did Trotsky reject the idea that the bureaucracy was a ruling class. The bureaucracy was, he thought, a parasitic growth on the continuously degenerating forms of collectivised economy rooted in the 1917 revolution. By the end, the time span Trotsky projected was very short. "Might we not place ourselves in a ludicrous position if we affixed to the Bonapartist oligarchy the nomenclature of a new ruling class just a few years or even a few months prior to its inglorious downfall?", he wrote in "The USSR in War".

His refusal to conclude that the ruling bureaucracy was a ruling class was fundamentally and explicitly tied to and dependent on that time scale. In that sense only, and for that reason only, did Trotsky deny that the bureaucracy was a ruling class. Far from his refusal to call it a ruling class expressing softness towards the bureaucracy, Trotsky, as we saw, compared it unfavourably with Nazism.

The policy of "unconditional defence of the USSR" was part of this complex of ideas expressing the concept of an "interregnum economy". Degenerating from the revolution, but not yet overthrown by bourgeois forces, it retained the potential of regeneration by way of a new working-class 'political revolution'. It was not, in Trotsky's view, a degenerated workers' state in stable equilibrium, but continually degenerating. Else — he had said it only tentatively — it was a new form of class society, whose features were its own norm, not a degeneration of something else.

Yet, though this gave unmistakable signs of direction, it left the theoretical questions at Trotsky's death in a state of chaos and flux. Nothing could be more unsatisfactory than a political legacy which argued passionately for political conclusions that flowed from the bureaucratically-statised economy when seen in one framework (degenerated workers' state) while at the same time its proponents accepted that an alternative framework (new ruling class) — from which other conclusions would follow — might prove to be better: and would, moreover, have to be adopted if the phenomenon lasted much longer in its present form! Yet that is how things stood when Stalin's assassin Mercador struck Trotsky down.

The USSR did last, coming out of the world war intact and in occupation of vast tracts of eastern and central Europe. However, the conclusions drawn then by Trotsky's most loyal "disciples", his partisans of 1939-40, were not those that Trotsky indicated for such an eventuality, but their very opposite — views akin to those Trotsky had long ago been forced to jettison. What was to be "official" Trotskyism by the mid-1950s had been called Brandlerism and Bauerism in Trotsky's lifetime. On the class nature of the Soviet Union the theoretical identity of the Trotskyists had not been disentangled from that of the Stalinists, who also "defended the Soviet Union". Political conditions existed for the international Trotskyist movement, after Trotsky's subtleties died with him, to repeat the political collapse of the Left Opposition in 1928-30. Continuing to criticise, they nevertheless accepted as "progressive", despite everything, the expansion of Stalinism. They translated Trotsky's defence of the Soviet Union into partisanship for the USSR empire. This pattern would last as long as the USSR did, and longer.

The neo-Trotskyist solution to the problem of the post-war Russian empire — restricting the word empire to mean monopoly-capitalist empire — obfuscated but could not resolve the problem. Without being defined, it would be one of the issues that split the forces of orthodox neo-Trotskyism in 1953 at the time of the East German workers' uprising.

Trotsky's failures to understand Stalinism fully are not difficult to understand. Faced with nineteenth century industrial capitalism, for generations the critics and rebels against the bourgeois system had not fully understood it. Some tended to understand capitalism and the exploitation of the working class as a mere extension of landlordism and age-old land-based robbery. Myths about exploitation originating in the Norman Conquest did widespread service as general explanations well into Chartist times. It is no cause for wonder that in the first years of the new phenomenon of Stalinism, there was not instant clarity. Columbus tried to sail to the Indies and found an unexpected, unknown continent rising out of the sea before him. He died without ever understanding or accepting that it was not the Indies but a "New World" he had found. So with Trotsky and the unexpected social system that was Stalinism.

Trotsky too had a false map of history. Though he understood so much about Stalinism, he postponed defining it as the distinct socio-economic formation it was. Much of the difficulty was to cease seeing it in terms of either capitalism or socialism and to examine it as something new, having a "finished", settled character.It was strange, new and evolving.

At the end of his life he would talk of the USSR as a counter-revolutionary workers' state displaying "elements" of imperialism. But he still saw it in terms of other formations — capitalism, socialism — and only tentatively, and as if through a shifting mist, as what it really was, a socio-economic formation distinct both from capitalism and socialism: distinct from

116

capitalism, although the bureaucracy was not a mere parasitic growth on a backward workers' state, but a formed exploitative class which, as Trotsky put it towards the end, seized and disposed of all the social surplus product; and distinct from working-class socialism, although it was anti-capitalist and, in its own bureaucratic way, "collectivist" and a "planned" economy.

II. "IN DEFENCE OF MARXISM"

IN SEPTEMBER AND October 1939 Trotsky, as we have noted, tentatively accepted that the USSR as it was could be seen in a radically different theoretical framework — "bureaucratic collectivism". He said it was too early actually to reach such a conclusion; but irrevocably he had accepted it in principle. Then, close on this radical theoretical break with the past — hypothetical, conditional as it was, but a fundamental departure nonetheless — Trotsky engaged in a bitter political struggle against Burnham and Shachtman. His polemics then for "unconditional defence of the USSR", against Max Shachtman, Martin Abern, James Burnham, and about half of his American comrades, had the catastrophic effect after his death of half-burying what was new in his final position and obscuring the direction of his thought. His "orthodox" disciples would erect and freeze as "Trotskyism" ideas and attitudes with which Trotsky was, probably, breaking, and add for good measure ideas he (see below) had spent his last 17 years fighting.

The drama of the 1939-40 faction fight and split would be both the Nativity and the Easter Resurrection story for post-Trotsky Trotskyism. Its literature, by Cannon and Trotsky — kept "authoritative" by non-publication of Trotsky's other, vehemently anti-Stalinist, articles on the USSR of the same time — would educate and miseducate generations, and be the cultural medium of a tendency whose perspectives of workers' revolution were elaborations (not without criticism, to be sure, and, for the Soviet Union, calls for political revolution) on hopes for the success of Stalinism.

Trotsky's polemics from the faction fight were collected in a book, *In Defence of Marxism*, first published in December 1942. "The USSR in War", wherein for the first time he accepted the possibility that the USSR, as it was, without any transformation, might have to be reconceptualised, is the first major item in the 1942 collection. It is followed by a large collection of polemics against those who questioned unconditional defence of the USSR when Stalin was Hitler's partner in carving up Poland, and then invaded bourgeois-democratic Finland, and against those who said, or implied, that the USSR was already to be defined as a bureaucratic-collectivist (or state-capitalist) state.

In *In Defence of Marxism*, the heavy emphasis is on the idea that the Soviet Union is not, or not yet, to be given up. This book, and a companion volume by James P Cannon from the same factional struggle, came to embody "orthodox Trotskyism". Around *In Defence of Marxism* was built the alleged continuity with Trotsky's movement of the politically reconstructed and radically changed post-war "Trotskyism". From 1942 to 1969-70, when the first "scrapbook" versions of Trotsky's collected writ-

117

ings from the 1930s began to appear, working backwards from 1940, *In Defence of Marxism* was the main account of Trotsky's views on the Soviet Union known to English-language readers, apart from *The Revolution Betrayed*, written before the Moscow Trials.

If you take the articles on Stalinism from Trotsky's last 18 months and read them in sequence, putting the pieces in *In Defence of Marxism* in their proper place in the series, you get a very different picture of what Trotsky was saying and where he was going, and a radically different balance. You could, carefully picking through "The USSR in War", get an idea of what Trotsky was saying, or half-saying "for now", and where he might be going; but the countering, numbing, neutralising effect of the rest of the unbalanced collection, with its harsh denunciation of the "petty-bourgeois opposition" of Shachtman and the others, weighed massively, and for most people decisively, against doing that. By contrast, had "The USSR in War" been published in its proper place in the sequence, it would have been hard not to get Trotsky's drift, and hard to see his rather wild polemical sallies as the last word. And harder to take the road the official Trotskyists did take. But the selection in *In Defence of Marxism* was itself the result of decisions about which road to take.

What was put and kept in circulation embodied political selection and political alignment. From the death of Trotsky onwards his works were picked over and used instead of living theory, to garnish empirical political responses and never-again-coherent policies arrived at by means of adaptation to other forces.

In Defence of Marxism appeared in December 1942, as the SWP entered into a white heat of soviet patriotism — which was very popular in all the lands allied with Stalin, including the USA; in most people's minds it would have merged with the local patriotism, which the SWP of course rejected and repudiated. The publication of *In Defence of Marxism* and its slant reflected that wartime pro-sovietism and perpetuated it.

It was a time when *The Militant* was inclined to deny, or half-deny, that the Soviet-Nazi alliance had ever occurred, and when it was admitted, they argued that such an alliance was unnatural anyway, the place of the Soviet Union being, it was implied, naturally with the good guys. The book, with its extremely violent and unqualified condemnation of the "petty-bourgeois" opposition, appeared at a time when, one year after the USA's entry into World War 2, that condemnation had already been proven in life to be nonsensical at every level.

Shachtman's "petty-bourgeois" opposition had been accused of recoiling against the Hitler-Stalin pact because they were capitulating to American bourgeois democracy. In 1942, that opposition, organised in the Workers Party, stood before the American working class as defenders of neither the newly popular Soviet Union nor of the USA. The Shachtmanites preached stark opposition to the USA's war. Their young people had systematically gone into industry, where they would consistently have a higher profile than the SWP, whose trade unionists were told to "preserve the cadre" in industry during the war by keeping their heads down.

Faction fights generate exaggeration, suspicion, wild extrapolation. Events had shown by December 1942 what had been what in the old polemics. To publish these comments from late 1939 and early 1940, comments which flew in the face of the subsequent developments, was an act

118

of wilful and heedless factional libel. It is impossible to think that Trotsky would have approved.

And yet the story is worse still. If you read the reprinted records of the 1939-40 fight you are led to assume that the SWP in the war was always ardently for defence of the Soviet Union. *The Militant* and the SWP were for defence of the Soviet Union. But they became the passionate upfront public defenders of the USSR only after the tide of the war had turned in Stalin's favour at Stalingrad late in 1942. They were part of what CPers knew as "the Stalingrad draft". Before that, for a whole year, defence of the Soviet Union had had low priority in the pages of the paper.

Such is the origin of the compilation that shaped post-Trotsky Trotskyism for over 30 years, and still does so now that Trotsky's other writings of the time are in print. It was both symptomatic and central to the shaping of "orthodox" neo-Trotskyism. The element of accommodation to Stalinism's success is central and massive.

III. FREEZING "TROTSKY" INTO DOGMA

IN 1929, MANY members and leaders of the Left Opposition in the USSR surrendered to Stalin because, in erecting the totalitarian power of the new bureaucratic class and destroying what was left of the labour movement, he also kicked the feeble NEP bourgeoisie into its grave. Trotsky did not. Trotsky had had an independent axis, which his partially false conceptions of Stalinism twisted but did not uproot. So too at Trotsky's end. The neo-Trotskyists had no such axis. Nor had they Trotsky's political and theoretical culture. They made of Trotsky's "unconditional defence" of the "workers' state" a dogma which had less and less grip on the reality of Stalinism, and combined that blind incomprehension on the level of theory with opportunist adaptations. They did remain critics of Stalinism and advocates of working-class democracy — while supporting Stalinism "against capitalism". This combination of eyeless dogmatism and sometimes exuberant opportunist adaptation to successful and "victorious" Stalinism produced very bizarre results within two years of Trotsky's death, and would continue to do so for almost half a century.

By erecting Trotsky's conclusions of a particular time against his method, the official Trotskyists both expressed their own unwillingness to think, and sealed off the propensity to think of newcomers — for generations. Mummery displaced Marxism as a living thing.

Theoretical poverty, together with a religiosity rooted in fear to try to think along Trotsky's lines and face the real world, fear to look uncongenial reality in the eye, fear of "disillusionment", fear of not being "objective", fear of not being with the real "revolutions of our time", led to a hardening of the heart and of the mind. This produced a view of the world in the early forties, and then in the early fifties, akin to millenarian religion. It is not surprising to find the long-time British adherents of this sort of neo-Trotskyism, the Healyites — albeit in the 1970s after they had gone seriously mad — engaging in public ceremonies structured around Trotsky's death-mask.

Trotsky's tentative and questioning posing of an alternative to the workers' state framework unavoidably also implied a questioning, *pro tem* attitude to the old position. But the old position was frozen by his ardent disciples. They cut away Trotsky's last qualifications and questionings and hypothetical conclusions, and chose in due time to interpret the survival and expansion of Stalinism as proof that nothing in the USSR's "working-class character" had changed or required reconsideration. Trotsky had in anticipation said plainly that opposite conclusions would be indicated if the Stalinist system survived and had to be considered as stabilised. Trotsky had, at the end, set empirical and temporal tests for deciding that Stalinism was a new form of class society. Those who insisted they were the "orthodox" Trotskyists ignored and implicitly rejected these tests.

The events after Trotsky's death — when the Soviet Union survived, conquered great territories, became the second power in the world, and was replicated in foreign countries — were entirely outside what was even conceivable to him; but they pointed all the more forcefully to the conclusions Trotsky had indicated in the event that the USSR proved more stable than he had thought.

Having in the course of the faction struggle, which continued as rivalry between the two parties that resulted from it — the WP and the SWP — declared the alternative bureaucratic-collectivist framework which Trotsky had tentatively posed in September 1939 as the greatest heresy and "revision" of the "programme of the Fourth International", the neo-Trotskyists had boxed themselves off from resuming Trotsky's train of thought when time and experience of the USSR's survival in war made it imperative.

Whereas Trotsky had in anticipation said plainly that new conclusions would be indicated if the Stalinist system survived, his disciples, ignoring Trotsky's thought while using his words, still held that so long as nationalised property remained, and was being spread, nothing had changed or required reconsideration. Trotsky had broken with that position in September-October 1939. They were taken in tow by the Stalinist empire of countries which they soon discovered were "in transition to socialism".

IV. STALINIST SOCIETY IN TRANSITION TO SOCIALISM?

FACED WITH THE survival and expansion of Stalinism, Trotsky's real and evolving idea of Stalinism was destroyed amongst his followers even while they held to the letter of his pre-September 1939 reasoning. The new bureaucratic formations in China, etc. could not be understood, as Trotsky had said the USSR bureaucracy was, to be in conflict and contradiction with the collectivist property they created: bureaucratically collectivised property could not now be identified even obliquely with a form of working class property. James Connolly's mordant joke, "if state ownership is socialism, then the jailer and the hangman are socialist functionaries" had taken on a grim new meaning in the face of Stalinism. The old basic notion of socialism, that political power was decisive, logically came into its own, even if the confusions engendered by Trotsky's attempts to account for the USSR had been justified.

The neo-Trotskyists, who chose instead to hold to the letter of Trotsky's

120

ideas, did so because of the seeming resemblance of Stalinist society to socialist forms — nationalised economy and the elimination both of the capitalist mode of economic activity and of the bourgeoisie which personified it. And because attempts to analyse the world afresh threatened to collapse what they understood as the whole Marxist system. Within the verbiage of Trotsky, which they turned into a sacerdotal language, they radically altered Trotsky's ideas.

In substance, despite the forms of property, the USSR for Trotsky was not post-capitalist in the sense of being ahead of world capitalism. It could not be: the most basic ideas of Marxism on socialism's necessary relationship to capitalism in history ruled it out.

With its expansion, Stalinism had, said Trotsky's epigones, miraculously changed the direction of its social and class evolution, as Trotsky had seen them: where the USSR had inexorably been moving towards a convulsive restoration of capitalism, Stalinism in the USSR and its clones across an additional sixth of the world were now post-capitalist societies "in transition to socialism". Where socialism in one country had been in Marxist terms, as understood by the Communist International and the Trotskyist movement of Trotsky's time, a piece of illiteracy, expressing the world outlook of the bureaucracy, and in USSR life a gruesome mockery of socialism, a modified version of it became the operational idea of the neo-Trotskyists. It was, wrote Ernest Mandel, for example, no longer one country, but a cluster of countries. Most of them were backward (though not all: Czechoslovakia, East Germany) but they were evolving towards socialism by way of what earlier Marxists would have dismissed as utopian colony-building on a giant scale, on the periphery of world capitalism. Socialism was — "for now" — evolving not out of advanced capitalism and as its spawn and replica, but as its competitor, moving from the periphery to the centre.

Formal lip service, on ceremonial occasions and in ceremonial documents, to the idea that the world revolution would only be completed when capitalism was overthrown in the advanced countries could not make sense of this in terms of the Marxism of Marx, Lenin and Trotsky. That idea was for the future, more or less remote; and meanwhile the USSR, etc., were "societies in transition to socialism" side by side with capitalism. The "actually existing revolution" was a matter of "one, two, many socialisms in one country". On an international scale, it bore more than a passing resemblance to the vision of Michael Bakunin in the First International and after about the effective movement for revolution coming from the social fringes and the social depths. Not from the proletariat of advanced capitalism, on the basis of the best achievements of that capitalism, but from the "wretched of the earth" on the edges of capitalism.

In this way, Trotsky's ideas, proclaimed as "official" orthodox Trotskyism, were turned on their head, turned inside out and turned upside down. Socialism in one country — or "socialism in a number of backward countries", was proclaimed to be the permanent revolution.

The view that became dominant as neo-Trotskyism was already present in Trotsky's time. It existed in the communist movement, with the "Right Communists" (Brandler, Lovestone, etc.), but also among social-democrats. The old Fabian, George Bernard Shaw, for example, regarded both Stalinism and Fascism as progressive agents of the collectivist spirit immanent in 20th century capitalist society. Their ideas were brought into the fringes of the Trotskyist movement by the Italian, Bruno Rizzi, who is remembered because Trotsky polemicised with him in 1939-40. Like Shaw — who must have influenced him — Rizzi regarded the Stalinist system, which he defined as a new form of class society, as progressive; and, like the Right Communists and Isaac Deutscher, who would popularise their views mixed with elements of Trotskyism, he thought this system could grow organically and smoothly into socialism, without revolution. This idea of Stalinism as viable and progressive came to be adopted by the so-called official Trotskyists, those who, after Trotsky's death, made a palimpsest of his words and texts into which they interpolated alien ideas. The degenerated and deformed workers' state theories were Bruno Rizzi's progressive "bureaucratic collectivism", "Trotskyised"!

It is possible to argue that, faced with the reshaping of the world in and after World War 2, Trotsky would have abandoned the path of thought which he sketched in "The USSR In War", "Again and Once More...", and in his last articles, and agreed with his "orthodox" disciples. It is certain, on the literary evidence, that the "disciples", in elaborating what became official post-Trotsky Trotskyism, did not follow Trotsky's method and did not heed what he wrote. They erected part of Trotsky's tentative conclusions above reality, and for 30 years suppressed much that he wrote alongside *In Defence of Marxism*. Trotsky was flatly at variance with the positions that were, for decades after his death, falsely presented as his "last word".

The alleged continuity of "orthodox" neo-Trotskyism with Trotsky was not in fact continuity, but regression to the Trotskyism of before 1933, in a world where Stalinism had plainly moved on very far from the reality of the 1920s, which still shaped Trotsky's views up to 1933. Its angry criticisms of Stalinism were vitiated by its commitment to "unconditional defence" of the Stalinist state, and later the Stalinist empire, against capitalist forces.

Trotsky was receptive to events and their implications. The neo-Trotskyist movement used "Trotsky's position" in lieu of thought and real analysis. Neo-Trotskyist analysis was cut and tailed and topped and pruned to fit into a static frame made by taking a snapshot of one moment (one side of Trotsky's 1939-40 writings) out of what for Trotsky was a moving and evolving analysis.

When all the old conceptions of the nature of the Soviet Union and the bureaucracy had to be measured and reassessed against the survival, expansion and self-replication of Stalinism, the "official Trotskyists" — those who had taken Trotsky's side in 1939-40, led by James P Cannon, joined soon after the reflux of Nazi Germany by Ernest Mandel, Michel Pablo, and others — turned ideas such as defence of the Soviet Union into frozen dogma and let that dogma commit them to defence of the Stalinist empire, the second power of the world. They came, as we will see, to regard its expansion in war or its replication in Asia or Eastern Europe as advances for the working class. They turned Trotskyism back in its tracks, from what it was in 1940, into a critical adjunct of the full-blown Stalinist empires. They defined Stalinist expansion as the expansion of a deformed working-class revolution. They maintained the belief in the workers' revolution, which for Trotsky was a belief that the labour movement could be "turned round" so that it would play the necessary revolutionary role, by mystifying it out of all reality and beyond all tests of reality; they even rechristened Stalinist Chinese peasant armies as workers' parties.

In fact, this was only another way of declaring the whole real perspective of the Bolsheviks dead — everything that Trotsky had tried to avoid in the 1939-40 debate. It had the additional fault of not doing this clearly but by way of naming something else as the working-class revolution and even for the working class.

Their "revolutionary perspectives" came to have as their immediate protagonist the Stalinist movement. They evolved a variant of degenerated workers' state theory, supposedly Trotsky's, or developed from Trotsky, that switched all the directions, definitions, class affiliations, and lines of movement in Trotsky's actual theory, arriving at definitions of the Stalinist states — that these were societies in transition to socialism — that were the opposite of Trotsky's . They wound up accepting variants of the perspective of "socialism in one country", of socialism advancing from backwardness on the periphery of the world economy to the centre.

It was a procedure with the legacy of Trotsky belonging to the same order of things as the Stalinists' scholasticism and mummery over "Lenin", and with the same consequence, that words and terms lost their meanings and, filled with different content, acquired new and sometimes opposite meanings — except that those engaged in this work were sincere and honest revolutionaries who retained a democratic criticism of Stalinism and made propaganda for, and tried to organise to win, Trotsky's working-class programme against Stalinism. Suspicious of innovation and motivated at root by the desire to do the best they could, they were cautious about challenging Trotsky's authority for fear that they would thereby succumb to the pressure of their own ruling classes.

Neo-Trotskyism was rooted in the abortive factional dispute of 1939-40 and in the lines prematurely drawn and defended there. For the "orthodox" Trotskyists, who remained critical of Stalinism and advocates of either reform (as — anachronistically — for China until 1969, Yugoslavia, Cuba, etc., as if these were societies analogous to the USSR in the early period of degeneration in the 1920s) or political revolution — in the USSR and eastern Europe — it was a way to come to terms with the reality of Stalinism as a great collectivist anti-bourgeois power which was also and simultaneously an anti-working-class power. The Stalinist states, no matter how critical of them the neo-Trotskyists were, usurped the place in Marxist theory of the working class in the anti-capitalist revolution — in its first stage. All the typical word-play and all the mystified and mystifying assertions that the working class — crushed and enslaved by the new state and denied the most elementary liberties and civil rights — ruled, could not change that fact. But what else could these be but workers' states, degenerated like Russia or deformed at origin like the others?

For Trotsky, the "degenerated workers' state" idea existed within a complex web of ideas and perspectives. For his "disciples", the system within which Trotsky saw the USSR as a workers' state tended to shrivel to a "totalitarian economism". That is there in Trotsky, but there is a lot more. For post-Trotsky Trotskyism, the bare fact of nationalised property and a system modelled on Stalin's USSR, and the rule of Stalnist forces committed to this model, defined a workers' state whatever happened to the workers. It was, for this stage of history, carrying through the transition to socialism — and was to be valued above the lives and liberties of the workers. Words in defence of the workers, however sincere and deeply-felt, could not balance out this logic. From the late 1940s, as the "orthodox" accepted the extension of the Stalinist system in various ways as creating workers' states, they could do it only by taking nationalised property as the ultimate criterion of the alleged class character of those states.

V. MILLENARIANISM: "THIRD PERIOD" NEO-TROTSKYISM

THE LOGIC OF the neo-Trotskyists' conditionally positive assessment of the new Stalinist "revolutions" turned them to millenarianism — to the idea that socialist progress could be made by some force of "history" or "world revolution" above, beyond and outside the living working class.

Echoing the "Third Period" of Communist Party policy, 1928-34, when it was a dogma laid down by Stalinist command that revolution was imminent always and everywhere, the neo-Trotskyists professed certainty that the revolution was coming and, like seers seeking confirmation of prophecies, looked for or redefined events to fit their expectations. This too had roots in some of Trotsky's sweeping predictions of revolution when he could not clearly identify the agency, other than the working class in the most general terms — and in his final view that capitalism was "finished". The point is that the neo-Trotskyists were led, by extrapolation from the idea that the USSR remained a workers' state and the fact that Stalinist forces could create other similar states, to accept — for now — as substitute for the working class those who created in, for example, China, as much as "remained of 1917" in the USSR. There was logic in it. The first essay in millenarianism came out of World War Two.

In the period beginning with the end of the siege of Stalingrad (late 1942), the neo-Trotskyists turned to perspectives for socialist gains and capitalist defeats spun around the advances of the "Red" Army from the East to the very centre of Europe. The new approach was most preposterous in its attempts to claim the Russian Army as "Trotsky's Red Army" — a staple of *The Militant* throughout the war — and its promotion of the idea that it was the nationalised economy that was winning USSR victories and inspiring the Russian workers and soldiers to fight.

These bizarre fatuities, on the level of crude advertising-agency or public relations material, can too easily divert attention from the important and continuous core idea within the blatant nonsense — acceptance of a positive revolutionary role for what in fact was Stalin's army and Stalin's state. There was talk of the "Red" Army rousing workers and inspiring them — as there had been in 1939 at the start of the events in Poland and Finland — as if nothing had been learned from the fact that, in Trotsky's words, "the invasions immediately bring about the transfer of power into the hands of the local Stalinist candidates for totalitarian rule", and "not only the majority of the Finnish peasants but also the majority of the Finnish workers proved to be on the side of their bourgeoisie".

There was nonsensical pretence that there was not much to worry about in the (sometimes mentioned) counter-revolutionary character of the

Kremlin and, implicitly, of its "Red" Army, because that would be light-weight compared to the "revolutionary impulse" from Stalinist advance. There was utter unclarity about the relation between "progressive" nationalisations imposed by the "Red" Army, as in 1939-40 in Poland, and the working class as the agent of revolution. There was absolute subordination, in the last analysis, of all else to the supposed overriding principle of "defence of the USSR". As late as March 1945, only a few weeks before the end of the war in Europe, this fictitious view of the "Red" Army was the dominant one in the most important neo-Trotskyist publication in the world, the US *Militant*. (See chapter 6.)

The fundamental idea was, as we've seen, an identification of national-ised property with progress and of Stalinist policy, despite Stalin, as a mere reflex of that progressive economy. Everything else was faded into the background. Without dropping their criticisms — especially of the Communist Parties in western Europe, against which they fought bitter-ly — the US official Trotskyists and those they influenced took up the pos-ture of hopeful expectancy, of a push for socialist revolution connected with the advance of Stalin's army. The principle of "defence of the USSR" led directly to this; but to assert a straight line from Trotsky to the neo-Trotskyist politics of 1942-5 you have to ignore Trotsky's prognosis of 1939-40. This could not have been the policy of the Trotsky who wrote what he did in 1939-40. No, after Stalingrad the "orthodox" Trotskyists had taken a sharp fork in the road away from both the spirit and the let-ter of what Trotsky wrote. Post-Trotsky "Trotskyism" as it existed from 1942 was indeed part of the "Stalingrad draft" that led vast numbers to join the Communist Parties.

Foolish triumphalism about the victories of the workers' state was their response when history offered up the evidence that Trotsky had indicated would conclusively falsify the "workers' state" thesis: the bureaucracy remaining stable in the convulsions of a world war. The leader of the "orthodox", James P Cannon, had himself put the perspective most sharply, in a passage which I have already quoted from a letter to Trotsky: "Stalin could take the path of Napoleonic conquest not merely against small border states, but against the greatest imperialist powers, only on one condition: that the Soviet bureaucracy in reality represents a new tri-umphant class which is in harmony with its economic system and secure in its position at home, etc. If such really is the case, we certainly must revise everything we have said on the subject of the bureaucracy up to now" (*Struggle for a Proletarian Party*).

When Stalin did conquer a large part of Germany, however, Cannon made no such revision. What he revised, or licensed others to revise, while holding to Trotsky's words, were the framework and criteria of Trotsky's entire approach and Trotsky's root and branch rejection of socialism in one country.

Neo-Trotskyism became a chaos of crazily distorting mirrors. At the end of the war the workaday millenarian politics about "Trotsky's Red Army" were still clothed in shreds of the old Trotskyism. As the Russian Army consolidated itself as master of half of Europe, the USSR, though in fact the second power in the world, and the great power of Europe and Asia, was — so the ventriloquised Trotsky, used as Lenin had long been used in the USSR, told readers of *The Militant* — still in danger. "Only the world revolution can save the USSR for socialism. But the world revolution carries with it the inescapable blotting out of the Kremlin oligarchy".

Reading the coverage of current affairs in the files of the "Shachtmanite" *Labor Action* and *New International* and the "orthodox" Militant and Fourth International is like being with, on one side, people who live on the planet Earth and read bourgeois newspapers, and, on the other, citizens of the Moon peering at the affairs of Earth through a weak telescope and relying on old photographs and accounts of life on Earth thousands of years in the past to decipher what is going on.

Millenarianism is the all-tuning note in post-war "orthodox" Trotskyism. It was in full control by late 1942; by 1951 it was running riot, as the "Fourth International" looked to a Russian victory in an imminent nuclear world war (a "War-Revolution") to put an end to capitalism and begin the transition to socialism on a world scale. But there was not a straight line. In the 1940s there was an interruption, and perhaps the possibility of the "orthodox" evolving in a different direction.

VI. THE LESSONS OF ITALY

IN THEIR TIME Burnham and Shachtman had written almost all the policy statements and analytical articles for the SWP. After the split of April 1940, those who took over this work — but now with no help from Trotsky other than old texts — were Albert Goldman, Felix Morrow and John G Wright.

In the 1939-40 dispute Goldman had at first taken a flat and crass line of positive support for the Russian invasion of Poland (see chapter 7). No-one else had such a position. Morrow wrote daffy but logical extrapolations about "the class significance of the Soviet victories". But these were honest people, and thoughtful. Goldman's crassness in 1939 was evidently that of a downright man who wanted to say plainly and bluntly what he thought the position of his own side came down to. Soon Goldman, Morrow, and a number of others, including Jean van Heijenoort, Trotsky's secretary for seven years, became convinced that events were falsifying the perspective of "the Fourth International" (which at this time, though it had activists in Europe and throughout the world, was, as an organisation, not much more than a sub-committee of the SWP). When Italian fascism fell in mid-1943 they began to face up to realities.

Bourgeois democracy and Stalinism were the immediately powerful forces in Italy after two decades of fascist rule; the Trotskyists were a tiny force, facing immense difficulties. Trotsky had understood and written about the probability of illusions in bourgeois democracy being generated by fascism; he had counterposed to the ravings of Third Period Stalinism, for which "revolution" was everywhere and continuously imminent, a rational Marxist assessment of what it took to make a revolutionary situation (see chapter 9). Some of his general comments at the end of his life were vaguer. The Cannon group had "perspectives" for imminent European workers' revolution, as if it could be produced mechnically out of the war.

Working-class experience and Marxist and Bolshevik theory said that a socialist revolution could not be made and consolidated just by a sudden upsurge of raw working-class anger against capitalism, but required preparatory education and organisation. The Cannonites implicitly had a view of revolution as emerging spontaneously from working-class economic grievances. They occasionally paid lip-service to Marxist ABCs by talking of the super-rapid growth of Trotskyist groups to leadership of the workers in Europe — in abstraction from any real perspectives for the evolution and self-development of working-class politics. This mixture — an implicit view of revolution as produced by raw rage, combined with a sectarian drive to "build the party" which would unblock the spontaneous revolutionary lava — would become the central characteristic of certain neo-Trotskyist currents, in Britain of the SLL-WRP and its splinters. The Cannonites at first rejected democratic slogans. Talking as if victory was assured to the Trotskyists, they wanted to and did exclude from the reforming ranks of the Fourth International groups which did not share their views on the Russian question (see chapter 10). They were too busy trying to catch a little of the glory of "Trotsky's Red Army" to notice that mass Stalinist movements existed in Europe, or to think of what that implied for socialist revolution.

It was all deeply unrealistic, and in fact ultra-left, with implicit underlying assumptions more akin to anarchism than Marxism. The Third-Period-style ultra-leftism and the millenarianism — the expectation that other and non-human forces such as "crisis" and "history" would push through the revolution — would feed off each other for decades, in varying combinations and changing situations.

By contrast, the "Shachtmanite" Workers Party not only proposed more earth-grounded assessments of and responses to world events, but subjected the Cannonites to a running fire of criticism; and in 1943 and afterwards that criticism came to be echoed inside the SWP by Goldman and Morrow. They accused the SWP of ultra-leftism and unrealism, and of living on and purveying a lethal mixture of dogmatism and empirical opportunism. After the fall of Mussolini they advocated recognition of the realities of Europe and the use of democratic and transitional demands by the Trotskyists. Immediately, as in 1939-40, the political questions became snarled up with issues of party life and democratic procedure. Goldman and Morrow became an embittered opposition, and began, piecemeal and empirically, to see what the triumphs of Stalinism implied for the hopes of socialism in Europe; and they recognised the fact of Stalinist imperialism.

There was a more eminent critic of the SWP's "softness" on Stalinism: Natalia Sedova, Trotsky's companion of 40 years, who still lived in Mexico and participated in the affairs of the movement. After the siege of Stalingrad, Natalia veered slowly towards the opposite fork of the political road to that taken by the "orthodox" Trotskyists. She began to find the fantasies and delusions about "Trotsky's Red Army" distasteful and nonsensical, but also politically dangerous: the Stalinist advance was a mortal threat to the European workers' prospects of socialism, Natalia began to insist. Natalia's pressure slowly produced a certain shift in emphasis.

By the end of the war a Fourth International had been recreated in Europe. Real discussion developed — about what the future would be for Europe, the economic prospects for capitalism, assessment of the areas under Stalinist domination, and, once more, the nature of the USSR. The

Workers Party considered itself a section of the Fourth International and was accepted by the Europeans as such; there were radical anti-Stalinist currents in the small European parties. Unity discussions took place between the WP and the SWP in 1946 and '47; a group from the SWP joined the WP (Goldman and some of his comrades; Morrow, expelled from the SWP, dropped away from politics), and then a group from the WP joined the SWP (C L R James and Raya Dunayevskaya and five or six dozen people). The Workers Party participated in the Second World Congress of the Fourth International in March 1948, which made a formal distinction in one of its documents between "revolutionary bureaucratic-collectivists" like the Workers Party and "reactionary" ones like Dwight Macdonald.

VII. THE DILEMMAS OF 1945-8

THE THREE YEARS between the end of the war and Tito's break with Stalin in July 1948 were an interregnum in the evolution of "orthodox" neo-Trotskyism, at the end of which, much depleted in forces, it returned to the millenarian course of 1942-5 and developed it into a whole new system of politics. Afterwards it would develop by way of fraying, partial recoils, and eccentric movements from the doctrinal clarity around the perspective of "Stalinist-led world revolution" which it had by the "Third World Congress" of 1951. In 1945-8, however, there was real discussion and real fluidity.

The USSR's power had expanded enormously. In Eastern Europe, "Trotsky's Red Army" had repressed the workers and set up "coalition" regimes in which Stalinists had the key police-military, that is, state-controlling, ministries. Indigenous Yugoslav Stalinists won power in a long war against German occupiers, Croat fascists and Serbian monarchists. Having occupied Czechoslovakia and set up a "mixed" government, the Russian Army withdrew. Everywhere else (Poland, East Germany, Hungary, Bulgaria, Rumania) the Russian Army remained in occupation. Czechoslovakia had had a mass Communist movement before the war; the German Communist Party had been strong before 1933; nowhere else in these states were there strong CPs. There had been a strong independent Marxist tradition in Poland, but Stalinism had destroyed it, formally dissolving the CP in 1938, shooting its leaders who had taken refuge in Moscow from Polish military dictatorship. A new Polish party had to be created for Russia's purposes in 1942 after Germany invaded the USSR.

Everywhere, parties bred to rule were created out of old CPers, turncoat Social-Democrats, and nondescript careerists. The top-ranking Stalinists returned from Moscow "with pipes in their mouths" (like Stalin), as the saying went. After 1949, most of those Stalinist leaders who had been at home in the underground, and not in Moscow, during the war would be purged, tried for imaginary crimes, and hanged or jailed. The bourgeoisie was weak or had been heavily discredited or smashed by the Nazis. Chauvinism akin to the tribalism of the Dark Ages, and to Hitlerism, characterised these Stalinist-run states in their relations with each other. The USSR kept the areas of Poland it had taken in 1939 and gave to

Poland large areas of Russian-occupied Germany in return. Ten million Germans were cleared out of that territory at gunpoint, and with appalling suffering and many casualties. Three million Germans were driven out of the Sudetenland in the Czechoslovak state. Large numbers of Hungarians, too, were driven from Czechoslovakia.

How to evaluate these states? Plainly they, like the Baltic states in 1940, and the areas of former Poland Stalin controlled, were being "sovietised". Nobody paying attention and reading newspapers could doubt it. If the "orthodox" Trotskyists did doubt it, it was because this "sovietisation" presented them with all the questions that they had been avoiding since Stalingrad, or since 1939, or... since the Stalinist bureaucracy established its self-defined rule two decades earlier. The questions were writ too large to tolerate evasion, now that the USSR was the second power in the world, controlling a giant empire. The neo-Trotskyists would try to evade them in what was by now the traditional way: juggling with words and definitions, whose meanings were merely shifted.

The "orthodox" attitude on the Stalinisation of eastern Poland and the Baltic states had now to be reassessed. Why should it not be applied to the states now being turned into replicas of the USSR, and matching it for horrors with such things as the mass deportation of over ten million Germans? If the same approach were now applied to the vastly greater Stalinist expansion, would that not destroy whatever coherence remained to the "orthodox" position, compelling the neo-Trotskyists to see police-state repression of whole nations as somehow simultaneously being a form of socialist emancipation? But how, if the movement were not to fall into a gibbering lunacy, could it not be applied? Not applying it would disarrange the "orthodox" neo-Trotskyist position as much as applying it, only differently.

The hard fact was that anti-capitalist revolutions were being made. However the Stalinist transformations in Eastern Europe were defined, they were that, anti-bourgeois revolutions. For those who continued to see the USSR as a degenerated workers' state, the assimilation of the other countries into its model had to be defined as some variant of a workers' revolution — an anti-worker, counter-revolutionary, bureaucratic workers' revolution.

The labour movements were being subverted and destroyed by the Stalinist police states, and replaced by totalitarian entities in the service of the totalitarianising states. The working class was being subjugated at least as much as under fascism, and more than under the ramshackle pre-war loosely authoritarian regimes such as that of Hungary, for example. But if a categorisation as workers' states of the new Stalinist systems now congealing in eight East European countries and North Korea — and by 1948 the Maoist armies were on the road to control of all mainland China — was to be rejected, then how could such a rejection not logically imply that the whole "degenerated workers' state" assessment of the USSR was untenable?

If the dilemma were resolved by defining the new Stalinist states as being of the same nature as the USSR, that is as being workers' states of some sort, then another and more fundamental question was posed (though I don't think it ever was posed explicitly in those terms): what then was the theory according to which the USSR, with or without its empire of satellites, was a workers' state? The answer, "Trotsky's theory" — which became the "orthodox" Trotskyist answer, meaning that nothing basic had changed so long as nationalised property remained — would satisfy only those who had forgotten or not understood the whole trend of Trotsky's thought in the 1930s and what the terms of his workers' state theory had been.

The Soviet Union, even apart from its satellites and replicas, could not in 1945 be considered a workers' state according to the approach indicated in Trotsky's evolving and constantly-revised assessments in the 1930s. The bureaucracy had proved itself in the hardest possible test to be no mere malignant tumour on society, no collective bandit seizing the economy for a short transitional period in the reflux of the workers' revolution before it gave way either to capitalism or to renewed workers' power, no freak in the historical interstices between workers' power and capitalist restoration or workers' renewal. Events had made Trotsky's old theory impossible: a new one had to be developed and within the old name it was: that, as we have seen, came to be Bruno Rizzi's thesis of progressive bureaucratic collectivism as a stage on the road to socialism, renamed as "*degenerated* workers' states". Only a modified version of Trotsky's name for his very different theory of the degenerated workers' state would remain. The change took time.

Plain facts that could not be evaded had cancelled out the entire structure of reasoning according to which Trotsky had hung on to the "degenerated workers' state" theory in 1939-40. The facts of the mid and late 40s pointed imperatively to other conclusions, those provisionally indicated by Trotsky then: that the USSR was a species of new class society. The question in the discussion after 1944-5 was whether the collapse of Trotskyism into flat "totalitarian economism" — the idea that state ownership, or, in the given case, totalitarian state ownership, supposedly rooted, directly or more loosely (China, etc.) in the October Revolution, was necessarily working-class — would spread and prevail, or be reversed.

There was a large body of classical Marxist writing against the "totalitarian-economist" idea. It answered no real questions, but begged every question of working-class socialism. Such a reduction of the criteria to statised economy was always the "bottom line", the hard-fact basis, of Trotsky's theory. Trotsky was dealing with something new in history and compelled to measure it by comparison with known phenomena and by the pattern of previously existing modern class societies. Even so, his denial of the autonomy of the autocracy after 1928 was wrong; was by the mid-1930s blamably wrong. The war-time fantasies were an abandonment of the responsibility to think realistically about the world. But not even the war-time fantasies about "Trotsky's Red Army" completely and flatly replaced the working class with some other agency. The "Red" Army was supposed to stimulate working-class action. There was still some rational notion of ends and means hovering, or flapping loosely in the air, around the "Trotsky's Red Army" fantasies. Now there were only hard brute facts. For a period, the hard facts undid the millenarianism of 1942-5.

It needs to be stressed and kept in mind that the people involved were sincere and honest advocates of working-class socialism. They understood — and in a way that later generations of neo-Trotskyists often would not — the monstrous aberration from any sort of socialism that the Stalinist system was. With fascism a recent and vivid memory, they understood the horror of even contemplating the notion that the fascist-style states that the USSR was erecting in Eastern Europe (in part, with police forces staffed by recent fascists) could be accepted as a variant of workers' state. But they needed to make sense of the world. They needed to ward off the conclusion of despair some drew from the repeated defeats of the working class, the idea that the working class could not play the role indicated in Marxist theory. The lessons of history proved the opposite — the Paris Commune, the 1917 revolution, the workers' struggles in Spain in the 1930s, and many others — lessons that are indelible. But they saw depression and defeats of the working class, side by side with victories against the bourgeoisie by people calling themselves "communists" — victories that achieved as much as remained of the October 1917 Revolution. Revolutionary Stalinism beckoned as well as threatened. They needed to preserve hope for socialism, and paradoxically many of them — like the notorious US general who said he had destroyed a Vietnamese city "in order to save it" — preserved their hope for socialism in this epoch by killing the old idea and perspective of socialism and substituting for it something else (for "now", for "this stage") .

These dilemmas opened a period of discussion in the reorganising Fourth International. Max Shachtman could at the end of the war write that the "degenerated workers' state" thesis was withering and dying. He was wrong, but that seemed to be the trend. (He was right too: the last echoes of *Trotsky's* workers' state theory were dying; it would be replaced, by quite different theories. The death of the old workers' state was surely the only consistent and logical development of Trotsky's final position. In June 1946 the international centre, newly re-located in Europe, declared for the withdrawal of the USSR army — what had been so recently and for so long "Trotsky's Red Army" — from Europe. The 1948 Congress document talked about "defending what remained of the conquests of October 1917" in place of "defending the Soviet Union". This reflected a very much changed mood.

VIII. THE BRITISH REVOLUTIONARY COMMUNIST PARTY

ILLUMINATING HERE IS the case of the British Revolutionary Communist Party. At its peak around 1945 this organisation had 500 members; thereafter it steadily declined. By 1946 its leaders, Jock Haston, Millie Lee and Ted Grant, had provisionally decided that the USSR, its satellites and its Yugoslav replica, were of a similar class character — state-capitalist. After mulling this over for a while they changed their minds. The USSR and the others were, they still thought, of the same sort, but they were... workers' states. The RCP became the major proponents of this position in the Fourth-Internationalist movement, representing the opposite pole to the Workers Party, which was arguing that Stalinism was a form of class system, bureaucratic-collectivist (the WP majority) or state-capitalist (the minority). The RCP held that the Stalinist satellites partook of the same class nature as the USSR and were thus workers' states. For this phenomenon a new adjective would be coined: they had

131

not degenerated, as the USSR had, from a workers' revolution, so these were "deformed" workers' states.

The majority supported neither pole, and the RCP were much despised and much condemned for their position. The Shachtmanites said that the RCP were at least logical; the other supporters of the thesis that the USSR remained a workers' state spurned the RCP for creating a *reductio ad absurdum* of it. The RCP leaders were regarded as people who had gutted Trotskyism and bestowed on Stalinism undeserved recognition as a progressive anti-capitalist force. Ernest Mandel and others dealt with the issue by declaring the satellites — most of them occupied, except Czechoslovakia, by Russian troops, and with governments dominated by Stalinists — to be state-capitalist, while the USSR remained a workers' state. Mandel, the major academic theoretician of neo-Trotskyism from the late 1940s, managed to combine these two positions with a third: great enthusiasm for the victorious Chinese Maoists.

IX. TITO

THE MARCH 1948 second world congress, in Paris, consisted of 50 delegates and represented 22 organisations in 19 countries, including the Workers Party of the USA. The shape of the world which would last with secondary modifications until the collapse of the USSR 43 years later was now plain. Capitalism had stabilised and begun to revive, though much of Europe was still in ruins. The main changes still to work their way through would come from a range of anti-colonial struggles.

Just before the Congress, on 25 February 1948, the Stalinists in Czechoslovakia organised a coup which was the last act in the Stalinisation of all of Russian-occupied Eastern Europe — a coup in which mass working-class support allowed the Stalinists, who already controlled the key ministries, to stage something, with mass demonstrations, like a parody of a workers' revolution.

The tone of the 1948 congress resolutions is that of defeat and perplexity[39]. The USSR remained a workers' state. How, why? "The social revolution still lives in what remains of the conquests of October [i.e. the nationalised property] and in the vanguard layers of the working class", declared the congress document. Fourteen years after the start of the Great Terror, and twenty years after the consolidation of totalitarian rule, the idea of the "vanguard layers of the working class" still being able to determine the class character of the state was surreal. The congress resolution placed much stress on the "instability of the social relations" and the need to study the trends by which "the progressive character of the Russian economy... tends to become eliminated by the bureaucracy" and "the pos-

---

39. The Congress launched the slogan for the transformation of the small Trotskyist propaganda groups (some very small) into "parties of mass working-class struggle". The same call had been made by a previous conference in 1946, but this time it was made in the face of a major decline of all the groups. About half the membership of the French group, which was the largest in Europe, quit soon after the Congress, and its paper, previously weekly, appeared only three times between April and November 1948; the British RCP was also on the point of collapse.

sibilities of reaction and regression in all fields, including the economic, within the framework of these [nationalised] property relations, have been shown to be infinitely vaster than anyone could have thought". With the experience of Nazi rule fresh in their minds, the congress delegates described the USSR as "the most totalitarian police dictatorship in history". All the welter of qualifications and contrived arguments reflected minds at the end of their tether, about to flip back into the plain "totalitarian economist" definition of a workers' state by nationalised property alone.

In fact the congress solved nothing. By holding to the position that the USSR was a workers' state it indicated how the mainstream would solve the problem: but the congress itself stood between two open doors on either side of that final bivouacking of the old Trotskyist movement. Within three months the "orthodox" neo-Trotskyists would troop — no, stampede — through the one marked "Stalinism is revolutionary".

Tito's Yugoslavia was a fully-formed smaller replica of the USSR: if, as the congress said, it was capitalist, then it was a fascist state. Tito had won power with no dependence on the Russian army. In July 1948 Yugoslavia and the USSR fell out violently. Yugoslavia resisted the predatory — imperialist — relations that the USSR imposed on the satellites. Overnight, for the Russian propagandists, Tito became a fascist, a long-time "agent" in the Communist movement, and the new Trotsky. Tito acted to repress pro-Stalin people in his own state. A war of propaganda opened up. The Stalinists called for the removal of Tito. Russian invasion seemed a distinct possibility. Tito had a mass base of support, and appealed to the Yugoslav people. Not immediately, but over time, the Tito dictatorship, while retaining all the Stalinist basics, including the Byzantine cult of the leader, loosened up, and organs of (firmly controlled) popular representation appeared. The Yugoslavs criticised Russian Stalinism: they would soon designate the USSR as state-capitalist, and the "orthodox" Trotskyists would polemicise with them in defence of the working-class character of Stalin's state; they would denounce the orthodox Trotskyists for being soft on the USSR!

Now millenarianism — looking to other forces half-miraculously to make the revolution for the workers — came back to the "official" Trotskyists with a force and an all-conquering logic that showed the period of "Trotsky's Red Army" to have been a mere experimental half-rehearsal of a half-written play. Immediately the leaders of the Fourth International recognised that what on its merits had seemed a Yugoslav fascist, capitalist state was really a socialist state. All Tito's typical Stalinist talk of socialism and workers' power, which had been dismissed as cant at the March 1948 congress, was now understood to be good stuff. The recent fascist, capitalist state was to be supported against the degenerated workers' state. Everything was redefined. An open letter was quickly dispatched to the "comrades" at the head of the Yugoslav CP. Speculation on the possibility of fishing in the pro-Tito current which emerged in the Western left were part of it, but this was a genuine new "revelation".

At the congress, the "world revolution" had seemed to be in a cul-de-sac, apart from the colonial struggles. Now everything was on the move. By April 1949 the International Executive Committee was ready to recognise that the countries where Russian Stalinism had overthrown capitalism and created societies in its own image were after all workers' states — deformed workers' states. They had adopted the position of the long-despised and much-derided RCP majority. Their all reshaping idea now was that they should not be "sectarian" towards the "living revolution". None of the implication that had led them to despise the RCP had disappeared. Now they drew conclusions that repelled even the British. Alone of all the Trotskyist currents in the world the British RCP, in a front page article in *Socialist Appeal* by Jock Haston, had welcomed the Stalinists' final coup in Czechoslovakia in February 1948: now Haston could with justice criticise the "orthodox" for Tito worship!

Acceptance of the "living revolution" in Yugoslavia toppled the "orthodox" neo-Trotskyists over into acceptance of Stalinism as revolutionary. Now they saw that the Russian bureaucracy had played a tremendous international revolutionary role — as in the USSR after 1928. So had Tito played a great revolutionary role; so would Mao; so would others. Implicitly, this acceptance of the revolutionary role of the Stalinist bureaucracy internationally was a long-ranging backward revision of Trotsky's view of the bureaucracy, and implied a much-needed understanding of its independent role after 1928; but it was accompanied by positive acceptance of the Stalinists' new international achievements, and led not to a criticism and correction of Trotsky's conclusion that the USSR was a workers' state but to a thoroughgoing revision of his account of how and why it was a degenerated workers' state. The label "workers' state" was kept from Trotsky; little else was.

In the new millenarian world-view, the socialist revolution was moving forwards. It had made tremendous strides in the suppression of capitalism.

Hesitantly and with zig-zags, the "orthodox" had levered the "workers' state" theory up away from Trotsky's whole method of analysis, so that eventually it rested on a single point, nationalised property. Then, pivoting on that single point, the theory was turned round so that it came to be, not a one-sided version of what Trotsky had argued, but in many respects its opposite.

A nationalised economy defined a workers' state. The Stalinists created nationalised economies. Therefore, the Stalinists were a force who made workers' states. Therefore, for some, Stalinist power defined a workers' state, and was in fact the political core of it, nationalised economy being only the economic result — as in Trotsky's theory nationalised economy was the economic result demonstrating the continued vitality of traces from the 1917 workers' revolution. China could be seen by many of the "orthodox" as a "workers' state" as soon as the Stalinists took power, long before they got round to comprehensive statisation of the economy — and, in the terms of the "orthodox", rightly so!

Though the "orthodox" still upheld a norm of democratic workers' power, what they meant by "workers' state" in immediate politics was a state where the workers were crushed uninhibitedly by a monopolistic bureaucracy. The inversion of meanings was as complete as any that Stalin had worked.

The "orthodox" Trotskyists had saved their "belief in socialism" by altering their socialist perspective and by redefining socialism — for now — out of recognition; now they regained their vision of a world revolution by raising it above and separated from the real labour movements. They hitched their hopes to the Stalinist movement, and cut loose from the only possible agency of real socialism, the working class.

The wide variety of Trotskyist groups permuting basic positions proves how much freedom there is to juggle in the framework of the "new Trotskyism" defined in 1949-51. Yet there was in all the strands a logical connection with the basic theory on the Soviet Union. If the USSR was any sort of workers' state or advance beyond capitalism and towards socialism, then the states modelled after it by the "Red Army" or Tito or Mao were advances beyond capitalism — perhaps only a first stage of advance, but a decisive one. History had found its way out of the impasse of the 1930s. One could not be "subjective" about it. In plain language, this meant that other forces were doing at least the first stage of the job that was the workers' in Marxist theory. In backward countries, the solution, *pro tem*, to the crisis of leadership of the working class was to accept that history, for now, had dispensed with the working class.

X. THE "THIRD WORLD CONGRESS": A NEW TROTSKYISM IS FOUNDED

IN THE NEXT few years after 1948, the "orthodox" neo-Trotskyists would reconceptualise the world as one of ongoing struggle between the proletarian class camp — the USSR's empire and its allies — and imperialism. Russian *imperialism* was revolutionary anti-imperialism. All the signs were turned round. Trotskyism experienced as profound an inner transformation of ideas as the Communist International after 1923.

We have seen that one reason for the great difficulties that Trotsky experienced with understanding Stalinism was that he had thought of the autocracy's rule not as a regime "in and of itself" but as a freak short-term phenomenon of transition. Since the expected rupturing of forms (of state property by the bourgeoisie, or of bureaucratic political power by the working class) had not happened, only reconceptualisation of the USSR opened a way out of the cul-de-sac. Mesmerised by the survival and success and the challenge to capitalism Stalinism embodied, and fearful of innovation, Trotsky's followers, when they came to the unavoidable reconceptualisation, veered off in the opposite direction to that indicated by Trotsky in 1939: to critical but positive reassessment of Stalinism.

Between Tito's break with Stalin and their April 1949 decision that the states of the Russian empire were all workers' states, they performed a spectacular reconceptualisation. The only changes had been the transition there from the looser post-1945 regimes to the full-scale airtight Stalinist totalitarian terror system. Yet what the second world congress had defined as state-capitalist systems, with fascist-style regimes, became progressive variants of working-class rule, and would be designated as "in transition to socialism". Regimes in which, since 1945 the fascist-like destruction of labour movements, of civil liberties and of all workers' rights by Russian quisling regimes had been observed, condemned and summed up in the resolutions of the 1948 congress, were now "reconceptualised". You would have to look to the most spectacular voltes-faces of the Stalintern for a parallel switch.

Here there were not the complexities and difficulties that Trotsky had unavoidably faced in analysing the stage-by-stage degeneration of the Russian Revolution. Evolving, open-ended, seeming to be radically unstable by all available measures, the USSR could not look to Trotsky as it does in retrospect to those who know the whole story and approach it as history. The 1948-9 "official" Trotskyists approached their analysis from the other end.

They had seen the systems for something like what they were: and then they "saw" them again in a blinding light of revelation. So far had norms and standards been pulped. For the satellite states the neo-Trotskyists advocated the same programme as for the USSR: they did not abandon the working class. For the autonomous "workers' states" — Yugoslavia, China, Cuba[n] — they would not do that. They would adopt the posture of loyal critics with suggestions to make for reform. When some Chinese Trotskyists fled to Hong Kong from the Maoists — those who did not were killed or incarcerated for three or four decades — Michel Pablo, secretary of the new "Fourth International", dismissed them as "refugees from a revolution". Comradely open letters were written to the victorious Chinese Stalinists, too — and would be written to the central committee of the Communist Party of the Soviet Union as late as 1962.[40] Bowing down before success was part of it; so was a supine attitude to history that was the opposite of that appropriate to representatives of a revolutionary class at bay.

The reconstituted Fourth International consisted of very small groups (mostly only a few dozens strong) with an international leadership dependent on the bestowed authority of James P Cannon raised as a literary apparatus of commentators and fantasy strategists above a very weak movement. As it turned out, they would not long remain tractable to Cannon's bidding or long let themselves be held in check by Cannon's "old Trotskyist" inhibitions.

The implications drawn from the 1948-9 turn and its working-through were now that the transition to world socialism was moving forwards of its own momentum. It was surging forwards and seizing on and using any organisational instrument to hand.

As Ernest Mandel put it in January 1951: "The worldwide revolutionary upsurge continues to expand and deepen, even if between 1948 and 1950 it saw a temporary retreat in Europe: today it pulls all Asia in its wake, tomorrow it will cross the Atlantic and attack Capital in its last bastion. The development of this upsurge is the almost automatic product of the extreme decomposition of capitalism. It is in the absence of a sufficiently powerful revolutionary leadership that this revolutionary upsurge temporarily takes new and transitional forms, like those we have seen in Yugoslavia and we see now blooming in Asia.

"For ten years the advance of the world revolution has taken the most diverse and unexpected forms, the most outlandish and confusing combinations... Not to understand this concrete development of the world revolution, and to retrench behind schema of an 'ideal' world revolution, is to

---

40. It was 1969 before the Mandel Fourth International came out for a "political revolution" in Mao's China.

turn one's back on the real movement in the name of a chimera, to push communism back from the level of science to that of utopia" ("Ten Theses").

There was an ongoing, evolutionary-revolutionary, process. It no longer depended on the workers, at least not for now. Where democracy and every sort of self-determination or self-rule had been eliminated — not because to the neo-Trotskyists it was undesirable; but events had proved that for now it was inessential and unnecessary for the creation of this sort of workers' state — so now too was the action of the working class itself. Even the action of revolutionary socialists substituting for the working class — which would itself be far from Marxism — was eliminated: in its place were peasant armies or the Russian army. For Trotsky the bureaucracy was a corrupt, usurping stop-gap locum: for neo-Trotskyists it came to be the prime agency.

The evolution-revolution was an ongoing, self-moving process, raised out from reality and abstracted from the actualities of Stalinist revolutions, which in true Third-Period, or religious prophet, style were merely phenomenal expressions of the Grand Design. This process was seen as something that moved as though "striving" teleologically towards some goal already determined. The "transition to socialism" was moving forward, and continuously, of its own momentum, taking many and varied forms and with varying types of protagonist. The ongoing World Revolution, as if impatient with delay, abstracted from actual revolutions. The actual revolutions were given the name of proletarian revolution, but in the old meanings of such words they were nameless and classless — manifestations of a process elevated into a shadowy historical actor, a spectre stalking the Earth.

This was ideologising the "historical process", rationalising and prettifying reality, not Marxist analysis. A man like Ernest Mandel rationalised "the historical process", including Stalinism as, earlier, Karl Kautsky had rationalised the doings of the dominant parliamentary and trade union leaders in German Social-Democracy. Natalia Sedova wrote bitter words when she broke with the new Fourth International:

"In 1932 and 1933, the Stalinists, in order to justify their shameless capitulation to Hitlerism, declared that it would matter little if the fascists came to power because socialism would come after and through the rule of fascism. Only dehumanized brutes without a shred of socialist thought or spirit could have argued this way. Now, notwithstanding the revolutionary aims which animate you, you maintain that the despotic Stalinist reaction which has triumphed in Europe is one of the roads through which socialism will eventually come. This view marks an irremediable break with the profoundest convictions always held by our movement and which I continue to share.

"Most insupportable of all is the position on the war to which you have committed yourselves. The third world war which threatens humanity confronts the revolutionary movement with the most difficult problems, the most complex situations, the gravest decisions. Our position can be taken only after the most earnest and freest discussions. But in the face of all the events of recent years, you continue to advocate, and to pledge the entire movement, to the defense of the Stalinist state. You are even now supporting the armies of Stalinism in the war which is being endured by the anguished Korean people. I cannot and will not follow you in this.

"I know very well how often you repeat that you are critizing Stalinism and fighting it. But the fact is that your criticism and your fight lose their value and can yield no results because they are determined by and subordinated to your position of defense of the Stalinist state. Whoever defends this regime of barbarous oppression, regardless of the motives, abandons the principles of socialism and internationalism."

What might be called the peak experience the clearest possible proof that the picture painted here is not false or artificial, was the neo-Trotskyists' preparations for war. A Third World War was almost universally expected. Instead, the USSR developed an atom bomb, and the era in history characterised by a balance of nuclear terror began — though that is a view in hindsight. In June 1950 a proxy war began in Korea, when the Stalinist North invaded the South. World War seemed imminent — all-out, partially nuclear war. What did it mean for socialists? Basing themselves on the experience of Stalinist resistance movements in the Second World War, and on the militant discipline of the non-Russian Communist Parties, the apparatus of the Fourth International developed the following thesis: a Third World War will in fact trigger the European socialist revolution. The "Red Army" and the indigenous Communist Parties will conquer Europe and make that revolution. It will be a combined War-Revolution. Michel Pablo, who was by now the main international leader of the current, would speculate that this would lead to "centuries of deformed workers' states". What others feared as Armageddon, and what Trotsky, writing about the prospect of a world war after the Second World War, said would be "the grave of civilisation", was for these millenarians, now they had hitched themselves firmly to the Stalinist empire and its world-conquering mission, the socialist revolution. The Red Flag decorated with a picture of Trotsky in military uniform in front of a hammer and sickle, and the red flag waving behind the four horsemen of the Apocalypse — fire, famine, pestilence and war — would have properly emblematised this vision.

Michel Pablo explained in 1949: "The two notions of Revolution and of War, far from being opposed or distinguished as two markedly different stages of evolution, are brought closer and interlaced to the point of being merged in place and time. In their place, it is the notion of the Revolution-War, the War-Revolution, which emerges, and on which should be based the perspectives and the orientation of the revolutionary Marxists of our epoch.

"Such language may perhaps shock the lovers of dreams and 'pacifist' bluster, or those who are already lamenting the apocalyptic fate of the world which they foresee as following an atomic war or an expansion of Stalinism. But these sensitive hearts have no place among the militants, and especially among the revolutionary Marxist cadres of this epoch, the most terrible of all, where the sharpness of the class struggle has risen to its paroxysm. It is objective reality which pushes this dialectical complex of the Revolution-War to the first place, which implacably destroys 'pacifist' dreams, and which leaves no respite in the simultaneous gigantic deployment of the forces of the Revolution and of War, and their battle to the death...

"To the efforts of the bourgeoisie and of imperialism to mobilise the masses in their war against the USSR, the 'people's democracies', China, and the other Asiatic revolutions under way, and to crush the Communist

Parties and the revolutionary movement of their respective countries, broad layers will respond by revolt, open struggle, armed struggle, the new Resistance, but this time with an infinitely clearer class character. It is possible that on the basis of these mass reactions, and of the chaos and aggravation that such a war would rapidly create, different Communist Parties will see themselves obliged to undertake, pushed by the masses, pushed by their own base, a struggle which would go beyond the soviet bureaucracy's own objectives.

"Such a war, far from stopping the struggle which is currently going on to the disadvantage of imperialism, would intensify it and bring it to its paroxysm. It would shatter all balance, pulling all forces into the struggle, accelerating the process which has already begun namely that of the convulsive transformation of our society, which will only subside with the triumph of international socialism. The fate of Stalinism will be decided precisely in this period of gigantic overturns.

"People who despair of the fate of humanity because Stalinism survives and even wins victories are cutting down History to their measure. They had wished that the whole process of transformation of capitalist society into socialism should be accomplished in the span of their short lives, so that they could be rewarded for their efforts for the Revolution. As for us, we reaffirm what we wrote in the first article we devoted to the Yugoslav affair: This transformation will probably take a whole historical period of some centuries, which will be filled in the meantime with transitional forms and regimes between capitalism and socialism, necessarily distanced from 'pure' forms and norms...

"Those who think they can respond to the anxiety and the embarrassment of some people at the so-called victories of Stalinism by minimising the objectively revolutionary significance of these facts are obliged to take refuge in a sectarianism, anti-Stalinist at all costs, which scarcely conceals under its aggressive appearance its lack of confidence in the fundamental revolutionary process of our epoch. This process is the most certain pledge for the inevitable final defeat of Stalinism, and it will be realised all the more rapidly, the quicker the overthrow of capitalism and of imperialism progresses and gains a bigger and bigger part of the world". ("Where Are We Going?")

Pablo restated the perspective in a pamphlet of August 1952, "The Coming War". The war would be "that of united imperialism, led by Washington, against the Revolution in all its forms... The forces which threaten the capitalist regime are... those of the Revolution in all its forms: the non-capitalist states, the colonial revolution, the international revolutionary movement. In all these elements is expressed... directly or indirectly, in more or less clear and conscious forms, the fundamental, objective process of the world socialist Revolution of our century".

This drum-tight vision of apocalyptic Stalinist-led world revolution would change as tension relaxed in 1953 and after, and the world settled into the long years of nuclear stalemate. The method of relying on forces other than the working class would not change, though the forces would change and proliferate. The pattern has been set out, and there is no point in tracing it further. The number of permutations it produced is immense.

ONE BREAK IN the pattern, which created its own kaleidoscopic variations, remains to be indicated. Against the logical drift there would be recoil. The Pablo-Mandel current itself would recoil from the wild speculations of 1949-52. These were sincere socialists and anti-Stalinists, however inadequate their ideas seem with hindsight. The most important recoil was that of James P Cannon.

In 1953 he led a split in the Fourth International — the mono-factional and very shrunken rump that had in effect refounded itself as a different movement in mid-1951 at the so-called "Third World Congress". It was an utterly incoherent recoil, which kept all the basic ideas of the 1951 congress but demanded more emphasis on the building of Trotskyist parties. Cannon, who had pioneered millenarianism in the 1940s, reshaped the Fourth International after the war, and erected the "world leaders", now recoiled from them. 1953 was an incoherent and hysterical lurch towards what had been "Shachtmanism" in the early 1940s — the emphasis on the centrality of building Trotskyist parties. But Cannon and his comrades were held as by a chain to over a decade of confused history that had culminated in the "Third World Congress".

In his own way, incoherently, Cannon tried to do what Shachtman and his comrades had begun to do in 1939. There is evidence that Cannon thought he could "lift his finger" and Pablo would fall. Cannon was mistaken. The significance of Cannon's break (joined by groups in Britain and France) is that all coherence was lost.

Like ripples spreading out from a stone dropped in still water, the reverberations spread. Groups proliferated, some quite mad. A useful distinction in sorting out these groups is between people honestly trying to understand the world and trying to function politically — and both Cannon and his opponents in 1953 were that — and the charlatans. An increasingly conspicuous section of the neo-Trotskyist movement consisted of charlatans, groups like the French "Lambertists", the later British "Healyites", the Morenists in Latin America — people who would say or do anything for catchpenny advantage, for whom the old idea that the political programme builds the party had been inverted and for whom the exigencies of party-building dictated politics and "programme".

XII. CONCLUSION: THE COMMUNIST MANIFESTO AND TROTSKYISM

"History does nothing; it 'possesses no immense wealth', it 'wages no battles'. It is man, real living man, that does all that, that possesses and fights; 'history' is not a person apart, using man as a means for its own particular aims; history is nothing but the activity of man pursuing his aims." Marx and Engels, *The Holy Family*.

TROTSKY TRIED TO make sense of the bureaucratic-collectivist Stalinist society in terms of classical Marxism and the 1917 Bolshevik version of those ideas. His tardiness in drawing the sharp and clear conclusions which can be seen now as necessary wreaked havoc with the Marxism he set out to defend. He was forced to follow in the steps of Stalinism, putting his own gloss on events while critically accommodating to the brute reality of the USSR. In Trotskyism and then neo-Trotskyism there was a transformation, often out of recognition, of the ideas and language of Marxism. Throughout the 1930s, Trotsky stretched and adapted the old Bolshevik and Marxist ideas and terminology to accommodate the new things, adding qualifying adjectives and using terms with implied quote-marks, such as "caste" for the USSR's rulers. Beyond very narrow limits, such a procedure could not but corrupt meaning and confuse definition. By the end it had become a scholastic game or even a form of juggling with words akin to word magic and superstition. For example, what more than superstition was the idea that to hold back from giving the USSR bureaucracy a name — ruling class — implied in all Trotsky's concrete descriptions of its reality would somehow ward off the disturbing implications of that reality for the old Marxist schemes of history?

The toll taken by this attempt to "save the old theory" was that the meanings of most of the terms of that theory were changed. For example, "defence of the USSR" against a small non-imperialist nation, in the USSR-Finnish war, the "defence" that led anti-Stalinists to back those whom Trotsky had called "the rapists in the Kremlin" in their attempt to take over Finland, was not the same thing as the old "defence of the USSR against imperialist attack".

Within the old terminology, there took place what in other fields has been called a "shift of paradigm". This happened again and again as events shunted brutally into each and every one of Trotsky's theoretical positions on Stalinism, pushing them off what had seemed solid ground. Trotsky was working within a false theoretical frame from as early as the mid-1920s, when he saw the Stalinist "centre" as a minor threat compared to the Bukharinite "right wing". Trotsky's frame and the impact of reality on it combined to create doctrinal havoc with the very basics of communism. It was not enough that Trotsky conscientiously restated those basics from time to time. The fact that Stalinist society, calling itself socialist, was misidentified by its most bitter critics as a workers' state, inevitably debased the meaning of all the key words involved.

There was a further infusion of new meanings into old words as Stalinism spread after 1944. This process in Trotskyism paralleled what Stalinism did to Marxism and represented a degree of ideological conquest by Stalinism of its most consistent critics. By around 1950, neo-Trotskyism had stood on its head the Communist Manifesto and its basic ideas, that is, the foundation of Marxism as it was in 1917.

1) Marx and Engels made socialism "scientific" by converting it from a moral scheme, counterposed to capitalism, into a logical, although revolutionary, dialectical development from material preconditions created by capitalism. In neo-Trotskyism (that is, mainstream revolutionary socialism, for a whole era) a pre-Marxist sectarian rejection of capitalism on a world scale, and an identification with Stalinist states as a progressive alternative (because they were anti-capitalist), had replaced this idea of the relationship of capitalism to socialism.

The idea that capitalism (and even on some levels imperialism) is progressive was excised from Marxism. So was the idea that to reject and negate the progressive work of capitalism (technology, bourgeois civilisation, the creation of the working class) is sectarian and backward-looking. Marxists reverted to the spirit of those who in the mid-nineteenth century wanted to go backwards from industrialism and of those against whom Lenin polemicised for their "petty-bourgeois" desire to unscramble imperialist concentrations of industry back to an earlier stage of capitalism.

The neo-Trotskyist idea that the Stalinist states were "in transition to socialism", following in the tracks of Stalin's "socialism in one country", turned elementary Marxism on its head. The "movement" was from the periphery to the centre. This was the politics of Marx's anarchist-populist opponent Mikhail Bakunin, not of Marx himself, or Lenin or Trotsky. Even reactionary alternatives to capitalism, and not Stalinist ones alone, were seen as progressive, even though they destroyed the fruits of world civilisation since the Renaissance. World history was seen teleologically as a process with an outcome — world socialism — mechanically fixed in advance, irrespective of what living women and men did or failed to do.

2) The patently false notion that capitalism had reached its historic end was used in the spirit of utopian socialists who felt they had discovered "the last word". That Stalinism was replacing capitalism was supposedly proof of this proposition.

Acceptance of the mid-nineteenth century idea of socialist colony-building, which would compete with advanced capitalism and replace it, was at the heart of post-1951 "Third World Congress" neo-Trotskyism — acceptance of Stalinism as representing a viable "transition to socialism", albeit one that would eventually need drastic working-class reform, or even "political revolution", to perfect it.

3) The idea that the proletarian revolution is made by the proletariat and cannot be made for them had been displaced by the idea of a locum acting to create, if not socialism, then the first decisive step towards socialism — the creation of a "workers' state". Working class rule was seen to inhere in the forms of bureaucratically nationalised property. A totalitarian economism — a fetish of nationalised economy, separated off from all the social and political conditions that might give it a working class socialist character — was substituted for the traditional politics of Marxism.

Actual working-class political rule — "to win the battle for democracy and make the workers the ruling class", as the Communist Manifesto put it — was pushed to the margins and relegated to the future by the ongoing "revolutionary process" that was spreading worker-enslaving and labour-movement-destroying "workers' states" across the globe. That "process" was the first and immediate stage of the socialist revolution. Workers' rule would be a second and subsequent stage.

The old communist centrality of democracy — even during the dictatorship of the proletariat — went. Democracy was a desirable extra. It could be done without in the "workers' revolution", at least in the first and immediate stage.

The idea of socialist revolution was detached from Marx's notion of the organised, self-aware working class as the force that could make it, and reduced to millenarianism, the hope for a superhuman agent of liberation. Marxists became millenarians scanning the horizon for the revolutionary agency. Again, Stalinism was central; it was the prototype of the non-proletarian force which nonetheless, through a perverse twist of history, becomes the agent of proletarian progress.

4) Marx and Engels in the Communist Manifesto saw the development of the organised, conscious communist political party as integrally interlinked with the self-development of the whole working class. The communists would "represent the future of the movement in the movement of the present". This was replaced by the notion of a "party" self-defined by the possession of an esoteric doctrine and revelation. The Marxists were those who could see the hidden and secret process leading to a socialist future within the horrors of Stalinism. Having once discovered that truth, their job was primarily to gain enough forces, anyhow, to present themselves as "the leadership" to the elemental working-class revolt guaranteed by the decay of capitalism.

Neo-Trotskyism, rationalising from Stalinist reality and building its "revolutionary perspectives" around it, regressed back behind the political level attained in 1848 at the dawn of Marxism.

4. MAX SHACHTMAN AND JAMES P CANNON

I. MAX SHACHTMAN

THE AUTHOR OF most of the material in this volume is Max Shachtman. His texts champion the Russian Revolution and revolutionary socialist politics with incomparable verve. Through most of the 1930s Max Shachtman had played a role second only to Trotsky in propagating revolutionary Marxism. But by the time he died in 1972 he had moved far from such politics. Sometime in the later 1950s Shachtman became convinced that revolutionary politics in the USA were not "operational" in the foreseeable future.

Like the Workers Party, which he and others founded in 1940 after breaking with Trotsky over Russia, and its successor the Independent Socialist League, Shachtman believed it to be his duty to help the American working class develop a mass political party, of the sort the British Labour Party then was, but with better politics. In 1958 the ISL liquidated itself into the tiny Socialist Party, and soon Shachtman and his friends controlled that party. The Democratic Party, since Roosevelt, had had the active support of most of the trade union movement. Soon the Socialist Party was working in the broad Democratic Party for a strategy devised by Shachtman: they would take the American working class a giant stride forward in politics, by transforming the Democratic Party into a labour-controlled party, in effect a Labour Party. How? The racist southern Democrats, whose affiliation to the Democratic Party dated back to the Civil War, would be hived off. Shachtman became a sort of operational Fabian, working behind the scenes to manipulate developments in the trade unions and the Democratic Party in the direction he thought would best serve the next stage of working-class development on the road to a socialist consciousness. In this guise of American Fabian, Shachtman helped organise the civil rights movement.

He had at the beginning described this Democratic Party realignment strategy as "foul and discreditable work", but necessary. In pursuit of an "opening to the right" which dominated the labour movement, he himself moved on to the right wing's political terrain. How much was initially a pedagogical adaptation, I do not know. He worked with the existing trade union leaders, whom he had once justly described as agents of the ruling class — the labour lieutenants of capital.

In an exact replication of the fate of the USA's "Right Communist" grouping of the 1930s, headed by Jay Lovestone, many of Shachtman's supporters became part of the trade union bureaucracy. Shachtman ceased to believe in a "Third Camp" of the working class and oppressed people throughout the world, and opted — like the "orthodox" Trotskyists, only on the other side — for one of the two great camps in the world. He chose the camp led by the USA.

Like the working class itself, as a revolutionary political force, the "Third Camp" existed only as a potential, as something to be won, worked for, propagandised about, wrought in the class struggle. Shachtman had insisted on that against those who felt impelled to stand, with however critical a demeanour, in Stalin's camp. After the crushing of the Hungarian rising by Russian tanks in 1956, increasingly Shachtman gave up on it. He accepted liberal capitalism as a "lesser evil" to Stalinism. He believed that the imposition of Stalinist regimes, which would stifle and destroy the labour movement and democratic freedoms won over decades and centuries, as Stalinism did everywhere it ruled, was to be resisted, on pain of death for the labour movement — resisted, even in alliance with liberal bourgeois and American imperialist forces.

ii

In the post-war world where the USSR was the second great global power, recognition that the USA and Western Europe — advanced capitalism — was the more progressive of the contending camps, the one which gave richer possibilities, greater freedom, more for socialists to build on, was, I believe, a necessary part of the restoration of Marxist balance to socialist politics. It was a pre-requisite for the reconstruction of Marxism after the systematic destruction of concepts over a whole period. That destruction began with the early 1920s conversion of Bolshevik civil-war exigencies into revolutionary law and culminated in the final ideological convulsions of Trotsky. But reconciliation with capitalism in the manner of Shachtman in his last years was no necessary part of it, any more than it was for Karl Marx in *The Communist Manifesto* when he rejected the "reactionary socialists". Marx was able to analyse the progressive work of British rule in India while also opposing it; Lenin could write "Can anyone in his senses deny that Bismarckian Germany and her social laws are "better" than Germany before 1848?... Did the German Social Democrats ... vote for Bismarck's reforms on these grounds?".

For Marx, for Lenin, and for the classical Marxists, to recognise something as "objectively" progressive did not at all necessarily entail supporting it or endorsing it politically; their task, as they saw it, was to educate, organise and mobilise the working class and to help it to utilise its opportunities — not to promote progress in general in abstraction from the class struggle.

Thus the idea of defending even bourgeois liberty against Stalinism, which was an international extension of the tacit alliance revolutionaries might enter into with liberal bourgeois forces against threatening reaction, did not necessarily imply surrender of working-class independence, or demand of revolutionary socialists that they should commit *hara-kiri* for its sake.

Shachtman drew conclusions he had never drawn in the fight against fascism. He joined the democratic capitalist camp. At the time (1962) of the CIA-backed Cuban émigré invasion of Cuba at the Bay of Pigs, Shachtman broke with those of his comrades, Hal Draper and Phyllis and Julius Jacobson, and others who would continue to stand on Workers Party and ISL politics. Shachtman thought that a Stalinist Cuba, where no real labour movement could exist, was the greater evil, and backed the invaders.

Shachtman's hopes for the development of the Democratic Party into a party controlled by the labour movement floundered as Lyndon B

145

Johnson's America got drawn deeper and deeper into war in Indochina — a war of mechanised slaughter wreaked from the air indiscriminately on Vietnam and Cambodia. Shachtman believed that only behind the bulwark against Stalinism which the USA thus provided could the forces that would resist Stalinism on the basis of progressive politics and democracy be given a chance to emerge. He backed the USA.

He died of a heart attack on 4 November 1972, as the USA was preparing to "bomb Cambodia into the Stone Age" — which it did, leaving the ultra-Stalinist Khmer Rouge as murdering kings of the ruins. The folly of relying on US imperialism against Stalinism could not have been more horribly proven. At his end Shachtman stood as a negative example of the need for the politics he had defended for four decades — socialist, working-class independent politics. Yet his writings continue to stand as an immensely valuable positive embodiment of such politics.

iii

IT IS only from the point of view of the so-called "Third Camp" — that is, of the consistently independent working-class politics which he did so much in his time to clarify and defend — that Shachtman can properly be evaluated or justly condemned. Those who opted for Stalinism, however critically, as a progressive anti-capitalist, anti-imperialist force, were Shachtman's mirror image, only in the other "camp". Those who supported Vietnamese self-determination against the USA were right to do so, but many of us too blithely dismissed the concerns that led Shachtman to his "foul and discreditable" course because, in the last analysis, we accepted that Stalinism, the force, for now, fighting imperialism in Indo-China, was also progressively anti-capitalist.

Nor were Shachtman's machinations to find a road forwards for the mass labour movement necessarily discreditable. Even if one thinks the strategy for turning the Democratic Party into a labour party unlikely to succeed, or simply fantastic, and the techniques employed by Max Shachtman and his friends to help engineer it suicidal for socialists, it does not follow that dawdling in sectarian aloofness — still less doing that while basking in imaginary reflected glory from foreign Stalinist dictatorships — is thereby certified to be the best socialist politics. Shachtman's efforts to avoid relegation to the role of passive propagandist have merit, even if one emphatically disagrees with his actions. Nonetheless, Shachtman at the end was deeply mired in conventional American dirty bourgeois politics.

The man who had with some justification denounced James P Cannon's conception of the revolutionary party as owing too much to conventional American machine "boss" politics, died in the company of the real machine-politics "bosses". His section of the Socialist Party in effect supported Richard Nixon in the election that was held a week after Shachtman's death.

This end to Shachtman's political life must for socialists cast a dark shadow on his memory. There are those eager to make sure it does, who use it to discredit his ideas and his struggle in the '40s and '50s for rational revolutionary working-class politics — that is, to develop the real heritage of Trotsky. It is not so simple or straightforward. The position of Hal

Draper and his comrades, their resistance to Shachtman's course, and their break with him would alone refute the canard that Shachtman's end was implied in his differences with Trotsky.

Shachtman, when he took himself into the camp of American imperialism, did not take his life's work with him. He could not. Against his future self, he had laid down immense barriers of passionate reason, unanswerable logic, truthful history, righteous contempt for turncoats and fainthearts and scorn for those who in middle age make peace with the capitalism on which in their braver youth they had declared war to the death. Shachtman's "Third Camp" writings are the best commentary on, and the best condemnation of, Shachtman at the end. Those writings, and the writings of Shachtman's comrades, are an important, indeed a unique part of the capital of revolutionary socialism. Arguably — I would so argue — they are the lineal defence, elaboration and continuation of Trotsky's ideas, that is of unfalsified Marxism, as they really were and as they really were developing at Trotsky's death. These writings are a precious part of the heritage of revolutionary socialism: in the post-Stalinist world they are no small part of the seed from which an unfalsified socialism will be reborn.

There are parallels. Lenin advocated that the literary remains of George Plekhanov should be kept in print and studied by socialists. Plekhanov, one of the greatest and the first of Russian Marxists, had backed the Russian Tsar's war in 1914-18.

Lenin also advocated that the pre-World War One work of Karl Kautsky should be treated in the same way. So should Shachtman and his work.

Isn't it to aggrandise Shachtman and his comrades too much to bracket them with Plekhanov and Kautsky? On the contrary, it is to risk understating their importance. Plekhanov and Kautsky were very talented and accomplished participants in a large school. The group of which Shachtman was the political leader and the outstanding writer were the rearguard of an overthrown and ruined political civilisation, which they worked to preserve and restore. It was a political world in which Stalinism fostered amnesia, charlatanism, spiritual darkness, a world in which socialism was eclipsed by vile fraudulence and the old socialist movement had been engulfed by political barbarism. Shachtman and his comrades kept alive Marxist method, culture, political memory, and the aspiration to working-class liberty in that age of political barbarism. Even their nearest brothers and sisters, the "orthodox" Trotskyists, who, despite their faults and inadequacies, had great merit of their own, were infected and tainted by the forces dominant in the labour movement during the Stalinist dark age.

Neither Plekhanov nor Kautsky was irreplaceable in his time: there were others as good or better and a large movement from which they could be expected to emerge. The work Shachtman and his friends did was irreplaceable in their time and place. No-one else did it. They were part of no big school of thought. They had to resist the gravitational pull of the far more numerous forces of "official" Trotskyism, itself caught in the gravitational pull of "Communism", in order to do their work. Most who called themselves Trotskyists misrepresented them then, and have since tried to obliterate the memory of the work Shachtman and his comrades did. Making these writings accessible is a necessary part of rebuilding socialism in our time.

147

Nor are the literary remains of Shachtman tainted, except in the eyes of those who want them to be tainted, by his political end: it was not in his power to taint them. As far as I know Shachtman made no serious attempt to repudiate his earlier work.

The small prefaces he wrote in his later years to editions of Trotsky's books put out by the Ann Arbor Press — *Terrorism and Communism* and *Problems of the Chinese Revolution* — make criticisms of the Bolsheviks no more stringent, though one-sidedly put, than what he said (I think justly) in "The Mistakes of the Bolsheviks" in November 1943 (chapter 1 of this book).

iv

IN THE NATURE of things revolutionary politics is generally a young person's game. Hope wells; reality is perceived raw; indignation is untempered by the sense of powerlessness and resignation; sensibility is uncalloused, raw human responses uncowed, courage naive and unchastened by fear of consequences or a sense of its own insufficiency.

Age and experience cow, make callous, teach resignation. They impress the painful cost of banging yourself against walls that for now may be impregnable, of pitting yourself against things you cannot soon change, of forgoing the sustaining and comforting community of the acquiescent; of living with a raw sharp awareness, like a nail in your shoe, that ours is a world of iniquity and intolerable injustice — the world which, yet, even when you struggle to change it, you must live in. The sense of powerlessness replaces the youthful idea that anything is possible. Vulnerability replaces the youthful sense of indestructibility. The brutal foreshortening with age of personal time and perspective dims or blots out the longer perspective of a collective socialist struggle. That is especially so when that struggle against capitalism and for socialism is narrowed down to maintaining a small group of socialists now and preparing the future. Then especially, the sense of personal impermanence and weakening infects and saps the idea of an ongoing struggle. The desire to achieve something becomes seductive and warps and replaces the fresh, clean, young sense of what is *necessary* and worth striving to achieve, whatever the cost and however long the struggle. The long view and the overview give way to shorter, discrete, unintegrated views. Impatience breeds opportunism and induces indifference to the seemingly less immediate concerns. The business of achieving a little bit now displaces the old goal, or pushes it beyond the horizon. So it must have been with Max Shachtman, who in addition saw the world threatened with engulfment by Stalinist barbarism.

Julius Jacobson, a long-time associate of Max Shachtman's before 1961, wrote in an obituary of Shachtman in *New Politics* that, by the end, it was an abuse of language to call him a socialist at all.

Yet there is continuity, despite the waning and attrition of individuals. There is a movement, whether a great mass movement or a faltering and struggling cluster of little groups. There is an accumulation of texts and literature and ideas that, once created, once put into circulation, are independent of the mind and the personality in which they originated and of the fate of that individual. Though individuals backslide, grow old and tired, or cowardly or corrupt, they cannot always undo what they did, unwrite what they wrote, erase the criticisms they made of class society, dim the socialist vision they conjured up, even though it has now grown dim for them — nor can they snuff out the activities of those they won and inspired and set to work to win others to the old ideals. Capitalist society has at root not changed even if its old critic has. And so it is with Max Shachtman, as with Karl Kautsky, as with George Plekhanov and many others.

That it is so with Shachtman is of tremendous importance. For Shachtman with his comrades, bore, for almost two decades, the main burden of ensuring the continuity of socialism. They knew themselves to be the survivors of a subverted socialist civilisation that had almost vanished; and they knew that it could eventually be recreated by the will, energy and dedication of socialists like themselves, acting in accord with the inner logic of history and basing themselves on the struggles of the working class. In that sense, Max Shachtman remains a great force for socialism.

II. JAMES P CANNON

IN MANY OF the polemics in this volume, J P Cannon is not only antagonist but villain: he is what Shachtman is to the "orthodox" Trotskyists. Lucifer, Satan. Since Cannon did more than anyone else to determine the fate of the "official" Trotskyists — those who stood with Trotsky in '39-'40 — there is, I think, some justice in this. Nonetheless, it is one-sided, inadequate and essentially unfair.

Cannon was no villain. He was and remained a Marxist working with ideas on Stalinism he took from Trotsky, and conceptions of socialist organisation that proved wrong or inadequate. He insisted on calling himself an "agitator", indicating perhaps a too modest conception of his own capacities; at the same time he had too much confidence and too much self-assurance that he knew what was what in the field of socialist organisation — and far too much assurance that it could be sufficient.

Cannon would, according to Shachtman, say to his intimates that he was a Trotskyist in his politics but a "Leninist" in organisation. Shachtman plausibly argued that Cannon's organisational notions had been shaped by the mid-'20s Zinoviev-led Communist International.

The factional battle in 1939-40, and Trotsky's death, left Cannon the undisputed leader of the biggest Trotskyist organisation, and the one around which the FI would regroup at the end of the war. To Cannon and those he could find for the work fell the task, if they could do it, of liquidating Trotsky's political errors and repairing his tardiness in re-evaluating the USSR.

But Cannon was tied as by an iron shackle to the logic of the locum workers' state that would remain a comparatively progressive force no matter what it did so long as the economy remained nationalised. In response to the World War experience of Stalinism, he might have chosen to follow through on Trotsky's 1939 — and his own — indication of the need to revise the whole position: he chose instead to follow the logic of "totalitarian economism" through to the end. Possibly, he was a late casualty of the

149

'39-'40 faction fight: he had spent too much energy denouncing the indicated changes as criminal "revisionism" and betrayal of "the programme of the FI" to find it easy work.

The continuing competitive struggle with the "Shachtmanite" Workers Party did not make it easier. There is perhaps a suggestion of relief in the way in which Cannon in late '41 seems to have accepted that the destruction of the USSR had virtually been accomplished. There can be no doubt that Cannon hated and taught others [the writer, for example] to hate Stalinism. But ultimately, Cannon chose to tie himself and those for whom he had the authority of guardian of Trotsky's legacy, to "progressive" Stalinism; he chose to freeze the movement politically and theoretically at the point Trotsky died. He used his authority after the war to "appoint" and back official theoreticians who extrapolated and developed in a scholastic spirit socialist perspectives from the existence of the anti-capitalist Russian Stalinist empire and the new autonomous Stalinist states such as China.

He reconstructed the FI (after the close of discussion in the three-year transitional period after 1945) as a mono-tendency sect around the frozen Trotsky of 1940, in a world that had not remained frozen. Cannon played little traceable part in the theoretical re-evaluation after 1945. He could not have done worse than those he licensed and endorsed.

The Catholic Church is a mutated piece of the bureaucracy of the later Roman Empire, that has floated down to our time through a number of different types of society; the typical "official" Trotskyist organisations shaped and influenced by Cannon's organisational conceptions can be seen collectively as a fragment of the mid-20s Zinovievist Communist International. Even where comparatively sizeable organisations have been built, they have been politically sterile.

5. TROTSKY AND THE FUTURE OF SOCIALISM

"To face reality squarely; not to seek the line of least resistance; to call things by their right names; to speak the truth to the masses, no matter how bitter it may be; not to fear obstacles; to be true in little things as in big ones; to base one's programme on the logic of the class struggle; to be bold when the hour for action arrives — these are the rules". Leon Trotsky

THE OCTOBER REVOLUTION showed for all time what the working class is capable of achieving, what working-class socialists, democratically organised and clear-headed, can do. It proved that the idea of working-class socialism is no chimera.

But the real October has been buried for decades, first under the foundation stones of the autocratic Stalinist system and now under the ruins of Stalinism. Together with other bankrupt Stalinist stock, the bourgeois victors have taken over Stalinism's great lie — one of the most poisonous lies of the twentieth century — that Stalinism was Bolshevism. In the war of ideas, the ghost of Stalin is enlisted now on the bourgeois side, still insisting that Stalinism was Bolshevism.

The bourgeoisie proclaim that history has ended and that they are the victors. But do they believe it themselves? Marxist socialism is the conscious expression of the underlying unconscious processes of history. Those processes go on. Whatever the fond ideologues of capitalism say, the laws of capitalism uncovered by Marx have not been suspended or superseded. The class struggle goes on: it is ineradicable.

Despite the triumphant crowing of the bourgeoisie, socialism now and in the period ahead has a better chance of being revived than at any time in 75 years. Stalinism as a force in the working-class movement is dead! Socialism is rooted in capitalism itself: in the beginning of socialism is the critique of capitalism from the point of view of its exploited victims, the working class. The bourgeois claim to have killed socialism is the claim to have frozen history. No-one can do that. All the contradictions of capital remain. The bourgeoisie must abolish the class struggle before it can eliminate socialism. It can't.

The bourgeoisie have won the long cold war with their Stalinist competitors. But capital has, in Stalinism, merely seen off a backward, inestimably more primitive competitor. *Their ideological victory over "socialism" is an imaginary victory.*

The texts in this book establish what the real relationship of unfalsified socialism and historical Bolshevism was to Stalinism, and therefore what value is to be placed on the capitalist version of the old Stalinist myths and lies — right now, the lie that Stalinism was socialism, and that socialism died with the collapse of the USSR.

Class struggle is ineradicable because the working class is ineradicable. It is the law of life of capitalist society, because capitalism cannot do without the proletariat. Capitalism repeatedly revolutionises technology and the organisation of production. Thereby it changes the proletariat. It disrupts working-class organisations by technological change and by blows in the class struggle. But the labour movement too revives, reorganises, redefines itself. The handloom weavers and others who made the first mass labour movement, The Chartists in the 1830s and 40s, were no longer a social force when the modern labour movement was created. The working class, renewed, changed, augmented, was. The exploitation of labour by capital — the basic cell of capitalist society — continues generating class struggle and self-renewing labour movements. It will continue until the working class abolishes capitalism.

ii

Marxists criticise the waste, the irrationality and the savage inhumanity of capitalism, but at the same time see capitalism as the necessary forerunner of socialism. That, not that capitalism is vindicated, is the proper conclusion from the experience of the defeat of the Russian Revolution and of the collapse of the society set up by its Stalinist gravediggers, who tried in their own way and for their own reasons to "by-pass" and "dispense with" capitalism.

Capitalism has not ceased to be irrational and inhuman, nor have market mechanisms ceased to be blind and wasteful, just because of the failure of the Stalinist experiment in "state socialism". Wage slavery and exploitation have not ceased to be at the heart and root of capitalism. *Millions of poor children die needlessly under this system eevery year.* In the United States, the richest capitalist country in the world, thousands of people sleep on the streets, or get a living only through the drug trade. Third World slum conditions exist side by side with obscene opulence in its leading cities. In Latin America unemployment runs at 40% in many cities. Cocaine gangsters rule huge areas. Malnutrition and even starvation are widespread. That Stalinism's "authoritarian state socialism" failed to bypass capitalism and emerge as a historical alternative to it does not mean that socialism has ceased to be the answer to capitalism!

Stalinism was an experience on the fringes of world capitalism, arising out of the defeat of a working class revolution, and stifling under its own contradictory bureaucratic regime. Stalinism was part of the pre-history humankind must grow beyond. So, still, is capitalism!

The idea that only the market system of the West can be the basis for democracy is the idea that only wage slavery for the masses together with the phenomenal concentration of wealth — and therefore power — at the top of society can be the basis of democracy! It is a prize example of the crazy logic satirised by George Orwell according to which war is peace and lies are truth. It has a lot in common with the old Stalinist habit of asserting that black was white, truth was lies, bureaucratic tyranny was socialism.

Even such democracy as we have in the West owes its existence to decades and centuries of struggle by the working people. Democracy in capitalism is limited, imperfect, and frequently not very stable. Mass self-rule by the producers, dominated neither by a bureaucratic state monopoly nor by the economic rule of the multimillionaires and their officials, is a better form of democracy. It is democracy worth the name. It is socialist democracy.

The model of socialism restored to its proper shape and colour by the disintegration of Stalinism and the open disavowal of socialism by the Stalinists is the only model of socialism that ever deserved the name — the fight to organise the working class as a clear conscious force, a class for itself, to break bourgeois state power and abolish wage slavery. "To raise the proletariat to the position of ruling class, to win the battle of democracy... to centralise all instruments of production in the hands of the State, i.e. of the proletariat organised as the ruling class... In place of the old bourgeois society, with its classes and class antagonisms, we shall have an association, in which the free development of each is the condition for the free development of all". *The Communist Manifesto*

Socialism will revive as a mass force. The only questions are what sort of socialism, and how soon will it revive? And how free will it be from the defects that have rendered it a nullity or worse for most of the twentieth century — since the crushing of the Bolshevik Revolution in the 20s? That depends to a considerable extent on the socialists themselves, on what they do. That in turn depends greatly on how we come to terms with the twentieth century experience of socialism.

In the 1880s in Britain less than 200 socialist pioneers set to work to win over the working class, to expand the labour movement and transform it into a *socialist* workers' movement. Their inadequacies need not detain us here. Work like that will be done again: and we start on a very much higher level, with a mass trade union movement. Here tradition is very important. Tradition is our collective memory. The Marxists are the memory of the working class. The historical memory of a class is worked and reworked; learned from or forgotten, lost and regained, relearned and reinterpreted, and put to work as part of the political capital of the movement. Much depends on the socialists. Not "history", or "capitalist crisis", nor any mechanical agency will do it, but living, conscious, determined, remembering people.

iii

This book is a relentless criticism of the "Trotskyist" tradition that for decades has in a hundred permutations been the most widespread variant of revolutionary socialism. *It is criticism from within that current.* A large part of the introduction is a systematic criticism of Trotsky's thought on the USSR all through the 1930s: but it is *Trotskyist* criticism of Leon Trotsky, and it is, I hope, loyal criticism in the spirit of Trotsky himself. The publishers of this book are proud to name themselves in politics with Trotsky's name. However, we refuse to mistake piety for political rigour or mimicry and mummery for fidelity to Trotsky. Trotsky mimicked no-one; and he had the contempt of a reasoning human being for all mummery and all mumbo-jumbo. Trotsky made grievous mistakes on the USSR. In the light of history this is indisputable. The serious Trotskyists are those who critically apply themselves to rectifying and renewing the ideological fabric with the help of which a renewed mass revolutionary socialist movement will be built. That demands a critical, and self-critical, appraisal of the history of socialism.

Trotsky once asked rhetorically: What do we do when the "good old books" fail to give the necessary answers? *Try to manage with one's own head!*

After Trotsky's death, his mistakes on the USSR were frozen in the work of pious but uncomprehending or irresponsible disciples into something inimical to his whole spirit. Trotsky was thereby lost.

The real Trotsky was both the hero of the workers' victory and the embodiment of the Russian workers' resistance to the Stalinist counter-revolution. He is not only the Trotsky but also the Spartacus and the Blanqui of the twentieth century. Trotsky personified a whole epoch of proletarian culture, tradition, experience, and unbreakable belief in the rational and humanist traditions of Marxism and of the proletariat.

Trotsky has come to symbolise and personify revolutionary communism itself, the elemental drive for freedom of the slaves of capitalist class society.

Trotsky's writings embody the lesson of working-class struggles that ended in unprecedented victory, and of struggles that ended in catastrophic defeat. Trotsky's writings constitute our best link with the Russian Revolution and the early Comintern: here Trotsky is the Buonorotti of the twentieth century, the passer on of great tradition, the link between the past and its future renewal on a higher level. His writings, mistakes on the USSR aside, embody the lessons of the greatest struggles in working-class history. They are an irreplacable part of the political, theoretical and moral resource of extant socialism.

But Trotsky's legacy will necessarily have to be assimilated critically, and reworked in the light of new experiences and new realities — just as Trotsky himself reworked and developed the heritage of his teachers, as, for example, on the theory of permanent revolution. He can *only* be reappropriated critically. Trotsky, rescued from the posthumous captivity in which for so long he has been imprisoned by well-meaning disciples, offers guidance, tradition and an incomparable example. He cannot think for socialists today, but he can help us learn to think better for ourselves. Not misplaced piety — loyal Marxist criticism!

It is in this spirit and to contribute to that work that people who think of themselves as Trotsky's people have subjected Trotsky's writings on the USSR to severe criticism. Trotsky is infinitely more than his mistakes.

iv

History is unending struggle — economic, political and ideological. The truth of history is on the side of socialism. This volume will, we hope, make that clearer. That the bourgeoisie should now be triumphant is natural. It is shortsighted. All around the globe, wherever capitalism has created a modern economy it has raised up a militant working class — in Korea and Indonesia, for example. Even when most successful, capitalism only creates its own gravediggers. The paths of capitalist glory lead but to the grave! Class war goes on.

What socialists do in this war can be decisive. What they are able to do depends on how they see the world, how they come to terms with the past, how well they resist the pressure of the conservative anti-socialist classes — in short, how they fare in the battle of ideas. The ideas in this book are a contribution to that battle.

6. THE PURPOSE OF THIS COLLECTION

THIS COLLECTION HAS a number of purposes. We aim to put into circulation certain key documents of revolutionary Marxism, long lost to anyone not prepared to rummage in libraries, and unavailable even in most good libraries. Though some of the publications in which these texts first appeared had a small circulation in Britain and Ireland, even the most important of them, such as "Is Russia a Workers' State?", were never printed or given any decent circulation here. Neither was Shachtman's collection of articles *The Bureaucratic Revolution,* (1962). Without being too fanciful, and indulging in no more than a little permissible exaggeration, one could call these documents the Dead Sea Scrolls of 20th century revolutionary Marxism.

We want to provide an approach to the real history of Trotskyism, that is, of unfalsified Bolshevism and Marxism, and its post-Trotsky mutations; to give as comprehensive as possible an account of the dissident Trotskyists who continued along the basic lines indicated by Trotsky in "The USSR in War", and the trajectory of his concrete descriptions and political responses to the USSR, from "The Theory of Degeneration" (1933) to "The Comintern and the GPU" (1940). We want to put these texts into the living stream of a reviving left, one of whose pre-requisites is a proper coming to terms with the experience of the Russian Revolution and its gravedigger, Stalin, and with its own real political history.

It is not a matter here of imagining that one can go and find and put on a tradition, like an old garment found in an attic. Revolutionary politics is not like that. It is not a Disney theme park where you can choose: today we are in the Wild West, or the Middle Ages, or the American or French Revolutions. Maoists in the 1960s and '70s did that with various past periods of the Stalinist movement — the Third Period, the Northern Ireland Communist Party's World War 2 Unionist period, Popular Frontism... It does not work. Real political tradition is a living thing, made up of the practice and assumptions and mutual relations of active militants.[41]

These texts are an irreplaceable element in the work of re-elaborating a living Trotskyist tradition.

It should not be thought that one has to take or leave the political legacy of the Workers' Party and the ISL as a whole. Nothing could be more foreign to the spirit of that organisation. The Workers' Party was not a "monolithic" party; nor are the organisations of those who want to learn from it (for example, some of those who have worked with me to produce this volume would find "state capitalism" — though not as understood by the Workers' Party minority — a better framework for understanding the Stalinist states than "bureaucratic collectivism"). There are things to criticise and reject in that tradition.

They got the overall perspective of Stalinism wrong. From our vantage point it is plain that Trotsky, and then Shachtman until 1946 or '47, were right to regard the Stalinist phenomenon as an aberration in the broad

---

41. For example, the tradition of Workers' Liberty/Phoenix Press is an evolution from the tradition of James P Cannon, an evolution that has led us to criticise and rethink, but not to repudiate and disavow.

sweep of history. It is understandable that the spread of Stalinism after 1944 to a further sixth of the Earth should have led Shachtman to misunderstand. Nonetheless it is plain now that the Stalinist systems emerged as parallels to capitalism, not as its successor. They were historical blind alleys.

Apart from the historical importance of some of the pieces reprinted here, the labour movement can learn a very great deal from these texts about what living Marxism is and is not.

PART I

REVOLUTION AND COUNTER-REVOLUTION IN RUSSIA

1. FOR THE BOLSHEVIK REVOLUTION!

Max Shachtman

THE FIRST GREAT WORKERS' REVOLUTION

ONE MUST JUDGE A REVOLUTION out of the circumstances from which it sprang. The social structure of Czarism, the most reactionary and outlived in Europe, was in a state of complete collapse. The imperialist war was bleeding the country white; a consciousness of the futility of continuing it deepened not only among the people at home but also among the soldiers at the front. At the top in official and court circles, bigotry, corruption and every conceivable form of social and intellectual leprosy was eating into the régime. At the front, a bloodletting that was as useless as it was incredible; at home a veritable orgy of war-profiteering among the capitalist classes and an unendurable growth of hunger among the working classes.

In February 1917 the Czarist régime appeared to be the most powerful in the world, with the world's biggest army at its disposal, with a subject people at once docile and impotent. Shortly after, the régime was overthrown by the same people and the same army. It was an imposing example to all statesmen and politicians that the patience of the people is not inexhaustible and that, once they are determined to rise in the struggle for liberty, for their aspirations, they stand on no ceremony, on no formalities. They take action directly and stop waiting for the promises of their well-wishers to be fulfilled in some distant and indefinite future. The example was also instructive to statesmen and politicians capable of learning from the people. As it soon turned out, not many of them are capable of learning very much.

Democracy does not consist in imposing upon the people what their rulers, by themselves, decide is a good thing for the people. It consists in the free expression of the desires of the people and their ability to realize these desires through institutions manned by their freely-chosen representatives. What then did the people who had just put an end to czarist rule want? It would be a bold man who contended that two opinions are possible on this score.

They wanted (1) an end to the imperialist war; (2) the convocation of a national, democratically-representative Constituent Assembly; (3) an end to the rule of the predatory landlords and a distribution of land among the peasants; (4) a radical change in industry, beginning with the 8-hour work day and the assuring of the beginning of the end of completely arbitrary rule of industry by the capitalist class by the establishment of workers' control in industry; (5) the right of national self-determination for the nationalities oppressed by czarism.

Not a single one of these desires is, by itself, the equivalent of socialism. Every single one of the demands of the Russian people was democratic

Max Shachtman's presentation in a debate on the Russian Revolution with the leader of the government overthrown by that Revolution, Alexander Kerensky. *Labor Action*, February 19, 1951. Abridged.

through and through. And yet, as we shall see, they required a socialist revolution for their realization. Virtually from the first day the revolution established what were tantamount to two governments, two powers, contesting with one another for political supremacy. One was the soviets; in 1917, as in 1905 they were spontaneously established. More democratic institutions it would be hard to imagine. They were directly and freely elected and sat in permanent session as direct representatives of the workers, peasants and soldiers. They were not the creation or invention of the Bolsheviks. While they were spontaneously formed without waiting for instructions from anybody, they were dominated by the right-wing socialists and the Socialist-Revolutionists. The Bolsheviks started as a tiny minority in the soviets.

While the soviets were the only elected body on a nation-wide basis in the land, and only they could thus speak authoritatively for the people, being referred to even by Kerensky as the "revolutionary democracy," they did not seek to become the government of Russia under their compromising leadership. But they were the real power, recognized by all: by the czarist generals who wanted to crush them and restore reaction; by all the provisional governments; by the Bolsheviks who wanted them to take all governmental power; and above all by the people. Not a single significant political or military step could be taken by the official government without their support.

Appearing to stand above the soviets were the various provisional governments. These were not democratic, if by that term is understood a government elected by popular suffrage in regularly fixed elections and submitting its conduct to the control of any popularly elected democratic body. The provisional government was constructed exclusively from the top, bureaucratically, by agreements among party leaders, self-constituting and self-perpetuating. Unstable by its very nature, it had no independent power of its own. It depended for its existence on the unpreparedness, and therefore the tolerance, of the reactionary forces on the one side and the revolutionary forces on the other. While the soviets mistakenly thought the government could be the vehicle for the advancement of the revolution, they watched its every step, particularly its reactionary wing and allies, and tried to control each step, reflecting the attitude of the whole people. The provisional government tried to maintain itself by satisfying both the *real* social and political forces, the reaction and the revolution. This aim was *utopian;* the two forces could not be reconciled. Both forces realized their life and future depended on the other's destruction. The governments became more and more governments of chaos, sure to produce nothing but that.

The 8 months' record of provisional governments in this stormy period when the desires of the people were urgent and manifest consisted of the following:

(1) The main body of the czarist officialdom remained intact, only few changes being made at the top. Czarist officers primarily remained at the head of the army, doing everything to undermine the soldiers' soviets, soldiers' rights, and even keeping enough power to threaten this same government. Cossacks, symbol of the czarist knout, were kept intact.

(2) The Constituent Assembly was not convened, on the basis of all kinds of pretexts. The real reason for this, as the bourgeoisie openly declared,

was that the election results would not be acceptable to them and would mean that the régime might refuse to continue the imperialist war.

(3) While the people wanted peace, the provisional government, in obedience to Czarist commitments made to the Anglo-French allies, drove the army into the June offensive at a horrible cost in lives and against conservative military opinion that it would be doomed. The people did not want to fight for the Czar's secret treaties, authentic agreements made among imperialist pirates. While Kerensky had been told by Miliukov about them, he never repudiated them and refused to publish them, since such would be a "discourtesy to the Allies".

(4) While the rule of the landlords continued, the peasants who wanted the land received promises. But they were taking the land, carrying out the revolution themselves in the traditional style of every great agrarian revolution. The provisional government forbade them to act, instead of carrying out its own reforms. It sent Cossacks against the peasants, who had never seen a Bolshevik in their lives but who were taking things into their own hands.

(5) No changes in industry. While the capitalists sabotaged production by locking out workers, the government failed to intervene. The 8-hour work day decreed by the government was not enforced. Everything was promised for *after* the "Constituent Assembly" met, but its convocation was constantly delayed. Workers saw that their soviets' influence in the government declined as that of the capitalists and Czarists grew.

(6) The treatment of oppressed nationalities represents the "acid test" for a democrat. The Finnish social-democrats obtained a majority in early June and declared for their autonomy, enjoyed previously under the Czars. The provisional government dissolved the Finnish parliament, barring its doors with Russian soldiers... In June Kerensky prohibited the holding of the Ukrainian Soldiers Congress called by the nationalist Rada. Vinnichenko, head of that body and an anti-Bolshevik, attacked the provisional government for being "imbued with the imperialist tendencies of the Russian bourgeoisie". In October Kerensky demanded an explanation of alleged criminal agitation started there for a Ukrainian Constituent Assembly and an investigation of the Rada was ordered.

On the basis of this record of failing to meet the continuing demands of the revolution, the provisional government of Kerensky fell. It also explains why the power of the compromiser Menshevik-SR leadership in the Soviets likewise fell. They had urged confidence in the provisional government, which showed it did not deserve the masses' confidence.

After the Kornilov affair, the Bolsheviks won uninterrupted victories in the soviets, while the Mensheviks and SRs split up and declined. Bolshevik influence was won fairly, openly, democratically, in spite of huge handicaps. Their leaders were arrested or driven underground, presses and headquarters smashed, press outlawed, forbidden entry to the garrisons and a lynch spirit aroused against them as German agents.

On November 7 the soviet congress, whose convocation had been delayed by its compromising leadership, was called together by that same leadership. The Bolsheviks had a clear majority. The congress endorsed the uprising led by the Military Revolutionary Committee of the Petrograd Soviet under Trotsky by electing a new government of Bolsheviks holding soviet power. Two weeks later the Peasant Soviet Congress, called by the compromisers, gave a majority to the Left SRs and the Bolsheviks, and the Left SRs entered the new soviet government.

In a few days the soviet government did all the things the provisional government had failed to do: (1) gave the land to the peasants; (2) offered peace by broadcast to all governments and peoples, starting with proposals for a 3 months' armistice; (3) inaugurated workers' control of production to stop bourgeois sabotage of industry; (4) decreed freedom for all nationalities, beginning with Finland and the Ukraine; (5) denounced and published all secret treaties and Czarist rights in China and Persia; (6) wiped out all Czarist power in the army and began creation of new workers' and peasants' army; (7) abolished special Cossack privileges and caste position; (8) inaugurated the new soviet régime of direct representation, with full right of recall.

The Constituent Assembly finally met in January; and because of its then unrepresentative character, big changes having occurred in mass thinking since its lists were drawn and the election held, and its refusal to recognize that the revolution had conferred full power on the soviets, it was dissolved. No champions could be found among the people for it — only reaction supported it. The country rallied to the soviet power as the only guarantee of the great democratic achievements consolidated by the Bolshevik Revolution.

The future proved to be a difficult one. The country was plunged into civil war by the dispossessed classes, landlords, bankers, bondholders, monarchist and reactionary scum in general who sought to arouse the wealthier peasants against the régime, and by all the imperialist powers who forgot their differences in the face of the socialist enemy. This civil war brought devastation to the country from which it took years to emerge. It forced upon the soviets a harsh régime, and laid the basis for the eventual rise and triumph of a counter-revolutionary bureaucracy which is in power today.

But in spite of that these achievements are immortal; nothing that happened afterwards can eradicate that from history or from the thoughts of mankind. They are a monument and a guidepost.

The road out of the blind alley into which society is being driven more and more, lies in the struggle for democracy. The struggle for democracy receives its clarity, purpose and guarantee in the struggle for socialism; the struggle for socialism lies in the hands of the working class — the beast of burden, the despised of the earth — whose will to victory was forever underlined by their first great revolution, the Bolshevik Revolution in Russia.

Max Shachtman

OCTOBER IS OURS!

THE BOLSHEVIK REVOLUTION WAS the great dividing line between socialism in theory and socialism in practise — it was not yet socialism, but the end of socialism as mere theory and the beginning of socialism as living social practise. In the Paris Commune, the people ruled their own destinies for the first time in history, but only for ten weeks, without support from France, without support from Europe, without the strength, the time, the possibility of mustering such support; without clear consciousness, without clear leadership. It was the dawn, but a false dawn.

In the Russian Revolution, the people ruled for years, the socialist proletariat ruled with understanding of its status and its role, with a leadership such as no class in history ever equalled. They proved — in a backward, three-quarters ruined country! — and proved it once and for all, that the socialist proletariat itself can take power in its own name, hold power, and proceed to put the inherited chaos into socialist order. Beset by every conceivable foe, handicapped by every conceivable difficulty, they proved it beyond anybody's dreams, beyond what they were required to prove, beyond what a working class encircled and isolated in one backward land could be expected to prove.

They proved at long last that the proletariat does not have to have a master to exploit and oppress it, that there is no quality inherent in the proletariat that precludes its taking power for itself. They proved that in the dark mass for which all rulers and their retainers have such lordly contempt are hidden deep and powerful springs of resourcefulness, idealism, passion for liberty, capacity for brotherhood, enormous creative genius, which await only revolutionary release to inundate and fructify the social soil corrupted by the rule of man over man until it blooms for a peaceful world.

They not only proved that this dark mass, once lighted up by revolutionary fires, can govern itself, but they found once more, to an infinitely higher degree than the Paris Commune or the Revolution of 1905 in Russia, that natural state form which the working class needs for its own rule until there is no rule by anyone over anyone — the Commune type of state, the Soviet type of state. It was there to be found, not because it had been invented and artificially imposed upon the people by some doctrinary, but because it developed naturally in their class struggle first as a fighting weapon and then also as the form of their rule. With this new and highest form of democratic representative government, they passed above and beyond bourgeois parliamentarism just as surely as parliamentarism had in its time passed above and beyond monarchical rule by divine right. And even after they succumbed to powers beyond their strength, the proof

Abridged from "Under the Banner of Marxism", an internal bulletin of the Workers Party, January/March 1949, replying to Ernest Erber, a leader of the Workers Party who had suddenly renounced Bolshevism.

was not undone, for they succumbed not because the socialist proletariat had dared to take power but because the proletariat in other countries had not dared.

Practically every bourgeois in the world recognized whose revolution it was and who ruled Russia. Millions of workers and colonial slaves recognized it too. That is why revolutionary Russia was able to light the fires of freedom all over the world. That is why it aroused passions and hopes, combativity and confidence in millions and tens of millions who were never before inspired. History does not know of another event like it; this old world was never before shaken as it was by the triumph in Russia.

It was our revolution. It remains our revolution, our victory and vindication — even now! Even now when it has been killed, strangled by its imperialist encirclers, deserted by those who should have been its socialist comrades-in-arms, speared in the back by its Stalinist assassins, dragged in the mud by every backslider and faintheart, it is our revolution.

How easy and contemptible it is to draw near the slain Achilles and kick his head now and spit on him. Every craven, every deserter, every dilettante can now track his dirty boots on to the imperishable page and relax his wretched bowels over it. That is cheap, it is popular in the most respectable quarters, it requires no courage.

The defense of the Russian Revolution moves along with the attack on it in the same way and with the same aim that the fight for socialism goes on by the side of the fight against socialism. Read all the "socialist" attacks on the Revolution that have been written in recent times, including Erber's. If their authors have the slightest awareness of what is really involved, they give no evidence of it. The attack upon the Russian Revolution conducted nowadays by the traditionally anti-socialist and anti-working-class bourgeoisie is not different in a single essential from what it was beginning with 1917-1918. All that is new in it is the ammunition that Stalinism has provided it with. Otherwise, the attack remains the same. It has a political meaning determined by its class aim and the class interests that prompt it. What does it boil down to? We have indicated that before:

"You workers, whatever else you do, *do not take state power,* do not even think in such terms! We have been warning you against it since the days of Marx. In Russia, they didn't listen to us, and look what happened. Lenin carried through a Marxian revolution. We are even ready to admit that Lenin himself was a noble idealist, but that didn't mean very much. Once started on the road, the movement had an iron logic of its own. Its inevitable outcome is the Stalinist state they have today, which even the radical Trotskyists say is an inferno for labor.

"Once you abolish private property, once you put all economic power into the hands of the state, we are all done for, you as well as we. Socialism is a Utopia. Capitalism is not absolutely perfect, but so long as we have free enterprise and democracy, you can get as much out of it as we can. Go ahead with all the reforms you want to. We will disagree with you here and there. But learn from Russia! Do not think of revolutionary socialism!"

That is the *only political meaning* of the "theoretical struggle" to prove that Stalinist totalitarianism was the inevitable outcome of the Russian Revolution, that Stalinism flowed "logically" from Leninism which the

165

bourgeoisie understands perfectly to have been nothing but revolutionary Marxism. That "theoretical struggle" is part and parcel — a very, very big part today — of the bourgeois struggle *against socialism and against the working class*. You have to be a permanent resident of one of the remoter planets not to see this demonstrated a hundred times over in the daily ideological and political life of our times.

When we defend the Russian Revolution, its great principles and its great achievements, it is not because we are hopeless stick-in-the-muds. We are not idol-worshippers or iconoclasts in principle. We are not traditionalists or innovators in principle. We do not believe that what is old is gold or what is new is true. Our defense of that Revolution, even more than our defense of its pioneer, the Paris Commune, is nothing but the continuation of our fight for the socialist emancipation of the people. And whoever does not know ought to know that the *whole line* of the bourgeois attack on the Revolution is the continuation of the century-old fight against socialist liberty and part of the century-old fight against the working class.

"Come now, are you saying that *any* attack on the Russian Revolution or criticism of it is reactionary, bourgeois, a blow to socialism and the working class? Isn't that dangerously close to the method of argument used in the notorious Stalinist amalgams?" We anticipate the familiar question. Since that is not what we said, we are no closer to the Stalinist method than we ever were.

Lenin submitted the Russian Revolution and its course to criticism; Trotsky had his criticism, during the great days and later in his life; Rosa Luxemburg criticized it; we ourselves have a critical reëvaluation to make. Marx criticized the Paris Commune, but so also did the British bourgeoisie. It all depends on what you are criticizing, what you are attacking, how you criticize or attack it, on what is your political point of departure, on what is your political conclusion. We do not even dream of denying *anyone* the right to criticize the Russian Revolution or the labor movement in general. We hope in turn that we shall not be denied the right to criticize the critics. There is the proletarian, the socialist or Marxist criticism of the Russian Revolution; there is the bourgeois criticism of it. And there is the "intermediate" criticism which renounces or rejects the struggle for socialism without yet adopting in full the position of our class enemy.

Read Marx's memorial to the Paris Commune. It was not an uncritical eulogy of everything the Communards thought or did — far from it. Indeed it was written by a man who, a few weeks before the establishment of the Commune, regarded the idea as preposterous! But every line vibrated with a challenging defense of the revolution.

"Workingmen's Paris, with its Commune, will be forever celebrated as the glorious harbinger of a new society. Its martyrs are enshrined in the great heart of the working class. Its exterminators, history has already nailed to that eternal pillory from which all the prayers of their priests will not avail to redeem them".

Read Rosa Luxemburg's criticism of the Bolshevik Revolution which she set down in 1918 in her fragmentary prison notes. She did not draw back from what she felt she had to say about the régime of Lenin and Trotsky. But she was blood-kin of Marx, she was a revolutionist to her finger-tips

who never for a moment relaxed the struggle against the enemy for socialist freedom. What right — political, moral or any other — do the backsliders and tired and retired radicals have to pull into their camp the revolutionist who ended her critical notes with these clarion words:

*"What is in order is to distinguish the essential from the non-essential, the
kernel from the accidental excrescenses in the policies of the Bolsheviks…
It is not a matter of this or that secondary question of tactics, but of the
capacity for action of the proletariat, the strength to act, the will to power
of socialism as such. In this, Lenin and Trotsky and their friends were the
first, those who went ahead as an example to the proletariat of the world;
they are still the only ones up to now who can cry with Hutten: 'I have
dared!'*

*This is the essential and enduring in Bolshevik policy. In this sense theirs
is the immortal historical service of having marched at the head of the
international proletariat with the conquest of political power and the practical placing of the problem of the realization of socialism, and of having
advanced mightily the settlement of the score between capital and labor in
the entire world. In Russia the problem could only be posed. It could not be
solved in Russia. And in this sense, the future everywhere belongs to
'Bolshevism'."*

It is no great problem to attack the Bolshevik Revolution today. Buy any
of a dozen such attacks and you find all the raw materials required by an
enterprising person. For a modest investment, you get two or three standard blueprints plus a wide range of parts to choose from for the finished
product. You get: what Trotsky said about Bolshevism before the revolution; what Luxemburg said about Bolshevism after the revolution; what
Lenin said about the revolution before and after; a few loose facts and figures about the Constituent Assembly; a selection of stories about
Kronstadt by any number of people who weren't there, authenticity guaranteed or your money back, plus a choice of figures on how many sailors
were murdered by Lenin or Trotsky or Dzerzhinsky (one, one hundred,
one thousand, ten thousand — whichever looks better); a selection of quotations from Lenin and Trotsky about (1) dictatorship and (2) democracy;
a calendar showing that Stalin took power after Lenin died, proving with
actual dates that Stalinism flowed from Leninism; differently colored bits
of gossip, all very spicy and revealing, about various Bolsheviks, certified
by a number of political Peeping Toms; labels marked "Cheka Terror",
"Secret Police", "Suppression of Socialists", all lithographed in scarlet to
imitate bloodstains and scare children; an assortment of wiring, string,
nails, screws, matchsticks, nuts and bolts, and a bottle of rubber cement.

All the quotations are easily pasted together, for they come carefully
chopped out of context and cut down to convenient size. No special skill or
training is required; any child can follow the directions and assemble all
sorts of articles from the kit, including a full series for the *New Leader*
which can be expanded, with the aid of a little more work and ingenuity,
into a full-length book for a venturesome publisher.

Once you have this handy little kit (more elaborate ones are available if
you want to invest in more of these second-hand books), you can write a
critique of the Bolshevik Revolution. We urge the reader to believe that
very little skill is required for this sort of job. They will all come out looking about the same. In the beginning, there was the Error. At the other

end are the woes of the world today. The shortest distance between two points is a straight line. You draw a straight line between the beginning and the end, and you get a clear and complete understanding not only of the development of the Russian Revolution but of all world politics for the past thirty years. It is a triumph for one of the elementary principles of plane geometry.

But where is the three-dimensional reality of the country known as Russia in all this, with its class stratifications and their reciprocal relations, with its economic and social situation and the urgent political and social problems it posed at a given time, with its relations to the rest of the capitalist world in which it actually lived? Doesn't exist. It is just a discrete point on the straight line.

Where are the classes in Russia at the time of the revolution and afterward, what was their position, what were they thinking, what were they doing, what did they want? Were there other political groupings in Russia, apart from the Bolsheviks, and did they play any role in the development of Bolshevik policy, in the development of the Revolution? Not important. Each class and each party gets no more than one discrete point on the straight line.

The same question with regard to the classes and their struggle outside of Russia, the political groupings, especially the Social-Democratic parties, and their policies, and what effect they all had on the Bolsheviks and the Revolution, gets the same answer. Not worthy of note. A few more discrete points on the straight line.

But at least the straight line is made up of all these discrete points? No sir! Got nothing to do with it! The line projected itself by a logic of its own right out of the heart and substance of the Error itself, just as mundane wickedness emanates from original sin. What about the interaction of the multitude of economic and political forces which affected the development of Bolshevism and the Revolution? Not important. Waste of time. What about Trotsky's studies and analysis of the course and the causes of the degeneration of the Revolution? Of no value. Don't have to be refuted. Don't even have to be mentioned. Waste of time. I'm working with my kit.

Max Shachtman

THE "MISTAKES" OF THE BOLSHEVIKS

THE CAUSES FOR THE DECAY of the Russian Revolution are often sought in the "mistakes of the Bolsheviks." If only they had not suppressed freedom of speech and press! If only they had not suppressed the freedom of political organization and all the non-Bolshevik parties! If only they had not established a one-party dictatorship! If only they had not set up a Communist International to split the Western European labor movement! Had they acted otherwise, we would have no fascism today, and no Stalinism, but instead a progressive development toward democratic socialism inside Russia and out.

From *New International*, November 1943

That is the tenor of most of the criticism leveled at the Bolsheviks in the labor movement. Consistently thought out, they boil down to the idea that the real mistake was made in November 1917 when the Bolsheviks took power. This judgment is based essentially on the same factors that generated the fundamental theory of the Stalinist counter-revolution — "socialism in one country" — and differs from it only in that it is not on so high a level.

The bonds by which Czarism held together the Russian Empire were brittle in the extreme. Under the stress of so minor a struggle as the Russo-Japanese war of 1904 and the revolutionary rehearsal a year later, the bonds almost shattered. Twelve years later, under the much heavier stress and pounding of the World War, they exploded beyond repair and tore Czarism to bits like the shot from shrapnel.

With Czarist despotism gone as an integrating force, who was left to keep the nation together and maintain it as a power, economic as well as political? One or two hundred years earlier in similar circumstances, it was the bourgeoisie. In one country after another, it united the nation on a new basis, eliminated or repressed the disintegrative forces, expanded the wealth and power of the country, and vouchsafed democracy to the masses in one measure or another. In Russia, however, the bourgeoisie had come too late. The solving of the problems of the democratic revolution had been too long postponed to permit a repetition of the French Revolution. This was the theory held in common by Lenin and Trotsky.

The period of the revolution in which Czarism was overturned tested the theory to the end. The bourgeoisie did come to power, but it was quite incapable of mastering the centrifugal tendencies which Czarism, in the comparatively peaceful days, had been able to hold in precarious check. The empire was falling apart. Be it in the person of Lvov, or Miliukov, or Kerensky, or Kornilov, the bourgeoisie made desperate, violent, but vain efforts to keep the subjected peripheral countries like Finland, the Ukraine, Poland, the Caucasus, inside the old empire with a new nameplate. It is unbelievable, but it is a fact, cried Lenin, that a peasant uprising is growing in a peasant country, "under a revolutionary republican government that is supported by the parties of the Social Revolutionists and the Mensheviks". The peasant rising did not come to strengthen the bourgeoisie and its pallid democracy, but was directed against it. The bourgeoisie was unable to deal with it in any better way than the Czar had discovered. At the same time, a proletarian power, the Soviets, not at all Bolshevik, grew up spontaneously by the side of the bourgeois power and threatened its existence.

The bourgeois democracy was incapable of seriously approaching a single one of the social and political problems at home. Given the collapse of Czarism, all the long-standing, outer-Russian imperialist tendencies to reduce Russia to a colony — tendencies most vigorously represented by the Germans, but not exclusive with them — received free rein. The country ruled by the bourgeois republicans was about to be overrun by foreign imperialism as a prelude to its partition among the great powers. This problem, too, the "revolutionary democracy" was unable to solve, or even undertake seriously to solve. The country faced complete economic ruin, political disintegration, chaos, dismemberment and subjugation from abroad, the imminent triumph of counter-revolution and reaction, with all the consequences flowing from them. The bourgeoisie, the bourgeois democracy, was impotent in dealing with the situation, notwithstanding the support it received from the Mensheviks and Social Revolutionists.

To say that they might have solved these problems democratically if the Bolsheviks had not interfered is not only to ignore an overwhelming mass of facts, but to stand the question on its head. The "interference" of the Bolsheviks was made possible only because the bourgeois democrats, plus the social democrats, could not solve the problems.

Political action can be understood, not in the abstract, but in the concrete conditions in which it occurs. It cannot be rationally appraised by itself, but only in terms of the alternative. The alternative to the "risky" seizure of power by the working class under Bolshevik leadership was not the painless flowering of "democracy" but the triumph of savage counter-revolution and the partitioning and colonialization of the country.

The "mistake" of the Bolsheviks in taking power when they did and where they did, not only saved the honor of international socialism and gave it a new and powerful lease on life, but it saved Russia. Without this "initial mistake", the greatest likelihood is that long ago German imperialism would have been ensconced in Petrograd and Moscow, French imperialism in Odessa, British imperialism in the Caucasus, Japanese imperialism throughout Siberia, Kerensky in a clerk's chair, with the Mensheviks running errands for them all.

The Bolsheviks cannot, and therefore must not, be judged as if they were uncontested masters of a situation in which they could calmly and undisturbedly plan a campaign of social reorganization. The disdainful critics like to overlook the fact that they, or at least their friends and patrons, left no stone unturned or unhurled to prevent the new state power from working out its destiny. Class interest came before "scientific interest" in the "new social experiment."

Both Czar and bourgeoisie left the Bolsheviks, who took power almost without shedding a drop of blood, a heritage of chaos and violence and multitudinous unsolved problems.

The sabotage of the bourgeoisie, loyal patriots of the fatherland who were ready to sell it to foreign imperialism rather than have it ruled by the proletariat, forced the Bolsheviks to resort to the most radical socialist measures from the very beginning. The Bolsheviks were anything but Utopian. Their program was modest and realistic. If they took what would otherwise have been premature steps, it was done under the compulsions of the bitter class struggle immediately launched by the counter-revolution.

Decrees permitting capitalists to continue owning their factories under workers' control are impotent against shells loaded and fired at these factories by their departed owners. Terroristic attacks upon the government and its officials cannot be effectively met with sermons on the superiority of oral agitation and moral suasion. Freedom of the press cannot be extended by a government to "critics" who come to overthrow it with arms and battalions furnished by Czarists and foreign imperialists. Freedom must be defended from such critics, and with all available arms.

Not only the bourgeois democrats like Kerensky, but the Mensheviks and SRs resorted to arms against the democratic Soviet power. Nor were they too finicky about the company they kept in their crusade against the Bolsheviks. Alliance with the Bolsheviks against their reaction was inadmissible in principle and beneath the integrity of these democrats. Alliance with reaction, with the Czarist generals, the Cossacks, the Clemenceaus and Churchills against the Bolsheviks, that was good, practical politics, realistic, tolerable by democracy.

In any country, such "practical politics" are commonly known as treason and treated accordingly. Against the Soviet power, this was not merely "treason to the nation," but treason to the working class and the working-class revolution. Those who tolerated the traitors, who even collaborated with them in a common party, who did not join the Bolsheviks in crushing them, were not much better. The Soviet power had no alternative but to outlaw these elements and their political institutions. This can be contested only by those who ignore facts — we say nothing of the class interests of the proletariat, of the interests of socialism! — including the fact that civil war is not conducted in accordance with the rules recommended in finishing schools for young ladies of good breeding.

What is downright outrageous is the impudence of the criticism of Bolshevism's dictatorial measures leveled by the very persons or groups which acted in such a manner as to leave the Soviet power no alternative but stern decisions of sheer self-defense.

This holds true also for the organization of the Communist International. The picture of Lenin as some sort of wild and irresponsible "professional splitter" is three-fifths myth and two-fifths abysmal misunderstanding. The social democracy during the war had led the working class into the cattle corrals of the bourgeoisie. The Communist International was organized to restore the class independence of the proletarian movement, of which it had been robbed by the leaders of the Second International. It was organized to unite the proletariat once more around a revolutionary socialist banner, to have it serve itself again, instead of serving the Kaiser, the French Steel Trust or the British Empire.

Above all, however, it was organized as an indispensable weapon of the Russian Revolution itself. The Comintern was the general staff of the world revolution. Its task was the organization of the victory of the proletariat in the capitalist countries. This was assigned to it by the Bolsheviks, not out of considerations of abstract internationalism, but out of the thousand-times-repeated conviction that without the revolution in the West, the Russian workers' state could not hope to survive, much less solve its fundamental problems.

This fact is well known and widely acknowledged. Its full significance is not always grasped. The Russian Revolution was the first act of world revolution. That is how it was conceived by its authors. That was the starting point of all their policies. The heart of the question of the "mistakes of the Bolsheviks" is reached when this is thoroughly understood. Everything remains mystery and confusion if the question is studied from the standpoint of Stalin's nationalist theory.

The program of the Bolsheviks called for establishing the widest possible democracy. The Soviet régime was to be the most democratic known in history. If a state power, that is, coercion and dictatorship, was needed, it was to be directed only against a counter-revolutionary bourgeoisie.

Was so much concentration of dictatorial power and violence needed against the Russian bourgeoisie, that is, against a bourgeoisie described as helpless and hopeless? *On a Russian national scale*, the answer could easily have been in the negative. But as the world bourgeoisie understood, and immediately showed, the Russian Revolution was directed at international capitalism. Without world capitalism, the Russian bourgeoisie could have been disposed of by the Soviet power with a wave of the hand. With world capitalism behind it, the bourgeoisie of Russia, which is only another way of saying the danger of a victory for the counter-revolution, was a tremendous force against which the greatest vigilance was demanded.

Because the problem was only posed in Russia but could be solved only on a world scale, the Bolsheviks counted on the international revolution. Because they counted on the international revolution, the Bolsheviks allowed themselves all sorts of infringements upon the standards of political democracy, and even upon the standards of workers' democracy.

The suppression of democratic rights for other working-class organizations, even of those which were not directly engaged in armed insurrection against the Soviets, was first conceived as a temporary measure dictated by the isolation of the Russian Revolution and in virtue of that fact by the dangers to which it was immediately subject. The victory of the revolution in the West would have meant a vast relaxation of suppressive measures. To this day the best of the Russian Mensheviks (if there are any left who have not gone over to Stalin) do not understand that the primary responsibility for their disfranchisement in Russia (and, more important, the degeneration of the revolution) falls upon the shoulders of their German co-thinkers, who so effectively prevented the German proletariat from coming to power.

In other words, if the October Revolution is looked at as a purely Russian revolution; if the world revolution on which the Bolsheviks reckoned is looked upon as a Utopia doomed in advance to failure; or if the world revolution is looked upon as a movement that *should* have been suppressed, as was done by the reaction and its social-democratic supporters; or if the world revolution is looked upon from the standpoint of the Stalinist theory of nationalist reaction — then the dictatorial and suppressive acts of the Bolsheviks (the Bolsheviks, not the Stalinists) become a series of mistakes and even crimes. If, however, these acts are regarded as measures imposed upon the Bolsheviks seeking to hold out at all costs while the world revolution was maturing — the world revolution on which they had every right to count — then their true nature is revealed. They are then understandable, not as something "inherent" in Bolshevism, as that which "unites" Bolshevism with Stalinism (or fascism!), or as that which produced the degeneration of the revolution; but as temporary measures aimed at overcoming the effects of an enforced isolation and superfluous to the extent that this isolation was relieved by socialist victory abroad.

However, if this is so, an important conclusion follows. The proletariat that triumphs in the next wave of socialist revolutions and triumphs in *several* of the *advanced* countries will have neither wish nor need to repeat all the measures of the Russian Revolution. It is absurd to think otherwise. It is much more absurd for the revolutionary movement to adopt a program advocating the universal repetition of all the suppressive measures of the Russian Bolsheviks. This injunction applies most particularly against the idea of a single, legal, monopolistic party, or as it is sometimes (and inaccurately) put, a "one-party dictatorship".

The workers' power in the advanced countries will be able to assure the widest genuine democracy to all working-class parties and organizations, and (given favorable circumstances, which mean, primarily, no attempt at counter-revolution) to bourgeois parties, and this assurance must be set down in advance. The assurance cannot be confined to a ceremonial pledge on holiday occasions, but must be reflected in the daily political practice of the revolutionary vanguard party. In the concrete case, the "daily practice" includes a critical reëxamination of the Russian experience.

There were "mistakes" imposed upon the Bolsheviks by the actions of their opponents and by conditions in general. There were mistakes, without skeptical quotation marks, that cannot be sheltered under that heading.

The most critical and objective reconsideration of the Bolshevik revolution does not, in our view, justify the attacks made upon Lenin and Trotsky for the violence they used against their violent, insurrectionary adversaries. Nor, even after all these years, can the excesses in repression and violence be regarded as having been weighty factors in the degeneration of the Soviet state. To condemn a revolution for excesses is to condemn revolution; to condemn revolution is to doom society to stagnation and retrogression.

But after having been compelled to overthrow all the non-Bolshevik parties, the leaders of the party in power made a virtue, and then a principle, out of a temporary necessity. "There is room for all kinds of parties in Russia", said one of them, Tomsky, if we rightly recall, "but only one of them in power and all the rest in prison". Tomsky merely expressed what had become the rule and principle for the other leaders.

The idea of one party in power is one thing, and not at all in violation of either bourgeois or workers' democracy. The idea that all other parties must be, not in opposition, with the rights of oppositions, but in prison, violates both bourgeois and workers' democracy, and it is with the latter that we are concerned here.

Even if every non-Bolshevik group, without exception, had resorted to armed struggle against the Soviet power, it was a disastrous mistake to outlaw them in perpetuity. From every point of view that may legitimately be held by a revolutionary party or a revolutionary government, it would have been wise and correct if the Soviet power had declared:

"Any political group or party that lays down its arms, breaks from the foreign imperialists and the counter-revolutionary bourgeoisie at home, adapts itself in word and deed to Soviet legality, repudiates armed struggle against the government and those who resort to armed struggle, will enjoy all democratic rights in the country, equal to those of the party in power."

The Bolsheviks made no such declaration. Instead, the kind made by Tomsky gained prevalence. There can be no question in our mind that the adoption and enforcement of the "Tomsky policy" contributed heavily to the degeneration of the revolution and the victory of Stalinism. From the prohibition of all parties but the Bolshevik, only a step was needed to the prohibition of all factions inside the Bolshevik Party at its tenth congress. Anyone acquainted with the history of the subsequent developments knows that this decision, also taken as an "emergency" measure, was a most powerful weapon in the hands of the bureaucracy against the Left Opposition. Disloyally construed, disloyally used, it smoothed the road to the totalitarian dictatorship of the bureaucracy.

The whole Bolshevik Party was politically miseducated and ideologically intimidated against the very idea of more than one party in the country, and for this miseducation none of its leaders can escape his share of responsibility. It is enough to recall that from the time of Zinoviev's first capitulation to Stalin in 1927 to the time of the last of the capitulators, every desertion from the Opposition was motivated to a considerable extent by the cry, "No two parties in the country!"

The Bolshevik revolution was betrayed and crushed by the Stalinist counter-revolution. It is not right to say that nothing remains of the revolution. Much remains: its great tradition is still alive in millions of men; its ideas and teachings remain fundamentally sound for the much greater socialist revolution to come; its experiences are still before us and so are the lessons to be learned from them.

Not the least important lesson is the need to return to the principles set forth by Lenin in *The State and Revolution*. Especially in the light of what has happened the heaviest emphasis must be laid upon the dictatorship of the proletariat as the democratic rule of the workers; as the widest and most genuine democracy the workers have ever had; as the equitable enjoyment of democratic rights by small groups, political opponents of the government included, and military opponents alone excluded; as the safeguard of the principle of electivity of officials, above all of the trade unions and the soviets.

The revolutionary Marxists must learn, and then must teach, that the struggle for democratic rights is not just a clever device for embarrassing the undemocratic bourgeoisie, that the struggle is not confined to the days of capitalism. On the contrary: it is precisely when the new revolutionary power is set up that the struggle for democratic rights and democracy acquires its fullest meaning and its *first* opportunity for complete realization. The revolutionists after the overturn of capitalism differ from the revolutionists before that overturn not in that they no longer need democratic rights and no longer demand them, but in the fact that they are for the first time really and fully able to promulgate them and to see to it that they are preserved from all infringement, including infringement by the new state or by bureaucrats in it. The right of free speech, press and assembly, the right to organize and the right to strike are not less necessary under the dictatorship of the proletariat, but more necessary and more possible.

Socialism can and will be attained only by the fullest realization of democracy. The dictatorship of the proletariat must be counterposed to the dictatorship of the bourgeoisie in this sphere because the latter denies the people access to and control over the very material bases whose monopoly by the bourgeoisie makes its "democracy" a formality not really enjoyed by the great masses.

That is what the revolutionary Marxists should teach. But first of all they must learn it, and thoroughly. It is one of the most important lessons of the Russian Revolution and its decay.

Max Shachtman

A DEMOCRATIC REVOLUTION

ACCORDING TO ERBER, the ruination began, in the theoretical field, "with Lenin's revision of the traditional Marxist concept of the relationship of democracy to socialism in favor of the anti-democratic view of the party ruling on behalf of the masses", and it gathered real momentum in the political field "once the Bolsheviks had dispersed the Constituent Assembly and decided to rule alone".

What is the traditional Marxist concept which Lenin, says Erber, held to firmly up to 1917 and revised in that year and afterward? We will repeat from Erber the quotations wherein it is set forth:

"If there is anything that is certain, it is this, that our party and the working class can only come to power under the form of a democratic republic. This is, what's more, the specific form for the dictatorship of the proletariat, as the great French revolution has already shown".

That from Engels. And this from Rosa Luxemburg:

"Democratic institutions — and this is of the greatest significance — have completely exhausted their function as aids in the development of bourgeois society... We must conclude that the socialist movement is not bound to bourgeois democracy, but that, on the contrary, the fate of democracy is bound up with the socialist movement".

And further, from her *Reform or Revolution?*: *"We must conclude from this that democracy does not acquire greater chances of life in the measure that the working class renounces the struggle for its emancipation, but that, on the contrary, democracy acquires greater chances of survival as the socialist movement becomes sufficiently strong to struggle against the reactionary consequences of world politics and the bourgeois desertion of democracy. He who would strengthen democracy should want to strengthen and not weaken the socialist movement. He who renounces the struggle for socialism renounces both the labor movement and democracy".*

The quotation from Engels is taken from his long-concealed criticism of the draft of the Erfurt program of the German Social Democracy in 1891. It is not directed at some over-radical opponent of parliamentarism, but at the opportunists in the party. In a letter to Kautsky accompanying the criticism, Engels writes that he "found an opportunity to let fly at the conciliatory opportunism of *Vorwärts* [the German party organ] and at the cheerful, pious, merry and free 'growth' of the filthy old mess 'into socialist society'." This gives us a hint of what Engels would let fly today at Erber. What occasioned Engels' reference to a democratic republic? Perhaps someone in the German party who wanted to disperse a Constituent Assembly and set up a Soviet government? Quotations from our teachers do not *decide* political questions for us; but if they are used, they should be used in context so that their real sense and purpose is conveyed. Engels complained bitterly about: *"the inroads which opportunism*

This and the next four sections, abridged from "Under the Banner of Marxism".

is making in a great section of the Social-Democratic press. For fear of a revival of the [Bismarckian Anti-]Socialist Law and from recollection of all manner of premature utterances which were let fall during the reign of that Law, the present legal position of the party in Germany is now all of a sudden to be treated as sufficient for the carrying out of all the demands of the party by peaceful means. People talk themselves and the party into the belief that 'the present society will grow into socialism' without asking themselves if for this it is not equally necessary that society should grow out of its old social constitution and burst its old shell just as violently as the crab bursts its old shell — as if in Germany society had not in addition to smash the fetters of the still semi-absolutist and moreover indescribably confused political order..."

This already gives us quite a different picture from the one our muddlehead wants to draw for us! We will not grow gradually into socialism, insists Engels. The old shell will have to be burst. And the opportunists are keeping quiet about the need to destroy in the very first place the semi-absolutist political order, *the Hohenzollern monarchy.* That is why he concludes that "our party and the working class can only come to power under the form of the democratic republic". Engels is simply posing the democratic republic in opposition to monarchical semi-absolutism! Not an inkling of this from Erber.

Was the democratic republic synonymous, for Engels (and Marx), with bourgeois democracy and parliamentarism? If *that* is the concept Erber wants to convey, it is his right; if he wants to make Engels responsible for it, it is not his right. Engels, in his *Origin of the Family*, calls the democratic republic the "highest form of the state", adding that "the last decisive struggle between proletariat and bourgeoisie can only be fought out under this state form. In such a state, wealth exerts its power indirectly, but all the more safely". In his letter to Bernstein on March 24, 1884, Engels writes that:

"The proletariat too requires democratic forms for the seizure of political power, but, like all political forms, these serve it as means... Further, it must not be forgotten that the logical form of bourgeois domination is precisely the democratic republic, which has only become too dangerous owing to the development already attained by the proletariat, but which, as France and America show, is still possible as purely bourgeois rule... the democratic republic always remains the last form of bourgeois domination, that in which it is broken to pieces".

It is under bourgeois democracy that we have the last form of bourgeois domination, and under bourgeois democracy that the rule of the bourgeoisie is broken to pieces. And that is precisely what the Paris Commune almost succeeded in demonstrating, and what the Russian Commune did succeed in demonstrating to the full! Not, as we shall see, if the Russian Commune had followed the free advice of the eminent Marxist Erber, but because it followed the leadership of Lenin.

Does the shattering of bourgeois rule mean that the proletariat dispenses with a democratic republic? Not at all! That follows only for parliamentary cretins who cannot absorb the idea that there can be any democratic republic other than the bourgeois democratic republic and the bourgeois parliamentary system. The Paris Commune was not a bourgeois state. Engels called it a dictatorship of the proletariat. *But the Paris*

Commune was a democratic republic nevertheless, and a thousand times more democratic than the finest bourgeois democracy! The democratic republic is "the specific form for the dictatorship of the proletariat, as the great French revolution [the Paris Commune] has already shown".

That is precisely what the great Russian Revolution also showed. The Russian Commune was not a *bourgeois* democracy, but a *democratic republic*. Neither in 1871 nor in 1917 did the revolutionary proletariat, in establishing its own democratic republic, set up a parliamentary state, but *a Commune type of state*.

Engels calls the Paris Commune a democratic republic in full knowledge of the fact that it was not a parliamentary régime. How does Erber explain that? He doesn't. He gives no sign of realizing that there is something here that merits explanation. Democratic republic and bourgeois democracy become synonymous with parliamentarism and inseparable from it. He sees the bourgeois republic and parliamentarism as a tremendous advance over autocracy and despotisms of all kinds, he sees the great advantages they offer the working class. But he cannot see beyond bourgeois democracy and parliamentarism to a workers' republic which is neither bourgeois nor parliamentary.

Lenin quotes striking and illuminating sections of Marx's study of the Commune:

"The Commune was to be a working, not a parliamentary body, executive and legislative at the same time... Instead of deciding once in three or six years which member of the ruling class was to represent the people in Parliament, universal suffrage was to serve the people, constituted in Communes, as individual suffrage serves every other employer in the search for workmen and managers of his business".

Lenin opposed parliamentarism not because it was democratic and not because he was "for dictatorship", not in order to replace democratic by anti-democratic institutions, but for contrary reasons. "The way out of parliamentarism", wrote Lenin, "is to be found, of course, not in the abolition of the representative institutions and the elective principles, but in the conversion of the representative institutions from mere 'talking shops' into working bodies". On what grounds did Lenin attack parliamentarism? Because of its inferiority to despotism or because of its inferiority — from the working-class point of view, of course — to the Commune type of state?

"Take any parliamentary country, from America to Switzerland, from France to England, Norway and so forth — the actual work of the 'state' there is done behind the scenes and is carried out by the departments, the offices and the staff. Parliament itself is given up to talk for the special purpose of fooling the 'common people'."

The real government machine of the bourgeois-democratic state is the locust horde of bourgeois and bourgeois-minded bureaucrats, growing in number, power, arrogance and contempt for the masses every year. Even an Americanized "Marxist" ought to know this by now. If the American people as a whole do not know it better than the people of other countries, they are being forced to learn fast.

Of all the bourgeois democracies, the American is the most reactionary and the least responsive to the will of the masses. No other bourgeois democracy has a political system so cunningly calculated to thwart the

will of the people: with its states' rights, its division into a bicameral legislative body, its enormously bureaucratized executive with unprecedented powers, its appointed judiciary with law-making and law-breaking
powers, its outrageously undemocratic system for amending the
Constitution, its broken-field system of electing Congressmen every two
years, Presidents every four and Senators every six, with its boss-patron-
age political machine which parallels and mocks the legal government
machinery from top to bottom — to mention only a few of the *traditional
and fundamental* characteristics of our bourgeois democracy. The mass
proposes; the bureaucracy disposes. The mass is allowed to vote once a
year and to "petition" the government at all times. The rest of the time, it
has *nothing* to do with running the government, with the adoption of the
laws of the land, and even less to do with carrying them out. The parliament talks; it adopts the laws; the executive, the locust-horde of the
bureaucracy, carries them out in its own fashion. That is in the very
nature of parliamentarism. And that is why the Paris Commune and the
Soviet system marked such an enormous advance in genuine democracy.
In the Paris Commune, Lenin noted,

*"Representative institutions remain, but parliamentarism as a special
system, as a division of labor between the legislative and the executive functions, as a privileged position for the deputies, no longer exists. Without
representative institutions, we cannot imagine democracy, not even proletarian democracy; but we can and* must *think of democracy without parliamentarism, if criticism of bourgeois society is not mere empty words for
us, if the desire to overthrow the rule of the bourgeoisie is our serious and
sincere desire, and not a mere 'election cry' for catching workingmen's
votes, as it is with the Mensheviks and the SRs, the Scheidemanns, the
Legiens, the Sembats and the Vanderveldes".*

This was written by Lenin in the middle of 1917, before the Soviets took
power, while the Bolsheviks were calling for the convocation of the
Constituent Assembly which the bourgeoisie and the Mensheviks and the
SRs and all the later champions of the Assembly were sabotaging with all
the strength and tricks at their command. It was not written after the
Bolsheviks dispersed the Assembly and in order to give a "theoretical
cover" to their action. It was written in broad daylight, for everyone to see,
and no political person had the right to misunderstand what the
Bolsheviks stood for.

So far as Luxemburg is concerned, again Erber just doesn't understand
what he reads and so imprudently or inappropriately quotes. Luxemburg
is attacking the Bernsteinites, the revisionists, the opportunists. If any
criticism is to be made of Luxemburg's formulation, it is that it tends to be
a little absolute. But that does not concern us at this time. As a general
statement of the Marxist view it is unassailable. It does not in the least
speak against Lenin or the Russian Revolution; it speaks against the
muddlehead! "We must conclude that the socialist movement is not bound
to bourgeois democracy, but that, on the contrary, the fate of democracy is
bound up with the socialist movement".

Luxemburg is a Marxist. She distinguishes between bourgeois democracy and... democracy. She is saying nothing more than this (it is a good
deal!): The victory of socialism does not depend upon the preservation of
bourgeois democracy; genuine democracy depends upon the victory of

socialism, upon strengthening the socialist movement, upon the independence and militancy of the proletariat, upon the unrelenting struggle for the socialist goal, on no compromise with bourgeois politics. "He who renounces the struggle for socialism renounces both the labor movement and democracy".[1]

"The Bolsheviks", writes Erber, *"rose to power in the Russian Revolution on democratic slogans: 'Down with the Kerensky Dictatorship! Only the Soviet Power Will Convene the Constituent Assembly!' However, after the Bolsheviks dissolved the Constituent Assembly, democratic slogans became a weapon of their socialist opponents, while they tried to give the relationship of democracy to socialism a new interpretation: Not through political democracy, but through its overthrow, would socialism be achieved, ran the new Bolshevik doctrine. Democracy was considered the fortress of the bourgeoisie, dictatorship the weapon of the working class. Democratic processes and institutions were described as bourgeois weapons to blind the masses"*.

Lenin, Erber explained to us, first revised the Marxian concept on democracy and socialism in the early and middle parts of 1917. In its place, he adopted the "anti-democratic view of the party ruling on behalf of the masses". But, continues Erber's explanation, after adopting the anti-democratic view Lenin still put forward democratic and not anti-democratic slogans. Why? Was there a "cultural lag" in Lenin's mind? No, democratic slogans were the only ones by which the Bolsheviks could rise to power. A supremely clever trick! For, once in power by exploiting the democratic sentiments of the masses, the Bolsheviks dropped their mask and showed in practise what their revision of Marxism really meant. It meant the destruction of political democracy and the establishment of dictatorship. Democracy was denounced as bourgeois, so were democratic institutions and processes; and "democratic slogans became a weapon of their socialist opponents".

Because the Bolsheviks attacked *bourgeois* democracy as *bourgeois* and defended *proletarian* democracy as *a thousand times more democratic*, it follows, like apricots from acorns, that the Bolsheviks were against democracy. Because the Bolsheviks attacked *bourgeois* representative institutions and the *bourgeois* democratic process as *bourgeois*, it follows, like an oak tree from an apricot pit, that they were against democratic representative institutions and processes. Because the Bolsheviks attacked the twisted, subverted, formal political democracy that exists under bourgeois rule, under the ownership of the means of production and exchange by an exploiting minority which gives it the power of life and death over the masses; because they supported the Soviet system of government as one which gives the masses real control and power — it follows, like Erber follows Marx, that they were for destroying political liberty.

The poor fellow simply cannot think in any but bourgeois terms. His mind is tightly boxed in by them. Proletarian democracy, soviet democracy, is a blank space to him; he cannot see it. The minute you are opposed to bour-

---

1. The reader is referred to the rewarding study of at least three basic documents without which a serious discussion of the question is impossible: Lenin: *State and Revolution*, Karl Kautsky: *reply to Lenin*, and the indispensable sequel by Lenin, *The Proletarian Revolution and Kautsky the Renegade*.

geois democracy, not from the standpoint of despotism or Fascism, but in the name of a Soviet democracy, you are in for it so far as Erber is concerned. He cannot forgive you. It is clear to him that opposition to bourgeois democracy is opposition to democracy — full stop. That's the only kind of democracy there is. No other democracy is possible, and don't try to fool *him*. The minute you are opposed to parliamentary representation, it doesn't matter what you are for — Erber knows you are against representative government, democratic institutions and processes, and political democracy in general. And don't try to confuse him with a lot of talk about classes and class antagonisms, because you'll be wasting your time too.

Let us see just what it was that the Bolsheviks did do, and what happened with the "democratic slogans [which] became the weapon of their socialist opponents".

The key to the first door of the mystification is given in the second part of the sentence above. How is it that "democratic slogans" *became* the weapon of the Mensheviks and Social Revolutionists *only after* the Bolshevik Revolution? It was certainly a powerful weapon *before* November 7, 1917. These slogans were certainly popular with the masses of the workers and peasants. In fact, they were so powerful and popular that the Bolsheviks were able to rise to power with their aid, as Erber notes. How is it that the "socialist opponents" didn't use this weapon against the Bolsheviks before they came to power, in order to prevent them from coming to power and bringing our whole world to its present dismay? Weren't they in an exceptionally favorable position to raise these slogans *and* to carry them out in political life? They were chiefs of Kerensky's Provisional Government and at the same time they were the chiefs of the Workers' and Soldiers' and Peasants' Soviets. They enjoyed, for months after the overturn of Czarism, the undeviating and enthusiastic support of the masses. They had all the political power and support that anyone would need to do anything he wanted to, certainly so far as raising democratic slogans and carrying them out is concerned.

They didn't do anything of the kind. They refused to convene the Constituent Assembly. They refused to give the Finns, Ukrainians and other peoples yoked by Czarism their national independence. They suppressed the peasants who tried to throw off the landlords and take the land. They persisted in carrying on the Czar's imperialist war which had bled and sickened and tired the people. They did nothing of consequence against the bourgeoisie which was sabotaging and crippling the economy. They did nothing of consequence to crush the counter-revolutionary monarchist nests in the country. But they did what they could to crush the Bolsheviks, their press and their freedom of action.

Strange, isn't it! What inhibited these unterrified democrats? Were they lured away from the Marxist concept of the relation between democracy and socialism by Lenin's revision of it? Maybe the Bolsheviks, or the workers and peasants themselves, prohibited these "socialist opponents" from becoming champions of democracy? That, too, is worth considering, but obviously not for long.

The "socialist opponents" did not fight for democratic slogans and democracy when they were in the best position to fight for them. Why? Because to fight consistently and militantly for democracy under conditions of the sharpest conflict between the classes, that is, under conditions of revolution, required a break with pure-and-simple parliamentary methods and modes of thought, a break with the *bourgeois* democrats and *bourgeois* democracy. Because *such a fight required, for the realization of its objectives, the installation of the working-class state power and led inexorably to this state power.*

There is the hitherto well-kept secret of the failure of the "socialist opponents" and the success of the Bolsheviks.

Erber writes: *"Against the Menshevik policy of subordinating the aims of the Revolution to the imperialist program of the bourgeoisie, Lenin advanced the policy of subordinating the Revolution to the full or maximum socialist program of the proletariat".*

What [Erber] says about the Menshevik policy has the distinguishing merit of being a fact, and shows that he has some notion of the "secret". Now, if we adopt the daring hypothesis that a policy of subordinating the Russian Revolution to the program of the bourgeoisie — its imperialist program, no less! — was not quite the right thing to do, what, in the opinion of the Wise One, was the right policy for Marxists to pursue? On this question, we can call on Marx himself for a suggestion. Scared to death of being denounced as Marx-worshippers, we hasten to say that Marx's words do not "settle" the problems of the Russian Revolution. But they do help to "settle" them and, at the very least, they show how Marx (not Lenin the revisionist, but Marx the Marxist) would have approached these problems.

Marx is writing about the *bourgeois-democratic* revolution in Germany, in his famous and all-too-little-known Address to the Communist League in 1850.

"As heretofore, so in this struggle the mass of the petty bourgeoisie will maintain as long as possible an attitude of temporizing, irresolution and inactivity, and then as soon as the victory is decided take it in charge, summon the workers to be peaceful and return to work in order to avert so-called excesses, and so cut off the proletariat from the fruits of the victory. It does not lie in the power of the workers to prevent the petty-bourgeois democrats from doing this, but it does lie in their power to render their ascendancy over the armed proletariat difficult, and to dictate to them such terms that the rule of the bourgeois democrats shall bear within it from the beginning the germ of its destruction, and its displacement later by the rule of the proletariat become considerably easier. Above all things, during the conflict and right after the battle, the workers must to the fullest extent possible work against the bourgeois measures of pacification, and compel the democrats to carry into action their present terroristic phrases. They must work to prevent the immediate revolutionary excitement from being promptly suppressed after the victory. They must keep it going as long as possible. Far from setting themselves against so-called excesses, examples of popular revenge against hated individuals or public buildings with only hateful memories attached to them, they must not only tolerate these examples but take in hand their very leadership. During the struggle and after the struggle the workers must at every opportunity put forth their own demands alongside those of the bourgeois democrats. They must demand guarantees for the workers the moment the democratic citizens set about taking over the government. They must if necessary extort those guarantees, and in general see to it that the new rulers pledge themselves

to every conceivable concession and promise — the surest way to compro-
mise them. In general they must restrain in every way to the extent of their
power the jubilation and enthusiasm for the new order which follows every
victorious street battle, by a calm and cold-blooded conception of the situ-
ation and by an open distrust of the new government. Side by side with the
new official governments, they must simultaneously set up their own revo-
lutionary workers' governments, whether in the form of municipal commit-
tees, municipal councils or workers' clubs or workers' committees, so that
the bourgeois democratic governments not only immediately lose the sup-
port of the workers, but find themselves from the very beginning supervised
and threatened by authorities behind which stand the whole mass of the
workers. In a word: from the first moment of victory our distrust must no
longer be directed against the vanquished reactionary party, but against
our previous allies, against the party which seeks to exploit the common
victory for itself alone. But in order to be able energetically and threaten-
ingly to oppose this party, whose betrayal of the workers will begin with the
first hour of victory, the workers must be armed and organized. The arm-
ing of the whole proletariat with muskets, rifles, cannon and ammunition
must be carried out at once, and the revival of the old bourgeois militia,
directed against the workers, resisted. Where this cannot be effected, the
workers must endeavor to organize themselves independently as a prole-
tarian guard with chiefs and a general staff elected by themselves and put
themselves under orders not of the state but of the revolutionary municipal
councils established by the workers. Where workers are employed in state
service, they must arm and organize in a separate corps or as a part of the
proletarian guard with the chiefs elected by themselves. Arms and muni-
tions must not be given up under any pretext; every attempt at disarma-
ment must if necessary be thwarted by force. Destruction of the influence of
the bourgeois democrats upon the workers, immediate independent and
armed organization of the workers, creation of the most difficult and com-
promising possible conditions for the momentarily unavoidable rule of the
bourgeois democracy — these are the main points which the proletariat,
and consequently the League, must have in mind during and after the com-
ing uprising".

This utterly amazing document — amazing for the compactness and unequivocalness of its summary of Marx's views on the bourgeois-democratic state and bourgeois democracy, on the role and tactics of the proletariat in the bourgeois-democratic revolution, and amazing for its almost uncanny word-for-word anticipation of the course of the Bolsheviks in the Revolution — deserves reading in full, down to the last line in which the German workers are told that "Their battle cry must be: the Permanent Revolution!"[2]

---

2. If we may be permitted a "personal note", we add the incidental information that it is to be found complete in a compilation of Marx's most important writings made by Max Eastman in 1932, which we helped to assemble, translate and edit. In his introduction, Eastman, referring to Marx's Address of 1850, says that "it will perhaps more than anything else written by Marx convey a full sense of the degree in which he was the author and creator of all the essential outlines of what we call 'Bolshevism'." Right, a hundred times over and over again! Eastman's advantage over Erber lay in his knowledge, understanding and attempt at consistency. When, therefore, he repudiated the Russian Revolution and Bolshevism, he also repudiated Marx and the fight for socialism. It was a triumph for logic and what he called "the Anglo-Saxon mind".

Let us jump from Marx in Germany in 1850 to Lenin in Russia in 1917. The Wise One [Erber] writes:

"The Kerensky régime had done its utmost to block its further advance by frustrating the efforts of the masses to end the war and divide the land. The régime sought to stretch out its undemocratic authority as long as possible by repeatedly postponing the election of a Constituent Assembly. If the revolution was to advance, Kerensky had to go. Only the Bolshevik Party was able to show the way to the teeming, creative, democratic Soviets of 1917. The revolution broke through the impasse and opened a road toward a resolution of the land and peace questions. Far from carrying out a coup d'état, as their opponents charged, the Bolsheviks rode to power on the crest of an upsurge that sought to realize the long-promised objectives of land and peace".

We are beginning to get an idea of what the Marxist policy should have been, and it's not bad as a starter. "If the revolution was to advance, Kerensky had to go." Right is right. But Kerensky alone? Really, now, would that have been fair? Should Kerensky have been made the scapegoat for the "Kerensky régime," that is for the Kerensky government? What about the "socialist opponents" — the Mensheviks and SRs — who made the existence of the régime possible, who were part and parcel of it, who were fully co-responsible with Kerensky in trying to "stretch out" the "undemocratic authority" of the régime "as long as possible," and doing "its utmost to block" the advance of the revolution "by frustrating the efforts of the masses to end the war and divide the land"? What gives them immunity and not Kerensky? Whatever our opinion may be, we know the opinion of the Russian workers and peasants; the whole kit and caboodle had to go! Their place had to be taken by — write it down again! — "the teeming, creative, democratic Soviets of 1917." Led by whom? By Lenin and Trotsky, because — write this down, too! — "only the Bolshevik Party was able to show the way" to the Soviets. Only the Bolsheviks.

That way was the seizure of power by the workers' and peasants' Soviets, which proceeded to give the land to the peasants, control of the factories to the workers, peace to the whole country, and to usher in the greatest victory for the socialist working class in all its history.

THE CONSTITUENT ASSEMBLY

BUT WHAT ABOUT the Constituent Assembly — didn't the Bolsheviks demand that it be convened and then, after tricking the workers into giving them power on the basis of this democratic slogan, didn't these same Bolsheviks disperse the Assembly when it did convene? This brings us to Erber's second pontifical bull against the Bolsheviks, the second error which brought about the subsequent 30 years' horror. And for a second time, Erber is counting on the possibility that his reader's ignorance is greater than his own.

The Bolsheviks, along with the Left Social Revolutionists, did indeed disperse the Constituent Assembly. But this means that they refused to disperse or dissolve the revolutionary workers' and peasants' Soviet government in favor of a counter-revolutionary and unrepresentative parliament. That's the first point and the main point!

What was the revolutionary Soviet power? It was "far from… a coup d'état," it was the triumphant revolution of the "teeming, creative, democratic Soviets" which "broke through the impasse and opened a road toward a solution of the land and peace questions." This impasse was broken through against the opposition and resistance not only of Kornilov and Kerensky, but above all of the Mensheviks and SRs. The workers and the peasants, in their democratic Soviets, repudiated the two old parties and their leadership. They turned to the leadership of the left wing of the SRs and above all the leadership of Lenin's party, because — we are still quoting from the Wise One — "only the Bolshevik Party was able to show the way." That way was lined with the slogan, was it not, of *All Power to the Soviets!*"

What was the Constituent Assembly that finally convened in 1918, after the Soviet revolution? It was a faint and belated echo of an outlived and irrevocable political situation. It was *less* representative and *less* democratic than the Kerensky régime had been during most of its short life. During most of its existence, the Kerensky régime was supported by the bulk of the workers, soldiers, and peasants who were democratically organized in their Soviets. It was supported by the Menshevik and SR parties and party leaderships which, at that time, dominated the soviets, had their confidence and support, and represented (more or less) the actual stage of political development and thinking of the masses at the time. Given the change in the political development and thinking of the masses, this régime had to go, says the Wise and Stern One.

But what did the Constituent Assembly represent when it finally came together, despite the months of Kerenskyite, Menshevik and SR sabotage? It was elected on the basis of *outlived* party lists. It was elected by a working class and peasantry that — politically speaking — no longer existed. The SR party, which held about half the seats, had already split in two. But while the official party, controlled by the right wing, held most of these seats, the new left-wing SR party which was collaborating with the Bolsheviks in the Soviet power and which already had or was rapidly gaining the support of the great majority of the peasants, held very few of the SR seats. The official SR list had been voted by the peasants before the tremendous revolutionary shift had taken place in their ranks. The official SR peasant supporters no longer existed in anything like the same number that had, earlier, cast their vote for the party list. Substantially the same thing held true for the Menshevik group in the Assembly, which represented the votes of workers who had since turned completely against the Mensheviks and given their allegiance to the parties of the Soviet Power, the Bolsheviks or the Left SRs. The composition of the Assembly, on the day it met, no longer corresponded even approximately to the political division in the country. The sentiments and aspirations of the masses had changed radically since the party lists for the Assembly were first drawn up and after the voting had taken place. By its composition, we repeat, the Assembly was less representative than the Kerensky government in its heyday.

It is not surprising, then, that the Constituent Assembly turned out to be a counter-revolutionary parliament. The Bolsheviks and the Left SRs called upon the parties of the Assembly to recognize the Soviet Power. The Mensheviks and right-wing SRs, to say nothing of the bourgeois Kadets, refused. Understandably! They had opposed the democratic slogans which brought about the revolution. They had brought the revolution against the monarchy to an impasse. They resisted tooth and nail the attempts to "open a road toward a solution of the land and peace questions." They had opposed the slogan of "All Power to the Soviets!" Their leadership had been repudiated and overturned by the "teeming, creative, democratic Soviets" which turned to the Bolsheviks as the "only" ones able to show the way. They had "subordinated the aims of the Revolution to the imperialist program of the bourgeoisie." They capped this not very glorious, not very socialist, not very democratic record by presenting a little amendment to the Soviet Power, namely, that it give up power and all claim to power, and take its orders henceforward from them! They asked the revolution to renounce itself, dig its own grave, jump into it and cover itself with earth hallowed by bourgeois democracy. From its very beginning, the Constituent Assembly declared war upon the Soviet Power.

Erber, the democrat, is merciless in his criticism of the Bolsheviks for dispersing the counter-revolutionary Assembly. But nowhere does he even indicate that what was involved was the demand by the Assembly to disperse and dissolve the revolutionary Soviet Government installed by the "teeming, creative, democratic Soviets of 1917"! Erber is for the Soviets so long as they confine themselves to teeming, but not if they exercize their democratic rights and mission to create a proletarian, socialist power. What is the difference between the Russian Assembly, which he accepts, and the German Scheidemann whom, he says, he rejects? Only this: Scheidemann succeeded in crushing the German Soviets and the Assembly failed to crush the Russian Soviets — that's all.

It may be asked: "Even if it is granted that this Assembly was unrepresentative, why didn't the Bolsheviks call for new elections which would have made possible the convocation of a parliament corresponding democratically to the political division in the country?"

The Bolsheviks preferred the Soviet (Commune-type) form of government to the parliamentary form from the standpoint of the working class and democracy and as the only state form under which the transition to socialism could be achieved. The Bolsheviks did not invent the Soviets, they did not create them. The Soviets developed spontaneously among the masses and, without asking anybody's approval, became organs for the defense of the demands of the masses *and organs of power*. The wisdom and superiority of the Bolsheviks consisted in understanding the full meaning and social potentiality of these democratic organs which they themselves did not fabricate artificially but which they found at hand as a natural product of the revolution. Among the Bolsheviks, it was Lenin who understood them best. His views were not concealed, hidden in his pocket to be brought out only after the masses had been tricked into giving the Bolsheviks state power. Immediately upon his return to Russia, Lenin saw that the Soviets were already a state power, a unique power, *dual to the official state power and in immanent conflict with it*. Almost the first words he wrote on the subject (*Pravda*, April 22, 1917) were these:

"It is a power entirely different from that generally to be found in the par-

liamentary bourgeois-democratic republics of the usual type still prevailing in the advanced countries of Europe and America. This circumstance is often forgotten, often not reflected on, yet it is the crux of the matter. This power is of exactly the same type as the Paris Commune of 1871. The fundamental characteristics of this type are: (1) the source of power is not a law previously discussed and enacted by parliament, but the direct initiative of the masses from below, in their localities — outright 'usurpation', to use a current expression; (2) the direct arming of the whole people in place of the police and the army, which are institutions separated from the people and opposed to the people; order in the state under such a power is maintained by the armed workers and peasants themselves, by the armed people itself; (3) officials and bureaucrats are either replaced by the direct rule of the people itself or at least placed under special control; they not only become elected officials, but are also subject to recall at the first demand of the people; they are reduced to the position of simple agents; from a privileged stratum occupying "posts" remunerated on a high-bourgeois scale, they become workers of a special 'branch', remunerated at a salary not exceeding the ordinary pay of a competent worker. This, and this alone, constitutes the essence of the Paris Commune as a specific type of state".

Lenin prized the Soviet type of state, from the very beginning of the revolution, for its superiority from the standpoint of the workers and of genuine democracy. His view on the Constituent Assembly, furthermore, is most concisely and clearly set forth in the first two of his theses on the subject:

"1. The demand for the convocation of a Constituent Assembly was a perfectly legitimate part of the program of revolutionary Social Democracy, because in a bourgeois republic a Constituent Assembly represents the highest form of democracy and because, in setting up a parliament, the imperialist republic which was headed by Kerensky was preparing to fake the elections and violate democracy in a number of ways. 2. While demanding the convocation of a Constituent Assembly, revolutionary Social Democracy has ever since the beginning of the revolution of 1917 repeatedly emphasized that a republic of Soviets is a higher form of democracy than the usual bourgeois republic with a Constituent Assembly".

Lenin wrote his views about the Soviets, and repeatedly stated that "Humanity has not yet evolved and we do not as yet know of a type of government superior to and better than the Soviets of Workers', Agricultural Laborers', Peasants' and Soldiers' Deputies," not after the Soviets had rallied to the support of his party, but from the very start, in April, when the Soviets were overwhelmingly under the leadership and control of the Mensheviks and SRs, with the Bolsheviks as a small minority among them. Lenin wrote his views on the Soviets and the Constituent Assembly, on the Commune type of state and the parliamentary type of state, for the entire political public to see and read. Anyone able to understand anything in politics was able to understand Lenin.

Once the Soviet power had been established with the decisive support of the masses of workers and peasants, the Constituent Assembly could not represent anything *more* than a throwback to bourgeois democracy, a throwback in the course of which the new Soviet power would have to be crushed, as it was crushed later on in Germany, Bavaria, Austria and Hungary. To have tried to bring into life a "good" bourgeois parliament when life had already made a reality of a *far more democratic form of government* established by the masses themselves and enjoying their support and confidence, would have meant a victory for reaction. That in the first place.

In the second place, we do not hesitate to say that, *abstractly*, a second and a third or fourth attempt to establish a more democratic parliament, could not be ruled out as impossible, or unnecessary, or contrary to the interests of the working class — *abstractly*. Similarly, you cannot rule out a decision by the revolutionists themselves, under certain circumstances, to dissolve Soviets that came into existence under different circumstances. The Soviets may be too weak to take supreme power in a country but strong enough to prevent the bourgeoisie and the petty-bourgeois parties from consolidating their power on a reactionary basis; the bourgeoisie may be too weak to crush the Soviets but strong enough to hold on to its rule. The revolutionists or the Soviets may not enjoy sufficient popular support; the bourgeoisie may hesitate before a civil war in which everything is at stake. Decisive sections of the people may believe insistently in the possibility of finding a solution in a more democratic parliamentary system and at the same time refuse to allow the new proletarian democracy to be destroyed. History knows all sort of combinations of circumstances and is very fertile in creating new combinations. How long it would be possible for revolutionary Soviets (a semi-state) to exist side by side with an uncertain bourgeois parliament (another semi-state) under any and all conceivable circumstances, cannot be answered categorically or in advance. All we need to say is this: there are historical laws of revolution, we know these laws, and we also know that there have been and will probably continue to be *exceptions* to these laws.

However, it is not this abstract question that is being discussed, important though it is in its own right. We are not saying that in *every* socialist revolution, *regardless* of the country, the period, the economic and political conditions in which it develops, Soviets will arise; or if they do that they will develop just the way they did in Russia, that the workers' organs will come into existence in head-on conflict with the bourgeois parliamentary system, that these workers' organs will have to disperse or dissolve the parliament in the same way that we saw in Russia, that the bourgeoisie will have to be overturned by violence, that the ousted bourgeoisie is absolutely certain to resist with armed force, that a civil war is absolutely inevitable. It is *conceivable* that the rise of the socialist proletariat is so swift, mighty and irresistible; that the economy is in such a state of disorder and the bourgeoisie in such a demoralized, depressed and hopeless state, that it decides to throw in its hand without a real fight. It is *conceivable* that under such or similar circumstances the classical bourgeois parliament can be so drastically revised from within its own organs that it becomes transformed into something radically different. All laws, including historical laws, have their exceptions. But again, that is not what we are discussing here. We are discussing what actually happened in the Russian Revolution.

And what *actually* happened, that is, the way the social and political forces actually meshed and drew apart and clashed in Russia during the revolution, shows that the Bolsheviks acted as revolutionary socialists in the struggle around the Constituent Assembly and not like political sci-

187

ence professors drawing diagrams on a high school blackboard.

Which brings us to the third place — the political reality. Once the Soviets took power, the counter-revolution instantly adopted the slogan of the Constituent Assembly even before the Constituent actually convened. The true representatives of the *classes* regarded neither the Soviets nor the Constituent Assembly as abstractions. For the reaction as well as for the petty-bourgeois democracy (each from its own standpoint), the Constituent Assembly became the rallying cry, the banner, the instrument for the struggle to overthrow the Soviet Power of the workers and peasants, which also meant to overthrow all the achievements obtained by this power and expected from it. The conflict between "Soviet" and "Assembly" on the blackboard is one thing. In the Russia of 1917-1918, it was *a violent and irreconcilable conflict between the classes*. In Erber's document, it need hardly be added, the class struggle does not exist. Or if it does, why, it can easily be straightened out by men of good will. The Assembly demanded the capitulation of the Soviets; it could not exist without such a capitulation. Men of good will were of little use in this conflict. A civil war broke out and, as the German phrase has it, the weapon of criticism gave way to the criticism of weapons.

THE CIVIL WAR

THE CIVIL WAR THAT FOLLOWED is clearly the fault of the Bolsheviks. Of that, there is no doubt in Erber's mind. It's notoriously true, too! If the Bolsheviks had not taken power, there would have been no need for a civil war to crush them! Even before the Bolsheviks took power, as a matter of fact, if the Soviets (we mean, of course, the teeming, democratic Soviets) had not existed at all, there might not even have been a Kornilovist-monarchist plot to drown them in a bloodbath. Indeed, we may even state it more generally: If workers were not so insistent and militant in trying to impose their modest demands on obstinate and reactionary employers, the latter would find no need of subsidizing thugs and fascists to beat and shoot workers. You can hear that philosophy expounded in any high school (third term), from a thousand pulpits and ten thousand newspaper pages: If labor gets unreasonable in its demands and doesn't know its proper place, well then, we don't like it, you know, but if that happens, Fascism just is inevitable. Yessirree! It's notoriously true. It is also true that if you stop breathing altogether, not even your worst enemy will dream of strangling you.

Oh, wait a minute! Erber is not defending the bourgeoisie and the reaction! He's really radical, and he doesn't care much about what is done to the bourgeoisie. What upsets him is that the Bolsheviks took power and dispersed the Assembly in opposition to the *workers*. Do you see now? Listen to this little sneer, lifted right out of the literature of the professional anti-Bolshevik (and the professional anti-unionist, we might add):

"As for the masses who constituted the Soviets, Lenin held that they would be won to the idea in time. It was for the vanguard to act and explain later. Those of the workers who refused to accept this concept of the

dictatorship of the proletariat had to be handled firmly, for their own good".

Our little animal is a vicious one, isn't he? Lenin was for imposing his dictatorship upon the masses and explaining to them later. And if they didn't go along, why, shoot the rabble down — for their own good! He turned out pretty bad, this Lenin. Fights for months with democratic slogans; fools everybody, including the democratic Soviets which brought him to power on the crest of their upsurge and without a coup d'état on his part, and then, a very few weeks later, the mask is off! He acts for their own good; he shoots them for their own good. There's an authentic portrait of Lenin for you, an unretouched photograph of him!

What is the proof for this insolent charge? One proof is the famous "demonstration" of January 18, 1918, organized by the reactionary City Duma of Petrograd against the Soviet Power and for the Constituent Assembly. The "demonstration" was dispersed by Red Guards. To show the magnitude of this Bolshevik atrocity, Erber quotes an article by Maxim Gorky, "whose honesty as a reporter of the events can be accepted." We hear Gorky burning with indignation at the charge that this was a bourgeois demonstration and denouncing the Bolsheviks for encouraging "the soldiers and Red Guards [to] snatch the revolutionary banners from the hands of the workers."

Gorky's honesty, guaranteed by Erber personally, makes him a good reporter of events! Gorky was, to be sure, an honest man and a socialist. But on revolutionary problems, he had no more qualification than the next man, except perhaps that he was warmly sentimental, almost always confused in the political conflicts of the Marxian movement, and a bitter enemy of the Bolshevik Revolution for a long time, above all, at the time it occurred. If Erber picks him out as his reporter of events, it is a clear case of like calling unto like. Erber is attracted by Gorky's impressionism and by his confusion, which he likes to think is no greater than his own muddleheadedness.

You read Erber's lurid quotation from Gorky, and your mind's eye conjures up the image of Scheidemann, Noske and Ebert mowing down the German workers with machine guns. Erber has his countries, parties and men mixed up a little. Who was involved in this huge demonstration which, if you follow Erber, you might think was terminated with workers dead and dying by the thousands? Three days before Gorky's anguished article, his own paper, *Novaia Zhizn*, reported the demonstration as follows: "About 11.30 some two hundred men bearing a flag with the words, 'All Power to the Constituent Assembly,' came across the Liteiny Bridge." There is the imposing number of the Petrograd population that followed the clarion call of the bourgeoisie, the Mensheviks and the SRs to proclaim the sovereign rights of the Constituent Assembly which they had so successfully sabotaged for six months. One hundred plus one hundred, making a grand total of two hundred, all good men and true!

The other proof is this: "Gorky is quite correct in asking what the bourgeoisie had to cheer about in the convocation of a Constituent Assembly in which the bourgeois party, the Kadets, held only fifteen seats out of 520, and in which the extreme right Social Revolutionaries, who had been identified with Kerensky, were thoroughly discredited".

We will even try to explain to this innocent what the bourgeoisie had to cheer about. A Constituent Assembly with only 15 Kadets out of 520 seats and a majority for the SRs, even right-wing SRs, would give the bourgeoisie very little to cheer about, *if* this Constituent were proclaiming its sovereignty against the Czarist Duma. The same Constituent, however, in proclaiming its sovereignty against the revolutionary power of the democratic Soviets of the workers and peasants, would give the bourgeoisie, *inside Russia and all over the world*, plenty to cheer about. *And it did cheer about it!!* How explain that mystery? And how explain a few other mysteries?

Between them, the right-wing SRs and the Mensheviks had the majority of the seats in the Constituent. Since it was an ever-so-democratic Constituent, this must have meant that the two parties were supported by the majority of the population. The Constituent is dispersed by the Bolsheviks, who do not have the masses but who act for them and explain later, and who shoot them down for their own good. So far, so good. The outraged SRs and Mensheviks return to the outraged masses, with the declaration, as one of them put it, that "The Constituent Assembly alone is capable of uniting all parts of Russia to put an end to the civil war which is speeding up the economic ruin of the country, and to solve all essential questions raised by the revolution." The masses want democracy and the solution of all these essential questions. The Mensheviks and SRs promise to solve them. In fact, Erber tells us, they are now really for peace and for land to the peasants. What is more, the rôles are reversed on the matter of democracy. The Bolsheviks are for the despotic dictatorship over the masses and "democratic slogans became a weapon of their socialist opponents."

We are in 1918. The Bolshevik power is established in only a very tiny part of Russia and consolidated in none. The anti-Bolsheviks have political control in a multitude of localities — the great majority — and they even have considerable armed forces at their disposal. The Bolsheviks do not have what Stalin, for example, has today: a huge, tightly-knit political machine, hordes of privileged bureaucrats, a tremendous army, an all-pervading and terrifying GPU, and the like. They cannot simply dispose of their opponents by force or terror, as Stalin does. It is still a fair and square political fight, with the big odds still apparently in favor of the "socialist opponents" who now have democratic slogans as their weapons and the democratic Constituent Assembly, in the flesh, as their banner.

The unexplained mystery, hidden to Erber behind seven of his own fogs, is this: How account for the fact that the "socialist opponents" get nowhere with their "democratic slogans" and their Constituent Assembly? Aren't they the parties of the workers and peasants, as proved by the majority they registered at the opening of the Constituent? Aren't they now armed to the toes with "democratic slogans" which, only a day ago, were so vastly popular with the masses that the cunning Bolsheviks won power with their aid? Thorny questions, aren't they? But Erber is not going to get any thorns in his fingers if he can help it. Solution? He leaves the questions strictly alone.

That's a solution for him, but it does not answer the questions. The answer gives us the second key to the mystification: The bourgeoisie had everything to cheer about in the convocation of the Constituent Assembly — *everything*. It could not expect to restore its power in its own name in the Russia of 1917-1918. But it could hope to restore it behind the stalking horse of bourgeois democracy, the Constituent Assembly and its Menshevik-SR champions. Shall we look into this point for a minute?

Here, for example, we have the report of the US Consul Dewitt Poole to the American Ambassador in Russia, written in Petrograd exactly one week after the final session of the Constituent. He is reporting on his visit five weeks earlier to Rostov-on-Don "to investigate the question of the establishment of an American Consulate in that city." During his visit, Mr Poole meets with notorious monarchist and Cossack counterrevolutionists like General Kaledin, General Alexeyev and others connected with General Kornilov. The anti-Bolshevik united front is being formed into a "Council" in the Southeast of Russia immediately after the Soviet Power is established and before the Constituent even assembles. Let us read, and with profit, every one of the lines that we have room to quote from Mr. Poole's report:

"Negotiations are in progress for the admission to the Council of three representative Social Democrats, namely, Chaikovsky, Kuskova and Plekhanov; and two Social Revolutionaries, namely, Argunov and Potresov.

"On the conservative side the Council, as now constituted, includes, besides the three generals (Alexeyev, Kornilov and Kaledin), Mr Milyukov; Prince Gregory Trubetskoy; Professor Struve; Mr Fedorov, representing the banking and other large commercial interests of Moscow; two other Kadets or nationalist patriots yet to be chosen; Mr Bogayevsky, the vice ataman of the Don Cossacks; and Mr Paramonov, a rich Cossack. The Council will undoubtedly undergo changes in personnel, but a framework of an equal number of conservatives and radicals, not counting the three generals, appears to have been adopted.

"In pursuance of the agreement with Mr Savinkov, a proclamation to the Russian people has been drafted… It refers to the suppression of the Constituent Assembly and asks for the support of the people in defending that institution. It is sound on the subject of the continuance of the war. The proclamation will be issued in the name of the league, unsigned, because it is frankly admitted that it has not yet been possible to obtain the names of persons who, it is thought, would be thoroughly acceptable to the people at large".

Isn't every line of our wonderful Mr Poole covered with mother-of-pearl, even though he never, we suppose, read Engels' letter to Conrad Schmidt? What did the bourgeoisie have to cheer about in the convocation of the Constituent Assembly? Gorky didn't know. Erber doesn't know yet. False modesty prevents us from saying we know. But Generals Alexeyev, Kornilov and Kaledin — they know. Prince Trubetskoy — he knows. Gospadin Fedorov, "representing the banking and other commercial interests of Moscow" — he knows. Gospadin Paramonov, a Cossack who happens also to be rich — he knows. Alas, every one of them has passed from our midst to enjoy the reward of the pious; not one of them is alive today to tell Erber what he knows. And that's a double pity, because the proclamation of the Council was so "sound on the subject of the continuance of the war" — which is another subject that is of interest to Erber.

General Denikin issued a proclamation on January 9, 1918, before the hideous Bolsheviks dispersed the Assembly, proclaiming the aims of his

"Volunteer Army."

"The new army will defend the civil liberties in order to enable the master of the Russian land — the Russian people — to express through their elected Constituent Assembly their sovereign will. All classes, parties, and groups of the population must accept that will. The army and those taking part in its formation will absolutely submit to the legal power appointed by the Constituent Assembly".

This Czarist General did not have much luck either. He was ready to "absolutely submit" to the Constituent, but he couldn't find anyone else who panted to follow his inspiring democratic lead. "The volunteer movement," he wrote later in his souvenirs, "did not become a national movement... At its very inception... the army acquired a distinct class character." Erber should be compelled by law — democratically enforced — to read this. There are classes in society and their interests are irreconcilable. Above all in revolutionary times, all groups, movements and institutions *"acquire a distinct class character."* So distinct that a Czarist general finally sees it. But not Erber.

Here is another Czarist general, Kornilov, and here are five instructive points from his program of February, 1918:

"(3) To reëstablish freedom of industry and commerce and to abolish nationalization of private financial enterprises.

(4) To reëstablish private property.

(5) To reëstablish the Russian Army on the basis of strict military discipline. The army should be formed on a volunteer basis... without committees, commissars, or elective officers...

(8) The Constituent Assembly dissolved by the Bolsheviks should be restored...

(9) The government established by General Kornilov is responsible only to the Constituent Assembly... The Constituent Assembly, as the only sovereign of the Russian land, will determine the fundamental laws of the Russian constitution and will give final form to the organization of the state".

It's a double pity that Kornilov joined his ancestors in the unsuccessful attack on Yekaterinodar a few weeks later, so that *he* can't explain what the bourgeoisie had to cheer about, either.

Maybe we can find a hint from the other paladin of the Constituent, General Alexeyev, who is also armed to the teeth with "democratic slogans" (*after* the Bolsheviks take power but not, we regret to note, before), plus 100,000,000 rubles appropriated for his democratic efforts by the no less democratic government of France. In a perplexed and gloomy letter to the Chief of the French mission in Kiev, the General writes in February, 1918:

"The Cossack regiments coming from the front are in a state of complete moral dissolution. Bolshevik ideas have found a great many followers among the Cossacks, with the result that they refuse to fight even in defense of their own territory. [Alexeyev means, of course, that these stupid Cossack regiments refuse to fight for the French banks.] *They are firmly convinced that Bolshevism is directed solely against the wealthy classes... and not against the region as a whole, where there is order, bread, coal, iron and oil".*

We have found the hint! In the eyes of the masses, even of the politically backward and privileged Cossacks, the Constituent Assembly, the fight for it, the men and groups leading that fight, represent not democracy but the wealthy classes, the restorationists, the reaction and, at best, the compromisers and confusionists. In the eyes of the masses, the Bolsheviks and the Soviets represent the fight for freedom and the assurance that it can be won. They represent the movement "directed solely against the wealthy classes."

That is why the Mensheviks and SRs, with all their votes, and with all their "democratic slogans" and their Constituent Assembly, never and nowhere inspired the masses, never and nowhere recruited them to the banner of struggle to overturn the Soviet Power, and succeeded only in bringing the most shameful discredit upon themselves. That is why the "anti-democratic" Bolsheviks consolidated the Soviet Power among the democratic masses in spite of odds almost without historical parallel. The "theoretical dispute" was decided *freely* by the masses, decided in struggle.

So far as *main lines* are concerned, could the Bolsheviks have followed some other course? Erber has an alternative to suggest. He writes: "It is one of the unquestioned myths of our movement, that the Bolsheviks, once they were in power, had no other alternative but the course they pursued". Instead of dispersing the Assembly, the Bolshevik course should have been:

"A government that was responsible to the Constituent Assembly, either an SR government or a coalition of the worker and peasant parties (Bolshevik, Menshevik, Left SR and Right SR parties)... It would have experienced many internal crises and may have found it necessary to refer the disputes to the people in the form of new elections. However, such a government would have had a much wider base than the Bolshevik régime and the victory over the Czarist and bourgeois counter-revolution would have been far easier, quicker and less costly".

This is no commonplace genius we have here! What dazzling audacity and sweep of thought, hammerlock grip of logic, boulder-crushing simplicity, graceful persuasiveness of argument, blade-edge keenness of concept, anxiously-concealed modesty! How avert the conflict of the parties and its consequences? By stopping the conflict! By uniting the parties! By forming a coalition! Where? In the Constituent Assembly, the Temple of the Faith and Fountain of All Blessings.

How simple that would have been, had anyone been gifted enough to think of it in 1917-1918! Just take, as the first two ingredients for the coalition — the Mensheviks and the Bolsheviks — and mix them together thoroughly. The Mensheviks, Erber told us, had the "policy of subordinating the aims of the revolution to the imperialist program of the bourgeoisie". Lenin "advanced the policy of subordinating the revolution to the full or maximum socialist program of the proletariat". After all, is that so much of a conflict in policy as to prevent men of good taste and good will from getting together? After all, don't you have to be practical in politics? After all, when there's a difference of opinion you can't go biting a man's head off. You compromise on a little point here and a little one there. You take a little, you give a little. All you needed, then, was for the Mensheviks to give a little to the "socialist program of the proletariat", and for the Bolsheviks to give a little to the "imperialist program of the bourgeoisie".

That would be the least any reasonable person could do in all fairness to both classes.

Naturally, such a coalition "would have experienced many internal crises". If not many, then at least a few. Erber is a statesman of the new day, and such things do not throw him into unseemly panic. A way can always be found by men of good will. If, for example, the first question on the agenda of the wonderful coalition, with its "much wider base", was what to do with the Soviet Power, that could easily be disposed of. The Mensheviks and the SRs make a motion to dissolve the Soviet Power. The Bolsheviks and, let us say, the Left SRs oppose the motion. There is a fair and square discussion, two speakers on either side, with equal time for all, and then — the democratic vote.

It is carefully counted by two impartial tellers. The Soviet Power is dissolved, so is the Red Guard. The revolution is buried in a simple but dignified casket. The Bolsheviks, democrats to the marrow of their bones, shrug their shoulders. "Guess we lost that one", they say with perfect good humor. "What's the next point on the agenda?" The first little internal crisis of the coalition, and just see how easily it was overcome! All we needed was men of good will, a sense of humor, and a thorough knowledge of Engels' letter to Conrad Schmidt with glossary notes by Erber.

Well and good, the Grand Coalition is formed. The Mensheviks do not demand as the price for collaborating with the Bolsheviks that Lenin and Trotsky be kicked out summarily (as they *did* demand). The Left SRs promise that if there is a disagreement over signing a peace treaty with the Germans, they will not rush into the streets with rifles to overthrow the Bolsheviks or the coalition as a whole (as they *did*). The Right SRs also swallow themselves whole and agree to the coalition if the Soviets are suppressed. At last, the coalition is here. Now, "what", asks Erber, "would have been the nature of the state that would have emerged under such a régime, and what would have been its social basis?" To this he answers:

"In its essentials it would have been what Lenin had in mind for Russia until February 1917, under the formula of a 'democratic dictatorship of the proletariat and peasantry'; a state which would have cleansed Russia of the vestiges of feudalism and curbed the power of the big bourgeoisie through the nationalization of monopolies and trusts, while leaving private enterprise and the market undisturbed. The participation of the workers in economic life through collective bargaining and measures of workers' control of production would have been far more extensive and democratic under such a régime, despite capitalist economic relations, than was the case after a year of Bolshevik rule..."

One of the *unique* features of Russian social and political life lay precisely in the inseparability of the landlords and capitalists. It is precisely this feature of Russia that brought Marxists like Lenin, Trotsky, Luxemburg, Mehring *and* (the pre-war) Kautsky on one common side, against the Mensheviks on the other side. The real Marxists all agreed on at least this much: The coming *bourgeois-democratic revolution* in Russia cannot be carried out under the leadership of the bourgeoisie because the *real* class and economic relations in Russia prevent it from conducting a struggle against the feudalist landlords with whom they are either *identical* or inseparably identified in a hundred social and economic ways. The *democratic* revolution can be carried out in Russia only under the leader-

194

ship of the proletariat. Up to that point — agreement.

The disagreements began only after that point, and it is after that point that Trotsky developed his now familiar theory of the permanent revolution. Trotsky has *demonstrated* — which is of course the reason for Erber's prudent silence on this score — that whatever Lenin's formula may have been before the revolution, the actual course of events forced the workers, supported by the peasants, to take power. He has *demonstrated* in numerous writings that nobody has successfully challenged that, once in power, the working class and the Bolsheviks, who had *not* advanced the policy of the "full or maximum socialist program of the proletariat" (as Erber ignorantly or maliciously states), found themselves compelled to pass over to the "maximum program" *in order to carry out the program of the democratic revolution.* What compelled them? Among other things, and not least of all, *the uncontrollable class reaction of the bourgeoisie.* It understood what neither the Mensheviks nor their dim feeble echo understood: that the assault upon "the vestiges of feudalism" and the "curb" upon their own power, if carried through *seriously*, could not but be an assault upon its own class position, could not but mean the end of all its economic and social power. The only way to maintain "capitalist economic relations", now so dear to Erber, was to abstain from a real cleansing of the stables of feudalism in Russia.

Why, *at bottom*, didn't the Mensheviks use the "democratic slogans" as their weapons before 1918? Because they were wicked men without good will? No, they loved the workers and loved democracy. But to carry out the democratic slogans against the "vestiges of feudalism" and despotism, would have brought them into violent conflict with the bourgeoisie. It would have forced them to break with the bourgeoisie. It would have forced them to lead in the establishment of a democratic republic without the bourgeoisie and against it. But that is exactly what they could not do and did not do because *they were tied to their dogma* that, since the Russian Revolution is a bourgeois-democratic revolution, it must remain under the leadership of the bourgeoisie and within the framework of capitalist society. They remained captives of this dogma throughout the revolutionary storm. Result: they were paralyzed in the struggle for freedom, they lost the support of the workers, and came out of the revolution eternally and shamefully compromised.

LENIN, TROTSKY, LUXEMBURG

ALL OUR MUDDLEHEAD proposes, with that insight you get only from hindsight, is that the Bolsheviks should have followed exactly the same course as the Mensheviks. The high revolutionary role which he asks that the revolutionary party should have assigned itself in the Russian Revolution boils down to this: Maintain capitalist economic relations (in plain English: capitalism) which *the workers themselves* were smashing; and smash the state power of the "teeming, creative, democratic Soviets" which *the workers themselves* were maintaining. And what, we ask in a conspiratorial whisper, what if some of the workers resisted the execution of this modest program? No problem! It would be, to quote the muddle-head, "for the vanguard to act and explain later". The workers would have "to be handled firmly, for their own good". The only trouble is that when the Mensheviks and SRs, with a little help from Kaledin, Alexeyev, Kornilov, Churchill, Wilson and Poincaré, did try to execute this program, for the good of the workers and peasants — the rabble didn't know what was good for them.

"Lenin subjected to merciless ridicule Trotsky's theory of the permanent revolution right up to the outbreak of the February Revolution". Thus Erber. If Lenin had kept up this merciless ridicule, and stuck to the theory of the "democratic dictatorship of the proletariat and peasantry", the Constituent Assembly would be going full blast to this day and "despite capitalist economic relations", the world would be a distinctly pleasant place to live in, free from Fascism and above all from Stalinism. But what happened? We don't know exactly *why* it happened or *how*, we don't know *what* got into Lenin's democratic head, but that which did happen was the worst thing imaginable: Lenin took over Trotsky's mercilessly ridiculed theory. From then on Russia, along with the rest of the world, was a gone goose. The Bolsheviks "set foot on a course from which there was no turning back".

Now you know everything, for just as no secret can be kept from Erber, so Erber keeps no secrets from you. We have Stalinism today (and Lord alone knows what else) *because of the theory of the permanent revolution*. All you Social Democrats, liberals, ex-Marxists, ex-Trotskyists and other professional anti-Bolsheviks, take note! Do you still think Stalinism flowed from Leninism? You are wrong! From Leninism, the authentic, the genuine, the unrevised and unretouched, would have flowed milk, honey, democracy and a world of other blessings. *Stalinism flows from Trotskyism!*

Why from Trotskyism alone? The course of the Bolsheviks, seduced by Trotsky, followed very strictly (more strictly than even they knew at the time) the prescriptions of Marx and Engels on the course that revolutionary socialists should follow in the bourgeois revolution, the course they will have to adopt toward "democracy". In this connection, a few highly revealing words from Engels will suffice to show where the responsibility for the Error really lies, where it all began. We quote from his letter to August Bebel on December 11, 1884:

"As to pure democracy and its role in the future I do not share your opinion. Obviously it plays a far more subordinate part in Germany than in other countries with an older industrial development. But that does not prevent the possibility, when the moment of revolution comes, of its acquiring a temporary importance as the most radical bourgeois party... and as the final sheet-anchor of the whole bourgeois and even feudal régime. At such a moment the whole reactionary mass falls in behind it and strengthens it; everything which used to be reactionary behaves as democratic... This has happened in every revolution: the tamest party still remaining in any way capable of government comes to power with the others just because it is only in this party that the defeated see their last possibility of salvation. Now it cannot be expected that at the moment of crisis we shall already have the majority of the electorate and therefore of the nation behind us. The whole bourgeois class and the remnants of the feudal

landowning class, a large section of the petty bourgeoisie and also of the rural population will then mass themselves around the most radical bourgeois party, which will then make the most extreme revolutionary gestures, and I consider it very possible that it will be represented in the provisional government and even temporarily form its majority. How, as a minority, one should not *act in that case, was demonstrated by the social democratic minority in the Paris Revolution of February, 1848.*

In any case our sole adversary on the day of the crisis and on the day after the crisis will be the whole collective reaction which will group itself around pure democracy, *and this, I think, should not be lost sight of".*

An absolutely remarkable letter! An absolutely remarkable anticipation of what happened in Russia in 1917-1918 and of just how it happened! No wonder we revolutionists have such tremendous esteem for our two great teachers, Marx and Engels. Such intellectual titans come but once a century, and not always that often. And what did Engels means by how "one should *not* act in that case"? What was his reference to the February, 1848 revolution in Paris? He explained in a letter to the Italian socialist, Turati, on January 26, 1894:

"After the common victory we might perhaps be offered some seats in the new government — *but always in a* minority. Here lies the greatest danger. *After the February Revolution in 1848 the French socialistic democrats (the* Reforme *people, Ledru-Rollin, Louis Blanc, Flocon, etc.) were incautious enough to accept such positions. As a minority in the government they involuntarily bore the responsibility for all the infamy and the treachery which the majority, composed of pure Republicans, committed against the working class, while at the same time their participation in the government completely paralyzed the revolutionary action of the working class they were supposed to represent".*

Now perhaps Erber will know, *from Engels,* who was not present in the Russian Revolution, but who, in exchange, had over Erber the advantage of revolutionary understanding and revolutionary spirit — what the bourgeoisie and the "whole collective reaction" had to cheer about when it "grouped itself around pure democracy" in the form of the Constituent Assembly and its struggle against the Soviet Power. Now perhaps he will know why the Bolsheviks refused, in advance, his kind proposal that they enter as a minority in the Grand Coalition he dreamed up. Perhaps he will also understand why Eastman and others like him, in rejecting the Bolshevik Revolution, also and necessarily reject Marx, why they do not come to a ridiculous halt after condemning Lenin and Trotsky but go right back to the "source" of the Error. Once they have rejected the Russian Revolution and Marx, they have the elementary decency not to pretend that they are still interested in the fight for socialism.

We will dwell even less upon Erber's third "charge" against Lenin — that he gambled *everything* on a victory of the revolution in Germany. Not only because the charge is false and was *specifically repudiated more than once* by Lenin himself, as everyone who has read Lenin's writings *knows* and as everyone who takes the right to talk about the question *ought to know,* but because it does not deserve more than a few contemptuous words.

To Lenin, you see, the whole Bolshevik revolution, the whole course he pursued in it, was a gamble. "If Lenin won, history would absolve the Bolsheviks of all the charges their socialist opponents made against them". A fine democrat's morality this is! A fine piece of gross and typically "American" success-philistinism this is! If the revolution had triumphed in Germany, all Lenin's crimes against Marxism, against socialism, against democracy, all his anti-democratism and contempt for the masses who have to be shot for their own good, all of this and more would have been pardonable. Scheidemann, who saved Germany from the socialist revolution, therewith saves our stern judge from the unpleasant task of pardoning the criminal.

Contrast this low-quality philistinism with Marx, whose revolutionary spirit Erber will never see in a mirror — with Marx writing about the Paris Commune, which, we may recall, he was at first *opposed* to establishing. "World history would indeed be very easy to make, if the struggle were taken up only on condition of infallibly favorable chances", he wrote to Kugelmann. Give Erber infallibly favorable chances, and he'll plunge into the revolution with only the least bit of hesitation. And not he alone...

Contrast Erber and *every word he writes* with the *critical* appraisal of the Bolsheviks written in prison by Rosa Luxemburg, who is invoked against revolutionary socialism nowadays by every turncoat and backslider who wouldn't reach up to her soles if he stood on tiptoes:

"That the Bolsheviks have based their policy entirely upon the world proletarian revolution is the clearest proof of their political farsightedness and firmness of principle and of the bold scope of their policies".

You will never see *that* quoted by the turncoats who have drafted Luxemburg into the crusade against Bolshevism against her will. Nor will you see *this* quoted: *"The party of Lenin was the only one which grasped the mandate and duty of a truly revolutionary party and which, by the slogan — 'All power in the hands of the proletariat and peasantry' — insured the continued development of the revolution... Moreover, the Bolsheviks immediately set as the aim of this seizure of power a complete, far-reaching revolutionary program: not the safeguarding of bourgeois democracy, but a dictatorship of the proletariat for the purpose of realizing socialism. Thereby they won for themselves the imperishable historic distinction of having for the first time proclaimed the final aim of socialism as the direct program of practical politics".*

We can see now how much right Erber has to drag Rosa Luxemburg into court as a fellow-detractor of the Bolsheviks, how much right he has to mention her views in the same breath with his own. Fortunately, Luxemburg is not a defenseless corpse. She left a rich political testament to assure her name from being bandied about by soiled lips. Read this:

"The real situation in which the Russian Revolution found itself narrowed down in a few months to the alternative: victory of the counter-revolution or dictatorship of the proletariat — Kaledin or Lenin. Such was the objective situation, just as it quickly presents itself in every revolution after the first intoxication is over, and as it presented itself in Russia as a result of the concrete, burning questions of peace and land, for which there was no solution within the framework of bourgeois revolution".

This is a *revolutionist* writing — not an idol-worshipper of Lenin and the Bolsheviks, but still a *revolutionist*, a tireless, defiant, unflinching champion of the proletariat in the class struggle.

"In this, the Russian Revolution has but confirmed the basic lesson of every great revolution, the law of its being, which decrees: either the revo-

lution must advance at a rapid, stormy and resolute tempo, break down all barriers with an iron hand and place its goals ever farther ahead, or it is quite soon thrown backward behind its feeble point of departure and suppressed by counter-revolution. To stand still, to mark time on one spot, to be contented with the first goal it happens to reach, is never possible in revolution. And he who tries to apply the home-made wisdom derived from parliamentary battles between frogs and mice to the field of revolutionary tactics only shows thereby that the very psychology and laws of existence of revolution are alien to him and that all historical experience is to him a book sealed with seven seals".

Read it over again, especially that wonderfully priceless last sentence!

"Still, didn't Rosa criticize the Bolsheviks for dispersing the Constituent Assembly?" No, she did not. She criticized them for not calling for elections to a new Constituent; she criticized them for the arguments they made to justify the dispersal. But in the first place, her criticism has next to nothing in common with that of the latter-day anti-Bolsheviks (or, for that matter, of the anti-Bolsheviks of the time). And in the second place, she was wrong, just as she was wrong in her criticism of the Bolshevik position on the "national question" and of the Bolshevik course in the "agrarian question". And in the third place, what she wrote in prison, on the basis of "fragmentary information" (as the editor of the American edition of her prison notes admits), was not her last word on the question. Before her cruel death, she *altered her position* on the basis of her own experiences, on the basis of the living realities of the German revolution. Lenin's *State and Revolution* was checked *twice* — first in the Russian Revolution and then in the German revolution! We will give the reader an idea of what she wrote before her death so that he may see why our present "champions" of Luxemburg never find time, space or inclination to *quote her to the end.*

The German workers, a year after the Bolshevik Revolution, overturned the Hohenzollern monarchy and, just as spontaneously as did the Russians before them, they formed their Workers' and Soldiers' Councils (*Räte*, Soviets). The German Mensheviks — Scheidemann, Noske and Ebert — feared and hated the Councils just as much as did their Russian counterparts. They championed the National Assembly (German counterpart of the Russian Constituent) instead, calculating thereby to smash the Councils and the struggle for socialism. Haase and Kautsky, the centrists of the Independent Socialists, oscillated between the Councils and the Assembly. What position did Rosa Luxemburg take, what position did the Spartacus League and its organ, *Die Rote Fahne*, take? Here once more was the problem of workers' democracy versus bourgeois democracy, the democratic republic of the Councils versus the bourgeois republic, dictatorship of the proletariat organized in the Councils versus the National Assembly — not in Russia but in Germany, not in 1917 but a year later, not while Rosa was in Breslau prison but after her release.

Here is Rosa Luxemburg in *Die Rote Fahne* of November 29, 1918, writing on the leaders of the Independents:

"Their actual mission as partner in the firm of Scheidemann-Ebert is: to mystify its clear and unambiguous character as defense guard of bourgeois class domination by means of a system of equivocation and cowardliness. This role of Haase and colleagues finds its most classical expression in

their attitude toward the most important slogan of the day: toward the National Assembly.

Only two standpoints are possible in this question, as in all others. Either you want the National Assembly as a means of swindling the proletariat out of its power, to paralyze its class energy, to dissolve its socialist goal into thin air. Or else you want to place all the power into the hands of the proletariat, to unfold the revolution that has begun into a tremendous class struggle for the socialist social order, and toward this end, to establish the political rule of the great mass of the toilers, the dictatorship of the Workers' and Soldiers' Councils. For or against socialism, against or for the National Assembly; there is no third way".

On December 1st, Luxemburg spoke on the situation at a meeting of the Spartacus League in the hall of the Teachers' Union. At the end of the meeting, a resolution was adopted setting forth her views and giving approval to them:

"The public people's meeting held on December 1st in the Hall of the Teachers' Union on Alexander Street declares its agreement with the exposition of Comrade Luxemburg. It considers the convocation of the National Assembly to be a means of strengthening the counter-revolution and to cheat the proletarian revolution of its socialist aims. It demands the transfer of all power to the Workers' and Soldiers' Councils, whose first duty is to drive out of the government the traitors to the working class and to socialism, Scheidemann-Ebert and colleagues, to arm the toiling people for the protection of the revolution, and to take the most energetic and thorough-going measures for the socialization of society".

In her first editorial in *Die Rote Fahne* of November 18, she writes under the title, "The Beginning": *"The Revolution has begun... From the goal of the revolution follows clearly its path, from its task follows the method. All power into the hands of the masses, into the hands of the Workers' and Soldiers' Councils, protection of the work of the revolution from its lurking foes: this is the guiding line for all the measures of the revolutionary government...* [But] *What is the present revolutionary government* [i.e. Scheidemann and Co.] *doing? It calmly continues to leave the state as an administrative organism from top to bottom in the hands of yesterday's guards of Hohenzollern absolutism and tomorrow's tools of the counter-revolution. It is convoking the Constituent Assembly, and therewith it is creating a bourgeois counterweight against the Workers' and Peasants' representation, therewith switching the revolution on to the rails of the bourgeois revolution, conjuring away the socialist goals of the revolution.*

From the Deutsche Tageszeitung, *the* Vossische, *and the* Vorwärts *to the* Freiheit *of the Independents, from Reventlow, Erzberger, Scheidemann to Haase and Kautsky, there sounds the unanimous call for the National Assembly and an equally unanimous outcry of fear of the idea: Power into the hands of the working class. The 'people' as a whole, the 'nation' as a whole, should be summoned to decide on the further fate of the revolution by majority decision. With the open and concealed agents of the ruling class, this slogan is natural. With keepers of the capitalist class barriers, we discuss neither the National Assembly nor about the National Assembly.... Without the conscious will and the conscious act of the majority of the proletariat — no socialism. To sharpen this consciousness, to steel this will, to organize this act, a class organ is necessary, the national par-*

200

liament of the proletarians of town and country. The convocation of such a workers' representation in place of the traditional National Assembly of the bourgeois revolutions is already, by itself, an act of the class struggle, a break with the historical past of bourgeois society, a powerful means of arousing the proletarian popular masses, a first open, blunt declaration of war against capitalism. No evasions, no ambiguities — the die must be cast. Parliamentary cretinism was yesterday a weakness, is today an equivocation, will tomorrow be a betrayal of socialism".

It is a pity that there is not space in which to quote far more extensively from the highly remarkable articles she wrote in the last few weeks of her life, before she was murdered by those whose "parliamentary cretinism" became the direct betrayal of socialism — by those for whom Erber has now become a shameful apologist by "showing" that the defeat of the revolution in Germany was as much the responsibility of the masses as it was of the Scheidemanns and Noskes! The articles as a whole show the veritable *strides* that Luxemburg took away from her prison criticism and toward a policy which was in *no* important respect different from the one pursued by the Bolsheviks toward the bourgeois and petty-bourgeois democrats, toward the Mensheviks and other "socialist opponents", toward the Constituent Assembly and the Soviets. With these criticisms of hers in print, to mention her today as an enemy of the Bolsheviks, as a critic of their attitude toward bourgeois democracy and the Constituent, is excusable only on the grounds of inexcusable ignorance.

The course of the German Revolution, life, the lessons of the struggle — these left us the heritage of a Rosa Luxemburg who was, in every essential, the inseparable comrade-in-arms of the leaders of the Russian Revolution. To claim that this firm solidarity did not exist, is simply an outrage to her memory. What is worse, it shows that nothing has been learned of the lessons of the Russian Revolution and nothing of the lessons of the German Revolution — the two great efforts of the proletariat to test in practice what is, in the long run, the question of life and death for us: the state and revolution. And on this question, with Lenin *and* with Luxemburg, the real Luxemburg — we remain under the banner of Marxism.

REVOLUTION AND VIOLENCE

ERBER IS STILL A LITTLE RESTLESS over the traces of what he learned when he was a Marxist. So he comes to the noteworthy conclusion that: "Even the most perfect organization of the workers in industry, transport, communications, etc., will not guarantee a non-violent accession to power. Since the working class may be challenged by force on the democratic road to socialism, let it be prepared to take up arms not to overthrow a democratic state but to 'win the battle of democracy'. Standing as the defenders of the best traditions of American democracy, its cause will be immeasurably strengthened. A Marxist in the United States can commit no greater folly than to view the workers' road to power as culminating in an armed insurrection against a state that rests on political democracy".

Against whom is all this pomposity directed? Against the Bolsheviks, perhaps? What democratic state did they overthrow with arms in hand? The state of Kerensky and Company ("Company" meaning the Mensheviks and SRs). And what was this state? We turn to the most authoritative reference work on the subject, Erber's document, and read that the Kerensky "régime sought to stretch out its undemocratic authority as long as possible by repeatedly postponing the elections of a Constituent Assembly. If the revolution was to advance, Kerensky had to go". Very well, go he did, along with everyone whose teeth were sunk in his coat tails.

Is it directed, perhaps, against Erber's newly-acquired chums and exemplars, the Mensheviks and the SRs? They did indeed take up arms to overthrow a democratic state, the state of the "teeming, creative, democratic Soviets". Is it directed against the Left SRs, that minority which sought to impose its will on the Soviet government with arms in hand because it disagreed with the decision to sign the Brest-Litovsk peace treaty? Or against the still tinier minority of anti-Bolshevik anarchists who likewise sought to overthrow the régime?

Or maybe it is directed against us here? Maybe he wants *us* to give a solemn pledge not to resort to armed insurrection against "a state that rests on political democracy"? Very well, we do not hesitate to give our pledge to Citizen Pompous Muddlehead, and therewith to state once more our credo.

We do not and will not call for armed insurrection to overthrow a "democratic state", a "state that rests on political democracy". It is an oath. The political infants who led the early communist movement in this country and who had little in common with Marx or Lenin — they issued such calls and advocated such a course. We — never! Not yesterday, not today, not tomorrow. We are not for violence in principle any more than we are for parliamentarism in principle. If anything, our principles call for an abhorrence of violence, as a capitalistic and uncivilized means of settling disputes among people. We are compelled every day to defend ourselves, with whatever organized strength we can muster, from the violence, open or concealed, with which the ruling classes impose their exploitation upon the masses. We are not putschists because we are not bureaucrats — and in every putschist, who has no confidence in the people, is concealed the bureaucrat, who has contempt for the people. Overthrow the bourgeois state by armed insurrection! Who, we? Not today and not tomorrow, and not if we had a hundred times as many members and followers as we have now!

The bourgeois state, bourgeois democracy, still has the confidence and support of the overwhelming majority of the people, including the working-class people. They think bourgeois democracy can solve all their basic problems. We Marxists do not. We believe that such a solution requires a working-class democracy, the rule of the proletariat, which develops into a more extensive and even more genuine democracy, the rule of *all* the people, which in turn develops into the end of *all* rule (democracy is a form of rulership) by dissolving into the classless society of socialism and communism. The workers do not share our belief. Can we even dream of imposing our views, the views of a tiny minority, by merely wishing, or by decree, let alone by armed insurrection?

Without abandoning our views for a moment, we say to the workers: Unite into your own economic and political organizations, free from the control and influence of your sworn class enemy. You have confidence in bourgeois democracy? Then organize your own political party. Challenge your enemy not only on the economic field but also on the political. Send your own representatives into the legislative bodies to work and fight for your interests. We say, with Engels, that "universal suffrage is the best lever for a proletarian movement at the present time". We say, with Engels, that "universal suffrage is the gauge of the maturity of the working class". We will therefore do everything we can to raise the red line in that thermometer which measures the maturity of the working class. "On the day when the thermometer of universal suffrage reaches its boiling point among the laborers, they as well as the capitalists will know what to do".

But what Marxist would try to displace the bourgeois state with a workers' state before that boiling point has been reached? Certainly no intelligent and educated Marxist would think of it, any more than he would think of walking out into the street with only his shirt on in winter time. A "state that rests on political democracy" is a state which, deservedly or not, still enjoys the confidence of the masses. To think of overturning such a state by armed insurrection under such conditions is putschist madness and adventurism, not revolutionary Marxism.

When the masses no longer have confidence in the bourgeoisie and the bourgeois state, when they have reached the point where they are ready to take the state into their own hands, ready to undertake a radical solution of the social problem, ready to take control of their own destinies — the situation changes! Once the masses have expressed their decision to take power and expressed it clearly and democratically — be their will expressed in the organs of parliament *or* in organs of their own which they find at hand *or* in organs of their own which they create spontaneously in the course of the struggle — the situation changes! *If* the bourgeoisie and the bourgeois state bow to the democratic will of the people, so much the better! As we wrote before, nobody would be more delighted than we and with us the whole working class. Up to now, however, history has been very frugal with examples of such bowing to the democratic will of the revolutionary people. But if there is nevertheless one chance in a thousand of that happening, then it is possible *only* if the working class confronts the bourgeoisie not with votes alone (the "boiling thermometer") but with serried class strength, with organized power. Such power is nothing else than *potential violence*, that is, violence that can be summoned the minute the democratically rejected bourgeoisie tries to perpetuate its domination over the people by the use of armed force.

But what if the bourgeoisie and its state *do not* bow to the will of the people? What if the régime seeks "to stretch out its undemocratic authority as long as possible"? With all due respect to the fanatical democratism of the bourgeoisie and its state, we think such an alternative is... quite possible. If it occurs, we will manage to say what Erber says about the Kerensky régime: *It has to go!* And if it does not go quietly, it will have to be pushed a little.

We, followers of Marx and Lenin, want to make sure that on the day the thermometer boils over — not today, not tomorrow, but on *that* day — "the laborers... as well as the capitalists will know what to do". We want to make sure that on that day the laborers not only have enough votes in their hands, but enough power to enforce their will. Is that the folly of viewing "the workers' road to power as culminating in an armed insurrection against a state that rests on political democracy"? Not at all! Erber is just repeating the drivel of the social democrats. What we Marxists call for is the good common sense of the workers' road to power culminating in the armed dispersal — *if the stubborn bourgeoisie insists on it* — of the state which no longer enjoys authority among the workers, which no longer has the confidence or support of the people, which, therefore, no longer "rests on political democracy" in the real sense of the term. It is with this view that we want to imbue every socialist militant, every vanguard fighter, every worker whom we can reach with our voice and pen.

That, stated for the hundredth time, is our credo. Take note of it, O Pompous Muddlehead! Take note of it, all workers! Take note of it, too, Mr Public Prosecutor!

Why are we so impassioned and tenacious in our defense of Marx, of Lenin, of Luxemburg, of Trotsky, of the Paris Commune, of the Russian Revolution, from all their falsifiers and detractors? Out of academic considerations? Because we are mere historians concerned with an accurate record of our past? Because we are Talmudists with our noses buried in the ancient books of wisdom? We are revolutionary socialists, and the fight to keep our heritage clean is an indispensable part of our fight for socialism. Does anyone think we would consume all this paper just to prove that this one is a liar, that one a deserter, that one a muddlehead, the other one a traitor? There are more pleasant and important things to do in life.

We are fighting for socialist freedom, and in this fight we are now on the defensive. The working class is on the defensive all over the world. It is lacerated by defeats, it is confused and disoriented, it has lost a lot of confidence in its power. It has been backed into a corner like the quarry in a hunt. It is surrounded by baying hounds.

The hunters challenge it: "Give up! Surrender!" The Stalinist dogs bark: "You cannot free your own self. Wherever you tried it yourself, you failed. You are too weak, too stupid, too undisciplined if left to your own democratic devices. You need an iron hand over you, an iron hand with a whip. Under Lenin's Soviets, the state was feeble. Under Stalin's GPU, the state has been consolidated and enormously strengthened. We have extended it over Europe and Asia. You must have a bureaucracy to lead you out of the wilderness!"

The bourgeois dogs bark: "You cannot free your own self. Wherever you tried it, you failed. You failed because there have always been the rulers and the ruled, and that is how it will always be. Look what happened in Russia! You tried, and you failed. Socialism is an ideal, but a Utopian ideal. Marx brought you Lenin. Lenin brought you Stalin. Under our rule you will at least have a bed to sleep in and unemployment insurance".

The reformist dogs bark: "Learn the lessons of the Russian Revolution! Revolution brought you only misery. Lenin was a gambler and he lost. Don't take power into your own hands. All evil flows from that. Just send enough of us to parliament and we will patch up the bourgeois state without you having to do a thing. Collaborate with the decent bourgeois elements, in plant and government and war, and don't lose your temper and get violent. It will do you no good. Revolution only brings Stalinism".

Erber whimpers: "Woe is me and woe is the world. Lenin ruined us all. I really don't know what to say or do about it. I really don't know what road you should take to get out of this universal ruin. Wait here, don't budge. I'll figure out something presently. But whatever you do, don't follow Lenin, don't take the road of revolution, don't take power into your own hands".

Hook nods philosophically: "Lord Acton was right, dear pupils. Power corrupts and absolute power corrupts absolutely. I want no part of it".

Social interests shape ideas. Ideas serve social interests. The ideological campaign against Marxism is still what it always was: an integral part of the fight against socialism and the interests of the working class. The campaign against Lenin, the Bolsheviks and the Russian Revolution is still what it always was: an integral part of the fight to turn the working class away from the idea of taking their fate into their own hands. The attempt to bind and gag Rosa Luxemburg and kidnap her to an alien camp, so that we cannot hear what she really said and wanted, is still what it always was: an integral part of the turncoats' campaign to dirty the great Russian Revolution so that their capitulation to democratic imperialism will look clean.

The defense of the Russian Revolution is the defense of Marxism. The defense of Marxism is the fight for socialism, the fight to drive away the baying hounds, to enable the working class to leap forward again with renewed confidence in its own strength, in its great emancipating mission, in its eventual triumph.

We are not idol-worshippers. We are not uncritical eulogists of Marx or Lenin or Trotsky or Luxemburg or the Russian Revolution itself. From its grandeur, we have learned what to do. From its decay, what not to do. We think we understand now more than we ever did before why Lenin, for all his disagreements with Rosa, called her an eagle. Even in her prison notes she wrote these words which are so timely thirty years later:

"Everything that happens in Russia is comprehensible and represents an inevitable chain of causes and effects, the starting point and end term of which are: the failure of the German proletariat and the occupation of Russia by German imperialism. It would be demanding something superhuman from Lenin and his comrades if we should expect of them that under such circumstances they should conjure forth the finest democracy, the most exemplary dictatorship of the proletariat and a flourishing socialist economy. By their determined revolutionary stand, their exemplary strength in action, and their unbreakable loyalty to international socialism, they have contributed whatever could possibly be contributed under such devilishly hard conditions. The danger begins only when they make a virtue of necessity and want to freeze into a complete theoretical system all the tactics forced upon them by these fatal circumstances, and want to recommend them to the international proletariat as a model of socialist tactics. When they get in their own light in this way, and hide their genuine, unquestionable historical service under the bushel of false steps forced upon them by necessity, they render a poor service to international social-

ism for the sake of which they have fought and suffered; for they want to place in its storehouse as new discoveries all the distortions prescribed in Russia by necessity and compulsion — in the last analysis only by-products of the bankruptcy of international socialism in the present world war.

Let the German Government Socialists cry that the rule of the Bolsheviks in Russia is a distorted expression of the dictatorship of the proletariat. If it was or is such, that is only because it is a product of the behavior of the German proletariat, in itself a distorted expression of the socialist class struggle. All of us are subject to the laws of history, and it is only internationally that the socialist order of society can be realized. The Bolsheviks have shown that they are capable of everything that a genuine revolutionary party can contribute within the limits of the historical possibilities. They are not supposed to perform miracles. For a model and faultless proletarian revolution in an isolated land, exhausted by world war, strangled by imperialism, betrayed by the international proletariat, would be a miracle...

"In Russia the problem could only be posed. It could not be solved in Russia. And in this *sense, the future everywhere belongs to 'Bolshevism'."*

"The danger begins when they make a virtue of necessity". That danger is inherent in every great revolution and every great revolutionary party suffers from it. The Bolsheviks were no exception. They could not be, especially given a socialist revolution, for which there was no blueprint worked out in advance and could not be. Improvization was imperative. What is remarkable is that in all this convulsive turbulence, so much order prevailed, so much was done according to plan, so much was done to turn the helm when the ship of state hit uncharted and unexpected reefs. In that respect, *no* revolution, no social transformation in history, even equalled the Russian Revolution.

"*Es schwindelt*", said Lenin to Trotsky when the storm lifted the Bolsheviks to the first socialist power in history — it makes you dizzy. Everybody was made dizzy. The Bolsheviks alone kept their heads. The others lost them completely. The bourgeoisie, the landlords, international capital, plunged into their mad and sanguinary adventure to crush the revolution. The Mensheviks and SRs joined with what Engels predicted would be "the whole collective reaction which will group itself around pure democracy". In the wild civil war that followed, in which millions of ordinary workers and peasants proved to be far fiercer and more intolerant toward the opponents of the Soviet power than the Bolsheviks themselves, there was no room for the "home-made wisdom derived from parliamentary battles between frogs and mice". One by one, the parties and groups that took up arms against the Soviet Power were outlawed. No one has found another solution in civil war.

The Bolsheviks performed no miracles; they promised none. They were summoned to hold the first revolutionary citadel against frenzied and maddened besiegers until the relief columns of the Western proletariat could be brought forward. They held the citadel, better and longer than anyone expected, even they themselves. Julius Martov, the Menshevik leader, wrote in October 1921 that "The political tactic of our party in 1918 and 1920 was determined primarily by the fact that history had made the Bolshevik Party the defender of the foundations of the revolution against the armed forces of the domestic and foreign counter-revolution". Alas, what he says about the Menshevik party is not true in its entirety, but only for a tiny part of it. What he says about the Bolshevik party is true in its entirety. But the Bolsheviks were not gods. In seeking to master necessity, they also had to bend to it. War, especially civil war, especially when your enemies on a world scale outnumber you a hundred to one, is not the ideal culture medium for democracy to flourish in. "The Bolsheviks have shown that they are capable of everything that a genuine revolutionary party can contribute within the limits of the historical possibilities. They are not supposed to perform miracles. For a model and faultless proletarian revolution in an isolated land, exhausted by world war, strangled by imperialism, betrayed by the international proletariat, would be a miracle".

Once the civil war came to a triumphant end for the Soviet Power, necessity became more and more a virtue. What was imposed on the Bolsheviks by the exigencies of war was gradually transformed into an article of faith for the period of peace as well. One-party government, which is anything but abnormal in all countries at all times, and was just as normal and unexceptionable in Russia, was transformed to mean: Only one party can enjoy legal existence in the country. To this, Stalinism succeeded in adding: Only one faction can enjoy legal existence in the party. The extension of full democratic rights — not the right to armed putsches but full democratic rights — to *all* parties, without exception, would have strengthened the country and reinvigorated the Soviets themselves. It should now be clear that without the presence of other political organizations capable of freely debating (debating, not shooting at) the proposals presented to the Soviets by the Bolshevik party, the Soviets would rapidly and inevitably deteriorate to the position of a *superfluous duplicate* of the ruling party, at first only consulted by the latter, then disregarded by it, and finally discarded altogether for the direct rule of the party alone (the bureaucracy of the party at that!) In this process, the decay of democracy within the Bolshevik party and the decay of Soviet democracy went hand in hand, each having the same deleterious effect upon the other until both were suppressed completely and, along with them, all the achievements of the revolution itself. Deprived of the saving oxygen of revolution in the West, the democratic organism was suffocated. Poisons accumulated throughout the whole system which could not be thrown off, new poisons were added (necessity becoming virtue), and the Revolution moved tragically toward its death.

Of the period of decay, much has been written — in advance by Luxemburg, in his time by Lenin, later by Trotsky. Much more can be written and much more will be written as the distance of years sets off the Revolution in clearer perspective. We close no doors. We file away nothing as an absolutely closed case. But it does not follow that no conclusions at all can be drawn from the great revolution. It does not follow that anybody's conclusions, no matter how superficial or trivial or reactionary, are as valid as any others. Our struggle has been hurled back — that is now a commonplace. But it does not follow that we start with *tabula rasa* — knowing nothing, learning nothing, believing nothing. From the grandeur of the Russian Revolution, we have learned something: the superiority of proletarian democracy to bourgeois democracy. From the decay of the Russian Revolution we have learned something: that proletarian democracy cannot exist for long if it is confined to one faction or one party, even if it be the revolutionary party, that it must be shared equally by all other working-class and even — under favorable circumstances — bourgeois parties and groups, for without it the proletarian party and the proletarian democracy both die and with them die the prospects of socialism.

These are not the happiest days for socialism. We know that. We know that the grotesque outcome of the Russian Revolution, the failure of the proletariat anywhere else to come to power, has raised more than one gloomy doubt about the *social ability* of the working class to reorganize society rationally, about the very possibility of a socialist future.

It is precisely in this regard that the Russian Revolution is our lasting triumph! It is precisely in this regard that the Russian Revolution continues to fortify our convictions!

What the Marxists *claimed* for decades, the Russian Revolution *proved*. What did it prove? That the rule of the capitalist class is not eternal. That the power of the capitalist class is not invincible. That the working class *can* overthrow the rule of capital and the bourgeois state, not in the books of Karl Marx, but in the living struggle of organized workers. To this day and hour we say: If the Russian working class could take power, the working class can take power in any other country under similar circumstances. This we consider *proved*. To disprove it, it is only necessary to show that the Russian proletariat had national or racial characteristics which determined its victory and which are not to be found in any other proletariat. Or, it is only necessary to prove that no other country can ever reproduce a combination of circumstances similar to those which made possible the triumph of the Russian Revolution. Nobody has done this up to now. Until it is done, we regard as *proved* the ability of the working class to take power in its own name and for its own self. That's a tremendous acquisition for the Marxian and working-class movements. Why should any socialist or even a non-socialist worker be fool enough to bagatellize this acquisition, let alone relinquish it?

"But surely you cannot claim that the Russian Revolution also proved that the working class can *hold* power and use it to usher in a socialist society!" We make no such claim. *That*, the Russian Revolution did not prove and, by itself, could not prove. But to prove that the proletariat has some basic and inherent social incapacity to hold power and establish socialism, you must be *concrete*, and not confine yourself to going from concept to concept to concept without once touching material ground. To be concrete, dear skeptic, to be *scientific*, you have to show why the *Russian* proletariat lost power. Merely to point to *the fact* that the proletariat, one hundred years after the *Communist Manifesto*, has not yet liberated itself, is not one whit more serious an argument to prove that it cannot liberate itself than pointing to *the fact* that the failure of generations of scientists to find a cure for cancer proves that cancer cannot be cured.

This brings us back to what is, after all, the very essence of the dispute over the Russian Revolution: *Why* did the proletariat lose power and, therewith, lose the indispensable instrument for constructing socialism?

Exactly ninety-nine per cent of the critics of Bolshevism answer the question in this way, at bottom: *The Russian workers lost power because they took power.* Stalinism (the destruction of the Russian workers' power)

208

followed ineluctably from the seizure of power by the proletariat and Lenin's refusal to surrender this power to the bourgeois democracy. Exactly ninety-nine per cent of the revolutionary Marxists answer the question in this way, at bottom: *The Russian workers lost power because the workers of the other countries failed to take power.*

There is the difference. It is fundamental and yields to no compromise.

We also know that *our* "proof" is not final. There is *no* way of making it final in the realm of concepts. It can be made final *only in struggle*. By ourselves, we cannot provide this final proof. We will not even attempt it. The proletariat alone can provide this proof, in the course of the struggle which it must carry on in order to survive, and in which it must triumph if it carries it on to the end. The Russian proletariat, the Russian Revolution, proved all it could prove. The rest will come. And one of the not unimportant reasons why it will come is that we remain loyal to the fight for socialism. We remain defenders of the imperishable Bolshevik Revolution. We remain under the banner of Marxism.

Leon Trotsky

WHO MADE THE REVOLUTION?

WITHOUT THE ARMED INSURRECTION of 7th November 1917 the Soviet state would not be in existence. But the insurrection itself did not drop from Heaven. A series of historical prerequisites was necessary for the October Revolution.

1) The rotting away of the old ruling classes — the nobility, the monarchy, the bureaucracy.

2) The political weakness of the bourgeoisie, which had no roots in the masses of the people.

3) The revolutionary character of the agrarian question.

4) The revolutionary character of the problem of the oppressed nationalities.

5) The significant social burdens weighing on the proletariat.

To these organic preconditions must be added certain highly important connected conditions.

6) The Revolution of 1905 was the great school, or in Lenin's phrase "the dress rehearsal" of the Revolution of 1917. The Soviets, as the irreplaceable organizational form of the proletarian united front in the Revolution, were created for the first time in the year 1905.

7) The imperialist war sharpened all the contradictions, tore the backward masses out of their immobility, and thus prepared the grandiose scale of the catastrophe.

But all these conditions, which fully sufficed for the outbreak of the revolution, were insufficient to assure the victory of the proletariat in the revolution. For this victory one condition more was necessary.

8) The Bolshevik Party.

When I enumerate this condition last in the series, I do it only because it follows the logical sequence, and not because I assign the last place in the order of importance to the Party. No, I am far from such a thought. The liberal bourgeoisie can seize power and has seized it more than once as the result of struggles in which it took no part; it possesses organs of seizure which are admirably adapted to the purpose. But the working masses are in a different position; they have long been accustomed to give, and not to take. They work, are patient as long as they can be, hope, lose patience, rise and struggle, die, bring victory to others, are betrayed, fall into despondency, bow their necks and work again. Such is the history of the masses of the people under all régimes. To be able to take the power firmly and surely into its hands the proletariat needs a Party, which far surpasses other parties in the clarity of its thought and in its revolutionary determination.

The Bolshevik Party, which has been described more than once and with complete justification as the most revolutionary party in the history of mankind, was the living condensation of the modern history of Russia, of all that was dynamic in it. The overthrow of Tsarism had long been recognized as the necessary condition for the development of the economy and culture. But for the solution of this task the forces were insufficient. The bourgeoisie feared the Revolution. The intelligentsia tried to bring the peasant to his feet. The moujik, incapable of generalizing his own miseries and his aims, left this appeal unanswered. The intelligentsia armed itself with dynamite. A whole generation was wasted in this struggle.

On March 1st 1887, Alexander Ulianov carried out the last of the great terrorist plots. The attempted assassination of Alexander III failed. Ulianov and the other participants were executed. The attempt to make chemical preparation take the place of a revolutionary class came to grief. Even the most heroic intelligentsia is nothing without the masses. Ulianov's younger brother Vladimir, the future Lenin, the great-

From Leon Trotsky's November 1932 lecture on the Russian Revolution, in Copenhagen.

est figure of Russian history, grew up under the immediate impression of these facts and conclusions. Even in his early youth he placed himself on the foundations of Marxism, and turned his face toward the proletariat. Without losing sight of the village for a moment he sought the way to the peasantry through the workers. Inheriting from his revolutionary predecessors their capacity for self-sacrifice, and their willingness to go to the limit, Lenin at an early age became the teacher of the new generation of the intelligentsia and of the advanced workers. In strikes and street fights, in prisons and in exile, the workers received the necessary tempering. They needed the searchlight of Marxism to light up their historical road in the darkness of absolutism.

Among the émigrés the first Marxist group arose in 1883. In 1898 at a secret meeting the foundation of the Russian Social-Democratic Workers' Party was proclaimed (we all called ourselves Social-Democrats in those days). In 1903 occurred the split between Bolsheviks and Mensheviks, and in 1912 the Bolshevik fraction finally became an independent Party. It learned to recognize the class mechanics of society in its struggles during the events of twelve years (1905-1917). It educated groups equally capable of initiative and of subordination. The discipline of its revolutionary action was based on the unity of its doctrine, on the tradition of common struggles and on confidence in its tested leadership. Such was the Party in 1917. Despised by the official "public opinion" and the paper thunder of the intelligentsia press, it adapted itself to the movement of the masses. It kept firmly in hand the lever of control in the factories and regiments. More and more the peasant masses turned toward it. If we understand by "nation" not the privileged heads but the majority of the people, that is, the workers and peasants, then the Bolsheviks became during the course of 1917 a truly national Russian Party.

In September, 1917, Lenin, who was compelled to keep in hiding, gave the signal, "The crisis is ripe, the hour of the insurrection has approached." He was right. The ruling classes faced with the problems of the war, the land, and liberation, had got into inextricable difficulties. The bourgeoisie positively lost its head. The democratic parties, the Mensheviks and Social Revolutionaries, dissipated the last remaining bit of confidence of the masses in them by their support of the imperialist war, by their policy of compromise and concessions to the bourgeois and feudal property-owners. The awakened army no longer wanted to fight for the alien aims of imperialism. Disregarding democratic advice, the peasantry smoked the landowners out of their estates. The oppressed nationalities of the far boundaries rose up against the bureaucracy of Petrograd. In the most important workers' and soldiers' Soviets the Bolsheviks were dominant. The ulcer was ripe. It needed a cut of the lancet. Only under these social and political conditions was the insurrection possible. And thus it also became inevitable. But there is no playing around with insurrection. Woe to the surgeon who is careless in the use of the lancet! Insurrection is an art. It has its laws and its rules.

The Party faced the realities of the October insurrection with cold calculation and with ardent resolution. Thanks to this, it conquered almost without victims. Through the victorious Soviets the Bolsheviks placed themselves at the head of a country which occupies one-sixth of the surface of the globe.

211

Leon Trotsky

THE PARTY RÉGIME

IN 1923, THE CAMPAIGN AGAINST FACTIONALISM proceeded mainly from the argument that factions represent the embryos of new parties; and that in a country with an overwhelming peasant majority and surrounded by capitalism, the dictatorship of the proletariat cannot allow freedom of parties. In itself, this postulate is absolutely correct. But it also requires a correct policy and a correct régime. It is clear, however, that such a formulation of the question signified the discarding of any extension to the communist parties in the bourgeois states of the resolution adopted at the Tenth Congress of the ruling CPSU. But a bureaucratic régime has a devouring logic of its own. If it tolerates no democratic control within the Soviet party, then it tolerates it all the less within the Comintern which stands formally above the CPSU. That is why the leadership made a universal principle out of its rude and disloyal interpretation and application of the resolution of the Tenth Party Congress — which met the specific requirements at the time in the USSR — and extended it over all the communist organizations on the terrestrial globe.

Bolshevism was always strong because of its historical concreteness in elaborating organizational forms. No arid schemes. The Bolsheviks changed their organizational structure radically at every transition from one stage to the next. Yet, today, one and the same principle of "revolutionary order" is applied to the powerful party of the proletarian dictatorship as well as to the German Communist Party which represents a serious political force, to the young Chinese party which was immediately drawn into the vortex of revolutionary struggles, and to the party of the USA which is only a small propaganda society. In the latter, no sooner did doubts arise as to the correctness of the methods foisted upon it by a Pepper, in command at the time, than the "doubters" were subjected to chastisement for factionalism. A young party representing a political organism in a completely embryonic stage, without any real contact with the masses, without the experience of a revolutionary leadership, and without theoretical schooling, has already been armed from head to foot with all the attributes of "revolutionary order," fitted with which it resembles a six-year old boy wearing his father's accoutrement.

The CPSU has the greatest wealth of experience in the domain of ideology and revolution. But as the last five years showed even the CPSU has been unable to live with impunity for a single day on the interest of its capital alone, but is obliged to renew and expand it constantly, and this is possible only through a collective working of the party mind. And what, then, need be said of the communist parties in other countries which were formed a few years ago and are just passing through the initial stage of accumulating theoretical knowledge and practical ability? Without a real freedom of party life, freedom of discussion, and freedom of establishing their course collectively, and by means of groupings, these parties will never become a decisive revolutionary force.

Prior to the Tenth Party Congress which prohibited the formation of factions the CPSU had existed two decades without such a prohibition. And precisely these two decades so trained and prepared it that it was able to accept and endure the harsh decisions of the Tenth Party Congress at the time of a most difficult turn. The communist parties of the West, however, proceed from this point at the very outset.

Together with Lenin, we feared most of all that the CPSU, armed with the mighty resources of the state, would exert an excessive and crushing influence upon the young parties of the West that were just being organized. Lenin warned tirelessly against premature strides along the road of centralism, against the excessive tendencies of the

By Leon Trotsky, from *The Draft Program of the Communist International: A Criticism of Fundamentals*, written in 1928.

ECCI and the Presidium in this direction and, especially, against such forms and methods of assistance as transform themselves into direct commands from which there is no appeal.

The change began in 1924 under the name of "Bolshevization." If by Bolshevization is understood the purging of the party of alien elements and habits, of social democratic functionaries clinging to their posts, of freemasons, pacifist-democrats, idealistic muddleheads, etc., then this work was being performed from the very first day of the Comintern's existence; at the Fourth Congress, this work with regard to the French party even assumed extremely sharp combat forms. But previously this genuine Bolshevization was inseparably connected with the individual experiences of the national sections of the Comintern, grew out of these experiences, and had as its touchstone questions of national policy which grew to the point of becoming international tasks. The "Bolshevization" of 1924 assumed completely the character of a caricature. A revolver was held at the temples of the leading organs of the communist parties with the demand that they adopt immediately a final position on the internal disputes in the CPSU without any information and any discussion, and besides they were aware in advance that on the position they took depended whether or not they could remain in the Comintern. Yet, the European communist parties were in no sense equipped in 1924 for a rapid-fire decision on the questions under discussion in Russia where, just at that time, two principal tendencies were in the formative stage, growing out of the new stage of the proletarian dictatorship. Of course, the work of purging was also necessary after 1924 and alien elements were quite correctly removed from many sections. But taken as a whole, the "Bolshevization" consisted in this: that with the wedge of the Russian disputes, driven from above with the hammer blows of the state apparatus, the leaderships being formed at the moment in the communist parties of the West were disorganized over and over again. All this went on under the banner of struggle against factionalism.

If a faction which threatens to paralyze its fighting ability for a long time does crystallize inside the party of the proletarian vanguard the party will then naturally always be confronted with the necessity to decide whether to allot more time for a supplementary re-examination or to recognize immediately that the split is unavoidable. A fighting party can never be the sum of factions that pull in opposite directions. This is incontestably true, if taken in this general form. But to employ the split as a preventive measure against differences of opinion and to lop off every group and grouping that raises a voice of criticism is to transform the internal life of the party into a chain of organizational abortions. Such methods do not promote the continuation and the development of the species but only exhaust the maternal organism, that is, the party. The struggle against factionalism becomes infinitely more dangerous than the formation of factions itself.

At the present time, we have a situation in which the actual initiators and founders of almost all the communist parties of the world have been placed outside of the International, not excepting even its former chairman. The leading groups of the two consecutive stages in party development are either expelled or removed from leadership in almost all the parties. In Germany the Brandler group today still finds itself in the position of semi-party membership. The Maslow group is outside the party. In France are expelled the old groups of Rosmer, Monatte, Loriot, Souvarine, as well as the leading group of the subsequent period, Girault-Treint. In Belgium, the basic group of Van Overstraeten has been expelled. If the Bordiga group, the founder of the Communist Party in Italy, is only half expelled that is to be accounted for by the conditions of the Fascist régime. In Czechoslovakia, in Sweden, in Norway, in the United States, in a word, in almost all the parties of the world we perceive more or less similar phenomena which arose in the post-Leninist period.

It is incontestable that many of the expelled committed the greatest mistakes, and we have not been behindhand in pointing them out. It is equally true that many of the expelled, after they were cut off from the Comintern, have to a great extent returned to their former points of departure, to the Left social democracy or syndicalism. But the task of the leadership of the Comintern by no means consists in driving the young leaderships of the national parties into a blind alley every time, and thus dooming their individual representatives to ideological degeneration. The "revolutionary order" of the bureaucratic leadership stands as a terrible obstacle in the path of the development of all the parties of the Communist International.

Organizational questions are inseparable from questions of program and tactics. We must take clearly into account the fact that one of the most important sources of opportunism in the Comintern is the bureaucratic régime of the apparatus in the Comintern itself as well as in its leading party. There cannot be any doubt after the experience of the years 1923-1928 that bureaucratism in the Soviet Union is the expression and the instrument of the pressure exerted by the non-proletarian classes upon the proletariat. The draft program of the Comintern contains a correct formulation on this score when it says that bureaucratic perversions "arise inevitably on the soil of an insufficient cultural level of the masses and of class influences alien to the proletariat." Here we have the key to the understanding not only of bureaucratism in general but also of its extraordinary growth in the last five years. The cultural level of the masses, while remaining insufficient has been rising constantly in this period (and this is incontestable); therefore, the cause for the growth of bureaucratism is to be sought only in the growth of class influences alien to the proletariat. In proportion as the European communist parties, i.e., primarily their directing bodies, aligned themselves organizationally with the shifts and regroupings in the apparatus of the CPSU, the bureaucratism of the communist parties abroad was for the most part only a reflection and a supplement of the bureaucratism within the CPSU.

The selection of the leading elements in the communist parties has proceeded and still proceeds mainly from the standpoint of their readiness to accept and approve the very latest apparatus grouping in the CPSU. The more independent and responsible elements in the leadership of the parties abroad who refused to submit to shuffling and reshuffling in a purely administrative manner, were either expelled from the party altogether or they were driven into the Right (often the pseudo-Right) wing, or, finally, they entered the ranks of the Left Opposition. In this manner, the organic process of the selection and welding together of the revolutionary cadres, on the basis of the proletarian struggle under the leadership of the Comintern was cut short, altered, distorted, and in part even directly replaced by the administrative and bureaucratic sifting from above. Quite naturally, those leading communists who were the readiest to adopt the ready-made decisions and to countersign any and all resolutions, frequently gained the upper hand over those party elements who were imbued with the feeling of revolutionary responsibility. Instead of a selection of tested and unwavering revolutionists, we have frequently had a selection of the best adapted bureaucrats.

All questions of internal and international policy invariably lead us back to the question of the internal party régime. Assuredly, deviations away from the class line in the questions of the Chinese revolution and the British labour movement, in the questions of the economy of the USSR, of wages, of taxes, etc., constitute in themselves a grave danger. But this danger is increased tenfold because the bureaucratic régime binds the party hand and foot and deprives it of any opportunity to correct the line of the leading party tops in a normal manner. The same applies to the Comintern as well. The resolution of the Fourteenth Party Congress of the CPSU on the necessity of a more democratic and more collective leadership in the Comintern has been transformed in practise into its antithesis. A change in the internal régime of the Comintern is becoming a life and death question for the international revolutionary movement. This change can be achieved in two ways: either hand in hand with a change in the internal régime in the CPSU or in the struggle against the leading role of the CPSU in the Comintern. Every effort must be made to assure the adoption of the first way: the struggle for the change of the internal régime in the Comintern and for the preservation of the leading ideological role of our party in the Comintern.

For this reason, it is necessary to expunge ruthlessly from the program the very idea that living, active parties can be subordinated to the control of the "revolutionary order" of an irremovable governmental party bureaucracy. The party itself must be restored its rights. The party must once again become a party. This must be affirmed in the program in such words as will leave no room for the theoretical justification of bureaucratism and usurpatory tendencies.

A LENINIST DEBATES KERENSKY

SELDOM DOES HISTORY record the former head of a government, deposed by social revolution, facing up in an open debate 34 years later to a modern representative of the same ideological current which swept him from power. This was the situation in the February 8 [1951] debate at the University of Chicago where Max Shachtman confronted Alexander Kerensky, the head of the régime which was overthrown by the great Russian Revolution.

The intervening years since the revolution have witnessed the rise in Russia of the totalitarian bureaucratic oligarchy of Stalinism. Grabbing onto this bare historical fact, Kerensky sought to bury the anti-democratic crimes of his own régime by pointing an accusing finger at Lenin and the Bolsheviks as those responsible for Stalin's monstrous despotism. Shachtman thus faced a double task in this debate, one familiar enough to genuine socialists: that of establishing historical truth against the combined opposition of both capitalist and Stalinist falsifiers of the past 34 years.

This is the reason that Shachtman, in opening the discussion, found it necessary to remark: "The Stalinist régime never slackens in its efforts to portray itself as the legitimate successor of the Bolshevik Revolution. It needs this great authority to help befuddle the thinking of people and to maintain itself in power... It came into power as the result of a *counter-revolution* which systematically destroyed not only every single one of the great achievements of the Bolshevik Revolution but likewise exterminated all its founders, builders and defenders".

Kerensky based himself on the necessity for the provisional government to "defend Russia" during the war, opposing the elements of extreme monarchist reaction who favored a separate peace with Germany and likewise opposing the desire of the people to get out of the disastrous war. He took the stand that the social reforms demanded by the people must be postponed until the war was over. The government could legitimately adopt measures such as its land reforms, the 8-hour day, the need for a Constituent Assembly, the right of self-determination for oppressed nationalities — but (and it was a very big but) nothing could really be done until the Constituent Assembly met, and it would be better for that body to meet only after the conclusion of the war. After all, the organization of a Constituent Assembly is a "big job".

The aim of Bolshevism, according to Kerensky, was to exploit the country in totalitarian fashion. The real question here, he announced, is what happened *after* the revolution. Lenin, Trotsky and Stalin, he said, were playing a double game of trickery on the country and the government. Lenin sent various "secret instructions" to his central committee. (Kerensky, without pointing it out, was referring to the period when his own government had jailed Trotsky and other Bolsheviks and had forced Lenin to go into hiding!) Another aim of Bolshevism, Kerensky charged, was "to distract the freest country in the world from preparing a base for the future world socialist movement." So, Lenin concluded, the provisional government had to be stopped. "For this they ruined Russian democracy," he cried, after having made clear that he understood nothing about the urgent desire of the Russian masses for the democratic and socialist reforms which only the Bolsheviks were fighting for.

Striking a personal note, Kerensky drew some applause when he cried: "Maybe my government was unpopular but I needed no bodyguards. In Kiev when I took a walk the people liked to gather around me and speak to me". Kerensky was presumably referring to *Stalin's* secluded and guarded living habits; but while he was supposed to be discussing Lenin and the days of the Russian Revolution, he made no mention of the fact that Lenin and the other Bolshevik leaders continually mingled with the

Report from *Labor Action*, February 19, 1951, on the Shachtman-Kerensky debate from which Shachtman's opening speech is at the start of this chapter.

workers at all kinds of meetings and elsewhere, guarded at other times as the crisis neared only against the police vengeance of Kerensky himself.

The fight in 1917, said Kerensky, was "not a fight between capitalism and socialism, but between freedom and slavery." And "Stalin is the most faithful, most able, most talented disciple of Lenin."

Shachtman demanded to know "who elected" the supposedly "democratic" provisional government — which, of course, had been put into power by no popular vote of any kind. In contrast, he pointed out, the Bolshevik government took power with the support of a free vote of the broadest and most representative body ever assembled in Russia or for that matter in the world — the soviets (councils) of the workers, peasants, and soldiers of the country — in a congress organized and prepared by enemies of the Bolsheviks. He stressed the absurdity, not to speak of the slanderousness, of Kerensky's claim that the Bolsheviks were able to lead a vast, tumultuous, surging mass revolution of the people through "trickeries."

2. THE STALINIST COUNTER-REVOLUTION IN THE USSR

Max Shachtman

REVOLUTION AND COUNTER-REVOLUTION IN RUSSIA

NOT A SINGLE Bolshevik leader considered it possible for the Soviet power to endure for a long period of time, much less for Russia to achieve the classless socialist order, unless the workers of one or more advanced capitalist countries came to its aid.

"When we began the international revolution" [said Lenin at the Third Congress of the Communist International in 1921] *"... we thought, either the international revolution comes to our aid and then our victory is quite assured, or else we do our modest revolutionary work and do it in the knowledge that in the event that we suffer defeat, we are thereby of use to the cause of the revolution, because we make it possible for other revolutions, made shrewder by our experiences, to do it better. It was clear to us that without the support of the international world revolution, the victory of the proletarian revolution is impossible. Even before the revolution and also afterwards, we reflected: either the revolution in the other countries, in the capitalistically more developed countries, comes immediately or at least in very swift succession, or we must succumb".*

Neither the hope nor the prognosis was realized, as is known. Yet the Soviet state has not perished. At first blush, this seems to confirm Stalin's nationalistic thesis that a socialist society can be established within a single country regardless of whether the revolution triumphs in other lands. But only at first blush. For while the Soviet state has not succumbed despite its enforced isolation, it has not only been unable to achieve its socialist goal but it has been corrupted from within by the deadly cancer of degeneration. The canal through which the poisons have flowed to the heart and head of the régime is the Stalinist bureaucracy.

Even before it expropriated the economic power of the bourgeoisie, the Russian revolution deprived it of its political power. Its place was taken by the rule of the working class, a proletarian democracy, Lenin wrote, "a million times more democratic than any bourgeois democracy, and the Soviet régime... a million times more democratic than the most democratic régime in a bourgeois republic." The Soviet democracy was based on the abolition of a professional governmental bureaucracy divorced from the people, on the indivisibility of the legislative and executive bodies, on the direct rule of the toilers through their deputies to the Soviets, subject at all times to recall, on the armed people as against a professional body of armed men divorced from the masses, and on the privileged position of the proletariat as the vanguard of the toiling masses. While the Bolshevik party, as the tested and trusted revolutionary vanguard of the proletariat, was the ruling party, it maintained a live and sensitive contact with the toilers through the Soviets, the trade unions, the factory committees, the

From *New International*, January 1938, "The 20th anniversary of the Bolshevik uprising and the degeneration of the Soviet power".

committees of poor peasants, the coöperatives, and similar institutions. The existence of a wide freedom of discussion and decision in all these bodies, of genuine workers' democracy, made of this interlocking system of institutions the living reality of the political rule of the proletariat — never ideal or flawless, to be sure, but decisive.

The counter-revolution of the Stalinist bureaucracy consists in nothing less than this; it has effectively destroyed all these institutions in the last fourteen years and thereby it has just as effectively expropriated the proletariat *politically*.

LENIN ATTACHED, even if not uncritically, a tremendous significance to what was called the Old Guard of the Bolshevik party. He regarded those veterans who had passed through three revolutions, the World War and the civil war, as one of the main assurances that the revolution would continue along its indicated path. "It must be recognized," he wrote to the Central Committee in March 1922, "that at the present time the proletarian party policy is determined not so much by its membership as by the unlimited and powerful authority of that thin layer which we may name the old party Guard." The Stalinist bureaucracy, in the course of its reaction to the revolution, its traditions and its ideology, has destroyed the Old Guard which embodied them.

Take but one example which comes to hand, the Central Committee elected at the 9th Congress in 1920: Artem, Dzerzhinsky, Lenin, Bukharin, Zinoviev, Kamenev, Krestinsky, Preobrazhensky, Rudzutak, Radek, Rakovsky, Rykov, Serebriakov, I N Smirnov, Tomsky, Trotsky, Andreyev, Kalinin and Stalin. The first three died of natural causes. Of the rest, Zinoviev, Kamenev, Serebriakov and I N Smirnov were murdered by the Stalinists; Tomsky was killed or driven to suicide; Trotsky is in Mexican exile; Bukharin, Krestinsky, Preobrazhensky, Rudzutak, Radek, Rakovsky and Rykov are imprisoned or disgraced — all thirteen of them as fascists or wreckers or assassins. Only Stalin, Kalinin and Andreyev remain, which is like saying that only Stalin remains.

Important to note in this devastating and uninterrupted purge is the fact that it is not only the generation of defenders of the October Revolution that has been crushed. The Trotskyists or Zinovievists — men like Trotsky, Zinoviev, Kamenev, Rakovsky, Mdvani, Piatakov, Smirnov, Smilga, Preobrazhensky, Bieloborodov, Muralov — were removed long ago by the Thermidorian generation that brought Stalin to power. Now even the men of the Thermidorian reaction have gone or are going: Bukharin, Rykov, Rudzutak, Tukhachevsky, Bubnov, Postyshev, and hundreds less well known. Their places are taken by entirely colorless unknowns like Beria, Eikhe, Zhdanov, Khrushchev who are not so much party leaders as Stalinist governor-generals who rule the provinces like old Turkish Walis; they are made or un-made in a day by simple decree, and their coming and going are like the shadows of a guttering candle flame.

WHATEVER ELSE it may be, a political organization that does not have a free and rich inner life is not a revolutionary proletarian party. In Lenin's time, even after the Mensheviks and Social Revolutionists had placed themselves outside the Soviet pale by their counter-revolutionary course and left the Bolshevik party with a monopoly of political rule, the party led an intense and active inner life, discussing freely at all times, debating all questions openly, electing, criticizing and removing its leadership and deciding the party line at will. Under the gun-fire of the Kronstadt mutiny and the echoes of the peasant risings in Tambov and elsewhere, the 10th Congress adopted the entirely exceptional and temporary emergency measure prohibiting separate factions with separate platforms. This unprecedented limitation on party democracy, however, was adopted with numerous significant reservations. The adopted resolution stated:

"It is necessary that every party organization takes rigorous care that the absolutely necessary criticism of the shortcomings of the party, all analyses of the general party direction, all appraisals of its practical experience, every examination of the carrying out of the party decisions and of the means of correcting the mistakes, etc. — shall not be discussed in separate groups standing upon any 'platform', but rather in the meetings of all the party members. Toward this end, the Congress decides to publish a periodical Discussion Sheet *and special periodicals. Everyone who comes forward with a criticism must take into consideration the position of the party in the midst of its encircling enemies, and he must also strive, in his direct activity in Soviet and party circles, to correct the mistakes of the party in practise. While the Congress orders the Central Committee to exterminate all factionalism, the conference declares at the same time that those questions which attract the special attention of the party membership — e.g., on the purging of the party of unproletarian, unreliable elements, on the struggle against bureaucratism, on the development of democracy and the broader participation of the workers, etc. — and in general all objective proposals, must be examined with the utmost possible scrupulousness and tested practically. All party members must know that the party cannot take all the required measures in these questions, since it encounters a whole series of the most varied obstacles, and that while the party decisively rejects an un-objective and factional criticism, it will continue tirelessly to test new methods, and to fight with all means against bureaucratism and for the extension of the democracy of the self-active masses, for the uncovering, exposure and expulsion of all unreliable elements from the party"* (*Russische Korrespondenz*, Nr. 5, May 1921, p. 323.)

Not aimed at suppressing democracy, even the restrictions of the 10th Congress were designed to extend discussion and criticism, to organize it, to ferret out bureaucratism, and to do all this in a manner that would be less dangerous and factional under the concrete conditions. When, at the same congress, Riazanov moved an amendment prohibiting elections of delegates to coming congresses on the basis of factional platforms, Lenin, quick to sense the danger, replied:

"I think that the desire of comrade Riazanov is unfortunately not realizable. If fundamental disagreements exist on a question, we cannot deprive members of the Central Committee of the right to address themselves to the party. I cannot imagine how we can do this. The present congress can in no way and in no form engage the elections to the next congress. And if, for example, questions like the Brest-Litovsk peace arise? Can we guarantee that such questions will not arise? It cannot be guaranteed. It is possible that it will then be necessary to elect by platform. That's quite clear". (*Minutes of the 10th Congress*, p. 292. Russ. ed.)

And again, elsewhere, during the same period, Lenin wrote:

"But if deep, fundamental disagreements of principle exist, we may be told: 'Do they not justify the sharpest factional action?' Naturally they justify it, if the disagreements are really deep, and if the rectification of the wrong policy of the party or of the working class cannot be obtained otherwise". (*Works*, Vol. XVIII, Pt. 1, p. 47, Russ. ed.)

In the period of acute danger to the Soviet régime, when it had to make the painful and hazardous transition to the New Economic Policy, and when the party imposed certain organizational restraints upon itself, Lenin nevertheless called for freedom of discussion and criticism, for internal discussion organs, and acknowledged the permissibility and even inevitability of factions, platforms and the "sharpest factional action". By this he was merely testifying to the existence of a *living party*.

The Stalinist bureaucracy has changed all that. It started with the Trotsky-Zinoviev Opposition. In 1927, it prohibited the publication of their *Platform*, arrested those leaders and militants who mimeographed it for circulation in a pre-congress discussion period, and expelled all those who defended it. It demanded not only that the Opposition supporters cease *advocating* the views in their *Platform*, but that they cease believing those views! In 1932, Stalin demanded the execution of the old Bolshevik, Riutin, for circulating a "platform" which ended with Lenin's demand that Stalin be removed from his post; Riutin was "merely" imprisoned by the GPU. In the last few years — the years of Stalinist domination — not one single word of criticism of the party leadership has been uttered; not one single proposal different from the proposals of the Führer. Nobody dares. Yet there are differences of opinion, whispered about and muttered in tiny grouplets. Only, the party does not decide these differences. The party is dead. The GPU decides them in accord with the instructions of the Secretariat.

The congress of the party is its highest and most authoritative instance, selecting the leadership to carry out the line of policy which the congress adopts. At least, so it was in Lenin's time. The question of seizing power, the Brest-Litovsk treaty, the New Economic Policy, the trade union question — all these were decided at party congresses, after the fullest discussion of all the conflicting standpoints. In the Stalinist epoch, congresses no longer take place. In their stead, the bureaucracy organizes palace assemblies of hand-picked lieges who listen without discussion to the Throne Speech of the Führer. The lesser bureaucrats appear only for the purpose of burning frankincense to Stalin and of giving him assurances of their blind fealty in terms reminiscent of the fawning speeches made by provincial princelings to an Oriental potentate.

Just think: In the days of illegality and thin purses, under Tsarist despotism, the Russian party nevertheless held four regular congresses between July 1903 and May 1907. (Of party conferences under Tsarism, there were eight, from the Tammerfors meeting in 1905 to the Poronino meeting in 1913.) In the revolutionary period, between the overthrow of the Tsar and the death of Lenin, the party held eight regular party congresses (and seven conferences). The Stalinist record is quite different. The first real post-Lenin congress was the 14th, in December 1925; the 15th was held 2 years later; between it and the 16th, 2½ years were allowed to elapse; between the 16th and the 17th Congress — the last to be held, in January 1934 — more than 3½ years went by. The statutes adopted by the Stalinists themselves at the 17th Congress provided (§27) that "regular congresses are convened no less than once in three years". In cynical violation of its own statutes, the bureaucracy has let four years pass and the fiction of a party is not even allowed to hold its fiction of a congress. And what four years these have been! What drastic changes the bureaucracy has made without even going through the formality of consulting the party! Under the Stalinist bureaucracy, the Bolshevik party (if it may be called that) has been allowed to meet in congress (again, if it may be called that) only four times in more than thirteen years. The party met more often under the Tsar! The bureaucracy has crushed the old party.

IN THE EARLY DAYS of the revolution, the Bolsheviks regarded the trade unions as a school of Communism, and as one of the institutions through which the workers ruled in the factories and the Soviets. The Bolsheviks did not fear debate and discussion, and as late as 1920, almost three years after the revolution, Dalin and Martov could still appear as the official representatives of the Menshevik party at the 3rd Congress of the trade unions to present their views and debate the Bolshevik spokesmen. But even more: the Bolsheviks regarded the trade unions as an indispensable instrument for the defense of proletarian interests from the transgressions, abuses and wantonness of the state itself, and especially of its bureaucracy. It was only in 1927 that Molotov put forward the bigoted, bureaucratic conception that since Russia is a workers' state there can be no question of defending the workers from it. Lenin had nothing in common with this bureaucratic idealism. Speaking before the party fraction of the 8th Soviet Congress on December 30, 1920, during the discussion on the trade union question, he said:

"Comrade Trotsky speaks of the workers' state. Permit me, that is an abstraction. When we wrote about the workers' state in 1917 that was understandable; but when it is said today: Why defend, defend the working class against whom, there's no longer a bourgeoisie, don't we have a workers' state — then an obvious error is being committed. The whole joke is that it is not quite a workers' state. That's where the basic mistake of comrade Trotsky lies! We have passed over from general principles to objective discussion and to decrees, but that's where we are being held back from practical objective work. That will not do! Our state is in reality no workers' state, but a workers' and peasants' state. A whole lot follows from that... But still more. From our party program it follows that our state is a workers' state with bureaucratic deformations. We have to paste this — how shall we call it? — sorry label on it. That is the reality of the transition!... Our present state is such that the organized proletariat must defend itself and we must utilize these workers' organizations for the defense of the workers against their state and for the defense of the state by the workers". (*Der Kampf um die soziale Revolution*, pp. 593f.)

What a decisive rôle Lenin assigned to the trade unions in this profoundly dialectical concept of the interrelations between the economic organizations of the workers and the *real* — not idealistically perfect — workers' state, a concept beyond the grasp of superficial minds accustomed to abstract and absolute categories. The trade unions are an instrument for the defense of the workers' state and for the defense of the workers from that state! And if the latter was necessary seventeen years ago, how infinitely more urgent is it today that the trade unions defend the workers from a régime in which the bureaucratic cancer has grown to monstrous, undreamed-of proportions? What, for example, has happened to the right to strike, solemnly recognized by the party congress in Lenin's time? Most likely it has not been abolished by law; only, the exercise of that right is rewarded by a prompt visit by the GPU.

The right to intervene in the question of hiring and firing and of management in general was taken from the trade unions, from the factory committee and from the party nucleus in the factory, in September 1929. The trade unionists and the unions themselves are silent in the face of the most abominable abuses of the factory directors. The bitterness of the average worker against the growing disparity between his wages and the salary of the industrial bureaucrat or the labor aristocrat who carries the title of Stakhanovite, is felt in the heart and muttered in the most discreet privacy, but is not expressed in or through the trade unions.

The trade union leadership is composed of case-hardened bureaucrats, appointed from above and removed just as easily. They know they have neither obligations nor responsibilities to the ranks; nor are they under their control. As a result the Soviet press is compelled to print countless depressing reports of wantonness, irresponsibility, embezzlement, brutality and degeneration among the trade union officialdom. The worker does not know today who will be the head of his trade union tomorrow; he is not consulted and, knowing quite well that he has a union in name only, he cares precious little. He is aware that the armed guard who watches over him in the mine pit is far more real and far more powerful than the empty shell that was once the Russian trade union movement.

The first All-Russian congress of the trade unions met in January 1918; the second early in 1919; the third in April 1920. The 9th Congress met towards the end of 1928; the 10th Congress early in 1932. Since then — that is, for almost six crucial years — there has been no congress. If one knew nothing else about the Russian trade unions, the comparison between the two sets of dates would suffice to indicate the difference between a living movement, a real foundation stone in the structure of proletarian democracy — and a fiction. But behind the fiction stands the usurpatory bureaucracy.

THE RUSSIAN REVOLUTION laid bare the Soviets — the councils of workers, soldiers, peasants — as the most natural, most democratic, most efficient form of proletarian state rule in the transition period between capitalism and communism. In all other countries where a revolutionary situation matured, Soviets, just like the Russian or slightly varied in form, developed spontaneously as the embryonic organs of insurrection and power, and not as a product artificially imported from Russia.

The original Soviets *were* a million times more democratic than any bourgeois republic precisely because they smashed the monopoly of the professional capitalist politician and bureaucrat whose relationship with the masses is confined to electoral campaigns once a year or less often. The Soviets made it possible for the masses to throw off the yoke of "voting cattle" which bourgeois rule imposes upon them, and to act as the direct, independent administrators of their own affairs. Unsatisfactory representatives could be recalled at will and replaced by others. Lenin saw especially in the right of recall not only one of the main pillars of Soviet democracy but also a guarantee of the peaceful settlement of conflicts and disputes in the country. Four weeks after the Bolshevik uprising, he said at a session of the All-Russian Central Executive Committee of the Soviets:

"Various parties have played a dominant rôle among us. The last time, the passage of influence from one party to another was accompanied by an overturn, by a fairly stormy overturn, whereas a simple vote would have sufficed had we had the right of recall . . . The right of recall must be granted the Soviets, which are the most perfect carrier of the state idea, of coercion. Then the passage of power from one party to another will proceed without bloodshed, by means of simple new elections". (*Izvestia*, No. 233, Dec. 6, 1917.)

The whole course of the Stalinist bureaucracy, climaxed by a "democratic election under the new democratic Constitution" which is gruesomely mocked by the never-ceasing purge, has proceeded by trampling under foot every one of the conceptions of the place and function of the Soviets which prevailed in the early years of the revolution. From the local Soviets to the Central Executive Committee itself, the administrations are appointed and removed at will by the corresponding party apparatus-bosses, and without the slightest intervention of the masses themselves. The right of recall exists, to be sure, but it is exercised only by the Stalinist bureaucracy. What Soviet institution, what mass organization or movement intervened, for example, to remove the recently condemned People's Commissars of White Russia, of the Ukraine, of Georgia, of the RSFSR, of the Soviet Union, and to put others in their place? Only the GPU, acting as administrative agent of the party secretariat. What "democratic" significance have the new constitutional rights of free speech, free press and free assembly when they are enjoyed exclusively (and even then limitedly) by the myrmidons of the bureaucracy who are themselves under the constant surveillance of the secret police? What value has the secret ballot when there is but one candidate to choose from, and he hand-picked by the apparatus? The elections to the Soviets and all other alleged legislative and executive bodies are classic examples of Bonapartist plebiscites; they are an abominable caricature of Soviet democracy, the very negation of it.

The bureaucracy has strangled the Soviets of the revolution. The political rule of the workers and peasants has been supplanted by the political rule of the bureaucracy and those social strata which are its direct props. What a revealing story there is in the social composition of the guaranteed-to-be-elected candidates to the Council of the Union! Of actual workers and peasants, there are none or next to none. The overwhelming majority of the candidates is made up of party officials, factory directors, labor aristocrats (Stakhanovites), GPU and army officers, well-to-do farmers, that is, the reactionary bureaucracy and its associated social layers. The Soviets were to make it possible, in Lenin's words, for any charwoman, for the lowest and most despised, to become the administrators of the state, so that it would no longer be, properly speaking, a state in the old sense of a bureaucratic apparatus of oppression with special bodies of armed men separate and apart from the people. The triumph of the Stalinist bureaucracy has been accomplished by the political expropriation of the charwomen, of the proletariat. It signifies the victory of the *political counter-revolution*.

AT HOME, THE BUREAUCRACY has not yet been able to free itself from the confines of the economic basis achieved by the Russian revolution, about which more later. But abroad, it has a free hand, so to speak, and there its course is openly counter-revolutionary. It is the gendarme of law and order, of the *status quo* throughout the capitalist world. A comparison between the situation even in 1923, when the reactionary tumor was already apparent in the Soviet body, and 1937, when the totalitarian bureaucracy is celebrating its triumph, will indicate the profound change.

In 1923, when the German revolution was expected, the Soviet Republic stood at attention to aid it. The harbor of Petrograd was filled with grain ships ready to sail for Stettin so that the German Soviet republic would not be starved out by the Entente. Representatives of the Comintern and the Russian party were active on German soil, preparing for the uprising as best they could under the leadership of Brandler and Zinoviev. Specialists of the Red Army were assigned to give expert assistance to the German communists. The close diplomatic alliance existing at that time between the Soviets and the German bourgeois republic had not converted the International into the main prop of German capitalism — quite the contrary.

In 1937, all the diplomatic moves in Europe, all the aid sent by the Soviet Union to the Spanish loyalists (in the form of munitions, arms, military experts, GPU agents, *etc.*), are directed towards crushing the proletarian revolution in Spain, preserving Spanish bourgeois democracy as an instrument in the hands of Anglo-French imperialism. The policy of Stalin in Spain is distinguished from that of Noske and Scheidemann in the Germany of 1919 only by its more systematic savagery.

All the policies of the Soviet bureaucracy are based upon its self-preservation. Abroad, at the very least, in the international labor movement and class struggle, it is indisputable that the interests of the Soviet bureaucracy come into head-on conflict with the interests of the working class. These interests produce not the policies of the Mensheviks of 1905, nor even of 1917, but of those Mensheviks who took up arms, in alliance with Anglo-French imperialism in 1918-1919, to overthrow the young Soviet republic. They are not just non-revolutionary policies, they are the policies of counter-revolution.

WHAT REMAINS of the Russian revolution? Why should we defend the Soviet Union in case of war? A number of realities still remain. The conflict between German fascism (and fundamentally, also, of the capitalist world as a whole), and the Soviet Union, still remains no less a reality than, let us say, the conflict between fascism and social-democracy or the trade unions, regardless of how corrupt may be the leadership of the latter, regardless of how it may compromise and capitulate, regardless of how much it may seek to place itself under the protection of one capitalist force (as did the Austrian social democracy) against another. The conflict can be resolved only by the capitalist world being overturned by the working class, or by the Soviet Union, its present bureaucracy included, being crushed and reduced to the status of a colonial or semi-colonial country, divided among the world's imperialist bandits.

Another great reality is the economic foundation established by the October revolution. Despite bureaucratic mismanagement and parasitism, we have the prodigious economic advances made by Soviet industry, the great expansion of the productive forces in Russia (without which human progress is generally inconceivable) in a period of stagnation and retrogression in the capitalist world, the principle and practise of economic planning. All these were possible only on the basis of the abolition of socially operated private property, of the nationalization of the means of production and exchange, their centralization in the hands of the state which is the main prerequisite of an evolution towards the classless society of universal abundance, leisure and unprecedented cultural advancement.

Outraged by the brutality of the reactionary usurpers, by their blood purges, by their political expropriation of the toilers, by their totalitarian régime, more than one class conscious worker and revolutionary militant has concluded that nothing is left of the Russian revolution, that there are no more grounds for defending the Soviet Union in a war than for defending any capitalist state. The professional confusionists of the various ultra-leftist grouplets prey upon these honest reactions to Stalinism and try to goad the workers into a reactionary position. Some of these philosophers of ignorance and superficiality prescribe a position of neutrality in a war between the Soviet Union and Germany; others, less timid, call for the strategy of defeatism in the Soviet Union. At bottom, the ultra-leftist position on the Soviet Union, which denies it any claim whatsoever to being a workers' state, reflects the vacillations of the petty bourgeoisie, their inability to make a firm choice between the camps of the proletariat and the bourgeoisie, of revolution and imperialism.

Class rule is based upon property relations. Bourgeois class rule, the bourgeois state, is based upon private ownership, appropriation and accumulation. The political superstructure of the bourgeois class state may vary: democratic republic, monarchy, fascist dictatorship. When the bourgeois can no longer rule directly politically, and the working class is still too weak to take power, a Bonapartist military dictatorship may arise which seeks to raise itself "above the classes", to "mediate" between them, But it continues to rule over a *bourgeois state* (even though, as in Germany, it has politically expropriated the bourgeoisie and its parties), because it has left bourgeois property relations more or less intact.

The October revolution abolished bourgeois property relations in the decisive spheres of economic life. By centralizing the means of production in the hands of the state, it created new property relations. The counter-revolutionary bureaucracy, although it has destroyed the political rule of the proletariat, has *not yet* been able to restore capitalist property relations by abolishing those established by the revolution. This great reality determines, for Marxists, the character of the Soviet Union as a workers' state, bureaucratically degenerated, it is true, usurped and therefore crucially imperilled by the Bonapartists, but still fundamentally a workers' state. This great remaining conquest of the revolution determines, in turn, our defense of the Soviet Union from imperialist attack *and* from its Bonapartist sappers at home.

Because it is not a simple question, Lenin pointed out at the 9th Congress of the party in 1920, we must be careful not to sink into the morass of confusion.

"Wherein consists the rule of the class? Wherein consisted the rule of bourgeoisie over the feudal lords? In the constitution it was written: 'freedom and equality'. — That is a lie. So long as there are toilers, the property owners are capable and, as such, even compelled to speculate. We say that there is no equality there, and that the sated are not the equals of the hungry, the speculator is not the equal of the toiler. Wherein does the rule of the class express itself? The rule of the proletariat expresses itself in the abolition of landed and capitalist property. Even the fundamental content of all former constitutions — the republican included — boiled down to property. Our constitution has acquired the right to historical existence, we did not merely write down on paper that we are abolishing property, but the victorious proletariat did abolish property and abolished it completely. — Therein consists the rule of the class — primarily in the question of property. When the question of property was decided in practise, the rule of the class was thereby assured; thereupon the constitution wrote down on paper what life had decided: 'There is no capitalist and landed property', and it added: 'The working class has more rights than the peasantry, but the exploiters have no rights at all'. Therewith was written down the manner in which we realized the rule of our class, in which we bound together the toilers of all strata, all the little groups. The petty bourgeois proprietors were split up. Among them those who have a larger property are the foes of those who have less, and the proletariat openly declares war against them when it abolishes property....

The rule of the class is determined only by the relationship to property. That is precisely what determines the constitution. And our constitution correctly sets down our attitude to property and our attitude to the question of what class must stand at the head. He who, in the question of how the rule of the class is expressed, falls into the question of democratic centralism, as we often observe, brings so much confusion into the matter that he makes impossible any successful work on this ground". (*Russische Korrespondenz*, Nr. 10, July 1920, p. 8.)

Liberal apologists have distorted Lenin's concepts into an argument for the compatibility of the bureaucratic dictatorship, and even a personal dictatorship, with a consistent development toward the new social order. "So long as industry remains nationalized and the productive forces expand," runs their apology, "what does it really matter if Stalin maintains a bureaucratic despotism, which we civilized liberals would not tolerate but which is good enough for backward Russians?" It is of course quite true that Lenin saw no absolute incompatibility between proletarian democracy and "individual dictatorship" in industry under given conditions. A year before his quoted speech at the 9th Congress, he observed:

"That the dictatorship of single persons in the history of the revolutionary movements was very often the spokesman, the carrier and the executant of the dictatorship of the revolutionary classes, is evidenced by the incontestable experience of history... If we are not anarchists, we must acknowledge the necessity of the state, i.e., of coercion, for the transition from capitalism to socialism. The form of coercion is determined by the degree of development of the given revolutionary class, furthermore, by such special

227

circumstances as, e.g., the heritage of a long reactionary war, furthermore, by the forms of the resistance of the bourgeoisie or of the petty bourgeoisie. Therefore there is not the slightest contradiction in principle between Soviet (i.e., socialist) democracy and the application of the dictatorial rule of individual persons". (*Sämtliche Werke*, Bd. XXII, pp. 524f. Ger. ed.)

But in order to make clear his real thoughts, he hastened to add the following indispensable supplementary statement, without which everything is one-sided and therefore false:

"The more resolutely we now come out in favor of a ruthlessly strong power, for the dictatorship of individual persons in definite labor processes *during certain periods of* purely executive functions, *the more manifold must be the forms and methods of control from below in order to paralyze every trace of a possibility of distorting the Soviet power, in order to tear out, incessantly and tirelessly, the weeds of bureaucratism".* (Ibid., p. 532.)

It is precisely those manifold forms and methods of *democratic control from below* which the bureaucracy has destroyed in its development toward despotic rule. In destroying proletarian democracy and the political rule of the working class, the bureaucracy has lifted itself beyond the reach of the masses out of which it emerged. Having abandoned its original class base, it must find a new one, for it cannot last long as a thin bureaucratic stratum hanging, so to speak, in mid-air. The social layers with which it has linked itself are the well-to-do farmers, the factory directors and trust heads, the Stakhanovite aristocracy, the officialdom of the party, the Soviet apparatus, the Red Army and the GPU. But none of these, nor all of them taken together, represents a *class*, with a distinctive function in the productive life of the country, or with specific property forms upon which to build a firm class and firm class rule. Their whole *tendency* is to develop into a new property-owning class, that is, into a capitalist class based on private property. Blocking the road to the realization of this yearning stands the still powerful reality of the nationalization of the means of production and exchange, centralized planning, and the protection of nationalized industry which is afforded by the monopoly of foreign trade.

The bureaucracy, closely interlinked with these restorationist strata of Soviet society and embodying their social aspirations, is now driven by inexorable forces to take its next big step backward. Hitherto, the reaction has been confined essentially to the destruction of the whole political superstructure of the workers' democracy established by the revolution, and to the physical annihilation of all those who were the living connection between today and the revolutionary yesterday. From now on, the anti-Soviet bureaucracy will, and in a certain sense must, seek its self-preservation by an assault upon the economic foundations of the workers' state: nationalized property, planning, the monopoly of foreign trade.

In our opinion, it cannot and will not succeed in establishing the rule of an independent, new Russian capitalist class, even if we arbitrarily exclude the possibility, *by no means exhausted*, of the crushing of the counter-revolutionary bureaucracy by a resurgent proletariat. The new strata of society gathered around the ruling Soviet clique *may* prevail over the Russian proletariat in the period to come. But we do not believe that they are strong or solidly rooted enough to develop into a national neo-bourgeoisie capable of resisting, on a capitalist basis, the infinitely stronger bourgeoisie of the foreign imperialist countries. In other words, the Stalinist bureaucracy and its satellites are doomed regardless of the outcome. They cannot develop into an independent ruling capitalist class in Russia. Either they are defeated by the proletariat which carries through a political revolution for the purpose of restoring workers' democracy and of safeguarding the economic basis of the workers' state which still exists. Or they are defeated by powerful foreign imperialism, which would wipe out that old economic basis, reduce the Union to a semi-colonial country, and convert the restorationist strata not into a ruling capitalist class for Russia but merely into a compradore agency of world imperialism, occupying a position not dissimilar from that of the Chinese national bourgeoisie.

The class conscious workers will place all their hopes and bend all their efforts toward the realization of the former outcome of the struggle. The building of the revolutionary party to lead the Russian masses in the battle to save the Russian revolution is dependent upon the success of the revolutionary movement in the capitalist world. The depression and reaction in the ranks of the Russian proletariat was created by the defeats of the working class in the rest of the world, by the feeling of the Russians that they had no powerful allies in the capitalist world. The growth and victories of the Fourth International will galvanize the latent revolutionary strength of the Russian masses and set it into irresistible motion. Everything depends on the speed with which we accomplish our indicated task.

THE CRISIS OF THE RUSSIAN revolution has emboldened all the critics of Bolshevism, that is, of revolutionary Marxism — all of them, old and new. But all their hoary argumentation leaves the Marxist unrepentant for his solidarity with those principles and ideas which made the Russian revolution possible. For in abandoning these ideas, he would have to adopt others, and what others are there? Should he adopt those of the Mensheviks? It is true: had they triumphed, the proletarian revolution in Russia would not have degenerated into its Stalinist caricature for the simple reason that there would have been no proletarian revolution. Should he adopt those of the Western European confrères of the Mensheviks, the parties of the Second International? It is true: they did not let the proletarian revolution in Germany and Austria and Italy degenerate, and that by the simple device of crushing it in the egg and thus facilitating the consolidation of their famous bourgeois democracy which brought the working class directly under the knife of Hitler and Schuschnigg and Mussolini. Should he adopt those of the anarchist politicians who have become so clamorous of late, especially about the Kronstadt rebellion? But the lamentable collapse of anarchist politics in Spain, the servile collaboration with the bourgeoisie, the heaping of capitulation upon capitulation and the yielding of one position after another without a struggle, are not calculated to attract us away from Marxism.

It is not in place here to dwell on the flawlessness of Bolshevism and all its policies in the great period of the revolution. Its defects may be freely granted. But the oppressed and exploited of the world have not yet been offered a scientific guide to action in their struggle for freedom which can even remotely claim to serve as a substitute for the party and principles of Lenin. In the face of enormous obstacles — not the least of which were created, with arms in hand, by the present-day bourgeois and reformist critics — Lenin and the Bolsheviks carried through the first conscious proletarian revolution. They laid the economic foundation for the new society without class rule, without iniquity or exploitation or oppression. They — and nobody else — gave us a picture of the truly breath-taking prospects for human advancement and human dignity which are open to us as soon as capitalism is sent to the rubbish-heap.

Rash indeed would he be who forecast the immediate future of the Russian revolution. But whatever it may be, its historical achievements are already imperishable. The first steam engine may not have been much faster than the old-fashioned stage-coach, if it was able to move at all. But the country's network of rails is today skimmed by speedy, advanced, stream-line locomotives, while the stage-coach can be found only in museums. The creation of the steam engine was a monumental contribution to human progress. The creation of the first Soviet republic was an even greater contribution. History will give little place to the period of Stalinist counter-revolution, for it will treat it as a passing historical episode. But the Bolshevik revolution of 1917 and its enduring achievements will never be wiped out of the consciousness of man, for it sounded the knell of all class rule, marked the beginning of the end of man's pre-history, the inauguration of a new era for a new man. In this sense, Lenin and his party of revolutionary Bolsheviks could say with Ovid: *Jamque opus exegi: quod nec Jovis ira, nec ignes, Nec poterit ferrum, nec edax abolere vetustas.*

"I have now completed a work which neither the wrath of Jove, nor fire, nor the sword, nor the corroding tooth of time, shall be able to destroy."

Max Shachtman

WHY STALIN DEFEATED TROTSKY

NO WAR THAT WAS LOST, but could and should have been won, fails to produce an aftermath of criticism of the strategy and tactics employed, of recrimination, and sometimes of apostasy. So it has been with the war launched almost twenty years ago by Trotsky and his comrades in the effort to save the Russian Revolution from the degeneration that finally destroyed it.

If only Trotsky had made Lenin's Testament public in time! If only he had attended Lenin's funeral in Moscow! If only he had arrested Stalin with a corporal's guard of Red Army men before he was driven out of the War Commissariat! If only he had made a bloc with Zinoviev from the very beginning (or — other version — if only he had never made a bloc with him)! If only he had formed a new party fifteen years ago, instead of nine years ago! If only he had possessed, or shown, some of Stalin's skill at "machine politics"! If only he had gotten along better with people! If only...

If it were not for the fact that these lamentations come from self-styled friends of the cause Trotsky represented, and that they sometimes find an echo in the ranks of militants in the movement, they would not even be worth recording. But no; on second thought, they merit recording and commentary in any case, for there is much to be learned from a criticism of the critics.

The first thing that strikes the commentator on the criticisms of the way Trotsky conducted the struggle against Stalinism is the common characteristic that unites nearly all the critics. With few exceptions they are all people who have never had any experience in the work of the revolutionary political movement, and have only a book-knowledge about working class organization, based in most cases on the wrong books at that. If some critics differ from others in that they have spent more than ten minutes observing the movement from the outside or in that they have been direct participants in the movement, they are composed almost exclusively of the most mediocre kind of failures.

This apparently *ad hominem* argument might be set aside as unjust and therefore invalid if it were not that the political and "organizational" character of the critics is literally translated into their criticism, and gives it its literarious, academic, abstract, unreal and erroneous character. They have never been able to understand why their comments appear so ludicrous and preposterous to the more experienced militants in the movement.

Timing is one of the most difficult aspects of that complicated art known as political struggle. To exaggerate, you could almost say that the art of politics is proper timing. With the best principles and program and intentions in the world, a party can break its neck if it takes the beginning of a process as its end, the peak of a process for its ebb, or its ebb for its flow.

From *New International*, August 1942, "Trotsky's struggle against Stalinism: On the second anniversary of the assassination".

231

Proper timing is connected inseparably with proper focusing. If the time is ripe and the place is wrong, all is wrong. You must not start shooting in the valley when you want to take by surprise an enemy entrenched at the top of a mountain. You must not start fighting in one sphere if that means an immediate transfer of the struggle, for which you are unprepared, to another sphere, which is not prepared as a battlefield. Timing and focusing depend in turn upon the relationship of forces. To launch a battle when defeat is assured in advance is seldom superior to the kind of warfare which consists in retreating at all times. It is permissible only when retreat would lead to complete demoralization or decimation of your forces, whereas a fight, even with defeat as the sure outcome, would offer the chance of keeping a diminished force intact for a later attack. The participant in the struggle must assimilate organically these, and a hundred other, vital "commonplaces." The literary observer of the struggle does not even think of them.

Should Trotsky have launched an open struggle against the Triumvirs (Zinoviev, Kamenev, Stalin) long before he actually did, while Lenin was still more or less active? Should he have appealed right off the bat to the rank and file against the leadership, instead of confining the dispute for so long to the narrow ranks of the party's upper stratum? There isn't a second-guesser, or any other kind of *besserwisser*, who hesitates to speak up boldly, twenty years later, and answer: Yes!

The problem involved was not, however, one so easily and simply disposed of. In the first place, to have expected anybody except a crystal gazer to perceive at that time that the bureaucracy would develop to the point it reached twenty years later would require a degree of unreality attainable only by the most foggy-minded. It would have been necessary, before anything else, to look forward to a long and unbroken line of defeats for the working class throughout the world, a long recession in the strength and morale of the international revolutionary movement on the basis of which the bureaucracy was able to arrive at its present position. There *were* no serious grounds in 1922-23 for such a perspective. In the second place, the bureaucracy at that time resembled its present-day successor in only the most general and superficial way. There *were* serious grounds to believe that what was involved was a deviation, an aberration, a deformity that could be cured without *too* much difficulty and not a full-fledged counter-revolutionary line. If Trotsky had not been merely the most far-sighted thinker of his time but a man gifted with supernatural powers of insight into the future, everyone would have regarded as utter insanity any effort by him to delineate the future of the bureaucracy as it was to develop twenty years later.

What Trotsky had to fight against were the universally apparent signs of fatigue, of "revolution-weariness," among the population of the country. The people had undergone the most strenuous sufferings. Their nerves had been kept keyed to the highest pitch for several years. Their bodies had been steadily worn down. To the inferno of normal life under Czarism had been added three terrible years of the World War, then the convulsing straits of two revolutions, one right after the other, then years of the peculiar horrors of civil war, the exhausting rigors of "War Communism," the ghastly famine, the disappointing failure of the world revolution to triumph in the West. It is not so much that they finally began to break down

232

under all this that deserves to be noted, but rather that they held out so long before breaking down, that they showed such marvelous powers of endurance, such vast reservoirs of revolutionary and idealistic confidence.

The powers of endurance of the masses are not so limitless as the capacity for wind-jamming by dilettantes. The change in the moods of the masses corresponded to the inauguration of what Trotsky so aptly called the period of social, political and ideological reaction in Russia. The new moods of the masses, in which all sorts of reactionary ideas were able to multiply and flourish, were not communicated to them by the Bolshevik Party. The masses communicated their moods to the party. Not even its immunity to the virus of degeneration was absolute, especially by 1922, when many of its best elements had already been killed off in the series of battles the party had led since 1917, and been replaced in large measure by bandwagon-climbers who became the ward-heelers and the voting blocs of the bureaucracy.

The first task, therefore, was to restore the domination of revolutionary ideas in the party, in order that it, in turn, could re-inculcate the masses with them. But the party itself was not a uniform, homogeneous aggregation. When the internal fight broke out, it was composed overwhelmingly of new recruits, new and untrained. Compared with the broad masses of workers, these recruits were still an élite; but compared with the trained and hardened older revolutionists, they were anything but an élite. Another section was composed of the "pre-October" Bolsheviks, but not much older in their party membership than early in 1917. And then there was the real élite, commonly known as the "Old Guard" of the party, who went back to the early years of the struggle against Czarism, many of them as far back as the first revolution (in 1905) and even earlier.

Lenin attached the greatest importance to preserving the political and organizational integrity — and, to put it bluntly, the party leadership — of the Old Guard. He had no great illusions about it, and we, who have lived longer and seen more, have found no reason at all for illusions about it. Trotsky had no illusions about it; indeed, one of the reasons for his first clash with the bureaucracy was the warning he issued that the Old Guard might degenerate, as had old revolutionary generations before it. But with all its defects, all its weaknesses, there was no force in the country that compared with it even remotely — provided it was a force capable of preserving the revolution that you were looking for.

Trotsky should have appealed "directly" to the non-party masses against the "case-hardened" party, and "over its head"! How easily such a criticism rolls off the pen of the supercilious and superficial dilettante. But such a course would have been almost like appealing to a superstitious person to help persuade an erring scientist not to become a medicine man. The masses represented the *conservative pressure on the party*. It is no accident that one of the first public steps taken by the bureaucracy to weaken the revolutionary spirit of the party was the notorious "Lenin Levy", in which the doors of the already diluted party were thrown open to a flood of raw, ill-educated workers (and not a few ex-Menshevik and ex-SR intellectuals, and worse) who easily became the tools of the Stalinists in the work of smashing the Bolshevik Opposition.

Substantially the same can be said of the idea of precipitating a rank and file struggle from the very beginning. The first task of the intelligent and responsible revolutionist was to win the maximum possible support from the trained and *tested* cadre of the party, the party that was responsible for the revolution and stood at its head. Trotsky wisely set himself that task. It should not be imagined that this cadre was confined to a handful of leaders at the top. No, it embraced thousands, and even tens of thousands. And in the first period of the struggle, despite the pretensions of the Stalinists that they represented the "Old Guard of Bolshevism," it is a fact that in addition to the revolutionary-minded student youth (largely composed of young proletarians studying in the party political schools) Trotsky rallied the support of hundreds of the most honored and firmest militants in the party. In 1925-26 when the Zinovievist opposition united with Trotsky and his comrades, this held true to an even greater extent. The Old Guard was to a large extent in the ranks of the army fighting the bureaucratic degeneration of the revolution. To have proceeded in accordance with the rules gratuitously provided by the light-minded critics would have meant vastly facilitating and accelerating the triumph of the bureaucracy.

The experience of the masses can very seldom be anticipated, or substituted for by one's own experiences or convictions. The triumph of the bureaucracy in the party, and in the country in general, was required before a call could be issued seriously for a new party. The revolutionists had to be convinced that it was no longer possible to use the official party as a base, that it could no longer be reformed. It had to become clear in the eyes of the best militants that the official party had become nothing more — literally nothing more — than an ossified instrument of the counterrevolutionary bureaucracy. But above all, the call for the second party — that is, the formation of a new organization out of revolutionary forces *outside of* the official party as well as directed against it — had to wait until, unlike 1922-23, the revolutionary workers were outside the ranks of the Stalinized party. It had to wait, in other words, for a situation in which an appeal to the "mass" against the "party" was an appeal to the revolutionary, or potentially revolutionary forces against the conservative or counter-revolutionary force — the official party. Whether Trotsky should have issued such a call on the day he did, sometime in 1933, after the German disaster, or a day or week or month or year earlier or later, is of pretty small importance, and of less interest. Important is the *basis* on which Trotsky proceeded: the *method* he employed in reaching a decision on such questions.

He lost the war, we said at the outset. But what Stalin won was the victory of the counter-revolution. What Trotsky preserved, even in defeat, was the indispensable, the imperishable. He was not allowed by Stalin to live to see his vindication; he did not succeed in reaching his goal. That is true. But he saved the honor of the revolution. He set up in himself a model of fortitude, of intransigence, of persistency, of superb selflessness, of revolutionary principle and revolutionary integrity. He handed over to the next generation an arsenal of political weapons, not merely intact, but greatly enriched by the most gifted mind of our time. And if all of that was salvaged after a defeat, what greater assurance is needed that the defeat was only for a day and that the coming victory will hold for good?

PART II

WHAT SORT OF COUNTER-REVOLUTION?

3. THE TWO SOULS OF TROTSKYISM

On 23 August 1939, Stalin signed a pact with Hitler. It was clear from the start, and soon became clearer, that this was not just another defensive treaty of the sort that the Soviet Union had signed with many imperialist governments right back to 1918. Stalin was directly helping Hitler in imperialist conquest — and taking his own share of the plunder, too. The Marxists who fought the Stalinist counter-revolution and yet still felt obliged to defend the Soviet Union's statised economy against capitalism, had reached a fork in the road: what did the old "defence" of the USSR mean now? Albert Goldman argued for supporting the Stalinist invasion of Poland as a legitimate defensive move, and in any case a lesser evil than Nazi conquest of the whole country. Max Shachtman and others said that their former policy of "unconditional defence of the Soviet Union, despite Stalin" must be modified to allow for unequivocal opposition to the USSR in its conquest of eastern Poland and, later, Finland. Leon Trotsky, and with him the majority of the American Trotskyists, insisted on maintaining "unconditional defence of the Soviet Union" while condemning the Stalinist invasions. The implicit assumption was that the invasions were secondary and marginal events in a context dominated by a World War in which the USSR would surely soon be under attack. The ensuing political dispute divided Trotskyism into two currents which would diverge further as Stalinist imperialism grew and expanded.

James Burnham

THE MASK IS OFF!

THE MASK IS OFF, at last. The blood-stained, monstrous face of Stalinism is exposed, now, for the whole world to see quite clearly. The illusions, the veils, the deceptions are abandoned. Stalin, as the press of the Fourth International has consistently predicted since Munich[1], has capitulated to Hitler. For the Russian bureaucracy and the new exploiters which it represents and of which it is an integral part, there was no other course. Driven by an unbroken series of defeats for its external policy, knowing its utter failure within, faced with the universal hostility of the Russian masses, motivated solely by the desperate wish to save somehow its own power and privilege, the bureaucracy seeks a respite by throwing itself at the feet of the Nazi giant.

The text of the "non-aggression pact", put together with the previously signed trade and commercial agreement, proves it to be in reality an alliance. There is no escape clause, such as in all analogous treaties provided for cancellation if either party were guilty of aggression against a third state. Hitler and Stalin each binds himself against any agreement

---

Editorial from *New International*, September 1939.

1. "Stalin Agonises", editorial note from *New International,* November 1938:
   The cost of Stalinism, not simply to the workers of the world but to the Soviet Union itself, becomes suddenly clearer after Munich. What will the Kremlin do? Stalin cannot make a revolutionary turn, if for no other reason, because the first victim of such a turn if actually made would be himself. The parties of the Comintern cannot make such a turn, if for no other reason, because they are no longer political parties in the genuine sense of the term: they are merely groups of agents of the foreign office and the GPU. If they now begin to *appear* occasionally to jerk to the left, this does not at all express a real political movement toward the left but the momentary exigency of the counter-revolutionary foreign office of the Kremlin. We do not interpret a momentary progressive vote by a stool-pigeon in a union as signifying that he is moving leftward; we know that it merely answers the orders of his employer.
   The Kremlin has already made a preliminary sounding of what it is going to *try* to do, through its mouthpiece Duranty. In an article given to the world press, Duranty wrote in the most brutal prose that the era of "Litvinov diplomacy" was finished, and that Stalin must now come to an agreement with Hitler. In an unbelievably cynical sentence, omitted from the version published in New York City but included elsewhere, Duranty reminded his readers — and unquestionably above all it was intended for his Nazi readers — that more Jews had been killed in the last two years in the Soviet Union than in all the years of Hitler's regime.
   There can be nothing startling in such an attempted orientation. It is a perfectly consistent development of the Stalinist course; indeed, in 1933 the Kremlin also attempted but failed to secure a rapprochement with the then young Nazi regime. Stalin's aim is to preserve "socialism in one country"; i.e., to maintain Russia's territorial boundaries; i.e., to keep himself and his gang in power. To serve this aim it was proper to come to agreement with the class enemy as represented by the democratic imperialisms — this was the policy of the Popular Front. Then why not, when that fails, by agreement with the class enemy as represented by the fascist imperialisms? And, in point of fact, there is no fundamental difference between the two tactics.

with any power or group of powers directly or indirectly threatening the other. Unquestionably there are secret pledges attached to the pact which go far beyond the public document.

The Russian bureaucracy capitulates to Hitler in order to try to save its own neck. But it capitulates in vain. Far from bringing salvation, the signing of the pact only seals the doom of the bureaucracy. The sole question for the future is whether it will be put in its grave by Hitler, once the treaty is no longer of use to him (an alliance, Hitler explains in *Mein Kampf*, is simply one of the weapons wherewith to crush an enemy), or by the Russian people once more rising in triumphant revolution to sweep away their tyrants and exploiters.

The pact makes everything clear, throws everything to the surface. The meaning of the Trials; how clear it is now why Stalin had to wipe out every vestige of the living tradition of the revolution, had to murder the whole generation of those who made the revolution. The end of the Spanish Civil War: how clearly we can know now why Russian aid was withdrawn from Spain shortly after Munich, why Catalonia was abandoned without a fight, why the Spanish Stalinists accepted the Prieto-Negrin surrender terms... perhaps also why Miaja was never expelled from the Communist party. The dismissal of Litvinov, the speeches of Stalin and Molotov to last winter's party congress, how clear they all are now. And no wonder Stalin had to rule his state and his parties by an iron monolithism: he had to try to manufacture subordinates ready to embrace Hitler at his nod.

But the Stalin-Hitler pact, that ultimate betrayal of the masses of the entire world, is itself today swallowed up in the war crisis, is itself in fact only one part of the war crisis. When this issue leaves the press, the war may already have begun. If it is postponed another week or month or two months, what has changed? The world, the capitalist, imperialist world, is rotted through. There is no medicine. The crisis will not end, will not end until it is settled. If Chamberlain and Roosevelt and Hitler and Daladier and Stalin have their way and their war — for that is all that is left for them — it will be settled by the destruction of the very foundations and roots of civilization. Against them and that prospect can be launched only the masses of the peoples of the world, in unremitting and final struggle within *every* nation against the rulers and the oppressors.

The Stalin-Hitler pact strengthens every sector of reaction. As it gives a free hand and concrete aid to Hitler, so it gives a new impetus and a new lie to Chamberlain and Daladier and Roosevelt. Under the new circumstances which it creates, Roosevelt aims to hurl the United States far sooner than would have been otherwise necessary into the war. But it is imperialism, Roosevelt's and Chamberlain's as well as Hitler's imperialism, which is the foul mother of the pact, and of Stalinism itself for that matter. To denounce and reject the pact — and who but the utterly depraved could conceivably accept it? — is wholly meaningless unless that rejection is coupled with the thousand-fold renewal of the international struggle against world imperialism. For every worker in every nation, the main enemy remains — the enemy at home.

Max Shachtman

HITLER AND STALIN INVADE POLAND

I: 5 September 1939

THE HITLER-STALIN PACT is the most sensational news to come out of Moscow in many years. Up to yesterday, it was the general belief that Stalin was moving heaven and earth in an earnest attempt to establish a "peace front" of the "democracies" against the "fascist aggressors", especially against Fascist Germany. The friends and supporters of the Stalin régime said this repeatedly, and in so many plain words. Suddenly, right in the midst of the Anglo-French-Russian military discussions in Moscow, came the news that Hitler and Stalin had made a very important trade agreement. [Then] came the news that a "non-aggression" pact had been negotiated between the two countries. Forty-eight hours later, the Nazi Minister of Foreign Affairs and author of the Anti-Comintern Pact had flown to Moscow where he was greeted with swastika flags, and the pact was promptly signed.

The newspapers which reported that the pact had "staggered" and "stunned" and "stupefied" most of the world did not exaggerate in the least. Most bewildered and shocked of all were the members and sympathizers of the Communist Party, whom the news hit over the head like a metal-studded club. One organization, however, was not caught off guard and shocked by the news of the Stalinazi pact — the Socialist Workers Party, and the Fourth International with which it is affiliated, the so-called Trotskyist movement. This is simply a matter of fact and it is not stated in a boastful vein. Our movement foresaw the alliance and predicted it as early as a year ago. In the *Socialist Appeal* of October 8, 1938, Leon Trotsky wrote: "We may now expect with certainty Soviet diplomacy to attempt *rapprochement* with Hitler at the cost of new retreats and capitulations which in their turn can only bring nearer the collapse of the Stalinist oligarchy". In the same paper of March 17, 1939, the present writer said: "The democratic front on which all Stalinist policy hinged — the 'united front of the democracies against the fascist aggressors and warmongers' — Stalin has dropped overboard without a splash. In its place is something so 'new' that it must have had a stunning effect upon the Stalinist parrots all over the world. Stalin holds out the olive branch to the fascist powers, to Germany primarily".

They denounce as slanderers the Trotskyists, or anybody who even hinted a year, or a month or as little as two weeks ago that Stalin and Hitler would come to terms. "It is a great contribution to the cause of world peace", [US CP leader Earl] Browder says now. It helps the cause of democracy and the Democratic Front! It helps Poland! What happened directly after the Stalin-Hitler pact? Not only vast expansions of the armed forces of all governments, but mobilization of troops and marching

Abridged from *Socialist Appeal*, September 1939.

orders on a scale unknown since the World War broke out in 1914. The Moscow-Berlin pact is exactly the opposite of a contribution to the cause of peace.

In exchange for a Hitlerite promise not to attack the Soviet Union, Stalin has given Hitler a free hand in Poland! Poland has been ruthlessly sacrificed to the brutal imperialistic ambitions of Nazi Germany in the hope of saving the hides of the Kremlin autocrats.

There cannot be the slightest doubt on this score. Why was the pact signed just at this moment — just when Hitler has declared in the most insolent manner that he demands the absorption of Poland into Nazidom, just when France and England threatened to take armed action against Germany? A non-aggression pact between Germany and the Soviet Union has been in existence for 13 years, signed in 1926 by Foreign Minister Gustav Stresemann and Soviet Ambassador Nikolai Krestinsky. This pact is still formally in force. Why was it necessary to have *another* "non-aggression pact" at this particular time?

In order to deliver a *demonstrative blow* against Poland! In order to explode, as publicly, as sensationally, as thoroughly as possible, any Polish hope that a Hitlerite invasion would encounter not only the Polish army, but the joint armed resistance of England and France on the one side, and the Soviet Union on the other.

II: 12 September 1939

PUBLICLY, THE STALINIST PATRIOTS from Moscow to New York and back again have shouted for a united military front of England, France and the Soviet Union *against* Germany and the Axis. Not *with* Germany, we repeat, but *against* her. They insisted that it was more than ever urgent, following the tragic Czechoslovakian experience, in order to save Poland.

Now we Trotskyists, like revolutionary socialists everywhere, never agreed with the chauvinistic campaign of the Stalinists for the "defense of Poor Little Poland". *Their* agitation meant, in reality, the commission of two crimes: the recruiting of cannon-fodder for one gang of imperialist bandits (the slave-holding "democracies" of England and France) as against another, and the meek submission of the Polish workers, peasants and national minorities to the rule of the reactionary Polish autocracy. The primary and principal task of the Polish masses was and remains the overturn of the clique of Generals and Colonels who rule the land, who club down the workers, squeeze the peasants to the bone, keep the Ukrainian and other national minorities in an inferno of persecution and discrimination, and practise a vicious anti-Semitism which is second only to Hitler's.

Yet, while we did not join in the Stalinist cattle-herding for war, we were not and are not indifferent to the fate of the Polish people or even of the Polish nation — and we mean the *Polish* nation, not the Polish *Empire* in which the old and upstart Polish aristocracy rules by military force over millions of people of other nationalities. The hope for aid which the Polish masses threatened by Nazi subjection could rightfully and not vainly place in a revolutionary workers' government, if that existed in Russia today, was betrayed by the perfidious Bonapartist gang in the Kremlin when it capitulated to Hitler.

Stalin capitulated to Hitler? Exactly! And that brings us to the question of *why* Stalin felt obliged to sign the shameful pact. The Stalin régime enjoys only the bitter hatred of the Soviet masses. Its basis continues to narrow every day. And the capitalist world, largely thanks to Stalinism's criminal policies, is far more sure of itself as it faces the working class in 1939 than it was in 1919. Scratch beneath the surface of the optimistic fairy tales told in the Stalinist press and you find that, under Stalin's rule, the Soviet Union is in an advanced state of degeneration. Stalin's clique is at once the product and the producer of this degeneration.

Now we are in a position to deal with the question: Which of the two partners in the Stalinazi pact was the stronger, which is in the better position to gain from the pact? It is a bitter truth for us to observe, but we must not refuse to see that in the past six years Hitler has not only consolidated but has vastly expanded his power. He took power in Germany without meeting with the slightest resistance by the Social Democrats or the Stalinists (1933 marked Stalin's *first* capitulation to Hitler!) He denounced the Versailles Treaty limitations on German armaments in 1935, and nobody stopped him. He reintroduced conscription without opposition. He remilitarized the Rhineland and nobody stopped him. He won the Saar territory in a plebiscite. He succeeded in smashing to bits the whole labor and revolutionary movement. In March 1938 he annexed Austria without firing a shot. Six months later, Czechoslovakia was raked in. Another six months passed, and he took Memel, without a fight. He won his fight in Spain. By the time this appears, he may have Danzig [Gdansk] and the Corridor, if not all of Poland.

Against this indubitable strengthening of the Nazi régime, Stalin has only defeats to record. He lost the German and Czechoslovakian Communist Parties — each with hundreds of thousands of members — in two Hitlerite blows. The Polish Communist Party he himself suppressed while he wooed the Polish Colonels. Ethiopia, despite Litvinov's tearful pleas to the League of Nations, fell to Mussolini, whose airplanes flew with Russian oil and whose soldiers fed on Russian wheat. His whole policy in Spain cracked up. Czechoslovakia, ditto. His policy in the Orient lost him the Chinese Eastern Railway and is ending with "ally" Chiang Kai-shek driven further and further into the interior. His big "Popular Front" in France breathed its last when it produced Daladier and Bonnet, voted into office by the Communist Party. All of Stalin's foreign policies have proved bankrupt; all his foreign enterprises have suffered shipwreck.

At home, his position is no better. The last six years in particular have seen Stalin's rule in a state of almost uninterrupted crisis, each convulsion more violent than the one before it. The overwhelming majority of the people — the simple people, the small people, the toiling people — hate Stalin as bitterly as Czar Nicholas the Bloody was hated, and with just as good reason. How else explain the continual purges, the imprisonments, the exilings, the executions, the endless mass terror? What truly popular government has ever had to resort to anything like it outside a period of civil war? And that's exactly what Stalin is engaged in: a civil war of the bureaucratic caste against the masses of the people.

Stalin has wiped out the whole Old Guard of the Russian Revolution, except Trotsky who has been sought by more than one GPU assassin's bullet. The prisons, the God-forsaken corners of exile, the vast concentration camps are chock-full of Stalin's victims. There are more political prisoners in some provinces of the country today than there were in the whole empire under the Czar. All the liberties won by labor's blood and rifle in the revolution have been abolished by the bureaucracy. The worker is tied to his job and cannot shift to another job or another city without being granted permission, duly recorded in the internal passport he is compelled to carry. The disparity between the wages of the low-paid worker and the salaries of the upper crust is stupendous and on the rise. So is the disparity between the income and conditions of the poor peasants and the bosses of the "collective" farms. Science, art, and culture are prostituted to the power-interests of the narrowminded gang in power. Conditions in the non-Russian national republics — Ukrainian, Georgian, White Russian, Uzbekistan, *etc.* — are a replica of the relations that existed between the Czarist imperial Russians in Moscow and the national minorities at the periphery of the empire. The secret police (GPU) and the army machine keep Stalin in power with the aid of jail-keys, pistols and bayonets.

Stalin rules and can only rule by means of terror. As the country moves closer to the monstrosity which he misnames "socialism" the purges and the terror increase in intensity. Everywhere about him, Stalin sees plots and conspiracies, real and alleged, against his domination. The reign of terror during which millions, literally millions, have either been deported, imprisoned or murdered, is Stalin's own confession to immense unpopularity. The rule by terror means that Stalin and the bureaucracy he personifies, are themselves terrified. What do they fear? War! The fear of war, in this case as in so many others, is the fear of mobilization. The fear of mobilization is the fear of arming the masses of people. The fear of arming the masses is *the fear of revolution*.

The reasons behind the Stalinazi pact cannot be fully understood, however, unless the reader grasps the fundamental standpoint of the Kremlin régime, and grasps, further, the fact that it is in irreconcilable opposition to the fundamental standpoint of the original Lenin-Trotsky régime which Stalin and Co. finally succeeded in overthrowing in the course of a running fight that began as early as 1923.

Lenin, Trotsky and the real Bolshevik party led the masses to victory in 1917 on the basis of the proposition that the Russian Revolution was only one part of an *international* working-class revolution. The Bolshevik leaders repeated a thousand times to the Russian and world masses that Red Russia could not establish socialism by itself, with its own forces, and unaided by the triumphant workers of other, more advanced countries. This was not only in conformity with Marxian theory, but with modern world realities. Russia might hold out for a time, and even lay the foundations of socialism, but it could not keep going for a long period of time without help from revolutionary states in the other lands. As for achieving a classless socialist society, with security and plenty for all, that was out of the question entirely if revolutionary Russia remained isolated in a capitalist world.

In 1924, however, when the European revolutionary wave subsided for a while, Stalin coined the theory of "socialism in a single country". Russia, he argued, *could* establish socialism by itself *provided only* there was no armed intervention from abroad.

Now this theory, while totally unsuited to the interests of the Russian and international revolutions, was ideally suited to the interests of the growing Soviet bureaucracy. The officials — corrupted oldsters and upstart youngsters — had lost all faith in the power of the world working class to free itself from capitalist misrule — at least not for another hundred years! Meanwhile, they argued, let's hold on to what we have in Russia.

That sounded plausible to many people, especially those who had grown weary and discouraged and didn't see that new and stormier waves of revolution would break throughout the world in the years to come. Only, the officials really meant: Let's hold on to what *we* have in Russia — and to what *we* can get. As for the rest of the world, the task of the working class is confined primarily (later it became exclusively) to preventing foreign intervention. In other words, instead of concentrating on getting rid of their own capitalist despots at home, the workers in other countries were to be limited to acting as border patrols for the Soviet bureaucracy.

Leaving aside for the moment the theoretical aspects of the question, the practical results of this policy were disastrous both for the official Communist International and that section of the labor movement that followed it, *and for the Soviet Union itself.* All that a labor skate or capitalist political shyster had to do to get the unqualified support of the Communist movement for some shady enterprise or a downright sell-out, was to take a cheap oath in favor of "defending" the Soviet Union. As Stalinism went from bad to worse, and the Kremlin went in for superclever diplomatic tie-ups with imperialist Powers, the official Communist International, from which every critical, honest revolutionist was expelled, was changed from a militant fighter against world capitalism into an anti-revolutionary instrument, a cheap pawn in the hands of Stalin's Foreign Office.

III: 19 September 1939

IN LENIN'S TIME, THE SOVIET GOVERNMENT made more than one diplomatic or commercial agreement with capitalist countries. That was unavoidable then, and remains unavoidable so long as a workers' government is surrounded by a hostile world. But if Lenin made a diplomatic agreement with Germany or France, he did not compel the revolutionary movement in those countries to stop fighting its own capitalist class and government.

Stalin changed all that. While he was seeking an alliance with England, France and the United States, especially in the past four years, the Communist Parties in those countries tried with might and main to make an alliance with the home capitalist government and urged the labor movement as a whole to follow suit. Where the Communist Parties had once been the champions of labor's independence and militancy, Stalin converted them into the champions of labor's subordination and docility to capitalism. In practise, therefore, especially in recent years, "socialism in one country" meant that Stalin traded off Communist Party support to any government, no matter how reactionary, no matter how many millions of colonial slaves it oppressed, so long as it promised to be an "ally" in protecting the Soviet bureaucracy.

In practise, also, Stalin's Russian nationalism meant putting the fate of the Russian Revolution into the hands of cynical imperialist diplomats who pretended for a moment to be friendly, instead of where it belongs — into the hands of the Russian and international working class. In practise, this working class was confused, demoralized, and driven under the yoke of its enemies. Thus, the interests of the ruling bureaucracy in Russia have come into ever sharper and finally irreconcilable conflict with the interests of the Russian masses, of the Soviet Union itself, and of the international working class.

Stalin fears war. But he fears especially such a war as the Soviet Union and its bureaucracy are involved in, for that would in all likelihood spell his doom. It would, however, be wrong to jump to the conclusion that Stalin is a real prop of peace. The same reasons that dictate his yearning for peace for Russia, *dictate a policy of war-mongering in all the other important countries of the world!*

The Soviet Union is immediately and directly threatened on two sides: by Japan on the East and by Germany on the West. The principal Soviet enemy [is] Hitler. It has therefore been Stalin's policy at bottom, since the Nazis came to power in 1933, to "appease" Hitler, to come to terms with him, to make an alliance with him. Russia would then be in a position to deal comparatively easily with Japan in the East.

If this basic point is borne in mind, much that was obscure in Stalinist policy becomes clear. It will be easier, for example, to understand why the Stalinist press in France, instead of solidarizing itself with the despairing young Jew, Herschel Grynzspan, who sought to protest Hitlerite anti-Semitism by shooting Von Rath, denounced him as a Nazi or Trotskyist spy! To understand the shameful silence from Soviet officialdom on the occasion of Hitler's barbarous pogroms against the Jews. To understand why Jewish refugees could find no haven in the Soviet Union. To understand what Walter Duranty meant when he cabled the *New York Times* that after all Stalin has killed off as many Jews as Hitler did. To understand why Litvinov was purged (how could a sensitive "Aryan" like von Ribbentrop shake hands with a Jewish Foreign Commissar?). The concentration on making a deal with Hitler has frequently been interrupted, so to say, for two reasons: one, by the hope of making an alliance with the "democracies" to squeeze Hitler into a corner and prevent him from assaulting Russia; and two, by the hope that the negotiations with the "democracies" would frighten Hitler into speeding up an agreement with Stalin.

The first hope, illusory and utopian from the beginning, was completely shattered at Munich. The "democratic" imperialists showed that they would much rather give Hitler free rein in his drive to the East, that is, against Russia, than they would make an alliance with Russia to smash Hitler and Mussolini. Especially when they reflected that *after* fascism cracked up in Germany and Italy, revolutions would break out and spread rapidly to France, England and God knows where else! Stalin therefore had to come to terms with Hitler. And Hitler chose the moment for springing the announcement of the pact which would give him the best position in starting his next conquest, Poland.

But though he capitulated to Hitler, it does not follow that Stalin would object violently to having another World War explode, with the "democracies" fighting the "fascist aggressors" and the Soviet Union staying out of the war as long as possible. Quite the contrary! Stalin continues to drive in just that direction. Although he has made his peace with Hitler for a short time, as we shall see later on, he continues to instigate a war in which he will not participate. While he is a "pacifist-out-of-fear" at home, he is a warmonger abroad.

Keep ourselves in the saddle, preserve ourselves by hook or crook, and everything else — the labor movement, the Communist International, the colonial peoples, the twaddle about "democracy" and "peace" — can go hang!

Will the bureaucracy succeed in keeping itself in the Soviet saddle? Not the slightest hesitation need be felt in replying categorically: *no!* The only point to be resolved is this: the abominable Stalinist clique will be crushed at a later stage by Hitlerism, in which case, a new era of reaction will open up from which the world may not emerge for a long, long time; or it will be swept into the discard by a resurrected revolutionary movement of workers and peasants inside the Soviet Union itself. All our hopes and all our energies must be directed toward the latter solution of the mortal crisis the Russian Revolution is experiencing.

Will Hitler really attack the Soviet Union? Whoever examines the situation intelligently must reply, Yes! The feeble Stalinist arguments that the "pact has weakened the Axis" are so much nonsense, and dangerous nonsense at that.

What Stalin gave away in the pact we have already seen. What did Hitler abandon? His designs upon Russia, especially on the granary of the Ukraine and the mineral riches of the Urals? Not for a moment! His idea of immediately attacking the Soviet Union? He didn't have to give up that idea, for the simple reason that he did not contemplate such an attack *at this time*. His objective, for the time being, is more modest — the conquest of Poland — and Stalin gave him invaluable aid in achieving his goal.

He *did* abandon Japan, of that there is no doubt. And the Stalinist press presents this as a tremendous victory. Hitler abandoned Japan *for the time being* and only for the time being, in exchange for a much solider ally. And he did abandon the so-called "Anti-Comintern Pact". Small consolation! The "fight against the Communist International" was as much a fraud with Hitler as the "fight for democracy" was with Stalin. *Hitler has known for years that Stalin himself liquidated the Communist International*. The Hitlerites know what Stalinism represents: they know where the real threat of working-class revolution comes from. It is not the discredited pawns of Stalinist diplomacy, the Communist International, that Fascism fears. As the banner-bearer of the working-class revolution, of the revolution for socialism, it sees the "Trotskyists" — the Fourth International. And it is right, for the Fourth International is the mortal, implacable foe of Fascism, of imperialism in general, of capitalist oppression, and as their foe it shall triumph! That is why the Socialist Workers Party summons every militant worker who is conscious of his class interests, who is imbued with the real spirit of internationalism, to rally to its great banner and to fight in the great cause. Our call is addressed in particular to the rank and file of the Communist Party and the Young Communist League and their sympathizers.

The Soviet Union is not relieved of the threat of attack; that threat is aggravated. Hitler had a non-aggression pact with Poland not so long ago. Stalin's policy facilitates the coming attack upon Russia because, by giving Hitler a free hand through Poland, he grants him a highly important strategical base of operations against the Soviet Union. Tomorrow or the next day, Hitler will seek to repay Stalin for the pact in even more ringing coin than he is repaying Poland. Every worker, every Communist worker, must understand that.

Every worker must be also clearly aware now of the monstrous crime that was perpetrated by Stalin in his series of "trials" and purges. How many thousands of revolutionists did he send to their deaths in the last few years on the charge of being "Trotskyist agents of Hitler"! We called the trials frame-ups, and now, by signing the pact with Hitler, Stalin draws the black pencil of emphasis under our charge. While he was framing up and assassinating all opponents, all critics — past, present or potential — with the accusation of "Hitlerite agents" he was busily engaged in becoming *the principal agent of Hitler!* The Moscow Trials, the horrible purges, the nightmare of terror — these were all part of the preparations for an alliance with Adolph Hitler and his bandits.

Together with Ribbentrop, Molotov and Stalin signed the death-warrant of the Communist Parties. Stalin long ago drained the revolutionary blood out of them. Now he is smashing them bodily. Their organizational disintegration is taking place at a terrific rate before our very eyes.

Where will those sincere and devoted workers go who are now abandoning the Communist Parties by the thousands in England, France and the United States?

We know where the bureaucrats will go. They will remain the paid lackeys and scribblers of the Kremlin despot, or they will become full-fledged servants of their own imperialist overlords.

But the Communist workers? Will they go over to capitalism? Will they become the dupes of that fantastic fraud known in capitalist society as "democracy"? Will they abandon the class struggle entirely, and become docile serfs of the rulers of industry and finance, willing cannon-fodder of the coming war?

The Stalinist party is through, and nobody will mourn at its burial. Nobody will try to defend the Stalinazi pact in a serious trade union, in a Jewish organization, or for that matter wherever intelligent workers are assembled. What then?

We say: there is a need, greater than ever today, to struggle against reaction, against the capitalist offensive, for socialism and freedom, for peace and plenty. There is a road to struggle, too. That road was broadly marked out by the great teachers of the working-class movement, Marx and Lenin. That road the workers must take if they are to survive as human beings, if they are to rise to new heights of human dignity.

That road is the revolutionary struggle for socialism!

All the professional "democrats" and the "social democrats" and the "liberal intellectuals" who only yesterday approved the Moscow frame-ups or covered them up, and who presented Stalin as a noble, worthy ally of the

Great Democracies, are turning tail now and scurrying off like rats. Now they no longer declare that "Soviet democracy" and bourgeois democracy are practically the same thing and make natural allies; now they expound the new wisdom that "communism" and "fascism" are the same thing and make natural allies.

Their conclusion? Their road? On to a new War to Make the World Safe for Democracy? On to the trenches! Long live the divine goal of modern humanity — the battlefield graveyard!

Our road was never theirs. Our road leads to the great socialist society. Our methods are the methods of militant and uncompromising class struggle against all exploitation and iniquity. Stalin has succeeded only in — discrediting Stalinism. The banner of revolutionary struggle, of the Fourth International, continues to fly without a shameful spot upon it.

On to the victory of socialism and freedom!

Editor's note The SWP Political Committee minutes of September 3, 1939, record: "Reading by Cannon of two quotations from the article by Shachtman in the September 4th issue of the Appeal, which is article designed for publication as a pamphlet. Quotations as follows: 'In exchange for a Hitlerite promise not to attack the Soviet Union, Stalin has given Hitler a free hand in Poland! Poland has been ruthlessly sacrificed to the brutal imperialistic ambitions of Nazi Germany in the hope of saving the hides of the Kremlin autocrats'. 'Why was it necessary to have another "non-aggression pact" at this particular time? In order to deliver a demonstrative blow against Poland! In order to explode, as publicly, as sensationally, as thoroughly as possible, any Polish hope that a Hitlerite invasion would encounter not only the Polish army, but the joint armed resistance of England and France on the one side, and the Soviet Union on the other'. Motion by Cannon: That the printing of the pamphlet be held up until the material as a whole can be studied and approved by a subcommittee of the PC of which Comrade Shachtman will be a member. Carried, Carter abstaining".

Max Shachtman

THE SOVIET UNION AND THE WORLD WAR

THE OUTBREAK OF THE SECOND World War has once more put prominently at the top of the order of the day the "Russian question". The signing of the Hitler-Stalin Pact was followed by the joint invasion of Poland; by the reduction of Lithuania, Latvia and Estonia to the state of vassals of the Kremlin; by the invasion and seizure of part of Finland by the Red Army; and by speculation and prediction of coming events which, a year ago, would have been waved aside as preposterous.

In bourgeois-democratic circles, these events furnished the occasion for more pious homilies about the identity of communism and fascism. In the labor movement, the patriots skilfully exploited the workers' indignation against Stalin's crimes in order to promote the cause of the democratic warmongers. Among the revolutionary Marxists, however, the events provoked an intense and thoroughgoing discussion, resulting in a re-evaluation of the role of the Soviet Union in the war and in a revision of the traditional slogan of the Fourth International, "For the unconditional defense of the Soviet Union." It is with this discussion that the present article is concerned.

The views of the Fourth International on the question of defense of the Soviet Union in a war, put forward up to the time the present war broke out, may be summarized as follows:

The Soviet Union, existing on the basis of state property and dominated by a counter-revolutionary bureaucracy, is a degenerated workers' state which must be defended (by internationalist, class methods independent of those employed by the bureaucracy) in any war with a capitalist power, regardless of which side appeared to be the "aggressor" and regardless of the immediate cause of the war. This defense is "unconditional" in the sense that it is not conditioned on the abdication or overthrow of the Stalinist bureaucracy, or even upon its acceptance of a revolutionary policy. The Soviet Union must be defended in a war with a capitalist power not because of the Stalinists but in spite of them; must be defended, however, with our own independent policy which is aimed, among other things, to overthrow the bureaucracy because we have no faith in *its* ability to organize an effective defense of the Soviet Union. Should the Soviet Union, in a war against one or more capitalist powers, find itself in alliance with one or more other capitalist powers, the slogan of defensism retains its full validity, just as the slogan of defeatism retains its validity both in the countries Russia is allied with and at war with; the only difference in policy in the two capitalist countries would be tactical and practical (for example, we would not oppose the shipment of munitions to Russia from the factories and ports of one of its capitalist allies).

Why is it necessary to revise this point of view, it is asked, above all now, when the war has actually broken out? Is it because Stalin has allied him-

From *New International,* April 1940.

self with a fascist imperialism instead of with a "democratic" imperialism? Can Marxists allow themselves to make a fundamental distinction between the two? And if such a distinction is made with respect to alliances with the Soviet Union, does it not imply a patriotic position toward the "democracies" with respect to their war with Germany? What, in a word, has changed so fundamentally as to justify a change in our position on the defense of the Soviet Union?

The change which the Marxists must make in their position has nothing whatsoever to do with all the petty-bourgeois lamentations over Stalin's shift from "democrats" to fascists. While allied with France, Stalin was already allied, at least indirectly, with a number of totalitarian régimes and military dictatorships in the orbit of French imperialism. The alliance of the notorious butcher Chiang Kai-shek with the equally notorious butcher Stalin does not eliminate the duty which every revolutionist has to defend China from Japan. The change in position is dictated by far more profound and real considerations.

The discussion of the role of Russia in the war during the period of the Franco-Soviet Pact was based on hypotheses and prediction. Reference to the policy proposed by Lenin in 1917 for an "alliance" with France and England against Germany was invalid, and in any case not decisive, among other reasons because the "alliance" never seriously materialized. It was therefore false to generalize from this experience which was never experienced. The discussion of the role of Russia in the war during the Hitler-Stalin Pact is based upon tangible realities. These realities make it as mandatory upon us to reconsider our slogan of "unconditional defense of the Soviet Union" as the realities of the March, 1917, Revolution in Russia made it mandatory upon Lenin to reconsider the traditional and, up to that point, intransigently defended Bolshevik slogan of a "democratic dictatorship of the proletariat and peasantry."

The 1935 Pact with France was a defensive alliance for the Soviet Union. It was directed against a rising and truculent German imperialism but it was calculated essentially to maintain the status quo, to keep Germany from precipitating war. The status quo policy of People's Frontism was adopted by the Comintern in accordance with this objective.

Stalinist capitulation to Hitler in 1939 took the form of an *aggressive military alliance*. This is precisely what was *not* foreseen or allowed for by us in the past, as Trotsky himself acknowledged at the beginning of the war. In general, it is true, the possibility of a rapprochement between Hitler and Stalin had been envisaged in our literature, but not an aggressive military alliance. The difference between the two pacts does not lie in the fact that one was made with such an illustrious democrat as Pierre Laval and the other with an undemocratic fascist. It lies in the real difference between the two imperialisms, French and German. This difference is in no wise of such a fundamental character as to warrant supporting one against the other, in the manner of the war-mongering social-democrats. But it is sufficiently important to change the character of the alliance made by Stalin. In the past, too, it was sufficiently important for us to distinguish between Hitler and Laval, not fundamentally, not so far as their social role is concerned, but to the extent of characterizing Hitler and not Laval as the "super-Wrangel", that is, the spearhead of world imperialist assault upon the

Soviet Union. This difference was not based upon a feeling of tenderness on the part of Laval for Russia, but upon the fact that German imperialism, for a series of historical reasons, was dynamically aggressive and forced, in the most immediate and direct sense, as Hitler himself has said, to "expand or die" (just as England, for example, is forced to hold on to her empire or die).

The role of the Soviet Union can be followed and understood only if one is clear about the *predominant character of the war*. It is not a war of imperialist attack upon the Soviet Union; it is not a "mixed war". It is a war between two big imperialist camps for the redivision of the world, with the Soviet Union as an integral part of one of the imperialist camps.

The strategy of the imperialist camp to which Stalin is subordinated is fairly clear. It is to keep all sides of Germany protected by herself and her allies, to confine the front to the comparative safety of the Westwall-Maginot lines; to destroy the British Empire for the benefit of the Rome-Berlin-Moscow axis, primarily for the Berlin section of it. Stalin's role in the war, from the very beginning, has been that of auxiliary executant of this strategy.

Hitler did not descend upon Poland until he had assured himself not of Stalin's neutrality but of Stalin's active support. Poland was defeated and partitioned jointly and by pre-arrangement with Hitler, in accordance with the real relationship of forces between the partners, getting the lion's share and Stalin the jackal's. The work of covering Hitler's eastern flank from possible attack by the Allies or their vassals, was then completed by Stalin's invasion and subjugation of Latvia, Lithuania and Estonia. Far from meeting resistance from Hitler, Stalin was encouraged to proceed along the indicated line in order that Germany might have at its Baltic rear governments no longer subject to the manipulations of Anglo-French imperialism but sterilized governments kept in escrow for him by his friendly sub-partner of the Kremlin.

Of the same order and in accordance with the same imperialist strategy was Stalin's invasion of Finland, presented to us so cynically by the Stalinist press as a "defense of the Soviet Union from imperialist attack" and characterized so naively by the *Socialist Appeal* in the same terms. Whoever did not understand the real meaning of the Finnish invasion at the time, should surely understand it in the light of subsequent events. The middle-class journalistic muttonheads who still talk about Hitler being Stalin's captive in the pact, sought to present the invasion of Finland as a "blow at Germany". The truth is just the opposite. Hitler wanted Stalin to invade Finland and Trotsky is without doubt right in saying that Berlin "obviously pushed" Stalin toward Helsinki. Why? For two reasons which are really one. In the first place, the action involves Stalin more deeply in the war on Hitler's side. In the second place, the occupation or subjection of Finland was needed by Germany as the first step toward closing to the Allies a northern front they were seeking to open against Hitler. Only after Stalin had crushed Finland and enormously weakened Sweden, did Hitler feel able to take those brutal and decisive measures which are calculated to guarantee his northern flank. Denmark and Norway fell to German instead of to Anglo-French imperialism only because Finland fell to Germany's partner. It goes without saying that if Hitler consolidates himself in Norway (as he appears to be doing at this writing), the fate of Sweden, hemmed in between Hitler and Stalin, is a foregone conclusion.

Thus, in two big moves, Hitler, with the Soviet Union at his orders, has succeeded in doing what the Kaiser and Hindenburg were unable to do in the first World War: to confine the conflict to a momentarily "defensive" war of position on a single well protected front, the West. With Stalin's aid, Hitler has fairly well assured his eastern, northeastern and northern flanks. With Stalin's aid — today in the form of a threat, tomorrow in the form of active military intervention — he is assuring his southeastern flank, in the first place in Romania. The day after, it is not at all excluded that Germany, Italy and the Soviet Union will be fighting jointly for the "defense of the Soviet Union" in the southeast and the Near East — in actuality, for the partitioning of the Balkans and the Near East among the members of the Rome-Berlin-Moscow axis. What the Moscow *Izvestia* said about Hitler's invasion of Norway, really holds true here: War has a powerful logic of its own.

Alongside of this parallelism of military action, there is a corresponding parallelism of political agitation. Moscow echoes every claim of Berlin, every diplomatic lie, every self-justification. The same "war-guilt" explanation is given by both. The diplomatic offensives which precede military action are carefully synchronized in both capitals. The Stalinist parties, it goes without saying, do their part loyally for the Axis, concentrating all their attacks upon England and France, to the exclusion of Germany. In the colonies Hitlerite and Stalinist agents, whether by formal agreement or by the internal logic of their war alliance, conduct a harmonious campaign for the "liberation" of the oppressed peoples from Anglo-French imperialism (that is, for subjecting them to the yoke of the Axis). This is what the participation of the Soviet Union in the war looks like in reality. Under these conditions the slogan of "unconditional defense of the Soviet Union" is tantamount to giving objective political aid to one imperialist camp against another. It is therefore imperative that the slogan be radically altered to read "defense of the Soviet Union in a progressive war".

Wherein is Russia's participation in the war reactionary? In two respects (1) it is acting primarily as agent of German imperialism in the war; (2) it is itself fighting a war of bureaucratic expansion, of subjugation and oppression of other peoples. From these follow the reactionary social and political consequences of its participation in the war: instead of the class consciousness of the workers being heightened, their bourgeois-patriotic feelings are intensified; instead of being brought closer to the revolution, they are driven into the arms of their own ruling class, and not the most liberal sections of it, at that (Poland, Finland); instead of becoming more sympathetic toward the principles and achievements and defense of the Russian Revolution, they become more antipathetic toward them; instead of advancing the interests of the world revolution and weakening world imperialism, the participation of the Soviet Union in the present war retards enormously the former and strengthens enormously the latter.

The two respects in which Russia's war is reactionary are not contradictory or mutually exclusive. In the partnership of the Pact, Stalin is very much the subordinate; it is indeed quite accurate to say that the Stalinist bureaucracy capitulated to Germany in the hope (a) of buying itself off from an immediate attack by Hitler upon the Soviet Union and (b) of escaping complete involvement in the world war. The first hope has been realized, of that there is no doubt. But it has been realized precisely at the expense of the second hope. The very conservatism, the provincial pacifism, the timidity and national-narrowness that have characterized the Stalinist bureaucracy, are precisely the forces that drag it deeper into the war as a tool of one of the imperialist powers. It is no mere literary paradox but a political fact of primary importance that the very fear of war which has dominated the course of the Stalinist bureaucracy has led it progressively further into war. Not less important is the fact that while serving as an agent of a big imperialist power, the Kremlin bureaucracy pursues an imperialist (expansionist) policy of its own.

The programmatic documents of the Fourth International, in all its prehistory and since its foundation, have never taken into account the possibility of a war of expansion by the Kremlin. Quite the contrary. Our analysis of the Stalinist bureaucracy emphasized its national conservatism, its characteristic of staying-at-home-at-all-costs epitomized in Stalin's famous phrase about not fighting for an inch of foreign soil and not yielding an inch of Soviet soil. Throughout our political history, one can find only one or two purely incidental remarks about the possibility of the Kremlin seizing new territory; in our programmatic documents, one cannot, we repeat find any whatsoever. This explains, at least in part, the silence, confusion and equivocation that characterized the press of the Fourth International throughout the initial period of Russia's invasion of other countries. We had not been prepared for such a development. But there is no reason why such a state of affairs should be perpetuated in the revolutionary Marxian movement.

Is the imperialist policy of the Kremlin of the same nature as the imperialism of Germany, Japan, France, England and America? No, for it has different origins, different bases, different paths of development. Is it based upon the dominance in economy of finance capital, the export of capital and other characteristics of modern imperialism, we have been asked with misplaced sarcasm? No, it is an imperialism peculiar to the Stalinist bureaucracy in its present stage of degeneration.

The opposition to our characterization of Stalinist imperialism (it is not at all "red imperialism" as the social-democrats would say; there is nothing red about it), is based in large measure on a mis-reading or misunderstanding of Lenin's conceptions of imperialism. *Modern* imperialism is characteristic of the last stage of capitalism, of capitalism in decay. But Lenin did not and could not say that imperialism, imperialist policy and imperialist war are possible only under decaying capitalism. Thus, of prewar Czarist Russia, Lenin declared that "the prevailing type of Russian imperialism is military and feudal", in distinction from the modern capitalist imperialism of England and Germany which he described so fully in his study, *Imperialism*. Thus, and even more pertinently to the present discussion, he insisted on a precise formulation of the question in his article "On the Revision of the Party Program" written in 1917 not as a casual piece of journalism but as a fundamental and critical programmatic document:

"Crises, precisely in the form of over-production or of the 'stocking up of market commodities' (if comrade S. prohibits the word overproduction), are a phenomenon which is exclusively proper to capitalism. Wars however,

are proper both to the economic system based on slavery and on feudalism
There have been imperialist wars on the basis of slavery (Rome's war
against Carthage was an imperialist war on both sides) as well as in the
Middle Ages and in the epoch of mercantile capitalism. Every war in which
both belligerent camps are fighting to oppress foreign countries or peoples
and for the division of the booty, that is, over 'who shall oppress more and
who shall plunder more' must be called imperialistic. When we say that
only modern capitalism, that only imperialism brought with it imperialist
wars, that is correct, for the preceding *stage of capitalism, the stage of free*
competition or the stage of pre-monopolist capitalism was predominantly
characterized by national *wars in Western Europe. But if it is said that in*
the preceding stage there were no imperialist wars in general, that would
be false, that would mean that the equally *imperialist 'colonial wars' have*
been forgotten." (Collected Works, German ed., Vol. XXI, pp. 387f.)

"Every war in which both belligerent camps are fighting to oppress foreign countries or peoples and for the division of the booty . . . must be
called imperialist," wrote Lenin. Does not the joint invasion of Poland by
Hitler and Stalin fall precisely into that category? Does not the joint invasion of Scandinavia (of Finland by Stalin and immediately thereafter of
Denmark and Norway by Hitler) also fall into the same category? The
Poles are brought under full enslavement by Hitler; the White Russians
and Ukrainians, according to Trotsky, under "semi-enslavement" by
Stalin. It may be argued, and it is, that in Eastern Poland Stalin carried
through the nationalization of property and in Finland he acquired military bases which are valuable to the defense of the Soviet Union from
imperialist attack, and that from the standpoint of the international
working class these measures are progressive. On October 18, 1939,
Trotsky wrote that "the economic transformations in the occupied territories do not compensate for this by even a tenth part!" — meaning by "this"
the antagonizing of the world proletariat and oppressed peoples. Even if
we granted for the moment the above argument, we would reply, paraphrasing Trotsky: "The nationalization of property in Eastern Poland and
the acquisition of military bases in Finland do not compensate by even a
tenth part for the enormous strengthening of one of the imperialist camps,
for the demoralization of the world working class, for the subjugation of
millions upon millions of Ukrainians, White Russians, Lithuanians,
Karelians and Finns to the Kremlin yoke."

Space does not permit a complete elaboration of the question of Stalinist
imperialism, which must be reserved for another article. Let us conclude
here by touching on a few brief supplementary points:

1. What is the nature of Stalinist oppression in the Soviet Ukraine? In
that country, the Fourth International has *added to* the general, "All-
Soviet Union" slogan of a political revolution against the bureaucracy, the
special slogan of the independence of the Ukraine. We not only insist on
the Ukraine's *right* to separation from the Union, but we *advocate* its separation. This position, especially applied to the Ukraine, has meaning
only on the condition that the Ukraine suffers under *national* oppression.
And what is the nature of this national oppression? We characterize it as
a type of imperialist oppression peculiar to the Stalinist bureaucracy.

2. In the "USSR in War" (Sept. 25, 1939), Trotsky wrote: "We do not
entrust the Kremlin with any historical mission. We were and remain

against seizures of new territories by the Kremlin." It would be more accurate to say, "We *are* against seizures of new territories by the Kremlin," for the simple reason that the question of Stalin seizing new territories was never raised in our movement for either an affirmative or negative reply. That is, we never envisaged the possibility of a war of bureaucratic expansion. Now that we see both the possibility and reality of such a war, we declare our opposition to it. Why? We did not oppose "seizures of new territories" under Lenin (Georgia, 1920). We oppose them now because the Stalinist war of expansion, which we are today compelled to see as a reality, is reactionary, because, as Trotsky rightly says, we do not entrust the bureaucracy with any historical mission, and because we oppose the national oppression of new millions under the imperialist yoke of the Kremlin.

3. The Stalinist bureaucracy, we were told in the party discussion, is not imperialist, but an agent of imperialism. But that is true, in a sense, also of the imperialistically-corrupted labor aristocracy of the great capitalist powers. This aristocracy profited directly from the imperialist advancement of the bourgeoisie, although at the expense of the broad masses of the toilers. It is quite accurate to describe it as an imperialist labor aristocracy. The Stalinist machine is a labor aristocracy raised to the nth degree, to a new and unheard-of power. Naturally, its ambitions, hopes, appetites are limited, not merely by the economic base on which it rests, but above all by its subordinate position in world politics and economics. This "agent of imperialism" has its own imperialist aims and ambitions. These aims do not have, let us repeat, the same roots as British imperialism, but they exist. The Stalinist bureaucracy is not averse to acquiring oil wells in the Western Ukraine, copper and nickel mines in Finland, stocks of goods however modest, skilled and semi-skilled workers in occupied territories, and — far from least important — a wider basis for the extension of its bureaucratic power (at least a million hard-boiled Stalinist bureaucrats will be placed in power in the occupied East-Polish territories, inhabited by some 13,000,000 people).

The other arguments of the proponents of the traditional policy, are contradictory and untenable. "We condemn the invasion but we remain for the defense of the Soviet Union," that is, for the victory of the Red Army, they say in connection with Poland or Finland. They condemn the invasion, but support the invaders! They are against seizures of new territories by the Kremlin, but support those who are fighting to seize them! They are against the invasion *before* it takes place; they are against it *after* it has succeeded (once Stalin is triumphant, they will raise the slogan of an independent Soviet Finland); but they are *for* the invasion (for the victory of the Red Army) *while* it is taking place.

The attempt to draw an analogy with a conservative trade union on strike misses fire completely. We do not *condemn* any strike, even if conducted bureaucratically by a reactionary leadership; we may criticize the methods, the timing, etc., of a strike. We do not oppose the "seizure of new territories" (the organizing of the unorganized) even by a reactionary union; on the contrary, we condemn the bureaucrats for not "seizing enough territory" (for not organizing more and more of the unorganized). "It is not a question of 'little Finland'," we are told, "since Finland is only an episode in the Second World War. This war will inevitably turn into a war of imperialist attack upon the Soviet Union, aimed at reducing it to a colony of world imperialism." Essentially the same objection, made in reverse, was put forth by ultra-leftists against our policy in Spain. On Sept. 14, 1937, Trotsky replied to the argument about the "episode" as follows:

"It can be objected that the two imperialist camps (Italy and Germany on one side and England, France and the USSR on the other) conduct their struggle on the Iberian peninsula and that the war in Spain is only an "episode" of this struggle. In the sense of a historical possibility, it is true. But it is impermissible to identify a historical possibility with the actual concrete course of the civil war today. The intervention of the imperialist countries has indisputably great influence upon the development of the events in Spain. But until today it has not changed the fundamental character of these events as of a struggle between the camp of the Spanish bourgeois democracy and the camp of Spanish fascism." (Internal Bulletin, Oct. 1937, p. 3)

What is called an "episode" today is indeed an integral episode of the development of the second imperialist World War, in which the Soviet Union is fighting *primarily* the battle of German imperialism. The present war may be transformed, at a later stage, into an imperialist war against the Soviet Union, in which case it will be the duty of the international working class to defend the Soviet Union even under Stalin. But it is absurd to apply to the war today the policy applicable to the war into which it may be transformed.

"Only a sophist (wrote Lenin) could wipe out the difference between an imperialist war and the national war on the grounds that the one can be transformed into the other. The dialectic has not seldom served, even in the history of Greek philosophy, as a bridge to sophistry. We, however, remain dialecticians who struggle against the sophists, not through a denial of every transformation, but rather by means of a concrete analysis of the given instance, as much in its momentary situation as also in its development." (Gegen den Strom, p. 417.)

A concrete analysis of the given instance shows — it is imperative to repeat this time and again — that the Soviet Union under Stalin is participating in the present war as an integral part of one of the two imperialist camps. To defend the Soviet Union in *this* war, i.e., to be "the best soldier in the Red Army," to fight for its victory wherever it marches, means, objectively to work for the victory of one imperialist camp against the other.

"It is not Stalin we are defending, but the remaining conquest of October — nationalized property." In the *present* war, the nationalized property of the Soviet Union is not what is primarily involved. What is at stake is the world dominance of Anglo-French imperialism on the one side, and the imperialist ambitions of German imperialism and the concern for "power, prestige and revenues" of the Stalinist bureaucracy on the other. In a war between Daladier and De la Rocque the fascist, bourgeois democracy would be at stake; the trade union bureaucrats supporting the democratic side would be participating, whatever their motives or methods, in a progressive war against fascism. In a war between Daladier and Hitler, bourgeois democracy would not be at stake but rather the respective imperialist interests of France and Germany; the trade union bureaucrats supporting Daladier on the basis of desiring to defend the French trade unions from Hitlerism, would be participating — again regardless of motives and methods — in a reactionary, imperialist war.

The corollary argument that Stalin did, after all, nationalize property in the occupied territories is no more valid for the thesis of support of the Red Army. In the first place, property relations remain intact in Latvia, Lithuania and Estonia, so that the Soviet Union is in the unique position of commanding three capitalist colonies, or rather semi-colonies. In the second place, the fact that property was nationalized in Western Ukraine and Southern Finland only means that the proletariat in conquering those territories (as in the Soviet Union itself) would proceed from this new reality in its struggle to overthrow the Stalinist régime, that is, it would base itself upon statified property and give it a genuinely progressive, i.e., socialist significance. It does not have it in and by itself and under all circumstances. Arab or Irish nationalists might utilize, for their own purposes, material aid which German imperialism might give them for its own purposes; it would not follow that revolutionists must work for the victory of the German army. Finnish revolutionists will not only "accept" Stalin's nationalization but will extend and deepen and fructify it as they grow in power; but it does not follow that they should support the counter-revolutionary troops of Stalin. Capitalism itself, as Marxists have always pointed out, has found itself compelled time and again to take steps which had revolutionary consequences. *"Did not the fact that Guchkov and Shulgin* (Russian monarchists) *brought with them to Petrograd the abdication of Nicholas II play a revolutionary role,"* Trotsky once asked. *"Did it not arouse the most downtrodden, exhausted, and timid strata of the population?... Did not the entire activities of capitalism rouse the masses, did it not rescue them, to use the expression of the* Communist Manifesto, *from the idiocy of rural life? Did it not impel the proletarian battalions to the struggle? But does our historical evaluation of the objective role of capitalism as a whole or of certain actions of the bourgeoisie in particular, become a substitute for our active class revolutionary attitude toward capitalism or toward the actions of the bourgeoisie? Opportunist policies have always been based on this kind of non-dialectical, conservative, tail-endist 'objectivism'."* (*Third International After Lenin*, p. 175.)

The nationalization of property is not an abstraction and has no absolute merits in and of itself. "Its progressiveness is relative; its specific weight depends on the sum-total of all the other factors." (Trotsky.) In the present war, it must be considered in its social and political context. It must be considered in the light of the character of Russia's participation as an integral part of the imperialist war. The conception that since nationalized property is "progressive by its very nature" a régime based upon it must *automatically* be fighting a progressive war, has as much in common with Marxism as vulgar economic determinism has with historical materialism; the conception is, at bottom, nothing but a variety of immanent idealism.

To sum up briefly in conclusion: That "concrete analysis of the given instance" which Lenin demanded shows the imperative need of revising one of our traditional slogans. If, at a later stage, the present war between the imperialists should be transformed into an assault upon the Soviet Union, the slogan of defensism would have to be raised again, for it is not to the interests of the socialist world revolution and the working class to have one-sixth of the world, which the October uprising removed from the control of imperialism, restored to capitalist exploitation. In the present war, however, the world proletariat, the Russian included, cannot take upon itself a shadow of responsibility for the participation of the Stalinist bureaucracy in the imperialist conflict. The revolutionary vanguard must put forward the slogan of revolutionary defeatism in both imperialist camps, that is, the continuation of the revolutionary struggle for power regardless of the effects on the military front. That, and only that, is the central strategy of the third camp in the World War, the camp of proletarian internationalism, of the socialist revolution, of the struggle for the emancipation of all the oppressed.

Max Shactman

A NEW BANNER AND A NEW BEGINNING

OUR PARTY IS THE DIRECT PRODUCT OF THE SPLIT that took place in the Socialist Workers Party in 1940. Almost from the day of its birth, the Trotskyist movement in this country experienced recurring internal discussions and struggles not only over political and theoretical questions, but also over the question of bureaucratism. Underlying and clarifying these struggles was, at almost all times, a healthy reaction against the tendencies toward bureaucratism displayed with increasing obviousness by a section of the American Trotskyist leadership represented by Cannon and a little clique of permanent supporters and apologists.

It is not surprising that militants, young and old, who were attracted to the Trotskyist movement by its unrelenting struggle against Stalinist bureaucratism, or the old-style bureaucratism of the American trade union hierarchy, reacted vigorously against a diluted, or dressed-up, variety of bureaucratism in their own party. This reaction only gained in vigor, and in determination to fight, as it became clear that the clique in the leadership did not have sufficiently imposing political virtues to compensate for its bureaucratic rule. On the contrary, it was characterized — this is more so the case now — by its conservatism, political timidity or opportunism, adoration of internal maneuvers (both in the party and in the trade union movement), backwardness and in some cases outright indifference to Marxian theory, especially so far as its leader was concerned.

The outbreak of the Second World War took this leadership completely off guard and revealed its inability to deal with big and new events. It was at this point that its bureaucratic tendency showed positively disastrous results. The only party in the country committed to a program of consistent struggle against imperialist war found itself tongue-tied, because when the war finally broke out it did not take precisely the form that had been envisaged. The imperialist world did not launch an attack on Russia; Russia and Germany joined, instead, in an imperialist assault for the division of booty named Poland, and later on, of other countries of Eastern Europe.

In this situation, all the official leadership of the party could say, when it finally summoned up the ability to speak at all, was to repeat what was at best an utterly meaningless formula: "We are for the unconditional defense of the Soviet Union," and what was at worst a position of objective support to one of the two imperialist camps in the war.

Taken together, a majority of the membership of the party and the youth organization attached to it rebelled against this position, demanding first of all a broad, well organized and thoroughgoing discussion. To extract permission for such a discussion from the leadership was no small task in itself. Cannon even wrote that a discussion of the burning questions con-

From *Labor Action*, April 26, 1943, "Three years of the Workers Party and Labor Action. Join with us in the fight for socialism!".

259

nected with the war was a "luxury." The leadership pretended to act as if it directed a mass party of hundreds of thousands of members up to its hips in the trenches of a civil war, with little or no time for a democratic discussion — this in 1939, in the United States! In fact, the only three branches of the party which, to the very end, remained unanimously in favor of the official position (they were the only three that were unanimous, on either side of the dispute), never did have a debate on the contested questions throughout the internal fight.

Our group, then called the Minority, rejected the slogan of "unconditional defense" of Stalinist Russia in this war and raised instead the slogan of the victory of the Third Camp — not the camp of the imperialist Axis or the camp of the imperialist democracies (plus their more than one totalitarian ally!), but the independent camp of the working class of the world and the oppressed colonial peoples. We pointed out, and it has yet to be refuted, that it was impossible to do anything in the "defense of the Soviet Union" that did not mean aid and support of the imperialist camp of which it was an integral and subordinate part. It is not surprising that to this day, be it during the period of Stalin's alliance with German imperialism or of the alliance with Anglo-American imperialism, the Cannonites have found it impossible to advocate *doing* anything — anything! — for the "defense of the Soviet Union."

In one sense, the struggle in the party, insofar as it was a political and theoretical dispute, took place between us and Comrade Trotsky. Trotsky, as is known, was no small opponent, and he never shrank from a discussion. He did not refrain from this one! Virtually every single document that appeared in behalf of the leadership, on the Russian question, on the organizational question, and a number of other questions that were raised, rightly or wrongly, by both sides, was written by Trotsky. The majority leaders confined themselves to underlining their own sterility by trying to repeat Trotsky's arguments; but the imitation was not one-tenth as good as the original, which was not very adequate to begin with. Left to themselves, without Trotsky's counsel (regardless of whether or not it was good), the majority leaders proved to be a pretty helpless lot. The party membership could not help observing this fact.

The official leadership won a majority of the delegates to the special convention of the party early in 1940. That is not surprising. What is surprising is that its majority was so slim — a bare 55 per cent — in view of the tremendous, irreplaceable aid given it by Trotsky's long and well-earned prestige and authority in our movement. What their convention delegation would have amounted to without that aid is not even worth talking about. As it is, if the support we had in the party is joined with our support in the youth (which was overwhelmingly on our side), we had a clear majority of the united Fourth Internationalist movement in this country.

Recognizing, however, that we were formally in the minority in the party, we demanded, in view of the enormous importance of the differences, that we be permitted to publish a special periodical of our own, free from the control of the majority, in whom we had no confidence and could not have any. In this periodical, we would of course support the fundamental principles we held in common, the general party program, but present our own standpoint on Russia in a responsible manner.

260

There was nothing new or outrageous in such a proposal; on the contrary, it was the best method, under the circumstances, of preserving the unity of a party whose leadership had shifted away from a revolutionary internationalist position. It was a right we had all fought for when we were the Left Wing of the Socialist Party, and what we said about the Thomas bureaucracy when it denied us this right was a little too vigorous for public prints. It was a right long enjoyed by groups in the Russian Social-Democratic and Bolshevik movements before the war, under Lenin's leadership; and even during the most critical period of the revolution itself, the exercise of this right was not a basis for expulsion or other organizational sanctions. It was Stalin who abolished it, as early as 1925, when he hammered the Leningrad Opposition for attempting to exercise this right. The Cannonites, again acting as if they were right in the midst of a civil war, would not hear of it. Trotsky, unfortunately, with a complete misunderstanding of the situation in the party, and above all a misunderstanding of the character and composition of our group, supported the Cannonites in this matter.

For the bureaucratic clique in control of the party, our demand was of course only a pretext for action to get rid of a group of militants whose criticism they could not endure. They did not act as men confident of their position, and of the early verification that events would bring; and they did not act in panic. Quite coolly and deliberately, they split the Fourth International in half and thus relieved themselves of our embarrassing presence — to them, the one was worth the other.

Characteristically enough, we were not expelled for any violation of discipline! We were not expelled for publishing *Labor Action*, for example. Our expulsion occurred before *Labor Action* saw the light of day, before we were even accused of having violated party discipline. Immediately after the convention, our representatives in the Political Committee were confronted at a meeting with a prepared motion. It was in two parts. We have often challenged the Cannonites to make public this infamous improvement on Stalinist procedure. They have not accepted.

Recently, they published, in an introduction to a collection of Trotsky's articles against us, the *first part* of the motion; they are obviously sufficiently shamefaced to keep the second part secret. The first part pledged all members to abide by the convention decisions. The second part — observe this innovation in the revolutionary movement! — declared that anyone who does not vote in favor of the motion is... kicked out! A magnificent formula for getting unanimity in the leadership. Not even Stalin ever equalled this brilliant product of Cannon's brain. No wonder he permits his magazine to write of him repeatedly in this wise: "Marx, Lenin, Trotsky and Cannon" — an invincible combination if there ever was one.

We are not unaccustomed to bureaucratic measures, expulsions included. Bureaucrats live most uncomfortably in the presence of revolutionary ideas and of people capable of holding them and expounding them, and not being frightened out of them when small-time officials scowl and threaten. But we must say that when we were expelled, along with Cannon, from the Stalinist leadership and party, our "trial" lasted almost a week. When Cannon had us "finished off," he turned from his watch to his colleagues with the triumphant remark, "Only four and one-half minutes!"

Many wishfully gloomy predictions were made about our imminent doom when we founded the Workers Party and launched *Labor Action* and *The New International* under our auspices. You'll last six months, we were told by the most pessimistic of our expellers. Without regrets, we have refused to comply with their hopes. We draw profitable consolation from the fate of others who so prematurely predicted our doom: the leaders of the CP who expelled us and degenerated completely into reactionary, totalitarian bureaucrats: the Lovestonites, who directed our expulsion from the CP and ended at the boot tips of the imperialist war machine; the Socialist Party leaders who expelled their Left Wing and then completed the ruin of a once so promising party; and even the SWP leaders who have to explain constantly to their members that they are not really opportunists on the war question, on the question of their now-buried "military policy," on the trade union question.

In launching the new party, we merely continued the struggle for the proletarian revolution and socialism to which we have always been devoted and which is the only progressive cause in the world today. We have gained some modest but gratifying successes; under the pressure of the war situation we have suffered our share of setbacks and losses.

Immediately after the founding of the party, one of its most promising leaders, Burnham, quit its ranks, deserting the struggle for socialism. He proved incapable of measuring up to the task, and revealed that lack of character and stamina which is, alas, not uncommon in our time. The working class movement has a history studded with examples of desertion even of some of its most prominent spokesmen, and the Fourth International has not been and could not be immune from this malady in its ranks.

It is here, by the way, that was shown how sadly Trotsky misjudged our group, which he thought was led by Burnham, and was imbued with "Burnhamism." Nothing of the sort, of course. Burnham's desertion, as is always so in such cases, was a blow, but not a particularly serious one. The loss was his, not ours. Important was the fact that no one among us, not a soul, followed him into the void. There have been other losses, as we originally counted there would be, and there will undoubtedly be still others before we reach our goal. But all of them together have not been very important, and we have made up for them ten times over in different ways. Every one of us knows this, knows that our Workers Party today is by far and away more solid and more effective than it has ever been.

Our confidence in the party is strengthened by the fact that it has remained true to the banner of revolutionary internationalism and to the interests of the working man and working woman at a time when it counts — during the war. We have not retreated from our principles, we have not vacillated, we have not given up an inch of them or sought to gloss them over in the hope of gaining a deceptive and momentary popularity, or of winning "mercy" from our enemy. And that is how we shall continue to be.

Our *Labor Action* — and we call it ours because we are in the forefront of those who have made its existence and growth possible — has reached a point in popularity and distribution unknown to the radical labor press in our generation. Exact figures would show that more workers read *Labor Action* than read the *Socialist Call*, the *New Leader*, the *Militant*, the *Weekly People* and the *Industrial Worker* combined. And of the tens of thousands who read it, those who feel themselves in solidarity with the program it fights for, surely number in the thousands, at the very least.

Our membership is firmly established among the rest of their class — in the factories and mills and on the ships, for we record proudly that our party is made up of at least ninety per cent of proletarian men and women, who stand out from the rest of the working class only in their socialist convictions and in the degree of their determination to fight for working class interests night and day, without exception, on all occasions and in all places. Their activity is the kind that assures the future of a party that rightly calls itself the Workers Party.

APPENDIX: THE TROTSKYISTS' DEBATE IN 1939-40

i) BURNHAM'S THESES

Section I: The nature of the war as a whole

1. The Second World War, which has now begun, is, *as a whole*, imperialist and totalitarian in character. It is a war among the great powers for the re-division of the world; and is, from the point of view of both sides and of all participants in the conflict, directed against the interests of the masses.

2. In this war, "neutrality" is impossible for any nation. The nature of the war makes it certain that within a comparatively short time all nations will be compelled to line up with one side or the other: at the very least, economically; and in the case of most nations and of all the great powers, with military means as well.

3. From the imperialist, totalitarian character of the war as a whole, and the involvement of all nations in the war, it follows that from no point of view or in any respect can it be regarded as being fought for "the defense of the independence of small nations", "the rights of subject nationalities", or for any other progressive purpose. The conflict as a whole is reactionary, and all secondary or isolated features are subordinated to its reactionary nature.

4. This war marks the end of bourgeois democracy as a historically possible form of government. Under the conditions of the war, the democratic and fascist imperialisms lose their structural differences and reach identity, in all essential respects, in the totalitarian war dictatorships. Whatever the outcome of the war, it will never be possible for them to return to a bourgeois democratic form of government. This conclusion holds for the United States, as for the other nations. The only possible exceptions — which would prove in any case only temporary — would be one or two of the smaller and unimportant nations; and even such exceptions are doubtful.

5. From the character of the war, it follows that the warring powers are incapable of concluding a just or even a workable peace.

6. A just and lasting peace can be concluded only by the overthrow of world imperialism as a whole.

7. The task of the masses, confronted with the war, is *to stop the war*. This task can be accomplished by the masses only by the overthrow, within each nation, of the war-makers: that is, of their own rulers and oppressors.

8. Within the advanced nations, this task must be carried out through the conquest of power by the working class in the socialist revolution.

9. The colonial peoples and the subject nationalities can carry out this task by the struggle for freedom and independence from "their own" imperialist oppressors. This struggle must be firmly supported by the international working class. The struggle for the freedom of the colonial peoples and subject nationalities can be carried to success, however, only if the working class maintains in supporting it a socialist policy wholly independent of the native bourgeoisies and bourgeois nationalists, and only if the working class gains leadership in the struggle and succeeds in transforming it into the struggle for the workers' revolution.

10. The perspective of the struggle of the masses against the war is summed up in that of the United Socialist States of Europe, the United Socialist States of the Americas, a free Asia, a free Africa, and the world Federation of Socialist Republics.

Section II: The nature of the Russian state in the light of the war

1. The signing of the Hitler-Stalin Pact brought to a definitive climax the series of developments within the Soviet Union which began with the rise of Stalin and entered a stage of rapid transformation during the past five years.

Introduced by James Burnham at the SWP Political Committee on September 5, 1939, but later withdrawn.

2. Internally, the Soviet bureaucracy has carried through a political counter-revolution, which required for its achievement an undeclared but no less actual Civil War.

3. Within the Soviet Union, the present Soviet state has during the past period gone over to an imperialist or quasi-imperialist policy, in both political and economic relations, toward the minority nationalities within the Soviet borders.

4. During the past period, the Soviet Union has, partly through the destruction of the nationalized forms of economy and partly through the manipulation of them, assumed a definitely *exploitative* character in the economic realm. The ruling stratum of the population *systematically exploits* the masses of the people for its benefit.

5. It is impossible to regard the Soviet Union as a "workers' state" in any sense whatever.

6. The ruling stratum of the Soviet Union does not constitute a crystallized bourgeois class in the traditional sense, nor can it be predicted with assurance whether its evolution in the future — even if unchecked — will be toward such crystallization.

7. The *de facto* political and economic character of the present Soviet state, and the mode under which its oppression and exploitation is carried on, suggest the term *"bureaucratic state"* as its most adequate definition. Political and economic power and privilege, as well as the state apparatus, are the *property* of the bureaucracy and its affiliates.

8. This analysis is confirmed by an examination of the external policy of the present Soviet state. The armed and material intervention of the Soviet state externally, from having been revolutionary in its first period and what might be called passive or non-revolutionary in its middle period, has now become *counter-revolutionary* during the latest period.

9. The present Soviet state, as it functions both internally and externally, is no longer a bulwark, even partially or indirectly, of what remains of the socialized economy, but is exclusively a bulwark of the power and privilege of the bureaucracy, the interests of which are now in complete conflict with all progressive remains of the socialized economy.

10. In foreign relations generally, during the years since 1933, the policy of the present Soviet state, in serving the aims of the bureaucracy, has become wholly subordinated to one or another of the groups of imperialist powers — a development culminating in the pact with Hitler.

Section III: The question of defense of the Soviet Union

1. The policy of *unconditional defense of the Soviet Union* was predicated upon the proletarian character of the Soviet state and the conception of four possible types of war in which that state might be involved: (1) A war of defense against imperialist intervention; (2) a civil war; (3) an external war of liberation, in which the Soviet forces aided the toilers and oppressed of some nation or nations against their rulers and oppressors; (4) a so-called "mixed war", in which the Soviet state would be compelled to join military forces with one or another group of contending imperialist powers. All of these types of war occurred, and the policy was upheld for all of them.

2. Conditions are now altogether changed. First: an external war of liberation is now excluded. The external military intervention of the present Soviet state could now be, not revolutionary in character — in support of the toilers against their oppressors — but counter-revolutionary — in support of one or another set of rulers against the masses. In such cases, therefore, defense of the Soviet Union is social-patriotism, and must be abandoned for a defeatist policy.

3. In the case of internal war, revolutionists are now committed to support, not of the present Soviet state, but of the revolutionary struggle of the Russian workers and peasants against that state, and of the struggle for freedom of subjection nationalities from that state (e.g., as in the case of the struggle for a free Soviet Ukraine). Far from defending the Soviet state in such cases, we call upon the workers and peasants of Russia to overthrow and to reestablish their own socialist power; and we call on the subject peoples, joining with their brothers now under the rule of other nations, to fight for their freedom against both the rulers of those other nations and the rulers of the Soviet state.

4. The case of a "mixed war" is no longer abstract but concrete: it is the present war. The armed intervention of the Soviet Union in the present war is almost certain, and its political and economic intervention has already taken place. This intervention will be wholly subordinated to the general imperialist character of the conflict as a whole; and will be in no sense a "defense" of the remains of the socialist economy but on the contrary the sure means

toward the elimination of what progressive remains there still are. Under these circumstances, defense of the Soviet Union would be social-patriotism, and a major barrier also to revolutionary developments among the peoples of the other warring powers. Revolutionists must call upon the Russian workers and peasants to join hands with the workers and peasants of all the powers, of Poland and Germany and France and England and the United States, to stop the war and conclude a just peace by the overthrow of their own rulers and oppressors.

5. The one remaining case is that of combined imperialist intervention against an isolated Russia. To answer in advance what should be the policy of revolutionists in this instance is impossible, since the problem is abstract: the real war is not occurring in this manner, and an indefinite variety of changes might well occur before any such event took place, granted that there is any likelihood of it. If such an event had taken place yesterday, or took place today, the present Soviet state would occupy a role comparable to that of the local rulers of a semi-colonial or "comprador" nation, and, since the success of the imperialist interventionists would strengthen world imperialism and their defeat weaken it, material support of the Soviet state would be the mandatory policy.

[Section IV resumes, more or less, the common-stock ideas of the Trotskyists on anti-war agitation in the USA.]

ii) AFTER THE STALINIST INVASION OF POLAND

Albert Goldman, James Burnham, James P Cannon; Motions to SWP Political Committee.

"Special Club Executive [SWP Political Committee] meeting. September 18, 1939"

Present: Drake [George Breitman], Erickson [Ernest Erber], Wilson [B J Widick], Levine, Anton [Nathan Gould], Walsh [Joseph Carter], Stuart [Sam Gordon], Morris [Albert Goldman], Kelvin [James Burnham], Michaels [Max Shachtman], Charnis [Paul Bernick], Martin [James P Cannon], Stern [Morris Lewit], White [Bert Cochran]. By invitation: Cohen [C L R James].

Next issue of paper and war in Poland

Motions by Kelvin:

1. Through its invasion of Poland the Red Army is participating integrally in a war of imperialist conquest.

2. This estimate of the character of the war shall govern the news articles and editorials in our press.

3. Prior to the plenum the more general questions concerning the nature of the Russian state and the defense of the Soviet Union shall not be dealt with; but a statement of the committee shall be published to the effect that these are under discussion and consideration with the aim of arriving at the speediest possible decision.

For: Kelvin, Michaels, Walsh. Against: Drake, Levine, White, Morris, Stuart, Stern, Martin. Abstaining: Wilson, Erickson, Anton and Charnis. Motion Lost.

Motions by Morris:

1. Under the actual conditions prevailing in Poland we approve of Stalin's invasion of Poland as a measure of preventing Hitler from getting control of all of Poland and as a measure of defending the Soviet Union against Hitler. Between Hitler and Stalin, we prefer Stalin.

2. It is necessary to connect the invasion of Poland by the Red Army with the general policies of Stalin and to show that he is not motivated by any interest for the revolutionary proletariat but by his desire to protect the Stalinist bureaucracy.

3. It is necessary to urge the Polish, Ukrainian and White Russian workers and peasants to continue their struggle for national and social liberation against the Stalinist bureaucracy.

For: Morris. Against: all except Levine abstaining. Motion Lost.

Motions by Martin:

1. The party press, in its handling of Russia's participation in the war in Poland, shall do so from the point of view of the party's fundamental analysis of the character of the Soviet State and the role of Stalinism as laid down in the fundamental resolutions of the party's foundation convention and the foundation congress of the Fourth International.

2. The slogan of an independent Soviet Ukraine shall be defended as a policy wholly consistent with the fundamental line of defending the Soviet Union.

For: Morris, Stuart, Wilson, Anton, Levine, Erickson, Stern, Drake and Martin. Against: Walsh, Kelvin. Abstaining: Michaels and Charnis. Motion Carried.

iii) "A COUNTER-REVOLUTIONARY IMPERIALIST WORKERS' STATE?"

"For the Consideration of the Political Committee", by "Cohen" (C L R James), September 26, 1939.

I. I draw the attention of the PC to the fact that at the last convention I raised the question of "the nature of the Soviet State". I proposed that a discussion be initiated because of the obvious design of the Soviet State to establish "protectorates" over the Baltic States. It is necessary to emphasize that the reconsideration of this question was raised before the Russo-German pact.

II. For a Fourth Internationalist, the Russo-German pact marks no particularly shameful "betrayal", any more than a sudden retreat by Stalin from the German to the Anglo-French alliance would mark any regeneration. Such tendencies in our movement should be sternly opposed. This does not mean that the sentiment of disillusionment in the ranks should not be utilized in our press and propaganda, but it does mean that no abnormal political conclusions can be drawn from the mere signing of this pact.

III. The pact, however, does emphasize the direction in which the Soviet State was headed during the earlier negotiations with France and Britain. It is my opinion that the Soviet State has now incontestably reached a stage of political degeneration in which its foreign policy is indistinguishable from that of an imperialist state, and that it is prepared to conclude not only binding alliances with imperialist states, but in peace or war, will share in any partition of Poland and the allotment of spheres of influence in Eastern Europe or the Baltic States. In my opinion it would be a grievous error to entertain any illusions as to the action of the Soviet State if presented with any opportunities of this kind, and such action is of greater importance than breaches in the monopoly of foreign trade which may well be of a substantial character without causing any fundamental change in the present Soviet economy.

If we persist in denominating the Soviet Union as a "Workers' State" then we shall have added to Marxism a new category — the counter-revolutionary imperialist workers' state. To object that imperialism is the outgrowth of capitalism and therefore inapplicable in this instance is to make of the classical Marxist terminology not a starting point for the analysis and classification of new phenomena but a hindrance for those who attempt such investigations. I shall not argue about what name is to be given to the forcible subjection of a people by arms, police, and GPU of the Soviet State. A definition more precise than imperialism may be found. The fact would remain. I submit that to continue to call Workers' State any government from which action of that sort is not only possible but probable, is to use terms which are devoid of political meaning and fraught with an increasing danger to our movement.

IV. This with the allied question of the defense of the Soviet Union is no longer a matter of abstract theory but an urgent question of immediate practical importance.

(a) For comrades in Europe and Poland particularly may break their necks on this question.

(b) For great numbers of the workers, this question henceforth becomes one of the most urgent interest though they may not be able to formulate clearly their wish for clarification.

V. I therefore propose to the Political Committee that in view of the difficulties created for our international secretariat by the international situation, the discussion proposed at the PC Tuesday last take the following course:

(a) Our international sections be notified immediately and urged to participate.

(b) That the discussion should not take a discursive, meandering course, but that some reasonable limit should be imposed for the formal presentation of different points of view.

(c) That at some convenient time, formal resolutions should come before a joint meeting of the National Committee, available members of the International Secretariat, and members of the Pan-American Bureau, all with voice and vote, and that this body make such recommendations in regard to reaffirmation, modification, or repudiation of our position as may be demanded by the international situation. Such recommendations to deal with 1. the nature of the Soviet State; 2. the defense of the Soviet Union.

VI. It is regrettable that such a discussion should apparently be initiated by the signing of the Russo-German pact. It is more regrettable that it should be necessary at this time. But the plain fact remains that our movement, united on all other fundamental questions, is today seriously disturbed by our relation to the Soviet State and its effect on our struggle in the coming war. And a discussion, firm and precise, is needed if we are not to go into the hard conditions of illegality hesitant and doubtful on a question as decisive for the fate of the working class as it is for our cohesion and morale.

iv) MINORITY RESOLUTION, SEPTEMBER 28, 1939

"Resolution on the Soviet Union in the present war", drafted by Max Shachtman. From SWP Internal Bulletin, October 10, 1939.

The party has thus far failed to give a clearcut and unambiguous answer to the questions raised by Stalin's invasion of Poland. The result has been a serious weakening of the effectiveness of our press, a disorientation of the Party membership, and a corresponding reduction of our striking power against the American Stalinist machine and against the social-democratic and imperialist-patriotic forces who seek to exploit the events for their own reactionary ends and who can be counteracted most successfully only by an unequivocal revolutionary position on our part. This is all the more urgent in view of the Estonian events and the prospective extension of Stalin's invasion to other Baltic and to the Balkan countries.

The new questions raised cannot be and are not answered by a mere reiteration that "the Soviet Union is a workers' state" and that "we stand for the unconditional defense of the Soviet Union". The idea that these declarations provide an automatic reply to the concrete questions posed by the concrete military and political actions taken by Stalin is absurd, and has been proved absurd in practise. Without raising at this time the problem of the class nature of the Soviet state, it is necessary to give immediate answers to the concrete questions raised by the Hitler-Stalin Pact, the ensuing conquest of Poland and matters related thereto.

Considered abstractly, the Hitler-Stalin pact stands on the same level as the Franco-Soviet pact, and revolutionary Marxists have only contempt for the Popular Frontists and patriots of all stripes who endorsed the latter because it was made with democratic imperialists and condemn the former because it was made with Nazi imperialism. For our part, we reject and condemn both, without forsaking our basic position which recognizes the admissibility of temporary agreements between a Soviet state and a bourgeois state.

Considered concretely, however, the Hitler-Stalin Pact has meant the following, which was, in general, only potentially contained in the Franco-Soviet Pact:

(1) Stalin gave Hitler the signal for opening up the Second Imperialist World War — and linked his fortunes with those of the Nazi war machine;

(2) Stalin gave Hitler the signal for the brutal Nazi invasion of Poland;

(3) Stalin not only facilitated this imperialist invasion politically and militarily but jointly divided the spoils with the triumphant Nazis.

The Party must sternly reject any attempt, made inside or outside its ranks, to "explain away", to justify or to condone the Stalinist invasion of Poland and its partition in partnership with Hitler. The Party must reject the essentially capitulatory standpoint summarized in the formula, "As between Hitler and Stalin, the Poles should choose Stalin". We deny that the choice of the multi-national masses of Poland is limited to the rule of the Hitlerite bandits or the Kremlin slave-drivers. The Fourth International calls upon the masses of Poland to fight against both of them as well as against the Polish ruling class — for a Socialist Poland and for the united, independent Soviet Republics of the Ukraine and of White Russia. The Party also rejects the standpoint which, under the guise of an "objective explanation" and in the name of the "defense of the Soviet Union", makes the Stalinist invasion a matter of indifference to the masses of Poland or relegates it to the category of purely military-tactical considerations of the Red Army. It is not a question of military science but a political question, and it must be dealt with accordingly.

The Party condemns the Stalinist invasion and subjugation of Poland as acts of imperialist policy. Regardless of the illusions the Kremlin gang may feed the masses (or itself, for that matter), it is acting as the agent of German imperialism, just as it was ready to act as agent of Anglo-French imperialism yesterday and may act as such tomorrow. Produced by the same cause, German Fascism and Stalinist bureaucratism are now engaged in a joint campaign of imperialist expansion.

The Party must denounce the monstrous claims of the Stalinists that the Red Army is "liberating" the Ukrainian, White Russian and Polish people, just as it denounced the earlier Stalinist claim that the Polish masses would be fighting for democracy and freedom against fascism by supporting the ruling class of Poland and its régime. The war in Poland shows, to an infinitely greater and clearer extent than the civil war in Spain, the utterly counterrevolutionary role played by the Stalin bureaucracy. While we were not and could not be for the defense of "poor little Poland" — the imperialist Poland of yesterday — we recognized in the patriotism and the hatred of Hitlerism shown by the Polish masses something potentially progressive. With the inevitable collapse and flight of the rotten Polish military landowning clique and its government, arose the possibility of a revolutionary defense of Poland, if not a Polish October immediately, then an October reached after a Polish "February". In the chaos attending the collapse of the Polish Imperial Army, signs of such a possibility already could be discerned in parts of the country. Instead of helping in any way — even to the tiny extent to which it was done in Spain, where at least one Soviet rifle out of ten might be counted on to fire at Franco — to materialize this possibility, i.e., to promote an independent class war against the Nazi invader, Stalin wiped out this possibility completely in partnership with that invader. Stalin and the Red Army thus played a flatly counter-revolutionary role in Poland.

The bitter realities of the recent events, most particularly of the events in Poland, dictate a revision of our previous concept of the "unconditional defense of the Soviet Union". As understood by our movement, this concept meant not only that we call for the defense of the Soviet Union even if it is directed by the Stalinist bureaucracy, but also that we support the Red Army in any military struggle in which it engages, that we are for its victory under all circumstances, be it a so-called "defensive" or "aggressive" war. To be true to its revolutionary internationalist role, the Fourth International must now call upon the Polish workers and peasants to rise in revolutionary struggle and, with their own armed forces, drive out the oppressors of the people — Hitler in one-half of the country and the Stalin bureaucracy in the other. The same applies in similar situations elsewhere. This means a struggle both against the Reichswehr and against the Red Army. In this struggle, the revolutionary internationalists cannot and will not be for the victory of the Red Army which the Stalinist Bureaucracy has compelled to act as an agent of imperialism and an oppressor of the people. Instead, the Fourth International will call upon the workers and peasants of the Soviet Union, those in the Red Army included, to help their revolutionary brothers in Poland — just as we call on them to help fight for the establishment of an independent United Soviet Ukraine — and to overthrow the Stalinist bureaucracy and its reactionary officer corps at home.

From this position — the only one compatible with the revolutionary interests of the international proletariat as well as of both the Polish and Soviet masses — does not necessarily follow the abandonment of the slogan of the defense of the Soviet Union. The collapse of the Franco-Soviet Pact demonstrated once more the fragility and temporariness of alliances between the Soviet Union and capitalist states. It is quite possible — even probable — that the Hitler-Stalin Pact will last an even shorter time. All of Stalin's hopes and ruses to the contrary notwithstanding, a change in the character of the war into direct imperialist attack upon the Soviet Union by one or more states is not at all excluded. Assuming that the bourgeois counter-revolution, which is now on the order of the day in the Soviet Union, has not triumphed, the defense of the Soviet Union, even under the rule of the bureaucracy, will again become an immediate and paramount task. In other words, just as wars of national liberation can change into imperialist wars and vice versa, and imperialist wars into revolutionary wars, so we cannot exclude the possibility of the present imperialist war turning into a war of intervention in the Soviet Union. The Party cannot adopt a position which may result in new events catching it unawares and it must therefore envisage the possibility of a radical change in the decisive nature of the present war and in the position occupied by the Soviet Union.

It is necessary to submit these questions immediately to the discussion of the Party membership — and of the International — in a sober, orderly and responsible manner. There is no other way of arriving at a firm and clear revolutionary position, thus enabling us to discharge the enormous responsibilities faced today by the Fourth International.

v) NATIONAL COMMITTEE PLENUM, SEPTEMBER 30-OCTOBER 1, 1939

"Motions on Russian Question", from SWP Internal Bulletin, October 10, 1939

The following motions were adopted by the Plenum of the National Committee, meeting on September 30th and October 1st, 1939.

1. That we reaffirm the basic analysis of the nature of the Soviet state and the role of Stalinism and the political conclusions drawn from this analysis, including the unconditional defense of the Soviet Union against imperialist attack, as laid down in the previous decisions of our party convention and in the program of the Fourth International.

2. The plenum endorses the political conclusions of the document of Trotsky on 'The USSR in War' and instructs the Political Committee to publish this document as an evaluation and elucidation of the new events on the basis of our fundamental position.

vi) THE EXPULSION OF THE MINORITY

"Minutes of the Club Executive [SWP Political Committee] no.2, April 16, 1940"

Club Exec. Members Present: Martin [James P Cannon], Stern [Morris Lewit], White [Bert Cochran], Stuart [Sam Gordon], Smith [Farrell Dobbs], Rand [George Clarke]. Late: Stone [Martin Abern], Michaels [Max Shachtman]. Club Exec. Members Absent: Kelvin [James Burnham], Charnis [Paul Bernick]. Club Members Present: Dorn [Murray Weiss], Drake [George Breitman], Cassidy [Felix Morrow], Joad [Joseph Hansen], Wilson [B J Widick], Erickson [Ernest Erber], Walsh [Joseph Carter], Anton [Nathan Gould]. Present by Invitation: Williams [Oscar Schoenfeld], Georges [George Novack], Manny. Chairman: Stern [Lewit].

Party situation. Motion by Martin: That the committee accepts the convention decisions and obligates itself to carry them out in a disciplined manner. Vote on motion: For: Rand, Smith, Martin, Stern, Cassidy, Dorn, Drake, Stuart, White. Abstaining: Stone, Michaels, Wilson, Walsh, Anton, Erickson. Motion carried.

Motion by Martin: Those members of the Club Executive and Club (NC) who abstain from voting on this motion stand suspended from the party and from all party functions, including the function as agents of the party and the New International Publishing Company and *Socialist Appeal* Publishing Association until such time as they have indicated to the satisfaction of the committee their intention to comply with convention decisions.

Question by Michaels: By what authority can this motion be made? Answer by Martin: By the constitution of the party as amended by the last party convention. Vote on motion: For: Rand, Smith, Martin, Stern, Cassidy, Dorn, Drake, Stuart, White. Against: Stone, Michaels, Wilson, Walsh, Anton, Erickson. Motion carried.

The minority members were thereby suspended and retired from the meeting.

4. WHICH CLASS RULES IN THE USSR?

Could the shift from "unconditional defence" of the Soviet Union to "conditional defence" be made as no more than an adjustment within the basic theory that the Stalinist bureaucracy was only a cancerous outgrowth on a workers' state? Trotsky thought not; and he was not yet ready to conclude that the bureaucracy was a new ruling class with its own role in history. He wrote: "Might we not place ourselves in a ludicrous position if we affixed to the Bonapartist oligarchy the nomenclature of a new ruling class just a few years or even a few months prior to its inglorious downfall? Posing this question clearly should alone in our opinion restrain the comrades from terminological experimentation and overhasty generalisations". By 1940 Shachtman and almost all his comrades had decided that the Soviet Union, a system where a totalitarian bureaucracy left no room for any political or social control by the workers, could not be a workers' state. Their positive conclusions diverged in detail. Joseph Carter said that the USSR was a new and entirely reactionary system of exploitation which he called "bureaucratic collectivism". Shachtman used the same term as Carter, but remained closer to Trotsky on the potentially progressive significance of the statised economy. C L R James called it state capitalism. None of them shared the views of the maverick Bruno Rizzi, whom Trotsky had polemicised against as the representative of "bureaucratic collectivist" theory in 1939. Paradoxically, the true heirs of Rizzi would, after the late '40s, be the "orthodox" Trotskyists. They would come to share his perspective of totalitarian statised economies bringing, despite everything, a whole new epoch of progress for humanity by their development of the productive forces.

271

Max Shachtman

IS RUSSIA A WORKERS' STATE?

THAT THE "RUSSIAN QUESTION" should continue to occupy the attention of the revolutionary movement is anything but unusual. In the history of modern socialism, there is nothing that equals the Russian
Revolution in importance. It is indeed no exaggeration to write — we shall
seek to reaffirm and demonstrate it further on — that this revolution does
not have its equal in importance throughout human history. For us, the
historical legitimacy of the Bolshevik revolution and the validity of the
principles that made its triumph possible, are equally incontestable.
Looking back over the quarter of a century that has elapsed, and subjecting all the evidence of events to a soberly critical re-analysis, we find only
a confirmation of those fundamental principles of Marxism with which the
names of Lenin and Trotsky are linked, and of their appraisal of the class
character and historical significance of the revolution they organized.
Both — the principles and the appraisal — are, and should remain, incorporated in the program of our International.

Our investigation deals with something else. It aims to re-evaluate the
character and significance of the period of the degeneration of the Russian
revolution and the Soviet state, marked by the rise and triumph of the
Stalinist bureaucracy. Its results call for a revision of the theory that the
Soviet Union is a workers' state. The new analysis will be found to be, we
believe, in closer harmony with the political program of the party and the
International, fortifying it in its most important respects and eliminating
from it only those points which, if they corresponded to a reality of yesterday, do not correspond to that of today.

In our analysis, we must necessarily take issue with Leon Trotsky; yet,
at the same time, base ourselves largely upon his studies. Nobody has
even approached him in the scope and depth of his contribution to understanding the problem of the Soviet Union. In a different way, to be sure,
but no less solidly, his work of analyzing the decay of the Soviet Republic
is as significant as his work of creating that Republic. Most of what we
learned about Russia, and can transmit to others, we learned from
Trotsky. We learned from him, too, the necessity of critical re-examination
at every important stage, of regaining, even in the realm of theory, what
was once already gained, or, in the contrary case, of discarding what was
once firmly established but proved to be vulnerable. The garden of theory
requires critical cultivation, re-planting, but also weeding out.

What new events, what fundamental changes in the situation, have
taken place to warrant a corresponding change in our appraisal of the
class character of the Soviet Union? The question is, in a sense, irrelevant.
Our new analysis and conclusions would have their objective merit or

From *New International*, December 1940. This is the full text, restoring cuts made by
Shachtman when he reprinted the article in his book *The Bureaucratic Revolution*, Donald
Press, NY, 1962.

error regardless of the signature appended to them. In the case of the writer, if the question must be answered, the revision is the product of that careful re-studying of the problem urged upon him by both friends and adversaries in the recent dispute in the American section of the International. The outbreak of the second world war, while it produced no fundamental changes in the Soviet Union in itself, did awaken doubts as to the correctness of our traditional position. However, doubts and uncertainties cannot serve as a program, nor even as a fruitful subject for discussion. Therefore, while putting forward a position on those aspects of the disputed question on which he had firm opinions, the writer did not take part in what passed for a discussion on that aspect of the question which related to the class character of the Soviet Union. The founding convention of the Workers Party provided for the opening of a discussion on this point in due time, and under conditions free from the ugly atmosphere of baiting, ritualistic phrasemongering, pugnacious ignorance, and factional fury that prevailed in the party before our expulsion and the split. The writer has, meanwhile, had the opportunity to examine and reflect upon the problem, if not as much as would be desirable, then at least sufficiently. "Theory is not a note which you can present at any moment to reality for payment," wrote Trotsky. "If a theory proves mistaken we must revise it or fill out its gaps. We must find out those real social forces which have given rise to the contrast between Soviet reality and the traditional Marxian conception." We must revise our theory that Russia is a workers' state. What has up to now been discussed informally and without order, should now be the subject of an ordered and serious discussion. This article aims to contribute to it.

Briefly stated, this has been our traditional view of the character of the Soviet Union: *"The character of the social régime is determined first of all by the property relations. The nationalization of land, of the means of industrial production and exchange, with the monopoly of foreign trade in the hands of the state, constitute the bases of the social order in the USSR. The classes expropriated by the October revolution, as well as the elements of the bourgeoisie and the bourgeois section of the bureaucracy being newly formed, could reëstablish private ownership of land, banks, factories, mills, railroads, etc., only by means of a counter-revolutionary overthrow. By these property relations, lying at the basis of the class relations, is determined for us the nature of the Soviet Union as a proletarian state".* (Trotsky, *Problems of the Development of the USSR*, p.3, 1931.)

But it is not a workers' state in the abstract. It is a degenerated, a sick, an internally-imperilled workers' state. Its degeneration is represented by the usurpation of all political power in the state by a reactionary, totalitarian bureaucracy, headed by Stalin. But while *politically* you have an anti-Soviet Bonapartist dictatorship of the bureaucracy, according to Trotsky, it nevertheless defends, in its own and very bad way, the *social* rule of the working class. This rule is expressed in the preservation of nationalized property. In bourgeois society, we have had cases where the social rule of capitalism is preserved by all sorts of political régimes — democratic and dictatorial, parliamentary and monarchical, Bonapartist and fascist. Yes, even under fascism, the bureaucracy is not a separate ruling class, no matter how irritating to the bourgeoisie its rule may be. Similarly in the Soviet Union. The bureaucracy is a caste, not a class. It serves, as all bureaucracies do, a class. In this case, it serves — again, badly — to maintain the social rule of the proletariat. At the same time, however, it weakens and undermines this rule. To assure the sanitation and progress of the workers' state toward socialism, the bureaucracy must be overthrown. Its totalitarian régime excludes its removal by means of more or less peaceful reform. It can be eliminated, therefore, only by means of a revolution. The revolution, however, will be, in its decisive respects, not social but political. It will restore and extend workers' democracy, but it will not produce any fundamental social changes, no fundamental changes in property relations. Property will remain state property.

Omitting for the time being Trotsky's analysis of the origin and rise of the Stalinist bureaucracy, which is elaborated in detail in *The Revolution Betrayed*, we have given above a summary of the basic position held by us jointly up to now. So far as characterizing the class nature of the Soviet Union is concerned, this position might be summed up even more briefly as follows: To guarantee progress toward socialism, the existence of nationalized property is necessary but not sufficient — a revolutionary proletarian régime is needed in the country, plus favorable international conditions (victory of the proletariat in more advanced capitalist countries). To characterize the Soviet Union as a workers' state, the existence of nationalized property is necessary and sufficient. The Stalinist bureaucracy is a caste. To become a ruling class, it must establish new property forms.

Except for the slogan of revolution, as against reform, which is only a few years old in our movement, this was substantially the position vigorously defended by Trotsky and the Trotskyist movement for more than fifteen years. The big article on Russia written by Trotsky right after the war broke out, marked, in our opinion, the first — and a truly enormous — contradiction of this position. Not that Trotsky abandoned the theory that the Soviet Union is a degenerated workers' state. Quite the contrary, he reaffirmed it. But at the same time, he advanced a theoretical possibility which fundamentally negated his theory — more accurately, the motivation for his theory — of the class character of the Soviet state.

If the proletariat does not come to power in the coming period, and civilization declines further, the immanent collectivist tendencies in capitalist society may be brought to fruition in the form of a new exploiting society ruled by a new bureaucratic class — neither proletarian nor bourgeois. Or, if the proletariat takes power in a series of countries and then relinquishes it to a privileged bureaucracy, like the Stalinist, it will show that the proletariat cannot, congenitally, become a ruling class and then "it will be necessary in retrospect to establish that in its fundamental traits the present USSR was the precursor of a new exploiting régime on an international scale."

"The historic alternative, carried to the end, is as follows: either the Stalin régime is an abhorrent relapse in the process of transforming bourgeois society into a socialist society, or the Stalin régime is the first stage of a new exploiting society. If the second prognosis proves to be correct, then, of course, the bureaucracy will become a new exploiting class. However onerous the second perspective may be, if the world proletariat should actually prove incapable of fulfilling the mission placed upon it by the course of

development, nothing else would remain except openly to recognize that the socialist program based on the internal contradictions of capitalist society, ended as a Utopia. It is self-evident that a new "minimum" program would be required — for the defense of the interests of the slaves of the totalitarian bureaucratic society. But are there such incontrovertible or even impressive objective data as would compel us today to renounce the prospect of the socialist revolution? That is the whole question." (Trotsky, "The USSR in War," *The New International*, Nov. 1939, p.327.)

That is not the whole question. To that question, we give no less vigorously negative a reply than Trotsky. There is no data of sufficient weight to warrant abandoning the revolutionary socialist perspective. On that score, Trotsky was and remains quite correct. The essence of the question, however, relates not to the perspective, but to the theoretical characterization of the Soviet state and its bureaucracy.

Up to the time of this article, Trotsky insisted on the following two propositions: 1. Nationalized property, so long as it continues to be the economic basis of the Soviet Union, makes the latter a workers' state, regardless of the political régime in power; and, 2. So long as it does not create new property forms, unique to itself, and so long as it rests on nationalized property, the bureaucracy is not a new or an old ruling class, but a caste. In "The USSR in War," Trotsky declared it *theoretically possible* — we repeat: not probable, but nevertheless theoretically possible — 1. for the property forms and relations now existing in the Soviet Union to continue existing and yet represent not a workers' state but a new exploiting society; and 2. for the bureaucracy now existing in the Soviet Union to become a new exploiting and ruling class without changing the property forms and relations it now rests upon.

To allow such a theoretical *possibility*, does not eliminate the revolutionary perspective, but it does destroy, at one blow, so to speak, the *theoretical* basis for our past characterization of Russia as a workers' state.

To argue that Trotsky considered this alternative a most unlikely perspective, that, indeed (and this is of course correct), he saw no reason at all for adopting it, is arbitrary and beside the point. At best, it is tantamount to saying: At bottom, Russia is a workers' state because it rests on nationalized property and... we still have a social-revolutionary world perspective; if we abandoned this perspective, it would cease being a workers' state even though its property forms remain fundamentally unaltered. Or more simply: it is not nationalized property that determines the working-class character of the Soviet state and the caste character of its bureaucracy; our perspective determines that.

If Trotsky's alternative perspective is accepted as a theoretical possibility (as we do, although not in quite the same way in which he puts it forward; but that is another matter), it is theoretically impossible any longer to hold that nationalized property is *sufficient* to determine the Soviet Union as a workers' state. That holds true, moreover, whether Trotsky's alternative perspective is accepted or not. The traditional view of the International on the class character of the USSR rests upon a grievous theoretical error.

In his writings on the Soviet Union, and particularly in *The Revolution Betrayed*, Trotsky speaks interchangeably of the "property forms" and the "property relations" in the country as if he were referring to one and the same thing. Speaking of the new political revolution against the bureaucracy, he says: "So far as concerns property relations, the new power would not have to resort to revolutionary measures." (p.252.) Speaking of the capitalist counter-revolution, he says: "Notwithstanding that the Soviet bureaucracy has gone far toward preparing a bourgeois restoration, the new régime would have to introduce into the matter of forms of property and methods of industry not a reform, but a social revolution." (p.253.)

When referring to property forms in the Soviet Union, Trotsky obviously means nationalized property, that is, state ownership of the means of production and exchange. It is just as obvious that, no matter what has been changed and how much it has been changed in the Soviet Union by Stalinism, state ownership of the means of production and exchange continues to exist. It is further obvious that no Marxist will deny that, when the proletariat takes the helm again in Russia, it will maintain state property.

However, what is crucial are not the property forms, *i.e.*, nationalized property, whose existence cannot be denied, but precisely the relations of the various social groups in the Soviet Union to this property, *i.e., property relations!* If we can speak of nationalized property in the Soviet Union, this does not yet establish what the property relations are.

Under capitalism the ownership of land and the means of production and exchange is in private (individual or corporate) hands. The distribution of the means or instruments of production under capitalism puts the possessors of capital in command of society, and of the proletariat, which is divorced from property and has only its own labor power at its disposal. The relations to property of these classes, and consequently the social relations into which they necessarily enter in the process of production, are clear to all intelligent persons.

Now, the state is the product of irreconcilable social contradictions. Disposing of a force separate from the people, it intervenes in the raging struggle between the classes in order to prevent their mutual destruction and to preserve the social order. "But having arisen amid these conflicts, it is as a rule the state of the most powerful economic class that by force of its economic supremacy becomes also the ruling political class and thus acquires new means of subduing and exploiting the oppressed masses," writes Engels. Under capitalism, "the most powerful economic class" is represented by its capitalist class state.

What is important to note here is that the social power of the capitalist class derives from its "economic supremacy," that is, from its direct ownership of the instruments of production; and that this power is reflected in or supplemented by its political rule of the state machine, of the "public power of coercion." The two are not identical, let it be noted further, for a Bonapartist or fascist régime may and has deprived the capitalist class of its political rule only to leave its social rule, if not completely intact, then at least fundamentally unshaken.

Two other characteristics of bourgeois property relations and the bourgeois state are worth keeping in mind.

Bourgeois property relations and pre-capitalist property relations are not as incompatible with each other, as either of them are with socialist property relations. The first two not only have lived together in *relative* peace for long periods of time but, especially in the period of imperialism on a world scale, still live together today. An example of the first was the almost one-century-old cohabitation of the capitalist North and the Southern slaveocracy in the United States; an outstanding example of the second is British imperialism in India. But more important than this is a key distinction between the bourgeoisie and the proletariat. The capitalist class already has wide economic power before it overthrows feudal society and, by doing so, it acquires that necessary political and social power which establishes it as *the* ruling class. Finally, the bourgeois state solemnly recognizes the right of private property, that is, it establishes juridically (and defends accordingly) that which is already established in fact by the bourgeoisie's ownership of capital. The social power of the capitalist class lies fundamentally in its actual ownership of the instruments of production, that is, in that which gives it its "economic supremacy," and *therefore* its control of the state.

How do matters stand with the proletariat, with its state, and the property forms and property relations unique to it? The young bourgeoisie was able to develop (within the objective limits established by feudalism) its specific property relations even under feudalism; at times, as we have seen, it could even share political power with a pre-capitalist class. The proletariat cannot do anything of the kind under capitalism, unless you except those utopians who still dream of developing socialism right in the heart of capitalism by means of "producers' co-operatives." By its very position in the old society, the proletariat has no property under capitalism. The working class acquires economic supremacy *only after* it has seized political power.

"*We have already seen* [said the *Communist Manifesto*] *that the first step in the workers' revolution is to make the proletariat the ruling class, to establish democracy. The proletariat will use its political supremacy in order, by degrees, to wrest all capital from the bourgeoisie, to centralize all the means of production into the hands of the State (this meaning the proletariat organized as ruling class), and, as rapidly as possible, to increase the total mass of productive forces.*"

Thus by its very position in the new society, the proletariat still has no property, that is, it does not own property in the sense that the feudal lord or the capitalist did. It was and remains a propertyless class! It seizes state power. The new state is simply the proletariat organized as the ruling class. The state expropriates the private owners of land and capital, and ownership of land, and the means of production and exchange, becomes vested in the *state*. By its action, the state has established new property forms — nationalized or state-ified or collectivized property. It has also established new property relations. So far as the proletariat is concerned, it has a fundamentally new relationship to property. The essence of the change lies in the fact that the working class is in command of that state-owned property *because* the state is the proletariat organized as the ruling class (through its Soviets, its army, its courts and institutions like the party, the unions, the factory committees, *etc.*). There is the nub of the question.

The economic supremacy of the bourgeoisie under capitalism is based upon its ownership of the decisive instruments of production and exchange. Hence, its social power; hence, the bourgeois state. The social rule of the proletariat cannot express itself in private ownership of capital, but only in its "ownership" of the state in whose hands is concentrated all the decisive economic power. Hence, its social power lies in its political power. In bourgeois society, the two can be and are divorced; in the proletarian state, they are inseparable. Much of the same thing is said by Trotsky when he points out that in contrast to private property, "the property relations which issued from the socialist revolution are indivisibly bound up with the new state as their repository." (*The Revolution Betrayed*, p.250.) But from this follows in reality, what does not follow in Trotsky's analysis. The proletariat's relations to property, to the new, collectivist property, are indivisibly bound up with its relations to the state, that is, to the political power.

We do not even begin to approach the heart of the problem by dealing with its juridical aspects, however. That suffices, more or less, in a bourgeois state. There, let us remember, the juridical acknowledgement by the state of private ownership corresponds exactly with the palpable economic and social reality. Ford and Dupont own their plants... and their Congressmen; Krupp and Schroeder own their plants... and their Deputies. In the Soviet Union, the proletarian is master of property only if he is master of the state which is its repository. That mastery alone can distinguish it as the ruling class. "The transfer of the factories to the state changed the situation of the worker only juridically," Trotsky points out quite aptly. (*Op. cit.*, p.241.) And further: "From the point of view of property in the means of production, the differences between a marshal and a servant girl, the head of a trust and a day laborer, the son of a people's commissar and a homeless child, seem not to exist at all." (*Ibid.*, p.238.) Precisely! And why not? Under capitalism, the difference in the relations to property of the trust head and the day laborer is determined and clearly evidenced by the fact that the former is the owner of capital and the latter owns merely his labor power. In the Soviet Union, the difference in the relations to property of the six persons Trotsky mentions is not determined or visible by virtue of ownership of basic property but precisely by the degree to which any and all of them "own" the state to which all social property belongs.

The state is a political institution, a weapon of organized coercion to uphold the supremacy of a class. It is not owned like a pair of socks or a factory; it is controlled. No class — no modern class — controls it directly, among other reasons because the modern state is too complicated and all-pervading to manipulate like a 17th century New England town meeting. A class controls the state indirectly, through its representatives, its authorized delegates.

The Bolshevik revolution lifted the working class to the position of ruling class in the country. As Marx and Engels and Lenin had foreseen, the conquest of state power by the proletariat immediately revealed itself as "something which is no longer really a form of the State." In place of "special bodies of armed men" divorced from the people, there rose the armed people. In place of a corrupted and bureaucratized parliamentary machine, the democratic Soviets embracing tens of millions. In the most difficult days, in the rigorous period of War Communism, the state was the "proletariat organized as the ruling class" — organized through the Soviets, through the trade unions, through the living, revolutionary proletarian Communist party.

The Stalinist reaction, the causes and course of which have been traced so brilliantly by Trotsky above all others, meant the systematic hacking away of every finger of control the working class had over its state. And with the triumph of the bureaucratic counter-revolution came the end of rule of the working class. The Soviets were eviscerated and finally wiped out formally by decree. The trade unions were converted into slave-drivers cracking the whip over the working class. Workers' control in the factories went a dozen years ago. The people were forbidden to bear arms, even non-explosive weapons — it was the possession of arms by the people that Lenin qualified as the very essence of the question of the state! The militia system gave way decisively to the army separated from the people. The Communist Youth were formally prohibited from participating in politics, *i.e.,* from concerning themselves with the state. The Communist party was gutted, all the Bolsheviks in it broken in two, imprisoned, exiled and finally shot. How absurd are all the social-democratic lamentations about the "one-party dictatorship" in light of this analysis! It was precisely this party, while it lived, which was the last channel through which the Soviet working class exercized its political power.

"The recognition of the present Soviet state as a workers' state," wrote Trotsky in his thesis on Russia in 1931, *"not only signifies that the bourgeoisie can conquer power in no other way than by an armed uprising but also that the proletariat of the USSR has not forfeited the possibility of submitting the bureaucracy to it, of reviving the party again and of mending the régime of the dictatorship — without a new revolution, with the methods and on the road of reform." (Op. cit.,* p.36.)

Quite right. And conversely, when the Soviet proletariat finally lost the possibility of submitting the bureaucracy to itself by methods of reform, and was left with the weapon of revolution, we should have abandoned our characterization of the USSR as a workers' state. Even if belatedly, it is necessary to do that now.

That political expropriation of the proletariat about which the International has spoken, following Trotsky's analysis — that is nothing more nor less than the destruction of the class rule of the workers, the end of the Soviet Union as a workers' state. In point of time — the Stalinist counter-revolution has not been as cataclysmic as to dates or as dramatic in symbols as was the French Revolution or the Bolshevik insurrection — the destruction of the old class rule may be said to have culminated with the physical annihilation of the last Bolsheviks.

A change in class rule, a revolution or counter-revolution, without violence, without civil war, gradually? Trotsky has reproached defenders of such a conception with "reformism-in-reverse." The reproach might hold in our case, too, but for the fact that the Stalinist counter-revolution was violent and bloody enough. The seizure of power by the Bolsheviks was virtually bloodless and non-violent. The breadth and duration of the civil war that followed were determined by the strength, the virility, and not least of all by the international imperialist aid furnished to the overturned classes. The comparative *one-sidedness* of the civil war attending the Stalinist counter-revolution was determined by the oft-noted passivity of the masses, their weariness, their failure to receive international support. In spite of this, Stalin's road to power lay through rivers of blood and over a mountain of skulls. Neither the Stalinist counter-revolution nor the Bolshevik revolution was effected by Fabian gradualist reforms.

The conquest of state power by the bureaucracy spelled the destruction of the property relations established by the Bolshevik revolution.

If the workers are no longer the ruling class and the Soviet Union no longer a workers' state, and if there is no private-property-owning capitalist class ruling Russia, what is the class nature of the state and what exactly is the bureaucracy that dominates it?

Hitherto we called the Stalinist bureaucracy a caste, and denied it the attributes of a class. Yet, Trotsky admitted in September a year ago, the definition as a caste has not "a strictly scientific character. Its relative superiority lies in this, that the makeshift character of the term is clear to everybody, since it would enter nobody's mind to identify the Moscow oligarchy with the Hindu caste of Brahmins." In résumé, it is called a caste not because it is a caste — the old Marxian definition of a caste would scarcely fit Stalin & Co. — but because it is not a class. Without letting the dispute "degenerate into sterile toying with words," let us see if we cannot come closer to a scientific characterization than we have in the past.

The late Bukharin defined a class as "the aggregate of persons playing the same part in production, standing in the same relation toward other persons in the production process, these relations being also expressed in things (instruments of labor)." According to Trotsky, a class is defined "by its independent rôle in the general structure of economy and by its independent roots in the economic foundation of society. Each class... works out its own special forms of property. The bureaucracy lacks all these social traits."

In general, either definition would serve. But not as an absolutely unfailing test for all classes in all class societies.[1] The Marxian definition of a class is obviously widened by Engels (*see footnote*) to include a social group "that did not take part in production" but which made itself "the indispensable mediator between two producers," exploiting them both. The merchants characterized by Engels as a class are neither more nor less encompassed in Trotsky's definition, given above, or in Bukharin's, than is the Stalinist bureaucracy (except in so far as this bureaucracy most definitely takes part in the process of production). But the indubitable fact that the bureaucracy has not abolished state property is not sufficient

---

1. Although, for example, the merchants would fail to pass either of the two tests given above, Engels qualified them as a class. "A third division of labor was added by civilization: it created a class that did not take part in production, but occupied itself merely with the exchange of products — the merchants. All former attempts at class formation were exclusively concerned with production. They divided the producers into directors and directed, or into producers on a more or less extensive scale. But here a class appears for the first time that captures the control of production in general and subjugates the producers to its rule, without taking the least part in production. A class that makes itself the indispensable mediator between two producers and exploits them both under the pretext of saving them the trouble and risk of exchange, of extending the markets for their products to distant regions, and of thus becoming the most useful class in society; a class of parasites, genuine social ichneumons, that skim the cream off production at home and abroad as a reward for very insignificant services; that rapidly amass enormous wealth and gain social influence accordingly; that for this reason reap ever new honours and ever greater control of production during the period of civilization, until they at last bring to light a product of their own — periodical crises in industry." (Engels, *The Origin of the Family*, p.201.)

ground for withholding from it the qualification of a class, although, as we shall see, within certain limits. But, it has been objected:

"If the Bonapartist riffraff is a class this means that it is not an abortion but a viable child of history. If its marauding parasitism is 'exploitation' in the scientific sense of the term, this means that the bureaucracy possesses a historical future as the ruling class indispensable to the given system of economy". (Trotsky, "Again and Once More Again on the Nature of the USSR," *The New International*, Feb. 1940, p.14.)

Is or is not the Stalinist bureaucracy "a ruling class indispensable" to the system of economy in the Soviet Union? This question — begs the question! The question is precisely: what is the given system of economy? For the *given* system — the property relations established by the counter-revolution — the Stalinist bureaucracy is the indispensable ruling class. As for the economic system and the property relations established by the Bolshevik revolution (under which the Stalinist bureaucracy was by no means the indispensable ruling class) — these are just what the bureaucratic counter-revolution destroyed! To the question, is the bureaucracy indispensable to "Soviet economy"? one can therefore answer, Yes and no.

To the same question put somewhat differently, Is the bureaucracy an "historical accident," an abortion, or viable and a necessity, the answer must be given in the same spirit. It is an historical necessity — "a result of the iron necessity to give birth to and support a privileged minority so long as it is impossible to guarantee genuine equality." (*The Revolution Betrayed*, p.55.) It is not an "historical accident" for the good reason that it has well-established historical causes. It is not inherent in a society resting upon collective property in the means of production and exchange, as the capitalist class is inherent in a society resting upon capitalist property. Rather, it is the product of a conjunction of circumstances, primarily that the proletarian revolution broke out in *backward* Russia and was not supplemented and thereby saved by the victory of the revolution in the *advanced* countries. Hence, while its concrete characteristics do not permit us to qualify it as a viable or indispensable ruling class in the same sense as the historical capitalist class, we may and do speak of it as a ruling class whose complete control of the state now guarantees its political and economic supremacy in the country.

It is interesting to note that the evolution and transformation of the Soviet bureaucracy in the workers' state — the state of Lenin and Trotsky — is quite different and even contrary to the evolution of the capitalist class in its state. Speaking of the separation of the capitalist manager into capitalists *and* managers of the process of production, Marx writes:

"The labor of superintendence and management arising out of the antagonistic character and rule of capital over labor, which all modes of production based on class antagonisms have in common with the capitalist mode, is directly and inseparably connected, also under the capitalist system, with those productive functions, which all combined social labor assigns to individuals as their special tasks... Compared to the money-capitalist the industrial capitalist is a laborer, but a laboring capitalist, an exploiter of the labor of others. The wages which he claims and pockets for this labor amount exactly to the appropriated quantity of another's labor and depend directly upon the rate of exploitation of this labor, so far as he takes the trouble to assume the necessary burdens of exploitation. They do

not depend upon the degree of his exertions in carrying on this exploitation. He can easily shift this burden to the shoulders of a superintendent for moderate pay... Stock companies in general, developed with the credit system, have a tendency to separate this labor of management as a function more and more from the ownership of capital, whether it be self-owned or borrowed". (Capital, Vol.III, pp.454ff.)

Even though this tendency to separate out of the capitalist class (or the upper ranks of the working class) a group of managers and superintendents is constantly accentuated under capitalism, this group does not develop into an independent class. Why? Because to the extent that the manager (*i.e.*, a highly-paid superintendent-worker) changes his "relations to property" and becomes an owner of capital, he merely enters into the already existing capitalist class. He need not and does not create new property relations.

The evolution has been distinctly different in Russia. The proletariat in control of the state, and therefore of economy, soon found itself unable directly to organize economy, expand the productive forces and raise labor productivity because of a whole series of circumstances — its own lack of training in management and superintendence, in bookkeeping and strict accounting, the absence of help from the technologically more advanced countries, *etc., etc.* As with the building of the Red Army, so in industry, the Russian proletariat was urged by Lenin to call upon and it did call upon a whole host and variety of experts — some from its own ranks, some from the ranks of the class enemy, some from the ranks of the bandwagon-jumpers, constituting in all a considerable bureaucracy. But, given the revolutionary party, given the Soviets, given the trade unions, given the factory committees, that is, given those concrete means by which the workers ruled the state, *their* state, this bureaucracy, however perilous, remained within the limitations of "hired hands" in the service of the workers' state. In political or economic life — the bureaucracies in both tended to and did merge — the bureaucracy was subject to the criticism, control, recall or discharge of the "working class organized as a ruling class."

The whole history of the struggle of the Trotskyist movement in Russia against the bureaucracy signified, at bottom, a struggle to prevent the crushing of the workers' state by the growing monster of a bureaucracy which was becoming increasingly different *in quality* from the "hired hands" of the workers' state as well as from any kind of bureaucratic group under capitalism. What we have called the consummated usurpation of power by the Stalinist bureaucracy was, in reality, nothing but the self-realization of the bureaucracy as a class and its seizure of state power from the proletariat, the establishment of its own state power and its own rule. The *qualitative* difference lies precisely in this: the bureaucracy is no longer the controlled and revocable "managers and superintendents" employed by the workers' state in the party, the state apparatus, the industries, the army, the unions, the fields, but the owners and controllers of the state, which is in turn the repository of collectivized property and thereby the employer of all hired hands, the masses of the workers, above all, included.

The situation of the young Soviet republic (the historical circumstances surrounding its birth and evolution), imposed upon it the "division of labor" described above, and often commented on by Lenin. Where a similar division of labor under capitalism does not transform the economic or political agents of the ruling class into a new class, for the reasons given above (primarily, the relations to capitalist private property), it does tend to create a new class in a state reposing on collectivized property, that is, in a state which is itself the repository of *all* social property. Trotsky is entirely right when he speaks of "dynamic social formations [in Russia] which have had no precedent and have no analogies." It is even more to the point when he writes that "the very fact of its [the bureaucracy's] appropriation of political power in a country where the principal means of production are in the hands of the state, creates a new and hitherto unknown relation between the bureaucracy and the riches of the nation." For what is unprecedented and new, hitherto unknown, one cannot find a sufficiently illuminating analogy in the bureaucracies in other societies which did not develop into a class but remained class-serving bureaucracies.

What Trotsky calls the indispensable theoretical key to an understanding of the situation in Russia is the remarkable passage from Marx which he quotes in *The Revolution Betrayed*: "*A development of the productive forces is the absolutely necessary practical premise [of communism], because without it want is generalized, and with want the struggle for necessities begins again, and that means that all the old crap must revive.*"

Both Lenin and Trotsky kept repeating in the early years: in backward Russia, socialism cannot be built without the aid of the more advanced countries. Before the revolution, in 1915, Trotsky made clear his opinion — for which Stalinism never forgave him — that without state aid of the western proletariat, the workers of Russia could not hope to remain in power for long. That state aid did not come, thanks to the international social democracy, later ably supplemented by the Stalinists. But the prediction of Lenin and Trotsky did come true. The workers of the Soviet Union were unable to hold power. That they lost it in a peculiar, unforeseen and even unforeseeable way — not because of a bourgeois restoration, but in the form of the seizure of power by a counter-revolutionary bureaucracy which retained and based itself on the new, collectivist form of property — is true. But they did lose power. The old crap was revived — in a new, unprecedented, hitherto-unknown form, the rule of a *new bureaucratic class*. A class that always was, that always will be? Not at all. "*Class,*" Lenin pointed out in April 1920, "*is a concept that takes shape in struggle — and in the course of development.*"

The reminder is particularly timely in considering the struggle and evolution of the Stalinist bureaucracy into a class. Precisely here it is worth more than passing notice (because of its profound significance), that the counter-revolution, like the revolution that preceded it, found that it could not, as Marx said about the seizure of power by the proletariat in the Paris Commune, "simply lay hold of the ready-made state machinery and wield it for its own purposes." The Russian proletariat had to *shatter* the old bourgeois state and its apparatus, and put in its place a new state, a complex of the Soviets, the revolutionary party, the trade unions, the factory committees, the militia system, *etc.* To achieve power and establish its rule, the Stalinist counter-revolution in turn had to shatter the proletarian Soviet state — those same Soviets, the party, the unions, the factory committees, the militia system, the "armed people", etc. It did not and could not "simply lay hold of" the existing machinery of state and set it going for its own ends. It shattered the workers' state, and put in its place the totalitarian state of bureaucratic collectivism.

Thereby it compelled us to add to our theory this conception, among others: Just as it is possible to have different classes ruling in societies resting upon the private ownership of property, so it is possible to have more than one class ruling in a society resting upon the collective ownership of property — concretely, the working class and the bureaucracy.

Can this new class look forward to a social life-span as long as that enjoyed, for example, by the capitalist class? We see no reason to believe that it can. Throughout modern capitalist society, ripped apart so violently by its contradictions, there is clearly discernible the irrepressible tendency towards collectivism, the only means whereby the productive forces of mankind can be expanded and thereby provide that ample satisfaction of human needs which is the pre-condition to the blooming of a new civilization and culture. But there is no adequate ground for believing that this tendency will materialize in the form of a universal "bureaucratic collectivism." The "unconditional development of the productive forces of society comes continually into conflict with the limited end, the self-expansion of the existing capital". The revolutionary struggle against the capitalist mode of production, triumphing in those countries which have already attained a high level of economic development, including the development of labor productivity, leads rather to the socialist society. The circumstances which left Soviet Russia isolated, dependent upon its own primitive forces, and thus generated that "generalized want" which facilitated the victory of the bureaucratic counter-revolution, will be and can only be overcome by overcoming its causes — namely, the capitalist encirclement. The social revolution which spells the doom of capitalist imperialism and the release of the pent-up, strangled forces of production, will put an end to the want and misery of the masses in the West and to the very basis of the misery of Stalinism in the Soviet Union.

Social life and evolution were slow and long-drawn-out under feudalism. Their pace was considerably accelerated under capitalism, and phenomena which took decades in developing under feudalism, took only years to develop under capitalism. World society which entered the period of world wars and socialist revolutions, finds the pace speeded up to a rhythm that has no precedent in history. All events and phenomena tend to be telescoped in point of time. From this standpoint, the rise, and the early fall, of the bureaucracy in the Soviet Union necessitates an indication of the limits of its development, as we pointed out above, precisely in order to distinguish it from the fundamental historical classes. This is perhaps best done by characterizing it as the ruling class of an unstable society which is already a fetter on economic development.

What has already been said should serve to indicate the similarities between the Stalinist and Fascist bureaucracies, but above all to indicate the profound social and historical difference between them. Following our analysis, the animadversions of all species of rationalizers on the identity of character of Stalinism and Fascism, remain just as superficial as ever.

Trotsky's characterization of the two bureaucracies as "symmetrical" is incontrovertible, but only within the limits with which he surrounds the term, namely, they are both products of the same failure of the Western proletariat to solve the social crisis by social revolution. To go further, they are identical, but again within well-defined limits. The political régime, the technique of rule, the highly-developed social demagogy, the system of terror without end — these are essential features of Hitlerite and Stalinist totalitarianism, some of them more fully developed under the latter than under the former. At this point, however, the similarity ceases.

From the standpoint of our old analysis and theory, the Soviet Union remained a workers' state despite its political régime. In short, we said, just as the social rule of capitalism, the capitalist state, was preserved under different political régimes — republic, monarchy, military dictatorship, fascism — so the social rule of the proletariat, the workers' state could be maintained under different political régimes — Soviet democracy, Stalinist totalitarianism. Can we, then, even speak of a "counter-revolutionary workers' state"? was the question posed by Trotsky early this year. To which his reply was, "There are two completely counter-revolutionary workers' Internationals" and one can therefore speak also of "the counter-revolutionary workers' state. In the last analysis a workers' state is a trade union which has conquered power." It is a workers' state by virtue of its property forms, and it is counter-revolutionary by virtue of its political régime.

Without dwelling here on the analogy between the Soviet state today and the trade unions, it is necessary to point out that thoroughgoing consistency would demand of this standpoint that the Soviet Union be characterised as a *Fascist workers' state*, workers' state, again, because of its property forms, and Fascist because of its political régime. Objections to this characterization can only be based upon the embarrassment caused by this natural product of consistency.

However that may be, if it is not a workers' state, not even a Fascist workers' state, neither is it a state comparable to that of the German Nazis. Let us see why.

Fascism, resting on the mass basis of the petty-bourgeoisie gone mad under the horrors of the social crisis, *was called to power deliberately* by the big bourgeoisie in order to preserve its social rule, the system of private property. Writers who argue that Fascism put an end to capitalism and inaugurated a new social order, with a new class rule, are guilty of an abstract and static conception of capitalism; more accurately, of an idealization of capitalism as permanently identical with what it was in its halcyon period of organic upward development, its "democratic" phase.

Faced with the imminent prospect of the proletarian revolution putting an end both to the contradictions of capitalism and to capitalist rule, the bourgeoisie preferred the annoyance of a Fascist régime which would suppress (not abolish!) these contradictions and preserve capitalist rule. In other words, at a given stage of its *degeneration*, the *only* way to preserve the capitalist system in any form is by means of the totalitarian dictatorship. As all historians agree, calling Fascism to political power — the abandonment of political rule by the bourgeoisie — was the conscious act of the bourgeoisie itself.

But, it is argued, *after* it came to political power, the Fascist bureaucracy completely dispossessed the bourgeoisie and itself became the ruling class. Which is precisely what needs to be but has not been proved. The system of private ownership of socially-operated property *remains basically intact*. After being in power in Italy for over eighteen years, and in Germany for almost eight, Fascism has yet to nationalize industry, to say nothing of expropriating the bourgeoisie (the expropriation of small sections of the bourgeoisie — the Jewish — is done in the interests of the bourgeoisie as a whole). Why does Hitler, who is so bold in all other spheres, suddenly turn timid when he confronts the "juridical detail" represented by the private (or corporate) ownership of the means of production? Because the two cannot be counterposed: his boldness and "radicalism" in all spheres is directed towards maintaining and reinforcing that "juridical detail," that is, capitalist society, to the extent to which it is at all possible to maintain it *in the period of its decay*.

But doesn't Fascism control the bourgeoisie? Yes, in a sense. That kind of control was foreseen long ago. In January 1916, Lenin and the Zimmerwald Left wrote: "At the end of the war a gigantic universal economic upheaval will manifest itself with all its force, when, under a general exhaustion, unemployment and lack of capital, industry will have to be regulated anew, when the terrific indebtedness of all states will drive them to tremendous taxation, and when state socialism — militarization of the economic life — will seem to be the only way out of financial difficulties." Fascist control means precisely this new regulation of industry, the militarization of economic life in its sharpest form. It controls, it restricts, it regulates, it plunders — but with all that it maintains and even strengthens the capitalist profit system, leaves the bourgeoisie intact as the class owning property. It *assures* the profits of the owning class — taking from it that portion which is required to maintain a bureaucracy and police-spy system needed to keep down labor (which threatens to take away *all* profits and *all* capital, let us not forget) and to maintain a highly modernized military establishment to defend the German bourgeoisie from attacks at home and abroad and to acquire for it new fields of exploitation outside its own frontiers.

But isn't the Fascist bureaucracy, too, becoming a class? In a sense, yes, but not a new class with a new class rule. By virtue of their control of the state power, any number of Fascist bureaucrats, of high and low estate, have used coercion and intimidation to become Board Directors and stockholders in various enterprises. This is especially true of those bureaucrats assigned to industry as commissars of all kinds. On the other side, the bourgeoisie acquires the "good will" of Nazi bureaucrats, employed either in the state or the economic machinery, by bribes of stocks and positions on directing boards. There is, if you wish, a certain process of fusion between sections of the bureaucracy and the bourgeoisie. But the bureaucrats who become stockholders and Board Directors do not thereby become a new class, they enter as integral parts of the industrial or financial bourgeoisie class which we have known for quite some time!

Private ownership of capital, that "juridical detail" before which Hitler comes to a halt, is a social reality of the profoundest importance. With all its political power, the Nazi bureaucracy remains a bureaucracy; sections of it fuse with the bourgeoisie, but as a social aggregation, it is not developing into a new class. Here, control of the state power is not enough. The bureaucracy, in so far as its development into a new class with a new class rule of its own is concerned, *is itself controlled* by the objective reality of the private ownership of capital.

How different it is with the Stalinist bureaucracy! Both bureaucracies "devour, waste, and embezzle a considerable portion of the national income"; both have an income above that of the people, and privileges which correspond to their position in society. But similarity of income is not a definition of a social class. In Germany, the Nazis are not more than a bureaucracy — extremely powerful, to be sure, but still only a bureaucracy. In the Soviet Union, the bureaucracy is the ruling class, because it possesses as its own the state power which, in this country, is the owner of all social property.

In Germany, the Nazis have attained a great degree of independence by their control of the state, but it continues to be "the state of the most powerful economic class" — the bourgeoisie. In the Soviet Union, control of the state, sole owner of social property, makes the bureaucracy the most powerful economic class. Therein lies the fundamental difference between the Soviet state, even under Stalinism, and all other *pre-collectivist* states. The difference is of epochal historical importance.

Of epochal historical importance, we repeat, for our analysis does not diminish by an iota the profound social-revolutionary significance of the Russian proletarian revolution. Starting at a low level, lowered still further by years of war, civil war, famine and their devastations, isolated from world economy, infested with a monstrous bureaucracy, the Soviet Union nevertheless attained a rhythm of economic development, an expansion of the productive forces which exceeded the expectations of the boldest revolutionary thinkers and easily aroused the astonishment of the entire world. This was not due to any virtues of the bureaucracy under whose reign it was accomplished, but in spite of the concomitant overhead waste of that reign. Economic progress in the Soviet Union was accomplished on the basis of planning and of the new, collectivist forms of property established by the proletarian revolution. What would that progress have looked like if only those new forms, and property relations most suitable to them, had been extended to the more highly developed countries of Europe and America! It staggers the imagination.

Fascism, on the other hand, has developed to its highest degree the intervention of the state as regulator, subsidizer and controller of a social order which *does not expand but contracts* the productive forces of modern society. The contrary view held by those who are so impressed by the great development of industry in Germany in the period of war economy, is based upon superficial and temporary phenomena. Fascism, as a motor or a brake on the development of productive forces, must be judged not by the tons of war-steel produced in the Ruhr, but on the infinitely more significant policy it pursues in the conquered territories which it seeks to convert, from industrially advanced countries, into backward agricultural hinterlands of German national economy.

Both bureaucracies are reactionary. Both bureaucracies act as brakes on the development of the productive forces of society. Neither plays a progressive rôle, even if in both cases this or that act may have an abstractly progressive significance (Hitler destroys Bavarian particularism and "liberates" the Sudetens; Stalin nationalizes industry in Latvia). In the Soviet Union, however, the Stalinist bureaucracy is the brake, and its removal would permit the widest expansion of the productive forces. Whereas in Germany, as in other capitalist countries, it is not merely the Fascist bureaucracy who stand in the way, but primarily the capitalist class, the capitalist mode of production. The difference is between increased state intervention to preserve capitalist property and the collective ownership of property by the bureaucratic state.

How express the difference summarily and in conventional terms? People buying canned goods want and are entitled to have labels affixed that will enable them to distinguish at a glance pears from peaches from peas. "We often seek salvation from unfamiliar phenomena in familiar terms," Trotsky observed. But what is to be done with unprecedented, new, hitherto-unknown phenomena, how label them in such a way as to describe at once their origin, their present state, their more than one future prospect, and wherein they resemble and differ from other phenomena? The task is not easy. Yet life and politics demand some conventional, summary terms for social phenomena; one cannot answer the question — What is the Soviet state? — by repeating in detail a long and complex analysis. The demand must be met as satisfactorily as is possible in the nature of the case.

The early Soviet state we would call, with Lenin, a bureaucratically deformed workers' state. The Soviet state today we would call — bureaucratic state socialism, a characterization which attempts to embrace both its historical origin and its distinction from capitalism as well as its current diversion under Stalinism. The German state today we would call, in distinction from the Soviet state, bureaucratic or totalitarian state capitalism. These terms are neither elegant nor absolutely precise, but they will have to do for want of any others more precise or even half as precise.

From the foregoing analysis the basis is laid not only for eliminating the discrepancies and defects in our old analysis, but for clarifying our political position.

Political or Social Revolution? Here too, without falling into a game of terminology or toying with abstract concepts, it is necessary to strive for the maximum exactness. As distinct from social revolution, Trotsky and the 4th International called up to now for a political revolution in the Soviet Union. "History has known elsewhere not only social revolutions which substituted the bourgeoisie for the feudal régime, but also political revolutions which, without destroying the economic foundations of society, swept out an old ruling upper crust (1830 and 1848 in France, February 1917 in Russia, *etc.*). The overthrow of the Bonapartist caste will, of course, have deep social consequences, but in itself it will be confined within the limits of political revolution." (*The Revolution Betrayed*, p.288.) And again, on the same page: "It is not a question this time of changing the economic foundations of society, of replacing certain forms of property with other forms."

In the revolution against the Stalinist bureaucracy the nationalization of the means of production and exchange will indeed be preserved by the proletariat in power. If that is what is meant by political revolution, if that is all it could mean, then we could easily be reconciled to it. But from our whole analysis, it follows that the Stalinist counter-revolution, in seizing the power of the state, thereby changed the property relations in the Soviet Union. In overturning the rule of the bureaucracy, the Soviet proletariat will again raise itself to the position of ruling class, organize its own state, and once more change its relations to property. The revolution will thus not merely have "deep social consequences," it will be a social revolution. After what has been said in another section, it is not necessary to insist here on those points wherein the social revolution in Germany or England would resemble the social revolution in Russia and wherein they would differ from it. In the former, it is a question of ending capitalism and lifting the country into the new historical epoch of collectivism and socialism. In the latter, it is a question of destroying a reactionary obstacle to the development of a collectivist society towards socialism.

Unconditional Defense of the USSR? The slogan of "unconditional defense of the Soviet Union" assumed that, even under Stalin and despite Stalin, the Soviet Union could play only a progressive rôle in any war with a capitalist power. The Second World War broke out, with the Soviet Union as one of the participants, now as a belligerent, now as a "non-belligerent." But, "theory is not a note which you can present at any moment to reality for payment." Reality showed that the Soviet Union, in the war in Poland and in Finland, in the war as a whole, was playing a reactionary rôle. The Stalinist bureaucracy and its army acted as an indispensable auxiliary in the military calculations of German imperialism. They covered the latter's eastern, northern and southeastern flank, helped in the crushing of Poland (and along with it, of the incipient Polish Commune), and for their pains, received a share of the booty. In the conquered territories, it is true, Stalin proceeded to establish the same economic order that prevails in the Soviet Union. But this has no absolute value, in and of itself — only a relative value. One can say with Trotsky that "the economic transformations in the occupied provinces do not compensate for this by even a tenth part!"

From the standpoint of the interests of the international socialist revolution, defense of the Soviet Union in this war (*i.e.,* support of the Red Army) could only have a negative effect. Even from the more limited standpoint of preserving the new economic forms in the Soviet Union, it must be established that they were not involved in the war. At stake were and are what Trotsky calls "the driving force behind the Moscow bureaucracy... the tendency to expand its power, its prestige, its revenues."

The attempt to exhaust the analysis of the Stalinist course in the war by ascribing it to "purely military" steps of preventive-defensive character (what is meant in general by "purely military" steps remains a mystery, since they exist neither in nature nor society), is doomed by its superficiality to failure. Naturally, all military steps are... military steps, but saying so does not advance us very far.

The general political considerations which actuated the Stalinists in making an alliance with Hitler (capitulation to Germany out of fear of war, *etc.*) have been stated by us on more than one occasion and require no repetition here. But there are even more profound reasons, which have little or nothing to do with the fact that Stalin's master-ally is German Fascism. The same reasons would have dictated the same course in the war if the alliance had been made, as a result of a different conjunction of circumstances, with the noble democracies. They are summed up in the lust for expansion of the Stalinist bureaucracy, which has even less in common with Lenin's policy of extending the revolution to capitalist countries than the Stalinist state has with the early workers' state.

And what is the economic base of this lust for expansion, this most peculiar imperialism which you have invented? we were asked, sometimes with superior sneers, sometimes with genuine interest in the problem. We know what are the irrepressible economic compulsions, the inherent economic contradictions, that produce the imperialist policy of finance capitalism. What are their equivalents in the Soviet Union?

Stalinist imperialism is no more like capitalist imperialism than the Stalinist state is like the bourgeois state. Just the same it has its own economic compulsions and internal contradictions, which hold it back here and drive it forward there. Under capitalism, the purpose of production is the production of surplus value, of profit, "not the product, but the surplus product." In the workers' state, production was carried on and extended for the satisfaction of the needs of the Soviet masses. For that, they needed not the oppression of themselves or of other people but the liberation of the peoples of the capitalist countries and the colonial empires. In the Stalinist state, production is carried on and extended for the satisfaction of the needs of the bureaucracy, for the increasing of its wealth, its privileges, its power. At every turn of events, it seeks to overcome the mounting difficulties and resolve the contradictions which it cannot really resolve, by intensifying the exploitation and oppression of the masses.

We surely need not, in a serious discussion among Marxists, insist upon the fact, so vehemently denied a year ago by the eminent Marxologist at the head of the SWP, that there are still classes in the Soviet Union, and that exploitation takes place there. Not *capitalist* exploitation — but economic exploitation nonetheless. "The differences in income are determined, in other words, not only by differences of individual productiveness, but also by *a masked appropriation of the product of the labor of others*. The privileged minority of shareholders is living at the expense of the deprived majority." (*The Revolution Betrayed*, p.240. My emphasis — MS.) The *driving force* behind the bureaucracy is the tendency to increase and expand this "masked [and often not so masked] appropriation of the product of the labor of others." Hence, its penchant for methods of exploitation typical of the worst under capitalism; hence, its lust to extend its dominion over the peoples of the weaker and more backward countries (if it is not the case with the stronger and more advanced countries, then only because the power, and not the will, is lacking), in order to subject them to the oppression and exploitation of the Kremlin oligarchs. The *de facto* occupation of the northwestern provinces of China by Stalin is a case in point. The occupation and then the spoliation of eastern Poland, of the three Baltic countries, of southern Finland (not to mention the hoped-for Petsamo nickel mines), of Bessarabia and Bukovina, tomorrow perhaps parts of Turkey, Iran, and India, are other cases in point. We call this policy Stalinist imperialism.

But are not imperialism and imperialist policy a concomitant only of capitalism? No. While crises of over-production are unique to capitalism, that does not hold true either of war or of imperialism, which are common to divers societies. Lenin, insisting precisely on the scientific, Marxist usage of the terms, wrote in 1917:

"*Crises, precisely in the form of overproduction or of the 'stocking up of market commodities'* (comrade S does not like the word overproduction) *are a phenomenon which is* exclusively *proper to capitalism. Wars, however, are proper both to the economic system based on slavery and the feudal. There have been imperialist wars on the basis of slavery (Rome's war against Carthage was an imperialist war on both sides) as well as in the Middle Ages and in the epoch of mercantile capitalism. Every war in which both belligerent camps are fighting to oppress foreign countries or peoples and for the division of the booty, that is, over 'who shall oppress more and who shall plunder more,' must be called imperialistic."* (*Sämtliche Werke,* Vol. XXI, pp.387f.)

By this definition, on which Lenin dwelled because comrade S had made an "error in principle," it is incontestable that the Stalinists in partnership with Hitler have been conducting an imperialist war "to oppress foreign countries or peoples," "for the division of the booty," to decide "who shall oppress more and who shall plunder more." It is only from this standpoint that Trotsky's statement late in 1939 — "We were and remain against seizures of new territories by the Kremlin" — acquires full and serious meaning. If the Soviet state were essentially a trade union in power, with a reactionary bureaucracy at its head, then we could not possibly oppose "seizures of new territories" any more than we oppose a trade union bureaucracy bringing unorganized workers into the union. With all our opposition to their organizing methods, we always *insisted* that Lewis or Green organize the unorganized. The analogy between the Soviet state and a trade union is not a very solid one...

The theory that Soviet economy is progressive and therefore the wars of the Stalinist bureaucracy against a capitalist state are, by some mysticism, correspondingly and universally progressive, is thus untenable. As in the case of a colonial or semi-colonial country, or a small nation, we defend the Soviet Union against imperialism when it is fighting a progressive war, that is, in our epoch one which corresponds to the interests of the international socialist revolution. When it fights a reactionary, imperialist war, as did "little Serbia" and China in the last world war, we take the traditional revolutionary position: continue implacably the class struggle regardless of the effects on the military front.

Under what conditions is it conceivable to defend the Soviet Union ruled by the Stalinist bureaucracy? It is possible to give only a generalized answer. For example, should the character of the present war change from that of a struggle between the capitalist imperialist camps into a struggle of the imperialists to crush the Soviet Union, the interests of the world revolution would demand the defense of the Soviet Union by the international proletariat. The aim of imperialism in that case, whether it were represented in the war by one or many powers, would be to solve the crisis of world capitalism (and thus prolong the agony of the proletariat) at the cost of reducing the Soviet Union to one or more colonial possessions or spheres of interest. Even though prostrated by the victors in the last war, Germany remained a capitalist country, whose social régime the Allies did their utmost to maintain against the revolutionary proletariat. In the present war, we find victorious Germany not only not undertaking any fundamental economic changes in the conquered territories but preserving the capitalist system by force of arms against the unrest and revolutionism of the proletariat. There is no reason to believe that victorious imperialism in the Soviet Union would leave its nationalized property intact — quite the contrary. As Germany now seeks to do with France, imperialism would seek to destroy all the progress made in the Soviet Union by reducing it to a somewhat more advanced India — a village continent. In these considerations, too, the *historical significance* of the new, collectivist property established by the Russian Revolution, again stands out clearly. Such a transformation of the Soviet Union as triumphant imperialism would undertake, would have a vastly and durable reactionary effect upon world social development, give capitalism and reaction a new lease on life, retard enormously the revolutionary movement, and postpone for we don't know how long the introduction of the world socialist society. From this standpoint and under these conditions, the defense of the Soviet Union, even under Stalinism, is both possible and necessary.

To revise one's position on so important a question as the class character of the Soviet Union, is, as the writer has himself learned, no easy matter. The mass of absurdities written against our old position only served to fix it more firmly in our minds and in our program. To expect others to take a new position overnight would be presumptuous and unprofitable. We did not arrive at the views outlined above lightly or hastily. We neither ask nor expect others to arrive at our views in that way. It is, however, right to ask that they be discussed with the critical objectivity, the exclusive concern with the truth that best serves our common interests, and the polemical loyalty that are the best traditions of Marxism.

Max Shachtman

SHACHTMAN CONTRA BURNHAM

I AM THE LAST ONE to claim that the validity of my point of view is based on some "brand new" conception which nobody ever thought of. But the interests of clarity demand that wherein it differs from previous standpoints receive at least the same emphasis as wherein it resembles them.

Let us take first the famous Burnham position, stated only as recently as September, 1939, when the fight in the SWP broke out. Carter, who knows his position as well as I, quite properly considers the statement that I now have Burnham's position as entirely ludicrous. Wherein is the difference? Burnham proceeded from the same fundamental premise as did the Old Man, and as the Cannonites do today. That may sound odd, but it is true. The Old Man said, for 15 years, the Stalinist bureaucracy aims to destroy nationalized property, that it is the channel through which the bourgeoisie will restore private property, and as late as his *Revolution Betrayed* he insisted that the new constitution was deliberately constituted to lay the juridical basis for the restoration of capitalism.

Substantially, said Burnham, that is correct. Only, he continued, it has already gone so far in wiping out nationalized property that we can no longer speak of the Soviet Union as a workers' state. It is highly interesting to read even now Burnham's resolution of September 1939, which ostensibly served to precipitate the fight. Still accepting Trotsky's premise, Burnham declared that the de-nationalization of property, especially in land, had gone so far as to change the class character of the Soviet Union.

Now, both the Old Man and Burnham were wrong. Looking back upon the past 15 years, and allowing for the Stalinist zig-zags, the indubitable historical fact is that the bureaucracy has done an enormous work in strengthening and expanding the nationalization of

From a letter by Max Shachtman, early 1941.

property. Moreover, granted all the contradictions inherent in its work, it far outstripped all predictions so far as industrialization was concerned. We used to say, to put it crudely: there is an inherent contradiction between nationalization and the Stalinist bureaucracy's rule. This proved to be utterly false, at least in the sense in which we meant it. The preservation of nationalized property and the intensified industrialization resulted in an enormous hypertrophy of bureaucratism. (From this, it doesn't of course follow, as stupid people like Eastman believe, that industrialization and nationalization "inevitably" strengthen a bureaucracy.)

Again, if we look back, we must establish it as an historical fact, that the bureaucracy's relationship to nationalized property is roughly comparably to the relationship of social democracy to bourgeois democracy. By its written class-peace program and its practice the social democracy paves the way for fascism, that is, for the destruction of bourgeois democracy. But this does not change the fact that the social democracy stands or falls with bourgeois democracy. When we say, correctly, that it paves the way for fascism, we don't mean, as the Stalinists used to say, that it is for fascism, and that it is against bourgeois democracy. For the contrary is the fact. Similarly with the Stalin bureaucracy. We used to think that this bureaucracy is, so to speak, consciously and deliberately aiming to restore private property, capitalism. This has not proved to be the case. It rests and can rest only upon nationalized property. It stands and falls with it. To continue the comparison: by its policy of class-peace it so weakens the independent class position of the proletariat as to facilitate the victory of capitalism and world imperialism. That is by no means equivalent to saying that it wants the victory of capitalism and the end of nationalized property. With this as one of my points of departure, you can more easily understand how it is impossible for me to accept Trotsky's position on the class character of the Soviet Union, or the revision of it by Burnham and the others holding the same view. I might add parenthetically that Carter doesn't hold Burnham's view any longer, and has not held it for more than a year. Indeed, at the very beginning of the fight in the SWP, there were in fact four positions on the Russian Question, and not three, as the Cannonites thought. I mean among us. There was the traditional position, there was Burnham's position, there was Carter's position which he didn't get a chance to formulate on paper, and there was the notorious Shachtman school of doubters, which I am trying to liquidate.

In one sentence, the Marxian concept of the state is: the state is the machinery of repression in the hands of the economically dominant ruling class, calculated to preserve its social rule, its property relations. I continue to hold to this concept. What I think I do — and it is anything but contradictory to the Marxian concept — is to show that these property relations take one form in a social order where property is private (feudalism, capitalism) and another form where property is no longer private; and necessarily so. Where property is private the relations to it are expressed with comparative clarity and simplicity. In the United States or Germany, your relations to property, and mine, are, alas, only too clear. We don't own it! All we have is our labor power. Ford's relations to property or Krupp's are no less clear. They own the property.

Where property is state property, then property relations become, so to speak, "state relations". The Russian bourgeoisie ceased to own the state as well as the property. The Russian proletariat took over state power. The state took over property. That made the proletariat the ruling class. Then, after a long, drawn-out civil war, the proletariat lost the state power, the bureaucracy took it over. Trotsky says the bureaucracy owns the state as its private property, "so to speak" — that is, in appearance. In appearance *and in fact*, as everybody knows or should know. By virtue of its ownership of the state, its relations to state property are clearly established for it — and for me. What are the relations to Soviet property of the Soviet proletariat? I quote from an authoritative source, an editorial that appeared a few weeks ago in the *Socialist Appeal*. It said, literally: the Soviet factories are penitentiaries to which the Russian workers are sentenced for life. My dear friend, I could not express the Russian proletariat's relation to Soviet property more brutally or crudely. The eminent Marxists of the *Appeal* may not know it, but in their characterization they are speaking precisely of property relations. There — there and nowhere else — is my own little contribution to the analysis of the Russian question for which I have no particular desire to lay claims for originality.

Joseph Carter

BUREAUCRATIC COLLECTIVISM

IN THE PRESENT ARTICLE I propose to discuss the class character of the Soviet Union, particularly the views of Leon Trotsky, and present my own position in positive form. The origin of the Russian-Trotskyist Opposition dates back to the sharp factional fight which broke out in the Bolshevik Party after the death of Lenin. Trotsky analyzed this struggle as follows: In view of the fact that the Bolshevik Party had a complete monopoly of political power (that is, excluded all rival parties), the interests of the conflicting classes sought expression through factions of the ruling party. The Right Wing represented the Thermidorian faction; the pressure of the capitalist restorationist elements (the kulaks, Nepmen, the old petty-bourgeois specialists) and the labor aristocracy (the better paid workers, white collar employees, and trade union officialdom). On the other hand, the left opposition represented the interests of the working class. In between these two class forces was the Stalin faction, the "bureaucratic Centrist" wing of the party, representing no independent class, but wavering between the two fundamental factions, veering in the long run towards the right, viz., towards bourgeois restoration. The defeats of the West European socialist revolutions strengthened both the Right and the Center; these two united against the Left on the basis of "socialism in one country alone."

Early in 1928 Trotsky wrote: *"... the socialist character of industry is determined and secured in a decisive measure by the role of the party, the voluntary internal cohesion of the proletarian vanguard, the conscious discipline of the administrators, trade union functionaries, members of shop nuclei, etc. If we allow that this web is weakening, disintegrating and ripping then it becomes self-evident that within a brief period nothing will be left of the socialist character of state industry, transport, etc. The trusts and individual factories will begin living an independent life. Not a trace will be left of the planned beginnings, so weak at the present time. The economic struggles of the workers will acquire a scope unrestricted save by the relation of forces. The state ownership of the means of production will be first transformed to a juridical fiction and later on even the latter will be swept away".* (The Third International After Lenin.)

Trotsky's prognoses were refuted by history. The First Five Year Plan, put into effect a few months after he had penned the above lines, strengthened and centralized state ownership and control over the trusts

"Bureaucratic collectivism", from *New International*, September 1941. This version is taken from *Neither Capitalism Nor Socialism: Theories of Bureaucratic Collectivism*, edited by Ernest Haberkern and Arthur Lipow, Humanities Press, New Jersey, 1996, where the full text can be found. The parts omitted here are mainly polemic against Shachtman's position of the time, arguing that Shachtman's is "an illogical, eclectic combination of... the position that Russia is a new, reactionary economic system with the opposite view that it is a progressive economy established by the Russian workers' revolution but distorted by bureaucratic domination."

and factories and extended the planned economy on a scale never reached before. The Bolshevik Party was destroyed, both its Left Wing and Right Wing liquidated politically and physically. The proletarian "web" was broken, but the Stalinists extended their totalitarian control over the economy. At the same time the bureaucracy destroyed virtually all the old capitalist elements in the economy. Contrary to Trotsky's predictions, the destruction of the Bolshevik Party did not mean the end of state property and planning; Russia did not travel the road of Thermidorian, capitalist restoration. On the contrary the Stalinist counter-revolution took a new, hitherto unknown path, the road of bureaucratic absolutism.

Yet Trotsky in the above quotation (and on innumerable other occasions) stated that "the *socialist* character of industry is determined and secured in a decisive measure by the role of the party, the voluntary internal cohesion of the proletarian vanguard, etc." That is, the socialist character of state industry was determined by the domination of the proletarian party in the state and through it in the economy. Or, put in another way, the economic power of the proletariat rested on its political power.

Confronted by the unexpected development of the destruction of the political power of the working class *and* the strengthening of state power and planning, Trotsky faced the dilemma: either to maintain his old criterion and affirm that Russia is no longer a workers' state and its economy no longer "socialist"; or to revise completely the Marxist conception of the workers' state. He chose the latter course, and thereby abandoned the Marxist view he had held until then. He now affirmed that it was the state-owned character of property which determined the socialist character of the economy and the proletarian nature of the state. The bureaucracy's expropriation of the political power of the working class, he added, only signified that Russia was a "degenerated" workers' state, politically dominated by a Bonapartist bureaucracy.

Unfortunately, Trotsky never subjected his old analyses to a thorough critical examination. He never sought to explain why, contrary to his predictions, Russia did not travel the Thermidorian, capitalist road of counter-revolution even though the political power of the working class was destroyed. It is true that he often declared that "the bureaucracy after a stubborn resistance, found itself compelled by the *logic of its own interests* to adopt the program of industrialization and collectivization." (*The Kirov Assassination,* Emphasis in original.) But this would only indicate that the logic of the bureaucracy's own interests was not capitalist restoration (or socialism) but its own absolutist rule in state and economy.

And in retrospect, was the Right Wing of the Bolshevik Party the "Thermidorian" faction? Here again Trotsky never reëxamined this question in great detail. However, he did write in 1938:

"The latest judicial frame-ups were aimed as a blow *against the Left*. This is true also of the mopping up of the leaders of the Right Opposition, because the Right group of the Bolshevik Party, seen from the viewpoint of the bureaucracy's interests and tendencies, represented a *Left* danger". (*Program and Resolutions of the Founding Conference of the Fourth International,* Emphasis in original.)

This correct appraisal of the relation between the Right Wing and the Stalinists involves a serious revision of the old view as to the "class struggle" in the Bolshevik Party. It is strange indeed that the Right Wing, the

"Thermidorian" faction, whose policy was that of resistance to rapid industrialization, was to the left of the bureaucracy which "by the logic of its own interests" adopted the program of rapid industrialization and collectivization. Strange, that is, from the viewpoint of those who hold that Russia is a workers' state.

Trotsky defended his new position, that the Stalinist state is a workers' state though the working class has no political power, by citing the bourgeois Bonapartist régimes. Under Bonapartism (and fascism) the bourgeoisie is deprived of all political power and is in fact politically oppressed. Despite this, the bourgeoisie remains socially the ruling class and the régime is bourgeois in character. Stalinist-Bonapartism, according to Trotsky, has an analogous relation to the Russian working class.

The analogy would be valid only if the political expropriation of the working class had been accompanied by the strengthening of its economic and social power, its domination of society. Such was the case under all Bonapartist régimes: the political expropriation of the bourgeoisie was accompanied by (or more exactly, was the precondition for) the strengthening of its economic and social power. (In a more complex form this holds true for fascism.) Marxists have adduced abundant empirical evidence to prove this contention.

But what does the evidence show as regards Russia? Simply this: that the working class has been deprived of all economic and social power as well as political power. The strengthening of state property and planning, which allegedly signifies the social rule of the proletariat, resulted in the increased economic, social, and political oppression of the working class. Here is a process which is the exact opposite of what occurs under Bonapartism!

By this analogy, however, Trotsky revealed an important methodological error which permeates his writings on Stalinist Russia. In seeking to explain the different forms of bourgeois rule, Trotsky failed to give adequate recognition to the decisive, qualitative differences between proletarian and bourgeois rule. In other contexts, for example in his theory of the permanent revolution, Trotsky proceeded from the basis of the totally new character of proletarian rule as compared to all previous class rule, to whit, the working class must first conquer political power, and through its own state organize the economy. (And with successful socialist revolutions internationally, build a world socialist economy which would lead to the dissolution of the workers' states and the proletariat as a class, to the triumph of a world socialist classless society.)

Every ruling class has its own laws of development and its own forms of economic, social, and political domination. The bourgeoisie, for example, first develops its economic power (capitalist ownership of the means of production and exchange) in the womb of feudalism, and then struggles for political and social power. In bourgeois society, in other words, the rule of the capitalist class rests basically on bourgeois private property. The state power defending this property may be in the hands of a semi-feudal aristocracy, a military clique, a parliamentary government controlled by the big bourgeois or petty-bourgeois parties, a Bonapartist bureaucracy, a fascist bureaucracy, etc. Quite the contrary is the case of the proletarian revolution and proletarian state. The proletariat is a propertyless class. Its control over the economy and its domination in society is possible only through first winning political power. It is through state power that the working class becomes the ruling class and develops the conditions for the abolition of all classes, the socialist society. Without political power the working class cannot be the ruling class in any sense.

Of course, the workers' state may assume different forms. But whatever the form the state must express the political power of the proletariat. Once it is acknowledged, as Trotsky and everyone in our movement has, that the Russian workers have no political power whatsoever, that is tantamount to saying that Russia is no longer a workers' state.

But can there not be a sick, degenerated workers' state? History has given the answer: the régime of Lenin and Trotsky was a sick, bureaucratized, revolutionary workers' state — as Lenin and Trotsky themselves often affirmed. In a healthy workers' state there would be complete democracy, the working class exercising its power democratically through Soviets, trade unions, rival parties. This state of affairs, as is known, never existed in Russia. The political rule of the working class was expressed almost exclusively through the dictatorship of the proletarian party, the Bolsheviks (with extreme limitations on Soviet and union democracy from the earliest days). The administration of the state and the economy in culturally backward and isolated Russia, while controlled by the Bolsheviks, was in the hands of a bureaucracy. The Bolsheviks expected, and worked for, the extension of the Russian Revolution into the more advanced industrial countries which would break the capitalist encirclement, raise the Russian industrial and cultural level, and thus create the preconditions for complete workers' democracy. When these conditions did not materialize the Stalin faction which controlled the party apparatus expressed the dominant desire of the bureaucracy for a peaceful and stable national existence. The old Bolshevik (and bourgeois) elements of the bureaucracy were eliminated, and a new bureaucracy created. The theory and practice of national socialism, "socialism in one country alone," was developed as the great social rationalization ("ideology") of the bureaucracy. With the Stalin faction as its representative it utilized its centralized administrative control of the state and economy to conduct a civil war to destroy its internal opponents, proletarian and bourgeois. On the one hand, it destroyed the limited workers' democracy that had existed, liquidated the old Bolshevik Party and converted the Communist International into the world detachment of Stalin's Foreign Office and GPU. On the other hand, it wiped out virtually all remnants of the old capitalist elements in the economy, strengthened state property, and extended the industrialization and collectivization of the country. Thus when the Stalinists announced "the complete and irrevocable victory of socialism," they were indeed proclaiming to the world the triumph of bureaucratic collectivism.

Stalinist Russia is thus a reactionary state based upon a new system of economic exploitation, bureaucratic collectivism. The ruling class is the bureaucracy which through its control of the state collectively owns, controls and administers the means of production and exchange. The basic motive force of the economy is the extraction of more and more surplus labor from the toilers so as to increase the revenue, power, and position of the bureaucracy. The economy is organized and directed through state totalitarian planning and political terrorism. The toilers are compelled by the state (as well as economic necessity) to labor in the factories and fields. Forced labor is thus an inherent feature of present-day Russian productive relations.

The relations within the ruling class — the share which individual bureaucrats receive of the wealth produced, their relative power and position, the manner in which persons enter or are forced out of the ruling class — are determined by noneconomic, primarily political factors.

Through the state monopoly of foreign trade the bureaucracy has a complete monopoly over the internal market; for the exploitation of the abundant material and human resources of the country, for the investment and for sale of goods. This monopoly is indispensable for the Stalinist imperialist exploitation and oppression of the national minority peoples of the Soviet Union (the Ukrainians, the Georgians, etc.).

While bureaucratic collectivism has succeeded in raising the industrial level of the country, its productive relations are tremendous obstacles to the real growth of the social productivity of labor, the raising of living standards of the masses, and the economic and political freedom of the workers and peasants. Despite the organizational advantages of state-owned monopoly and the vast internal market, and totalitarian planning (aided by the importation of advanced capitalist technique), Stalinist Russia has experienced a growing decline in the annual rate of increase of industrial output and an increasing disproportion between the income of the bureaucracy and the "new intelligentsia" on the one hand, and the income of the mass of workers and peasants on the other. (In recent years the yearly rate of increase of industrial production has been, according to official figures, only twice the rate experienced under Czarism.) The terroristic régime which is an integral part of bureaucratic planning (the bureaucratic productive relations) leads to constant disruptions in production; disproportions in the output of the various industries dependent on one another and therefore large-scale economic waste; low efficiency of production. The constant purges of the bureaucracy lead to vast disruptions of planning and production. The low wages, speed-up and poor housing have led to such large turnovers of labor, despite laws restricting labor mobility, that far stricter laws carrying penalties including the death sentence, had to be proclaimed to maintain production. The progressive, organic, and long-range development of the productive forces, the real growth of the social productivity of labor, and the raising of the standard of living of the masses demand scientific planning, that is, democratic planning by and of the masses. This is the antithesis of Stalinism.

Then again, bureaucratic collectivism is a nationally limited economy (or, more accurately, confined to a single backward "empire," Stalinist Russia). In relation to the capitalist imperialist states, Russia occupies the position of a huge national trust, which by monopolizing the home market intensifies the contradiction existing within these countries between the tendency for unlimited increase of the capitalist productive forces and the growing limitations of the markets for capital investment and the sale of commodities. From the standpoint of Russian industrial and cultural development, the overthrow of world capitalism is an indispensable condition for the liberation of its own nationally confined productive forces, so that it could benefit fully from advanced Western technique and take its place as an integral part of a progressive world economy. Here also, bureaucratic collectivism reveals its socially reactionary character in its role as an assistant of outlived capitalist imperialism in the task of destroying the independent working-class movement for socialism.

Thus, from the day of its birth the new Stalinist society is a reactionary obstacle to the development of Russian and world society toward socialist freedom and security. From a historical viewpoint, Russia has taken a bastard path backward from the régime established by the Bolshevik Revolution. It is from the start torn by contradictions and antagonisms which exclude its assuming a progressive road comparable to early bourgeois society. It arrives on the scene of history as an expression of world social reaction; at a time when the world economic conditions already exist for a great leap forward from class exploitation to socialist freedom and plenty; and when the working class is the only social power which can bring about the progressive transformation of society.

The class conscious workers have no interest in common with this new system of exploitation and oppression, bureaucratic collectivism. In wartime as during peace the revolutionary socialists must not give any support to the Stalinist state. Our task is that of awakening the working class to socialist struggle against bureaucratic collectivism, fascism, and democratic imperialism; and for working-class power and socialism.

WHO OWNS THE STATE?

TROTSKY'S LETTER TO BORODAI, which we publish here for the first time in English, is of special interest and importance. The document is undated, but it was evidently written during Trotsky's exile in Alma-Ata, toward the end of 1928, shortly before the author was banished from the Soviet Union to Turkey by the Stalinist régime. The importance of the letter lies in the fact that it is the first document known to us in which Trotsky debates with a Bolshevik anti-Stalinist the question of the class character of the Soviet state: Is it still or is it no longer a workers' state?

Borodai, whose subsequent fate is unknown to us, was a militant of the Democratic-Centralist group, or "Group of the Fifteen," as it was sometimes known, who was expelled from the Communist Party by the bureaucracy in 1927 along with all his fellow-thinkers, and sent into exile. The Democratic-Centralist group was founded as far back as 1920 by a number of left-wing communists in the Russian party, who sought to break through the rigid walls of the War-Communism régime and restore a democratic system in the party. The conditions of civil war were not conducive to their victory, and the one-sided emphasis they placed upon the democratic principle earned them the opposition of the most authoritative Bolshevik leaders, Lenin and Trotsky included.

In 1923, when Trotsky and his comrades launched the post-civil war struggle against a meanwhile swollen bureaucracy and for party democracy, they were joined by many of the original Democratic-Centralists, among them their outstanding leader, Timofey V Sapronov, proletarian, trade union leader, and old, pre-war Bolshevik of high standing. It was Sapronov who took the initiative in bringing together and presiding over the first joint meeting of the representatives of the Trotskyist (or Moscow, or 1923) Opposition and the Zinovievist (or Leningrad, or 1925) Opposition. This meeting and the ones that followed led to the formation of the famous United Opposition Bloc, composed of the Trotskyists, the Zinovievists, the remnants of the old Workers' Opposition (led by Shlyapnikov and Medvedyev) and of the Democratic-Centralists (Sapronov and Vladimir M Smirnov).

Shlyapnikov and other Workers' Opposition leaders soon capitulated to Stalin, as did virtually all the leaders of the Zinovievist Opposition in 1927-28. Most of the Democratic-Centralists, and outstandingly their leaders Sapronov and Smirnov, remained, in exile, incorruptible adversaries of the bureaucratic counter-revolution. There is no reason to believe that any of these militant revolutionists is still alive; they were murdered, gradually or outright, by the GPU.

Written as an introduction to the next item, "Trotsky's Letter to Borodai", from *New International*, April 1943. We restore small changes made by Shachtman when he republished the article in 1962 and delete only a paragraph where Shachtman lists other relevant articles he has written in *New International*.

In 1926, the former Democratic-Centralists broke away from the United Opposition Bloc because of the famous declaration in the middle of that year in which the Opposition pledged itself to refrain from factional activities — provided, of course, that a more-or-less normal internal régime was established in the party. The insurgents elaborated a platform of their own and set up a completely independent group. It became known as the "Group of Fifteen," from the number of signatories to the platform. They were: T V Sapronov, V M Smirnov, N Savaryan, V Emelyanov (Kalin), M N Mino, M I Minkov, T Kharechko, V P Oborin, I K Dashkovsky, S Schreiber, M Smirnov, F I Pilipenko, F Duney, A L Slidovker, L Tikhonov.

At the Fifteenth Party Congress in November-December, 1927, adherence to the views of the Democratic-Centralists was declared incompatible with membership in the Russian party, as was adherence to the views of the Trotskyist Opposition. All supporters of both groups were expelled and the most prominent leaders and militants first sent into exile and, years later, shot. In exile, a rapprochement between the two groups proved unrealizable and, except for individual shifts from one group to the other, they remained as far apart as they had ever been.

What was the evolution of the political ideas of Sapronov and Smirnov, there is now no way of judging, and there probably never will be until the day the Russian proletariat makes public the confiscated documents in the secret archives of the Stalinist police. But what the ideas of the Democratic-Centralists were in the days of the following letter by Trotsky, that is, around the year 1928, is implicit in the questions put by Borodai. In a word, they were: The proletariat has already lost power; the triumph of Stalin over the Opposition marks the triumph of the Thermidor, that is, the counter-revolution; the working class does not rule in Russia and Russia is no longer a workers' state; it is necessary to prepare a new social revolution to restore the proletariat to state power.

These contentions Trotsky denied, as is clear from his reply to Borodai. It is the arguments he employed in refuting Borodai's views that are interesting and important, both for a knowledge of the situation in the Opposition in those days and, much more to the point, for a Marxian evaluation of the present situation in, and the class character of, the Russian state.

In the discussion and polemics over the class character of the Soviet or Russian state, Trotsky, *years later*, found himself obliged to alter his criterion radically from what it had previously been, not only for him but without exception for the entire revolutionary Marxian movement. "Found himself obliged," we say, because of his insistence on maintaining his characterization of Russia as a workers' state long after the objective basis for it had been destroyed by the Stalinist counter-revolution. Trotsky, in later years, argued that Russia is a workers' state because the ownership of the principal means of production is vested in the state, that is, because property is nationalized.

The radical alteration of the criterion lay in converting nationalized property from a *necessary* characteristic of a workers' state into an *adequate* characteristic. In other words, Trotsky began to argue that no matter how degenerated and anti-proletarian and even counter-revolutionary the political régime in the country, Russia nevertheless remained a (degenerated or "counter-revolutionary") workers' state so long as property (the means of production and exchange) remained nationalized or state property.

It should be borne in mind that Trotsky *did not* hold that the existence of nationalized property was in itself adequate for a consistent *development toward socialism*. That required, he rightly emphasized, a socialist proletariat in political power and the victorious revolution in the advanced countries of the West. And, he added, given the absence of the political power of the workers and the revolution in the West, the workers' state would continue to degenerate and eventually collapse entirely. But so long as nationalized property remained more or less intact, Russia still remained a workers' state.

To repeat: for Trotsky, nationalized property was transformed from a *necessary* characteristic into the *adequate* characteristic, and the *decisive* one, at that.

This theory not only cannot withstand a fundamental Marxist criticism, but conflicts with the theory, with the criterion, originally and for a long time put forward and defended by Trotsky himself. The letter to Borodai is one of the many available evidences of this fact.

In his letter, aimed at refuting the thesis that Russia is no longer a workers' state, Trotsky does not once so much as mention the existence of nationalized property! He employs a different criterion, entirely correct and fully decisive, namely, *does the working class still have political power, in one sense or another, even if only in the sense that it is still capable of bringing a straying and dangerous bureaucracy under its control by means of reform measures?*

Why is this criterion correct and decisive? Because without *political* rule, the *proletariat* simply does not rule at all, and whatever you call the state or government under which it lives and works, it is not a workers' state. This is an iron law that derives from the fundamentally different *nature* of the class rule of the proletariat as contrasted with the class rule of *any private-property-owning class*. For example: Under a Bonapartist régime, be it of the early (Napoleon I or III) or the modern (Brüning or outright fascist) variety, the class rule of the bourgeoisie is maintained and fortified by virtue of two interrelated reasons:

(1) Although the bourgeoisie does not enjoy full or direct political power, it continues *to own*, as individuals and as a class, the means of production and exchange, and to draw profit and power from this ownership, and

(2) The régime which deprives the bourgeois class of full or direct political power uses that power to strengthen, to consolidate, to expand the social order of capitalism, to benefit the bourgeoisie in the most easily ascertainable tangible manner. Similarly, though not identically, under feudalism, where ownership of land was in private hands.

The proletariat, however, is not, never was and never will be a private-property-owning class. It comes to power, and lays the basis for an evolution to socialism, by nationalizing property and vesting its ownership in the hands of the state, making it state property as a preliminary to transforming it into *social* property. The state is not a class, but the complex of institutions of coercion (army, police, prisons, officials, etc.). Once the means of production and exchange have been made state property, the question, "Who is the ruling class" is resolved simply by answering the question: "In whose hands is the state?" It cannot be resolved by answering the question: "In whose hands is the property?" because no class then owns the property, at least not in the sense in which all preceding classes have owned property. To put it differently, the question must be posed in this way (because no other way makes sense): "In whose hands is the state which owns property?" Still more simply and directly: "Who rules politically?"

That is why a Marxist may argue, on the basis of empirical evidence, that Trotsky was right, or was wrong, in saying to Borodai that the workers in Russia (in 1928) still ruled politically, or could "regain full power, renovate the bureaucracy and put it under its control by *the road of reform of the party and the Soviets.*" But he must acknowledge that Trotsky's criterion, his methodological approach to the question of the class character of the Russian state, was incontestable. All that is necessary and correct is stated by Trotsky when he writes to Borodai:

"The question thus comes down to the same thing: Is the proletarian kernel of the party, assisted by the working class, capable of triumphing over the autocracy of the party apparatus which is fusing with the state apparatus? Whoever replies in advance that it is incapable, *thereby speaks not only of the necessity of a new party on a new foundation, but also of the necessity of a second and new proletarian revolution."*

Trotsky did not mean by this last a "political" revolution, as he said years later. He simply and rightly meant a *social* revolution. That is, the test of whether Russia was still a workers' state could be made by asking if the proletariat could still reform the political régime. If not, Russia is no longer a workers' state; a new party is needed, and a new social revolution to overthrow the ruling class and put the workers into power again. The idea is unambiguously stated.

And nationalized property? It is, we repeat, not even referred to. Why not? Because, obviously, it is assumed as a *necessary* feature of a workers' state, its indispensable economic foundation, but not by itself *adequate* or *decisive* for a workers' state. That is right, and nothing Trotsky wrote years afterward can effectively refute his original and unassailable standpoint.

The formulation of the question in the letter to Borodai is not accidental. It is to be found in any number of Trotsky's writings of that period and prior to the self-revision of his view. In his letter to the Sixth Congress of the Comintern, on July 12, 1928, he wrote: *"...the socialist character of industry is determined and secured in a decisive measure by the rôle of the party, the voluntary internal cohesion of the proletarian vanguard, and conscious discipline of the administrators, trade union functionaries, members of the shop nuclei, etc. If we allow that this web is weakening, disintegrating and ripping, then it becomes absolutely self-evident that within a brief period nothing will remain of the socialist character of state industry, transport, etc."* (*Third International After Lenin*, page 300.)

That is, the class character of the political power is not determined by industry (nationalized property), as he later contended, but conversely, "the socialist character of industry is *determined* and *secured in a decisive measure*" by the party, that is, in Russia, by the political power. From which it follows that if that political power has been *utterly* destroyed, as Trotsky later acknowledged and insisted on, the class character of "industry" (nationalized property, again) has been *fundamentally* altered.

303

Again, in his theses on Russia, on April 4, 1931, he returned to the same question, and from fundamentally the same standpoint:

"If we proceed from the incontestable fact that the CPSU has ceased to be a party, are we not thereby forced to the conclusion that there is no dictatorship of the proletariat in the USSR, since *this is inconceivable without a ruling proletarian party?*" (*Problems of the Development of the USSR*, page 34. My emphasis. — S.)

"This is inconceivable!" Why, then, is it a workers' state notwithstanding? Because, wrote Trotsky, there still remain powerful and firmly-rooted elements of the party, traditions of the October, *etc., and* by virtue of these the bureaucracy can be submitted to the proletariat and its revolutionary vanguard *by means of reform.*

"*The recognition of the present Soviet state as a workers' state not only signifies that the bourgeoisie can conquer power in no other way than by an armed uprising but also that the proletariat of the USSR has not forfeited the possibility of submitting the bureaucracy to it, of reviving the party and of mending the régime of the dictatorship — without a new revolution, with the methods and on the road of reform*". (*Ibid.*, page 36.)

It follows unambiguously and inexorably that to recognize — as the further degeneration of the Russian Revolution compelled us all, Trotsky included, to recognize — that the bureaucracy *cannot* be submitted to the proletariat, that the so-called Communist Party *cannot* be revived, that the régime *cannot* be reformed, that a new revolution *must* be organized — is to recognize that Russia is no longer a workers' state.

What is worth noting, however, is that the Cannonites, who insisted three and a half years ago on discussing the "class character of the state" and nothing else, have maintained a most prudent silence since the day we began to develop our criticism of Trotsky's fundamental position and to present our own analysis. They confine themselves to muttering simple and undigested ritualistic phrases, which have no meaning to them, which they cannot explain coherently and which they justify by one final and unanswerable appeal: "Well, Trotsky said so." Fortunately, Trotsky also said that it is necessary for a Marxist to "learn to think."

To the question, "Why is it a workers' state?" they answer, "Because the state owns the property." To the question, "But what is the class character of this state that owns the property?" they answer, "A workers' state"! In this hopelessly vicious circle, the workers are reduced from a living, propertyless, stateless, oppressed and exploited class to a... decorative adjective.

To the question, "What are the property relations at the basis of present Russian society?" they answer, "Nationalized property." That is like asking the question, "What are the marital relations under feudalism?" and being given the answer, "Male and female." That is, the answer says nothing. The whole question lies in this: "Just what are the relations of the classes or, if you wish, the social groups to the property? Just what are the production relations? Just what are the social relations?" But the answer, given with an increasingly mysterious look, remains, "Nationalized property."

"The Stalinist Bonapartist régime preserves the nationalized property in its own way," it is said. Correct! But why does that fact testify to the existence in Russia of a workers' state? The bourgeois Bonapartist or fascist state preserves private property not primarily for the bureaucracy (although for it, too), but above all for the very tangible benefit of the ruling class, the bourgeoisie, whose economic and social position it protects, consolidates, expands. Does the Bonapartist régime of Stalin preserve nationalized property for the tangible benefit of the working class? If so, what benefit? Does it protect, consolidate, expand the economic and social (to say nothing of the political) position of the proletariat? If so, what sign (not signs, just one sign) is there of it? The present bourgeois Bonapartist state reduces the proletariat to slavery and enormously increases the wealth and power of the capitalists. Which class does the Stalinist Bonapartist régime reduce to slavery, and which class does it accord vast increases of wealth, social position and power, while it is at work preserving nationalized property "in its own way"?

It would be interesting to hear something in detail on these matters from the Cannonites — not apart from abuse (that is utopian) but, let us say, in addition to it. Our interest, we fear, is doomed to remain unsatisfied. To all that was said, Poe's raven intransigently answered with two words, "Never more!" To all we have said in the past two years about Russia, the Cannonite raven has answered, when he did answer, with two words, "Nationalized property"! It is doubtful if he will some day become more articulate or logical.

Leon Trotsky

"OUR DIFFERENCES WITH THE DEMOCRATIC CENTRALISTS": LETTER TO BORODAI

I HAVE JUST RECEIVED after almost a month's delay, your letter of October 12 from Tyumen. I am replying immediately by return mail, in view of the importance of the questions you put to me. Taking your point of departure from the standpoint of the Democratic-Centralist group to which you belong, you put seven questions and demand that the answers be "clear and concrete" and "not nebulous." An altogether legitimate wish. Only, our way of being concrete should be dialectical, that is, encompass the living dynamics of evolution and not substitute ready-made labels which, at first sight, seem very "clear" but are in reality false and devoid of content. Your way of putting the questions is purely formal: yes, yes — no, no. Your questions must first be put upon a Marxian basis in order that correct replies may be made.

1. After setting forth the character of the social composition of the party and its apparatus, you ask: "Has the party degenerated? That is the first question." You demand a "clear" and "concrete" reply: Yes, it has degenerated. However, I cannot answer that way, for at present our party, both socially and ideologically, is extremely *heterogeneous*. It includes *nuclei* that are entirely degenerated, others that are still healthy but amorphous, others that have hardly been affected by degeneration, etc. The régime of apparatus oppression, which reflects the pressure of other classes upon the proletariat, and the decline of the spirit of activity of the proletariat itself, renders very difficult a daily check upon the degree of degeneration of the various strata and nuclei of the party and of its apparatus. But this check can and will be achieved by activity, especially by our active intervention in the internal life of the party, by mobilizing tirelessly its living and viable elements. Naturally, such intervention is out of

the question if the point of departure is that the party as a whole has degenerated, that the party is a corpse. With such an evaluation of the party, it is absurd to address oneself to it, and still more absurd to wait for it, or for this or that section of it, that is, primarily, for its *proletarian kernel*, to heed or to understand you. To conquer this kernel, however, is to conquer the party. This kernel does not consider itself — and quite rightly — either dead or degenerated. It is upon it, upon its tomorrow, that we base our political line. We will *patiently explain* our tasks to it, basing ourselves upon experience and facts. In every cell and at every workers' meeting, we will denounce as a falsehood the calumny of the apparatus which says that we are plotting to create a second party; we shall state that a second party is being built up by the Ustrialov-people in the apparatus, hiding behind the Centrists; as for us, we want to cleanse Lenin's party of the Ustrialovist and semi-Ustrialovist elements; we want to do this hand in hand with the proletarian kernel which, aided by the active elements of the proletariat as a whole, can still become master of the party and save the Revolution from death, by means of *a profound proletarian reform in every field...*

2. "Is the degeneration of the apparatus and of the Soviet power a fact? That is the second question," you write.

Everything that has been said above applies equally to this question. There is no doubt that the degeneration of the Soviet apparatus is considerably more advanced than the same process in the party apparatus. Nevertheless, it is the party that decides. At present, this means: the party apparatus. The question thus comes down to the same thing: Is the proletarian kernel of the party, assisted by the working class, capable of triumphing over the autocracy of the party apparatus which is fusing with the state apparatus? Whoever replies in advance that it is *incapable*, thereby speaks not only of the necessity of a new party on a new foundation, but also of the necessity of a second and new proletarian revolution. It goes without saying that it can in no way be stated that such a perspective is out of the question under all circumstances. However, it is not a question of historical divination, but rather of not surrendering to the enemy but — on the contrary — of reviving and consolidating the October Revolution and the dictatorship of the proletariat. Has this road been tried to the very end? Not at all. At bottom, this methodical work of the Bolshevik-Leninists to mobilize the proletarian kernel of the party in the new historical stage has only begun.

The arid reply — "Yes, it has degenerated" — that you would like to get to your question about the degeneration of the Soviet power, would contain no clarity in itself and would open up no perspective. What we have here is a developing, contradictory process, which can be concluded in any way or the other by virtue of the struggle of living forces. Our participation in this struggle will have no small importance in determining its outcome.

3. "Taking the present situation in the country and the party as a whole, do we still have a dictatorship of the working class? And who possesses the hegemony in the party and in the country? That is the third question," you ask further.

From the preceding replies it is clear that you put this question also inexactly, not dialectically but scholastically. It is precisely Bukharin who presented this question to us dozens of times in the form of a scholastic alternative: *Either* we have the Thermidor and then you, Opposition, should be defeatists and not partisans of defense, *or*, if you are really partisans of defense, then acknowledge that all the speeches about Thermidor are nothing but chatter. Here, comrade, you fall completely into the trap of Bukharinist scholastics. Along with him, you want to have "clear," that is, *completely finished* social facts. The developing, contradictory process appears "nebulous" to you. What do we have in reality? We have a strongly advanced process of duality of power in the country. Has power passed into the hands of the bourgeoisie? Obviously not. Has power slipped out of the hands of the proletariat? To a certain degree, to a considerable degree, but still far from decisively. This is what explains the monstrous predominance of the bureaucratic apparatus oscillating between the classes. But this state apparatus depends, through the medium of the party apparatus, upon the party, that is, upon its proletarian kernel, *on condition that the latter is active and has a correct orientation and leadership*. And that is where our task lies.

A state of duality of power is unstable, by its very essence. Sooner or later, it must go one way or the other. But as the situation is now, the bourgeoisie could seize power only by *the road of counter-revolutionary upheaval*. As for the proletariat, it can regain full power, renovate the bureaucracy and put it under its control *by the road of reform of the party and the Soviets*. These are the fundamental characteristics of the situation. Your Kharkov colleagues, from what I am informed, have addressed themselves to the workers with an appeal based upon the false idea that the October Revolution and the dictatorship of the proletariat are already liquidated. This manifesto, false in essence, has done the greatest harm to the Opposition. Such declarations must be resolutely and implacably condemned. That is the bravado of adventurers and not the revolutionary spirit of Marxists.

4. Quoting from my Postscript on the July victory of the Right wing over the Center, you ask: "Are you thus putting entirely within quotation marks 'the Left course' and the 'shift' that you once proposed to support with all forces and all means? That is the fourth question." This is a downright untruth on your part. Never and nowhere have I spoken of a *Left course*. I spoke of a "shift" and a "Left-zig-zag," contrasting this conception to a consistent proletarian line. Never and nowhere have I proposed to support the alleged Left course of the Centrists, nor did I promise to support it. But I did propose and promise to support by all means every step that Centrism really took toward the Left, no matter if it was a half-measure, without ceasing for a single instant to criticize and unmask Centrism as the fundamental obstacle in the way of awakening the spirit of activity of the proletarian kernel of the party. My "Postscript" was precisely a document exposing the political capitulation of the Centrists to the Right wing during the July Plenum. But I did not and I do not hold that the history of the development of the party and particularly the history of the struggle of the Center against the Right wing came to an end at the July Plenum. We are right now witnesses of a new Centrist campaign against the Right-wingers. We must become independent participants in this campaign. Naturally we see right through all the hypocrisy and duplicity, the perfidious half-wayness of the apparatus in the Stalinist struggle against the Right-wingers. But behind this struggle we see profound class forces which seek to break a path for themselves through the party and its apparatus. The driving force of the Right wing is the new evolving proprietor who seeks a link with world capitalism; our Right-wingers are timid and mark time, for they do not yet dare to straddle this warhorse openly. The functionary of the party, the trade unions and other institutions, is the rampart of the Centrists: in spite of everything, he depends upon the working masses and seems to be obliged in recent times to take these masses into account more and more: hence, the "self-criticism" and "the struggle against the Right." *It is thus that the class struggle is refracted and distorted*, but nevertheless manifested in this struggle; by its pressure, it can transform the quarrel between the Centrists and the Right-wingers in the apparatus into a very important stage in the awakening and enlivening of the party and the working class. We would be pitiable imbeciles if we took the present campaign against the Right-wingers seriously. But we would, on the other hand, be pitiable scholiasts and sectarian wiseacres if we failed to understand that hundreds of thousands of workers, party members, do believe in it, if not 100 per cent then at least fifty or twenty-five per cent. They are not yet with us, to be sure. Do not forget that, do not become ensnared in sectarian trivia. Centrism holds on not only because of the oppression of the apparatus, but also because of the confidence or the half-confidence of a certain part of the worker-party members. These workers who support the Centrists will enter the struggle against the Right much more readily than they did in the struggle against the Opposition, when they had to be dragged along with a rope around their neck. A serious and intelligent Oppositionist will say, in any workers' cell, in any workers' meeting: "We are summoned to fight against the Right wing — that's a wonderful thing. We have called on you to do this for a long time. And if you're thinking of fighting seriously against the Right wing, you can count upon us to the limit. We will be no strikebreakers. On the contrary, we'll be in the front lines. Only, let us really fight. The leaders of the Right wing must be named out loud, their Right-wing deeds must be enumerated, etc." In a word, the Oppositionist will push the proletarian kernel of the party forward like a Bolshevik, and he will not turn his back upon it on the pretext that the party has degenerated.

5. "Is it still possible to entertain illusions about the ability to defend the interests of the revolution and of the working class? That is the fifth question."

You put the fifth question just as inexactly as the first four. To entertain illusions about the Centrists means to sink into Centrism yourself. But to shut your eyes to the mass processes that drive the Centrists to the Left means to enclose yourself within a sectarian shell. As if it was a matter of whether Stalin and Molotov are capable of returning to the road of proletarian policy!. In any case, they are incapable of doing it by themselves. They have proved it completely. But it is not a question of divining the future fate of the various members of the Stalinist staff. That doesn't interest us at all. In this field, all sorts of "surprises" are possible. Didn't the former leader of the Democratic-Centralists, Ossinsky, become an extreme Right-winger, for example?... The correct question is this: Are the tens and hundreds of thousands of workers, party members and members of the Communist Youth, who are at present actively, half-actively or passively supporting the Stalinists, capable of redressing themselves, of reawakening, of welding their ranks together "to defend the interests of the revolution and of the working class"? To this, I answer: Yes, this they are capable of doing. They will be capable of doing this tomorrow or the day after if we know how to approach them correctly; if we show them that we do not look upon them as corpses; if, like Bolsheviks, we support every step, every half-step, they take toward us; if, in addition, we not only do not entertain "illusions" about the Centrist leadership but expose them implacably, by dint of the daily experience of the struggle. At the moment, it must be done by the experience of the struggle against the Right wing.

6. After characterizing the Sixth Congress [of the Communist International] and describing certain phenomena inside the party, you write: "Is not all this the Thermidor with the dry guillotine? That is the sixth question." This question has been answered concretely enough above. Once more, do not believe that Bukharinist scholastics, turned upside down, is Marxism.

7. "Do you personally," you ask me, "intend to continue in the future to call the comrades belonging to the Group of Fifteen by the splendid epithet of 'honest revolutionists,' and at the same time to separate yourself from them? Is it not time to terminate the petty quarrel? Is it not time to ponder the consolidation of the forces of the Bolshevik guard? That is the seventh and last question."

Unfortunately, this question is not put quite correctly either. It is not I who separated myself from the Democratic-Centralists, but it is this grouping that separated itself from the Opposition as a whole to which it belonged. It is on this ground that a subsequent split took place in the Democratic-Centralist group itself. That is the past. Let us take the very latest phase, when the most serious exchange of opinions took place among the exiled Opposition, resulting in the elaboration of a whole series of responsible documents that received the support of 99 per cent of the Opposition. Here, too, the representatives of the Democratic-Centralists, without contributing anything essential to this work, once more separated themselves from us, by showing themselves to be more papist than the Pope, that is, than Safarov. After all this, you ask me if I intend to continue in the future to "separate" myself from the Democratic-Centralists! No, you approach this question from the wrong end. You represent things as if, in the past, the Zinovievs, the Kamenevs and the Pyatakovs, hindered the unification. You are mistaken on this score, too. One might conclude from your remarks that we, the 1923 Opposition, were for the unification with the Zinovievists, and the Democratic-Centralist group was against. On the contrary. We were much more cautious in this question and we were much more insistent in the matter of guarantees. The initiative for the unification came from the Democratic-Centralists.

The first conferences with the Zinovievists took place under the chairmanship of Comrade Sapronov. I do not say this as a reproach at all, for the bloc was necessary and a step forward. But "our yesterdays must not be distorted." After the Democratic-Centralist group separated itself from the Opposition, Zinoviev was always for a new unification with it; he raised the question dozens of times. As for myself, I spoke up against it. What were my reasons? I said: We need the unification, but a lasting and serious unification. If, however, the Democratic-Centralist group split away from us at the first clash, we ought not to rush into new corridor-fusions, but leave it to experience to check the policies and either deepen the split or prepare the conditions for a genuine, serious, durable unification. I hold that the experience of

1927-28 ought to have shown how absurd were the suspicions and insinuations of the Democratic-Centralist leaders toward the 1923 Opposition. I counted above all on the principled documents we addressed to the Sixth Congress facilitating the unification of our ranks. That is what did happen in the case of a number of comrades of the Democratic-Centralists. But the recognized leaders of your group did everything in their power not only to deepen and sharpen the differences of opinion but also to poison relations completely. For my own part, I take the writings of V Smirnov calmly enough. But in recent times I have received dozens of letters from comrades who are indignant to the highest degree over the character of these writings, which sound as if they were specially calculated to prevent a coming-together and to maintain at all costs a separate chapel with a pastor of its own.

But apart from the whole past history of who separated from whom, of how it was done, of who honestly wants unity in our ranks and who seeks to keep a parish of his own, there still remains the whole question of the *basis in ideas* of this unification. On this score, Comrade Rafael wrote me on September 28: "Our friends of the Group of Fifteen have begun to conduct a furious campaign especially against you, and there is a touching harmony between the editorial in *Bolshevik*, No. 16, and Vladimir Mikhailovich Smirnov and other comrades of the Group of Fifteen. The fundamental error of these comrades is the fact that they attribute too great value to purely formal decisions and combinations in the upper spheres, particularly to the decisions of the July Plenum. They do not see the forest for the trees. Naturally, these decisions are, during a certain phase of development, the reflection of a certain relationship of forces. But in any case, they cannot be looked upon as determining the outcome of the struggle that continues and will continue for a long time. Not a single one of the problems that provoked the crisis has been resolved; the contradictions have accentuated. Even the official editorial in *Pravda,* on September 18, had to acknowledge this. In spite of the 'steel hammer' that drives an 'aspen-wedge' into the Opposition every day (how many times already), the Opposition *lives* and has the will to live; it has cadres tempered in battle, and what cadres! To draw, at such a moment, conclusions like those of the Group of Fifteen, is false to the bottom and exceptionally harmful. These conclusions create a demoralizing state of mind, instead of organizing the working class and the proletarian kernel of the party. The position of the Fifteen cannot but be passive, for if the working class and its vanguard have already surrendered all their positions and conquests without a struggle, then on whom and on what can these comrades count? You do not organize the masses to revive a 'corpse,' and as to a *new struggle*, given the situation of the working class as they picture it to themselves, the time it will take is much too long and this will lead inevitably to the position of Shlyapnikov." I think Comrade Rafael is perfectly right in characterizing the situation the way he does.

You write that the proletariat does not like nebulous half-measures and diplomatic evasions. That is right. And that's the reason why you must finally cast up a balance. If the party is a corpse, a new party must be built on a new spot, and the working class must be told about it openly. If Thermidor is completed, and if the dictatorship of the proletariat is liquidated, the banner of the second proletarian revolution must be unfurled. That is how we would act if the road of reform, for which we stand, proved hopeless. Unfortunately, the leaders of the Democratic-Centralists are up to their ears in nebulous half-measures and diplomatic evasions. They criticize our road of reform in a very "Left" manner — a road which, I hope, we have shown by deeds is not at all the road of Stalinist legality; but they do not show the working masses any other road. They content themselves with sectarian mutterings against us, and count meanwhile on spontaneous movements. Should this line be reinforced, it would not only destroy your whole group, which contains not a few good and devoted revolutionists, but like all sectarianism and adventurism, it would render the best service to the Right-Centrist tendencies, that is, in the long run, to bourgeois restoration. That is why, dear comrade, before uniting — and I am for unification with all my heart — it is necessary to establish the ideological delimitations, based upon a clear and principled line. It is a good old Bolshevik rule.

With communist greetings, Leon Trotsky

Louis Jacobs

STALIN'S SLAVE LABORERS

HISTORY RECORDS NO GREATER CRIME than that of the Stalinist régime in its treatment of the victims in the concentration camps. Hitler's methods were not original. They ran parallel with, if they were not mere copies of those utilized by Stalin. If Hitler sent millions of people, primarily the Jews, into the gas chambers, the Russian camps have crushed, dehumanized and done to death more victims than all other concentration camps combined. For a time the war brought a decrease in the slave labor population of the *lagiers,* as Stalin's hell-holes are called. But this was only because the Kremlin found it necessary to use many of the male prisoners as a stopgap in the front lines, where they were quickly mowed down. This was part of the price paid by Russia for Stalin's being taken by surprise despite all the warnings that the Nazis would invade Russia. The end of the war once again reversed the trend. The far-away Siberian wastes are filling up anew. The slave labor enterprises of the MVD (the GPU) are operating full blast. There is, nevertheless, a distinct difference so far as the outside world is concerned. Humanity has, to all appearances, remained quite indifferent over a period of years to the stifled cry of slave laborers of the GPU. The evidence of the frightful conditions maintained in the *lagiers* came out before the outbreak of the war in a thin trickle only. But the fog created by Stalinist propaganda is being dissipated by the quantitative weight of unimpeachable testimony. Hitler and Mussolini have disappeared from the scene, leaving behind only the despicable Franco. Now the workers of the world will be brought face to face with the Soviet dictator Stalin and his methods.

There was one practice among others that Stalin and Hitler had in common. Their armies carried with them in their conquests lists of "undesirables" who were to be arrested immediately. It is hardly surprising that both lists were headed by revolutionists. First on Stalin's lists were Trotskyists, members of pre-revolutionary parties such as the Mensheviks, the Social Revolutionaries and anarchists. One such list that fell into foreign hands had fourteen categories. The eighth included refugees and political émigrés from other countries; the tenth any persons who had traveled abroad. Last of all came aristocrats, landowners, wealthy merchants, bankers and industrialists. Stalinism reintroduced Asiatic justice into Russia, for it takes not individuals who are wanted but their entire families. It goes even further. In the course of raids on some house or other in search of an individual, frequently enough the GPU arrested everybody in the house for whatever reason. The mass deportations from Poland were planned by the GPU in four great waves: in February, April and June of 1940, and again in June, 1941. The first waves caught in the net representatives of all political parties of whatev-

From *New International,* July 1947, "The extent and significance of a modern phenomenon", by Louis Jacobs (Jack Weber).

er shade of opinion, including the leaders of all Polish, White Russian, Ukrainian and Jewish socialist organizations and of socialist trade unions, members of working-class committees, organizers of working class, peasant and other youth institutions.

The utter cynicism of these "purges" is summed up in that which took place in June, 1941. Up to that time the GPU had utilized local committees of Communists and sympathizers, and even workers' militias. These local Communists had often enough helped choose those to be deported to Siberia. Their own turn came last! All those who had had any kind of dealings whatsoever directly with the Red Army, all known Communists, were shipped off in the fourth series of raids. What a curious light (let us say it mildly) this throws on the policy advocated by some Trotskyists to have Polish workers in partisan militias place themselves under the direct command of the Red Army generals! That policy certainly facilitated the task of the GPU of uprooting every vestige of working-class independence.

The description of the deportation trains is poignant and tragic beyond words. The utter indifference to considerations of common humanity evinced by the Red Army guards is a measure of the dehumanizing effects of life under Stalinism. The Poles thought first that this was due to the Russian hatred of Poland. Not at all! "It was still very difficult for people coming from outside the Union to understand that such things could be everyday sights; that members of these people's own families, their fellow workers or neighbors, might as easily have been transported in similar trains to similar destinations... It was still some time before they understood that all this was not some otherwise unheard-of proceeding against themselves as foreigners, but that the whole system and the institutions to which they were being taken had, in fact, come into existence and continued to exist as a normal part of life for Soviet citizens."

All Russian literature of Czarist times — it is the profound contribution of that literature to the world — is permeated with the deepest feelings of humanity, to the very point of inward torture. Stalinism has, at least outwardly, registered its greatest success in creating the complete atomizing of society in place of solidarity. Each is intent on his own salvation and is trained by terror to show utter lack of any concern for the suffering of his neighbor. This is true of ordinary life. It is trebly so in the *lagiers*, where the sheer problem of survival brutalizes every living soul. A survivor gives this description of the long march from the detraining center to the camp: "A nineteen year old boy with blood pouring from his lungs, fell for the last time and was so savagely beaten with rifles that, in the words of the witness reporting it, 'he was beaten into the ground'." Since law meant nothing at all, the GPU being a law unto itself, everything was arbitrary. The crowding of prisoners in trains, then in prison cells, was something incredible, a country-wide practice of the black hole of Calcutta. Is it surprising that in prisons also the terms used by the wardens have become once again identical with those used in Czarist times? A well-known Socialist sums up the treatment of prisoners as follows: "The prisoner is to get it into his head as soon as possible that he is nothing but a thing and that nobody has any reason to be particular about the way he treats him."

Stalinism is shown at its "purest" in the slave labor camps. Here is the final outcome of the GPU system. The Russian prisoners have a saying: "Nobody leaves *lagier* behind. *Lagier* is forever!" Yet occasionally a medical commission makes the rounds and releases from labor the total wrecks who have not yet died. "In September and October, 1941, a medical commission from Magadan visited some of the Kolyma mining and lumber camps. A long procession of human phantoms appeared in the town and were put into ships. Those who saw them go aboard could hardly believe they were human. It was a procession not of human beings, but of corpses and trunks. The majority had neither noses, lips nor ears; very many were armless and legless. Among these was a handful only of Poles. The rest were all Soviet citizens. The Magadan commission had recognized them as being unfit for work! In Magadan it was said that, once aboard ship, they were taken out to sea and drowned, but there is not any proof of this."

There is a Soviet "opera" unknown to the rest of the world. It is just the kind of grotesque and gruesome occurrence that one would expect under the rule of Stalin. In many of the camps the slave laborers are accompanied to work each morning by a Russian orchestra! The prisoners sing to its accompaniment a mournful dirge:

"And if you don't accomplish the norm
They give you only three hundred grams of bread."

Food is distributed by "Kettle," of which four or more categories are prescribed, from the punishment kettle up to the special kettle of the trustee. The kettle depends upon the amount of work accomplished, the unit being an impossible norm rarely if ever achieved. The slaves must put in twelve hours of hard labor besides the hours of exhausting marching to and from the places of work. After the invasion of Russia by the Nazis, there were never any free days. No political prisoners were allowed to hold any sort of administrative posts, even the most minor. Such posts when held by prisoners were given to the common criminals of the underworld. These brigade leaders became bestial slave drivers in order to protect their own few privileges, above all those connected with food. One survived, under a system bound to be corrupt from top to bottom, only through "blat," inadequately translated as graft.

It is the extent of the slave labor camps that freezes one's blood as much as the unmitigated blackness of their administration. "From this first-hand evidence it is known that vast regions about Kuibyshev, in northern Siberia and in Kazakstan, with, to the north, the whole of the Komi Republic up to Archangel, with Novaya Zemlya, have camps of this kind along almost every kilometer." In all this territory the MVD holds complete sway. There exist only guards and guarded! This tremendous GPU state is divided into zones, each territory enclosed within barbed wire, patrolled by armed guards and their dogs, and made doubly secure by lookout towers and storks' nests containing sentries. The population of these camps has never been divulged but is estimated anywhere from ten to twenty millions of souls. All these slaves are engaged in the building of canals, railroads, roads and bridges, factories, towns, ports, mining, forest clearing, or in cultivating gigantic state farms of ten to twenty thousand hectares.

The concentration camps of Stalin, euphemistically called "corrective labor camps," are the index of the fear in the hearts of the Russian rulers, and of the terror required to hold down the Russian population. A régime built on measures of this kind and on so vast a scale is inevitably one of profound crisis. But like all such phenomena, it takes on an independent development of its own with its own "vested interests." It is a source of vast profit to the state rulers and to the GPU. The Gulag, the labor camp administration, tries to fill in the glaring gaps due to failures in the bureaucratic five-year plans. The interstices of these plans, based on the most intense exploitation of the Russian proletariat, are cemented with slave labor outright. The turnover of labor in the giant clusters of camps is an important factor to be reckoned with in its effects on Russian life. Twenty to thirty per cent of deaths each year in the mines of the Far East and the Far North are common. Those who are released after serving their terms, are required to stay put in the places of exile, but are still counted as "lost" to the GPU. Replacements are ordered by the Gulag from the country-wide collection centers. Kravchenko showed how these demands from above influence arrests and rearrests on any available pretext or none at all. In colonial days the English resorted to impressment for their navy or for colonizing of the New World. But never in all history has there been outright enslavement in any country on such a scale. *Uncle Tom's Cabin* made a great appeal against the separation of families under slavery. This is a commonplace of Soviet life. In fact there is a special camp in the Karaganda cluster in Central Asia known as the "Wives' Camp" and used for the wives and widows of former Soviet leaders.

It is clear why Stalin needs an Iron Curtain. He has much to hide. Not all that he would like to keep hidden has to do with military secrets. When the Poles began their trek back after their belated release — the big majority of them remain buried in Russian earth — Stalin did his best to force them to become Soviet citizens in order not to let them out with the information they possessed. Stalin claimed that the Jews taken from Poland were Soviet citizens (as in the case of Ehrlich and Alter). He finally permitted the one hundred and fifty thousand of them, survivors of over half a million, to emigrate. The loss to the camps in this process was made up with German, Italian and Japanese prisoners of war. It was also made up with those Russian prisoners of war who were repatriated from Western Europe, those of them who were not shot outright for having committed the crime of seeing too much of the outside world. Stalin is fearful concerning the Russians who have fled abroad, including a large number of Red Army deserters. They may become the new centers of resistance, just as did the exiles under the Czar.

The challenge to humanity that exists in such glaring form in the Russian slave labor camps cannot be ignored without extreme peril to the working class of the entire world. If it is the workers everywhere who must free themselves and all the oppressed, it is certainly the workers of all other countries who must come to the aid of the workers ground into the dust in Russia. There are those who would remain silent on this question because they fear that any agitation against Russian slave labor will become a weapon in the hands of the imperialists who seek in time to wage war on Russia. There is no better weapon with which to arm these imperialists than working class silence on this life-and-death matter. If the vanguard of the workers is unable to rally the working class in fierce protest against such inhumanity, then reaction will seize on the issue for its own purposes at a suitable time. To fail to raise this issue without let-up because of a fear that reaction will profit from it means only that one does not know how to make use of the issue in Marxist fashion. Silence means to participate in the worst crime in all history. It is hard to believe that the working class, with the facts already known, can allow another May Day to pass without the cry: "Down with Stalin's slave labor camps!"

We Trotskyists owe a special duty to those comrades who gave so heroic an example to the world (it is now revealed in the testimony gathered by S Mora and P Zwierniak in *La Justice Soviétique,* as quoted by the Menshevik Dallin, whose factual gathering of material is most praiseworthy, though his motives fall under the shadow of imperialism) at the camp in Vorkuta. Several dozen of them, while they were still together, "decided to eternalize the people's memory of them by a last manifestation of their inflexible will, and thus remain victorious even if condemned to hard labor." They presented demands claiming the right of political prisoners to be separated from the criminals, the right to be employed only for work corresponding to their professions, and the right not to be separated. They then started a hunger strike until success or death, a hunger strike lasting for 120 days without interruption! Many died despite forced feeding. "When all the efforts to break their spirit proved ineffective, the Trotskyites were separated with the help of a pack of fierce dogs unleashed in their barracks." All were certainly shot later. The memory of these brave ones is surely eternal! Their challenge to us must be met.

The Russian phenomenon of slave labor is a challenge also to our theories. Never forget that the camps control vast sections (states within a state) of "nationalized property." This nationalized property — mines, factories, forests, railroads — is completely in the hands of the GPU. Such nationalized property has become completely identified with direct state slave labor. It is a kind of "pure form" of the tendency that exists under completely reactionary Stalinism. It is the most urgent warning that the mere words "nationalized property" or any formula using these mere words without complete and concrete analysis is dangerous and misleading. Nationalized property under Stalinism, in or out of the concentration camps, is permitted to serve the masses not in the slightest degree. Our deepest sympathies go everywhere to the exploited and oppressed masses. We defend them, their welfare, *their* conquests, not those of the privileged and exploiting minority. The concentration camps in Russia with their millions of forced laborers, are an important part of the evidence that the nationalized property taken by the masses in the October Revolution, has been wrested completely from the hands of the working class. That property today serves the interests of the rulers completely. The Wallaces, fearful of any new revolution inside Russia because such a revolution will endanger the entire capitalist system which they defend, shut their eyes to the existence of bestial slave labor in Russia. But only such a revolution can free the millions of political prisoners from the *lagiers* and prisons. Only such a revolution can restore the nationalized property to the masses from whom it was usurped. The American working class can help their suffering Russian brothers and sisters along the path to the renewal of the socialist revolution by protesting in one mighty voice against the retention of the concentration camps for slave labor in Russia.

James M Fenwick

THE MYSTERIOUS BRUNO R

THE MYSTERIOUS "BRUNO R" is one of the many persons who are remembered today only because their ideas were attacked by Leon Trotsky. The conceptions developed by Bruno R in his book *La Bureaucratisation du Monde* (*The Bureaucratization of the World*) were first introduced to the Marxist public in the United States by Trotsky in 1939, during the great polemic on the Russian question between himself and the minority of the Socialist Workers Party which subsequently became the Workers Party. The book itself was unknown.

Who then was Bruno R? What were his ideas? What relation do they bear to the theory of bureaucratic collectivism as advanced by the Workers Party? It has been assumed by some comrades both here and abroad that Trotsky's attack on Bruno R's theory of bureaucratic collectivism was in fact directed against the Workers Party's views. This is an error in chronology. Actually the very first draft of what was to become the WP position did not appear until December 1940, i.e., after Trotsky's death. In the 1939 dispute Trotsky tried to use Rizzi's book as a stalking-horse, in his opening gambit, when he thought that the axis of the discussion was going to turn on the theory of the Russian state. However, the discussion which ensued revolved around the political-programmatic question of *defense* of Russia in the war. Rizzi therefore disappeared from view; he is not even mentioned in the last two-thirds of Trotsky's *In Defense of Marxism*, for example.

Bruno Rizzi, Trotsky informs us, was an Italian who at one time belonged to the Fourth International. Because of the ease with which he was able to get around, his lack of Italian revolutionary "references", and his heterodox political views, he was treated with caution by comrades with whom he came in contact. Of his subsequent fate nothing is known.

The evolution of his political ideas is related by Rizzi in his book. He first began to re-examine the Russian question in 1936, when he published *Whither the USSR?* in Italian. This book was confiscated by the Fascist government, which, says Rizzi, "certainly did not understand the real objective of our work". (This curious statement will become clear when we elaborate upon Rizzi's views.)

He returned to the question in *Is This the Twilight of Civilization?*, written "to combat opportunism and to lead workers to the Fourth International". In this work he "dwelt on the question of the new ruling class in the USSR". Rizzi relates: "At London in November 1938 we attempted to pose the question of the nature of the Soviet state in the English section of the Fourth International. Unfortunately the comrades — totalitarians, also! — had already had 'plenty of discussions' and were all in agreement with Trotsky. We succeeded in being heard even in a limited way only by the East London comrades. They took us for a petty bourgeois, and obstructionism closed the development of the discussion".

The Bureaucratization of the World was conceived and written between the end of 1938 and the middle of May 1939. He believes that a new type of state, which he calls bureaucratic collectivist, has emerged in Russia. This state, which is neither proletarian nor capitalist, is ruled by the bureaucracy, which has assumed a class character.

As far as these two sentences go, they coincide with our own views. Beginning from such an insight into the nature of the Russian phenomenon, however, one can proceed in various directions. And from this point, the Workers Party parts company with the views of Rizzi. We shall see how far afield he goes in his own direction.

For Rizzi, bureaucratic collectivism is *historically progressive*. This indeed is the prime dividing line. For him, it is a world phenomenon intermediary between capital-

From *New International*, September 1948, "Footnote on the history of the 'Russian Question'," (abridged).

ism and socialism, partially achieved in Nazi Germany and Fascist Italy and existing in embryonic form in the New Deal in the United States. This new society, whose historic function is to raise the level of world production through the cooperation of several large autarkies, has been made mandatory by the bankruptcy of the working class. The chief task of the working class of England, France and the United States is, therefore, to put pressure on their governments to relinquish living space and raw materials to Germany and Italy — which would permit the dictatorships to relax and world production to rise.

With this birds'-eye view of Rizzi's conceptions on Russia, we can proceed to a more detailed examination of his ideas. The book opens with a synoptic view of the rise and decline of the Russian Revolution. "What is the USSR today?" Rizzi asks. "Its economy is not capitalist, nor is it based on private property, but it is based upon the collective ownership of the means of production". Exploitation takes place through the extraction of surplus value. The cause of this condition lies in the fact that "the country was basically constituted of manual laborers and of illiterates, its industry was greatly inferior to the necessities of a vanguard economy". Behind this lies the failure of the world revolution.

A new class neither bourgeois nor proletarian has appeared on the horizon. This class is fully formed in Russia and "it is also visible in Italy as well as in Germany. The first indications... are apparent everywhere, even in the countries of the great democracies". The purges which took place following the assassination of Kirov were "only the civil war necessary for the new class to solidify its power. It is not a question of this being a sign of weakness, but of its being a demonstration of the strength of this class".

Rizzi then takes up some of the arguments advanced against this thesis, in particular those used by Trotsky in 1938 in his article "Neither a Workers' Nor a Bourgeois State?".

"Can the nature of a state always be judged", asks Rizzi, "without taking into account its political forms?" He replies: "It is a question of seeing to what end the expropriated and nationalized property in Russia is safeguarded from imperialism..." If "a proletarian state with a bourgeois economy has existed" — as was the case immediately after the revolution — "could not a non-proletarian state with a nationalized economy also exist?"

Why should the new class attempt to denationalize property? "For if the nationalized property and planned economy remain it is because both are in consonance with the régime which holds power". Even bourgeois states tend more and more to plan and to nationalize property.

We are confronted with a *class*. An exploiting class exists in Russia, having in its hands the means of production and acting as its owner. If "property is nationalized in a non-proletarian régime it also loses its potential character of socialist property; it remains only class property".

The author next takes up the bogey of capitalist-restorationist trends which haunt Fourth Internationalist thinking. He argues that historically progressive organizations, which increase the volume of production, do not go backward. "Did feudalism ever have the intention of going back to slavery?" Even if Russia were invaded by the Anti-Comintern Pact forces, there would be no reason for the destruction of an "economic system which is in the process of construction precisely in their own countries..." Why think of the return of the bourgeoisie? "If a new class has formed, it is because, historically or accidentally, it has a role to play in the historic ascent of humanity... it is charged with organizing production on the basis of collective property in planning the economy within the state framework, while for socialism there will remain only the problems of international 'nationalization' and the socialist distribution of products".

Thus far Rizzi. As we have indicated, our common starting point is that Russia is neither a workers' state (however degenerated) nor a capitalist state, but rather a state ruled by a new class which is extensive, entrenched and showing no serious tendencies toward capitalist restoration. We likewise label this "bureaucratic collectivism". It must be admitted that Rizzi develops this part of his thesis with not inconsiderable skill and originality.

What *distinguishes* Rizzi's views, however, is his acceptance of bureaucratic collectivist Russia as a *progressive* phenomenon. This idea — that nationalization of the means of production is, in and of itself, progressive — is the widespread fallacy of our day.

A significant rise in the level of production over previously existing levels (the criterion for judging the progressive character of a given set of property relations) must, in the period of declining capitalism, be decided on a world basis. Seen from this point of view, the expression "politics is concentrated economics" takes on real meaning. The effect of Stalinist politics in the past twenty-five years has been to hold back the establishment of international socialism (a superior mode of production); to facilitate the outbreak of World War II (which has seriously lowered even world *capitalist* production); and to make World War III virtually inevitable — which, given the present constellation of forces, means the victory of US imperialism and, consequently, neo-barbarism. Only if socialism intervenes can the war be resolved on a progressive basis. From our vantage point we can see the concrete outcome of what to many, nearly a generation ago, seemed a theoretical quibble — the theory of "socialism in one country", i.e., Stalinist nationalism.

Actually, despite the limited resemblance between the Russian position of Bruno Rizzi and that of the Workers Party, in estimating Russia's historic role *he is much closer to the position of Trotsky and the Socialist Workers Party, for whom also the nationalized means of production form the decisive criterion of historical progressiveness*, than he is to us.

Rizzi: "Our conclusion is that, in Italy as well as in Germany, capitalist society is being destroyed day by day, while the corresponding crystallization of a new society replaces it, with economic characteristics identical with Soviet characteristics, even if they are still partial". This does not prevent Rizzi from speaking elsewhere as if his bureaucratic collectivism were a finished formation in these and other states. He says, for instance: "Nevertheless, while the work of Stalin, Mussolini or Hitler is everywhere described as socialism or capitalism, it is a question only of bureaucratic collectivism".

Unlike Rizzi, we cannot consider bureaucratic collectivism a world phenomenon intermediary between capitalism and socialism. We concur with Trotsky that state intervention in the fascist countries was primarily to co-ordinate the interests of the capitalists — and mainly for war purposes. Certainly to date bureaucratic collectivism bears the label "Made in Russia".

Our author moves on to the plane of Historical Generalization. Russia is the archetype of the new autarkic bureaucratic-collectivist state. It needs neither "further territory nor raw materials, but only to work tranquilly and intensely, exploiting the natural riches found in its domain". Japan is following the same course. If Germany and Italy are threatening to overrun the world it is because they lack living space and raw materials. Small states are being engulfed. "But if world peace and the increasing development of production are desired, a peaceful means must be found to give living space and the necessary raw materials for the building up of the German and Italian autarkies". The new ruling class must not seek to amass individual riches but be satisfied with good salaries while seeking an absolute increase in production. "Its historic function will end when it reveals itself incapable of pursuing this end".

"Nationalization, statification of the major means of production, economic planning, and production for non-individualistically speculative ends represent the trump cards of bureaucratic collectivism. In a political climate of reciprocal confidence among the autarkies, founded on sure economic bases, all possibilities for increasing production are offered to the new ruling class. From a historic point of view this class has the task of increasing the total world production in an organized manner..." This bureaucratic state is historically necessary, but the "last ruling class in history is so near to the classless society that it denies its class and ownership characteristics".

Rizzi agrees that the working class must have the right to strike, and the unions must be free of state control. They will serve as instruments of social control and criticism. State control of the unions in totalitarian countries must be relinquished... This serves to remind one that Rizzi is *trying* to think like a socialist.

The first task of the working class, then, says Rizzi, is to secure a redivision of the living space and raw materials of the world. To achieve socialism the world must first be rationally industrialized. This new cycle between capitalism and socialism is historically necessary. The workers of France, England, and the United States must "make themselves master of their state and impose at least a workers' and technicians' bureaucracy" but one which "will always permit proletarian control of the basic bodies". The seven or eight autarkies could then arrive at a working agreement with each other.

This progressive step is being threatened by world capitalism, which is opposing the fascist movement. The real enemies are not Hitler and Mussolini, who have, after all, "set out with the German and Italian workers on the new social road to the new world". "All feelings of bitterness or of hate" in regard to Stalin, Hitler and Mussolini must disappear. "They too will begin to pardon and to preach the law of Love which is the great law of Life, as well as social collaboration". Blinded by party passion we have failed to understand and to honor the fascist fallen. The job of the French, English and US working class is to force their capitalists to relinquish living space and raw materials to Germany and Italy. These latter countries would then reintroduce democratic régimes. Workers and the new rulers could then rationalize production. Bankers would be pensioned off. Rizzi concludes this frenzied rapture: "Mussolini and Hitler extend their hand to Lenin". The Hitler-Stalin pact is predicted. "The workers will never be a ruling class... they will only have the supreme honor of 'ruling' a classless society!" "The Russian experience shows us that the dictatorship of the proletariat changes into a new ruling class: that of the bureaucrats, while the proletarians are transformed into *citizen* workers". "The fascists have committed the theoretical error of wishing to collaborate with the bourgeoisie, whereas they should liquidate it and have already half killed it". When "the new class has provided for its material, intellectual and moral needs, it will obviously take pleasure in continually elevating the working class materially, intellectually and morally". This section contains the essence of Rizzi's *program: a "socialist" rationale for fascism.*

Next in Rizzi's film of free association is a short subject, titled "The Jewish Question". "All the racial theories of Rosenberg, Hitler, Italian racists, etc., have not been able to resist the slightest scientific attack. Questions of blood, of origin, etc... are, in our modest opinion, only empty words". Nevertheless, it must be said that the Jews are the "most jealously racist nation in the world and they have even claimed to be more intelligent than the others". In a big majority of cases Jews have been capitalist types. The struggle against capitalism must therefore be strongly identified with the struggle against the Jews. A mass campaign against the Jews must be initiated. "Hitler is right and we are wrong". But this should not be understood as advocacy of pogroms. Workers should not fall into the trap of treating *all* Jews alike. Jewish workers must be taken in marriage in order to regenerate them more rapidly and to eradicate them from the face of the earth! "We respect and honor Marx and Trotsky and a few others of our obscure friends of the Jewish race. Certain isolated and very beautiful flowers can grow in dung heaps, but as a whole the Jewish people have become a capitalist dung heap".

It is clear to what vile lengths of anti-Semitism Rizzi is led by his fatal acceptance of the "progressiveness" of Stalinist nationalization and fascist "statism". Of the degeneracy of his thinking it is enough to remark as did Dean Meeks of Grant's Tomb: "It's a tour de force, gentlemen. You cannot alter it in any way without improving its proportions".

Rizzi concludes with "An Appeal to Mankind". He asks the bourgeoisie to repent, for they must know that a collapse is coming if they do not grant 'living space' and raw materials to Italy, Germany and Japan. If this is done, the dictators will relax their régimes. "We do not believe that in the bottom of their hearts, and as men, Stalin, Hitler and Mussolini are happy with their régimes.... The New World which we desire will liberate even these great prisoners..."

And so, as all good films should, it is on this note of Love that we come to *The End* of the film of meditations of an isolated man who tried to think like a socialist under fascism — unsuccessfully.

C L R James

THE USSR IS A FASCIST STATE CAPITALISM

FOR MANY YEARS the fact that in Russia the means of production were state property was sufficient for the Fourth International to characterize the working class as ruling class and the Russian state as a workers' state. Today, however, 1941, side by side with a tremendous but declining rate of industrial expansion in Russia, the working class has been reduced to a state of pauperization, slavery and degradation unequalled in modern Europe. The real wages of the workers are approximately one-half of what they were in 1913. A bureaucracy holds all economic and political power. To continue to call the Russian workers the ruling class is to make a statement without meaning.

Yet Trotsky never wavered from this position. It led him, the direct successor of Marx, Engels and Lenin, into calling upon the workers of Russia to be the best soldiers in an army that was, according to his own statement, acting as the tool of an imperialist power. The Workers Party, in refusing to accept this position, and in calling upon the Russian workers in this war to turn the guns in the opposite direction, made a profound break not with all that we have thought on the Russian question, but with something far more important, with *how* we have thought about it. So profound a difference must convince the party that what we face is not a re-hash or manipulation of our previous ideas but a fundamental revaluation...

Marx rests his theory of society upon the technical level of the instruments of production under given historical circumstances. "Assume a particular stage of development in the productive forces of man and you will get a particular form of commerce and consumption. Assume particular stages of development in production, commerce and consumption and you will have a corresponding social order, a corresponding organization of the family and of the ranks and classes, in a word, a corresponding civil society". These are Marx's own words. The purely historical, i.e., the chronological analysis of society places property first. The logical method of Marx examines the actual historical relations always as an expression of the logical analysis, which begins with the technical level of the instruments of production. This determines the relation of the people to each other and the division into classes, which then determine the relation of the classes to the instruments of production and the results of labor. These last, usually expressed in laws, are the relations of property, which, from his earliest writings, Marx always defined as an *expression* of the mode of production. This is the strict Marxian terminology and the strict Marxian sequence as can be seen from a casual reading of the Preface to the *Critique of Political Economy* and *The Communist Manifesto*.

Applying this method to Russia we find that in 1941 the technical level of production, unsupported by one or more powerful socialist states, compels a social relation of exploited wage-laborers and appropriating capitalists. In order to achieve the bourgeois-democratic revolution in 1917 the proletariat was compelled to seize power. But this seizure of political power was due chiefly to the incapacity of the ruling class and the conjunctural historical circumstances. The working class lacked the maturity in production of a proletariat which was a majority of the population and had been trained and disciplined by large-scale capitalism. All political power rests in the last analysis on and is determined by production relations. This was the reason for the insistence of Lenin and Trotsky that without the proletarian revolution on a world-wide scale, the Russian proletariat was doomed to sink back to the position of wage-slaves, i.e., the restoration of Russia to capitalism. This is exactly what has happened. The whole society has turned itself slowly over and once more the working class has been pushed back into that submissive role in production which is determined by the low technical level of the productive forces judged on a national scale. The bureaucracy is completely mas-

Abridged resolution on the Russian question to the 1941 Workers Party convention by C L R James (J R Johnson), dated September 1941.

ter in the productive process and that is the basis of its political power.

No more convincing exposition of Marx's theory of a society resting on the technical level of production can be wished for.

Contrary to expectation the role of managers of production has not been seized by members of the old ruling class. The definition of the class which is today master of Russia must rest on an analysis of the mode of production which now prevails. The historical conditions of capitalist production are as follows: (1) the existence of the world market, (2) the existence of a class of "nominally free" wage-laborers, (3) the ownership or monopoly of the means of production by a class which rules production and disposes of the property, (4) production by private persons for a free and uncertain market. Such a society produces a certain type of product, the *capitalist* commodity which has its own special commodity characteristics. The labor contained in it has the double aspect of both use-value and exchange-value. To use Marx's own words, "*all* understanding of the facts depends upon this...", and any analysis of Russia which describes it as a society "unforeseen" by Marxists but yet omits a consideration of this and other aspects of the law of value is so inadequate as to be not only misleading but valueless. The law of value can be rejected. It cannot be ignored or allowed to go by default in a Marxist party.

The Marxian law of value, however, is merely an expression of a certain type of society. This society, contrary to all other societies we have known and expect to know, makes the extraction of surplus labor (called in this instance surplus-value) the main aim of production. For Marx "the capitalist mode of production (is) essentially the production of surplus value, the absorption of surplus labor". This is crucial. "It must never be forgotten, that the production of this surplus-value — the reconversion of a portion of it into capital, or accumulation, forms an indispensable part of this production of surplus-value — is the immediate purpose and the compelling motive of capitalist production. It will not do to represent capitalist production as something which it is not, that is to say, as a production having for its immediate purpose the consumption of goods, or the production of means of enjoyment for capitalists. This would be overlooking the specific character of capitalist production, which reveals itself in its innermost essence". This is the main aim of production in Stalinist society, a capitalist society. All other societies produced for consumption and enjoyment.

All previous societies produced surplus-labor, but, except in isolated instances, wants or use-values were the *main* purpose of production. It is only in a society where labor is free of all contact with the means of production, within the environment of the world market, that the contradiction between production for use and for surplus value dominates the whole society. Marx speaks of the difference between the use-value and the exchange-value of the commodity as the antithesis of the commodity. The contradictions and antagonisms of capitalistic society are merely embodiments of this antithesis, which is to be resolved by the synthesis of socialism, i.e., by the reuniting of the man of labor and the means of labor, and the abolition of the capitalist world market. International socialist society will produce surplus labor but it once more has as its sole aim the production of use-values.

Today this antithesis between production for use and production for surplus-labor can be seen nowhere so clearly as in Stalinist Russia. And that stamps this society as being of the same inner essence as capitalism. Up to 1928, the use-value of the commodity predominated to the limited extent that this was possible in a backward society in the environment of the world market. The industrial proletariat in that year lived, at the very least, up to the standard of 1913. The First Five Year Plan predicated doubling of the subsistence of the working class by 1932. But from 1929 a decisive change began. The lowering of agricultural prices in the world market threw the Russian plan into chaos. The competition on the world market, in its modern form of imperialist war, compelled the bureaucracy to reorganize the plan to meet the threat of Japan, at heavy cost; and with the coming to power of Hitler and his announcement that the main enemy was Russia, the change in Stalinist production and in Stalinist society became more uncontrollable. The bureaucracy was compelled to continue the process of industrialization at feverish speed. Under such circumstances, in a backward country, with an immature working class, the main aim of production inevitably must become the production of surplus-labor, for the sake of more production, for the sake of still more production. And all this at the cost of the working class. This is the specific characteristic of a capitalist

320

production. This *economic* necessity compelled an enormous increase in the repressive apparatus, the consolidation of the ruling bureaucracy by concrete privileges, honors and authority, and the destruction of persons and ideology connected with the October Revolution. The necessity of autarky, attempting to produce all that Russia needed within its own borders, resulted in further disruption of production, and the mounting indices of production as a consequence represented large uneconomic investment, thus increasing the strain upon the workers. Stakhanovism was a perfect expression of the qualitative change in Russian society. The climax came in 1936-1937 with the partial breakdown of the economy as exemplified by the charges of Trotskyite sabotage in every branch of production. In the historical circumstances of Russia, the antithesis between the production of surplus value and use-value has reached a stage unknown in other capitalist economies. The state of world economy today precludes any thought of a cessation of this mode of production. The economic power of the bureaucracy precludes that this can be done otherwise than at the continued and growing expense of the working class. The system has developed in every essential of production into a capitalist system and the parasitic bureaucracy has been transformed into an exploiting capitalist class. Henceforward its law of motion must be the same as that of other capitalist societies. An approximate date for the completion of the process is 1936, the year of the Stalinist constitution.

That the laws inherent in capitalist production in Russia manifest themselves in unusual forms is obvious. But their unusualness in Russia is not unique. It is exceeded by the capitalism which Marx himself invented. To deduce the laws of capitalist production, Marx constructed a capitalism such as never existed and never could exist. The very method on which *Capital* was constructed is a warning to all hasty and ill-based attempts to baptise societies as never before seen, from a consideration of their external forms of manifestation, and not from an analysis of their laws of motion.

The "free and uncertain" market of "pure" capitalism has been abolished before now in a national society. Lenin in 1917, before the revolution, stated that the immense majority of the capitalists in Russia were not producing for the market at all but for the State which advanced them money. It was not commodity production, which, he explained, was production for a free and uncertain market. It was not "pure" capitalism (the quotes are his own) but "A special type of national economy". In Germany today that process Lenin described is immensely more advanced than it was in Russia. It would be a perversion to assert that production in Germany is for a free and open market. It would be equally disastrous to see in this abolition of the traditionally free capitalist market, a basic change in the society. The law of motion is not thereby altered. To the contrary, it is in the nature of the law of motion to abolish the free market. In Russia the commodity is no longer the product of private individuals. But it is, however, the law of capitalist production to abolish the private character of capital. That Marx expected the revolution to occur before this was completed alters not one thing in his analysis of the movement of the society. The joint-stock company is "the abolition of capital as private property within the boundaries of capitalist production". The concentration of all available capital in the hands of the Bank of England "does away with the private character of capital and implies in itself, to that extent, the abolition of capital". The climax of this process is the ownership of all capital in the hands of the State. The bourgeoisie continues to draw dividends, but the drawing of dividends does not make a system capitalist. The dividends can be drawn from a Workers' State. It is the fact that the state acts as the entrepreneur and exploits the workers that is decisive.

An identical process of production in Russia moves inevitably to a similar result. The laws of capitalist production, always immanent in an isolated Workers' State and more so in a backward economy, have been forced into action, in the environment of the world market. The organic composition of capital in Russia mounts with the growth of industrialization. Year by year, however, the mass of surplus labor must grow proportionately less and less. Marx worked out his final theory of accumulation on the basis of the total social capital in the country and denied that this altered the economic and historical characteristics of the society. The expenses of an exploiting class within the environment of the world market, the privileges necessary to differentiate the classes, a vast military apparatus, increasing degradation and slavery of the worker, the lowering of his *individual* productivity at a stage when it needs to be increased, all these features of Russia are rooted in the capital-wage labor relation and the world-market environment. The advantages that Russia alone enjoyed in 1928, centralization of the means of production, capacity to plan, have today been swamped by the disadvantages of the quest for surplus labor. To its traditionally capitalist troubles the bureaucracy adds one of its own, an excessive waste due to the bureaucratic administration. But Stalin today, like Hitler, contends essentially with the falling relation of the mass of surplus value to the total social capital. That is the economic basis of the constantly growing persecution of the workers by the bureaucracy. The bureaucracy is no worse than any other ruling class. It behaves as it does because it must. This is the law of motion of Stalinist society. Ultimately the productive apparatus of Russia will stand as impotent as Germany's in 1932, and for the same reason, its incapacity to produce the necessary surplus labor which is the compelling motive of production for any modern class society. The struggle in Russia is not over consumption, as Trotsky thought, but over production, and the Stalinist state is organized nine-tenths, not for stealing, but for production. The party must make this clear in all its propaganda and agitation and correct this serious error.

This is the reply to all who see some new type of society superseding capitalism, and solving its contradictions. All of these theories are distinguished by their absence of economic analysis, or the flimsiness of their assumptions. If the party should adopt the same empirical method in its own analysis, it will completely emasculate its own capacity to answer and destroy the arguments of those who herald the managerial society, the "new" Fascist order, the garrison State, etc. This theory is the heritage that Marx left for the proletarian movement. And it is here that we must be clear or be always in confusion.

All imperialism was not necessarily of the particular type Lenin analysed. Japan and Russia were not, as he said, "modern, up-to-date finance-capital", but, as he explained, their military power, their domination of colonial territories, their plunder of China, etc., made them imperialist. By 1914 imperialism was therefore a struggle for all or any kind of territory, for the sake of the territory and in order to prevent rivals getting hold of it. This was done to control raw materials, to export capital, to expand the commodity-market, for strategic purposes, in fact *for any purpose which would contribute to the increase of surplus value*. That is the obvious economic basis of Stalinist imperialism. Like Hitlerism it will seize fixed capital or agrarian territory, tin-mines or strategic ports and transport manpower. Within its own borders the bureaucracy mercilessly exploits the subject nationalities. Should it emerge victorious in the coming war, it will share in all the grabbings of its partners, and for the same reason. Trotsky's idea that the bureaucracy seeks foreign territory merely to expand its power, prestige and revenues lays the emphasis on the consumption of the bureaucracy. That is false. The "greed" of the capitalist class is a result of the process of production, and the greed of the bureaucracy has the same roots. With a productivity of labor as low as it is in Russia, and the overhead expenses of an exploiting society within the environment of the world market as large as they are, equal to that of the most highly developed capitalist states, it is not possible for the bureaucracy to escape the same fundamental problems of production as an advanced capitalist state, and to move towards the same attempts at solution.

If the relations of production in Russia are capitalist then the state is Fascist. Fascism is a mass petty-bourgeois movement but the Fascist state is not a mass petty-bourgeois state. It is the political reflection of the drive towards complete centralization of production which distinguishes all national economies today.

Finance-capital and interlocking directorates are a result of the growing concentration of capital and the increasing socialization of production. The contradiction between this socialization and the appropriation of the product for the benefit of a few drives the few into a position where to survive they must act as one, against the workers and against the external bourgeoisie.

The Fascist state has deeper economic roots than we have hitherto acknowledged. In this respect the development of Russia is a signpost as to the future of capitalist society. In 1878 Engels (and Marx approved) made a statement of the most profound significance for the modern world: that the growing socialization of production would compel the capitalists to treat the productive forces as social forces, *so far as that was pos-*

sible within the framework of capitalist relations. How far is that possible? Today life and Marx's *Capital* teach us the probable extent and limits of this process... Today the capitalist class, impelled to treat the productive forces as social forces, so far has left the property relations intact but the group in control manipulates the surplus value more and more as a whole. Less and less capital is apportioned to production by competition. In Germany today capital is *consciously* directed to different branches of production. The process will continue. The capitalists abolish the free market and shape circulation as far as possible to their own purposes, rationing every commodity including labor-power. But the one fundamental condition of capitalist production, the sale and purchase of labor-power, and the process of production (Volume I), that they cannot alter without destroying themselves. Lenin (in the last two pages of *Imperialism*) as early as 1916 saw that with the increasing socialization of production "private economic relations and private property relations constitute a shell which is no longer suitable for its contents, a shell which must of necessity begin to decay if its destruction is postponed by artificial means". The Communist Manifesto of the Third International was written around the same thesis in the most pronounced form.

If Russia today has differences with a capitalist economy where the private property relations have decayed and *production* is nationalized, these points are not to be detailed for their own sake as being different. Nobody denies their difference. What is to be proved is that these differences alter the law of motion of the society. And this cannot be done, because the contradictions of the society are rooted in the class relations of production which are identical and determine all other relations. What was formerly private and uncontrolled by the very development of capitalist production becomes more and more state-controlled.

The antithesis of Stalinist society and capitalistic society being the same, the solution of their contradictions is the same. It can be stated in a sentence. The workers must take control of the process of production on a national and international scale; this achieved, automatically, according to the technical development and the relation with the world market, use values will begin to predominate. But with reasonable speed the same must take place on an international scale, or the quest for surplus-labor in the world as a whole will drag down the socialist state, unless it commands an exceptionally well-developed and extensive area. "We live", said Lenin, "not in a state but in a system of states". The consequences of this transformation will be:

1. The *individual* development of the laborer... The degradation of the Russian worker is an economic fact. Man is the greatest of all productive forces, and once his potentialities are released, the era of human freedom will begin. "Its fundamental premise is the shortening of the working day". Until then society will be increasingly like Russia and Germany, and plunging to destruction.

2. This release of the workers for creative labor in production will be immensely encouraged by the entry into productive labor of the millions of idlers and unproductive laborers who infest modern society.

3. Production will be for social needs. The idea that if the bourgeoisie should nationalize production and property, the hope for Socialism is a Utopia, that is a misunderstanding of the contradictions of capitalism which must be driven out of our movement. Such a transformation will solve nothing. The three points outlined above will be as far from realization as ever. A new society begins when the workers take power or when the world market is abolished by the domination of one capitalist state which would be an unspeakable barbarism. Marxism knows no other "new" society, far less any progressive new society. Either the emancipation of labor or increasing barbarism.

Only in the most abstract sense can state-property be said to be a higher form, as monopoly capitalism was a higher form than pre-monopoly capitalism. Today we have reached a turning point. The pauperization of the worker, which was formerly relative, is now on a world scale absolute. Today in the most advanced capitalist societies, he is on his way to slavery. In its present stage, capitalism, whatever its form, except in a few areas and for declining periods, can no longer maintain the worker even in the conditions of his previous slavery. Without the proletarian revolution the state-property form can be the vehicle of barbarism and the destruction of human society. Such terms as higher and lower forms have no meaning in the concrete circumstances. It is not the form of property but the social relations of production which are decisive. Today if the

323

working class is master the form is progressive. If it is not, the form is reactionary. "In bourgeois society living labor is but a means to increase accumulated labor. In Communist society accumulated labor is but a means to widen, to enrich, to promote the existence of the laborer". Any society today in which the aim is not to promote the existence of the laborer is doomed to crisis and disorder and will go always closer to barbarism until the workers take power. That is all there is to Marx, and, as he himself states, on an understanding of this, all comprehension of the facts depends.

On the basis of the above analysis certain political conclusions follow automatically. They are:

a) *No defense of Russia under any circumstances.* The first condition for working out a long term policy about Russia is to define the economic nature of the society and the historic character of the bureaucracy. It is bourgeois, and therefore has no rights over the struggles of the workers for their democratic rights. The struggle for socialism is the struggle for democracy, before or after the expropriation of the bureaucracy. The bureaucracy in Russia has to be expropriated, driven away from its stranglehold over the process and the means of production. To do this the proletariat mobilizes all the poor and all the oppressed of Russia. It is prepared without hesitation to restore private property to those peasants who wish it. It rejects a united front with Kerensky and all his scores of followers in Russia who ask the proletariat to fight for them so that they may each get a factory for themselves. With Mensheviks, and with any section of the working class movement, or any other section of society, it forms a united front for what it considers to be working-class demands, and for nothing else; it forms these on its own conditions and the revolutionary proletariat keeps its hands free and makes or breaks these attempts at united action as it sees fit in the interests of the struggle for power. Nothing in Marxism compels the proletariat to form a united front with any group at any time except it thinks to the advantage of the proletariat to do so in its struggle for power.

b) *Denunciation of the Communist Party as the agent of a Fascist power.* It appears that in the minds of some this excludes a United Front with the CP on a specific issue. The contention is not only stupid but dangerous. A United Front is formed with a section of American workers mainly on their intentions against the American bourgeoisie, or the world bourgeoisie, not on account of its belief in Stalinism. If it is not to be formed with them because the CP is the agent of a reactionary bureaucracy which is the enemy of the workers and of socialism, that excludes the United Front with the CP for all those who do not believe that the working class is still the ruling class in Russia. In the case of [CP leader] Browder whom the American government attacked for obvious reasons, the WP will offer a United Front. If the CP, however, had called for a mass protest against the war in 1939, then with our present policy the WP should have refused. But even that refusal is not definitive. For according to the temper of the American proletariat, the strength of the WP, the stage of development or disintegration of the CP, the strength of the bourgeoisie, the WP may even under similar circumstance decide even to support a specific anti-war action by the CP even though the call was dictated originally by the interests of the Russian bureaucracy. The sophistry which indulges in superficial arguments of the above type must be rigorously rejected. It would be most dangerous for the WP if it allowed itself to be driven into considering the United Front as a collection of fixed laws, instead of a tactical orientation within given circumstance toward a fixed goal.

c) *Propaganda for Socialism.* The WP must make it a first task, in its press, and all other propaganda and agitation, to preach the necessity of socialism, to explain that no modern society of any kind offers any solution to the problems of modern society, except a society in which the workers hold power. It must with special vigor denounce and expose the idea that Fascism, Managerial Society, or bureaucratic state-socialism, are in any concrete sense progressive societies or even could be, and it must do this by challenging their proponents on the fundamental economic categories and analysis of Marx.

d) The WP must initiate a serious study of Marxian economics.

5. RUSSIAN IMPERIALIST EXPANSION

In the course of World War 2 it became clear that the USSR had a full-scale program of imperialist conquest and plunder. The Stalinist rulers were participating in the war, not as unreliable or reluctant defenders of the statised economy against greedy capitalist predators, but as predators in their own right.

Max Shachtman

THE COUNTER-REVOLUTIONARY REVOLUTION

GENERAL PRINCE ALEXANDER Vassilivich Suvorov was a military figure of great renown who served throughout Europe under the Empress Catherine and, after her, under the Emperor Paul, in the latter half of the eighteenth century. He carried the banner of Czarist reaction to the Danube and threatened the power of the Turks. He fought the Napoleonic armies as far West and South as Italy, and learned Milanese remember that the day Suvorov's troops marched into their city marked the death of the Cisalpine Republic.

At the head of a greatly superior army of Russians and Cossacks, he defeated the Poles under Poniatowski and Tadeusz Kosciuszko in 1792, and opened the way for the second partition of Poland next year between Catherine and Frederick William of Prussia. In 1794, when Poland rose in insurrection under the banner of Kosciuszko, who had entered Cracow, proclaimed national independence, and then forced the besieging troops of the Prussian monarch to withdraw, Catherine again sent Suvorov into the field. He emerged triumphant with the capture of Warsaw, which inaugurated the third partition of Poland the following year and its effectual extinction as a nation.

Czarist Russia was the principal pillar of European reaction, the staunchest support of all the black forces that sought to stem the tide of revolutionary Jacobinism set in motion all over the continent by the Great French Revolution. Prince Suvorov was one of the ablest and most odious representatives of this reaction. He even came to be its symbol. The French counter-revolution in 1799 marched through Britanny and Normandy with the royalists shouting: "Long live Suvorov! Down with the Republic!" It was a name with a record and a meaning that it retains to the present day.

These recollections are evoked by the reports that the Order of Suvorov has now been established in Stalinist Russia, sometimes called, out of pure nostalgia (there is no other reason), the "workers' state." The Order of Suvorov, First Class, "may be awarded only to a commander of an army on the front, his chief of staff or departmental heads who have annihilated numerically superior enemy forces or accomplished break-throughs on major fronts. The Second Class of the Order is given to corps or divisional commanders and the Third Class to lower officers." There is now also an Order of Kutuzov, contemporary of Suvorov, and no less devoted a servant of Czarist despotism. Both of them and others of their kind adorn the breasts of any number of Stalin's marshals and generals.

"After two years of war with Germany. Notes on Russia in the war", from *New International*, July 1943. We have restored deletions and changes — all of them small and of a copy-editing function — made by Shachtman when he republished this article in his book *The Bureaucratic Revolution*. This is the first part of the article. The second part is in chapter 10 of this book.

It is a sign of the times in Russia, and not the first one, and far from the most important one. The old Red Army, which triumphed over the forces of all the imperialist powers sent against it, is gone, and gone of course is the socialist democratism, the internationalism, and the revolutionary spirit with which it was imbued from the start. Only people who do not think twice about how they are insulting the memory of the great founder of that army can refer to the Bonapartist levies that replaced it as "Trotsky's Red Army."

All the old grades and ranks which the Bolshevik Revolution abolished have been restored and new ones added. The comradely relationship between commandant and rank-and-file has been replaced by the hierarchical relationship between an officer corps and a disfranchised serf-in-uniform that prevails in all imperialist armies. Special guards' brigades and divisions have been created in direct imitation, not of the Red Guards of the revolution, but of the Praetorian Guards regiments set up by Czar Peter the Great. Officers are now prohibited from mingling with the ranks or maintaining an atmosphere of equality with them. Bristling with vulgar decorations, officers from the rank of platoon commander upward are now provided with flunkies, each one has an "orderly" who "takes his meals to his officer, makes tea for him and polishes his boots." A system of exclusive officers' clubs has been set up, thus formally acknowledging what was yesterday a thinly-disguised reality. Trotsky's Red Army knew no officers — the very name was done away with — and no permanent ranks, that is, no officers' corps.

The canonization of Suvorov in the Stalinist army is not altogether inappropriate. Suvorov and his army were the banner-bearers of the counter-revolution of their time. If Stalin harks back to the reaction of yesterday, it is because he represents the reaction of today. It is possible that under the name of Suvorov, the Stalinist army will win its battles; the proletariat will not. It is a class that differs from *all* others in history above all in the fact that it can conquer and rule only in its own name, and thereby put an end to all rule. In this statement there is not an ounce of sentimentality or abstract idealism; it is a profound and profoundly important social truth.

It is now possible to see much more clearly and fully what we saw incompletely and unclearly at the beginning of the war when we first rejected the slogan of "unconditional defense of the Soviet Union." The analysis of the problem of Stalinist Russia made by Trotsky in his last years, an analysis in irreconcilable conflict with one he had made originally, collapsed under the test of events. The Cannonites, who are less interested in critical Marxian analysis and re-analysis than in iconology, deem it sufficient to say their beads over and over again. But Marxism is not and never was a fully completed dogma, but a developing science.

Trotsky assigned to Stalinism, to the Stalinist bureaucracy, the rôle of undermining the economic foundations of the workers' state. By gradually de-nationalizing the means of production and exchange, loosening the monopoly of foreign trade, Stalinism would pave the way for the restoration of private property and capitalism. Indeed, it would not even survive this restoration, for that social act would be carried out by the forces of the Right Wing toward which the Stalinist Center leaned and repeatedly capitulated, and by which it would be crushed.

327

Nothing of the sort occurred. It was the Right Wing that was crushed by the Stalinist bureaucracy, and not the other way around. State property was not de-nationalized but, contrariwise, was more securely concentrated in the hands of the state and vastly expanded.

A year before World War II broke out, Trotsky found it possible to assert that the Right Wing, which the old analysis had described as the wing of capitalist restoration, represented a *Left* danger to the bureaucracy. The assertion was altogether abrupt, never motivated, not prepared by anything Trotsky had written previously, and to this day remains unexplained by the bead-sayers. It is nevertheless an assertion of first-rate significance.

As late as 1938, that is, in the same year, Trotsky not only saw an important fascist wing in the Stalinist bureaucracy (i.e., a *capitalist* wing), but declared that the political pendulum has swung more strongly "to the side of the right, the bourgeois wing of the bureaucracy and its allies throughout the land. From them, i.e., from the Right, we can expect ever more determined attempts in the next period to revise the socialist character of the USSR and bring it closer in pattern to 'Western civilization' in its fascist form." If by the "socialist character of the USSR" Trotsky was referring primarily to state-owned property — and he was — the last five years have not revealed a single sign of attempts by the bureaucracy or any important section to "revise" it, much less "ever more determined attempts," in the sense of restoring private property.

Again, it is the contrary that has happened. One can scrutinize most closely the serious political press, and even the often interesting summaries of the Russian press in the periodicals of the bead-sayers, but not a solitary concrete reference will be found to even the beginnings of a trend in the bureaucracy toward de-statification of property, toward the restoration of private property. A prediction which continues to be so completely refuted by events should be discarded, and if the analysis on which it was based is not discarded outright, it at least demands critical reëxamination. That is what we have sought to do in these pages on several occasions, without encountering any comment from the Cannonites. They continue to say their beads.

Upon the invasion of Poland, the Baltic countries and Finland, and the division of imperialist booty between Hitler and Stalin, we watched closely for the possibility, even the likelihood, that Stalin would maintain private property in the occupied territories. That attitude was based not only on the experience of the Spanish Civil War, in which the Stalinists were the most ardent defenders of private property, but on the old analysis, according to which the social rôle of the bureaucracy was to abolish, or to prepare the abolition of, nationalized property. We were profoundly wrong. After a slight delay, the bureaucracy established the same property relations in the occupied countries as in Russia itself. On this point, Trotsky was unmistakably right. But his statement that the bureaucracy would most probably nationalize property in the occupied territories only deepened the contradictions in his fundamental theory of Stalinist Russia as a workers' state.

In the course of the dispute which led to the split in the Fourth International, Trotsky developed his point of view on the "degenerated workers' state" to the stage of a "counter-revolutionary workers' state." We know, he said, of the existence of "two completely counter-revolutionary workers' internationals. These critics have apparently forgotten this 'category'. The trade unions of France, Great Britain, the United States and other countries support completely the counter-revolutionary politics of their bourgeoisie. This does not prevent us from labeling them trade unions, from supporting their progressive steps and from defending them against the bourgeoisie. Why is it impossible to employ the same method with the counter-revolutionary workers' state?"

But the difference, even from the standpoint of Trotsky's fundamental theory, or rather precisely from that standpoint, is irreconcilable. We are warranted in placing the label "counter-revolutionary" over the reformist organizations in the capitalist countries not because they are *for socialism* by "bureaucratic methods," but just because they are *against the socialist revolution*, and have given ample evidence of their opposition to it with rifle and machine gun in hand. They are counter-revolutionary because, at bottom, they base themselves upon and defend the capitalist social order and the capitalist property relations on which it stands.

That the Stalinist bureaucracy (and the state it completely dominates) is counter-revolutionary, needs no elaborate demonstration. That is, it opposes the proletarian socialist revolution, whose triumph would mean the end of Stalinism and its power. But its similarity with the bourgeois labor organizations in the capitalist countries goes no further. The Stalinist state is not only not a defender of bourgeois property and not based upon it, but has destroyed it with all the thoroughness at its command inside of Russia, and, as we now see, even outside of Russia, *provided it had the power to do so*. Its work in the occupied countries shows this sufficiently.

Just what was the nature and significance of this work? The Stalinist state, represented physically by its armed forces (the Russian army and the GPU) occupied a number of capitalist countries, and proceeded to expropriate the bourgeois proprietors, nationalize property under the control of the Stalinists, thus abolishing capitalist property and capitalist property relations. The transformation it effected in the occupied countries is not less than a social revolution. To say that the masses of workers and peasants effected this social change is an exaggeration, to say the least. It was carried out, and in the most thorough manner, by the Stalinist bureaucracy.

Trotsky does not characterize the transformation any differently. He speaks of the Stalinist expropriations of the bourgeoisie as "social revolutionary measures, carried out via bureaucratic military means"; and elsewhere remarks: "This measure, revolutionary in character — 'the expropriation of the expropriators' — is in this case achieved in a military-bureaucratic fashion."

What is the *class character* of this social revolution? By Trotsky's criterion, it must be characterized as *a proletarian, socialist revolution*, whether carried out "bureaucratically" or "militarily" or not.

We are able without difficulty to grasp the concept (it is more than that; it is a reality too often repeated in our time) of a counter-revolutionary labor organization, for example, the Second International, which fights to maintain capitalist society and fights against the inauguration of a socialist society. The concept of a counter-revolutionary workers' state which accomplishes a socialist revolution; which establishes thereby a workers' state without the working class and against the working class (Stalin converts the workers, wrote Trotsky, "into his own semi-slaves"); which makes the socialist revolution, establishes a workers' state and "degenerates" it all at the same time — there is a concept which, as Trotsky wrote, "did not disturb *our* dialectic," but which certainly destroys a number of fundamental teachings of Marxism, dialectical materialism included.

It would now be necessary to teach that there are not only counter-revolutionary *opponents* of the socialist revolution, but also counter-revolutionary *proponents* of the socialist (bureaucratic, to be sure, but from a class point of view, socialist) revolution. It would be necessary to modify the theory that the overthrow of capitalism and the laying of the foundations of socialism can be the work only of the proletariat, by adding that the same task can be accomplished, "via bureaucratic military means," without the proletariat and against it. The Marxian dialectic has often been abused in the revolutionary movement, as is known. But it has never been invoked in justification of a more fantastic theory than the one to which Trotsky was driven in presenting us with the counter-revolutionary socialist revolutionists.

The Stalinist bureaucracy did indeed carry through a social revolution in the occupied countries. A social revolution means a change in class rule. What class was put into power in the Baltic countries? The proletariat? If this is so, someone should bring it the good tidings to console it for the bitter memories of totalitarian enslavement it enjoyed while it "ruled" under Stalin. The new class that was really brought to power by the Russian army, the GPU, and its Bonapartist plebiscite, was the Russian bureaucracy, and the social régime it established, against capitalism but not less oppressive and exploitive of the masses than the latter, is best characterized as bureaucratic collectivism. Such a régime cannot exist without nationalized, or more accurately, state property; far from undermining it or weakening it, much less replacing it with private property, the new bureaucracy bases itself upon it, draws its sustenance and power from it, and employs it as the economic basis indispensable to the savage exploitation of the masses over whom it rules.

Max Shachtman

THE PROGRAM OF STALINIST IMPERIALISM

THE RULING CLASS IN RUSSIA is the Stalinist bureaucracy. It is composed of the leaders of all economic and political (including military) life in the country. They are organized, led and controlled by the political machine of the bureaucracy, the so-called Communist Party. This bureaucracy came to power in one of the bloodiest counter-revolutions in history. To achieve its unchecked totalitarian mastery of the country, it not only wiped out all the great achievements of the socialist revolution of 1917 but physically exterminated a whole generation of revolutionists with a thoroughness and cold-blooded cynicism unmatched by any reactionary power in the world, and reduced both worker and peasant to a new kind of state-serf.

This bureaucracy came to power under exceptionally favorable circumstances. Its domain was one-sixth of the world's surface, endowed with tremendous, barely-exploited resources and a population greater than that of any modern power. It was able to traduce the sympathy of toilers throughout the world by adopting as a guise some of the outward trappings of the great working class revolution of the Bolsheviks which it was itself destroying. Its consolidation was favored by the fact that the surrounding capitalist world was gripped for years by the most paralyzing economic crisis in history, and by the fact that there was relative peace in the world.

The causes and circumstances of the rise of this new class have been detailed by us elsewhere. Here it is enough to point out that the Stalinist bureaucracy came to power not only by overturning the power of the proletariat and reducing that class to its subject, but also by just as ruthlessly crushing the elements of capitalism in Russia and the classes representing it. Under Stalin, forced labor went hand in hand with the "extermination of the kulak as a class" and the wiping out of the NEP and the Nepmen. This point is of special importance in understanding Stalinist policy in and after the war. The collectivist bureaucracy does not tolerate sharing power with capitalism (to say nothing of the working class!) *wherever it has the strength to take power exclusively for itself.*

What is the economic basis of the Russian bureaucracy's power? The state-owned, state-centralized, state-managed, state-exploited property which belongs to it collectively and to it alone. From it, it derives its strength, its power, its privilege, its rule. Unless faced with a superior force (and none has yet presented itself), it will not divide this power with any other class, be it capitalist or proletarian.

To defend its rule and privilege, it must defend the economic basis upon which it rests, and repel all social forces that covet it. Throughout her history, Russia has been defeated by one power after another because she

---

From *New International*, October 194, "Notes on Russia in the war: the 'enigma' of Stalinist policy".

was weak — the master of platitudes and the bureaucracy once said in a speech — and that is why we must become strong. "To become strong" meant, for the bureaucracy as well as for any other modern class, to industrialize the country, to modernize it, to "catch up with and outstrip" the advanced countries. The bureaucracy proceeded to do just that and, as the war has shown, on a titanic scale and with unexpected success. A socialist success? In no way! For the successes of Russian economy were accomplished at the drastic expense of the social position of the working class and to the benefit of its exploiters and rulers. At the same time, however, the successes were accomplished without benefit to the capitalistic elements or classes in Russia, but rather to their detriment; more simply, to the point of their destruction. The bureaucracy will not share its power with any other class.

The Stalinist bureaucracy, at least as well educated politically as the other ruling classes of the world, understood all along that war is inevitable in the modern, capitalist world. In order to strengthen itself, it required time, and if possible, a time of peace. Its foreign policy was therefore directed to postponing the outbreak of the war as long as possible, but also to making such alliances with sections of the capitalist world, or maintaining such divisions and antagonisms within that world, as would reduce the magnitude of a possible attack upon Russia or, inasmuch as war must come sooner or later, to have it occur as an inter-capitalist conflict. Hence, Stalin's famous "pacifism," the Litvinoviad, the "collective security" policy, coupled with less publicized attempts to ally Russia with one bloc of capitalist nations against another.

That kind of "pacifism," however, is related to war as reactionary nationalism is related to expansion and conquest — it precedes it and prepares for it. The inevitable Second World War, as the rulers of the world, Stalin included, knew and know, would have for its aim the redivision of the world in favor of the victors. More clearly than any of the other powers, perhaps, the Stalinist bureaucracy understood that the war meant redrawing the map of Europe, of Asia and all the other continents. Hitler was a pacifist for years — in preparation for the war, a nationalist for years — in preparation for conquest. Similarly (though not identically) with American imperialism. Likewise, Russia.

Russia? Russia expand? Is that possible? What about Stalin's theory of "socialism in one country"? And his protestations that he does not covet an inch of foreign soil, any more than he will yield an inch of his own? He did yield; and he did covet. Now he intends to yield nothing, and to acquire as much of what he covets as possible.

To think of the Stalinist bureaucracy as guided strictly by some abstract formula ("socialism in one country"), is itself the sheerest abstractionism. It does not sit down before a meticulously drawn map of the Soviet Union and say: "We go as far as these frontiers and not an inch farther. Within them we shall always sit tight because our theory of socialism in one country will not let us go beyond them."

The Russian bureaucracy is inhibited by nothing but superior force — not by theoretical considerations or any other abstractions. And it is a ruling class whose rapacity has few equals in the world. In none of the democratic capitalist countries, at least, is labor so intensely exploited as in Russia. In none of them are the rights of the masses so shamelessly ignored. In none of them is the disparity between the social position of the aristocracy and that of the masses so great. But it is not mere desire, "free will," that impels the bureaucracy to expand wherever its strength makes expansion possible. There is a stronger, more compelling force.

No country in the world today, whatever its social character, can stand still and remain independent, at any rate, not for long. The present world tends more and more to be divided into a few of the advanced and powerful economic countries who enjoy independence, and the others that stagnate or retrogress economically and inevitably fall into economic and then political dependency upon the few. For a country (and the ruling class in it) to survive as an independent entity, in our time especially, requires an extension of its economic (and therefore its political) power. That holds for the capitalist countries. That holds for Stalinist Russia, which is not capitalist. (That would hold for a working class republic, even if in a different sense.)

The idea that Russia can expand its economic power indefinitely within the frontiers of what was the Soviet Union on August 22, 1939, and in disregard of the expansion of the big countries outside those frontiers, is a first-class illusion which is not, however, shared by the Stalinist bureaucracy. It understands the world situation; it realizes the problem; it knows better, even if some of its apologists do not.

Living amidst a hundred countries of more or less equal strength which would themselves be living a static existence within their own respective frontiers, Stalinist Russia would, or at least might, also continue a static existence within its former frontiers; that is, it would continue to "reproduce" itself or to expand only "internally." But this is of course a fantasy of fantasies. In actuality, Russia, like all other countries, lives in a world partitioned by a declining number of great powers, each of which can survive only at the expense of the others. That is what "expand or die" means for the old capitalist powers like Germany, the United States, England and Japan. Russia must keep pace with their expansion. In a physically limited world, this also means: resist, or confine, their expansion. Otherwise, Russia would eventually be overwhelmed by one or another of the powers that had succeeded in becoming the single, or one of two, super-giants in the world.

In other words, for all the social (not socialist!) differences that mark her off from the capitalist world, Russia is nevertheless confronted with the same problem and driven by the same impulsion as every other country in the world. The important difference between country and country (other considerations — like geographical position, for example — being equal) lies in comparative physical strength, backed, of course, by economic strength. Norway cannot dream of aspiring to the ambitions of Yugoslavia, or Italy to those of France, or France to those of Russia, or Russia to those of the United States.

It may be, and has been, said: Is it not a fact, however, that Russia's occupation of border countries is merely a defensive measure, aimed at acquiring strategical outposts that would discourage or blunt attacks from aggressor nations? And is it not a fact that these border countries were not really sovereign in the first place, or that, in any case, their occupation for defensive purposes by Russia saved their tenuous sovereignty from being overturned by aggressor nations? Is it better for Lithuania to be under

Hitler's domination, or Stalin's? Does Bessarabia really belong to Russia, not to Rumania?

Implicit in these questions are the arguments made by really innocent people, but above all by the Stalinists, by their apologists, by the liberals who trail them and, alas, by some "Trotskyists." But the arguments are replete with confusion, chauvinism, cynicism and downright mendacity.

If it could be shown that the seizure of these countries brought *freedom* to the peoples of the occupied territories, and thereby advanced the cause of freedom in other subject or semi-subject countries, it would be the right and duty of every real socialist, and even of every consistent democrat, to defend the action. But nobody in the world can show that.

Let us take the case of Poland. The incorporation of its eastern section into Russia reduced the inhabitants to slaves of the bureaucracy, or, as Trotsky put it with an incomprehensible modification, to "semi-slaves" of Stalin. What is more, it was accomplished as a by-product, or a joint product, of the reduction of Western Poland to "full-fledged slaves" of Hitler. The same holds true for the other seizures. The same will hold true for the other "defensive" conquests made by Russia in collaboration with its present imperialist allies.

Given the above consideration, the second argument stands out in its hoary reactionary nakedness. The United States occupied the Philippines to "protect" them from Spain and continued to occupy them to "protect" them from Japan. Japan now occupies them to "protect" them from the United States. Similarly, England protects India from other aggressors and, just incidentally, exploits and oppresses the Indians. Germany's "protectorate" over Czechoslovakia and the rest of Europe is equally notorious and instructive. In every such case, the imperialist apologists will say, informally, to be sure, "Granted, we are not ideal overlords. But the others who would take over if we withdrew are so much worse!" The more blatant imperialists say, "This is our mission." The language is classic. But we still believe that the Philippines belong to the Filipinos, who must have the right to rule themselves, and Bessarabia belongs to the Bessarabians, and not to a "Russia" which actually means a counter-revolutionary bureaucracy.

It is sometimes lamely argued by the more radical apologists: "But under Lenin, too, Russia crossed borders, conquered territories — in the Far East, in Tannu Tuva, in Georgia, in Poland. Where is your internationalism?" The similarity is only superficial. Under Lenin, the conquests of the Red Army brought freedom, or at least the beginnings of freedom, and extended the realm of socialism. Under the Stalinist bureaucracy, the conquests of the Russian army bring the end of all freedom for the working class. The difference, as Lenin used to say curtly, is enough for us.

The third argument is also classic and no less mendacious. Washington on the Potomac has to be defended by occupying the Gulf of Panama under the first Roosevelt, and by occupying Iceland under the second. To defend London on the Thames, England established a world empire, each part of which was occupied to defend the part preceding it in the series. To defend Berlin, Hitler first took the Rhine, then the Danube, then Danzig and found that he required for the defense of all of them — Cairo on the Nile. If the defense of Leningrad on the Neva and Odessa on the Black Sea requires the seizure of Kaunas on the Niemen and Ia si on the Pruth, why does not the defense of Kaunas require the occupation at least of Königsberg, if not of Warsaw on the Vistula, and so on and on and on?

If, as Stalin said in his 1942 May First order of the day, "We want to free our brother Ukrainians, Moldavians, White Russians, Lithuanians, Latvians, Estonians and Karelians from the insults to which they have been subjected by the German fascist beasts" — why not "free" in the same way the other peoples who have been subject to insults no less gross? What is the criterion? The 1939 frontiers of the Soviet Union? But that would exempt at least the Lithuanians, Latvians and Estonians from the blessed freedom. The frontiers of old Czarist Russia? But that would mean a "gay, prosperous and happy" life not only for the Lithuanians, Latvians and Estonians, but also for the Poles and Manchurians, and a virtual protectorate over Serbia and Bulgaria. "Blood brotherhood?" But the "racial" criterion would bring under Stalinist "freedom" half the populations of Europe and Asia. Are the Poles and Slovenes less racially akin to the Great Russians than the Lithuanians; the Hungarians and Finns less than the Karelians; the Chinese and Tibetans less than the Kirghiz and Buriats; the Turks and Iranians and Afghans less than the Turkmen, Kazakhs, Uzbeks, Tadjiks and Beluchistanians? (To mention the Volga Germans would be indelicate.)

The incorporation of any or all such countries and peoples into the USSR would be fitting, desirable and greatly contributive to progress and freedom, *if* it was a free Union, *if* it was Soviet, *if* it was Socialist, *if* it was a Republic. But it is none of these. It is as much a republic as Germany; it is the land where socialists are most fiercely hounded in the world; the soviets have been abolished in it; and the "Union" is an empire of the Great-Russian bureaucrats who have deprived the people of the peripheral "republics" of their most elementary rights, including autonomy and self-rule.

That the Russian ruling class wants the "border" countries for defense, is true, but not in the sense of its apologists. It aims to conquer and keep them for the defense and extension of the bases of its power, its privilege, its rule. It seeks their natural resources, their industrial plants and their populations — control, exploitation and militarization of which would enhance its wealth, its powers, its resistivity to attack, and the weight of its voice in world affairs. This should not be so hard to understand after the events of recent years.

Naturally, there are limitations to the imperialist ambitions of the Stalinist bureaucracy. But these are not limitations set by some fundamental principle, or an abstract theory or formula. They are determined concretely, at every given stage, by the relationship of forces. Specifically: by the relationship of forces between Russia and both its capitalist allies and opponents, on the one hand, and by the relationship of forces between Russia and the working class and revolutionary socialist movements, on the other. This dual relationship expresses itself in an apparent duality of foreign policy. It is this duality that creates the dilemma in the mind of the bourgeois politicians and analysts as to just what Russian aims are. The famous enigma is revealed when the duality is analyzed, separated into its parts. In doing so, we get a clearer idea of the radical difference between the policy of Stalinist imperialism and the policy of capitalist imperialism.

335

First part: Where the Stalinist bureaucracy does not dominate the working class and the labor movement, be it by persuasion or by violence; and where an attempt to overturn capitalism (we are assuming conditions when such an attempt is possible) would promptly bring reprisals against Russia by strong capitalist powers in a position to execute them; and especially where geographical remoteness makes the physical control of the country by Moscow extremely difficult — in such countries the Russia bureaucracy works to prop up capitalist rule, and to maintain a capitalist government. It prefers a democratic government, so that its agents, above all the Communist Party, may be free to work and exert pressure in its behalf, and a "strong" democratic government which will hold in check or suppress anti-Russian extremists from the right or working-class and revolutionary anti-Stalinists from the left. In any case, the government must be friendly to Russia, if not outrightly pro-Russian.

Thus, the Russian ruling class is interested in preserving capitalism only if a genuinely socialist revolution threatens. Against such a revolution, it always has and always will unite with the capitalist class. In this respect, as in all others, it shows that it is a thousand times closer to capitalism in its social type, its social inclinations, interests and instincts, than it is to socialism. The most striking example of how this policy worked out was the rôle played by Russia and its henchmen in the Spanish Revolution and the Spanish Civil War. It is playing the same rôle today in the revolutionary situation in France and Italy, and *may* (we shall soon see why the word "may" is used) follow the same rôle tomorrow in the revolutionary situation in Germany.

Second part: Where the Stalinists do dominate the mass movement; and where the world bourgeoisie is not in a very good position to prevent an overturn of capitalism by the bureaucracy; and where geographical conditions facilitate not only such an overthrow but also physical control by the Kremlin and its police — in such countries the bureaucracy tolerates neither the rule nor the existence of the capitalist class, democrats and fascists included. Such countries, under such conditions, it seeks to annex and subjugate. The well known examples are the three Baltic countries, Bessarabia, etc. It will be remembered that they were seized and, unlike Spain, capitalist property in them was wiped out, at a favorable moment, that is, when neither the Axis nor the Allies could do anything to prevent it.

Once this is understood, the heart of the enigma has been reached, the mystery is unveiled. Then, retracing our steps to the differences between Russia and her capitalist allies, we can see that they all pertain not so much to the "conduct of the war" as to the post-war period or, more specifically, to the repartitioning of the world after the war, to the division of the spoils. This applies as much to the difference over the "second front" as to the others.

Russia's imperialist program for the post-war world is not too difficult to ascertain. To describe it is to see how reactionary it is in every respect.

In Eastern Europe: The annexation of Lithuania, Latvia, Estonia, Southern Finland, the Western Ukraine and White Russia, Bessarabia and Bukovina is openly demanded and declared to be beyond debate.

But these annexations are not the limit. Always remembering the indispensable prerequisite of a favorable relationship of forces, Russia aims at having, as a minimum, vassal governments in Poland proper, in Finland, in Bulgaria and if not in all of Yugoslavia, then at least in Serbia. As a maximum, the complete occupation, domination and annexation of all these countries, including the expropriation of the native capitalist class (as well as, remember, the working class and peasantry) and the seizure of all property by the bureaucracy. Success in such an audacious program means also, as the map will immediately show, the finish of Rumania as well.

In the Near East: As a minimum, "free passage" through the Dardanelles and down to the Persian Gulf. As a maximum, return of the territory lost to Turkey through the Brest-Litovsk Treaty (Kars region), the occupation of bases on the Dardanelles and Bosphorus, and either a protectorate over or occupation of Iran, in whole or in part. The Russian demands on Turkey were revealed to Hitler and von Ribbentrop (according to these gentlemen) in the famous meeting they had with Molotov just before June 22, 1941. There is no particular reason, in the given case, for granting greater credence to Molotov's subsequent denials than to Hitler's and Ribbentrop's asseverations.

In Asia: A minimum of the northwestern provinces of China, including most of Sinkiang, Shensi, Suiyuan, Kansu, Chinghai, Ninghsia and Sinkiang, with a population of over 20,000,000. A maximum — provided there is a collapse and defeat of Japan — of most or all of Manchuria.

Is the realization of so breath-taking a program guaranteed? Let us underscore right here that we believe no such thing. Is it the *program* of the Stalinist bureaucracy? This we most decidedly believe. Is its realization *possible?* Yes, entirely possible, in our opinion — provided the Kremlin finds the circumstances favorable for it. The circumstances are of two kinds: one, the weakness of the revolutionary socialist and nationalist movements; two, inability, for any reason, of Russia's allies to stop her expansion.

What indications are there that this is the Stalinist program and that steps have been taken in the direction of realizing it?

1. Stalin has successfully maneuvered a break with the Polish "government in exile" in London. In Moscow, he has set up a completely servile Polish National Committee, with a full-sized apparatus, including a radio station and, what is more important, a now highly-trained, highly-mechanized Stalinist division of Poles, the Kosciuszko Division. How successful the agitation and organization work carried on among Polish prisoners and deportees in Russia has been, we do not know. But undoubtedly it has been intensive. Stalin can appear in Poland tomorrow with a well-integrated force, not only Polish, but backed by the vast apparatus (to say nothing of the "Red" Army of the Kremlin). How much resistance will the "government in exile" be able to offer? In any case, much more will be offered by the rank and file revolutionary underground movement. Just how much, remains to be seen.

2. Finland seems to be just about at the end of her rope. The fact that Stalin has remained ice-cold and silent to the recent all-but-public appeal by the Finns for a "decent" peace, is significant. Stalin is in no mood for a "decent" peace with the Finns. If the military situation continues to improve for him, tomorrow will find the Kremlin even more peremptory and exigent in its demands on Finland. For Germany, it does not ask "unconditional surrender." For Finland, it may very well ask just that.

Meanwhile, somewhere in the Kremlin files lies the easily-dusted-off "Finnish People's Government" of O W Kuusinen.

3. In Yugoslavia, from all reports, the Stalinists have been steadily gaining strength at the expense of the Greater Serbian imperialist force of Mikhailovich. The "Partisans" do not seem to be a Stalinist army, but the fact of Stalinist control (or at the very least, Stalinist decisive influence) in it seems to be well established. In one respect, the situation is more favorable in Yugoslavia for the Stalinists than in Poland — in the former country they have a substantial armed force right on the spot, with the only other armed native claimant for power, Mikhailovich, increasingly discredited, even though by no means a negligible force for that.

4. In Bulgaria, in spite of the savage persecutions to which it has been subjected for more than twenty years, the Communist Party, whose strength is difficult to judge, nevertheless seems to be the only organized force among the masses, apart from the army. Among the population in general, and even in higher circles, including the military, a pro-Russian orientation has not only been maintained but, it seems, strengthened. Bulgaria is not yet officially at war with Russia and very likely will not be. A collapse in that country, originating there or following a general European collapse, would undoubtedly create conditions favorable to Stalinist control or, at least, to decisive Russian political influence.

5. In Iran, something like half the country is already occupied by Russian troops and the "Iranian government" is just about as independent as the Slovakian government of Father Tiso. Although the other half is formally occupied by the British, there are indications that it is American influence and control that are growing in the country. Oil has an attractive smell. Nevertheless, Stalin is there and is fairly well entrenched. It is hard to believe that "after the emergency is over," the Russian troops and commissars will simply walk out of the country of their own accord and with a brief "Goodbye and thank-you."

6. The Stalinists — Russian, not Chinese — have been dominant in Sinkiang for several years now. Russian "advisers," who are to be found everywhere in this Chinese province, pretty much dictate all policy. Not only has the provincial army been built and trained by Russian officers and equipped with Russian armaments, but Russia has long maintained garrisons of her own troops in a number of strategic Sinkiang cities. Freedom of speech is generously allowed if you say nothing anti-Russian. How closely controlled Sinkiang's political life is may be judged from the fact that the "purges" in Russia are paralleled in the province. When the GPU head, Yagoda, was shot in Moscow, his man, head of the Bureau of Public Safety in Tihua, Sinkiang's capital, was shot immediately afterward! You can get into Sinkiang only with the approval of Moscow or the Russian diplomatic agent in Lanchow, and if any foreigner has succeeded in entering in the last few years, the fact is certainly not widely known.

The whole of Northwest China could be dominated without too much difficulty from a series of very well equipped Russian air bases, centering in Alma-Ata (where Trotsky was once exiled!), which is just inside the Russian border from Sinkiang, and directly related to the large air bases built by the Russians, with Chinese aid, at Lanchow, Ansi, Hami, Tihua and Ili, and largely manned by Russians. It is hardly necessary to mention the independent and powerful Stalinist Eighth Route Army, which dominates Yenan with reputedly 100,000 regulars and many times that number of coöperating partisans. For all its self-transformations and avowals of loyalty, it has remained what it was, an arm of the Stalinist régime, successfully exploiting the peasant discontent, and therefore a permanent thorn in the side of the Chinese bourgeoisie. It is noteworthy that just recently the Russian Stalinist press made a special point of its critical attitude toward the Chungking régime of Chiang and his circle, as if to go out of its way to emphasize that in China too, Russia is intent on playing an independent rôle, by no means confined to altruistic gifts of aid and best wishes to the Chungking government.

Even if all this is granted, it does not yet take up the question that has arisen recently to the top of people's thoughts, namely, what are Russia's intentions toward Germany? No matter how much importance is attached to such countries as Russia's border states, they are not of world-deciding significance. A country like Germany is.

Germany is the key to Europe. Will Russia be the key to Germany? Does Stalin aim to "communize" Germany, as the bourgeois press would say? Can he? Or does he merely want a good, strong, friendly, democratic neighbor in Germany? Just what is the meaning of the mystery-creating "Free German National Committee" set up in Moscow? Are Russia's differences with the Allies over the question of Germany's post-war fate irreconcilable? If not, along what lines may they be reconciled? What rôle may the German workers be expected to play in all this?

Obviously, these are vital questions. For Europe, they are becoming *the* vital questions, because at bottom Germany remains what she always was — the key to the European (and therefore to the world) situation. But to pursue our analysis along this line requires another article.

6. WHAT DID IT MEAN FOR SOCIALISTS TO "DEFEND THE USSR" IN THE SECOND WORLD WAR?

The contention of the "orthodox" Trotskyists was that the dissidents, in cutting loose from the established doctrine of "unconditional defence of the Soviet Union", were falling without a guide-rope into the swirling currents of middle-class democratic opinion. The war proved this charge false. Shachtman and his comrades opposed the war more boldly than the "orthodox"; their opposition to Stalinism was not softened when the Soviet Union became an ally of the USA and its cause became very popular in the West. It was the "orthodox" who became rudderless, because they had transformed Trotsky's hesitant "no fundamental change yet" position of 1939-40 into a timeless dogma which could have no adequate grip on events, and which had less and less grip on events after 1944. Into the vacuum created by false theory entered catchpenny opportunism: the slogan "defence of the Soviet Union" was used most when it put the Trotskyists "on the winning side", with the Stalinist armies on the offensive, and least when the USSR really was in danger of being overrun by the Nazis.

Committee for the Fourth International

THE WAR IN RUSSIA

THE DIE IS CAST. HITLER APPROACHES the gates of Moscow. Stalin's criminal contortion and maneuvers, which have led to the annihilation of the greatest revolution in history, are coming to an end. Year after year, Stalin has followed a continuous policy of concealed or undisguised treasons against the interests of the workers of Russia and of the world. His sole aim has always been that of his perpetuation in power. To impose upon the Russian people the rule of a bureaucratic oligarchy divorced from the masses, he committed all sorts of crimes, trampled upon the noblest feelings of the socialist workers, and courted every capitalist régime and government. In 1927 he sacrificed to the feudal lords of China the oppressed Chinese masses; shortly after that, he abandoned the German working class, delivering them to Hitler with hands and feet bound; fearing the consequences of this self-destructive policy, he proceeded to force the French workers into submission to Laval, Daladier & Co., thus demoralizing the French and the western working class and soiling the banner of communism. Finally, in a last and deliberate treason, he destroyed physically the best leaders of the Spanish revolution and so drowned in blood the first great revolution that came near to victory after the Russian Revolution of 1917. As a result of all this, we now have Franco in Spain, Pétain in France, Paris under the boots of Hitler's soldiers, and the European proletariat defeated and demoralized.

Seeing all the possibilities of a revolution in the West wiped out and Russia completely isolated, squeezed in the grips of Japan and Germany, Stalin began to court the Führer's good graces. This abomination reached its climax with the shameful German-Russian pact of 1939, which was the signal given to Hitler for the beginning of the Second World War. At that time Hitler seemingly paid a high price for the treason, but as it always happens, the treason money was earmarked and of no use. In order to obtain a few evanescent territorial advantages, the Kremlin's gloomy despot sacrificed the solidarity of the Polish, Finnish and Baltic masses, thus preparing the ground for invasion. And when Russia saw herself menaced these masses refused to participate in the defense, giving Hitler a free hand. If today the Finnish workers do not oppose the policy of their ruling class, which is sold to Hitler, this is due to the bureaucratic aggression against Finland in 1940, which was carried on with Berlin's acquiescence. If the Baltic masses did not rise against the Nazi invaders and facilitate the conquest of these countries, having even coöperated with the aggressor in a few cases, helping them to capture some cities, this is due principally to the bureaucratic tyranny.

That is how all this series of crimes and treasons are winding up in the most complete disaster. Stalin will definitely become known to posterity

"The War in Russia. Manifesto of the American Committee for the Fourth International", from *New International*, September 1941.

as the organizer of defeat for the international working class. Unable to appease the covetousness and the wrath of Berlin's victorious dictator, he submitted beforehand to everything, and if even today he is not "at peace" with Nazism and subordinated as a Quisling to the Führer's sovereign will, the cause of this lies in the fact that the Führer refused to accept Stalin's capitulation and thought it better to conquer by the power of his guns what was once the Soviet fatherland, to shatter the Red Army, and to eliminate all possibility of future resistance on his eastern front.

Driven to the wall, the Moscow dictator now has no one to appeal to but the same governments of the United States and England which even yesterday, to please his Berlin boss, he accused of being unfriendly to Russia, of being imperialists, warmongers, fascists and so on. Forced by circumstances to speak on the radio, addressing to the people of Russia and the world an appeal against the brutal aggression, Stalin loses his dictator's arrogance and stammers, speaking like a defeated man. Not the slightest reference is made in his speech to the world proletariat's solidarity; this force ceased to exist for him a long time ago. He did not dare to appeal to the revolutionary instincts or to the glorious traditions of the Russian working class. His only appeal was to the defense of the land and to patriotism, which he covered with an artificial layer of chauvinist and Pan Slavic nationalism. Outside of Russia, he only saw Churchill and Roosevelt.

We are now witnessing the end of his régime. For ten years the usurper has been destroying one by one the conquests of October; mercilessly he mowed down the revolutionary vanguard, and their remnants lie scattered, half destroyed, in the immense deserts and plains of Siberia, of Asia and the Polar Circle. Only a year ago the only great survivor of October — the last and most glorious living tradition of the Russian Revolution, Leon Trotsky — was infamously slain by direct command of Stalin.

However, in spite of Stalin, in spite of the totalitarian bureaucratic régime, in spite of the misery and oppression under which the Russian masses are held — under the impact of the bombs and tanks of the Nazi hordes the deep-rooted energies of the masses spring again to the surface. The anti-fascist hatred that lay smothered in the heart of the Russian workers, the old traditions of a proletariat who made three revolutions in one generation, come to life again, with heroic warmth, against the pestilential breath of the fascist beast. The muzhiks' ancient love for their soil awakens again in defense of the Russian land already razed by Hitler's dark legions. With fanatic courage, the best soldiers of the Red Army are sacrificing their lives against the Nazi tanks and cannons, in defense of what still remains of the October Revolution, or, rather, of a tradition. The Stalinist régime is thus given an appearance of cohesion and strength. The new Czar's adorers take advantage of this fact to boast about the people's response to the Leader's call. But this is only an appearance. It is not confidence in the false leader or love for the totalitarian régime oppressing them that moves the Russian masses. What moves them is their desire for liberation, their preservation instinct, the rekindled flames of the glorious traditions of October. However, it is no time now to foster dangerous and fictional illusions. With the Red Army beheaded of its best leaders, the working class oppressed by many long years of reaction and also beheaded of its vanguard, the numerous peasantry fatalistically passive but unresigned to the exploitation of the bureaucratic totalitarian state, even the greatest heroism of the masses is insufficient. Thanks to Stalin's maneuvers, the German attack against Russia was launched at the precise moment chosen by Hitler. Even if the political and military situation had been incomparably better than it is, even if the international working class had not suffered and were not still suffering from the consequences of a continuous series of defeats and catastrophes, even if the European proletariat were not, as they are today, subjugated by Hitler's totalitarian tyranny, even so the Soviet Union could never triumph in a war against foreign enemies as the result exclusively of strategic and military operations. In the Soviet Union, more than in any other country, victory in case of war will be assured mainly by the power of its ideals, by the international solidarity of the workers, by the revolutionary prospects in other countries, and not by the Russian guns, tanks or planes alone. And these ideological weapons have all been squandered by Stalin.

Now that Hitler's bayonets are against his breast, Stalin has lost the last vestige of independence. It is his fate to become an obedient instrument in the hands of the London and Washington governments. That is how the man whom the paid officials of the Communist International call "the leader of the world proletariat" finds it his fate, if he wants to survive, to become a Quisling in democratic or fascist attire, whatever turn war events may take. Stalin is now nothing else but an Asiatic despot forced to submit to the will of the Western imperialist governments in order to maintain his power. The agreement or, in Churchill's words, the "alliance" signed in Moscow by Molotov and the English ambassador, is nothing more than a compromise assumed by Churchill to maintain Stalin in power, trying to protract the existence of his government, hopelessly endangered in case of defeat; in return for this, Stalin promises to continue at war even if he will have to wage it from London or New York, at the service of his new bosses. Soviet diplomacy is already dictated by London. His principal aim is to defend his own régime by all possible means. Stalin may fall, however, and yet the struggle against the fascist invader may continue; Stalin may fall and yet the October Revolution will blossom again on the Russian soil.

The Stalinist bureaucratic gang now exploiting Russia's toiling masses both in the cities and the country, long ago forsook the aim of establishing socialism or defending the workers' interests, to adopt that of creating a new totalitarian régime in which this same bureaucracy would become a permanent new ruling class. This capital and transcendental theoretical historic question is going to be decided in fact by the present war.

Russia is now face to face with destiny. If the bureaucratic gang were able to go through the whole process of the present war uninjured, then the establishment of a new social class, based on a collective form of property, would be the clearly visible culmination of Russia's political and economic evolution. This would be the blazoned régime of bureaucratic totalitarianism in its final form. On the other hand, if Hitler wins or defeats the Stalinist régime, this same blow will destroy precisely his own future, the only possible and satisfactory conclusion to his adventure. With this victory, he will have wiped from the face of the earth the gloomiest prospect now darkening the horizons of the approaching proletarian and socialist revolution, that is, that of the victory of his "new order," the Iron

Heel régime, a "new" order of bureaucratic, obscurantist and neo-feudal totalitarianism, made possible only in case of symbiosis of the two régimes now closer to this "ideal" — the régimes of Hitler and of Stalin.

As the return or triumph of bourgeois capitalist "democracy" is a decrepit dream and a reactionary utopia, and as the present war will not come to its end if and when Hitler enters the Kremlin's gates, the only hope emerging from the ruins of the bourgeois civilization, the only spark that shines over humanity, is the banner of socialism.

Whatever may be the end of the Russo-German war, the régime of the Stalinist bureaucracy is doomed. Russian victory against Hitler would only be made possible by a profound revolution of the masses and the consequent restoration of the conquests of October and of the rights and benefits to the Russian working class that the Bolshevist revolution sought to give them in its beginning. If this fails to come, what the Soviet Union may expect is defeat by Hitler's guns or, possibly, dismemberment even in case of an Allied victory.

There is therefore no place in this war for defense of the present Soviet régime under Stalin's dictatorship. In the land of the Bolshevist Revolution, the struggle for national independence is tightly linked with the struggle for social freedom of the masses. This is due especially to the fact that there is no Czar, no prince, no descendant of the old dynasties, who can appear to the people in the Soviet Union as a symbol of this struggle. Neither can the future leaders or organizers of the country's defense against the invaders come from the circle of White Russian émigrés. Nor is this a task for Kerensky & Co.; or for other remnants of a defeated class inevitably doomed to be the agents of foreign powers, or for the present Russian military leaders like Timoschenko, who was boasting not long ago that his country was the only really and completely totalitarian country in the world; still less can it be a task for the military leaders of England and her allies, even if they are the victors in this war.

Preservation of Russian national independence will be the work of men coming from the people and bringing with them not only the idea of national independence but also the program of social liberation. They will come from the proletarian ranks of the Red Army, and from distant Siberia, an academy for revolutionists since the Czarist remote epochs. They will come from the inspired and oppressed layers of the young people; from the isolators, the concentration camps replete with those who have escaped death and who were thrown there by Stalin, or in other words, they will come from the heroic Old Guard of Bolshevism, the best part of the new generation, the authentic disciples, the real successors of Lenin and Trotsky. To them must go the solidarity of the workers of the world, for only they can lead the people to victory in their legitimate and sacred struggle against the fascist invader.

Stalin urged the peasants and soldiers to destroy everything in their way before retreating under the impact of the fascist blows, and to wage a guerilla war of partisans at the rear guard of the invaders. But the conditions today are not the same as in the first years of the civil war. At that time the peasants could wage a war of partisans against the White Russians and the capitalist invaders, because they had something concrete to defend: their land recently conquered by the October Revolution. In spontaneous uprisings, the workers of the cities marched to support the struggle in all fronts, and faced all situations, in a prodigious explosion of initiative from below, because they were impelled by the ideals engraved on the banner of Bolshevism and not defamed then by the Stalinist degeneration. They felt that they really had a new world to conquer, that they were really engaged in crushing the old world of oppression and misery and avoiding its return with the victory of counter-revolution.

Today the peasant, under the oppression of the totalitarian state, hates the Kremlin lord and feels that he is robbed of his labor's fruits on behalf of a privileged caste. The workers understand that they have been expropriated of their revolution and in the same factories taken by them in 1917 they now feel themselves under a new yoke, under the ferocious discipline of a new exploiter, the bureaucracy.

The surprising fact, however, that gives us all hope, is that even under these circumstances these heroic masses, refusing to accept the yoke of the new fascist invaders, resist them with great courage. They are moved by two profound and progressive feelings: an old natural patriotism of people who have only such elementary and legitimate things to defend as their bread and their land, and the anti-fascist hatred originated from the workers' old instinct of liberation.

The prolonged degeneration of the Soviet state has taken from Hitler the possibility of satisfying one of his great ambitions, as he offered himself too late to be the super-Wrangel of the international bourgeois class in an anti-communist crusade. When Stalin, ahead of Hitler, crushed the October Revolution, he made it impossible for Hitler's victory over Russia to be a victory over communism. By defeating Stalin, the gloomy Berlin Don Quixote will not defeat the follower or disciple of Lenin, but, on the contrary, the usurper of Lenin's banner. If the Nazi hordes find their way to the Kremlin, they will no longer find the banner of socialism unfurled over its walls. With their guns, they can conquer in the battlefield a corrupt totalitarian bureaucracy, or a decadent bourgeois class like that of France. Socialism, however, will not succumb to Hitler's bombs and cannons.

War will not end with Hitler's entry into Moscow. The decisive victory that he seeks flits on more rapidly than the advance of his *Blitzkrieg*. The sinister bandit of Berchtesgaden is continuously running after new victories that soon vanish as mirages of the desert. With the fatality of a stone rolling from a mountain, the capitalist world tumbles down day by day. It is not Hitler who makes history; on the contrary, it is the course of history that leads him inexorably to the abyss. Every day he is forced to improvise new issues, to invent new aims, to change directions, to make new attempts, the same as any impotent bourgeois government of a "democratic" country. Blind as a doomed man, he goes on undermining the ground under his own feet at every new "victory" and initiative. Carrying along misery, war and devastation wherever his reactionary legions tread, he saps the old capitalist order, but he does not establish any order, new or old: the only things he establishes are slavery, terror and chaos, masked with a tragic caricature of "revolution". In fact, what he carries along with him everywhere is a permanent counter-revolution.

Assaulting Russia, the most he can do, besides getting some immediate material advantages in case of an overpowering but transient victory, is to destroy a decayed régime and crush Stalinism. But the Russian land in its immensity will absorb his exclusively military victory and meanwhile the people, who are tempered by the traditions of their great revolution and brought up in anti-fascist hatred, are immune from internal poisoning by means of assimilation of the conqueror's ideology. By destroying with his guns the Stalinist totalitarian régime, Hitler, like the sorcerer's apprentice of the fable, will have set loose the forces of history, bringing forth the torrents of revolution. Socialism and the Russian proletariat will stand firm, and the future is theirs. Russia of October will resurge.

Stalinism, or what is still known as the Communist International, will thus disappear opprobriously under the heels of the fascist victor or under those of the "democratic" allies. It is now more necessary than ever to tell the truth to the millions of workingmen who are still deceived by Stalinism. It is necessary to keep them from being, through disillusionment or deception, led out of the struggle or into prostration or resignation in view of the triumph of the mortal enemy — fascism. Stalinism is doomed precisely because it betrayed the October Revolution. Socialism will not be crushed with it. The logic of history is often obscure. In the final crisis of the capitalist régime, the forces of reaction and of treachery are the first to be wiped from the scene by the social whirlwind. Stalinism, as a dead and decayed branch of Bolshevism, could not resist the lash of the war tempests. It is time now for unification of all the proletarian forces of the world to prepare for the final assault, when "democrats" and fascists, conquered or conquerors from the bourgeois camps, will have torn each other up in the war that they themselves unleashed. The thousands of Stalinist militants who are still misled by the tremendous machine of Moscow propaganda must now prepare to unite with the conscious revolutionary elements in order to reorganize the phalanxes of the revolutionary army of the workers of the world and to continue the glorious historical task only begun by the October Revolution in 1917. The banner of Marx, the banner of Lenin, the banner of Trotsky, will not fall with Stalin's defeat. Millions and millions of hands must now unite to hold it in order to unfold it over the ruins of the capitalist world. Even Hitler's victory over Russia, should it come, will have been but a passing though gloomy moment in the course of the final struggle for socialism and for real democracy. These will come along with total war as a last surprise in stock for humanity, but this time for its benefit.

Down with the fascist invader! Freedom for the thousands of political prisoners who are the victims of Stalinist totalitarian oppression! For a new workers' and peasants' government based on the soldiers', sailors', peasants' and workers' councils, to repel the fascist invader and restore the rights and liberties of the Russian people that have been taken away from them by the Stalinist bureaucracy!

For the Socialist United States of Europe!

For unification of all the socialist and revolutionary forces of the world in one party — the world party of socialist revolution, successor of the First, the Second and the Third Internationals!

For a new, for a Fourth International!

Max Shachtman

"DEFEND THE SOVIET UNION"?

I SHOULD LIKE TO TRY to make as plain and convincing as possible, the position I hold on the present stage of the war, with particular reference to Russia.

Some comrades argue that the character of the war has changed. Others even quote the article I wrote for *The New International* a few months ago, which says in effect that if the character of the war should change, then we should be for the defense of the Soviet Union whether it is attacked by one or more imperialist powers. But, while I still hold to that, the quoters are obliged to prove that the character of the war, that is, its *predominant* character (for there is no such thing as a war which is "purely" one thing or another) *has* changed. Here it must be said that the Cannonites are more consistent than some of our own defensists. And although B. is evidently losing all his bearings, from his point of view it nevertheless makes sense when he now says that the Cannonites are right now and were right a year and a half ago. One of the principal arguments of the Cannonites at the beginning of the war was that it did not matter who fired the first shot because you cannot, and it is not necessary to, decide between the "aggressor" and "defender" in a war. From a military point of view, this is of course, unassailable. Therefore, they could be for the defense of the Soviet Union when Stalin invaded Poland, the Baltic, Finland and the Balkans, *in anticipation* of the next stage of the war in which the conquests resulting from these invasions would serve as defensive outposts protecting the Soviet Union when it is attacked. In other words, if it is correct to defend the Soviet Union now, in the second stage of the war, then it was correct to defend it twenty months ago, and we would have to say that the genial Stalin showed a lot of foresight in providing himself in advance with protective armoring he acquired during the initial invasions. And *summa summarum,* that is now the big trump card Stalin's apologists are playing in this country. To a lot of simple people that even sounds convincing. For *supporters of the Stalin régime* this argument is and should be enough, and if I were such a supporter, all the petty lies and deceptions of Stalin would then recede into twentieth place.

Some of our comrades, however, fail to take into account that we are the revolutionary enemies of that régime. We are not its advisors, we are not out to reform it, we are out to overthrow it. We must therefore judge its "aggressive" and "defensive" measures not from a military, but from a social and political standpoint. We subordinate the former to the latter. The Cannonites subordinate the latter to the former. Example: they said the invasion of Poland or of Finland was a blow to the world revolution, that it was shameful and criminal. Presumably it was shameful and criminal primarily from a political and not a military standpoint. But, they said, they were for the defense of Russia, that is, for the victorious execution of this shame, this crime, this blow at the world revolution because it was militarily necessary. We said there is no conceivable abstraction in this world, not even the talk about nationalized property, that can get us to defend a blow against the world revolution, and a shameful and criminal one at that. We refused to be defensists because the Soviet Union was engaged in a reactionary war. Did that mean that the nationalized property of Russia was not at stake in the war? Of course it was. Would the fact that Leningrad would be more heavily protected if Stalin got southern Finland, help defend the nationalized property if Russia were attacked at a later stage? Of course it would. Isn't it also a fact that in the conquered territories Stalin abolished bourgeois property and nationalized it? Of course it is. But *our* basic criterion is the interest of the world proletariat and the international revolution. Stalin's war struck the most brutal blows at these interests. And, we said with Trotsky, the nationalization of property in the occupied territories does not compensate for these blows by one-tenth!

Just exactly what were these blows? 1. Capitulation to German imperialism. 2. The joint imperialist subjugation of the conquered territories, which should now be clear to anybody after the disclosures of Hitler and Von Ribbentrop a couple of months ago, was deliberately decided upon in advance and by agreement between the two bandits. 3. The political alliance between Stalin and Hitler, as exemplified, among other things

Excerpts from a letter to a West Coast comrade, from a Workers Party Internal Bulletin, August 1941.

by Stalin's white-washing of Hitler's war and of Hitler's peace. 4. The fact that Stalin drove the workers of Finland and of other countries, Germany and the United States included, deeper into the arms of their bourgeoisies. 5. That Stalin's army and GPU immediately suppressed all genuine revolutionary and Soviet manifestation of the masses in the territories he invaded. And so on.

All these either constituted or followed inescapably from the character of the war in which Stalin was engaged. We *never* condemned Stalin just because he and not the Finnish or Polish bourgeoisie fired the first bullet or because he was the first one to cross a boundary line.

Now let us see what has changed. The bureaucracy is now defending its imperialist conquests of a year and a half or more ago. We were against the Stalin bureaucracy's acquiring these conquests. Why should we defend it when it seeks to retain these conquests? We said with Trotsky, "We are and remain against seizures of new territories by the Kremlin." Why should we be for the Stalinists holding these territories after they have seized them? The Stalinists have changed imperialist camps. That is of great importance, but by no means of principled importance. In 1939 and 1940 their alliance with and subjugation to German imperialism drove the workers into the arms of the bourgeoisie. I contend that their alliance with Anglo-American imperialism in 1941 drives the workers into the arms of the bourgeoisie at least as much. The objective consequences of the bureaucracy's war in 1939 was the victory of one imperialism; now, of another imperialism. But, isn't the nationalized property, which is not bourgeois, "really" at stake in 1941, as was not the case in 1939? Allow me to return to the question at a later point. Right now I want to deal with the question of the famous "mixed war".

We used to speak a great deal in our movement, before the war broke out, of the "mixed war". It arose in connection with the Stalin-Laval pact in 1935 and it meant this: If Russia and France are allied in a war against Germany that would make it an imperialist war on the one side but not on the other. We cannot stand still in our own conceptions or be bound by the fetishism of words or memories. We must allow life to influence our conceptions. Life has proved that the degenerate Stalinist régime *cannot* fight a "mixed war" as a progressive or revolutionary war. By its very nature its agreements and alliances — alliances without quotation marks this time — with imperialism are reactionary through and through. And that again brings us to the character of the present war and the character of Russia's participation in it, even in the present stage of the war.

Again and again I repeat, we must judge our position of defeatism or defensism in any country by the interests of the socialist world proletariat, and not of the workers of one country. The victory of German imperialism in the war would have nothing but reactionary effects. The victory of Anglo-American imperialism over Germany, likewise. We are for the defeat of German imperialism — not by Anglo-American imperialism but by the German proletariat. We are for the defeat of the British empire — but not by Hitler. From the standpoint of our basic criterion what are the objective consequences of "defense of the Soviet Union" now? Taken on a *world scale*, and that is the only way we can take it, since we are not Russian nationalists, it means the imperialist victory of Washington and London over German imperialism, with all the tragic consequences that flow from that. The victory of Stalin in Poland was undoubtedly a "victory for nationalized property", if considered as an isolated national phenomenon. In the realities of present world politics and the present world war, however, this victory was a victory of German imperialism over its rivals. That is the fact and even children ought to know it. The same is true of the invasion of Finland. Trotsky said it was carried out at the dictates of Hitler. Correct. Did it help protect Leningrad? Of course. But from the international point of view, which is decisive, the invasion was a necessary part of the war strategy of German imperialism. What has changed now is that concretely "defense of the Soviet Union" means promoting the grand strategy of Anglo-American imperialism — objectively to be sure. Hence the dilemma of the defensists. I mean, of course, of revolutionary defensists like some of our comrades and the Cannonites. What *concretely* do they propose to *do* that we do not propose? I would like very much to hear that. In 1935-36 we used to say that in the hypothetical mixed war we would be for facilitating shipments to Russia but not

349

to France or Germany. In the present real and not hypothetical war I ask the follow-ing question of the defensists: Are you for facilitating American shipments to Russia today? Alas, the accursed realities of the war show that shipments to Russia mean convoys and that convoys, as our good president says, mean a shooting war. Is that a fact or not? Even Goldman is compelled to acknowledge this in the *Militant*. He tries to get around the dilemma by the poor lawyer's argument that he doesn't "urge" ship-ments, because that means convoys and they mean war, but his party will not oppose them. Isn't that a beauty of a position? Or will the defensists be proposing, for exam-ple, tomorrow, that we demonstrate before the Japanese consulates if hostilities break out between Japan and Russia? I doubt it. Because even they understand that such demonstrations, given the *real* and not hypothetical situation, would only be grist to the mill of American imperialism.

Or what will they do in the not at all inconceivable situation which may confront them tomorrow morning, so to speak, where British and Russian troops are fighting side by side in Afghanistan or Iran? Where do the British troops end and the Russians begin? Where does defensism end and non-defensism begin? Every intelligent observ-er knows that this is an entirely practical and immediate possibility. And where are the revolutionary compensations for the inevitably reactionary effects of Stalin's war, compensations which the Lenin-Trotsky régime could and did provide for? They do not exist and in the nature of the case cannot.

What about the workers in the Soviet Union? What about the defense of Nationalized Property? Nationalized property is not an abstraction any more than democracy is an abstraction. Nationalized property under the régime of Soviet democ-racy, that was a revolutionary workers' state. The nationalized property with the régime of the anti-soviet autocracy whether you call it a degenerated workers' state or bureaucratic collectivism, is certainly not equivalent to a revolutionary workers' state. On the basis of this very same nationalized property, in fact, during the very period when this property was consolidated and expanded enormously at the expense of bour-geois property, the proletarian and revolutionary movements in Russia were all but completely destroyed and the international proletarian movement frightfully under-mined. As you know, I consider nationalized property in the Soviet Union a historically superior form of property to any form of private property in history. But I do not attribute to it what Marx would call a supra-historical significance, any more than, for example, I would attribute such a significance to democracy. Is it worth defending? That depends on concrete circumstances, and not upon an evaluation of nationalized property in and of itself. It is dangerous to argue by analogy because people can easi-ly demonstrate that analogous situations are not identical situations. Yet to argue by analogy is also often illuminating. In the Spanish civil war there were elements of imperialist war and we pointed them out. But, we said, the war is *decisively* between bourgeois democracy and Fascism; and given the fact that the proletariat was not ready to take power in its own name, we supported bourgeois democracy as against Fascism — critically, to be sure. In the same manner, in a social war between world capitalism and the Soviet Union I would be a revolutionary, i.e., a critical defensist in Russia, because I do not want to see world imperialism get a new lease on life by reducing the non-capitalist Soviet Union to a capitalist colony. Isn't the nationalized property at stake in the present war too? Of course it is. But isn't the working class movement in the United States, its rights and institutions and in England too, also at stake in the present war? That is, if Hitler conquers the United States, would that not mean that in addition to the crushing of American imperialism the working class movement and the more or less democratic basis on which it can exist and progress, would also be destroyed? Of course it would. Yet, we are not defensists in the United States because however important the role this element plays, it does not alter the decisively imperialist and reactionary character of the war. But at the same time, even in the United States, we do not take a completely negative position. Without becom-ing defensists, or even flirting with defensism, we fight right in the midst of the impe-rialist war itself for the interests and rights of the working class. We fight to advance that which is worth defending. In the present situation in Russia, I would apply much the same policy. Would I tell the Russian workers not to fight the war? That advice is meaningless or stupid. I could not and do not tell them that in the United States. Do

I tell them in Russia not to obey their officers? Of course not. I am not an anarchist. In Russia and anywhere else the workers and especially the soldiers will obey their superiors until they have accumulated the organized power... not to obey if they so desire. In the Soviet Union now what would I fight for? You understand, of course, that "fighting for" anything in the Soviet Union today is, so far as our movement is concerned, a work of "patient enlightenment" as Lenin used to put it. I would say to the workers, organize and mobilize your strength to re-establish the Soviets, in the cities, in the army and on the land; to re-establish your trade unions; to take power again; to drive out the bureaucrats. Demand even now the diminution and eventual abolition of all bureaucratic privileges. Demand the release of all the revolutionary opponents of Stalin who were imprisoned. Demand the right of self-determination for the Ukraine (I notice that the Cannonites dropped this slogan out of their program of action for Russia), and so on.

Finally, it is necessary to have a little more clarity on the question of defeatism. You remember in the SWP dispute, the gifted Marxist, Cannon, explained to us that the Leninist theory of defeatism means that you *prefer* the victory of the enemy to the victory of your own government. That is, you *prefer* the defeat of your country by the enemy country, to the defeat of the enemy country by your country. Of course, Lenin never had such an idea, but trifles like that have never bothered Cannon in his theoretical flights. I personally think that so much confusion has been introduced in the concept of defeatism that I doubt if we would be losing too much if we dropped the *word* out of our vocabulary. However, be that as it may, let me try to specify what I mean by the content of this conception in the present situation. I am *not* for throwing open the front, so that Hitler can march in. Not at all. For that matter, in a considerably different situation, and for somewhat different reasons, I am not for throwing open the front in England either. By defeatism in Russia, if I may still use that word, I aim at the defeat of the Stalinist counter-revolution by the soviet working class. Right now, to talk realistically of revolutionary actions which endanger the front is phrase-mongering, playing with formulae, and nothing more. If ever a situation called for "patient explanation" it is the present situation in Russia. To the extent that anything can be done in Russia I would seek to direct the efforts of the Internationalists at reconstituting the independence and the integrity of the proletariat. Then one of two things. This would either facilitate the development of a favorable revolutionary situation, or else would be facilitated by the development of such a situation; more accurately, the one would influence the other. After such an independent proletariat became strong enough to have an influence on the front and on the military operations, then, given the continued existence of the Stalin régime you would have the beginnings of the dual power in Russia. In that case, without yet becoming a defensist, while continuing to denounce Stalin's reactionary war and reactionary war aims, I would try to appeal to the soldiers as Lenin did in 1917, not to engage in futile mutinies or riots or in any sporadic actions, *to hold the front*, so that the Germans do not break through and crush the proletarian elements of the dual power, and to speed the day when the Russian proletariat can crush the *Stalinist elements* of the dual power and change the war into a revolutionary war against imperialism.

I know that among certain comrades in the Party, a tiny minority I hope, there is what you might call a reactionary mood about the famous "Russian question". In their fury at Stalin and Stalinism and the Stalinists, some comrades are seeking some magic formula which will "rid them of the Russian problem" — and of Stalinism. I am firmly in favor of resisting and counter-acting such moods of desperation, because that is all they are. It is even reported to me that one comrade said that he is a "defeatist" in Russia, because, you see, if Russia is defeated we won't have the problem of Stalinism in the unions any more! I cannot, of course, vouch for the accuracy of this remark. But, I hardly need say that I have nothing in common with such a point of view. *I can understand* such a point of view only as a result of a reaction provoked by the hideousness of Stalinism and perhaps to a lesser degree by some extremist statements by defensists. It is necessary to be on guard against such extreme reactions, because even the best comrades, once they start on that road, will sure as fate go to hell. I appeal, rather, for the calmest and most objective judgement of the problem. I don't for a moment contend that it is a simple one. For the Stalinists of course, it is

351

simple. They don't even have to think. Anything Stalin does automatically merits support. For the Cannonites too, it is pretty simple. Any war that the "nationalized property" fights against capitalism, they defend it. The present Soviet state, said Trotsky, is a terrible monstrosity. It was never thought of or conceived by Marx or Engels or Lenin or Trotsky himself. It is unprecedented and unique and full of startling surprises and innovations. I consider it the height of stupidity to believe that every single problem connected with it can be answered by a simple formula. For my part I am ready to leave that travesty on Marxian politics to the Cannonites.

James P Cannon

DEFEND THE SOVIET UNION!

WE CONSIDERED THE WAR upon the part of all the capitalist powers involved — Germany and France, Italy and Great Britain — as an *imperialist war*. This characterization of the war was determined for us by the character of the state powers involved in it. They were all capitalist states in the epoch of imperialism; themselves imperialist — oppressing other nations or peoples — or satellites of imperialist powers. The extension of the war to the Pacific and the formal entry of the United States and Japan change nothing in this basic analysis.

Following Lenin, it made no difference to us which imperialist bandit fired the first shot; every imperialist power has for a quarter of a century been "attacking" every other imperialist power by economic and political means; the resort to arms is but the culmination of this process, which will continue as long as capitalism endures.

This characterization of the war does not apply to the war of the Soviet Union against German imperialism. We make a fundamental distinction between the Soviet Union and its "democratic" allies. We defend the Soviet Union. The Soviet Union is a workers' state, although degenerated under the totalitarian-political rule of the Kremlin bureaucracy. Only traitors can deny support to the Soviet workers' state in its war against fascist Germany. To defend the Soviet Union, in spite of Stalin and against Stalin, is to defend the nationalized property established by the October revolution. That is a *progressive war*.

The war of China against Japan we likewise characterize as a progressive war. We support China. China is a colonial country, battling for national independence against an imperialist power. A victory for China would be a tremendous blow against all imperialism, inspiring all colonial peoples to throw off the imperialist yoke. The reactionary régime of Chiang Kai-shek, subservient to the "democracies," has hampered China's ability to conduct a bold war for independence; but that does not alter for us the essential fact that China is an oppressed nation fighting against an imperialist oppressor. We are proud of the fact that the Fourth Internationalists of China are fighting in the front ranks against Japanese imperialism.

None of the reasons which oblige us to support the Soviet Union and China against

---

The "official" Trotskyist statement on the USA entering World War 2, from the *Fourth International*, January 1942. The Socialist Workers Party, whose leaders had been indicted under the "Smith Act" for "seditious conspiracy", and would eventually be jailed for sentences of up to 16 months, chose to speak through Cannon to reduce the risk of the party as a whole being banned. Abridged.

their enemies can be said to apply to France or Britain. These imperialist "democracies" entered the war to maintain their lordship over the hundreds of millions of subject peoples in the British and French empires; to defend these "democracies" means to defend their oppression of the masses of Africa and Asia. Above all it means to defend the decaying capitalist social order. We do not defend that, either in Italy and Germany, or in France and Britain — or in the United States.

The Marxist analysis which determined our attitude toward the war up to December 8, 1941 continues to determine our attitude now. We were internationalists before December 8; we still are. We believe that the most fundamental bond of loyalty of all the workers of the world is the bond of international solidarity of the workers against their exploiters. We cannot assume the slightest responsibility for this war. No imperialist régime can conduct a just war. We cannot support it for one moment.

We are the most irreconcilable enemies of the fascist dictatorships of Germany and Italy and the military dictatorship of Japan. Our co-thinkers of the Fourth International in the Axis nations and the conquered countries are fighting and dying in the struggle to organize the coming revolutions against Hitler and Mussolini. We are doing all in our power to speed those revolutions. But those ex-socialists, intellectuals and labor leaders, who in the name of "democracy" support the war of United States imperialism against its imperialist foes and rivals, far from aiding the German and Italian anti-fascists, only hamper their work and betray their struggle. The Allied imperialists, as every German worker knows, aim to impose a second and worse Versailles; the fear of that is Hitler's greatest asset in keeping the masses of Germany in subjection. The fear of the foreign yoke holds back the development of the German revolution against Hitler.

Our program to aid the German masses to overthrow Hitler demands, first of all, that they be guaranteed against a second Versailles. When the people of Germany can feel assured that military defeat will not be followed by the destruction of Germany's economic power and the imposition of unbearable burdens by the victors, Hitler will be overthrown from within Germany. But such guarantees against a second Versailles cannot be given by Germany's imperialist foes; nor, if given, would they be accepted by the German people. Wilson's 14 points are still remembered in Germany, and his promise that the United States was conducting war against the Kaiser and not against the German people. Yet the victors' peace, and the way in which the victors "organized" the world from 1918 to 1933, constituted war against the German people. The German people will not accept any new promises from those who made that peace and conducted that war.

In the midst of the war against Hitler, it is necessary to extend the hand of fraternity to the German people. This can be done honestly and convincingly only by a Workers' and Farmers' Government. We advocate the Workers' and Farmers' Government. Such a government, and only such a government, can conduct a war against Hitler, Mussolini and the Mikado in cooperation with the oppressed peoples of Germany, Italy and Japan.

Capitalism can offer no prospect but the slaughter of millions and the destruction of civilization. Only socialism can save humanity from this abyss. This is the truth. As the terrible war unfolds, this truth will be recognized by tens of millions who will not hear us now. The war-tortured masses will adopt our program and liberate the people of all countries from war and fascism. In this dark hour we clearly see the socialist future and prepare the way for it. Against the mad chorus of national hatreds we advance once more the old slogan of socialist internationalism: Workers of the World Unite!

Labor Action, Hal Draper, Max Shachtman

THE "ORTHODOX" DEFENSE OF THE SOVIET UNION IN PRACTICE

I

The Cannonite press has been fairly devoid of agitation to defend the Soviet Union. This would not be so startling were it not for the fact that defense of the Soviet Union in this war is supposed to be one of the leading slogans of the SWP — if not the leading slogan. One would expect a little more attention paid to a slogan of such importance! Emblazoned across the front page occasionally; hammered home in issue after issue. Especially inasmuch as *The Militant*, very properly, devotes considerable space to attacking the Stalinists — so much so that a worker picking up an average issue of the paper would hardly get the impression that here is an organization challenging the whole world with its defense of the Soviet Union. Can there be a reason? Can it be perhaps that some, let us say, trade union elements might have judged the slogan a little inappropriate to present-day needs? PS: When the Cannonites tried to enter the Stalinist May Day parade they brought with them a proposal that "Defend the Soviet Union" be included in the slogans of the parade. This, they explain lamely in the current issue of *The Militant*, was to put the Stalinists on the spot. But in this same issue there is printed a May Day manifesto. We looked in vain for the slogan, "Defend the Soviet Union". Good enough to propose to the Stalinist May Day parade. Not good enough to include in their own manifesto. How come?

II

THOSE VERY PRINCIPLED PEOPLE, the Socialist Workers Party (Cannonites), have re-discovered the "defense of the Soviet Union". This event occurs under very happy auspices for them. While Russia was busy grabbing Poland and Finland, they were also for its defense — but not so happily. The masses of people (not to speak of Churchill, Sumner Welles and Alexander Kerensky) were quite annoyed with Stalin in those days, so the principled Cannonites kept their slogan under their hats. In their public press they merely called the invasions a "crime" and "de-emphasized" the defense angle — to the extent of mentioning it practically only in internal argumentations and theses. As recently as their May Day manifesto, there was hardly a peep (in public, where somebody might hear them) from the SWP on this paramount task of "defending the Soviet Union". After all, it was so unpopular!

Now the "shamefaced defensists" of yesterday splash the headline "Defend the Soviet Union!" across the first page of *The Militant* and boldly write:

"German imperialism seeks to overthrow the October Revolution and to restore the capitalist system in its degenerate fascist form. This is the essential meaning of Hitler's attack on the Soviet Union... *Defend the Soviet Union at all costs and under all circumstances against imperialist attack!*"

As if "the politics of which this war is the continuation" is Hitler's desire to abolish nationalized property in Russia, rather than his very real desire to gain Russian resources to prosecute his war against Britain. The manifesto throughout is blind enough to speak as if Hitler's invasion is itself his goal, instead of a means to an end.

I Abridged from an unsigned article in *Labor Action*, May 5, 1941.

II From *Labor Action*, July 14, 1941, "From Shamefacedness to Solid Brass", by "Paul Temple" (Hal Draper).

The Militant, in addition, prints a ten-year-old quotation from Trotsky calling for the defense of the Soviet Union as *"the main fortress of the world proletariat"*. James P Cannon himself sends a telegram to Mr Stalin, via Ambassador Oumansky, calling for the release of Trotskyists from GPU jails so that they might "take their proper place in the front ranks of the defenders of the Soviet Union". (Naturally, he brings this up merely as a helpful suggestion, not as a condition for support, since the Cannonites are *unconditional* defenders of the Soviet Union.) In another column Russia is "this one bastion of socialism".

Shamefacedness being definitely thrown aside, Albert Goldman substitutes solid brass in the next issue of *The Militant* (July 5). Believe it or not, he blandly denies that there ever was an alliance between Hitler and Stalin; denies that the Cannonites ever *said* there was such an alliance; and remarks that the expression "Berlin-Moscow Axis" was used only by middle-class democrats and the Workers Party.

For outright forgery, this is equalled only by the Stalinists. We have room for only two examples: (a) One of Cannon's rare literary works, an article in the *Socialist Appeal* of September 29, 1939, denouncing "the joint policy of Stalin and his Axis partner, Hitler", and stating that "the pact of Stalin and Hitler is in fact a military alliance". (b) The article by Trotsky in *Liberty* of January 27, 1940, if anything, goes further, saying that Russia attacked Poland and Finland at Germany's behest.

Goldman explains the Stalin-Hitler pact (today) solely on the basis of Stalin's desire to avoid war and to strengthen his military position against Germany by taking over adjacent lands. This is a belated plagiarism from the *Daily Worker:* No alliance with Hitler, only a policy of peace and the defense of the Soviet Union! Like Churchill, Goldman, too, prettifies the Kremlin while calling for its defense.

Goldman attacks our own stand by asking, apparently seriously: If it is true, as the Workers Party claimed, that Hitler and Stalin were partners, how come one partner attacked the other? "For, if one claims that such a close partnership existed between Stalin and Hitler, then the fact that Hitler found himself in trouble need not and would not lead to his attacking the Soviet Union".

And he positively belligerently asks us to explain how "such an unusual change in imperialist partnerships" is possible! Of course, France changed partners, he admits, but that was because it was defeated, adopting its conqueror as partner. His memory being what it is, he forgets that Finland has changed partners too — this time not with its conqueror! In fact, there is hardly a country in the war that has not changed partners at least once. If Japan decides to pull out of the Axis in the event of successes by London-Washington-Moscow, Goldman will no doubt again be astonished at imperialist trickery, provided he doesn't deny that there was ever a Berlin-Tokyo Axis.

Two more notes on the SWP position: (1) We have said that the Cannonites are now very brash about proclaiming the "defense of the Soviet Union". But so far they have presented this slogan in a manner completely empty of any concrete meaning. Are they in favor of rendering "material and moral support to the Soviet Union" by the American workers? So far, they have indicated only that that's all right for the Russian Trotskyists — not a word to American workers on the subject. Their manifesto has only one sentence on the question of what to do: "The method to defend the Soviet Union is to continue the class struggle against the imperialists". If this is all the "defense of the Soviet Union" means in practice, in *this* war, it should be made unmistakably clear. But it is not all, as the CP can point out to them.

(2) *The Militant* appeals to the members of the Communist Party as follows: "You set the defense of the Soviet Union as your first task. We do likewise. On that basis we appeal to you to give sober consideration to the grave problems of this defense..." Follows an injunction to continue the struggle against capitalism and the war, and then: "This is the only real defense of the Soviet Union and in this defense we stand ready to join you in any action that will advance our common cause".

Since the defense of the Soviet Union is "the first task" of the SWP (here, in the United States, as Roosevelt drives into the war!) and since this is a "common cause" with the Stalinists, we presume that the SWP will immediately start a campaign for a united front with the Communist Party to render material and moral aid to the Soviet Union... Or will Cannon wait till the CP becomes more popular? If defense of Russia is the *"first* task", naturally everything else must be subordinated to it. In this connection, we note that *The Militant* has so far kept mum about the question of aid to Russia by the Roosevelt government. This *may* be an oversight (a pretty big one), but in any case it behooves the SWP to make clear its own attitude as well as specify what the defense of Russia means to it outside of literary exercises.

III

IN THE PAGES OF *THE MILITANT*, organ of the Socialist Workers Party, Albert Goldman has devoted more than a column to attacks on the position of our party, particularly with reference to the Soviet Union in the war, and to explanations of the position of his party on the same question. According to Goldman, the inside reason why our party took a position against the "defense of the Soviet Union" during the period of the Hitler-Stalin pact was because Stalin made the pact with a fascist imperialism instead of with a democratic imperialism; and we, collapsing under the pressure of the democratic bourgeois patriots, shied away from defending an ally of a fascist power. However, Goldman and his friends predicted, if Stalin were to make a pact with a democratic imperialism, which would not be displeasing to our democratic bourgeoisie and its apologists, we would turn about-face and become proponents of Soviet defensism. The theoretician of the SWP even wrote recently in its magazine that we were becoming defenders of American imperialism.

Like the other Cannonite predictions about us, this one too has proved to be slanderous and more than a little stupid. But let that pass for the moment, since we are presently interested in something else. What we would like is an explanation — please! This is what perplexes us:

In *The Militant* of July 12, Felix Morrow writes: *"Of course the Soviet Government could have rejected Hitler's offer of a pact in 1939. The Stalinist hirelings kept asserting, in the few days intervening between the pact and the outbreak of the Second World War, that the pact was bringing peace and was a blow at the Axis — fantastic gibberish, but they had to say something — but Stalin knew perfectly well that the pact was a go-ahead signal to Hitler, insuring him against an eastern front. 'Could the Soviet government have declined such a proposal?' Stalin now smirkingly asks. Yes, it had the elementary duty to decline, in order not to give Hitler a free hand. Nor is this hindsight on our part; we denounced the pact in precisely these terms at the time it was signed".*

Now, that's a lot of malarkey for the simple reason that neither Morrow nor his colleagues ever denounced the pact "in precisely these terms" or in any terms of recognizable similarity. Morrow cannot quote a single example to justify his remarkably tardy audacity. But let's let this pass, too, merely as proof that a man doesn't forget everything he learns in the Stalin school of journalism, and proceed with what's disturbing us — the explanation. In the issue of *The Militant* a week after Morrow's article, Michael Cort has an article too. This Cort is a specialist on imperialism, Soviet policy and pacts, and on the side he runs a funny column where he makes the most convulsing cracks about our party. He evidently does not read Morrow, so he writes: *"It is entirely correct for the Soviet Union to take advantage of conflicts among the imperialists. It is correct for the Soviet Union now to ally itself with capitalist opponents of Germany — sad necessity, the weakness of the USSR demands it. It is false and criminal, however, for the Stalinist bureaucracy to pay off its capitalist allies by stifling the class struggle within their borders".*

But has [Stalin] ever made, *or is* [he] *capable of ever making*, an alliance with a capitalist power which does not, by its every essence, stifle the class struggle in the camp of the ally? In other words, has the bureaucracy made, *or can it make*, an alliance which is not "false and criminal"? How can it be correct to make an alliance *that is sure to be "false and criminal"?* Explanation, please!

Then there are a few other questions, while we still have the floor. Was the pact with Hitler wrong because it was made with nasty fascist imperialists, whereas the pact with Churchill is okay because it is made with democratic imperialists who speak with

III From *Labor Action*, August 4, 1941, "Explanation, please!" by Max Shachtman.

such a nice Oxford accent? Was the pact with Hitler wrong just because the Stalinists claimed it "was bringing peace and was a blow at the Axis", as Morrow puts it? But don't they make the same claim for the pact with Churchill and Roosevelt — the pact that is "correct", as Cort puts it? Was the pact with Germany wrong just because it gave Hitler the "go-ahead signal... insuring him against an eastern front"? Is the pact with Churchill correct because it gives British imperialism the go-ahead signal for attacks on Germany and insures that the latter does have an eastern front? Was the pact with Germany wrong because it "made possible the subjugation of Europe by Hitler", as Morrow writes? Is the pact with British imperialism correct because it will make possible the, shall we say, emancipation of Europe by Churchill?

Is the pact with England correct because it helps Stalin "defend nationalized property" from imperialist attack? Then wasn't the pact with Hitler also correct, since it yielded new military outposts (Poland, Estonia, Finland, etc.) to the Soviet Union which would also help Stalin "defend nationalized property"? Was the pact with Hitler wrong because it was "a terrible blow to their (the workers') anti-fascist sentiments", whereas the pact with British imperialism is correct because it is less offensive to those many workers who are for Britain's victory? Would then the slogan of "defend the Soviet Union" have been wrong when Stalin invaded Poland or Finland with Hitler's support and thereby also struck "a terrible blow" at the anti-fascist sentiments of the workers? Who is right — Morrow or Cort? Or neither of them? Or perhaps there is something to be said for both of them?

Why do we ask Goldman? Because he has at least two qualifications. He admits that we are middle-class idealists, while he is a revolutionary Marxian materialist. In addition, *The Militant* announces him as the "attorney for the SWP". We cannot honestly swear to the first claim, but we'll vouch for the second. He surely is the attorney for the SWP. So we'll take a chance on him answering the questions, although our experience has been pretty gloomy.

Albert Goldman, *Labor Action*, Max Shachtman, Stanley Plastrik

THE BALTICS AND IRAN: THE EARLY STAGES OF USSR EXPANSION

I

By Albert Goldman: "Sovietization of the Baltic step forward".

WHEN THE SUPREME SOVIET of the USSR, at its next meeting, will grant the petitions of the Parliaments of Lithuania, Latvia and Estonia to be incorporated into the Soviet Union (and no doubt exists but that it will), it will once more be evidence of the fact that the foundations of the October Revolution are still operative in spite of Stalin. The basic achievement of the October Revolution, the nationalization of private property in the means of production, is extended to other territories and no class-conscious worker can raise any objection to that.

The Sovietization of the Baltic states reminds us of the controversy that raged in our party before the minority, unwilling to remain a minority and cocksure of the correctness of its fantastic theories, decided to set up a little shop of its own. When Stalin first sent the Red Army into the Baltic states and limited himself to stationing soldiers

I From *Socialist Appeal* — SWP — July 27, 1940.

at important bases, the minority gleefully pointed out that Stalin was leaving capitalist relations in those states intact. Which would prove, according to the leaders of the minority, that Stalin was not interested in destroying capitalism, a position which we never contradicted.

What the leaders of the minority failed to see was that once Stalin for any reason whatever acquires control over territory where capitalist property relations exist, the tendency must be for him to incorporate such territory into the Soviet Union and, upon incorporation, capitalist property relations must be destroyed and displaced by nationalized property. Stalin is not interested in extending the social revolution. He is interested primarily in the rule of the bureaucracy which he represents. But since Stalin heads a state based on nationalized property any territory acquired by that state cannot be left under capitalist property relations. The ruling clique in the Soviet Union cannot afford to divide its power with an alien ruling class. Should Stalin permit capitalism to function in any territory that had become part of the Soviet Union it would mean that he was actually determined to bring capitalism back to the Soviet Union.

How grotesque and senseless the "theory" of Soviet imperialism must appear to any one who thinks in Marxist terms. Every piece of territory into which Stalin sent his armed forces and which has been incorporated into the Soviet Union has been wrested *from* imperialism, the only kind of imperialism that Marxists know of as existing at the present time, the expansionist policy of finance capitalism. The resources of Latvia, Estonia and Lithuania are no longer open to imperialist exploitation unless they are taken away from the Soviet Union.

And superficial wiseacres will still contend that there is no difference between the Soviet Union and Nazi Germany! But these people have never yet explained why it is that Hitler has never called the Reichstag to proclaim the nationalization of land, banking and industry in any conquered territory. Individual capitalists, especially Jewish capitalists, run away from Hitler's rule. The capitalist class *as such* is expropriated under Stalin's rule.

We do not like bureaucratic socialization of industry. We would much rather prefer socialization of industry coming as a result of a social revolution than as a result of the conquest of territory by the Red Army under Stalin. And it is obvious that Stalin's bureaucratic method can only conquer small countries. But as against capitalism even bureaucratic socialization is a step forward and we shall support it as against all people who for any pretext whatever will defend capitalism.

That the working masses of the Baltic countries are as enthusiastic about their incorporation into the Soviet Union as the Stalinist press would want us to believe can be seriously doubted. They live too close to the Soviet Union and they therefore know too much about real conditions there to be enthusiastic about the happy life promised them under the leadership of the Kremlin despot. But the lot of the workers and peasants of Latvia, Lithuania and Estonia under capitalism has been a miserable one at best. Probably hundreds of thousands of them cannot picture anything worse than what they have experienced. The class-conscious workers of the Baltic countries, however, understand that capitalism throughout the world must be destroyed, that it offers nothing but fascism and war. These workers will support the nationalization of industry. And together with their class brothers in the Soviet Union they will continue the struggle against the Stalinist bureaucracy. The corruption of Stalinism must be destroyed in order to make the Soviet Union the powerful attractive force that it should be for the masses throughout the world.

"Stalin fastens hold on Baltic people. Liberation lies only on the path of socialist revolution"

STALINIST RUSSIA HAS ANNEXED the three small Baltic countries, Latvia, Estonia and Lithuania after controlled elections brought out close to a 100 per cent vote for "affiliation" to the Soviet Union.

This action concludes the process of Russian control over these states which began after the Stalin-Hitler Pact of last August and the establishment of Russian military and naval bases there. Last month whole divisions of Russian troops were sent into the Baltic countries, and with their aid the old national governments were ousted.

The new "Soviet Republics" have decreed the expropriation of the old landowning class and the state ownership of land. The declaration of the "Latvian Republic," for example, limits land ownership "at no more than thirty hectares" (about 75 acres).

"Any attempt to encroach on the private peasant property or to thrust on the laboring peasantry against their will the organization of collective farms will be strictly punishable as acts detrimental to the interests of the people and the state."

Whatever the pious promises of Stalin, the masses of the Baltic states who suffered under the brutal exploitation of their native landowners and capitalists and their reactionary dictatorships are now the subject peoples of the more powerful tyrant in the Kremlin. Land is now state property. Tomorrow the factories will also become the property of the state.

But the state machine is the instrument of the oppressive Russian bureaucracy. This ruling group can maintain and extend its power and revenue most effectively through such state ownership. In newly annexed territories it cannot tolerate the old ruling propertied classes, capitalist owners of factories and banks, and landowners for any extended period of time because this would mean a disruption of Russian statified economy, and future political opposition fostered by these old ruling elements. The expropriation of the reactionary property owning classes by Stalinist Russia is not undertaken in order to bring freedom and security to the masses, but rather to gain for the Russian bureaucrats themselves the results of the toil and sweat of the workers and peasants.

That is why revolutionary socialists, the genuine defenders of the interests of the workers and peasants, who are for the working people taking over the land and factories and banks from the big landowners and capitalists and collectively utilizing these resources for the common good of the people, condemn the reactionary annexations of these countries by Russia. In the Baltic countries, as in Russia itself, the masses can benefit from these resources only if they overthrow the despotic Stalinist government and organize their own workers' and peasants' government. At the same time revolutionary Socialists refuse to take seriously protests against Stalinist reactionary measures by the capitalist imperialist governments and their spokesman.

Last Tuesday, Sumner Welles, United States Acting Secretary of State, denounced the Russian annexation of the Baltic countries in a statement, according to the New York Times, "the vigor of which stamped it as one of the most exceptional diplomatic documents issued by the State Department in many years." No doubt Welles smiled cynically when he wrote that these states had "independent and democratic" forms of governments when everyone knows that they were organized after the World War as puppet buffer states against Soviet Russia, were controlled by one or another imperialist power, and had dictatorial governments.

However his statement correctly declares: "The people of the United States are opposed to predatory activities, no matter whether they are carried on by the use of force or by the threat of force. They are likewise opposed to any form of intervention on the part of one State, however powerful, in the domestic concerns of any other sovereign State, however weak."

The people — yes! Sumner Welles? Ask the people of Cuba who remember this gentleman who "by the use of force or by the threat of force" decided which group of rogues should control the Cuban government in the best interests of American imperialism!

II From *Labor Action*, July 29, 1940.

The Roosevelt Government? Ask the Latin American people about Yankee Imperialism! The people, above all the workers, must see through this fraud in order more effectively to struggle against all forms of reaction and oppression, and for freedom and security.

III

By Max Shachtman: "The Cannonites and Iran. Silence is golden".

THE SUBJUGATION OF IRAN by Anglo-Stalinist imperialism is all but completed now. The oil fields and refineries are already under the direct control of the invaders. So are the strategical railroads and highways. Hitler's agents and spies are on their way as fast as they can run or be deported. All that is left to Shah Riza Pahlevi, at this writing, is nominal police control of the capital and the assurance that he will continue getting his little rake-off on every barrel of oil pumped out of Iran's wells.

What is the essential difference between the assault on Denmark or Holland by Hitler and the assault on Iran by Churchill and Stalin? The professional democrats and warmongers in the United States wept tears of indignation at the former and shouted cheers of enthusiasm at the latter.

That is understandable, because they are people without honorable principle, scruples, or a sense of shame. In both cases, the invader claimed that the victim's territory was being converted by the enemy into a war base against himself. In both cases, the invader destroyed the sovereignty of the victim in the name of preserving its sovereignty. In both cases the invader claimed that his action was purely defensive. In both cases, the invader claimed that he was only helping keep the victim from being drawn into the war. In both cases, the invader declared that he was taking the initiative only in order to prevent the enemy from taking the initiative. And in both cases — lo and behold! — the invader was so surprised to find economic wealth in the territory of his victim that he promptly proceeded to loot it and to establish a military-police régime to protect him while the looting was going on. In a word, in both cases the imperialists acted as imperialists always have. Yet there is a difference so far as our "democrats" are concerned. What is it? Simply this: in the one case, it is "the other fellow's" imperialism, and in the other case it is "our" imperialism.

A reader might object by saying: What else can you expect from the apologists for imperialist depredation? The objection is well taken: Nothing else can or should be expected. But the same objection does not hold true of the Cannonites, for example. From them something quite different should be expected. But what is to be expected and what you actually get are two different things. The last issue of *The Militant*, the organ of the Socialist Workers Party, with all the space at its disposal, *did not have one single word to say about the invasion of Iran*, although it went to press in plenty of time after the event to make possible some comment — a paragraph, say, or at least a sentence. But we found neither a paragraph nor even a single syllable. For the Cannonites, the invasion of Iran does not exist.

Why not? When Stalin, in concert with Hitler, invaded Poland, the Cannonites (to be sure, only after we, and then Trotsky, had prodded them into it) were ready to denounce Stalin's act as "criminal and shameful." But when Stalin, in concert with Churchill, invades Iran, the Cannonites not only do not denounce it as "criminal and shameful" or as anything else, but they do not characterize it at all. They pretend it just isn't there. They stuff their ears, eyes, noses (yes, noses as well, because the invasion stinks of oil) and mouth with austere silence.

Can this be because the invasion of Poland was carried out in alliance with a fascist imperialism, whereas the invasion of Iran was carried out in alliance with a nice, popular, "democratic" imperialism? Can it be that the Cannonites "denounced" in 1939 because of bourgeois-democratic pressure, but do not "denounce" in 1941 because there is no bourgeois-democratic pressure upon them to do so now?

III From *Labor Action*, September 8, 1941.

We haven't had much luck with questions, similar to those asked above, which we have put to the Cannonites before. But perhaps persistence will yet succeed in piercing their awe-inspiring taciturnity. It is worth another try.

The Cannonites are for the "unconditional defense of the Soviet Union" in any war with a capitalist-imperialist country. Poland, for example, was such a country. Let us assume that Iran, a semi-colonial country, is in any case a tool of a capitalist-imperialist power. As a "defensist" Cannon is in favor of revolutionists being the "best soldiers" in the Red Army. He is also for revolutionists being the "best soldiers" in the American and presumably also in the British armies. We ask: what kind of soldiers should revolutionists be in the Iranian army?

Further: the "defensist" position is for the victory of the Red Army in the war; it is for political opposition in the army of Stalin's imperialist allies; it is for defeat, for military defeatism (with all that this implies) in the army of Stalin's enemy, for example, the army of Iran. Our question is: in what part of Iran and in what part of the Iranian army are the Cannonites for defeatism — in the north (which is invaded by Stalin), in the south (which is invaded by Stalin's ally, British imperialism), or in both? Also, which part of the Iranian army should be called upon to desert to the Stalinist army (which, according to one astrologer in *The Militant*, is now "Trotsky's Red Army"!), and which part, if any, should desert to Wavell's army?

Further: We think we know what the Cannonite position would be if and when the Iranian people were to rise in a revolutionary movement against imperialism. What we do not know is this: Would the "defensists" call upon the people of Iran *now* (or two weeks ago) to arm themselves and drive the British imperialists and/or the Stalinists out of Iran, and proclaim the full national independence of the country?

Such questions might have been set aside as "general" or "hypothetical" five or ten years ago. Today, however, they are specific, concrete and real. Will the Cannonites answer them? Or are suspicious people right in believing that the only way they can defend their position on Russia in the war is by swathing themselves in impenetrable layers of golden silence?

IV

By Henry Judd (Stanley Plastrik): "Once more on invasion of Iran".

BARRISTER ALBERT Goldman, leading spokesman for the Socialist Workers Party (Cannon group), devoted a lengthy column to Iran in *The Militant* of September 6. He waxes morally indignant — at the invasion as imperialist and reactionary? Heaven forbid! No, Goldman is indignant at those who *condemn* the invasion. They are "petty bourgeois moralists" who, as the *Daily Worker* tells us each day, cannot see that it is all for the good of "defending the Soviet Union!"

Here runs Goldman's argument: Russia is a "degenerated workers' state"; it is fighting for its existence against German imperialism; it must take "every measure necessary for its defense provided it does not conflict with the interests of the world revolution". The fact that Iran is invaded "at the same time" by British imperialism (notice how Attorney Goldman makes it appear that the joint invasion is merely coincidental in time, whereas *both* governments announced they undertook it as a *joint*, deliberately planned action) is not of "the slightest importance". Conclusion: All class-conscious workers and peasants (including those of Iran naturally) "will not permit anything to interfere with the defense of the Soviet Union". That is, the people of Iran should welcome their invaders and join with them (or is it only the Russian invaders who should be welcomed, Comrade Goldman?)

What does this position mean? *It is nothing but a total whitewash for Stalinism and its action in the war!* Is this a harsh judgment? Consider for a moment. Goldman is telling the people of Iran that they must subordinate themselves, *their interests as colonial slaves*, their interests as people who seek national freedom — to the military needs of Stalinist Russia *and*, by indirection, to the military needs of the British Empire. For the British Empire is *allied with* Stalinist Russia in the war; it conducts

IV From *Labor Action*, September 15, 1941.

joint military action with Russia. Any step taken by the people of Iran (or any other colonial country, for that matter) cannot but have an effect upon both Russia and Britain. If this is true for Iran, is it not also true for every other country that Germany threatens to drag into the war against Russia? Turkey, Iraq, India, etc.? Does Goldman contend that the 3,000 Germans in Iran were "threatening the defense of the Soviet Union?" Obviously, he must, or else there is no justification for Russia's Iranian invasion. But this is precisely the cynical excuse given by British imperialism for its share in the invasion. An excuse to cover up its *real* motives — namely, to secure its oil fields, to protect the road to its Indian colony, to establish air and naval bases, etc. Goldman would like to ignore the unpleasant fact — but Russia is *not* fighting its war in a vacuum; it is already up to its ears in the mud and filth of British imperialism and its dirty doings.

Nor is Goldman untainted by the Stalinist cynicism he now apologizes for. He refers to the treaty between the Soviet government and Iran in 1921. This treaty gives Russia the right to march troops into Iran if the Iranian government is unable to prevent an attack or a threatened attack upon the Soviet Union through Iran. Such is Article VI of the Constitution. But our barrister forgets Article II which (1) unqualifiedly rejects as a "criminal policy" the policy of the Czarist government toward Iran which consisted of concluding treaties with European powers "whose objective was a gradual annexation". Furthermore, (2) *"The Russian Soviet government declares its renunciation of participation in any measures which aim at a weakening or violation of the sovereignty of Persia (Iran) and declares that all conventions and agreements between the former government of Russia and third states injurious and relating to Persia (Iran) are abolished and nullified".*

To what disgraceful depths has Goldman stooped! Stalin in 1941 *jointly carves up* Iran with Churchill; Lenin in 1921 would have marched into Iran to stand by the side of the Iranian people *against* a British invasion. Stalin marches to meet Churchill in comradely embrace; Lenin would have marched to meet him in mortal revolutionary combat. And Goldman says these are one and the same thing!

Conclusions: (1) The Cannon group and its spokesmen here, as in other instances, act as shamefaced apologists for the crimes of Stalinism. (2) This apologism is being extended to include the momentary "allies" of Stalinist Russia — beginning with Great Britain. (3) The enslaved colonial peoples — victimized by both warring camps — are looked upon by the SWP as abject pawns in the World War. The colonial movement for independence, an essential part of the world revolution, is subordinated to "defense of the Soviet Union". (4) The logic of defensism in the present war appears to lead inescapably from "critical support of the Stalinist bureaucracy" to critical support (or should we say, *critical* support?) of the "democratic" imperialist war camp.

APPENDIX

THE STRANGE CASE OF THE MILITANT AND THE USSR IN THE FIRST 18 MONTHS OF WAR

EDITOR'S NOTE: It would seem obvious that there must be a straight line, a direct continuity, between the passionate polemics in 1939-40 about "defending the Soviet Union" and the record of "official" Trotskyism for the next 50 years. The files of the American Trotskyist papers, the *Socialist Appeal* and *The Militant*, tell a surprisingly different story. There is, during the year before Russian victory at Stalingrad, the year when the USSR seemed about to go down before the German onslaught, something like a break in continuity. In late 1941 the SWP — so the coverage in *The Militant* suggests — decided that the USSR was as good as done for. Anticipating it, they removed "defence of the Soviet Union" from the prominence it had had in *The Militant* since June 1941, when the Nazis invaded, and dropped the quotation from Trotsky which had appeared every week, insisting that the USSR was the "fortress of the world proletariat". Through most of 1942 *The Militant*, remaining "defencist", was fairly low-key and muted on the issue, though they still occasionally referred to Stalin's army as "Trotsky's Red Army". (See the strange keynote cartoon from August 1942, on page 410.) It was only after the tide turned at Stalingrad late in 1942 that *The Militant* "came back on board". Passion and ardour reappeared in their "defence of the Soviet Union". People who joined the Communist Parties then were known as "the Stalingrad draft". This was "Trotskyism's" Stalingrad draft. The facts are as follows.

Germany invaded the Soviet Union on 22 June 1941. *The Militant* responded (28 June 1941) with a front-page manifesto calling on workers to "Defend the Soviet Union at all costs and under all circumstances against imperialist attack!"

Although the German armies quickly conquered large areas, *The Militant* claimed that "Red Army morale astonishes its enemies... Soviet soldiers fight bravely because they have something worth defending" (9 August 1941). The vigour of the Red Army was traced back to the work of Trotsky in establishing it and leading it in the civil war ("Trotsky organized the Red Army", 16 August 1941, and repeated pictures of Trotsky in military uniform). From 9 August 1941 the editorial page carried a quotation from Trotsky (incongruously, from 1931!): "To defend the USSR as the main fortress of the world proletariat, against all assaults of world imperialism and of internal counter-revolution, is the most important duty of every class-conscious worker". *The Militant* advertised a pamphlet with a selection of Trotsky's writings between 1927 and 1937, entitled *In Defense of the Soviet Union*.

Stalinist propaganda pictures were sometimes used with uncritical captions ("Soviet collective farmers do their bit in defense of the Soviet Union by bringing in their harvests...", 20 September 1941). The paper did carry criticism of Stalinism. As the German armies moved up to Leningrad (September 1941) and Moscow (October 1941), *The Militant* carried a front-page lead by Natalia Sedova Trotsky: "Catastrophe faces USSR as result of Stalin's rule; Stalin's purges beheaded Red Army" (4 October 1941).

The USSR regained a small amount of territory in a counter-offensive in December 1941-January 1942, but was then driven back again by a new German offensive in summer 1942. *During this period, while the USSR's position seemed almost hopeless, The Militant did not renounce defence of the USSR, but gave it a very much lower profile.* On 17 January 1942 the quotation from Trotsky on defending the USSR was removed from the top of the editorial page. It did not reappear until the Russian armies were rolling back the German forces at Stalingrad. On 5 December 1942 *The Militant* had for the first time added a new point 9 to the eight-point policy statement it carried every week on its editorial page: "Defend the Soviet Union against imperialist attack". On 19 December 1942, the 1931 quotation, now with a portrait of Trotsky, reappeared on the editorial page.

As the USSR's military successes continued — and right up to 31 March 1945, while the Stalinist army was advancing through Eastern Europe — *The Militant* continued to carry the quotation and the policy-point. The SWP published *In Defense of Marxism*, a heavily one-sided selection of Trotsky's writings about the Soviet Union, in mid-December 1942. The references to Trotsky as the creator of the Red Army, and to "Trotsky's Red Army", would be a staple propaganda item for the rest of the war.

The SWP remained critical of "Stalinism". They organised a protest meeting when two Polish Jewish socialists were murdered by the Stalinist régime (*The Militant*, 13 March 1943). But the emphasis remained tilted heavily towards defence and glorification of the USSR, as if the social system there and the "Red" Army were things separate from the Stalinist rulers.

In 1944 Natalia Sedova Trotsky began to protest at the heavily pro-Russian line of *The Militant*. A decision was made in late 1944 to replace the regular Trotsky quotation with another. It would be March 31, 1945, when the Stalinist armies already controlled Eastern Europe and a large part of Germany, a few weeks short of the end of the war in Europe, before the 1931 quotation from Trotsky was replaced by another: "Only the world revolution can save the USSR for socialism. But the world revolution carries with it the inescapable blotting out of the Kremlin oligarchy". (The policy-point remained.) An editorial explained: "Whereas in the preceding period we correctly subordinated the struggle for the overthrow of the Stalinist régime to the needs of military defense, it is now imperative to subordinate everything else to the defense of the advancing European revolution".

Red Army Morale Asto...

But Soviet Soldiers Fight Bravely Because They Have Something Worth Defending

By GEORGE BREITMAN

on the basis of the weaknesses wrought by the Kremlin bureaucracy through its purges and repressions, and on the slow start of the Red Army in the 1939 Finnish war, a campaign toward which the Soviet masses for the most part had been lethargic. But they completely disregarded the other side of the picture.

Leon Trotsky, because he understood that whole picture, often stated that the outbreak of a capitalist war against the Soviet Union would at the very beginning bring forth the strong-...

and all oth...
because th...
want impe...
cause after...
same depre...
not the peo...
their maste...
soldiers are...
That i...

THE MILITANT
Formerly the SOCIALIST APPEAL

VOL. V—No. 32   Saturday, August 9, 1941

To defend the USSR as the main fortress of the world proletariat, against all assaults of world imperialism and of internal counter-revolution, is the most important duty of every class conscious worker.

—LEON TROTSKY

LENINGRAD

Masses Inspired By Memories Of October 1917

Kremlin Finally Compelled To Make Appeal To Traditions Of The October Revolution As Workers Rally For Defense To The Death

...in the hour of gravest dange...

A Tale Of Two Cities

A-D – The early months: big headlines backing the USSR, claims that "Soviet soldiers fight bravely because they have something worth defending."

A and **B** – August 9, 1941

C – August 30, 1941

D – September 6, 1941. The western Stalinists after June 1941 used to ask the rhetorical question: why, in contrast to France in 1940, was there no pro-Nazi fifth column in the USSR? And answered: because Stalin shot them all! This was retrospective justification for the Moscow Trials. Incongruously, *Militant* gets in on the act with its own gloss: in Leningrad the workers rule… In point of historical fact, over 90,000 members of the 'Red' Army defected and fought on the German side. Their leader Vlasov vainly tried to steer an independent course — like Poland's Pilsudski in World War 1 — between Russia and Germany.

F

E

G

H

THE MILITANT

Published in the interests of the Working People.

VOL. VI—No. 3   Saturday, January 17, 1942

JOIN US IN FIGHTING FOR:

1. Military training of workers, financed by the government, but under control of the trade unions. Special officers' training camps, financed by the government but controlled by the trade unions, to train workers to become officers.
2. Trade union wages for all workers drafted into the army.
3. Full equality for Negroes in the armed forces and the war industries—Down with Jim Crowism everywhere.
4. Confiscation of all war profits. Expropriation of all war industries and their operation under workers' control.
5. For a rising scale of wages to meet the rising cost of living.
6. Workers Defense Guards against vigilante and fascist attacks.
7. An Independent Labor Party based on the Trade Unions.
8. A Workers' and Farmers' Government.

THE MILITANT

Published in the interests of the Working People.

VOL. VI—No. 48   Saturday, Nov. 28, 1942

JOIN US IN FIGHTING FOR:

1. Military training of workers, financed by the government, but under control of the trade unions. Special officers' training camps, financed by the government but controlled by the trade unions, to train workers to become officers.
2. Trade union wages for all workers drafted into the army.
3. Full equality for Negroes in the armed forces and the war industries—Down with Jim Crowism everywhere.
4. Confiscation of all war profits. Expropriation of all war industries and their operation under workers' control.
5. For a rising scale of wages to meet the rising cost of living.
6. Workers Defense Guards against vigilante and fascist attacks.
7. An Independent Labor Party based on the Trade Unions.
8. A Workers' and Farmers' Government.

THE MILITANT

Published in the interests of the Working People.

VOL. VI—No. 51   Saturday, December 19, 1942

To defend the USSR as the main fortress of the world proletariat, against all assaults of world imperialism and of internal counter-revolution, is the most important duty of e v e r y class-conscious worker.
— LEON TROTSKY

JOIN US IN FIGHTING FOR:

1. Military training of workers, financed by the government, but under control of the trade unions. Special officers' training camps, financed by the government but controlled by the trade unions, to train workers to become officers.
2. Trade union wages for all workers drafted into the army.
3. Full equality for Negroes in the armed forces and the war industries—Down with Jim Crowism everywhere.
4. Confiscation of all war profits. Expropriation of all war industries and their operation under workers' control.
5. For a rising scale of wages to meet the rising cost of living.
6. Workers Defense Guards against vigilante and fascist attacks.
7. An Independent Labor Party based on the Trade Unions.
8. A Workers' and Farmers' Government.
9. Defend the Soviet Union against imperialist attack.

E, F, G – From late 1941 to late 1942: The USSR seems doomed and never more in need of defence (**E** October 18, 1941) — but from January to December 1942 the quotation from Trotsky about defence of the USSR is dropped.

H – December 1942: As the Stalinist army takes the offensive, the quotation reappears, with a new point in the paper's policy platform.

1 – The paper's cartoons by Laura Gray were consistently anti-Stalinist. This one appeared on March 17, 1945, while the paper was still carrying the Trotsky quote about defence and the "Defend the USSR" policy-point.

PART III

THE LONG "THIRD PERIOD": TROTSKYISM AFTER TROTSKY

7. THE OTHER TROTSKYISTS

For years, indeed decades, after the division of 1940, the "orthodox" damned the "other Trotskyists" by naming James Burnham as their representative figure. In fact they had distanced themselves from Burnham even before the split, and parted ways with him conclusively a few weeks after it. In 1956 Burnham would offer his help to an attempt by the government to keep Shachtman's group, then called the Independent Socialist League on the state's official list of "subversive" organisations. The "other Trotskyists" reaffirmed Bolshevism and the politics of the Russian Revolution against Burnham — and against what they saw as the stultified, "bureaucratic-conservative" notions of the "orthodox". The central task of a revolutionary party was to develop and promote creative political responses to living events — with a solid continuity of fundamental ideas — rather than just to build organisationally on the basis of an already-"finished" program. In the '40s they stressed the central need for revolutionary Marxist parties, while the Cannonites stressed spontaneous revolutionary working-class action.

Max Shachtman

THE PARTY WE NEED

THE RISE AND FALL of the Russian Revolution are both linked to the Bolshevik Party. Since 1917, revolutionary situations have developed in a dozen countries, with all the elements required for a working-class victory present to at least the same degree as in Kerensky's Russia — all but one: a revolutionary party prepared for just such a situation and capable of utilizing it to the utmost. This difference provides the decisive reason why the revolution triumphed in Russia and was defeated everywhere else. It also provides the basis for explaining the subsequent victory of the counter-revolution in Russia itself. The more generally this fact is acknowledged, the less trouble is usually taken to analyze it.

Political parties as we know them today are a comparatively recent development. They were quite unknown under feudalism. There were *partisans* of this or that group, of this or that idea, but there were no *parties* in the modern sense. That is understandable. Even though the young bourgeoisie created rudimentary political organizations in its struggle against feudalism in some countries, these were not an *indispensable* condition for the victory of the new society and its consolidation.

The revolution against feudalism and the socialist revolution against capitalism are alike only in that both bring a new class to power and organize a new social system. In every other respect, they are fundamentally different.

The bourgeois revolution takes place with the elements of capitalist economy already developed within, coëxisting with and constantly transforming feudalism itself. The revolution consists fundamentally in undoing the feudal shackles on the existing and growing capitalist organisms. Its task is not so much to "establish" capitalist relations as to liberate them for their freest unfoldment. The proletarian revolution does not find the socialist economic forms or relations at hand. All that dying capitalism provides it with — no trifle, to be sure! — is a tremendous economic machine, the socialization of production, and a modern working class capable of reorganizing society. Socialism itself does not exist; the revolution must first create it, establish it.

The bourgeois revolution need not necessarily be carried out by the bourgeoisie itself, that is, by the bourgeoisie as a class. The bourgeois revolution need not necessarily bring the bourgeoisie to political power. The basic requirements of this revolution are fulfilled when the main feudal shackles upon capitalist economic relations are broken. This can be accomplished by the bourgeoisie. But it can also be accomplished without the bourgeoisie and even against it. It can be carried out by the plebeian masses, with the bourgeoisie taking over power only later on by means of a counter-revolution; or it can be carried out "from above," in the

From *New International*, November 1944, "The Party that won the victory: Lenin's contribution to the revolution".

Bismarckian manner, by the aristocracy, by feudal or semi-feudal lords themselves. The bourgeoisie can maintain and consolidate the social system peculiar to it and nevertheless share political power with the outdated classes; it can even be cheated of political power by the latter. What is more, it can maintain itself to its dying day without necessarily destroying *all* "residues" of feudalism; in fact, in vast territories of the world, its continued power is based precisely upon the *preservation* of pre-capitalist economy. For the bourgeoisie it suffices that its economic system *predominates*.

The proletarian revolution, on the contrary, *cannot* be made by any other class but the proletariat itself, inasmuch as only the proletariat is capable of establishing the socialist society which is the only aim of this revolution. The *first and absolutely indispensable* condition of this revolution is "to make the proletariat the ruling class, to establish democracy." The bourgeoisie, on the basis of already existing capitalist economy, strives for political power. The proletariat, on the other hand, must *first* conquer "its political supremacy *in order*, by degrees, to wrest all capital from the bourgeoisie," and *then* organize socialist production. Capitalism, the capitalist state — these are conceivable without the political power of the capitalists. The very beginnings of the transition to socialism, however, are inconceivable without a workers' state, "this meaning the proletariat organized as ruling class."

The bourgeois revolution is not (not necessarily) the conscious revolution of a class. It is carried out with a false ideology (or to use the term in its original sense, simply ideology). Its victory over feudalism is assured by its fundamental nature, that is, the predominance of capitalist over feudal property is assured to the former by the "superiority of its productive methods." Capitalist production takes place, grows, goes through crises, declines, as a natural economic movement, regardless of will and in defiance of plan. The economy is automatically renewed (be it on a higher or lower level).

The proletarian revolution, on the contrary, cannot but be a conscious revolution, purposeful, planned, prepared, organized, timed. It does not have the automatic character of the bourgeois revolution. The transitional economy through which the revolution moves to socialism (above all if the revolution is surrounded by a predominantly capitalist world economy) is not automatically assured of a unilateral development to a classless society. Until the "administration of things" can replace the "administration of men," the *socialistic* character of the new economic relations depends entirely on the proletarian character of the state. Whereas capitalist production, based on "private property and competition, have been working out their own destiny," the development of the productive forces in a *socialist* direction, following the proletarian revolution, is "indivisibly bound up with the new state" as repository of the new property relations. "The character of the economy as a whole thus *depends upon* the character of the state power." The movement toward a socialist society can, therefore, take place *only* as a result of *conscious* planning. And inasmuch as a socialist society is based on production for use, planning can only mean plans elaborated by the "users," that is, democratic, socialist planning. Without consciousness and plan, the proletarian revolution is impossible; lacking them, a working class that seizes power will never hold it.

373

Without consciousness and plan, the establishment of socialism is impossible; if socialism is not consciously planned, it will never come. Consciousness and plan imply a *self-active, aware, participating, deciding* proletariat, which implies in turn a dying-out of coercion and bureaucratism.

Consciousness (*socialist* consciousness, that is) does not, however, come unfailingly to every worker at a given age, like hair on the head on a growing baby. Some acquire it early; some acquire it late; others go to their graves without it. The acquisition of a socialist consciousness equals the acquisition of an understanding of the indispensability of joint, deliberate and planned action for the fundamental task of reorganizing society. The ingenuity of man has not produced a vehicle or an instrument for this action that equals the *organized political party*.

The revolutionary proletarian party is the repository of the socialist consciousness of the working class. Composed of the *conscious* workers, the party is a means by which the working class is saved from existing permanently in a bourgeois stupor, from living intellectually from hand to mouth. It is the organized memory of the working class. It not only connects up yesterday with today, but today with tomorrow. In every activity of the working class it keeps before it its historic goal, thus helping to unify these activities, to rid them of distortions, to give them a progressive meaning and a basic purpose.

Of all the great contributions made by Lenin, *none* was as vitally important as the theory and practice of the revolutionary working-class political party which he evolved. It is true that the *elements* of Bolshevism-as-a-party (Bolshevism without a party means nothing) are to be found in Marx. But Marx did not, and could not work up these elements into the rounded, systematized, theoretically-motivated and practically-tested whole which they became under Lenin's leadership.

Lenin's whole conception of the party began and ended with the idea of an organization composed, trained and activated in such a way that it could be depended upon to lead the working class to power at the right time as the first step in the socialist reorganization of society. All critics and improvers of Bolshevism, of Lenin's party, who ignore this, are guaranteed to miss the mark

This conception meant, first of all, a party composed of *politically-educated fighters*, capable of subordinating all other interests and considerations to the cause of the socialist victory. If the party is to be the repository of the socialist consciousness of the working class, it must be made up of men and women whose *action* is based upon *understanding*. They had to understand the nature of the capitalist society whose overthrow they proclaimed; they had to understand the nature of the class that was to overthrow it; they had to understand the means, the strategy and tactics, by which it was to be overthrown.

Lenin's party was the best-educated political organization in the world. The Bolsheviks were intolerant of theoretical sloppiness; toward inattentiveness or neglect of theory, they were absolutely merciless. Lenin's "Without revolutionary theory, no revolutionary practice" was an organic concept with them. The sniggering at "theory" which became current in most other socialist parties of his time was never stylish in Lenin's party.

Lenin was an alert and ubiquitous polemist, and not a mild one. His polemically harsh and even violent language against adversaries used to shock (and still does) the delicate sensibilities of bourgeois and petty bourgeois politicians who considered it perfectly normal, however, to have the ruling class answer their "critics" with police clubs and prison sentences, to say nothing of disposing of "arguments" by slaughtering millions of "opponents" in a war. Lenin's violence in polemic was due to his uncompromising fidelity to the socialist revolution and the policy best calculated to achieve it. He was deadly serious about the revolution. Those whose theories and policies led the workers off the track, reconciled them with their class enemy, frustrated their efforts, had to be challenged with a vigor that matched the peril they represented. He helped train a party which, like himself, was sufficiently confident of the superiority of its program and views to engage anyone in debate without fear of coming off second best. He understood that you often teach more by polemical presentation and criticism than by "straight" exposition — the correctness of your own views standing out more clearly when counterposed to the views of others. He understood that mere reiteration of your own views is not enough to build a firm party. These views must be constantly defended in public (or revised when they cannot be defended!) against all critics — and defended successfully — otherwise your followers either begin to lose faith in your views or else continue to support them out of blind "party patriotism." Lenin, who was a party patriot if there ever was one, had no use at all for this kind of "patriot," any more than he cared for dopes in general. His own words were even blunter: "Whoever takes anything on faith is an idiot who can be disposed of with a wave of the hand." (The epigones of Leninism everywhere do far more, alas, to raise idiots than to raise Bolsheviks.)

Lenin's polemics, like all his writings, were meant to educate the party and the working class, to clarify, enhance and steel their consciousness. He did not *substitute* harsh words for logical substance. (The epigones believe they have destroyed an opponent's argument completely, and revealed themselves as living incarnations of Leninism, when they bark: "You are a prostitute! You are an agent of the bourgeoisie!" and then sit down, exhausted but content and triumphant.) The monger of platitudes, however orotund or shiny, bored Lenin to death; the demagogue, he detested as "the worst enemy of the working class."

The Bolsheviks built up a revolutionary party of action, not a pleasant company of salon habitués, dilettante socialists, or hair-splitting debaters. Their party was not a debating society, but a fighting army which had bloody battles to engage in and a world-renovating victory to win against the most powerful and deadliest enemy a class ever faced. Add to this the special circumstances of existence under Czarist autocracy and it is easy to understand why the Bolshevik Party was and had to be strictly centralized and disciplined. The right-wing socialists, especially of western Europe, who never envisaged battles or revolution, who looked forward to capitalist society gradually filling up with socialism by painless osmosis, shrank from Lenin's conception of centralism and discipline. The only discipline they wanted enforced was against the "ultra-leftist madmen." But Lenin, who understood to perfection the class enemy, its power, its savage capacity for self-preservation, its desperate unscrupulousness, knew that the revolutionary party challenging the enemy for nothing less than all-power itself would have to be a party of steel, disciplined, tested and re–tested, its ranks and program constantly checked for weakness, its fighting capacity kept at a high pitch.

What other conception of a party can you have *if* it is the socialist revolution you really aim for — a revolution that has not proved to be as easy as rolling off a log? Take, for example, our own Socialist Party in this country. Examine it from this standpoint and see why we cannot take it seriously (assuming that anyone else does). Pretty near anybody can be a member (except a real revolutionist — these are expelled). Anybody can put forward pretty near any view he wants to in public (except again, a real revolutionist). The party can adopt one position on a vital question, but the party leader, not caring particularly for this position, can put forward one of his own, even if it is the diametric opposite of his party's official stand. Pretty near any member can act as he pleases in the labor movement, follow whatever policy his heart and mind dictate, whether or not it conflicts violently with the policy followed by his fellow party-member in the same union or even with that officially advocated by his party. His party obligations are microscopic — he can attend meetings or not; if he drops into party headquarters once a month to exchange the time o' day with the other boys, he is not frowned on particularly; if his "party life" takes up two hours a month and the rest of his life is devoted to the bourgeois world, that is not a very black mark against him.

A fine, democratic and ever-so-non-fanatical a party! Of course, it never can and never will carry out the fight for socialism. It can never lead the workers in any serious struggle. In exchange, however, it offers these advantages over Bolshevism: A worker who wants to know, "Where do you, the Socialist Party, which wants to lead me, to have my support, stand on this or that vital question on the class struggle?" can always get his choice of half a dozen answers, each enjoying equal standing and validity, i.e., zero. A worker who wants to join the party need commit himself to nothing more serious than paying his dues, yawning over the pages of the party paper, and voting quadrennially for the party "standard bearer."

Joining the Bolshevik Party meant becoming a soldier in a revolutionary army. It meant discipline and centralization of efforts. It meant the ability to say: My party has this clear-cut policy, that clear-cut program, this answer to this problem; this is what it proposed to do about this situation; this is what it calls upon the people to do in that situation; if you agree with my party, support it, join it. My party means business; it is serious; it doesn't fool around with the interests and struggles of the working class; it calls upon labor to act as one man and it sets an example of how to act like one man.

In the last twenty years, there has been so much intellectual devastation in the revolutionary movement that Lenin's views on this point have been twisted and deformed beyond recognition. His insistence on discipline *in action* has been made to read discipline in *thinking*. His abhorrence of a "debating society," which he contrasted to a party capable of discussing policy thoroughly, coming to a decision by majority vote, and then unitedly executing the policy, has been made to read "no debates" in the party. The rich, even tumultuous, intellectual life of the Bolshevik party, for which there is no parallel anywhere; the continuous, passionate — and passionately interesting — and fruitful discussions of basic as well as topical questions which characterized it; the wide freedom of viewpoint which always prevailed in it as a matter of course, and not as a magnanimous bureaucratic dispensation once every two-three-four years, and even the freedom of political groupings and factions — all this has been wiped out by the not very sedulous apes of Leninism and its very opposite consecrated. Leninism, it now seems, boils down to this: We are rough and tough. We are hard people. We spit bullets. Shut up. Stop thinking. End debate — don't even start it. We know best. Our program is finished, amendments not admitted. Etc., etc. A party built on these "principles of Leninism" will do no more to bring about the socialist revolution than Norman Thomas' *laissez-faire, laissez-aller* party.

With the breaching of the world capitalist front in Russia, we have had, as Trotsky often noted, no lack of revolutionary situations. There has likewise been no lack of revolutionary initiative by the working class, resourcefulness, epic heroism, and repeated demonstrations that it is ready to extirpate the plague consuming civilization. This has showed that capitalism is doomed, inasmuch as it can no longer maintain peace, order and social equilibrium, and that the force called upon to dispatch it is irrepressible. All that has been and still is lacking is... a party of the Leninist type, not an artificial copy of the Bolshevist party, but a party of that *type*, built and schooled in the same way.

Having one, the Russian proletariat was able to accomplish more than anyone had a right to expect of the working class of any one country, and of a backward country, to boot. Having lost it, the Russian proletariat lost all its revolutionary achievements. That it lost its party is not due to that mysterious "fundamental defect" in Bolshevism which its critics have yet to explain to us, but to the fact that the working class of the advanced countries failed in time to build parties like it and remained under the domination of the anti-Bolshevik parties of labor.

With this loss, the center of revolutionary gravity has shifted further and further to the West. From Moscow there no longer come the liberating legions of the socialist revolution — as is unbelievably claimed by the self-patented "Trotskyists" — or the liberating ideas of Lenin, but the rolling waves of black reaction. Once, Leninist Russia almost freed the West. Now only the West can free the Russia of Stalin, not the West of today but of tomorrow. Success depends *entirely* upon how well and how soon a party of Bolshevism is built in countries like the United States. We have, it would seem, more time than many others. Every hour of it must be utilized to prepare for the inevitable revolutionary crisis.

If we do not succeed in having, at the crucial moment, the kind of party the Bolsheviks had in Russia in 1917, the absolutely inevitable catastrophe that would befall us all would have long-lasting effects. There is good reason, however, to believe that we shall not fail. The American working class has shown the most encouraging ability to move forward, not at a snail's pace but with leaps and bounds. It has not spoken its last word — only its first. Our bourgeoisie, "the most powerful in the world," has so little confidence in itself that it squealed with terror for months just at the sight of so limited and contradictory a step as the organization of labor into an independent political force in... bourgeois politics! How will it feel when labor really declares its political independence as a class?

The difference between how it feels and what it really gets, depends primarily and decisively upon the building of the revolutionary party. We have not been hurled back to the starting point. We have learned what is important to learn from Lenin in the period of the rise of Bolshevism; we have learned what is important from Trotsky, in the period of Bolshevism's crushing by the counterrevolution. The vanguard now knows more and knows it better. It must now clothe the skeleton of its program with the flesh and sinews of tens of thousands of workers who are breaking intellectually from capitalism. That is the task of tasks of the Fourth International today.

THE WORKERS PARTY: AIMS, TASKS AND STRUCTURE

"Resolution on the aims, the tasks and the structure of the party".

1. THE PARTY AIMS AT THE SEIZURE of state power by the American workers as part of the international proletarian revolution and for the purpose of establishing a classless socialist society. It bases itself on the revolutionary traditions of Marx, Engels, Lenin and Trotsky, whose fundamental ideas are crystallized in the program of the Fourth International. The aim of overthrowing the mightiest imperialist power in the world and reorganizing society on socialist foundations determines the nature, the tasks and the activities of the party.

2. The party bases itself unequivocally on the principles of Marxism, that is, the theory and practise of the proletarian revolution. Marxism is not a finished and immutable dogma, but a guide to action of the militant working class. Marxism, far from having been "refuted" by modern social developments and conflicts has been confirmed by them — if it is understood as a means of interpreting and changing society — and remains the only means whereby these new developments and conflicts can be understood. Since Marxism is by its very nature a revolutionary, living theory, and not a set of stone tablets, it must be constantly enriched and modified, in the spirit in which it has been developed up to now by its greatest proponents, and in the light of new events and experiences. In this sense, the party considers itself an aggressive champion of Marxism, a defender of its principles from the attacks of all its enemies.

3. The party emphasizes that, as a party of the international revolution, its main task is the organization and leadership of the struggle for socialism in the United States. Preoccupation with the position and problems of the labor movement in other countries has only too often meant ignoring the position and problems of the labor movement in this country, and has been the pretext for not analyzing and participating actively in the class struggle here. The party aims to break with this spirit of pseudo-internationalism. True internationalism means the application of the lessons learned from the world wide struggle against capitalism to the struggle against the main enemy of the working class at home as the best means of advancing the interests of the international revolution. The real test of the American revolutionist is not so much his opposition to British, French or German capitalism, or even to Stalinism, but to the ruling class and its social system in the United States.

4. In the sense indicated above, the party does not hesitate to call itself an American party, the party of the American working class fighting for the revolution in the United States. This demands, however, that the party have or acquire a thorough knowledge of the economic and political situation in the country in order that it may be able effectively to center its main activities in the American class struggle. The movement in this country has all too often displayed a more intimate knowledge of the situation in the Soviet Union or China or France than of the United States. It is imperative to make a radical change in this respect. If the party is to gain the confidence and leadership of the American workers, it must root itself in the American scene. It must study and analyze the history and the economic position of American imperialism; it must study and analyze American politics not only in general, but in their concrete and daily development; it must study and analyze the American labor movement. These studies and analyses, however, are worthwhile from only one standpoint, namely that they will enable the party to take active intelligent and effective part in the class struggle in this country, to intervene promptly and directly in American politics, and not merely to write about them as literary observers. What is said about the problem on a national scale applies with equal force to the problem on a local scale. The party must train its membership so that its knowledge of the situation "abroad" is surpassed by its knowledge of the labor movement and the political situation locally, so that in each locality the Party is able to participate directly and in time in the local labor movement and in local politics. From the lowest unit to the highest, the Party must learn to react with full energy to the needs and struggles of

the American working class. The respect, confidence and support of the American masses can be won in no other way.

5. Participation in the class struggle as an effective force is possible for the Party only if it is imbued with a spirit of action and combat. The working masses will not come to the party if it confines itself to telling them what they ought to do. It must show by example, by its own militant activity in the midst of the workers and side by side with them, that its program and leadership are worthy of their support. There is no other way for a propagandist group to develop into a party of the masses. This dictates an overwhelming emphasis upon party activism, day in and day out, and not limited to rare and isolated spectacular occasions. This means a constant training of the new (and old) members to the conception that the party demands of each and every comrade a basic minimum of activity on party assignment. This means constant selection and advancement of the active party members and a sifting out of purely book members who retard the work of others. A party facing such enormous tasks as does ours, must place corresponding responsibilities before its membership from top to bottom. It must be the aim of every branch to assign each member a specific task each week, thus doing away with the paralyzing division between "doers" and "non-doers". It is not necessary to approach every comrade, especially the new recruit, with such an attitude as will result in alienating him from the party immediately. But the orientation of a party of action and of individual responsibility must be kept firmly in mind until it is thoroughly established that the party is a serious organization of combat and not a casual discussion club for passing visitors. Otherwise the Party will surely decline into a futile reformist sect.

6. The Party cannot grow out of its present stage of a propagandist group unless its ideas, its program, its slogans are adopted by wide sections of the working class. Our party is the party of the working class. The socialist revolution is the revolution of the working class. The party can exert no influence at all in the American class struggle unless it exerts an influence in the working class. Hence, its main efforts must be directed towards winning workers to its ranks, primarily from the trade union movement. The proletarianization of the party is not only one of the most important guarantees of its revolutionary integrity, but is indispensable to its development as a decisive political factor in the country. The problem of acquiring an overwhelming working class predominance in the party is not to be solved mechanically or by the mere repetition of the wish. It is in the first place a political problem. It is solved by the political activity of the party. If the activity of the party, its slogans and campaigns, correspond to the needs and interest of the workers, the workers will respond to the appeals of the party. But this activity, these slogans and campaigns must be directed consciously and deliberately to the workers — primarily to those organized in the mass organizations, although not to the exclusion of the unorganized. Systematic, planned efforts must be made in every locality for members to establish contacts with individual workers and groups of workers. Every party member must consciously direct his efforts towards becoming a propagandist and organizer of his fellow-workers in the shop and neighborhood. Every party unionist must understand that his duty in the union — best fulfilled by being the ablest, most active and most class-conscious union militant — is to advance the influence and forces of the party in his organization. The party as a whole must concentrate on helping each individual member solve the problem of winning to its ranks those workers with whom he has contact. Experience, especially of the Stalinist party, shows that the initial isolation of the party from the workers in a given locality can be overcome by the selection of concentration points — factories and unions in the locality — at which a determined and systematic campaign of agitation and propaganda is conducted. A serious party of action must establish a network of such concentration points throughout the country. Without it proletarianization remains an empty phrase.

7. A revolutionary party functioning in present-day United States must direct its attention for the whole next period to two of the most downtrodden and dispossessed sections of the American working class: the Negro masses and the "locked-out generation", the Youth, each of which occupies a special position in the country and must be treated as a special problem. The neglect of the Negro problem is the disgrace of the American revolutionary movement. The extremely modest efforts made up to now show what a vast reservoir of recruitment and revolutionary potentialities is represented by the Negro masses. A branch functioning in a city with a Negro population is not worthy of the name

of a revolutionary organization unless it recruits Negro workers into its ranks. Special attention must be devoted to this problem by the press, literature, agitators and organizers of the party. Similarly with the Youth. The unrelieved crisis shows them that they have literally nothing to gain by maintaining capitalism and everything to gain by overturning it. A party branch which does not have a youth organization functioning side by side with it, is only half a branch. The youth, combining studies with activity in the class struggle, is the most important single reserve of the party and its indispensable auxiliary. The party must root out the rotten reformist attitude towards the youth expressed in a contemptuous superiority, in the attitude of seeking to confine the youth to doing the "dirty work" of the party and nothing more. At the same time, the party must help the youth organization overcome the tendency to decline into a sectarian "super-political" movement and aid it to become a broad mass movement of militant youth, a training ground for the party and the class struggle. The party must give special assistance to the youth in establishing contact with industrial workers and the mass labor organizations, where the talents and energies of the young militants best serve the movement. It is most significant that, except for the Stalinists, ours is the only organization that has a youth movement of any importance. This is a precious revolutionary acquisition which must be constantly expanded.

8. The tragic experiences of the international labor movement, and in the Soviet Union particularly, with the ravages of bureaucratism, have made all workers rightly concerned with the problem of workers' democracy. Bureaucratism is the product of the social influence, ideology and pressure of the bourgeoisie in the labor movement, undermining, corrupting and demoralizing it. As an unrelenting fighter against class-collaborationism, the Party must at the same time become the outstanding enemy of bureaucratism in the working class movement. Opposition to bourgeois democracy in no wise signifies opposition or indifference to workers' democracy; on the contrary, opposition to bourgeois democracy without counterposing workers' democracy is only grist to the mill of fascism. It must not allow the slightest taint of bureaucratism or tolerance towards bureaucratism stain and discredit its name. Above all, it must relentlessly combat the pestilence of Stalinism, which darkened the inspiring beacon light of the Russian Revolution and which has alienated millions of workers from the revolutionary movement and the cause of socialism. The socialist movement, socialism itself, cannot be built by bureaucrats or by bureaucratic methods, but only be destroyed by them. Socialism must be and can only be the achievement of the democratically-organized, class-conscious action of the working masses in power.

9. The party, therefore, is organized on the basis of democratic centralism. True party democracy is possible only on the basis of an active membership able to and capable of controlling its leadership, and a responsible elective leadership which justifies itself by the correct policies it pursues and the activities which it itself engages in. A party fighting the class war must be a centralized and disciplined organization, which demands unity in action on the basis of democratically determined policies. This concept must not, however, be debased into the bureaucratic dogma that since the party "is at war", a regime of military-barracks-discipline must prevail. The right of discussion and of free criticism of the party leadership and policy, is a membership right at all times, to be modified only by the strictly imposed requirements of party activity. Without a rich, free and variegated internal life, party democracy (and, in the long run, the party itself) is made impossible. A leadership which is satisfied with obedience, regardless of how obtained, has already abandoned the most elementary conceptions of party democracy. A membership which gives such obedience simultaneously surrenders party democracy.

10. An ignorant and uninformed membership is the bureaucrat's paradise. The first prerequisite of party democracy is an informed membership. An indispensable element of such information is a regular, all-year-round bulletin in which the party leadership gives a regular accounting of its stewardship, informs the membership of its important decisions and motivates them, informs the membership about important differences in the leadership or the ranks, and permits the free discussion of problems of party organization, activity and current policy. However, the discussion of important political questions is caricatured and rendered meaningless if it is carried on by an "educated caste" on the one side, and an uneducated membership on the other. The training of every party and youth member in the fundamental principles of Marxism, in the main elements of inter-

national and American politics, becomes, therefore, one of the best assurances for the preservation of meaningful party democracy. The arming of the party membership with the theory of Marxism is meant not only to equip it for more effective participation in the class struggle, but also for more effective participation in the inner life of the party, in the development of its policies, in constantly improving the relationships between the leadership and the ranks. A party member indifferent to continually learning more about the fundamental theoretical principles of the movement, is a party member who will be tolerant towards bureaucratism, or rather, who will become an easy victim of a bureaucracy, not only in the labor movement as a whole, but specifically, in his own party.

11. From this follows the need of constant attention to the theoretical development of the party. Every new member of the party, and especially all of the youth, must pass through at least an elementary series of study groups. Every branch of the party must set aside regular periods for educational discussion, either on a theoretical question or a problem of current politics. The educational work of the party must be guided and centralized by a special national department. The regular publication, distribution and study of the party's theoretical organ must have the attention of the entire party and youth, and not merely of a select group of "specialists." This organ must be one of the strongest pillars of the party. It must treat the fundamental theoretical problems of the movement from the Marxian standpoint. It must deal mainly, however, with the problems and position of American capitalism and the American labor movement, and demonstrate that the new generation of Marxists in this country are not only capable of repeating what Marx and Lenin said but of conducting independent and much needed investigations and analyses of new problems, of new political and social phenomena. It must not fear the discussion of new or even old problems on the grounds of an "orthodoxy" which has more in common with divine revelation than with genuine living Marxism. It should rather seek to continue the really best traditions of the Marxist movement, and its theoretical discussions, of the pre-war days in Germany and Russia, which made possible the enrichment of the arsenal of Marxism by such thinkers as Mehring, Luxemburg, Lenin and Trotsky.

12. Just as the theoretical organ of the party must devote itself mainly to propaganda, so the popular political press and literature of the party must devote themselves mainly to agitation, i.e., to concentration on the immediate political slogans and campaigns of the party. If these campaigns are to mean anything, however, it is necessary to make a sharp turn from the old, humdrum propaganda methods. The press must truly be a popular political press for the American worker. If it is to influence and to be read by the American worker, it must be written in a style and a language that will make our ideas accessible to him. That means, firstly, an end to the "professional jargon" of our movement which is unintelligible to him. It means an end to long and unread articles and to heavy, obviously labored propaganda efforts. It means writing about questions which not only concern him but in which he is interested — questions of American politics and the American labor movement, not to the exclusion of international questions, to be sure, but nevertheless with the main emphasis on what he sees about him and what he knows about. It means, also, a paper to which the workers and worker-readers contribute, the adoption and extension on a large scale of that "correspondence to the editor" which features in all the popular bourgeois papers. It means the attempt to center and continue the agitation of the paper on a central campaign for a given period of time, as contrasted to desultory, fitful agitation from week to week. This applies even more strongly to pamphleteering. The bulk of the party's pamphlets must be extremely cheap in price, extremely popular in presentation, devoted always to a single question, in most cases a question that is topical and related to the American scene. The party can well afford to model itself, in this field, on the best examples of agitational work in the pre-war socialist and syndicalist movements in this country. The lecture tours of party speakers, which must be systematically conducted, should also be arranged in the same spirit. In all its agitational and organizing work, the party must emphasize to the American workers that it is not a movement concerned primarily with things and problems which they now feel to be alien or remote from them, but primarily with the things and problems he feels are most acutely his, that it considers it to be, in a word, its task as internationalists to lead in struggle for the revolution in America.

THE WORKERS PARTY AND BURNHAM

THE LETTER OF RESIGNATION of James Burnham from the Workers Party makes it crystal clear that he has abandoned the struggle against the war and for socialism. The Political Committee does not consider it necessary, at this time, to enter into an exhaustive reply to his attacks on our program and movement. Much of what could be said can be found in the article "Intellectuals in Retreat" (*New International,* January 1939), written by Burnham in collaboration with comrade Shachtman. We urge all comrades to re-read the article.

However, some brief comments on Burnham and his letter are in order.

1. We assume to begin with, that the delegates to the national convention of the SWP (and our own conference) reported back to the members the frank and critical speeches of Comrade Shachtman on the question of Burnham. In those speeches it was explained that the part-time participation of Burnham in the leadership of the movement was due to his inability to break fully with his old manner of life, and to subordinate himself — his personal, social and cultural interests — to the needs of the working class movement. The task of the party, Shachtman added, was to utilize Burnham's talents and abilities to the maximum degree possible under the circumstance; and that time alone would tell what his future role in the movement would be. Burnham has now given the answer.

2. His letter informs us that he has become convinced that Marxism must be rejected. It is no secret that Burnham has never accepted dialectic materialism. However, until now he defended the Marxian theory of history (its sociological theories, and particularly its most crucial element from the viewpoint of the socialist revolution, the Marxian theory of the State). On February 1st, 1940, only a few months ago, he wrote that "it is a direct falsehood to say that I, or any other member of the opposition, rejects the Marxian theory of the State." ('Science and Style.')

Today he finds that the Marxian theory of "universal history" — a weaseled formula for the materialist conception of history and the Marxian theory of the state — has been disproved by scientific investigation. He has learned quite rapidly; and has so far kept the evidence for this conclusion a dark secret.

So also we are told for the first time that Burnham considers Marxian economics "false or obsolete or meaningless". When did he find this out?

3. Matters are worse when he presents his views on the political problems of the movement. It should be noted at the outset that Burnham falsifies his own previous position. For example, he writes: "The 'transition program' document seems to me — as it pretty much did when first presented — more or less arrant nonsense..."

How easily Burnham deceives himself! As, at least, all the leading comrades know, Burnham agreed with, and enthusiastically welcomed the general spirit of the transition program and the main ideas contained in it. He, as others, it is true, differed with certain formulations in the document, and insisted that its concepts and slogans be applied concretely to the American scene — but the criticism did not go beyond that. Now it appears that Burnham has convinced himself that he always considered the transition program as "more or less arrant nonsense"!

4. So it is in the matter of his attack on the "Leninist type of party". He finds that such a party is "incompatible with scientific method and genuine democracy", and gives the impression that this has always been his position.

Again he conceals the real meaning of his attack — which is a repudiation of any revolutionary socialist party — behind criticisms of "Leninism" and "Bolshevism".

Statement of the Political Committee on the Resignation of James Burnham from the Workers Party, May 31, 1940.

Precisely what is he against and what is he for? In the recent factional fight, Burnham, as our group as a whole, charged that Cannon had adopted the party theory and practice, not of Lenin, but of Zinoviev. He, as all of us, fought for a revolutionary socialist party in the best traditions of Lenin and the Bolsheviks, Luxemburg and Trotsky; a party with a Marxist program, democratically organized, united and centralized in common action. Are the theory and practise of the Workers Party "incompatible with genuine scientific method and genuine democracy"? Burnham wisely evades this concrete question, and takes refuge in the general clamor of those who desert the movement — against the "Leninist type of party".

This is understandable since what Burnham desires above all is freedom from all responsibility to any revolutionary party.

5. Burnham writes that since the Workers Party is a revolutionary Marxist organization the split from the SWP was not based upon anything "fundamental". Yesterday he understood that our conflict with Cannon and Trotsky was over the strategical orientation of the Fourth International in the second World War; and the character of the regime of the party, particularly in face of the war and the existence of two politically irreconcilable tendencies in the party. And that our struggle for the "third camp", against bureaucratic conservatism and for a democratically organized and centralized, activist Marxist party led to the split precisely because the differences went beyond "details and emphases".

We readily agree with his remark that "Nothing whatever in the faction fight indicated a decisive tendency away from this (Marxist) (Fourth International) orientation; on the contrary every sharp suggestion in such a direction was at once blocked".

His present view of the significance of the split is entirely comprehensible coming as it does from one who has broken with Marxism and the socialist movement; and has given up the struggle against the war.

6. He declares that he is in agreement with the Workers Party on the war, but also shares this position "with many other organizations". Which organizations? Where are they? Again: when did Burnham discover them?

More important is, what practical consequences does he draw from his "agreement" with our anti-war program? Only one... desertion of the movement against the war. And the retirement — his real program — is given a "scientific" basis. "Socialism would be a good thing if it can be achieved" but the next probable stage of development is a new system of exploitation, "managerial society". So why do we need any revolutionary party? Why conduct a hopeless struggle against the war and for socialism? Since this is the real meaning of Burnham's letter of resignation we can attribute his remarks on the war as a "psychological hangover".

7. As he suggests in his statement: "This letter may be an over-elaborate way of saying the single sentence: 'I feel like quitting politics'." And so it is.

The increased hardships of our small movement in face of the rapid developing war crisis — and the greater difficulties yet ahead — placed him (as every other comrade in the party) before a decisive choice: everything to the movement or personal passivity and retirement from revolutionary politics. The first choice requires confidence in the working class and the party; self-sacrifice, devotion and moral courage. Burnham, lacking these essential qualities, chose to give up the struggle. Where this will lead him tomorrow is yet to be seen.

8. After reading his letter it should be clear why he could not wage a fight for his views in our Party. He has nothing to offer the members, nothing to offer the working class. His attack on Marxism in the name of "scientific method and genuine democracy" and "truth and freedom" cannot be taken seriously since it is a pretext for quitting revolutionary politics. And why should he make any fight in the Party if his aim is to quit the movement?

9. The Workers Party is deeply concerned with the struggle for truth and freedom. Its methods are the methods of science and democracy. This struggle and these methods are inseparable from the struggle against the war and for socialism. They are an integral part of Marxism, the self-critical science of working class revolution, with the aid of which alone one can explain the past defeats of the movement, understand the events transpiring around us, and forge the instruments for proletarian victory. Burnham has abandoned scientific socialism, the socialist movement, the socialist

384

goal. He has thereby deserted the only meaningful struggle for truth and freedom.

10. Confronted with Burnham's letter of resignation, the Political Committee saw no reason to enter into an agreement with him, as suggested by his four alternative proposals. We accepted his resignation, effective immediately, and decided to inform the members as to the true facts in the case.

We are confident that the party members will understand the significance of Burnham's defection, and continue with increased energy our struggle against the war and for socialism.

A McCARTHYITE POLICE AGENT SPEAKS HIS LINES

THE ATTORNEY GENERAL'S OFFICE, whose attorneys began the present hearing with a show of confidence that they had a "case" for their listing, is bringing the hearing to an end with an all but open acknowledgement that their "case" against the organizations, after some five weeks of hearing sessions, has collapsed.

Twenty minutes of testimonials in favor of the government [were given] by its last-minute "surprise" witness and expert on the organizations, James Burnham. The appearance of this characterless turncoat in the first public performance of his new role as a police agent is an index to the degree of desperation reached by the government, in the brief course of the hearing which it was finally driven to grant the organizations after eight years of stalling. The fact is that not a single document introduced by the government as exhibit, or any other references emanating from the government, could be shown to sustain the claim that the organizations advocated the overthrow of the government by force and violence or that they were "communist" in any sense other than their support of a classless socialist society.

In contrast to the government's presentation, that of the organizations, as contained in the testimony of political opponents like Norman Thomas, Harry Fleischman, Daniel Bell and Dwight Macdonald, on the one hand, and ISL National Chairman Max Shachtman, on the other, was not only overwhelming against the government's case but stood up firmly under every attempt by the government attorney, in cross-examination, to break it down by so much as a hair's breadth.

So the government found it necessary to present the so-called "rebuttal", which was no rebuttal at all. It found it necessary to bring into the hearing, one way or another, a live witness who could at least claim familiarity with the organizations. That was the first big sign of the desperation of the government. All sorts of experts, real and alleged, were visited and pleaded with to testify against the ISL. Yet, opponents or not, there was not one of them that could be induced to forget his self-respect. So the government representatives sought a witness who would have none to forget.

That is how they found Burnham, ex-Marxist, ex-Trotskyist, ex-leader-of-the-Workers-Party-for-three-weeks, ex-admirer of Stalin, ex-democrat, now a frenzied champion of "preventive" war against Russia and Ivy League literary lawyer for the McCarthyite sewer. The testimony of the witness? Nothing but the spiteful offal of a well-coached turncoat.

"Was the Workers Party a Communist organization when it was formed in 1940?" The expert replies: "Yes, it was". "Have you seen any evidence since that time that it no longer is a Communist organization?" The expert replies emphatically, "None". "What form of Communism did you refer to in calling the organizations communists?" asks the examiner, Mr Morrissey. The expert replies with well-rehearsed promptness, "One that accepts the basic doctrines of Lenin".

And what would those be? They are four in number: the ultimate objective of a collectivized economy in a classless socialist society; the teaching that this objective can-

---

Unsigned article: *Labor Action,* July 9, 1956, "The government trots out J Burnham: A McCarthyite police agent speaks his lines". When he first appeared in court, Burnham went up to Max Shachtman and put his hand out; Shachtman turned his back on him.

not be achieved by reforms of the existing government; the teaching that a new form and structure of government must replace the existing government, that is, a proletarian dictatorship, or what Shachtman's *Fight for Socialism* calls a workers' government; and the formation of counter-organs of power, a new army and political institutions like soviets, workers' councils and the like, which are to carry through the transition to socialism.

Do these organizations then advocate force and violence to achieve their ends? asked Maddrix, the government attorney. To this question — asked more than once by Maddrix, and several times in the first part of the cross-examination by the organizations' counsel, John Silard — Burnham could not be induced to give a direct and honest answer. But then again, such an answer was not the purpose of his testimony. Do they advocate force and violence? Burnham replied, "It inevitably follows from the analysis of society made by the Workers Party". Does he know of such advocacy from any of the literature of the organizations? It is brought out in the hearing that his direct knowledge of the three organizations is limited to the three or at most four weeks during which he was a member of the Workers Party, that is, from the day he helped found it in April 1940 to the day he sent in his resignation from the party in May 1940.

Burnham testified that when he joined the Trotskyist movement he took the name of "John West". During the earlier cross-examination of Shachtman, Maddrix had tried to show that the organizations "ordered" members to take and use "false names", as part of the government's effort to create around the organizations the atmosphere of a secretive, conspiratorial, sinister movement. Burnham, in his new capacity as fiction writer for the government, tried to thicken this atmosphere for Maddrix, even though he knows more than enough about the organizations to know — not just assume, but know — that the charge is fraudulent and preposterous. In fact, it turns out that in those days he suffered from the "illusion" that he could not teach at New York University and be a member of the Trotskyist organization under one and the same name, and that was his final testimony on this score.

Under Rauh's relentless prodding, Burnham admitted that Waterman, the attorney general's man in charge of the case against the organizations, had visited him last September to ask him to testify for the government, but that he had declined the invitation on the ground that he "preferred not to". Waterman visited him a fourth time, a week or ten days before the session, according to Burnham. Waterman then "outlined the progress of the case", and told Burnham that Norman Thomas, Harry Fleischman, Daniel Bell and Dwight Macdonald had testified that the organizations did not advocate force and violence as the government charged.

Waterman said to Burnham: "Well, that's the trouble. Their side always gets its people to come down. Our side doesn't". Thereupon, testified Burnham, "I decided to come. It was my duty".

8. FROM "ORTHODOXY" TO MILLENARIANISM I: WHO WILL MAKE THE REVOLUTION?

As it turned out, the expectations held by all the Trotskyists — the "orthodox" and the others alike — of great revolutionary upheavals in Europe at the end of World War 2 were disappointed. There were upheavals, there was radicalisation, but the combined effects of the destruction of working-class political culture by Stalinism, Stalinist terrorism and astute concessions by the ruling classes kept the lid on. In hindsight, the perspective discussed in the texts in this chapter, of the Trotskyists winning the leadership of the anti-Nazi Resistance, was probably always unreal. Yet in these texts there is a debate of continuing relevance. One concept of what organised Marxian socialists can and must do in mass upheavals is counterposed to another. Al Glotzer's articles argue for active, creative tactics to regenerate a broad working-class socialist movement by agitation around democratic and immediate issues — in other words, for a strategy with a rational connection between ends (socialism) and means (development of the labour movements). The "orthodox" Trotskyists (together with a minority, around C L R James ("J R Johnson"), of the "unorthodox") upheld a concept which essentially saw the role of the revolutionary party as just being there — with strong organisation and a "finished" revolutionary program — to meet a revolutionary workers' movement which would develop almost automatically. They thus began to drift from rational politics to millenarianism — a politics based on hope for an all-transforming event to be brought about by some superhuman force — in this case "History".

Al Glotzer

FROM ANTI-HITLERISM TO SOCIALISM

THE IDEA THAT CAPITALISM has long ago outlived its progressive functions has been propagated for several decades by Marxian socialists. It has been the central theme of their world program described by the graphic term: capitalist barbarism or socialism. By capitalist barbarism is understood a condition where the social order, in a state of decay and disintegration, continues to exist without the prospect of its replacement by a new and higher order of society, namely, socialism. By counterposing these alternatives, revolutionary socialists placed on the order of the day the socialist revolution as a practical international goal.

Thus, Lenin characterized the present epoch as a period of "wars and revolutions." In this way he succinctly described the chaos of imperialist capitalism. The concept was thereafter embodied in all the writings and in the thinking of the modern generation of revolutionary socialists. Moreover, it has been and continues to be the central thesis of any Marxist analysis of the objective world situation which predetermines the active program for the realization of socialism.

On the basis of the above conception of modern capitalism as an outlived social order, the internationalists of the heroic period of the Communist International developed the slogan of the Socialist United States of Europe. This was the socialist solution to the impasse of European society in the 1914-18 post-war period. The slogan, adopted by the Comintern in 1923, was thereafter incorporated in the programs of the individual revolutionary parties. In this way was presented the progressive socialist way out of the morass of European society, in opposition to the bourgeois continuation of the chaos.[1]

The Russian Revolution was the first successful evidence of the new order emerging from this chaos. The Socialist United States of Europe would have marked a higher stage in the development of the new society; it would have insured the victory of world socialism. With this in mind, the Communist International during the years 1919-24 developed a strategy and series of tactics designed to win for it the support of the majority of the masses, to bring into harmony the activities of its affiliated parties with the revolutionary possibilities latent in the objective conditions of a moribund European capitalism. If the Comintern of Lenin and Trotsky

---

Abridged from *New International*, June 1943, "Issues on the National Question". This is a polemic against an earlier article by C L R James who, writing under the pen-name J R Johnson, criticised the WP's emphasis on national-liberation and democratic slogans for Europe, and counterposed the perspective of an immediate revolutionary struggle under directly socialist slogans.

1. The slogan was adopted after considerable dispute inside the Comintern. Lenin, for example, hesitated for a long time before he assented to the adoption of the slogan into the program because, under the conditions which existed at the time, he feared that the slogan might cause the revolutionary parties to overlook, modify or weaken their activities in their respective countries which were directed toward the organization of the masses with the specific aim of establishing the workers' power in the intensely revolutionary European

failed, it was due, not to the absence of the historical stage, "barbarism or socialism," or the lack of the essential complementary objective conditions, but solely to the failings of the revolutionary parties.

In consequence, Allied imperialism was able to create its reactionary system of small states, not only to establish a certain delicate balance between the capitalist powers in Europe, but equally to establish a barrier against the development of the indispensable Socialist United States of Europe.

The logic of the crisis of capitalist society, however, was so powerful that even sections of the bourgeoisie, their politicians and theorists, developed and advocated programs for a United States of Europe (naturally, not a *socialist* United States), which in their minds implied a "unification" under the domination of one or a set of imperialist powers. This idea, in its variegated forms, persists to this day. The inability of the democratic bourgeoisie to realize its program resulted from the specific relations between the national states and the fact that *its* kind of United States depended on a military struggle for power. Hitler, in form at least, has established a "unified" Europe: the unification of the sword and flame, wherein Germany, as the one economic, political and military power, exploits the Continent in the interests of the Reich's imperialist ruling class.

It is important to bear in mind that, however overripe the objective conditions of European capitalism have been for socialism, they did not automatically mean the *victory* of socialism. For, in the final analysis, the factor which is *all-decisive* is the *subjective* force — the organization, strength, intelligence and will to power of the revolutionary socialist parties, equipped with an unassailably correct program.

One important distinction must be borne in mind even when recognizing the fact that the Socialist United States of Europe was a central thesis of the Marxist program: this end aim for Europe was itself contingent upon the national victories of the parties of socialism. Even in the good days of the Comintern, the slogan of the Socialist United States of Europe was not the main active slogan of the revolutionary parties. It was a programmatic and ultimate European goal. Yet the necessity of the slogan and its urgency were just as valid and historically correct as they are now. Moreover, the Communist International had something with which to give substance and power to the slogan. The Comintern did not view the slogan as being achieved automatically, spontaneously and simultaneously. In the concept of Lenin, the Socialist United States of Europe would be inevitable only

---

situation which then existed. Lenin also feared, as a result of Bukharin's concept of the permanent revolution as a simultaneous European process in which the workers would seize power at once on a continental scale, that the entire international might become disoriented by the slogan. Bukharin's views had, at that time, great popularity. Once adopted, however, it was put in its proper place as outlined in this article. Why then was the slogan adopted in 1923? Because it was the belief and hope of the Comintern that a victory in Germany was virtually assured and therefore the whole question of the socialist reorganization of Europe would instantly became an *aktuel* question for the working class. It was the immediate possibility of state power in the West which made the slogan a reality in 1923. The defeat in Germany did not alter the programmatic place of the slogan, since it held true as long as decadent capitalism existed. But its utilization depended upon how close the proletariat, through its parties, was to *soviet* state power.

after the victory of the workers in a number of European countries. Again, in the minds of the Marxists, the subjective factor, in view of the decline and decay of capitalism, became in turn an objective factor of inestimable significance, nay, *of decisive importance*. This is a change from quantity to quality. For this reason, the question of the vanguard organization, its program and its transitional policies, its tactics and their application, was and remains today the fundamental problem of the epoch.[2]

In the resolution of the Workers Party (*The New International*, February, 1943), there is indicated the kind of epoch in which we live. It is upon this concept that the entire resolution is predicated. In proceeding on this basis, the resolution is in keeping with the tradition of Marxism.

What is new in this resolution? That the "unification" of Europe under German fascism, i.e., its conquest, which has reduced the European nations and the European masses to the state of oppressed and conquered peoples, has revived the national question on the Continent. This "unification" of the Continent by German arms has reintroduced the problem of national liberation as a burning question and need for the nationally oppressed European masses. The resolution points out that the "mass movements" in Europe today are largely movements which have been born around the single issue of national freedom from the yoke of a foreign oppressor; that this struggle for national liberation will rekindle the whole struggle between the classes for power, "for the old order or the new"; that there is a possibility of recreating the vanguard party through the instrumentality of these national movements; that these movements are plebian movements which, in the context of the European situation, are basically progressive; that national liberation, when and if realized, no matter if only for a few days, or a few months, can only pose the question of the workers' power; that revolutionary socialists must support these movements, integrate themselves in them, in order not to lose contact with the masses and to prevent these movements from becoming the instruments of an unchallenged imperialism; that the national movements are transitional in nature, and the participation of socialists in them is part of a transitional program leading to the struggle for socialism; that before the slogan of a Socialist United States of Europe can become a reality and an action slogan, we will see the reëstablishment of the national states, and, more important, this development will be necessary to reëstablish the International of Socialism as a genuinely functioning organization composed of a number of revolutionary socialist parties in the leading European countries; finally, that the Socialist United States of Europe remains a *central*, programmatic concept and slogan for revolutionary socialists.

In one place in his article Johnson makes reference to Trotsky for the purpose of proving that the national question in Europe does not exist. The case in point is an article written by Trotsky on the occasion of the Czechoslovakian crisis (*The New International*, November, 1938). Trotsky stated that the German seizure of the Czech Republic would not cause the

---

2. In "The Way Out for Europe" everything is stood on its head. Johnson shows by the development of his thesis that he has no comprehension of the main problem which the Marxist movement is confronted with in the present period of capitalist decline. The fact that the working class has suffered a series of uninterrupted and paralyzing defeats for twenty-five years, the fact that the working class movement as an *organized political force* in Europe does not exist, has completely passed him by, as we shall demonstrate by Johnson's own words.

working class movement to raise the slogan of national independence and organize for the defense of the bourgeois state. Johnson continues to quote Trotsky to the effect that there is no national question in Europe, ... unless a new war ends in a military victory of this or that imperialist camp, if the war fails to bring forth the workers' power, if a new imperialist peace is concluded, etc. In other words, Trotsky posed a number of *ifs* in a changing world situation. The war has not yet ended, but the conditions created by the conflict, the unforeseen Hitlerian sweep over the Continent have given rebirth to the national question. Trotsky, five years ago, dismissed these possibilities. And Johnson, not in 1938, but in 1943, says that none of these probable conditions posed by Trotsky have occurred. For emphasis, he adds: "Most obviously not."

Elsewhere he writes: "Behind any proposals to make a change (what kind of change, and who proposes it? — A. G.) in the application of the socialist slogan undoubtedly lurks some variant of the idea that Lenin put forward in 1915. Given certain conditions of continued reaction (!) and domination of Europe by a single power, a great national war is once more possible in Europe. *No such situation as Lenin envisaged is visible in Europe today.*" As clear as crystal; and therefore we shall return to this crucial selection from the Johnson contribution.

In his article, *The Pamphlet by Junius*, Lenin takes up the question of a probable return to national wars in Europe. What he says is also clear:

"It is highly improbable that this imperialist war of 1914-16 will be transformed into a national war.... Nevertheless, it cannot be said that such a transformation is impossible: *if the European proletariat were to remain impotent for another twenty years; if the present war were to end in victories similar to those achieved by Napoleon, in the subjugation of a number of virile national states; if imperialism outside of Europe (primarily American and Japanese) were to remain in power for another twenty years without a transition to socialism, say, as a result of a Japanese-American war, then a great national war in Europe would be possible. This means that Europe would be thrown* back *for several decades. This is improbable. But it is* not *impossible, for to picture world history as advancing smoothly and steadily without sometimes taking gigantic strides backward is undialectical, unscientific and theoretically wrong".* (Emphasis in original — A. G.)

It has not happened *exactly* as Lenin said, yet several important conditions cited by him have indubitably occurred. But Johnson says: "No such situation as Lenin envisaged is visible in Europe today." We have merely to ask: if this is so, why, then, do you say that you support the slogan of national liberation? Obviously, Johnson's support is merely formal. It has no great significance to him. He does not understand his responsibilities to such a slogan. For this reason, the agitational slogan and the programmatic slogan are consistently counterposed throughout his article. Wherever he declares the correctness of the slogan of national liberation, it is qualified by the declaration that the slogan of the United States is "on the order of the day," and all the emphasis is on the necessity of a *"ceaseless pounding, day and night, of the slogan, the Socialist United States of Europe."* (Emphasis mine — A. G.)

The source of Johnson's errors is to be found in his inability to understand the rôle of the subjective factor in world and European politics, the need of a revolutionary socialist party and the *indispensability* of such a party to a solution of any class problem. Instead, we are treated to generalities which in themselves are wrong because they have no relation to any vital concrete situation. He concerns himself with the end-aims, without resolving the many steps that must necessarily be traversed before the proletariat can be emancipated. In his presentation, everything is telescoped.

For example, the resolution of the Workers Party argues that there are powerful national barriers between the masses of Europe which must be overcome. Johnson says: "Today these powerful barriers . . . have been destroyed by declining capitalism." Under the subhead in his article, "The Abstract and the Concrete," the author commits three grievous errors, which explain a great deal about the whole contribution. In one place he writes in support of the argument that the Socialist United States is more urgent than ever that: "The most dangerous enemies of the militancy of the workers, the flourishing Social-Democratic and Stalinist bureaucracies, no longer exist." Whatever world he is writing about, it is certainly not our world, not on this planet. He adds to this erroneous statement another: "Our hypothetical half a dozen revolutionaries (in Lyon) have an opportunity *a hundred times greater than in* 1939, *so long as they do not counterpose theories and slogans to action.*" Against whom is Johnson polemizing? Against the workers who might "counterpose theories and slogans to action"? Obviously, Johnson does *not* mean the workers! And what theories and slogans should not be counterposed by the workers? Is it perhaps the slogan for national liberation? If it is not that slogan and the theory behind the slogan, what is the meaning of the sentence? The author of "The Way Out for Europe" unwittingly supplies the answer.

To say that the workers of Lyon have "an opportunity today a hundred times greater than in 1939," means that the possibilities of socialism are *today* a hundred times greater than in 1939, and that the power, strength and organization of the workers are a hundred times greater than in 1939. For the word "opportunity" has no meaning if organization, program, strength, tactics and strategy are not part of the concept of opportunity. The workers have an opportunity *in general*, in an *historical* sense. But the opportunity can never be realized unless it is fortified by the mass organization of the working class, by the existence of the revolutionary vanguard, by the existence of a correct program, and the proper application of this program! This is the idea, above all, which needs to be hammered home incessantly.

As if in anticipation of this argument, he says, in his third error, on page 153: "But, it is urged, the proletariat in the occupied countries is sluggish, it is not organized; the revolutionary movement is non-existent, etc. *But how much bigger was the revolutionary movement yesterday than it is today?*" Here again, Johnson has missed the whole lesson of the meaning of the fascist victories in Europe and their effect upon the proletariat and its organized movements. It seems odd to have to answer such an argument ten years after Hitler seized power, after the defeats in Spain and France, the victory of Stalinism and the realities of the Second World War.

Prior to the war, a large part of the European labor movement existed. Today it does not exist! Prior to the war, working class fraternal organizations were in existence. Today they have been wiped out. Prior to the war, there were large co-operative organizations. Where are they to be found on the Continent today? Prior to the war, there were revolutionary organizations in existence. Where are they today? Their size, their influence, their weight in the labor movement varied. It is true, they were not strong. But under the conditions of pre-war Europe, they *existed* and *functioned* and had the possibilities of enjoying growth and influence. Today, they do not exist!

The problem, to repeat, is one of reconstituting the workers' movement in Europe, and through it to reëstablish its organized revolutionary socialist wing. This the resolution of the Workers Party seeks to do. Johnson has an entirely different conception.

The theory which is implicit in his entire analysis of the historical epoch is not a new theory. It is as old as the socialist movement. I have already indicated what it is by saying that he visualizes the development in Europe on the basis of the "spontaneity of the masses." Otherwise, what is the meaning of the long, involved and stratospheric discussion of the general historical stage of present-day capitalism? To show that the crisis of capitalism must drive the masses along the socialist road. While this is true, *in general*, it is only the *beginning* of the problem. But for Johnson it is the *end* of the problem. To him, the process is *automatic:* the workers *must* become revolutionised! The workers *must* take the socialist road!

Yet between the compulsions created by the crisis of capitalism, which makes life for the masses a hellish nightmare, and the organization of the masses for the struggle for power, is a long road. It is the road of organization, education, training and preparation. Without the existence of strong mass parties of socialism, the working class is hopelessly doomed. Even a correct program is not enough. A correct program can *make it possible* to reach the masses, to win them to socialism, to organize them for the struggle. But the *vanguard party* is the indispensable link between the objectively ripe conditions for socialism and the establishment of socialism in one or more countries.[3]

Johnson's views are sectarian. In practice, they can never solve the one great problem of this stage, the reorganization and revitalization of the working class movement for socialism. That decisively fundamental idea does not become an integral element in his schema of the European situation.

Johnson has sought to create the impression that the position embodied in the resolution of the Workers Party means postponing the struggle for socialism for an impossibility: national liberation. He is for a Socialist United States of Europe *now*. What he does not comprehend is that the present situation in Europe has created a condition where the struggle for national liberation becomes interlinked with the struggle for socialism; that revolutionary socialists must be *in this movement* to lead on the high road of socialism.

---

3. In his *Strategy of the World Revolution*, Trotsky wrote: "Politics considered as a historical factor, has always remained behind economics." This observation has been accepted by all Marxists as an unassailable truth. It reveals why economics and politics do not develop simultaneously, why the economic collapse of capitalism does not bring about an automatic and immediate corresponding political response on the part of the masses. For the latter an additional series of experiences are necessary, plus an unprecedented activity by the vanguard socialist party to close the gap between "economics and politics".

Al Glotzer

THE "DEMOCRATIC INTERLUDE" AND
WORKING-CLASS LEADERSHIP

AS A RESULT OF THE PRESENT WAR, the Continent will be an even more devastated area: millions of dead, more millions crippled, a starved population, a new generation growing up on a starvation diet. Mass unemployment on an even larger scale than in the last post-war is more than likely. A European capitalism exploited by Washington will drive the masses to seek a radical solution of its impossible economic and political existence.

Whatever the nature of the military victory in Europe, it is easy to see that the post-war period in Europe will *approximate* the 1918-19-20 post-war period of the First World War. We can say with certainty then that the post-war period will see no end of revolutionary situations and revolutionary upheavals in which the masses will seek in their own way and by their own methods to resolve the capitalist crisis. We will undoubtedly witness many efforts on the part of the European proletariat to take power, on a national or provincial basis. There will undoubtedly be many examples of a dual power: the reëstablishment of the bourgeois democratic régimes in some occupied countries and the concomitant rise of workers' committees, factory committees, on a broad scale, embracing large areas of given countries and millions of workers and peasants. All of this merely attests to the revolutionary character of the epoch in which we live. For the revolutionary Marxist, however, the acceptance of this objective development in Europe is not enough, for the objective developments in bourgeois society is only half the question, and not, under the circumstances, the most important half.

More important than the specific conjuncture is the state of the proletarian movement, its organization, its program, its *strategy* and *tactics*. In the last analysis, this is the decisive factor. The objective situation may be ever so revolutionary, but so long as the subjective factor, the organization of the proletariat as a class, and not merely economically organized, but the organization of the socialist vanguard and a mass revolutionary-socialist movement which has the support of the majority of the proletariat and the whole population, is absent, it is not possible to talk about an impending struggle for socialism, let alone its victory.

The post-war period of the Second World War, while it will objectively approximate that of the First World War, presents an entirely different picture from the point of view of the class organization of the European proletariat. During the last war and in the post-war period, the grave problem of the Marxist movement was *primarily* the crisis of leadership in the Second International and in the left-wing groups. The task of winning the majority of the people to socialism was always present, but this

---

Abridged from *New International*, August 1944, "Tasks of the present period: The decisive role of the party", by "Albert Gates" (Al Glotzer).

task existed coincident with an enormous world socialist movement and mass national parties in the important European countries.

The degeneration of the Second International resulted in the development and growth of revolutionary Marxist groups, splits and parties throughout Europe. *This meant that there was a continuity in the theory and practice of genuine Marxism.* These groups, under the leadership of Lenin, in maintaining the great traditions of the movement, and most important of all, maintaining in every conceivable way the struggle, made possible the instantaneous mobilization of the revolutionary cadres and the revolutionary proletariat into the ranks of the Third International. Moreover, the Russian Revolution was an immense factor for the reorganization of the revolutionary movement. Consequently, the post-war period of 1919-20, irrespective of the fact that the proletariat in many important countries experienced defeat in their efforts to take power, witnessed a genuinely organized and purposeful struggle. The aforementioned defeats resulted, not from the existence of revolutionary parties and organizations, but from their weaknesses, from inexperience, from a lack of sufficient forces and from a failure to win the support of the majority of the people, an essential factor for victory.

Once the immediate post-war offensive of the working class ended, the tasks of the vanguard forces changed. The revolutionary international recognized after the defeats the need for a new policy, succinctly described as "winning the masses." *Here again the change was conscious, adopted by an organized movement to serve a certain end.* The whole revolutionary history of the Communist International is concentrated in those years and we shall refer to them elsewhere in this discussion.

The post-war period of the Second World War in Europe will unfold against the background of a destroyed workers' movement. Almost twenty years of Stalinism and more than ten years of Hitler have decapitated European labor. The existence of social democracy and Stalinism as organized factors is not something to be cheered. On the contrary, they are militating factors in the struggle to reconstitute the revolutionary movement in Europe. Both are linked to the bourgeoisie; both are active forces in defense of capitalism against the proletariat. There is yet no counteracting force on the Continent of sufficient strength, power or with the necessary foresight to understand what is now the main task in Europe.

There is no revolutionary party in any country in Europe, no substantial Marxist vanguard. This means that there is no force present which can educate the new layers of revolutionists which will undoubtedly arise. This means, too, that the task of clarification and reorganization is made more difficult, especially when it is understood what a welter of lies and miseducation has to be overcome. Even in the ranks of the Fourth Internationalist movement there is great confusion. The Cannonite Socialist Workers Party, for example, gives no consideration whatever to this, the most important question for Europe. It regards the revolutionary process and the struggle for power as something automatic and that is why its analysis of the European situation is so meaningless. It can apply to any period, twenty years ago, today, or twenty years hence. There is no sign whatever in its resolution on the European situation that it understands in the slightest what has happened to the European labor and revolutionary movement. Where there is a glimmer of the problem, it is stated in an offhand manner, as if it were of no importance. And this is of little wonder, for any organization which can regard Stalin's Red Army as an army of liberation, of socialist liberation at that, can hardly be expected to understand what the tasks in Europe are.

This attitude fortifies the new support given to concepts of spontaneity. The degeneration of the Second and Third Internationals, the weakness of the revolutionary groups, the crying need for a class solution to the capitalist crisis, all tend to strengthen the adherents of the theory of spontaneity in all its variety. Does this mean that the adherents of spontaneity are fully conscious that they espouse such a concept? Not necessarily. They may not even use the word. But the thought is there. They look upon Europe and say: capitalism is bankrupt; there is no solution to the capitalist crisis. Ergo, socialism will replace capitalism. The socialist revolution is the next stage of development in Europe. This is purely syllogistic reasoning. The basis for this attitude lies in an almost mystical certainty of the conscious *socialist* struggle for power on the part of an unorganized and leaderless working class.

Others understand that the post-war period in Europe will be accompanied by widespread class struggle, accompanied even by attempts to take power, and discuss the difficulties and prospects of that struggle. They speak of the "gestation of the European Revolution." In a general sense acknowledgment is made of the fact that *the party* will be necessary for a successful conclusion of that struggle. But even here, where recognition of the problem is present, it is not with a full conviction of what implications are involved.

I quote again from Lenin's attack on the Economists. If the quotation does not wholly apply to the present-day believers in spontaneity, it does in part. Moreover, it poses the whole question, in its proper light, of the relationship of the party to the struggle as a whole:

"Others, far removed from 'gradualness,' began to say: it is possible and necessary to 'bring about a political revolution,' but this is no reason whatever for building a strong organization of revolutionaries to train the proletariat in the steadfast and stubborn struggle. All we need do is to snatch up our old friend, the 'handy' wooden club. Speaking without metaphor it means — we must organize a general strike, or we must stimulate the 'spiritless' progress of the labor movement by means of 'excitative terror.' Both these tendencies, the opportunist and the 'revolutionary,' bow to the prevailing primitiveness; neither believes that it can be eliminated; neither understands our primary and most imperative practical task, namely, to establish an organization of revolutionaries capable of maintaining the energy, the stability and continuity of the political struggle".

This is for the old days! Let us agree that the struggles of the European working class today will not be merely economic struggles, but also political. Here again the political struggles that are inevitable in Europe are not automatically *socialist* struggles.

The state of decay of bourgeois society is so deep today, that the slightest economic struggle immediately becomes a political struggle; sharp economic struggles become political struggles of the greatest magnitude. But that is not enough. Again, it is necessary to give these intense political struggles a *socialist* character. This is what Lenin tried to teach the movement when he wrote:

*"The demand 'to give the economic struggle itself a political character'
most strikingly expresses* subservience *to* spontaneity *in the sphere of political activity. Very often the economic struggle* spontaneously *assumes a
political character, that is to say, without the injection of the 'revolutionary
bacilli of the intelligentsia,' without the intervention of the class-conscious
Social-Democrats. For example, the economic struggle of the British workers assumed a political character without the intervention of the Socialists.
The tasks of the Social-Democrats, however, are not exhausted by political
agitation in the economic field; their task is* to convert *trade union politics
into the Social-Democratic political struggle, to* utilize *the flashes of political consciousness which gleam in the minds of the workers during their
economic struggles for the purpose of* raising *them to the level of*
Social-Democratic *political consciousness"*.

I said in my first article that bourgeois production relations organize the
proletariat. This tendency, however, is contradicted first by the anarchy of
production and the general anarchy of bourgeois society, and secondly by
the severe dislocation of present-day declining capitalism. The only way
the proletariat can offset such disintegrating tendencies is by organization. In his *One Step Forward, Two Back*, Lenin wrote:

*"The proletariat has no other weapon in the fight for power except orga-
nization. Disorganized by the domination of anarchic competition in the
capitalist world, oppressed by forced labor for the capitalists, constantly
forced 'to the depths' of utter poverty, ignorance and degeneracy, the proletariat can become and inevitably will become an indomitable force only
because its intellectual unity created by the principles of Marxism is fortified by the material unity of organization which welds millions of toilers
into an army of the working class"*.

In all this discussion I have tried to show that spontaneity of the masses
is a fact, to one degree or another. But it is the kind of fact which produces
certain demands of the revolutionary party. Lenin did not deny the existence of spontaneity. What he tried to teach the movement was that spontaneity of itself could accomplish little; certainly it could not be the means
of taking power. He pointed out, however, that *"the spontaneity of the masses demands a mass consciousness from us Social-Democrats. The greater the
spontaneous uprising of the masses, the more widespread the movement
becomes, so much more rapidly grows the demand for greater consciousness
in the theoretical, political and organizational work of the social democracy."*

There is the whole relationship of spontaneity to the existing revolutionary party. The big danger in Europe today is that there will be many spontaneous movements of the workers, rebellions and putschist attempts.
But they will all be vanquished in the absence of strong revolutionary parties with correct theory, practice, strategy and tactics. Does this mean that
the existence of a revolutionary party is a guarantee against defeat? No,
but absence of the revolutionary party is a guarantee of certain defeat.
With a party it is possible to win. What has to be overcome in Europe is
the enormous gap between the inevitably rising revolutionary spirit of the
masses and the absence of revolutionary Marxist organization.

Let us approach the question from a somewhat different angle. The resolution of the Workers Party on the National Question in Europe
described the probable situation after a defeat of Germany in the following way:

"This first period after the overthrow of German rule will undoubtedly be the period of 'democratic illusions' to one extent or another, in one form or another. This is the clear lesson of the first 1917 revolution in Russia, the revolution in Germany of 1918, the Spanish Revolution of 1931. The power will, so to speak, lie in the streets. The masses will instinctively incline to take hold of it in its own name. Its difficulties will lie in the fact that it is just emerging from a period of non-organization, or only the most fragmentary organization. Organization is precisely what it needs for seizure and holding of power. The reformist and Stalinist organizations will of course not lead the proletariat to class power. In other words, some interval will undoubtedly elapse before a revolutionary party is properly organized and reaches the leadership of the organized proletariat".

What, exactly, does this mean? If it is true that the coming post-war period will witness enormous class battles, if the working class cannot hope to achieve a victory over the bourgeoisie without its organized party, and if it is impossible to build a party under the conditions of bourgeois dictatorship, as has been so abundantly demonstrated in the past twenty-five years, then the prospect of a "democratic interlude" in Europe should not only be recognized on the basis of the specific bourgeois relationship of forces, but ought to be planned for by the revolutionary Marxists, as favorable ground for the reëstablishment of the revolutionary party and the revolutionary international.

There is another aspect of this question of democracy which is equally as important as the fact that a "democratic interlude" will offer the opportunity for rebuilding the revolutionary movement. The chaos of bourgeois society has reached such a depth that democracy has become a luxury for it. The deep economic crisis, the political instability of the ruling classes, the permanence of the world social crisis secures the dictatorial and totalitarian tendencies of capitalism and makes the struggle for democracy an integral struggle for socialism. It is a vehicle by which the present small vanguard forces can build a mass movement. While the struggle for democracy in no way violates socialist principles and the struggle for socialism, it does clash with the most important interests of the bourgeoisie. The lesson in Italy is already clear. The American, British and Italian ruling classes and, of course, the Stalinists are doing everything in their power to prevent the establishment of genuinely democratic conditions in the country for fear of the consequent reëstablishment of the workers' organizations for the free workers' struggle. Conversely, the main force in the struggle for democracy in Italy is the working class, but this struggle cannot take place without the sharpest collisions with the bourgeoisie.

The problem there is how to link this struggle for democracy with the struggle for socialism. The link is the revolutionary organization and, consequently, the great weakness in Italy is the absence of proletarian organization. The weakness stands out because: "...the class struggle of the proletariat demands a concentrated propaganda, throwing light on the various stages of the fight, giving a single point of view, and directing the attention of the proletariat at each given moment to the definite tasks to be accomplished by the whole class". (Second Congress resolution of the Communist International on "The Role of the Party.")

Often in referring to the principles and experiences of the old Comintern we lose sight of the fact that its decisions and practices were based upon a given evaluation of bourgeois society and the prior or coincident existence of an organization in Europe, Asia and America, with a definite body of experiences. The old generation of Marxists knew that without a party there was no prospect of a victory of the working class; without a party there was no possibility of winning the masses. To win the masses meant the opportunity for a party to function in the day-to-day activities of the class, to provide leadership, to maintain closest relations with the masses, in order to prove by experience that it deserves the support of the working class. There is no other way to achieve the emancipation of humanity from capitalism.

It is, therefore, the height of sectarianism to discuss the prospects of a victorious struggle for power anywhere and everywhere in the absence of a single Marxist party in the world. It is just as if one would say: the smaller the revolutionary organization, the better the prospects for socialism; or, the total absence of revolutionary parties and class organizations guarantees the victory of socialism. To cite the fact that soviets, or workers' councils, arise spontaneously, is beside the point, because history has shown that soviets may be reactionary, i.e., under the influence and control of the bourgeoisie or their representatives. Soviets may and have existed without a party, but without a party their potential revolutionary and democratic force is limited or completely blocked. When the German Communist Labor Party (ultra leftists) proposed that, since the soviets were the historical form of proletarian rule, the party should dissolve itself into them, the Comintern rejected the proposal as "reactionary." It was reactionary because it sought the liquidation of the only force in bourgeois society that can bring about the preconditions for the development of the social order of socialism.

In *The Third International After Lenin*, Trotsky concerned himself with this very question, because before the complete degeneration of Stalinism had taken place, he had already observed impending the chaos in the developing crisis of leadership. Thus, he wrote:

"*If contradiction, in general, is the most important mainspring of progress, then the clear understanding of the contradiction between a general revolutionary maturity of the objective situation (despite ebbs and flows) and the immaturity of the international party of the proletariat ought now to constitute the mainspring for the forward movement of the Comintern, at least of its European section*". (Page 86.)

There are several points of interest here. First, the main essential question is posed. Secondly, it reveals that even with the existence of a world organization, the problem still existed of winning the conditions necessary for victory, i.e., the mere existence of the international parties did not automatically solve anything. What, in the main, was that problem? Trotsky continues:

"*When we looked forward at that time* [the first post-war period — A. G.] *to an immediate seizure of power by the proletariat, we reckoned that a revolutionary party* would mature rapidly in the fire of civil war. *But the two terms did not coincide. The revolutionary wave of the post-war period ebbed* before *the communist parties grew up and reached maturity in the struggle with the social democracy* [then having the majority support of the masses — A. G.] *so as to assume the leadership of the insurrection....* But it turned out that the determination of the leadership and the dissatisfaction of the masses do not suffice for victory. There must obtain a number of other conditions, above all, a close bond between the leadership and the masses and the confidence of the latter in the leadership. This condition was lacking at that time". (Pages 87f. Emphasis mine. — A. G.)

It becomes clear then why the Third Congress of the Comintern concerned itself, not with theory and principles, which had already been determined at the Second Congress, but with the questions of strategy and tactics. Had there been no Comintern, no revolutionary parties, it would have been impossible for such discussions to take place and yet have any concrete significance. The Third Congress therefore was really a gathering which dealt with the problems of building the International, working out the strategical and tactical line of the parties and preparing for the march "to power through a previous conquest of the masses." Lenin said at the congress that "the struggle for the masses is the struggle for power." There you have succinctly stated the correct relationship of the whole question which is so neglected, or completely forgotten, today.

To grasp even more thoroughly the meaning of the Third Congress, there is the dispute between Lenin and the ultra-leftists over the whole character of the struggle. In order to strengthen Bolshevik concepts, the resolution of the Third Congress emphasized the need to win "the majority." It stated:

"The Third Congress of the Communist International is proceeding to re-examine the questions of tactics under the circumstances that in a number of countries the situation has become acute in a revolutionary sense and that a number of Communist mass parties have been organized, none of which, however, have actually acquired the leadership of the majority of the working class in its genuinely revolutionary struggle".

Lenin led a most vigorous struggle against ultra-leftist and putschist concepts of the struggle for power, especially against the Italian representatives of this tendency! He said then, in 1921, not 1944:

"And they want to delete the words 'of the majority.' If we cannot agree about such simple things I fail to understand how we can work together and lead the proletariat to victory. That being so, it is not surprising that we cannot come to an agreement on the question of principles. Show me a party which is already leading the masses of the working class. It did not even occur to Terracini to quote an example.... He who fails to understand that in Europe... where nearly all the proletarians are organized — we must win over the majority of the working class — is lost to the Communist movement. If such a person has not yet learned this in the course of three years of a great revolution, he will never learn anything".

In the above is revealed the true Lenin, the revolutionist who could not think without having the masses in mind, who could not begin to conceive of a revolution without a party, and such a party without winning the majority of the masses. The whole early Comintern was of the same mind.

The Comintern, under the slogan, "To the Masses," and toward the "conquest of the majority," devised the tactic of the *united front* and adopted a series of *transitional demands* which could bridge the gap between the revolutionary party and the broad masses of the proletariat, peasantry and the middle class poor. It rejected Bukharin's mechanical concepts of the permanent revolution, his "mechanical understanding of the permanence of the revolutionary process."

In recapitulation we see the following situation in the capitalist world, i.e., the subjective situation. No revolutionary International, no revolutionary parties. At best there are revolutionary groupings. There are a body of principles and theories which guide these groupings. But there is as yet no adopted strategy or tactics applicable to concrete circumstances of the class struggle in the many countries of Europe, where the situation is most acute and where the prospects of a revolutionary resurgence may first occur. The absence of organization precludes the conditions which prevailed in the early years of the Comintern, the kind of decisions adopted by them. The main principles remain: build the revolutionary parties, win the majority of the working class and its allies. Without these there can be no serious discussion of a revolutionary victory.

Under the specific conditions of bourgeois society in the present period, the struggle for democracy is indispensable to the struggle for socialism, especially since the struggle for democracy is a struggle against present-day capitalist society and the decay which engenders indigenous tendencies of totalitarianism, becoming stronger the longer the social order exists. The working class needs a "democratic interlude" in order to recreate the socialist vanguard, to develop the struggle, and to guarantee a measure of success.

A whole new layer of revolutionaries is growing up. This new layer needs to be educated in the fundamentals of Marxism and in the principles of Lenin's and Trotsky's Comintern. And this requires a persistent and consistent struggle against any attempt to reintroduce into the movement those concepts which can only doom the working class to continued defeats and sterility. If such concepts gain credence and strength, the immediate future of the working class will indeed be black and dismal.

Herman Benson

NATIONAL LIBERATION AND FANTASY POLITICS

"Discussion on the National Question: National Liberation and Fantasy".

IN AN ARTICLE ENTITLED "Our Differences with the Three Theses" *(Fourth International,* December, 1942), Felix Morrow discusses the movement for national liberation in occupied Europe. Who the "our" refers to is not clear, but since this is the same Morrow who was the official defender of the line of the SWP on China we may assume it to be more or less an official defense or elaboration of the SWP on this question. At first glance the Morrow who confronts us here appears to be a new man. For China, he insisted that despite the fact that the war on its part is conducted in alliance with the imperialist war of the "democratic" camp by the bourgeois Chiang government, that war is a genuinely progressive war for national freedom. But how different is his approach to the European scene. No hint of his former "flexibility" is discernible. In reply to a group of European comrades who maintain that national liberation in Europe is a democratic demand deserving our support, Morrow, not without numerous distortions of their views, accuses them of working for the revival of the Third Republic in France, the Weimar Republic in Germany, of counterposing the "national movement to the workers' movement," and of committing a "nationalist deviation." It might appear that Morrow, who developed the opportunist line on China, has had a change of heart and is now the champion of a revolutionary policy for Europe as against nationalist deviators. Nothing could be more mistaken.

The opportunism of the Cannonite position on China consists in clinging to support of a war which in the past was a genuine war for independence but which is now part of the general imperialist war carried on by the United Nations camp. This is a social-patriotism concealed only by the fact that China formerly fought a real war for independence against Japan.

Morrow established a principle for himself in China: support to the war of a bourgeois régime in alliance with imperialism. He applies this principle because China is a semi-colonial country. But if he concedes that in Europe a genuine fight for national liberation exists, not under the leadership of revolutionary socialist elements he would be compelled to apply his principle to Europe as well.

Should the Norwegians, for example, succeed in overthrowing the domination of Hitler and permit the reëstablishment of a bourgeois régime which would continue a war in alliance with England and the United States, Morrow would be faced with an impossible difficulty. How could Morrow, who grants support to Chiang's war in alliance with imperialism, deny support to its counterpart in Europe? But such a policy for Europe would be clear and open social-patriotism and Morrow's entire article is permeated with the fear of facing the ultimate consequences, in Europe, of his line in China.

Morrow can extricate himself from this dilemma in one of two ways: 1) he can develop his China line for Europe and fall into a hopelessly pro-imperialist war line, or 2) since the development in real life of a progressive national struggle in Europe deals irreparable blows at his China position he can find refuge from life itself by falling back on principles eternally applicable "in this epoch." He chooses the latter as the lesser of the two evils. The opportunist Morrow finds refuge from his own opportunism

---

Abridged from *New International*, April 1943, by "Ben Hall" (Herman Benson). The "Three Theses" were written by German Trotskyists in exile, arguing that the workers' movement in Europe had been thrown back so that immediate politics must focus on democratic and national-liberation issues. The issue in dispute over China was whether to continue to support the Chinese national movement against Japan (as the SWP did) or to cease to do so because China's war had been clawed into the world war and the Chinese nationalists were now essentially only a subordinate part of the Allied side (as the WP argued). Until 1946 the US had a strong military presence, involving some hundreds of thousands of troops.

in the starry realms of sectarianism. Far from mitigating or nullifying the errors of his China line, Morrow's sectarian line for Europe reinforces them from another angle.

This article will concern itself not with Morrow's repeated and deliberate distortions of the Three Theses which he attacks but with outlining the essentially sectarian content of his whole treatment of the movement for national liberation in Europe.

Says Morrow: "The workers under the Nazi boot want national freedom. Good. The task is to explain to them that national freedom in this epoch is the task of the working class under the leadership of the Fourth International." This idea is unimpeachable as a general principle. *But it also applies to China* and for that matter everywhere else, and not only to the problem of national liberation but to all the important social problems "in this epoch." But in China, where this principle is equally valid, Morrow recognizes in addition the need to support what he considers a progressive, democratic, anti-imperialist struggle now not under the leadership of the Fourth International but of the Chinese bourgeoisie. In Europe, Morrow, confines himself to glittering universalities.

One might with equal validity proclaim to the Negro masses of the United States: "Full social, political and economic equality for the Negroes in this epoch is the task of the working class under the leadership of the Fourth International." But this hardly begins to define our relations to the Negro masses who fight today for equal rights under quite a different leadership.

What is at stake is the recognition of the progressive character of struggles which do not take place under your own socialist banner but which nevertheless in reality further the development of the socialist revolution itself. This is precisely what is occurring in occupied Europe today and exactly what Morrow contrives to dodge and to confuse throughout his whole article. Nowhere does he indicate the possibility of support to a not-yet-socialist struggle for national liberation in occupied Europe.

It is this attempt to substitute general principles applicable to "this epoch" for relations with a living mass movement that constitutes the hallmark of sectarianism.

Given a correct estimation of the fight for national liberation it becomes possible for revolutionists to lead it into a fight against not only the foreign oppressor but the native bourgeoisie as well. Morrow is forced to give a twist to this idea which transforms it into something entirely different and in fact altogether false.

"What is really new in the occupied countries is that the national sentiment of the workers and peasants is sharpening their class bitterness against the collaborating bourgeoisie. National oppression has given a new edge to the class struggle. National sentiment, hitherto serving only the bourgeoisie, today can be used *against* the bourgeoisie of the occupied countries. That is what is new".* (Emphasis in original.)

Morrow translates "bitterness" against the collaborating bourgeoisie into class-conscious opposition to the bourgeoisie as a whole. The class struggle has become more intense against the entire bourgeoisie as a class because a section of it collaborates with the Nazis. What this neglects is the fact that national oppression makes the masses, including the workers, prey to bourgeois elements of the de Gaulle variety and above all especially vulnerable to the bourgeois democracy of the labor reformists.

In pre-war France, the socialist proletariat was led into the People's Front of collaboration with the bourgeoisie by its socialist and communist leadership. The working class tolerated this policy only because unity with the bourgeois politicians appeared necessary to defend the workers and their organizations from fascism inside France and from Hitler on its borders. This enemy, fear of whom facilitated class unity, is now the master of all of France, both as a fascist ruler and a foreign oppressor. Morrow contends that this national oppression itself intensifies the class struggle. What is this but a pale reflection of the Stalinist pre-Hitler idea of "After Hitler come we." By a similar process of reasoning, the class struggle in Germany received a "new edge" after Hitler's rise to power, when it became clear that the bourgeoisie preferred fascism and that the socialists and communists could not fight it.

But if the class struggle has become more intense, and if the main content of our slogan is "under the leadership of the Fourth International," then there is really nothing new. There is no new element which in any way modifies the road taken by revolutionists in their approach to the masses. Morrow, uncomfortable in the Europe of 1943, seeks a formula which would miraculously return him to the pre-war days when his

China line had no application outside of Asia.

But there is something manifestly new. Before the war, the present struggle of the peoples of the occupied countries for national freedom did not exist. Now it does. Before the war the fight in all these countries was directly and first of all against the native bourgeoisie. Now, in order to carry on an organized, centralized and systematic struggle on a nationwide basis against the native bourgeoisie, the peoples of the occupied countries must get rid of the foreign oppressor. In this respect, the advanced peoples of occupied Europe are in the same position as the colonial peoples of Asia and their movement, like the latter, deserves our support.

Morrow has devised the theory of the "new edge to the class struggle" to escape the application of his China line to the European stage. In China, national oppression has led to a war for the democratic principle of self-determination which continues today, he maintains. Once he admits that this is the case in occupied Europe, the necessity of supporting bourgeois régimes in alliance with the imperialists inexorably follows.

The "Three Theses" have this merit: they emphasize the democratic nature of the fight for national independence in Europe. Morrow refuses to understand them, accusing their proponents of favoring the reëstablishment of the Weimar Republic in Germany and the Third Republic in France; similarly a confirmed sectarian might accuse us of favoring the establishment of a capitalist régime in Spain because we supported the war against Franco. This is not because the Theses are unclear on this point or because Morrow read them hastily. Morrow cannot permit himself to understand this point and cannot honestly reply to it because his own line on the democratic struggle for freedom as developed for China leads to social-patriotism. Does Morrow contend that the movement among the people of occupied Europe for national liberation is a conscious and direct struggle for socialism? We seek in vain for an answer to this question. Unwilling to characterize the movement as socialist and unable to characterize it as democratic, he seeks a new, ambiguous formula. It is a "workers' movement." But this cannot save Morrow. The vague phrase, "workers' movement," clearly indicates the class composition of the chief organizations and groups and individuals participating in the fight for national liberation but it says nothing about the immediate and direct aims of the struggle, nothing about its political character. A "workers' movement," which is based first of all on the struggle for national independence, is a movement for democratic rights — and the proletarian struggle is going through a democratic phase.

Says Morrow: "In discussions, the authors of the Three Theses have indicated that they consider national liberation as an immediate agitation slogan and the Socialist Unite States of Europe as a propaganda slogan, i.e., not suitable for immediate agitation. Their separation of the two slogans must be characterized as a nationalist deviation." Here again Morrow refuses to recognize any distinction between a democratic slogan — national freedom, and a socialist slogan — Socialist United States of Europe.

Presumably Morrow equates these two slogans because just as "national freedom in this epoch is the task of the working class under the leadership of the Fourth International", so national liberation is impossible without a Socialist United States of Europe.

This is a principle absolutely valid "in this epoch." In the long run, unless the revolutionary masses go over from the fight for national independence to a Socialist United States of Europe, it will be impossible for them to solve their pressing economic, social, and political problems. Imperialism persisting, the further intensification of national oppression is guaranteed.

But despite this general principle, the peoples of Europe fight now for national liberation. This is a just demand and moreover its realization is a prerequisite to the voluntary federation of the peoples as against the forcible unification by Hitler. This fight for national independence is the ideal of hundreds of thousands and millions. In that sense the demand for national independence is an immediate agitational slogan. The demand for a Socialist United States of Europe is the program of an infinitesimally tiny minority and a propaganda slogan.

Morrow *cannot* separate these two slogans. Just as he finds it impossible to distinguish between a socialist and a democratic demand, he finds it impossible to recognize the possibility of a struggle by masses striving for national liberation, not yet raising a socialist banner. Like all such movements it runs the danger of becoming a disciplined tool of the Allied war machine. But Morrow's China line prevents him from recognizing a genuine movement for liberation from one which has been subordinated to the imperialist war. Fearing to support the latter, he refuses to conceive of support for the former.

'We insist," he says, "that these two slogans must go together, otherwise the slogan of national liberation degenerates into mere bourgeois nationalism in the service of one of the imperialist camps." If we translate this idea into the truth it would read as follows and demonstrate the crux of Morrow's difficulty: "My China position supports a non-socialist, non-proletarian war for national liberation in alliance with imperialism. In Europe such a position would openly degenerate into mere bourgeois nationalism in the service of imperialism. To save myself, I 'insist' upon the possibility of and recognize only a socialist war for national freedom in Europe."

Morrow argues: "Only the working class can free the country by proletarian revolution." Had Morrow deliberately set out to confound and confuse he could never have discovered more suitable formulations on every point. The above is a typical example. Ordinarily the phrase "proletarian revolution" is quite clear and simple. We mean the *socialist* revolution. But the phrase may contain serious ambiguities.

There have been many proletarian revolutions in the last quarter of a century which did not solve the problems of national freedom, democracy, or any of the other major social problems of "this epoch." They were revolutions led by and dominated by the proletarian class and parties of the working class. But these proletarian revolutions stopped short of the socialist revolution, confined themselves within the framework of bourgeois democracy and consequently suffered ultimate defeat. Despite their failure to go to the end, great victories were achieved which made possible a speedy transition to the socialist revolution. Only in Russia did there prove to be a tested revolutionary party which could take advantage of such a proletarian revolution and lead it to the socialist revolution. The only kind of proletarian revolution which can really achieve lasting national liberation, which can free a nation economically and politically from imperialism, which can establish a genuine democratic régime and prevent the restoration of capitalist rule is a *socialist* proletarian revolution which spreads internationally to the powerful, advanced, industrialized nations. The socialist revolution aims at the complete destruction of the power and influence of the bourgeoisie and the expropriation of the industries under their control.

But between now and the time when such a proletarian, socialist revolution succeeds, many struggles and revolutions can and will take place which are not under the leadership of revolutionary socialist parties and revolutionary socialist slogans. One such struggle is the movement for liberation in occupied Europe which leads in the direction of a revolution which will facilitate the socialist revolution.

The phrase "proletarian revolution" is thus able to slur together two different, though closely related, aspects of the working class struggle. It is this ambiguity which makes the phrase ideally suited to Morrow, who is concerned above all with glossing over the democratic nature of the liberation struggle.

The difference between the *socialist* movement and the movement for national liberation which can also be carried on by revolutionary proletarian methods is that the former is directed toward the seizure of power by the proletariat for the purpose of expropriating the native bourgeoisie, while the latter sets as its first goal the ousting of the foreign oppressor as the precondition for organizing the socialist struggle of the masses on a systematic and centralized basis. Possible within the limits of still existing bourgeois property relations, the fight for national freedom is a *democratic* movement.

In order to achieve the ousting of Hitler the masses must be ready to struggle directly against their own collaborating bourgeoisie and the forces of Hitler occupation. In order to make the socialist revolution, the masses must be prepared to break with their own "democratic" bourgeoisie and its labor agents, to fight against the counterrevolutionary Stalinist régime which stands ready as the executioner of the Eastern European socialist revolution, and above all with the international bourgeoisie which as always stands ready with its tremendous economic and military resources to intervene in any one of the national sectors of its battlefront.

When Henry Wallace warns that if the Soviet Union agitates again for world communism there will be another war, he is really threatening war against all socialist revolutions; and when he promises food to those nations which string along with the Anglo-American camp, he promises blockade to its socialist enemies.

It is the power of the bourgeoisie on an international scale which makes it possible that the movement for national liberation will stop short of its logical and ultimate goal, the socialist revolution. The real alternative presented by international imperialism to the revolutionary people of Europe will be: "Restrain yourselves to a 'normal,' ordinary bourgeois government and we offer you economic assistance, food and temporary, benevolent neutrality. But go forward to a socialist revolution and we promise you economic blockade and military intervention." All kinds of concessions and compromises with capitalism and imperialism are possible provided the peoples "restrain" themselves and are "realistic." And it is to this realism and restraint that all the bourgeois democrats, reformists and Stalinists are dedicating themselves. These compromises are designed to withdraw the fruits of victory from the masses piecemeal until a firm basis for the bourgeois *status quo* is restored.

The thwarting of these "realistic" plans and the possibility of transforming the rising of the people for national liberation into an international socialist revolution on an all-European scale depends directly upon how rapidly the revolutionary, socialist proletarian party is organized and extended and obtains support from the masses. But this in turn is just as directly dependent upon the recognition by revolutionists of partial, progressive struggles which lead in their direction.

But all this is lost on Morrow. In his world, all is clearly black and white. All the reactionaries and imperialists line up clearly on one side and the revolutionary proletarians under the banner of the Fourth International line up on the other — and thus national liberation will be won. He must fear that if he recognized life with all its possible cruel compromises and betrayals, he would turn as opportunistic in Europe as he is already in China.

Leon Trotsky

WHAT IS A REVOLUTIONARY SITUATION?

FOR AN ANALYSIS OF A SITUATION from a revolutionary point of view, it is necessary to distinguish between the economic and social prerequisites for a revolutionary
situation and the revolutionary situation itself.

The economic and social prerequisites for a revolutionary situation take hold, generally speaking, when the productive powers of the country are declining; when the specific weight of a capitalist country on the world market is systematically lessened and
the incomes of the classes are likewise systematically reduced; when unemployment
is not merely the result of a conjunctural fluctuation but a permanent social evil with
a tendency to increase. This characterizes the situation in England completely, and we
can say that the economic and social prerequisites for a revolutionary situation exist
and are daily becoming more and more acute. But we must not forget that we define
a revolutionary situation politically, not only sociologically, and this includes the subjective factor. And the subjective factor is not only the question of the party of the proletariat. It is a question of the consciousness of all the classes, mainly of course of the
proletariat and its party.

A revolutionary situation, however, begins only when the economic and social prerequisites for a revolution produce abrupt changes in the consciousness of society and
its different classes. What changes?

(a) For our analysis we must distinguish the three social classes: the capitalist, the
middle class or petty bourgeoisie, the proletariat. The required changes in mentality
of these classes are very different for each of them.

(b) The British proletariat, far better than all the theoreticians, knows very well that
the economic situation is very acute. But the revolutionary situation unfolds only
when the proletariat begins to search for a way out, not on the basis of the old society,
but along the path of a revolutionary insurrection against the existing order. This is
the most important subjective condition for a revolutionary situation. The intensity of
the revolutionary feelings of the masses is one of the most important indications of the
maturity of the revolutionary situation.

(c) But a revolutionary situation is one which must in the next period permit the proletariat to become the ruling power of society, and that depends to some extent,
although less in England than in other countries, on the political thinking and mood
of the middle class: its loss of confidence in all the traditional parties (including the
Labour Party, a reformist, that is, a conservative party), and its hope in a radical, revolutionary change in society (and not a counter-revolutionary change, namely, a fascist).

(d) The changes in the mood both of the proletariat and the middle class correspond
and develop parallel to the changes in mood of the ruling class when it sees that it is
unable to save its system, loses confidence in itself, begins to disintegrate, splits into
factions and cliques.

At what point in these processes the revolutionary situation is totally ripe cannot be
known in advance or indicated mathematically. The revolutionary party can establish
that fact only through struggle; through the growth of its forces and influence on the
masses, on the peasants and the petty bourgeoisie of the cities, etc.; and by the weakening of the resistance of the ruling classes.

Economic development of society is a very gradual process, measured by centuries
and decades. But when economic conditions are radically altered, the delayed psychological response can quickly appear. Whether quickly or slowly, such changes must
inevitably affect the mood of the classes. Only then do we have a revolutionary situa-

From *The Militant*, December 19, 1931. Written by Trotsky after a discussion with Al Glotzer
about draft theses written by some revolutionaries in Britain.

tion.

In political terms this means: (a) That the proletariat must lose confidence not only in the Conservatives and Liberals, but also in the Labour Party. It must concentrate its will and its courage on revolutionary aims and methods.

(b) That the middle class must lose confidence in the big bourgeoisie, the lords, and turn its eyes to the revolutionary proletariat.

(c) That the propertied classes, the ruling cliques, rejected by the masses, lose confidence in themselves.

These attitudes will inevitably develop; but they do not exist today. They may develop in a short period of time, because of the acute crisis. They may develop in two or three years, even in a year. But today this remains a perspective, not a fact. We must base our policy on the facts of today, not those of tomorrow.

The political prerequisites for a revolutionary situation are developing simultaneously and more or less parallel, but this does not mean that they will all mature at the same moment — this is the danger that lies ahead. In the ripening political conditions, the most immature is the revolutionary party of the proletariat. It is not excluded that the general revolutionary transformation of the proletariat and the middle class and the political disintegration of the ruling class will develop more quickly than the maturing of the Communist Party. This means that a genuine revolutionary situation could develop without an adequate revolutionary party — but this is not inevitable. We cannot make an exact prediction, but it is not merely a question of a prediction. It is a question of our own activity.

9. FROM "ORTHODOXY" TO MILLENARIANISM II: THE RED ARMY AND STALINISM AS AGENTS OF SOCIALIST ADVANCE

The perspective of an almost-automatic revolutionary workers' upsurge and socialist victory at the end of World War 2 was nurtured, for the "orthodox", by the notion that the Russian armies were — at some deeper level than the visible reality of their brutality in crushing workers' and popular movements, which the "orthodox" Trotskyists knew about and condemned — agents of socialist advance. Repeatedly they described Stalin's army as "Trotsky's Red Army" — as if there were some mysterious ether in history, immune to the Stalinist purges which had destroyed mere human beings, able to transmit a revolutionary essence from 1917-21 forward to Moscow's military apparatus of the 1940s. Later this vision of Stalinist forces serving a process of World Revolution, despite themselves and despite the working class, would become the leitmotif of "official" Trotskyism. It would continue for forty years — until 1989, when the "accumulated conquests" of almost half a century of "rise of World Revolution" would be destroyed almost overnight by popular mobilisations, with the approbation and active participation of the working class.

"TROTSKY'S RED ARMY"

The Militant, August 15, 1942

Trotsky's Program Is The Banner of Socialist Victory

THE MILITANT

Trotsky Memorial Issue
AUTO MILITANTS PRESERVE
UNION DEMOCRACY
See page 2

PUBLISHED IN THE INTERESTS OF THE WORKING PEOPLE

NEW YORK, N. Y., SATURDAY, AUGUST 15, 1942 — FIVE (5) CENTS

TROTSKY'S WORKS LIVE ON IN HEROIC RED ARMY

Lewis Coser

THE POLICY OF "IF"

THE FOLLOWING CONSIDERATIONS are prompted by reports we
have received from the French Trotskyists with regard to their attitude
toward Stalinism and by a document of a French Trotskyist organization
which is contained in the March issue of the *Fourth International*. They
have been prompted by the conviction that a continuation of its present
attitude to Stalinism and the Soviet Union will doom the Trotskyist group
of France.

After declaring that the policy of the Communist Party has lost all working class character, the French comrades in the above mentioned document proceed: "Under conditions of illegality, the apparatus of the
Communist Party cannot directly control the rank and file groups. Thus
great possibilities for united action are open to us. *The common platform
for them and for us is the defense of the Soviet Union. Our common goal is
the proletarian revolution.* The unity of action will enable us to exercise a
friendly criticism and to detach the Communist workers from Stalinism"
(emphasis mine — E). These few lines contain an almost incredible
amount of confusion and denote a political blindness of the most dangerous sort. First we have the time-worn explanation of the "sane" membership and the "bad" leaders; the leadership and policy of the CP has lost its
working class character but the members fight for the "proletarian revolution."

This is an example of a scholastic approach, very typical of a certain kind
of political thinking in a period of decadence in Marxian thought. No
analysis is given of what are the real motives and reasons behind the attitude and thinking of members of the Communist Parties. No attempt is
made to clarify the changes which have occurred in the political motives
and the thinking of the rank and file members. This whole matter is dismissed by the formula: the good members and the bad leaders. It is, of
course, obvious that the aims and ideas of the leadership and members of
the CP may not coincide, but if it were true that the membership of the
CP stands for the proletarian revolution I cannot see why the founding of
a separate party was held necessary, years ago. The policy of working from
within would still be the only correct and workable one. But is this really
true? For example, do the average rank and file members have the same
ideas on the proletarian dictatorship that we do? We deny this most
emphatically.

"Politics is the art of the concrete," Lenin liked to say. But for many of
the would-be "Leninists" politics has become the art of the abstract. Not
the living reality is analyzed, but formulae are substituted for analysis.
Webster defines scholasticism as "close adherence to traditional teachings
and methods prescribed by schools and sects." And, indeed, no better definition could be found for this type of scholasticism prevalent among many

Abridged from *New International*, April 1942 by "Europacus" (Lewis Coser).

Marxists in our time. The "variable," in their explanation, is constituted by the different turns of Stalinist policy, whereas the "constant" is furnished by a repetitious roundelay about the sanity of the rank and file. But, has it not occurred to them that in fifteen years of undisputed reign of Stalinist theory inside the Communist movement, the basic thinking of the rank and file members also must have been heavily influenced? Has it not occurred to them that such a phenomenon is often observed in history (e.g., church, etc.)?

Fifteen years of Stalinist theory and practise have profoundly influenced the mentality of the average member of the Stalinist party. His ideas about socialism have been completely distorted by the example of the Soviet Union, his conception of proletarian morals has been fundamentally influenced by what is going on there, above all, the concepts socialism and democracy have been completely disassociated in his mind in these years. He has been led to imagine that the proletarian revolution is a product of a concerted drive by some leaders who conquer power and hold it. His concept of revolution is not that of spontaneous revolutionary activity of the masses but that of a "revolutionary" shepherd driving his herd where he considers it best and most suitable.

Does all this mean that we are in principle against a united front with local organizations of the Stalinists? Not at all. Just as we were for a united front policy with the social democracy in Germany before the Nazis came to power, so we are for united front actions in principle with Stalinist workers. It is impossible to decide from here whether or not this is warranted in the given concrete situation. But the decisive point is: do we make a united front with organizations, whose leadership we characterize as counter-revolutionary, on the basis of defending principles or in a general defense of the working class. There is a gulf between the two. Of course, we can make a united front against the rising cost of life, for better pay, for a common defense against the Nazified French police, against the Gestapo and for many other practical objectives. The contacts established in these common actions can then be utilized to make clear what is, and to fight for Marxian socialism as opposed to Stalinism. But what the French comrades propose is a quite different form of united front based presumably on common principles. Such a united front can only lead to self-destruction of the group itself, because its *raison de vivre* is to preserve certain principles of socialism which are or should be the exact opposite of principles fostered by the Stalintern.

The struggle inside the workers' movement should be confined to a dispute over "totalitarian" or "democratic" concepts of the proletarian revolution: are you for a workers' state which is based on democratic soviets as the basis of the proletarian power, or are you for a one-party system, with a bureaucratic apparatus controlling the destiny of the country in the name of the proletariat. Are you for a dictatorship from above, or from below? *Hic Rhodos hic salta.* This is the crucial question of the times to come. The crime of Stalin is not that he failed to do this or that; *his crime is anti-socialism.* The systematic deformation of the fundamental ideas of socialism, above all, is why we reproach Stalinism. What has to be restated as the root of revolutionary theory is the fact that there can be no socialism without democracy, that five-year plans of themselves have nothing in common with socialism. This is the message the young socialist revolutionaries must bring to the workers of Europe. Can this be achieved by "friendly criticism," by stating that, in fact, there is the common ground of the "proletarian dictatorship" upon which we both stand?

Only two explanations can be found for such an unprincipled attitude. One, either these comrades themselves do not clearly visualize the foregoing fundamental difference and still think in the manner of the by-gone days on the "right" or "left" deviations of Stalin. Or, two, while realizing this, they believe they are making a very "clever" strategical move. But strategical moves which abandon the very principles of our existence are criminal, especially when they are for the sake of "not hurting feelings." There are certainly many communists, especially among the younger generation, who are not by any means lost to the cause of the socialist revolution, but they can be won only by a clear-cut criticism, by a merciless pounding at the very heart of the counter-revolutionary theories of Stalinism. In periods of decline and defeat like the present, what is needed most is a clear vision of principles and a relentless fight for the preservation of the idea of democratic socialism. With the mounting tide of alien and hostile ideologies, it is urgently needed to state and restate them, not to regard them as matters which are to be taken for granted.

What is further required today is the understanding that Stalinism is not an ideological trend within the working class movement itself, but is really an ideology of an oppressor. To make this clear among the most advanced sections of the proletariat is one of the main tasks of the revolutionaries in Europe. It is a tragic misconception of their role if these revolutionaries think that they must concentrate on the CP, on gaining influence among this or that isolated group of communists. They continue to act as though there were still a powerfully established workers' movement, of which they are one tendency. They overlook the consequences of the great defeats of the European working class in the last ten years. It is necessary to understand first that what is needed in this dark hour is a constant restatement of the ideas of the *Communist Manifesto*, a restatement of the principles of socialism as the autonomous movement of the proletariat. Once that is understood the tactical question can be resolved.

Most of the theoretical material which is now produced by these people might come under the heading: the policy of "if." *If* there were a class-conscious proletarian movement, it must take this or that stand on concrete questions. They put the end at the beginning and try to write an "April Thesis" for a Bolshevik Party which does not exist. Such theories are bound to be entirely without value for the very simple reason that if there existed a movement of the kind they speak about, then the objective situation would be altered and the tactical problems would again be different. A small revolutionary socialist group which does not represent a real mass movement should not split hairs about this or that hypothetical turn in their tactical approach to a movement which is absolutely outside their reach. They ought to concentrate on the restatement and elaboration of the broad lines of socialist thought, on the propaganda for the socialist aim among the most advanced layers of the proletariat.

Max Shachtman

WAS STALIN'S ARMY "RED"?

THERE SEEMS TO be no end to the nonsense, and the downright fraud, that is written about Russia and her army in the war. When these scribblings appear in the capitalist or the "liberal" press, it is not very surprising. The writers and editors are either sublimely ignorant of what Russia really is and really is doing and aiming to do, or else they do know but will not say, because to tell the truth about Russia would help dispel some of the myths they have carefully created about the war in general and the so-called United Nations in particular.

What is not so easy to understand is nonsense — complete and very dangerous nonsense — about Russia when it is written in a paper that calls itself Trotskyist. For Trotskyism — that is, the consistent program of revolutionary, socialist internationalism, to which we firmly adhere — is the irreconcilable enemy of Stalinism, simply because working-class socialism is utterly incompatible with totalitarian tyranny.

In the report of a speech made in New York on "The Class Meaning of the Soviet Victories" by Felix Morrow, the February 27 issue of *The Militant* says: "The stranglehold of the Soviet bureaucracy, Morrow stated, has progressively weakened with every new Red Army victory and its consequent rise of morale among the Soviet masses. The Red Army is fighting for a socialist Europe as well as a socialist Russia, he declared, and they will never submit to any underhanded deal to preserve capitalism in Europe for the benefit of the very same imperialist powers that attempted to overthrow the October, 1917, Revolution".

It would, we suppose, be possible to compress into a few lines even more errors than are contained in the seventy words of the above quotation. But that would require a supreme effort, exerted by the organized collaboration of more than one person. To point out the errors, however, requires very little effort.

"The stranglehold of the Stalin bureaucracy has progressively weakened with every Red Army victory". Where, when, how? We are careful readers of *The Militant*, and we look through more than one other paper. Nowhere, thus far, not even in the pages of *The Militant*, have we read of a single important (or, for that matter, unimportant) fact to support this absurd contention. A weakening of the stranglehold of the bureaucracy would manifest itself in any number of concrete ways: sharp divisions in the upper circles, concessions of one kind or another to the masses, a moderation of the terror régime, increased independent class activity of the workers, etc. Will such things, especially the last-named, take place? Whoever understands the real situation in Russia is certain that they will. But as yet, there is no sign, no evidence, for Morrow's assertion.

What is more important is the radically wrong linking of the weakening of the bureaucracy with the victories of the army. In general, a totalitarian régime is weakened in wartime when it suffers military setbacks. For example, there is objective evidence that such was the case in Russia in the period when the army was standing still or losing ground in the first war with Finland (John Scott's book on Russia makes interesting reading in this regard). To speak now, especially now, of a weakening of the bureaucracy's stranglehold on the country and its people is, at the very best, wishful thinking. More simply, Morrow is talking up a spout.

This applies essentially to his words about the "consequent rise of morale among the Soviet masses". What, pray, is the evidence for this statement? If by "morale" Morrow is referring in general to the readiness of the masses to fight, to make sacrifices, then there is at least some evidence to warrant making the statement. But substantially the same thing could be said about the "morale" of the Germans and the Japanese, for instance. Didn't their morale hold up, and rise, with the big victories of their armies?

From *Labor Action*, March 15, 1943, "What is the Trotskyist position on Stalinism? The Victories of the 'Red' Army and the Struggle for Socialism".

And isn't it still pretty high, according to most reports? What does this fact, by itself, prove about Russia that it does not prove about Germany or Japan?

But Morrow spoke on "The Class Meaning of the Soviet Victories". If so, he should have dealt with the class morale of the Russian workers. If that is what he had in mind, his second statement falls into the same category as the first: nonsense. There is no evidence — again we emphasize, as yet — of any rise in the class morale of the Russian workers. Such a rise would show itself in the development of a class under-standing of (and therefore opposition to) the Kremlin's alliance with imperialism; in the development of organized opposition, however primitive, to the counter-revolutionary régime; in the development of an independent class movement, of a socialist consciousness, of internationalist spirit. That will come, we are utterly convinced. But where is there a single sign of it now? We, and others, would be obliged for a little information on this score. Until we get it, we must continue to say that Morrow's lips are still glued to a spout.

"The Red Army is fighting for a socialist Europe as well as a socialist Russia". What a gift he has for breath-taking, sweeping phrases! Not only is the "Red" Army fighting for a socialist Russia (which does not exist except in the lying propaganda of the Kremlin) but also (you really must believe this, for Morrow says so himself) for a socialist Europe. With all deference to the delicate eardrums of our readers, we say again: Nonsense! But this time, especially dangerous nonsense.

In the first place, there is no such thing as a Red Army. It once existed. It was orga-nized by Trotsky and the Bolsheviks. It was the army of the workers, of the people, of the socialist revolution. That is the spirit in which it was trained; that is the spirit that was drilled into every member of it, from commandant to raw rookie. That is the spirit in which it won its really great victories against the domestic and international counter-revolution. But Stalinism destroyed that army! Hasn't Morrow heard? If he hasn't "read it in the papers" in the last dozen years, he can find the whole story told and analyzed in Trotsky's writings.

What is "Red" (that is, socialist, internationalist, democratic) in the Russian army today? It would be interesting to know the answer. We disagreed with Trotsky on the question of the "defense of the Soviet Union" and on whether Russia today is a work-ers' state. But one thing we learned from him and we haven't unlearned it, namely: the Stalinist army is the army of the Bonapartist counter-revolution. Does Morrow get this? — the army of Bonapartist counter-revolution, not the army of socialism! It is controlled by the Bonapartist counter-revolution which is in power in the country; it is directed by it; it has been imbued with the poison of Stalinist chauvinism and Great-Russian nationalism; its program is the program of the counter-revolutionary bureau-cracy; its Praetorian "colonels" and "generals" and "marshals" (and its "orders of St George") differ in no important respect from their opposite numbers in the armies of capitalism; its discipline differs from that of a regular imperialist army like one egg from another. These are the truths that Trotsky taught. What Morrow says is, at the best, apologetics for Stalinism.

If it is "fighting for a socialist Europe as well as a socialist Russia", that is welcome news. But that would be a little more than just welcome news, it would be a miracle — and we don't believe in miracles. What is undoubtedly true is that there are many workers in the ranks of the Russian army who want socialism as much as they do not want Stalinism, who are revolted by the rule, the leadership, the aims of Stalinism because they are socialist internationalists, who hate capitalism, chauvinism and slavery of all kinds and who want freedom not only for the Russian masses, but also for all the people of Europe and the rest of the world. But how in the name of all that makes sense does this make the Stalinist army a Red Army, "fighting for a socialist Europe as well as a socialist Russia"? There are hundreds and thousands of workers in the British army who hate fascism, who hate imperialism and imperialist oppres-sion, who want an end of their own ruling class and of capitalism, who want a social-ist society for themselves and their brothers throughout the world. Does this indu-bitable fact make the British army an army of democracy? Does this indubitable fact make it possible to say that the British army "is fighting for a democratic (or social-ist) Europe as well as a democratic (or socialist) Britain"?

The British masses will really be fighting for a democratic and even socialist Britain

415

and Europe when they have first broken the control and fetters of imperialism in their own country, and established their control over the country, over the state, the government and the army. The Russian masses will really be fighting for a socialist Russia and Europe when they have first destroyed the rule of bureaucratic totalitarianism, rid themselves of the poison of Stalinist chauvinism, and taken control of the country, of the state, the government and the army. Not before! To disseminate the idea that the Stalinist army is fighting for a "socialist Europe as well as a socialist Russia" is to disseminate the most vicious pro-Stalinist propaganda, and thereby help destroy the prospects of a truly socialist Russia and Europe.

Morrow evidently does not know that the rule of Stalinism is the rule of slavery. Morrow evidently does not read *The Militant*, which so rightly said not long ago that Russia is a prison to which the workers are condemned for life. Morrow evidently does not read Trotsky, who wrote that the victory of the "Red" Army in Poland (which it divided with the Hitlerite pirates in 1939) meant the subjugation of the "liberated" masses to Stalinist slavery. Or if he did read it, it meant as little to him as the brash phrases he flings about with such abandon. A person who writes about Russia like Morrow deserves any name you want — apologist for the expansion of Stalinist slavery, for example — but not the name of revolutionary socialist. Precisely because of the dangerous illusions created among some workers here and in Europe by the "victories of the Red Army", the revolutionary socialist should and will emphasize: The extension of Stalinist rule means the extension of a new slavery. Call it bureaucratic collectivism, as we do, or "degenerated, counter-revolutionary workers' state", as Trotsky did, it is nevertheless a totalitarian slavery that Stalinist rule represents, a slave-master oppression which crushes everything that is noble, progressive, democratic, socialist and internationalist in the working class that comes under its heel.

The revolutionary socialist will emphasize: Socialism is the only hope of the world, and of the workers in particular. Be irreconcilable toward imperialism, be it in the form of fascism or "democracy". But be no less irreconcilable to Stalinism. Its maintenance or extension means a terrible setback to the inevitable socialist revolution, and not an aid to it. Neither the Stalinist bureaucracy nor its army will bring you socialism, or promote it by so much as a hair's breadth. The emancipation of the working class is the task of the working class itself, and there is not and cannot be a substitute for it. Whoever teaches differently is either an outright enemy of socialism, or a well-meaning obstacle in its path.

416

II

THE EX-SOCIALIST Max Eastman writes an article in *Readers' Digest* containing emphatic assurances of his desire for a Russian victory and for American collaboration with Stalin. But, as he suggests by the title of his article, "To Collaborate Successfully — We Must Face the Facts About Russia." Eastman is now a one hundred per cent imperialist patriot, but also an anti-Stalinist. We have nothing in common with his approach to the problem, with the purposes of his article, or with his political conclusions. That is not the point, however. The point is that on the whole the facts he gives about the régime and the vast concentration camp into which it has converted Russia, are commonplaces to the Marxist press and to informed people in general. The Stalin apologist, Professor Max Lerner, the new political writer of PM, sets out to answer Eastman, and he has one central refutation of the facts marshalled by the latter: "As I read Eastman on Russian poverty and the subjection of the people, I kept thinking: if these people are slaves, why do slaves fight so well" (PM, July 1.) There it is, the whole crushing reply, just as it was written by the learned Professor Lerner, who never heard in all of history, ancient or contemporary, of nations of slaves fighting well, at least for a certain time.

Germany is not a nation of free men but of slaves. What would Professor Lerner say about the state of its morale? Has the state of the morale of the Japanese army, which so often fights till the last soldier is dead, come to the attention of the Professor? Or doesn't he find time to read the public press?

The SWP prudently refuses to argue the theory that Russia is a workers' state merely because the state, which is completely in the hands of a counter-revolutionary, totalitarian bureaucracy, owns the means of production and exchange, and utilizes that ownership exclusively for its own benefit and to the social and political detriment of the proletariat. It prefers to argue the theory indirectly, and essentially on the same plane as Lerner and other pro-Stalinist Liberals.

"Those who deny that the Soviet Union is a workers' state," says the resolution adopted by the last convention of the SWP, "cannot explain the unprecedented morale of the Soviet workers and peasants." The same pathetic thought was repeated at a public meeting by the distinguished Marxian scholar who leads the party.

If this has become the criterion, or at least important proof, of the proletarian character of the Russian state — or, lest we forget, of its "counter-revolutionary proletarian" character — then objectivity demands that Germany be included in the category of workers' states of one kind or another, for there has thus far been no serious sign of a break in its "unprecedented morale." Nor would it be possible to exclude Japan, and one or two other countries.

The "deniers" may not be able to explain the "unprecedented morale." How do the "believers" explain it? We read: "Above all, the system of nationalized property provided the basis for the unprecedented morale of the Soviet workers and peasants. The Soviet masses have something to fight for. They fight for their factories, their land, their collective economy."

Such good tidings should not be kept from the people either. The "Soviet" masses should be informed that the factories, the land, the economy in general, is theirs, belongs to them. On second thought, it is not at all necessary for the Cannonites to bring the Russian people this news. The Stalinists have been feeding this treacherous falsehood to the masses for years. Trotsky, however, repeatedly denounced it as a falsehood. In 1936, for example, he wrote:

"The new constitution — wholly founded as we shall see, upon an identification of the bureaucracy with the state, and the state with the people — says '... the state property — that is, the possessions of the whole people.' This identification is the fundamental sophism of the official doctrine". (*The Revolution Betrayed*, page 236. Our emphasis.)

More of the same may be found in the chapter of Trotsky's work devoted to social

This is the second half of "After two years of war with Germany. Notes on Russia in the war", by Max Shachtman, *New International,* July 1943. We have restored small deletions and changes made by Shachtman when he republished this article in his book *The Bureaucratic Revolution.*

relations in Russia. But the quotation above will suffice to emphasize that the popular explanation of the "unprecedented morale" of the Russians is based directly upon what Trotsky rightly calls the "fundamental sophism" of the bureaucratic counter-revolution.

In the last issue of their magazine, the Cannonites strike a highly virtuous pose on the question of Russian morale. They compare their own writings and those of Souvarine to show that the predictions of the latter on the subject were wrong while their own were right. But that is not the only thing they "foresaw" and "forecast." In their voluminous and violently contradictory writings on the subject can be found all sorts of mutually-exclusive predictions precisely on the question of Russian morale in wartime. They have a wide choice to draw upon. For example, in the May, 1941, issue of the *Fourth International*, John G Wright, their specialist on Russian questions, quotes with evident approval from an article by Freda Utley as follows: "This method of [repressive] government can be successful only where there is no threat from abroad. A dictator who lacks popular support dare not risk a war in which weapons would be placed in the hands of the subjects who might be more anxious to use them against him than against the foreign enemy".

Miss Utley was expressing no more than the thoughts of Souvarine against which the June, 1943, issue of *Fourth International* fumes with such hypocritical piety and pretensions of superiority. In 1941, Wright did not find himself called upon to fume, but only to quote with approval. On the next page (125) of the same issue, Wright, commenting on another article in the bourgeois press, summarizes the situation as follows:

"The factor of morale is worst of all. The workers and peasants are no better than serfs. The cost of living is going up and wages down. Youth are now deprived of education. According to the Soviet press itself, the new decrees cut short the studies of some 600,000 students. Pupils in secondary schools have to pay 200 rubles per year, in universities and technical schools 400 rubles. This rule was applied even to pupils and students in their last year. In some provincial universities and technical colleges, eighty per cent were obliged to quit and seek employment. Boys of fourteen to seventeen were conscripted for labor. After one year's training they are obliged to work for four years anywhere they are sent. In short, Russia is a volcano ready for revolt". (Our emphasis)

Before venturing upon another spree of pompous self-adulation, the editor of the *Fourth International* could do worse than read a file of his own periodical. It will help tighten a loose jaw.

The appraisal of morale in wartime is an exceedingly difficult and complicated matter. This is especially true in the totalitarian countries where truth is an outlaw, statistics a court tool, and super-censorship is king. The conventional explanation says too little and too much at the same time. Yet it is possible to make an objective appraisal which approximates the truth as closely as that can now be done.

Wide sections of the Russian people entertain an active hatred of their régime. The rest are divided between those who tolerate it in one way or another, and those who are fanatically enthusiastic in support of it, either out of self-interest or out of persistent indoctrination (above all, this holds true of the youth). But the invader holds out no hope whatsoever for relief from tyranny. The masses are ready to resist him with whatever weapons are at their disposal, as is the case in so many other countries.

The Russian people have almost always fought well against a foreign invader, even when the odds against them were much greater than they are now. They are fighting better and with more conviction against the Germans now than they did during the adventure against Finland, when indifference and even cynicism was the rule. The feeling of attachment to the soil is very strong throughout Russia, even among the working class, which is not many years removed from the land. They do not want their country overrun and ruled by a foreign oppressor. And this is no ordinary foreigner, but a fascist. For long years, from Lenin's day through Stalin's, the Russian people have learned to feel a horror and hatred of fascism. The record of fascism's conquests in Europe has only deepened this feeling. Their feelings in this matter are more than justified, and correspond with the interests and ideals of the international proletariat. So, also, do the feelings of those British workers who support the war against

Germany because they fear a victory of fascism which would destroy their national independence and above all their democratic rights and working class institutions. The British worker has postponed, so to speak, his settlement of accounts with his own rulers until he has removed the threat of the Nazi knife at his throat. So has the Russian worker.

The task of the revolutionary Marxists can be fulfilled only by taking these progressive sentiments into full account, while continuing their "patient enlightenment" of the masses as to the imperialist and reactionary nature of the war itself, the harmfulness of political support of the war and the war régimes, the need of breaking with imperialism and the ruling classes, the urgency of an independent, internationalist road for the proletariat of all countries.

Are the Russian masses fighting "in defense of nationalized property"? Of course they are! The British workers are fighting willy-nilly in defense of capitalist property. The Russian people have shown no sign of wanting the restoration of capitalism, with its bankers and industrial monopolists. That is all to the good, for otherwise they would be the poor dupes of world reaction. The road to freedom for Russia does not lead backward but forward.

Right now, the "defense of nationalized property" means the defense of the economic foundations of bureaucratic totalitarianism and imperialist expansion — that is the point. The bureaucracy is perfectly well aware of this fact, and that is why it keeps its economic base intact. That is why it fights for it with such tenacity, with such indifference as to what alliance it makes with what capitalist-imperialist powers at the expense of the working class, with such cruel disregard for the legions of cannon-fodder it hurls wastefully into the breach against the enemy. That is why it fights to extend its base — and thereby its social rule — to whatever other country, from Sinkiang to Poland, from Finland to Turkey, that it has the power to take from its enemy and to be granted as its share of imperialist booty by its allies.

The morale of the Russians is high. Meanwhile, however, they are paying heavily with their life's blood for the rule of the bureaucracy and for the alliance with the capitalist imperialisms that were imposed on them. The older generation, which knows something about the great proletarian revolution, is too exhausted, on the whole, to carry out the task of liberation from the new despotism. The younger generation, again, on the whole, is for the time being fanaticized and blinded by the doctrines of the totalitarian régime. But it will learn, or re-learn. The war will teach it, and so will the social upheavals that the war accelerates. If proletarian revolution does not triumph, and thereby overturn the régime of the new autocrats, that is, if the rule of Stalin continues, it will make no difference to the masses whether Russia is victorious in the war or is defeated. Their work is as clearly cut out for them as is ours.

III

THE CANNONITES (the Socialist Workers Party and *The Militant*, which expresses its views) are not in a happy position with regard to the famous "Russian question." We refer specifically to the careful silence they feel obliged to preserve about our criticism of Trotsky's theory, which they share, that Stalinist Russia is a "degenerated workers' state."

In the party dispute in 1939, they would discuss nothing apart from the question of the class character of the Russian state. We, who were members of the SWP before the Cannonites expelled us, were not at that time challenging Trotsky's views on that question. Since then we have not only challenged it but worked out a criticism and our own positive position in a dozen published documents. But not a word of comment, much less critical discussion and refutation, has come out of the Cannonite camp.

The fact is that, against our criticism, their position is untenable. That is demonstrated both by their silence on the fundamental questions we have raised, and by the hopeless confusion into which they fall when they try to deal indirectly with our views on Russia — indirectly being the only way they have tried so far.

Here is the latest example: In the July, 1943, issue of *The New International*, the writer dealt with several aspects of the question under the title of "Notes on Russia in the War," The most important "note," particularly from the standpoint of Trotsky's final development of his theory, uncritically accepted by the Cannonites, dealt with his characterization of the Stalinist bureaucracy as one that carries out what can only be called the "counterrevolutionary socialist revolution." This position of Trotsky is treated in some detail in *The New International* and the interested reader is referred to it.

But, as usual, not a word from the Cannonites, who are not coy about calling themselves the only genuine Trotskyists.

In the August 21 issue of *The Militant*, however, M Morrison comments on my article[1]. On the important section of it, on the section dealing with the fundamental question, the question of the "class character of the Soviet state," which the Cannonites insisted was the beginning and the end of everything? Not for a moment. He ignores that as if it had never been mentioned. Instead, he spends two columns dealing with an altogether secondary question, namely, the question of the morale of the Red Army and the Russian people, about which his information and ours is not as extensive as it might be.

In my article, I argued that the apparently high morale of the Russians may be explained on many grounds, some (but not all) of which are mentioned. In any case, I wrote, it is preposterous to claim that their high morale is any kind of proof that Russia is a workers' state, for with such an argument you could likewise prove that Germany (or Japan or England) is also some kind of a workers' state.

This observation seems to have upset my somber critic violently. He writes that "it could be no other than Max Shachtman who would make a superficial wisecrack" like that. None other, you see, absolutely none other; and not only a wisecrack but a superficial one. This is not his most crushing answer. He has heavier ones.

"The morale of the Red Army," continues Morrison, "does not, of course, prove that the Soviet Union is a workers' state. The suggestion that someone said something to this effect is one of Shachtman's debating tricks, to make the opponent look ridiculous."

Well, now, let us see just how ridiculous the opponent really looks.

Here is a quotation from *The Militant* exactly one issue earlier, August 14, 1943: "The morale of the Soviet people, the recovery of the Red Armies from devastating defeat and now their tremendous victories testify to the unbounded vitality of the October Revolution."

By the "unbounded vitality of the October Revolution" the editor of *The Militant*, of course, means the "fact" that Russia is still a workers' state. Isn't the quoted sentence saying that the "morale of the Soviet people... their tremendous victories" prove ("testify to") that Russia is a workers' state?

Max Shachtman: "What class in Russia owns the nationalized property?"
1. "M Morrison" was a pen-name of Albert Goldman's.

An accidental article, perhaps. But here is Joseph Andrews, in *The Militant* of January 9, 1943: "This offensive testifies to the continued high morale and great vitality of the Red Army and the workers and peasants of the Soviet Union — a vitality such as no capitalist nation can summon, and a spirit such as no imperialist army can bring forth." (My emphasis, here and below — MS)

In plain English, isn't this a claim that the "high morale and great vitality" of the Russians are proof of the working class character of the Soviet state? "The suggestion that someone said something to this effect is one of Shachtman's debating tricks," wrote Morrison. Debating trick, or embarrassing fact?

But perhaps both quotations are isolated, and due only to "ridiculous" individuals. We fear not. Here is what the official political resolution "unanimously adopted by the convention of the SWP" has to say on the subject in question (*The Militant*, October 17, 1942):

"Those who deny that the Soviet Union is a workers' state cannot explain the unprecedented morale of Soviet workers and peasants."

Was Morrison present at the convention? Did he vote for this resolution? Did he at least read it? Or was he content then, as now, to let Cannon have his resolutions so long as he himself has his column in *The Militant*?

Unfortunately, there is more — by Morrison, and about him.

In the same article, he points to the difference between the fighting morale of the Russians in 1914 or 1917, and in 1942.

"What is the factor that explains this difference? Not because the Russian masses know that they own the factories and the state. They know too well that this is a fiction of the bureaucracy."

Whether the Russian masses know that it is a fiction or not, the fact is that the Cannonites do not know it. Proof? Here it is — not "debater's tricks," but proof!

George Collins, in *The Militant* of September 12, 1942: "But the workers and Red soldiers of the Soviet Union fight with a bitterness unmatched in this war because they are defending the socialist achievements of a workers' revolution. Factories, mines, mills, railroads, workshops belong to those who work them. The soil belongs to those who till it."

Editorial, in *The Militant* of July 31, 1943, on Russian morale: "Why? Because they [the Russian workers and peasants] have something to fight for: nationalized property, the land and factories which belong to them, their planned economy."

Again, straight from the fountainhead of the last SWP convention resolution, as printed in *The Militant* of October 17, 1942: "The Soviet masses have something to fight for. They fight for their factories, their land, their collective economy."

What are these statements? According to Morrison, and he is of course as right as two and two make four, they are simply the repetition of a bureaucratic fiction, that is, a fiction of Stalinism. Who has been spreading these Stalinist fictions? Morrison's comrades, Morrison's party, the party resolution for which Morrison and all the other absolutely genuine and one hundred per cent Trotskyists voted. Debater's trick, or embarrassing fact?

But if it is a Stalinist fiction to say that the Russian workers own the factories and the state, what is not a fiction? In other words, what is the truth? If they have neither the means of production nor the state, what do they have? The "nationalized means of production"? But these are entirely in the hands of the state, which the masses do not have but which the counterrevolutionary bureaucracy does have — and has exclusively. The masses, then, have nothing.

Excuse us. They do have something: a vast prison. *The Militant* once wrote literally (and correctly) that the Russian factories are a prison to which the workers are sentenced for life. Trick or fact?

The statement that the Russian "factories, mines, mills, railroads workshops belong to those who work them. The soil belongs to those who till it," is not the only bureaucratic fiction the Cannonites are guilty of spreading.

The Militant has written that the Stalinist army pursues "working class aims." Fiction. It has even called this instrument of counterrevolutionary Bonapartism in Russia "Trotsky's Red Army." Fiction. It has said that this army "is fighting for a socialist Europe as well as a socialist Russia." Fiction. It went so far a few months ago

(February 6, 1943) as to say that "the self-sacrificing Russian workers [are] producing under socialist methods." It was not the *Daily Worker* that wrote this, but *The Militant*. Wisecrack? Trick? Distortion? No, we state the simple, sickening facts.

But these are, after all, merely aspects of the biggest of the bureaucratic fictions: the theory that Russia is still some kind of workers' state. This theory can be tested only in practise. It would pass the test if it could be shown that in some meaningful way the Russian masses do own or control or have their interests represented by the state which has the means of production in its hands. That's just what cannot be shown.

Hence the confusion and embarrassment of the Cannonites. Hence their swinging from the dissemination of Stalinist fictions to Morrison's "repudiation" of the fictions. Hence the "ridiculous opponents." And hence their shyness at debating the question openly and directly with revolutionary critics.

IV

IT IS LITTLE short of amazing what people can do with the riches of modern vocabularies when they are hard put. Take, for example, the problem of announcing, in the least embarrassing way, the fact that your army has retreated instead of advanced or even held its own. Those responsible for issuing the war communiques do not simply say: "Our opponents won the battle, and we retreated". How would that sound back home? Instead, they write: "We have successfully disengaged our forces from the enemy", or "Enemy attempts to contact our rear guard were effectively thwarted", or "We have triumphantly evacuated the fortress because of a lack of adequate housing and sanitary facilities", or, more simply, "We have shortened our line". That sounds better. So it is in war nowadays; so, it seems, it is in political debate.

A good case in point is M Morrison, the Cannonite essayist of *The Militant*. A few issues ago in these pages we pinned him right to the board. He described as "one of Shachtman's debating tricks" the "suggestion that someone" in *The Militant* had said that the morale of the Red Army proves that Russia is a workers' state. I therefore proceeded, without tricks of any kind, to quote a half dozen occasions when writers in *The Militant* said precisely that. What does Morrison reply in a roundabout way, presumably in discussing a letter from a Chicago reader? In *The Militant* of October 2 he blandly writes: "It was a rather risky statement to make, I must admit, because it is quite possible that some comrade was guilty of making a bad formulation. I assumed the risk because Shachtman failed to cite any quotation justifying his assertion." (Emphasis mine — MS)

But once Shachtman has presented six or seven quotations "justifying his assertion", what does Morrison do? He "shortens his line", as they say in the war communiques. He repeats one of the quotations to create the impression that it was the product of some isolated and not entirely thoughtful or representative writer. "Shachtman", he says, "has to be grateful to the editors of *The Militant* for overlooking an incorrect formulation now and then" (my emphasis — MS). What Morrison does not tell his readers (who, he hopes, did not see the *Labor Action* article!) is that it was not a question of "overlooking" an "incorrect" formulation "now and then". Among other quotations we printed one from no less a document than the "unanimously adopted" political resolution of the convention of the Socialist Workers Party. What is more, I showed pretty plainly that this "incorrect formulation" was the sum and substance of every comment *The Militant* makes on Russian morale. But Morrison is shortening his line, and not only on that front.

In a still earlier issue, I addressed a few questions to the editor of *The Militant*. That paper has been repeatedly printing the outright Stalinist falsehood to the effect that the means of production in Russia belong to the workers and peasants, or the people. We asked the editor how he reconciled these statements, made in an "official" Trotskyist paper, with the assertion by Trotsky that the identification of "state property" with "possession of the whole people" is the "fundamental sophism of the official doctrine", that is, of Stalinism.

Morrison replied by "officially" ignoring my questions. In other words, and as usual, he dealt with them in a round-about way. But his answer was good enough, all things considered. Do the Russian workers own the factories, as *The Militant* has said repeatedly? No, replied Morrison, "they know too well that this is a fiction of the bureaucracy". And two weeks ago: "I must, however, admit that the expression 'the workers of the Soviet Union own the factories' was actually used in *The Militant*".

If Morrison were genuinely objective, and did not confine his indignation to the Stalinists for the mockery they make of self-criticism, he would have acknowledged that this "incorrect formulation" was not only "actually used in *The Militant*", but is contained, word for word, in the above-mentioned official convention resolution of the SWP. Perhaps my lordly critic didn't see it, either when it was written, or printed, or when he voted for it in the convention, or when it was reprinted. So here it is again, straight from the resolution: "The Soviet masses have something to fight for. They

Max Shachtman: "Who owns Stalinist property? Morrison 'shortens his line'. On what class owns Russian property".

423

fight for their factories, their land, their collective economy". (My emphasis — MS). Thus, as I once said, the very fountainhead of Stalinist fiction is the official position of the SWP, and not of an occasional writer whose repetition of it is "overlooked" by the editor "now and then". To be the disseminator of Stalinist fiction (and the fundamental one, at that) is a confoundedly bad thing for a "Trotskyist" party and paper to be. To be pilloried for it is even worse. Therefore? Therefore, Morrison "shortens his line" and condemns, not the resolution he voted for (pardon me — "overlooked"), but condemns... Shachtman. As the Germans say in their communiques: "Our forces were obliged to disengage themselves because the barbaric Russians were armed".

We would be done for the moment if Morrison had not retreated from the frying pan into the fire. Once forced to admit that the Russian working class does not "own the factories and the state," he has removed the only serious argument that Russia is a workers' state, degenerated or otherwise. The Chicago reader whom his October 2 article ostensibly answers without quoting directly, has obviously asked: If the workers do not really own the factories, what happens to our theory of the workers' state?

Morrison's explanation is a piece of muddled sophistry if ever there was one, and it goes without saying that it is smeared over with liberal layers of "dialectics."

We know, as Morrison does, that there is no capitalist class that owns the factories in Russia. We know, as Morrison now admits, that the working class does not own them. We also know that the working class has not the slightest degree of control over the state that does own Russian property.

Who, then, does own the land and factories in Russia? What class? We say: a new class developing out of special historical circumstances, the Stalinist collectivist bureaucracy. Morrison says: No class owns the means of production! That is all that his "answer" to the Chicago reader can mean. A magnificent sample of Marxian and dialectical thinking! For the first time in the long history of the class struggle we have a society in which no class owns the property and no class controls the state. The property is not owned by a class at all. It is merely nationalized, that is, it is owned by the state which is not a class. Is it any wonder that the Chicago reader is perplexed? What reader wouldn't be? And is it any wonder that the Stalinists declare Russia to be a classless, socialist state? Morrison abandons one Stalinist fiction only to approach another!

Morrison is still shortening his line. He refuses to say in simple or complex English what class owns the factories and (controls) the state, and then adds that the question is of no consequence! He quotes an entirely inappropriate paragraph from Trotsky, says: "It will of course not satisfy the doctrinaires who insist on a specific answer to the question: what class owns the nationalized property in the Soviet Union? The answer can only be to show that the Soviet state owns the factories and then proceed to give Trotsky's explanation of the nature of the Soviet state."

Morrison can "proceed to give Trotsky's explanation" from now till the end of time. He can write himself blue in the face with attacks on those who "insist on a specific answer to the question" as "doctrinaires" and "non-dialecticians" and "abstractionists." He can shorten his line to a pinpoint. But if he is to stop making a mockery of the fundamentals of Marxism, he must "proceed" from the premises that the state is the political instrument of a class which, fundamentally, controls it, and that there is no class society in which no class owns the property — be it slaves, land or factories.

Twist and turn, squirm and squeeze — you cannot evade an answer to the extremely concrete (by no means abstract or "legalistic") questions which Morrison readily answers for every country, in every period of history, except Stalinist Russia, namely:

What class owns the property (means of production and exchange) in Russia? Not the working class, not the capitalist class — then who?

What class controls (or "owns") the state machinery in Russia? Not the working class, not the capitalist class — then who?

What class is the social beneficiary of the present-day Russian state and the productive relations prevailing in it? In Kerensky's time, it was the capitalist class. In Lenin's time, it was the working class. And under the Stalinist bureaucracy?

If it is "doctrinaire" to "insist on a specific answer to the question of who "owns," then why is the capitalist class so infernally concerned about what class owns the factories (and controls the state) in America, England, Germany and Japan; why is it so concerned about changing the class ownership of the factories in Russia; and why are such "abstractionists" as Morrison (and ourselves) interested in changing the class ownership of the factories in the United States?

Is there perhaps another Chicago reader who will give Morrison occasion to explain further?

APPENDIX: THE CLASS MEANING OF THE SOVIET VICTORIES

GREAT MASSES THROUGHOUT the world are rejoicing at the victories of the Red Army. Without a rounded theory but nevertheless with a basically class loyalty, they understand that the Soviet victories are their victories too. They are definitely aware of a distinction between the Workers' State and its capitalist "allies." It is deeply symbolic that at Cardiff, Wales, in honor of the 25th anniversary of the founding of the Red Army, the miners from the surrounding valleys paraded with lighted lamps, the girl munition workers in overalls, while over the City Hall flew the red flag. Of course, the parade was officially sanctioned, Deputy Prime Minister Attlee was the chief speaker, and we can be sure that the Stalinists sought to identify the affair as a symbol of unity between the Soviet Union and British capitalism. But in the essence of the matter the red flag and the lighted lamps and overalls, so different from the symbols of the usual British celebration, signify that the workers were primarily celebrating for the Workers' State. Certainly no one can seriously pretend that the rejoicing in India over the Soviet victories is on behalf of Britain! No, at bottom it is a class phenomenon, the feeling of the oppressed toward the victories of the army established by the October revolution. Equally a class phenomenon are the first frank reactions of the "democratic" capitalists toward the Red Army successes. These — the very first victorious battles! — have already brought out into the press the anti-Soviet sentiments — and activities — of the "democrats." The Nazi armies are still deep in Russia, are still intact — yet already authoritative voices in the "democracies" indicate their dismay at the thought of a decisive Soviet victory over the fascist foe.

Felix Morrow, *Fourth International*, March 1943

10. BALANCE SHEETS

Max Shachtman

IT IS TIME TO UNDERSTAND

CONFUSION AS TO THE AIMS OF RUSSIA in the war is gradually dissipating from the minds of her Anglo-American allies. What antipathy there is in London and Washington is based on indignation at the thought that Moscow should aim, in general, at extending its oppression and exploitation to other lands and peoples, inasmuch as up to now this has been the exclusive prerogative of the capitalist imperialisms; and in particular that it should extend its rule over territories which Russia's allies believe ought to be *their* vassals or slaves. However, the military situation is such that the Honorable Allies find it extremely difficult, if not impossible, to translate their competitor's antipathy toward the unfolding of Russia's imperialist program into effective obstacles. They must make the best of a trying dilemma, and bide their time.

Confusion about Russia in the ranks of the Trotskyist movement, or, more accurately, in the part of it represented by the Socialist Workers Party, is not, however, being dissipated. The contrary is unfortunately the case. For it, Russia continues to be a workers' state, which has been degenerating day-in, day-out, for twenty years, which is now a life-long prison of the working class (to use the SWP's own words), which establishes not less than semi-slavery wherever it extends its sway (to use Trotsky's own words), but which does not cease for all that to be a workers' state which must be unconditionally defended and supported in the war.

Furthermore, according to the SWP, Russia is a "counterrevolutionary workers' state." The state is proletarian because property is nationalized; it is counter-revolutionary by virtue of the Stalinist political régime, the bureaucracy. What makes it counter-revolutionary? Is it for capitalism? Is it for restoring private property? No; the fact is that it defends nationalized property "in its own way." Is it for maintaining capitalism in the countries it conquers? No; the fact is that it abolishes capitalist private property in these countries and reorganizes the economy to correspond exactly with Russia's. Well then? Well, it is counter-revolutionary because it is a deadly enemy of the working class everywhere and a violent opponent of the proletarian revolution. But is not the essence of a social revolution the expropriation of the ruling class and a fundamental change in property relations? And is that not exactly what the Stalinist bureaucracy, its army and its police, do when they conquer new territory, as in the Baltic and Balkan countries? To this question the SWP replies with a triumphant affirmative. But then, what is the *class character* of this social revolution carried out by the Stalinist bureaucracy? The SWP rejects our theory that this bureaucracy is a new class (without as yet offering a single word of argument against it). Good. But the question still remains. Is this social

From *New International*, "It is time to understand. Continued confusion leads only to disaster", March 1944.

revolution a proletarian revolution? No answer — except Trotsky's above-quoted remark that when Stalin nationalizes the property of the conquered countries, he reduces the proletariat to semi-slavery. Is this *social* revolution a *socialist* revolution? No answer — except in the not very courageous form of the assertion that Stalin is carrying out "the extension of Soviet property forms." And the Russian army, which is the bureaucracy's completely controlled instrument in this "extension of Soviet property forms"? This army must be defended and supported, says the SWP. But — at the same time, "we are against the seizure of new territories" by the Kremlin!

What is clearly implicit in all this? The Stalinist bureaucracy is carrying out a revolution that is new in history, namely, a counter-revolutionary socialist revolution; we support the army which seizes the countries in which the bureaucracy carries out this revolution; we are opposed to the seizure of the countries in which this revolution is carried out; but this opposition is purely verbal inasmuch as we support, and call upon the workers to support, the army which is assigned to seize these countries.

The SWP has dug itself deep into the shelter of this galimatias of a dogma. But the realities of life, to which we have repeatedly added some wisely-unanswered critical remarks, have subjected it to such a merciless pounding that the position has become utterly untenable. Instead of abandoning it openly and in time, the SWP vacillates helplessly between clinging to it and the urge of some of its members to shift to a more easily held position. Fundamentally — and this is the source of the growing confusion — it represents vacillation between an objective capitulation to Stalinism and an advance to revolutionary Marxism. If these alternatives seem exaggerated, it can only be because documentation has not yet been supplied for the analysis. Let us supply it.

In *The Militant* of January 29 appears an article by the now dubiously renowned John G Wright called "Red Army Victories Alarm Stalin's Allies." It is sensational only in that it brings to a new low the position that *The Militant* has been developing on the question of Russia. In view of the startling views expressed in it — and it is written, let us note, by one of the Fiercest of the Fierce among the "Trotskyists" — the reader will surely not be bored by even a lengthy quotation:

"But the whole point is that the capitalists refuse to reconcile themselves to the price that Stalin needs and demands, that is, the strengthening of the Soviet Union in Eastern *Europe. Stabilization of capitalism in Europe is impossible without a capitalist Poland as a 'buffer' in order to keep the Soviet system isolated in preparation for its eventual destruction. Churchill and Roosevelt know this, and are working to this end.*

The establishment of the Curzon line, that is, in essence the reservation of the 1939 borders gained by Stalin through his previous deal with Hitler, would weaken Poland as the pivot of this indispensable capitalist 'cordon sanitaire.' Furthermore, implicit in the Kremlin's territorial demands is the extension of Soviet property forms to the whole of Poland. That this threat is not distant is borne out by the latest pronouncement by Stalin's Union of Polish Patriots calling not only for the inclusion of Silesia, Pomerania, East Prussia and Danzig in a 'New Poland,' but also for the seizure of Polish landed estates, their division among the peasants and 'the nationalization of industries and mines taken from the Germans' (Daily

Worker, January 28). Inasmuch as Polish industry is almost wholly in the hands of the Germans, the realization of this program would signify the complete destruction of Polish capitalism and a giant step in the inevitable extension of Soviet property forms far beyond the frontiers of 1939. *In its turn, this carries a twofold threat to capitalism: first, in addition to strengthening the USSR immeasurably, it would greatly hamper further attempts to isolate it. Second, the revolutionary wave in Europe, especially in Germany, would receive so mighty an impulsion from such developments in the territories of former Poland, let alone Silesia, East Prussia, etc., that the attempt to drown the coming European revolution in blood would be rendered well-nigh impossible.*

In any case, Roosevelt and Churchill will not voluntarily surrender to Stalin a single section of capitalism, no matter how tiny. Each advance of the Red Army, however, poses this issue pointblank and brings more and more sharply to the forefront the basic antagonism in the camp of the 'United Nations' — the irreconcilable class conflict between the 'democratic' capitalists and the Soviet Union, even in its degenerated condition under Stalin... But the irreconcilable class forces underlying the new crisis cannot be definitely suppressed or overcome by Stalinist intrigue and imperialist diplomacy. Inescapably they must and will manifest themselves in a life-and-death struggle between the forces of 'democratic' capitalism and the Soviet Union". (Emphasis in original.)

We ask the reader to overcome his revulsion and read the above a second and a third time so as to get its full flavor. It is the flavor of Stalinist degeneration — not of the "workers' state" this time, but of SWP theory and policy. What Wright says openly — poor fellow! — without the slightest feeling that it is shameful, is substantially identical with what the Stalinist bureaucrats say among themselves to the accompaniment of hilarious winks and jovial nudges in each other's ribs. That is how they justify their arch-hypocrisy and double-dealing to themselves and to the initiated and more reliable followers: "Of course we are still fighting for socialism, only with our new policy it is easier because we are fooling the bourgeoisie. Intrigue? Yes, but infernally clever and — successful. The working class? What is that, anyway?"

According to Wright (and remember, this is one of the most obstreperous of the self-appointed Genuine Trotskyists talking):

1) Stalin not only needs but *demands the strengthening of the Soviet Union.* It used to be said that he was weakening it. If this is no longer the case, why should not the thoughtful communist worker, who is also for the defense of Russia, say to himself: I will continue to support Stalin, but now with the approval of the Trotskyists.

2) Stalin is undermining the stabilization of capitalism in Europe, which means undermining capitalism itself. It used to be said by the Trotskyists that he is helping stabilize capitalism, that he is an agent of world capitalism, its tool, but they must have been joking. Stalin is actually "strengthening the USSR immeasurably" (immeasurably! says Wright, for he is no man to mince words). He and his so-called bureaucracy are giving a mighty impulse to the revolutionary wave in Europe, so mighty, indeed, "that the attempt to drown the coming European revolution in blood would be rendered wellnigh impossible." So, pursues the thoughtful communist worker, I will continue to support this underminer of capital-

ism, this strengthener — this immeasurable strengthener — of the Soviet Union, this mighty impeller of revolutionary waves.

3) Stalin is fighting for the "extension of Soviet property forms to the whole of Poland," and "'this threat is not distant,'" either. Stalin is fighting for an immediate, direct overthrow of capitalism in Poland, its "complete destruction," which means "a giant step in the inevitable extension of Soviet property forms." (Immeasurable strengthener; giant stepper; why not Man of Steel and Genial Leader?) No capitalist Poland means no capitalist stabilization anywhere in Europe. It used to be said that Stalin's role and goal were exactly the opposite of all this, but that was just a manner of speaking. Now the Marshal of Marshals is fighting for the socialist revolution against capitalism, with giant steps at that. The communist worker will continue to draw his conclusions — all, of course, provided he takes Wright seriously for the capitulator to Stalinism that he is.

4) Blank, blank, blank. These blanks used to be occupied by warnings that the triumph of Stalin not only "carries a twofold threat to capitalism," but a multiple threat to the working class, its interests and its aspirations. But what are such bagatelles compared to the "extension of Soviet property forms" by Stalin and the somewhat degenerated but highly nationalized GPU? And inasmuch as Wright is concerned only with big things and not with bagatelles like the enslavement or semi-enslavement of the workers by Stalin, the working class simply does not exist anywhere in his article. It need not be warned, it need not be guided, it has no particular function to perform or role to play, it does not exist in Wright's excited scheme of things. The advances of the Russian army (for no good reason in the world *The Militant* continues to call it the Red Army) poses "pointblank" the issue of... the struggle between capitalism and Stalin's property forms; they bring "sharply to the forefront" the irreconcilable class conflict, between irreconcilable class forces, manifesting themselves in a life-and-death struggle. Class conflict? Class forces? Life-and-death struggle? Between whom, do you think? The bourgeoisie and the proletariat? No, "between the 'democratic' capitalists and the Soviet Union," "between the forces of 'democratic' capitalism and the Soviet Union." The working class? What is that, anyway? That is something you leave out. Important is the fact that Stalin's "property forms are extended" over the working class of Poland and elsewhere, like a running noose over a mustang, so that it can be bridled and saddled with a "workers' state" which is degenerated, Bonapartist, counter-revolutionary, a prison for the workers, in which they do not rule, have nothing to say, and are totalitarian slaves, but which is, thank God, nevertheless a workers' state.

Where, the reader may now ask, is the confusion? Wright is not so much guilty of confusion as of splattering a ninety-nine per cent pure Stalinist poison on the pages of *The Militant*. The confusion of the SWP, we said, lies in the oscillation between Wright and the revolutionary Marxian position. Wright's article evidently evoked sufficient dismay to cause the editors of *The Militant* to attempt at least a partial disavowal of his views, without, of course, indicating by as much as a word that there are two views and a conflict between them. That falls under the heading of educating the reader, you see.

In the two issues following Wright's monstrous article, *The Militant* published two editorials, one unsigned, "Program for Poland," and the other more official yet, signed by "The Editors," and entitled "Stalinism and the Danger to Europe's Coming Revolution."

The first opens refreshingly enough with a highly deserved rebuke, and not just at bourgeois commentators, but at Wright, who is equally guilty. "In the current dispute over the Polish question, public attention has hitherto been concentrated exclusively upon the views and proposals of the various governments involved... Not one of these powers [England, the United States, the Polish government in exile, or Stalin] has signified any intention of permitting the Polish people to determine their future. They propose to settle all questions solely through the reactionary methods of traditional power politics."

So far, so good. What follows is even better. *"The Polish workers and peasants however have not suffered the horrors of the Second Imperialist War and fought against the Nazi beasts in order to pass under the yoke of any other dictatorship, whether it comes from the west through the restoration of the old régime backed by Anglo-American bayonets or whether it comes from the east in the person of the Bonapartist bureaucracy of Stalin. While the diplomats of the "United Nations" secretly bicker for the most advantageous terms, the Polish masses are waging their own independent fight for freedom against the national oppression of the Nazis and the social oppression of capitalism.*

The Polish people don't want any more lords and masters over them. They want to decide for themselves what system of society and what kind of government they shall have. And, despite the conspiracies and deals between the capitalist owners and the Stalinist bureaucrats, the Polish workers and peasants will speak the last word on these vital questions... In their struggle for such a free and independent socialist Poland, the Polish workers and peasants will find powerful friends and allies, not in the Anglo-American capitalists or the Stalinist bureaucrats who threaten to replace the fascist oppressors, but among the insurgent masses of the rest of Europe".

The words come late, but not too late. In any case, they are excellent. Wright should be compelled to write them on a blackboard one hundred times a day for three months before he is permitted to speak or write another word on any question relating to Russia. At the same time, however, the editors, and the SWP in general, cannot be permitted to continue with their evasions and double-talk, with putting forward a new line, or half line, without abandoning the old. In other words, they cannot be permitted to remain confused and, above all, to confuse others.

First: The editors tell us that "the advanced Polish revolutionists are anti-Stalinist, but they are pro-Soviet. They understand that despite Stalin, the Soviet Union is nevertheless unlike the capitalist world." Unlike in what way? In that it is a workers' state of one kind or another? The editors delicately refrain from saying. Not once, in either editorial, do they refer to Russia as a workers' state — the pen is beginning to stutter. Russia *is* unlike the capitalist world, not despite Stalin but precisely because of him (that is, Stalin as a synonym for the ruling bureaucracy). In Russia today we have neither a capitalist nor a workers' state but a new social system which we call bureaucratic collectivism. It is increasingly clear that the SWP has reached a complete blind alley in its attempt to maintain that this *anti-workers' state* is proletarian and at the same time

432

to maintain any kind of revolutionary policy for the situation in Europe. You cannot get out of this blind alley, as the two editorials try to do, by stressing the latter and remaining discreetly silent about the former. The contradiction is only ignored but not eliminated.

Second: The editors point out that the "capitalists are first and foremost concerned with the property forms in the occupied territories, they are concerned with the preservation of the capitalist system in Europe." Correct. And Stalin? Is he for maintaining the capitalist "property forms" in the occupied countries, or is he, as Wright quite correctly shows, for destroying them and substituting "Soviet property forms"? Now, *if* the mere existence or establishment of nationalized property in a country gives it a workers' state (degenerated or otherwise), as the SWP dogma reads, then does not Stalin's aim at a social revolution in Poland (i.e., the "extension of Soviet property forms") bear, fundamentally, a proletarian class character, which is, consequently, socialist in tendency?

The SWP can escape this inexorable conclusion from its dogma only in one of three ways: (a) by asserting that Stalin aims to maintain capitalist private property in the territories he conquers, a prediction it would be well-advised not to make; or (b) by claiming that a basic change in property forms and property relations, such as Stalin will clearly attempt, does not constitute the hallmark of a social revolution, a conclusion violating all history and all the teachings of Marx and Trotsky on the point; or (c) by agreeing with *us* that while it would mark a social revolution, it would be carried out by a new *class* which is neither bourgeois nor proletarian.

Third: The capitalists fear expropriation of their property not only by the socialist proletariat, but even by the Stalinist bureaucracy. Right. But the editors add: "The European peoples have aspirations and aims entirely different and opposed to those of Stalin." *Entirely* different? What about the "Soviet property forms" which are by themselves enough for a workers' state? Do not the European peoples, in so far as they are socialistic, have a common, if not an identical, aim with Stalin in the matter of "property forms"? That follows incontrovertibly from the SWP's theory, and to write about "*entirely* different" aims and aspirations is a mighty brash and cavalier way to dismiss one's own dogma!

The fact is that "entirely different" is fairly correct. Despite the argument of the SWP that nationalized property is what makes Russia a workers' state — an argument that implies a *fundamental* community of interests between the Stalinist bureaucracy and the socialist proletariat — nothing of the sort is true. Where property is state-owned, control of the state is control of society as a whole. Where the working class controls the state, as was the case in the early years of the revolution, it is a workers' state; the *form* in which property is owned (in this case, state ownership) is filled with one social content, one class content. Where the bureaucracy controls the state, and in a totalitarian way, as has been the case in Russia for almost a decade, the same property form is filled with a *fundamentally different* social or class content; entirely different property or social relations are established; the working class rules in no sense whatever, but is ruled over and exploited.

The failure to understand this simple idea is what is breaking the neck of the SWP. *Explicitly,* the SWP rejects this idea. *Implicitly,* it is dragged into giving the most reluctant, tongue-in-cheek acknowledgment of its validity. That is why it now feels obliged to support the workers of the capitalist countries, not only in fighting capitalism, but also in fighting against the "extension" of the rule of the "workers' state" over themselves. Example? Interestingly enough, it occurs in connection with Poland, as we shall now show.

Fourth: When Poland was first partitioned by the Berlin and Moscow gangster-imperialists, the question arose in the SWP of what attitude to take toward the Russian army (there was, of course, no dispute about the question of the German army). The majority said: Support the Russian army! We, of the then minority, said: Support neither army; organize the "third camp" of the independent proletarian struggle against the imperialist war and for workers' socialist power; teach the Polish masses that they must struggle against both oppressors who threaten them, even though the two are not socially identical, that they must *prepare*, beginning right now, for the uprising against both reactionary sides.

All of Trotsky's vast capacity for irony was tapped to ridicule this idea, to the uncontrollable chuckling of the majority. *"Shachtman began by discovering a philosopher's stone: the achievement of a simultaneous insurrection against Hitler and Stalin in occupied Poland. The idea was splendid; it is only too bad that Shachtman was deprived of the opportunity of putting it into practice. The advanced workers of eastern Poland could justifiably say: 'A simultaneous insurrection against Hitler and Stalin in a country occupied by troops might perhaps be arranged very conveniently from the Bronx; but here, locally, it is more difficult. We should like to hear Burnham's and Shachtman's answer to a 'concrete political question': 'What shall we do between now and the coming insurrection?'"*

The irony was, however, lost on us. In the first place, the Marxists had heard this same "annihilating" poser put (not by Trotsky, to be sure) about what the Czech workers should do "between now and the coming insurrection" while their country was occupied by troops, about whether a simultaneous insurrection against Hitler and Benes could be arranged very conveniently from the Bronx, from lower Manhattan, from Coyoacan, or even in Prague. In the second place, as in Czechoslovakia, it was not a matter of "arranging an insurrection" in Poland. The question was one of a political line of revolutionary socialist opposition to both reactionary war camps, one of training and preparing the workers in such a spirit, and of arming them with such a policy that they would not fall victim to Hitler's army or Stalin's, but move closer to the day when they could settle accounts with both.

Be that as it may, let us look at the SWP "Program for Poland" four years later. The Russian, alias the Red Army, is again approaching Poland. Where is *The Militant*'s courage? Why does it not say, as it did in 1939, that the Polish proletariat and peasantry should support the Russian army and work for its victory? There is not a blessed syllable about this in either of the two editorials! (There is indeed one vague, indirect and ever-so-mealy-mouthed reference to the Russian army, with which we shall deal below.)

The emphasis now, in 1944, bears no resemblance whatsoever to the emphasis in 1939. Now we are told that the Polish workers and peasants have not "fought against the Nazi beasts in order to pass under the yoke of *any* other dictatorship, whether it comes from the west... *or whether it comes from the east in the person of the Bonapartist bureaucracy of*

434

Stalin." Bravo! Late, but welcome nevertheless. (We were once denounced indignantly for "coupling" the two dictatorships, for putting them on the same plane. Now...) And the Poles *"will find powerful friends and allies, not in the Anglo-American capitalists or the Stalinist bureaucrats who threaten to replace the fascist oppressors, but among the insurgent masses of the rest of Europe."* Again, bravo! And the Poles *"are likewise aware of the counter-revolutionary role of Stalin and his clique. They know of the oppression of the nationalities and the peoples inside the Soviet Union. They understand that Stalin's Kremlin gang come into Poland not as liberators but as oppressors."* A double and triple bravo! The Poles, we are glad to see, understand, and the editors of *The Militant* also... finally... understand, at least in part.

Does this mean that the Polish vanguard elements should oppose both the Hitler forces and the Stalin forces? Does this mean that *The Militant*, too, has begun "by discovering a philosopher's stone: the achievement of a simultaneous insurrection [Ha-ha-ha!] against Hitler and Stalin [Ho-ho-ho!] in occupied Poland"? From the quotations above, one would think so. The Poles do not want to pass under Stalin's dictatorship; the Stalinist bureaucrats are not their allies or friends; they are counter-revolutionary; they come not as liberators but as oppressors. And one would think so, also, from the already mentioned fact that the editorials have nothing to say about supporting the Russian army, about helping it to victory, about being the "best soldiers in its ranks." Is silence on this key point supposed to reveal the superior political and revolutionary qualities of the editors over us, who have stated our views forthrightly and unambiguously for over four years?

And yet there *is* a sentence about the Russian army and Poland. Here it is, from beginning to end: *"They [the advanced Polish revolutionists] understand the great opportunities that are opening up for the Polish people and their struggle because of the victorious advance of the Red Army."* Here the bold editors bring up short. They add not a single word. Desperate reality pulls at their tongue, but the dogma has them by the throat! So, all they can emit is a mean little cowardly squeak that can be interpreted whichever way you please.

In what sense does the victorious advance of the Russian army offer great opportunities to the Polish revolutionists? In the same sense in which the victorious advance of Eisenhower's army offered opportunities to the Italian revolutionists? In the sense in which the victorious advance of the Japanese army offered opportunities to the Burmese? In other words, in the sense that the Russian advances so weaken the enemy, who is sitting right now on the necks of the Poles, that they can more easily deal a death blow to him, without in the slightest way doing anything to help seat the "liberating" Stalinist armies on their necks? Interpreted *this way* — and it was only in this sense that it was valid in the case of Burma, for example — what *The Militant* says is not untrue.

But does it follow from this, as *The Militant* editors have argued for so long, that the Polish masses should defend and support the Stalinist armies, work for their victory? It does not follow in the case of Russia in Poland any more than it did in the case of Japan in Burma, or in similar cases elsewhere. That *is* what followed for *The Militant* from 1939 onward. Does it still?

If it does, then *The Militant* might at least have the sorry courage of a Wright and blurt it out so that all may know that it still stands where it stood before — the ambiguous phrase, plus the enormous silence, give rise to doubts. In that case, let *The Militant* explain why the Poles must offer all resistance possible to the "Kremlin gang [who] come into Poland not as liberators but as oppressors," who are not "friends and allies," but must not resist — on the contrary, must defend and help to victory — the Russian army, even though this army is, in Trotsky's words, "an instrument in the hands of the Bonapartist bureaucracy." In other words, if *The Militant* holds to its old position, let it explain why Poles must oppose the executioner while helping him fire the gun (the "instrument") which is aimed right at them. If we may paraphrase Trotsky's irony about the "simultaneous insurrection," and paraphrase it for an idea to which, we think, it properly applies: "The idea is splendid! it is only too bad that the editors are deprived of the opportunity of putting it into practice."

However, if what once followed for *The Militant* no longer follows, it is doubly its duty to say so and to explain why. And if it no longer follows, away with these miserable subterfuges and double-talk! Instead of deceitful sentences such as we have quoted, *The Militant* should be saying to the Polish and all other workers that the Stalinist army is advancing under the banner of Stalin, Kutuzov and Ivan the Terrible for the purpose of reducing them to slavery! That would be a real step forward and lead directly to an even more important advance.

It is high time this step was taken. It is high time to understand. The European proletarian revolution is maturing. This is no longer the expression of a mere wish, in any sense. We have already seen the actual outbreak of the first stage of the revolution in Italy. With even one eye we can see the growth of the revolutionary forces in the popular underground movements in other countries.

The Militant sees, as the editors so correctly put it, that Stalin "threatens to dismember Germany; he threatens the German people with slavery. If the blood of the Russian and German masses continues to redden the territories of the eastern front, the responsibility in major measure rests on Stalin and his counter-revolutionary régime." It refuses to see, or to say, that its "workers' state" is precisely this Stalin and his counter-revolutionary régime; that the "nationalized property" is precisely the foundation of power of this Stalin and his counter-revolutionary régime; that the misnamed Red Army is precisely the instrument of this Stalin and his counter-revolutionary régime — of the state that threatens Germany and other lands with dismemberment, the people with slavery, and the revolution with such a bloodbath as even Anglo-American imperialism might well shrink from.

Up to now, all this preposterous and reactionary mumbo-jumbo about Stalin's Russia being a workers' state and Stalin's Bonapartist army being "Trotsky's Red Army" which is bringing socialism to Europe, has been little more than a tragedy. Tomorrow, for all that we hope for and work for in Europe, and for us here, it can become a first-class disaster.

Isn't it time to understand this? The question is addressed to those who have retained the capacity and the will to understand. They will not prove to be, we hope, too few.

Max Shachtman

A BLOW AT THE FOURTH INTERNATIONAL

THOSE OF US WHO ARE INTERESTED above all in the victory of international socialism have received exceptionally good news. We have waited with impatience and with confidence for the emergence of the genuinely revolutionary socialist movement in Europe. Our confidence has been justified; our patience rewarded. In Italy, where the imperialist front was first broken by the revolutionary uprising of the masses, the real socialists, the Trotskyists, have come together again and formed an organization of their own.

That is a sign of things to come. The treachery of the Stalinists, and the miserable capitulation of the right-wing socialists, has left the road clear to the growth of the revolutionary socialist movement represented in the United States by the Workers Party, in Italy by our new organization, and throughout the world by the Fourth International. In its growth lies the hope of tomorrow. Every worker to whom the ideal of socialism is dear follows its growth with passionate interest and the warmest solidarity.

We of the Workers Party greeted the formation of the new group with great enthusiasm, and immediately decided to give it the maximum aid. Our members and friends throughout the country have joined in this greeting with almost unprecedented vigor.

Like *Labor Action, The Militant,* which is the spokesman of the Socialist Workers Party, also printed the first manifesto to be issued by our Italian comrades. Here is how they headlined it in the April 8 issue of *The Militant*: Trotskyists in Italy Issue Call for Socialist Struggle. Denounce the Betrayals by the Second and Third International; Summon Masses to Fight for Socialist United States of Europe." The editors commented that this "very important document" was "issued by the Italian Trotskyists in the name of the Provisional National Center which has been constituted for the building of the Communist Internationalist Party (Fourth International). The text of this document is the first definitive proof that the genuine voice of revolutionary socialism is beginning to make itself heard amid the crucial events in Italy."

It is true that in reprinting the manifesto, the editors noted what they called "the vaguest and weakest section of the document," namely, the section on Russia. The reason for this was that the section indicates that our Italian comrades have not fallen into the reactionary trap of supporting Stalinist Russia in the war or designating that slave régime as a "workers' state." The document, while showing how Russia serves Anglo-American imperialism, does not refer to Russia's own imperialist ambitions and plans. But this defect is quite opposite to that of which the SWP complains. In any case *The Militant* did speak of the document on April 8 as *"the genuine voice of revolutionary socialism"* and of our comrades as "the Italian Trotskyists." That was good, that was right, that was wise, that was intelligent.

But since April 8, the editors have apparently received instructions that are neither good, right, wise nor intelligent. In their May 13 issue, they make a turn-about-face which is downright disgraceful. Under the imposing heading of "Trotskyism and the European Revolution," the editors suddenly find that the manifesto of our Italian comrades is no longer "the genuine voice of revolutionary socialism."

The editors are of course aware that members of the Socialist Workers Party, like members of our Workers Party, have responded with enthusiasm and sympathy to the news from Italy. They know, also, that many SWP members are beginning to reflect seriously and critically upon their disastrous party policy of supporting the Russian army as it advances to crush the coming European working class revolution under the weight of the GPU. The SWP policy of "unconditional defense of the Soviet Union" is

From *New International,* May 1944, "A blow at the Fourth International. *The Militant* and our Italian comrades".

not working out so well! So the editors proceed to pour an icy douche over this part of their followers:

"Nothing could be more fatal to the Trotskyist movement than to permit instinctive sympathy — for any insurgent groups fighting under the difficult conditions which exist in Europe today — to betray us into political conciliationism."

Political conciliationism with the counter-revolutionary Stalinist régime is all right for the SWP — but no "conciliationism" with the revolutionary socialists of Italy. The editors piously note that they can help the revolution in Europe and help "build a strong Trotskyist organization, only by drawing a sharp line of demarcation between the genuine Trotskyists and the impostors and muddleheads." In five short weeks, the Italian Trotskyists have ceased to be Trotskyists or to speak with "the genuine voice of revolutionary socialism" and have become "impostors and muddleheads."

Why? Because the "wiser" heads in the SWP have now realized what was always clear: *"The authors of this manifesto, who apparently wish to deny such defense* [of Russia] *felt the necessity of equivocating. No group can really be Trotskyist if it attempts to straddle the Russian question. The manifesto does not call for the defense of the Soviet Union. It does not characterize the Soviet Union as a workers' state. Therefore the manifesto is not an authentic Trotskyist manifesto."*

The language and style are typically Stalinist (even if used in the name of Trotsky), and so is the spirit of this excommunication.

Just think of this: After more than twenty years of fascist rule, after almost five years of the most devastating war in history, and in face of mountainous difficulties, a group of Trotskyists is organized and comes forward with a document which rings out as the "genuine voice of revolutionary socialism" even to the editors of *The Militant*. This group has what is so rare in the working-class movement right now — a sound position on the imperialist war and both camps in it. It has a correct position on fascism, imperialist democracy and the struggle for socialism. It has a correct position on Stalinism and the right-wing socialists, the Third and Second Internationals. Its position on the Socialist United States of Europe and world socialism is correct. So is its position on the struggle for democratic rights and demands in Italy, and the relation of this struggle to the fight for workers' power.

All this is of tremendous importance to the reviving revolutionary movement in Europe, and therefore to all of us here in the United States. On May 13, however, *The Militant* sees absolutely nothing of all this and has not a word to say about it. Its original greeting is replaced by a venomous denunciation. The "Italian Trotskyists" become "impostors and muddleheads." Workers are warned against yielding to their "instinctive sympathy" for the new Italian movement. The whole fundamental position of the Italian revolutionists fades into complete unimportance by the side of their unforgivable sin: *They do not adopt the SWP position on Stalinist Russia!*

The editors of *The Militant* are wrong on two counts (we politely use the word "wrong" instead of the more accurate term, "stupid and criminal").

First, so far as the "Russian question" is concerned, the Italian comrades are a thousand times more correct than the SWP. The latter can only help break the neck of the coming revolution in Europe. Today, the Russian army already stands on the threshold of Poland; tomorrow, perhaps, it will face Germany. The workers and peasants who will surely move to overturn their ruling classes and attempt to establish their own government power, will face an army which Trotsky once rightly called the tool of the Stalinist Bonapartes, the counter-revolution in Moscow. If the Polish and German masses follow the policy of the SWP, which calls upon them to work for the victory of the Stalinist army, they will facilitate the crushing of their revolution by this army and by the GPU — nothing less. *The SWP is simply asking these workers to dig their own graves.*

Our Italian comrades understand this; the SWP, with its mad fixation on "unconditional defense" of Stalinist Russia, refuses to understand it. We are entirely opposed to the SWP here, and entirely on the side of our Italian comrades and of all the other European Fourth Internationalists who have already taken or who will certainly take the same basic view.

Second, even if the Italian comrades were as wrong on Russia as *The Militant* says, since when has the position on this question become the *only* decisive test for partisans of a Fourth International? Who decided that, and when? We know that in the past many comrades were similarly "wrong" on the Russian question without being read out of the Trotskyist movement — and read out so shamefully at that. In 1939 and 1940, when half of the American Trotskyist movement was also "wrong" on the Russian question, in the opinion of *The Militant* and even of Trotsky, the latter strongly insisted that there was room in a united SWP for both groups and opinions, and that there should not be a separation over that question. If a split did nevertheless occur in the SWP, it was mainly because of the impossible conditions for membership the party leaders tried to make the opposition swallow.

Trotsky understood that the "Russian question" was not quite so simple as the SWP now holds it to be; that positions taken on it were much more subject to change than on any other important question in the revolutionary movement; that it was the Trotskyist movement itself, more than any other, which had modified its position on Russia a dozen times in accordance with changes in the situation and reconsiderations.

Trotskyism, for us, is modern revolutionary socialism. For us, all the fundamental principles of the socialist criticism of capitalist society, of the struggle for workers' power, of the building of the new society — the principles of socialist internationalism — are embraced by the word "Trotskyism," modern Marxism. Only idiots can reduce "Trotskyism" to one aspect of Trotsky's position — real or perverted — on Russia, and declare slavish adherence to this position the supreme test of a revolutionary socialist.

It is the SWP leaders who have introduced this new twist in the 'Trotskyist movement. We shall see what the other supporters of the Fourth International, as well as the SWP members themselves, have to say about this innovation. The SWP itself has changed Trotsky's position on Russia — *but in a reactionary direction, so that it becomes more and more the tail-end of Stalinism,* as we have repeatedly shown in these pages. The party leaders are blind and seek to blind everyone who listens to them. Their attack upon our Italian comrades is one of the rottenest examples of what we mean. Will they open their eyes only *after* the "defense of Russia" has brought about the crushing of the European revolution?

Max Shachtman

THE BUREAUCRATIC JUNGLE

THE PARTY AND ITS POLITICAL LIFE are directed, we said [in 1939/40],
by a clique led by Cannon which we characterized as *bureaucratically conservative*. The only amendment the new opposition [Morrison, Morrow,
Bennett] was obliged to introduce into this characterization is that the
party leadership is the carrier of the *"germs of Stalinist degeneration."* This
is the latest balance-sheet that the new opposition casts up after five years
in which the leadership of the SWP operated with a maximum of party
unity, a maximum of collaboration from all the party leadership, and a minimum of inner-party opposition, that is, none at all.

Our second main criticism in the 1939 dispute may be paraphrased as follows: "You have converted the theory that Russia is a workers' state, and the
slogan of the unconditional defense of Russia in the war, into abstractions
which make it impossible for you to deal correctly with the concrete political problems of the class struggle. When you do deal with them, they bring
you to a reactionary position. You base your central strategy on the defense
of the Stalinist régime which is an integral part of the imperialist coalition
in the war. We base ours on assembling, building and leading to victory the
'third camp,' the independent forces of the workers, peasants and colonial
peoples fighting for freedom against both imperialist camps. Our policy will
make it possible for the revolutionary Marxists to come to the leadership of
the inevitably upsurging movement of rebellion. Yours will make you the
apologist of Stalinism, the tail to its kite."

The Cannonites answered, as is their custom in such disputes, with a
minimum of argument and a maximum of imprecation: "We reiterate our
fundamental principles. We cling to our fundamental principles. We are
for unconditional defense of the Soviet Union. You have capitulated, in the
war, to the pressure of bourgeois democracy. You are petty-bourgeois opponents of Marxism."

Let us see how these "fundamental principles" have stood up in practice
(and this is the only decisive test) in the past few years, not in the light of
our criticism, so much as in the light of the criticism of the new oppositionists who joined, alas, in the condemnation of us in 1939 and later. For this
purpose, we have an invaluable document by A Roland, significantly entitled "We Arrive at a Line." Roland is an old party member, and unlike
Cannon and the court clique, knows something about Marxism. He was a
stout defender of Trotsky's position in 1939. His criticism is all the more
enlightening because of that.

In the very first place, Roland shows again that, all sophistry,
muddle-headed argument and "theory" to the contrary notwithstanding, it

Abridged from *New International*, March 1945, "From the bureaucratic jungle. The SWP
changes the line". "Morrison" here is a pen-name for Albert Goldman, who had gone into
opposition within the SWP; in 1946 he would leave the SWP and be a member of the Workers
Party for two years before leaving at the same time as Ernest Erber (see chapter 1). "Roland"
is Louis Jacobs. "A comrade with great prestige in the Fourth International" is Natalia
Sedova, Leon Trotsky's widow. "Frank" is Bert Cochrane.

is impossible, in the Cannonite party, to engage in a serious political dispute without coming into head-on conflict with the party régime which always defends its prestige and position by the methods it knows best, the methods of bureaucratism. His indictment of this régime is more damning than anything we wrote and said about it five years ago.

Now let us see what policy it is that this régime had to defend, and see it the way it worked out in practice. It cannot be over-emphasized that this is the decisive test. With the evidence assembled by Roland, let us apply the test to the "Russian policy" of the SWP. Roland's indictment on this score charges the leadership with hopeless confusion; hopeless inconsistency; inability to orient itself correctly or at all toward important events; painting up, apologizing for and tail-ending Stalinism; and in general, woodenness of thought, unthinking paraphrasing of Trotsky, perversion of political line for considerations of bureaucratic prestige. For every charge, he adduces more than enough of the necessary proof.

The SWP line, boiled down to essentials, was simply this, repeated week-in and week-out: Russia is a workers' state because the property in it is nationalized. In the war, the Stalinist bureaucracy is pursuing a role which is objectively revolutionary. Between Stalinist Russia and the capitalist world there are antagonisms which are irreconcilable. It is the primary duty of every worker to defend Russia — unconditionally.

The lengths to which these absurd and reactionary dogmas were carried, are given by Roland in some detail. Here is one example from the pen of one of the principal official spokesmen of the party, Wright, as set down in the April, 1943, *Fourth International*:

"But the same fundamental forces arising out of the irreconcilable clash between Soviet economy and world imperialism are driving the bureaucratic caste to measures which are revolutionary in their objective consequences... The Stalinist bureaucracy depends for its existence upon the maintenance of the workers' state created by the October Revolution. In desperation and as a last resort this bureaucracy has proved itself capable of acting in self-defense as to stimulate revolutionary developments..."

If Stalinism is *objectively revolutionary* and *"has proved itself"* able to stimulate revolutionary developments, the Marxian criticism of it ought to be reduced to fairly modest proportions. What else could a reader, who has not been immunized against such reactionary nonsense, conclude if he continued to read the SWP press? He would learn there that the Stalinist bureaucracy is not only taking measures that are revolutionary in their objective consequences, but that at one time "Stalin took preparatory steps for the Sovietization of Finland." (This pitiable muddlehead of a Wright does not even know the difference between nationalization of industry and *Sovietization*, i.e., the means by which the proletariat establishes and consolidates its class power. To him, the appointment of slave-drivers over industry by the GPU equals — Sovietization, the proletarian revolution.) And not only of Finland. Poland, too. In *The Militant* of January 29, 1944, the same Wright had these unbelievable things to say about the program of Stalin's Quislings in Poland: *"...the realization of this program would signify the complete destruction of Polish capitalism and a giant step in the inevitable extension of Soviet [again: Soviet!] property forms far beyond the frontiers of 1939. In its turn, this carries a two-fold threat to capitalism: first, in addition to strengthening the USSR immeasurably, it would greatly ham-*

per further attempts to isolate it. Second, the revolutionary wave in Europe, especially in Germany, would receive so mighty an impulsion from such developments in the territories of former Poland, let alone Silesia, East Prussia, etc., that the attempt to drown the coming European Revolution in blood would be rendered well-nigh impossible".

After this, nothing remains of the revolutionary struggle against Stalinism except a demand that it… carry out its program! Nothing more than this is required to destroy capitalism in Poland and Eastern Germany — that as a mere beginning! — by extending "Soviet" property to these lands, and then to give the proletarian revolution all over Europe such an impulsion as would practically guarantee its victory.

The Stalinist bureaucracy, the GPU factory bosses, and Osubka-Morawski are not the only guarantees of the victory of the European proletariat. There is also the Stalinist army. Trotsky called it the military arm of the Bonapartist counterrevolution. Wright, however, uninhibited by Trotsky's modesty and other qualities, has a different name for it. In a 1941 article, he wrote:

"It is not Stalin's Red Army that has successfully resisted the first two Nazi offensives. It is the Red Army of the October Revolution. It is Trotsky's Red Army, which was built in the fire of the Civil War, built not from the wreckage of the old Czarist armies but completely anew — unlike any other army in history… The Kremlin is of course trying to usurp credit for the heroic resistance of the Red Army, but Stalin will not succeed in this. We Trotskyists [Wright, it seems, calls himself a Trotskyist after all this!] *link up the present heroic resistance of the Red soldiers directly with the Russian October and the Civil War… Terrible as were the blows dealt by Stalin to the Red Army, it remains the one institution least affected* [!!!!] *by his degenerated régime".*

From this political delirium should follow, should it not, a clarion call to the workers throughout Europe: "Proletarians, welcome Trotsky's Red Army. Welcome the liberators of the toiling peoples! Welcome the Heroic Storm-Troop Divisions of the GPU, who are directly linked with the Red October!"

What has been quoted is not an individual aberration, although that is a contributing element in this case. It is the product of a political line. We have in addition, also quoted by Roland, the case of E R Frank. Frank is another of the party bureaucrats who has recently decided to turn a deft hand to "theoretical questions," under the impression that a snarl, pugnacious ignorance and phrasemongering are ample qualification. How, he demands in an article on December 4, 1943 — *"How is anybody going to explain today that amazing unity of Soviet peoples, that unprecedented vitality and morale which exists throughout the Red Army and the peoples of the Soviet Union, except on the theory that the October Revolution, though stifled and degraded, still lives…".*

Roland's comment on this panegyric to Stalinism is to the point:

"The complete unity of the Soviet peoples — under the totalitarian régime of Stalin! How could one possibly call for political revolution in that case? The unity of the Soviet peoples amidst the growth of inequality and an almost complete indifference of the bureaucracy to the lot and fate of the people during the war. The unity of the Soviet peoples — and the imprisonment even during the war not of tens of thousands, or hundreds of thousands, but

of millions in the concentration camps of the Kremlin! Could Stalin have wished for better propaganda in his favor? Stalin could have pointed to our press and asked what further proof was necessary that his killing off of all the oppositionists had united and strengthened the USSR".

We thereby get a very accurate definition of an "official Trotskyist," i.e., a Cannonite: He is a miserable epigone of Trotsky who cannot speak on Russia without carrying on, among revolutionary workers, better propaganda for Stalin than Stalin himself could hope for.

And by combining Wright and Frank, we get the following definition of Stalinist Russia: It is a country which is despotically oppressed by a totalitarian, counter-revolutionary Bonapartist autocracy that has converted the country as a whole into a prison for the people and is based upon Soviet property, an amazing unity of the Soviet peoples, and Trotsky's Red Army, all of which it employs to take objectively revolutionary measures that stimulate the world revolution — thus making Russia a workers' state, which is in irreconcilable antagonism to the imperialist world that is allied with it, gives it aid and comfort, and material and even political support, in return for material and political support received.

For the length of this definition, we are ready to take our share of responsibility; for its insanity, we share no responsibility and accept none.

The reader may think: After all, it is only Wright, or only Frank, who is involved. If he is an informed reader, he may add: And after all, who is forced to take them seriously as the spokesmen of the SWP? There is *some* validity to such reflections. What is wrong and misleading about them is shown by three facts: One, that their statements appear as the official view of the SWP. Two, that they are not rebuked or repudiated in any way by the party leadership, but were and are still being defended by the latter. And three, that the boss of the party himself is of a piece with them.

To prove the last assertion, we refer once more to Roland's precious document. Following page after page of evidence on the reactionary character of the official party policy on Russia, coupled with as much evidence on the preposterous vacillation and somersaults of the party press from week to week and month to month, he arrives at the period of the Warsaw uprising of last August. Under pressure of the stirring event, and of Roland himself, the SWP committee made another somersault in policy. It came out in favor of the Warsaw uprising, ranged itself with the revolutionists, warned them against Stalinist perfidy and counter-revolution, and called among other things for fraternization with the Russian army so as to help the Russian people "settle accounts with the bloody Bonapartist dictatorship of Stalin." Those of us who read the editorial in *The Militant* of August 19, 1944, recall with some satisfaction the policy presented in it. We recall also that it followed from the inspiring action of the Warsaw proletariat, and in no way whatsoever from anything in the analysis and policies defended up to then by the Cannonites.

The party boss, who was not at hand when the editorial appeared, reacted promptly, for a change. His letter of protest against the editorial is a monstrosity, but such a revealing one that we reprint it in its entirety, thanks to Roland, who did likewise in order to thwart the party bureaucracy's attempt to conceal it from the membership:

"The August 19 Militant *editorial, 'Warsaw Betrayed,' goes even further afield than the previous editorial we wrote about in muddling up our line of*

443

'Unconditional Defense of the Soviet Union' in the struggle against the Nazi-imperialist invaders. To call upon the revolutionary Polish workers to 'organize fraternization' with the Red Army soldiers, as the editorial does, is to think in terms of establishing contact with the rank and file of a hostile military force. But the Polish workers must be the allies of the Red Army in its war against Hitler's armies, *no matter how reactionary Stalin's policy is. Therefore, the task for the Polish revolutionaries is* to organize revolutionary propaganda *in the ranks of the Red Army, with which they will be in contact as allies, not to 'organize fraternization.' Secondly, the editorial adds that through this 'fraternization' the Polish workers will help the Soviet masses to 'settle accounts with the bloody Bonapartist dictatorship of Stalin.' Our program recognizes the vital necessity of overthrowing Stalinism in the Soviet Union and has always placed this task in order of importance second only to the defense of the Soviet Union against imperialist attacks. However, it is precisely the latter consideration that the editorial slurs over. Finally, the editorial again fails to put explicitly and unmistakably our slogan 'Unconditional defense of the Soviet Union' against all imperialists. The editorial also takes for granted a version of the Warsaw events about which there is little information, none of it reliable and many uncertainties. A full-scale battle against the Nazis by the Warsaw proletariat is assumed, as is the 'order of Stalin's generals' in halting the Red Army attack on the city. The Moscow charge that the London 'Polish government in exile' ordered the uprising without consulting the Red Army command is brushed aside without being clearly stated, much less analyzed in the light of the current Soviet-Polish negotiations. No consideration is given to the question of whether or not the Red Army was able at the moment to launch an all-out attack on Warsaw in view of its long-sustained offensive, the Nazi defensive preparations along the Vistula, the necessity to regroup forces and mass for new attacks after the not inconsiderable expenditure of men and material in reaching the outskirts of Warsaw, the fact that there was a lull along virtually the entire Eastern front concurrent with the halt before Warsaw, etc.* Nor does the editorial take up the question of the duty of guerrilla forces — and in the circumstances that is what the Warsaw detachments are — to subordinate themselves to the high command of the main army, *the Red Army, in timing such an important battle as the siege of Warsaw. On the contrary, the editorial appears to take as its point of departure the assumption that a full-scale proletarian uprising occurred in Warsaw and that Stalin deliberately maneuvered to permit Hitler to crush the revolt. A hasty, sketchy commentary on events, including the badly-limping Badoglio analogy, is then fitted into this arbitrary framework. We agree, indeed, as to Stalin's counter-revolutionary intentions. Moreover, one has the right to suspect or believe personally that the Warsaw events are just as the editorial pictures them. But we have no right to put in writing in our press, and in an editorial to boot, such sweeping assertions for which we have no proof and to draw conclusions based on such flimsy information. That is not the tradition of* The Militant. *We are deeply concerned about this carelessness in writing about such a crucial question and are anxious to hear the comments on our criticism*".

Let us not dwell on the style — it is as unnecessary as it is disagreeable. In any case, the political line is infinitely more important. The Warsaw proletariat was climaxing five years of unremitting struggle against its *nation-*

444

al and class oppressor with an epic effort. The Stalin régime was preparing its stab in the back not only with cynicism and cold-bloodedness, but above all with such obviousness as to move even the editors of *The Militant* away from this false line and toward a correct one. By defending the antithesis of what they had defended, they leaped over their own heads and — did their revolutionary duty. If, as the party boss said, they went "further afield... in muddling up our line of 'unconditional defense of the Soviet Union'," it was because the line was radically false; but in "muddling" it further, they at least made one progressive contribution amidst the hundred reactionary ones they had made in the past.

What did the party boss contribute? Instructions to the effect that *The Militant* should advise the Warsaw proletariat (contemptuously referred to as guerrilla forces! Stalin's army of counter-revolution is Trotsky's Red Army, but the insurrectionary Warsaw workers are... mere guerrillas) to "subordinate themselves to the high command of the main army, the Red Army." Or, to translate this pompous pseudo-military wisdom: the Warsaw workers must submit to the executioners of the GPU! In what name? In the name of "unconditional defense of the Soviet Union"!

Not even the Stalinists dared to carry out the crushing of the Polish proletariat under such a banner. The boss of the SWP deserves to be remembered if only for the fact that he was the one person in the whole wide world who called upon the Warsaw workers to "subordinate themselves" to their hangman, Stalin ("the high command of the main army"). There is the fruit, *in practice*, of the "defense of the Soviet Union."

The sequel to this letter is as revealing as the letter itself. At about the same time that it was written, another letter was being written and, unknown to the party boss, transmitted to the SWP leadership. It came from a comrade with great prestige in the Fourth International, a comrade whose opinions cannot be so easily dismissed by the Cannonites with personal aspersions, dirty gossip or imprecations (be it noted that we write, "cannot be so *easily* dismissed"). It, too, is worth reprinting in its entirety:

"I do not consider myself competent in political questions to the extent of condemning this or that line of your conduct. But in the given instance your mistaken course is all too clear to me. Permit me a few words in this connection. You seem to be hypnotized by the slogan of the 'defense of the USSR' and in the meantime profound changes, political as well as moral-psychological, have taken place in its social structure. In his articles, especially the last ones, L D [Trotsky] wrote of the USSR as a degenerating workers' state and in view of this outlined two possible paths of further social evolution of the first workers' state: revolutionary and reactionary. The last four years have shown us that the reactionary landslide has assumed monstrous proportions within the USSR. I shall not recount the facts, they are known to you — they bespeak of the complete moving away of the USSR from the principles of October. Soviet literature for the war years (Moscow magazines which I am receiving) confirm these facts; in current Moscow literature there is not the slightest echo of socialistic ideology; dominant in it are petty bourgeois, middle class tendencies; the cult of the family and its welfare. The Red Army, at the basis of whose organization were lodged the principles of the October overturn, and whose (the Red Army's) goal was the struggle for the world revolution, has become transformed into a nationalist-patriotic organization, defending the fatherland, and not against its bureaucratic régime but togeth-

er with its *régime* as it has taken shape in the last decade. *Do you recall the answer of L D to the question put to him in the Politburo in 1927: whether the Opposition would defend the USSR in case of war? 'The socialist fatherland — yes; Stalin's régime — no'.*

The 'socialist' has fallen away; the 'régime' has remained. A degenerating 'workers' state' presupposes that it is moving along the path of degeneration, still preserving its basic principle — the nationalization of private property. But just as it is impossible to build socialism in one country, so it is impossible to preserve inviolate this basic principle, if one pursues the reactionary road, destroying all the other conquests of 1917. It is necessary to explain this tirelessly day by day. It is impermissible to repeat an antiquated slogan by rote.

At the present time there is only one danger threatening the Soviet Union — that is the further development of black reaction, the further betrayal of the international proletariat. This is precisely the direction in which it is necessary to sound the alarm. To defend the Soviet Union against the régime of its 'master,' mercilessly laying bare the policy of the master who comes to the fore on the international arena in the capacity of a conciliator with bourgeois capitalism and as a counter-revolutionist in the European countries liberated from Hitler. (As far back as 1937 L D wrote in the Bulletin of the Russian Opposition *that not a single serious person believes any longer in the revolutionary role of Stalin.)*

You are correctly criticizing the foreign policy of the Marshal, but after all, foreign policy is the continuation of the domestic policy; it is impermissible to separate the one from the other. In your position there is a crying contradiction. It is necessary to hammer away at one point: to warn against the consequences of Russian victories; to warn, to sound the alarm on the basis of the elements that have already been disclosed with complete clarity, as well as to lay bare those elements which are about to be disclosed, and at the same time to point the way out".

This letter, which is blow upon blow at point after point of the SWP position, as Roland points out, caused a sensation and complete consternation among the SWP leadership. Their first reaction: how to conceal it from the membership! And not only from the membership, but even from those leading members, like Morrow and Morrison, who were in opposition! Their second reaction: how to maintain the prestige of the party leadership, and above all, of the party boss, who had *just written* in the directly opposite sense! Thanks in large measure to Roland, the leadership succeeded in neither case. It was not for want of trying.

The letter just quoted was promptly communicated to the party boss. With an agility nowhere revealed in his first letter, he prepared a retreat. He wrote a new letter to the committee which proposed, in effect, a change of policy on Russia, accompanied by all kinds of transparent "subtleties" to prove that it was not, after all, a change in policy. Like his previous letter, which said the opposite, it was couched in his customary Statesman-Tone, and intended for proclamation to the entire party membership. It prudently omitted (a) any reference whatsoever to his original letter, with which it did not jibe, and (b) any reference whatsoever to the letter we have quoted, which criticized the SWP line and urged a change in it. If any change is to be made in the party line, only One Man may initiate it — at least so far as the membership knows! What had changed in the world situation? What

446

had changed in the situation in Russia? For the boss, nothing. All that had changed was that someone with prestige and *authority* that cannot easily be torn down in the movement had proposed a change. In the SWP leadership, where, as Roland says, a "completely hierarchic attitude" reigns, it is not freely-expressed critical thought, not the unhampered exchange of views, not objective considerations, but "authority" and prestige-considerations that decide policy. There, and there alone, lies the secret of the recent (essentially meaningless) "change" in the SWP policy on Russia. To the complete surprise and dumbfoundment of the membership, without their having been prepared for it in the slightest degree — just the opposite! — the party leadership solemnly announced that the slogan of "unconditional defense of the Soviet Union" has been subjected to "a shift in emphasis."

How delicately put! What refinement! Now, you see, due to "the shift in objective conditions" (translation: the shift in emphasis recommended by the influential comrade and the need of preserving bureaucratic prestige), the old slogan is no longer "in the fore." It is "retired" to a secondary place. Nothing wrong with it, mind you, only it doesn't have the very, very first place now. In its place "We therefore push to the fore and emphasize today *that section* of our program embodied in the slogan: *Defense of the European Revolution Against All Its Enemies! The Defense of the European Revolution* coincides with the genuine revolutionary defense of the USSR." (SWP Convention Resolution.) Apparently, before today the defense of the European revolution did not coincide with the "genuine revolutionary defense of the USSR"; but from today onward it does. That is, now that the Cannonites have contributed their tiny mite to helping Stalinist Russia grow stronger against the European revolution (Warsaw worker, subordinate yourselves to the Marshal!), it is obviously high time to defend that revolution.

No open correction of errors; no honest explanation of changes and turns; politics as an instrument of organization instead of organization as an instrument of politics — that is how the Cannonites rule and ruin the SWP. It is not necessary to emphasize that the political education of the membership is utterly impossible under such conditions. This is not to say, necessarily, that it is also impossible to increase the membership of such a party. It is possible. But it will not be a revolutionary party that deserves the name of Trotsky. It is not by accident that Roland tells of what the "authoritative" comrade wrote in another letter to the SWP. The letter, says Roland, *"...reminded them (please tell us in what connection, Comrade Stein) of an incident way back in 1927 in which the Old Man and a Stalinist bureaucrat were involved. The Old Man was criticizing the Stalinists in the Executive Committee. One of them asked: 'Where is the party?' and Trotsky replied: "You have strangled the party!"* Idle reminiscence? No, the comrade is making a timely, pointed — and, in its nature, a deadly — reference to what is happening to the SWP under the Cannonite régime, which Morrison rightly called the bearer of the virus of Stalinism. The future of the SWP as a revolutionary organization is, at best, a dubious one. We recognized that five years ago. What has happened since has only made this fact plainer and caused many others to realize it. The number of those who understand this can only increase.

Max Shachtman

PRE-WAR PERSPECTIVES AND POST-WAR REALITIES

THE QUESTIONS WE POSED in the September *New International* have not remained unanswered. Our questions dealt with the theory that Stalinist Russia is a "degenerated workers' state," the theory set forth by Trotsky, and now thoroughly sterilized by the spokesmen of the Socialist Workers Party.

We quoted from a few of the declarations Trotsky had made before the war. He said repeatedly: *If a successful socialist revolution does not follow on the heels of the war, it will make no difference whether the Stalinist régime gains a military victory or suffers a military defeat* — "imperialism will sweep away the régime which issued from the October Revolution"; and "the inner social contradictions of the Soviet Union not only might, but must, lead to a bourgeois Bonapartist counterrevolution"; and "no military victory can save the inheritance of the October Revolution"; and "without the interference of revolution, the social bases of the Soviet Union must be crushed, not only in the case of defeat, but also in the case of victory."

No ambiguity, is there? No possibility of misunderstanding? One would think so. We simply asked the SWP people to say: Have events confirmed or refuted the analysis and predictions which Trotsky made in *inseparable* connection with his theory? If confirmed, how? If refuted, why? In any case, please answer.

Past experience with attempts to get the Cannonites to discuss the position which outstandingly distinguishes them in the revolutionary movement have not been encouraging. Being incorrigible optimists, we made the new attempt. In this case, patience has been rewarded by more than itself. We received not one answer to our questions, but two. Better than that. The two are not only not identical — thus sparing us the monotony of reiteration — but different, and not merely different, but different to the point of being mutually exclusive. Let whoever wishes to do so speak henceforth about the SWP as a monolithic party. Here, in any case, is living evidence of the fact that it not only permits the public avowal and defense of two different positions, but of mutually antagonistic positions, both of which bear the official stamp! We for our part never asked for that much. The most rabid democrat could not ask for more.

The first official answer is given by the leader of the party himself, in a speech delivered on the occasion of the 28th anniversary of the Bolshevik revolution (*Militant*, Nov. 17, 1945). We note first of all that Cannon does not once question the significance of Trotsky's prediction or its inseparable connection with Trotsky's theory. We note that he goes further — he reiterates the prediction. We note finally that he reiterates also the theory

From *New International*, December 1945, "Pre-war perspectives and post-war realities. An analysis of the politics of the Fourth International". This article refers to the proposals for WP-SWP reunification made at the time by the WP and the SWP minority. The SWP refused. In 1947 the WP and SWP agreed to reunite, but the agreement broke down.

that Russia is still a degenerated workers' state which every worker should defend against imperialism.

At first blush, this would seem to be impossible. The prediction said so plainly, didn't it, that if the war ends without a successful socialist revolution, the Russian workers' state, *in any form*, is done for. If Russia is defeated, the Stalin régime *and* nationalized property (the basis, so called, of the working-class character of the Russian state) will be wiped out. If Russia is victorious, then in the absence of the revolution, the "inner social contradictions not only might *but must* lead to a bourgeois Bonapartist counter-revolution." The revolution — it is hard but necessary to say — did not come. Russia was not defeated but victorious; the bourgeois counter-revolution did not come; private property has not been restored in Russia, nationalized property remains supreme. How does Cannon get over these not inconsiderable obstacles? By a leap which makes the nursery cow's jump over the moon look like a stroll through the meadow. Here is his *salto mortale* described in his own words:

"Trotsky predicted that the fate of the Soviet Union would be decided in the war. That remains our firm conviction. Only we disagree with some people who carelessly think that the war is over. The war has only passed through one stage and is now in the process of regroupment and reorganization for the second. The war is not over, and the revolution which we said would issue from the war in Europe, is not taken off the agenda. It has only been delayed and postponed, primarily for lack of leadership, for lack of a sufficiently strong revolutionary party".

There it is, with all the sweeping simplicity that distinguishes true genius! The prediction? Nothing wrong with it — absolutely nothing. Whoever thinks otherwise is a careless thinker. The trouble with such people is, you see, that they believe the war is over. Well, it just isn't. It has, you should understand, "only passed through one stage." What stage? The stage of armed, military struggle, the stage which twice-harebrained, careless thinkers have up to now called the stage of "war," but which must henceforward be called, among the careful thinkers of the SWP, by the simpler name of "one stage." Into what stage has it passed? Into the stage of the suspension of armed, military struggle, the stage which the thrice-ridiculous careless thinkers have up to now called the stage of "peace" or "imperialist peace," but which shall henceforward be called by the careful thinkers by the name of "the process of regroupment and reorganization for the second" stage. And the second stage? That cannot, it is clear, be called the resumption of the war, or the outbreak of a new war, since the war is not over in the first place. It cannot be called the Third World War, since the Second is not over (the Second, as a matter of fact, never existed — it was merely the continuation of the process of regroupment and reorganization which followed the First World War, which in turn is not over because it never came to an end).

All that is lacking is the names of the "some people who carelessly think that the war is over," so that the several hundred million other people who today have a somewhat similar notion may be better able to guard against them. That we are among them appears evident. But why should we be condemned to solitary confinement?

In the May, 1945, *Fourth International*, theoretical organ of the SWP, we read that "On the continent of Europe the agony of the imperialist war is

449

thus concluded; the agony of the imperialist 'peace' has begun." Cannon, out of restraints imposed upon him by solidarity with his own party comrades, may content himself with calling the editor of the *FI* a careless thinker. We see no need of such restraint. We call him *an idiot* for saying that the war is over in Europe. He is doubly an idiot for not keeping quiet till November when he could have learned from a real authority that the war is *not* over.

In the October, 1945, *Fourth International*, E R Frank writes that "The imperialist war in the Far East has ended." He writes that "The United States emerges out of the second world war as the strongest military power on earth." How can it emerge from a war when it is still submerged in the war which is not over? Careless thinker? No, not strong enough. Idiot!

In the November, 1945, *Fourth International* (the very eve of Cannon's historic pronouncement!), William R Warde writes that "The recently concluded war was a costly as well as risky enterprise for them." *What* recently concluded war? Idiot!

The press of the SWP is obviously written and edited by idiots. Who is not an idiot? Who thinks carefully? Differ with him all you want, but the truth is the truth, and the answer is: Cannon. For this, he deserves special recognition. For example, couldn't a sculptor be assigned the task of making a bust of the careful thinker to be set in a prominent place of honor in the headquarters of the SWP? Not an everyday bust, but a gilded one, of course. It may be objected that such an exhibition is not compatible with the dignity and morality of a revolutionary proletarian movement, that it is loathsome Byzantine icon-worship, that it is typical of Stalinism, that no revolutionist would assent to such a spectacle, especially if he were himself the subject of the bust. Are these objections really so cogent? Besides, hasn't the bust already been carved, gilded and placed? We ask the question with hypocritical innocence.

But enough! Let us try our luck with the second official answer, this time from the careless thinker who edits the *Fourth International*. His answer (November, 1945) is not only different from Cannon's, but, as we said above, exactly opposite in every respect but one: its studied disingenuousness. With E R Frank, the question is not as simple as it is with the careful thinker. He grants that the war is over; that the revolution did not triumph; that there has been no fundamental change in the Stalinist régime or in Russia; that Trotsky's prediction did not materialize. Consequently? Consequently — nothing more need be said on the matter. Everything is about the same as it was, except, perhaps, that Shachtman is more wrong than ever. But let us give a more detailed, more connected quotation from Frank, so that nothing is torn out of context, despite the certainty, based on rueful experience, that our critic will never reciprocate:

"But let us forcibly press the problem into Shachtman's narrow framework. It is true that Trotsky thought that the Soviet Union would not survive the second world war if there was no proletarian revolution; that the Soviet Union would succumb to capitalism either through intervention from without or counter-revolution from within. It is also true that hostilities between the major powers, have for the moment ceased; that imperialism still rules on a world scale and that the Soviet Union still persists under the Stalinist régime. From this Shachtman draws the sweeping con-

clusion that 'refuted... in our opinion, is the entire theory [of the degener-
ated workers' state] on which it [Trotsky's above quoted opinion] is based.'
How? Why? How does this follow? Argumentation must have some kind of
internal logic. The fundamental alternative which Trotsky analyzed as fac-
ing the Soviet Union: forward toward socialism in alliance with the world
proletariat or backward toward capitalism, remains the only possible his-
torical alternative. If one attempts to refute it by interjecting between the
proletariat and the capitalists a new bureaucratic class, one must declare
that Marxism, the science of socialism based on the internal contradictions
of capitalist society, has been proved in the light of experience, a utopia.
That is where Shachtman's 'fresh thoughts' are leading him, if he wishes to
be consistent.

All Shachtman has demonstrated, it appears to us, is that Trotsky thought
the tempo of development would be a little faster than it has proven to be.
No more. Shall we therefore overthrow his basic conception which has been
vindicated by the whole course of events? Marx thought the proletarian rev-
olution would follow fast on the heels of the bourgeois democratic revolu-
tions of 1848. But events moved more slowly. That did not invalidate the
basic conceptions of the Communist Manifesto, *did it? Marx thought the*
proletarian revolution would begin in France and the Germans would fol-
low. Instead, as we know, it was the Russians who began. Professorial
pedants and petty-bourgeois philistines have adduced these 'mistakes' time
and again as proof positive of the bankruptcy of Marxism. But Marxists
have shrugged their shoulders at such 'arguments' and have remained
unmoved even when the further accusation was hurled at them that they
had adopted a new 'religion'."

And more and more and more of the same, until you begin to wonder
whether he takes his opponent or his readers for numbskulls, or if the
obvious third possibility isn't the most likely one.

There are predictions and predictions. Trotsky's prediction about the proletarian revolution and the Second World War has about as much in common with Marx's prediction a hundred years ago as Frank's argumentation has in common with any kind of logic, internal, external, transverse
or transcendental.

Marx, Engels, Lenin, Trotsky and many others predicted, time and again,
revolutions which either did not take place or, if they did, were not successful. What has that to do with our present discussion? What has that to
do with the validation or invalidation of the "basic conceptions of the
Communist Manifesto"? Or with "proof positive of the bankruptcy of
Marxism"? Or with the abandonment of the perspective and fight for
socialism, which Frank slyly (and slanderously) suggests is the conclusion
we have drawn? Nothing! And where is the analogy with Trotsky's specific prediction which, we like to assume, is under discussion? Nowhere! To
prove this, it is fully necessary to *construct* an analogy.

Had Marx's prediction a hundred years ago about the imminence of a
socialist revolution been supplemented with the declaration: if this revolution does not take place at a certain time the military victory or defeat
of a bourgeois state in a war with a feudal state would make no difference
— we would have something analogous to Trotsky's prediction.

If Marx had declared: In the absence of a proletarian victory at the end
of such a war, either the victorious feudalists or the victorious bourgeoisie

451

will inevitably destroy bourgeois private property and restore feudal property — we would have an analogy with Trotsky's declaration.

If Marx had predicted: Should the war end without a proletarian victory, "the inner social contradictions of the bourgeois state not only might, but must, lead to a feudal counterrevolution" — we would have an analogy with Trotsky.

And if Marx had added: my prediction is *inextricably* connected with the theory from which I derive it, namely, the theory that the bourgeoisie is a passing phenomenon, a caste, not a class, that it is in immanent conflict with bourgeois private property, which it seeks to undermine in its historical capacity of agent of world feudalism, and this theory will be demonstrated *definitively* by the outcome of this war — then we would have an analogy with Trotsky.

Frank presents the matter as though we were engaged in some miserable carping over the date given in a prediction about proletarian revolution. We will not charge him with polemical dishonesty, but we have the right to protest against his hope that the reader is a fool. For who but a fool will believe that we, or anyone, could have more than a passing interest in an erroneous prediction of this kind, let alone base a theoretical conception upon it? Something far more serious and profound is involved.

At the very beginning of the war, Trotsky showed how intimately he linked his Russian theory with the outcome of the war. *"Might we not place ourselves in a ludicrous position,"* he wrote (*In Defense of Marxism*, p. 14), *"if we affixed to the Bonapartist oligarchy the nomenclature of a new ruling class just a few years or even a few months prior to its inglorious downfall?"* A few lines later, emphasizing that the outcome of the second world war will provide a test of *"decisive significance* for our appraisal of the modern epoch," he wrote:

"If contrary to all probabilities the October Revolution fails during the course of the present war, or immediately thereafter, to find its continuation in any of the advanced countries; and if, on the contrary, the proletariat is thrown back and everywhere and on all fronts — then we should doubtless have to pose the question of revising our conception of the present epoch and its driving forces. In that case it would be a question not of slapping a copybook label on the USSR or the Stalinist gang but of re-evaluating the world historical perspective for the next decades if not centuries: Have we entered the epoch of social revolution and socialist society, or on the contrary the epoch of the declining society of totalitarian bureaucracy?"

Does Frank know these passages? Certainly! For he quotes the passages that follow them immediately, but takes "scrupulous" care not to hint, much less to quote, Trotsky's full thought. Trotsky indicated pretty clearly the conditions under which "we should doubtless have to *pose the question* of revising our conception of the present epoch and its driving forces." In every way conceivable (and all their ways are a disgrace to the fine tradition of Marxian theoretical thought and debate), Frank and his friends are determined to prevent so much as a *posing* of the question, much less a discussion of it.

But whether there is "official" permission or not, the question *is* posed by events. Frank evidently believes it can be disposed of by brave bluster heavily dosed with demagoguery. "We don't believe that the defeats of the working class are definitive," he writes. "We don't believe…" Who does?

Names, please! "No one, in our opinion, has adduced sufficiently weighty evidence, however, to demonstrate that the working class has been *historically* defeated," he writes. In whose opinion *has* sufficient evidence been adduced? Shachtman's? The Workers Party's? The German comrades'? It is possible, from the comparative immunity of one's own editorial pages, to misrepresent an opponent's position, to falsify and twist it, to distort it by ripping sentences out of context, as Frank does, for example, and not for the first time, with an ironical sentence taken from an article in *The New International* by our German comrade, Arlins. But falsification and distortion are "sufficiently weighty evidence" of only one thing: the polemical and political morals of those who resort to them.

From a posing of the question that Trotsky raised, there do not necessarily follow the hypothetical conclusions that he indicated in 1939, namely, the disappearance of the perspective of proletarian victory and socialism. Nothing of the sort. But such a perspective cannot be maintained by people who, consciously or not, have lost or are losing a profound inner conviction about socialism that comes only from a well-grounded analysis of the actual development of society. It cannot be maintained by people who, losing this conviction, seem to be pressing back their own inner doubts by shouting "consolatory" promises, theories, slogans. "We have not lost it all; we still have the Soviet Union, and we cling to it." (The word "cling," used so often by the Cannonites in this connection, has a revealing significance!) "Our position and analysis has been confirmed and vindicated." "The revolution is on the order of the day." "The Red Army is bringing socialism to Europe." "Germany is on the eve of the revolution — it has broken out in the concentration camps." And more of the same. It is typical precisely of the *petty bourgeois radical* that he needs self-deceptions and consoling theories to bolster his fading convictions about socialism and the socialist perspective. Is it not, for example, to faint-hearted petty bourgeois radicalism, at least in part, that we owe the popularity in Russia to what Trotsky rightly called the "consoling doctrine" of "building socialism in a single country"?

The prospects and perspectives of working class struggle are inherent in modern class society, be it in semi-feudal, capitalist or bureaucratic-collectivist form. The ruling classes have shown nothing more than the capacity to repress or delay the struggle of the proletariat for a certain period of time. They have shown a great capacity to disorient and demoralize the working class and its struggle for a certain period of time. But they cannot wipe out the working class without wiping out the very foundations of their own power, and therefore society itself. The working class, on the other hand, *must* struggle, leadership or no leadership, socialist theory or no socialist theory. It *cannot* resign itself to accepting exploitive class rule even if it wanted to do so, because society has reached the stage where the irrepressible urge to live — not to prosper, but just to live — demands the resistance of the masses. As we have put it many times, the condition for the existence of the working class is the struggle against the conditions of its existence.

The prospects and perspectives of the victorious proletarian revolution are based above all upon the fact that no other class in modern society — not the bourgeoisie, not the petty bourgeoisie, not the collectivist bureaucracy in power in Russia — no other class but the proletariat is capable of halting the inexorable trend to barbarism and of leading all the exploited and oppressed strata of the population out of the increasing economic and political chaos and agony they now endure. It has been proved again and again that under the rule of any other class there is no economic orderliness, no lasting peace, no social stability, no progress (quite the contrary!) toward abundance, democracy, freedom, equality. The proletarian revolution can disappear from the social agenda only if there is a complete atomization of society, that is, barbarism.

The prospects and perspectives of socialism are based above all upon the fact that the proletariat, once in power, cannot even establish order and rationalize economic life without taking those political and economic measures which, in their full unfoldment, lead to the classless society of socialism.

For the revolutionary Marxist, these considerations are basic and sufficient. To be sure, they are not really sufficient from the standpoint of assuring the final victory of socialism. That requires an effective revolutionary party, without which socialism is inconceivable. Effectiveness for the revolutionary party requires a careful, concrete understanding of the given period in which we function, the given situation, the actual relationship of forces, the actual trend of social and political development; and the working out of policies corresponding thereto. Without that, no *real* progress toward the socialist victory is possible. And that is precisely what is not only lacking in the SWP leadership, but what it resists with a rare combination of dogmatic and ignorant narrow-mindedness, intellectual barrenness and petty factional malice.

Take its attitude toward our German comrades. The latter have made a contribution to our arsenal of exceptional value, especially in a period of the movement's history which is characterized by such sad theoretical sterility. At least, that is the opinion of the present writer. One can differ, as the writer does, with a number of the points in the analysis and the conclusions of our German comrades. These differences remain within the field of Marxism. What is important, however, for anyone who reads the contributions of the German comrades, especially their work on "Capitalist Barbarism," and reads it loyally and objectively, is their attempt to show the real, not the fictitious, revolutionary perspectives that are opened up before us not only in the very midst of the terrible decay of monopoly capitalism and the defeats of the proletariat, but precisely because of this terrible decay. They derive the perspective for struggle and victory, what they call the "good luck" for the revolution, not from the desirability of socialism, let alone from self-intoxicating shibboleths, but from a concrete analysis of the social development. One can debate their analysis and conclusions to his heart's content provided he does it loyally and objectively. What do the Cannonites, Frank prominently among them, do with regard to the contribution of the German comrades, whose loyalty to the cause of the Fourth International is unquestionable, whose seriousness in theoretical and political questions is too well known to be disestablished by anyone? They attempt to suppress the views of the Germans; they confine their "discussion" of these views to malignant abuse of their authors as... revisionists and... "People's Fronters"! (The Cannonites' authority for such severe condemnation no doubt comes from their advice to the Warsaw revolutionists to place themselves at the disposal of the GPU executioners.)

The same attitude has been displayed by the Cannonites toward the theoretical and political contributions of our Workers Party. We saw this in the case of our resolution on the national question a few years ago, in which, for the first time in this country during the war, a concrete analysis and perspective for revolutionary struggle was elaborated, and the tasks of the revolutionary Marxists set forth. We saw it and still see it in the case of our theory of the Russian bureaucratic-collectivist state.

The Cannonites commit two gross offenses against Marxism: they refuse to submit their own theory and policies on Russia to a reëxamination in the light of actual developments; and they refuse to engage in an objective discussion of our theory and policies on the basis of our real, not alleged, not misrepresented, not falsified, but real, position and in the light of the developments. The result is a ghastly miseducation and disorientation of their followers.

We have pointed out, many time and in unanswerable detail, that the Cannonite theory and politics on the Russian question suffered complete shipwreck during the war.

They started by being the "best soldiers" in the "Red" Army (our curiosity about what makes the counter-revolutionary Stalinist army "Red" — from Stalin's standpoint, or Trotsky's standpoint, or Cannon's standpoint, or anybody's standpoint — remains entirely unsatisfied). They advised the workers and peasants of Poland, Finland, Rumania, Iran and every other country that Stalin planned to seize, conquer and enslave, to work for the Russian army, to support it, to welcome it. They hailed every victory of the Stalinist army of counter-revolution, even to the point of maligning the Old Man by calling it "Trotsky's Red Army." They acclaimed this army as the advancing guard of socialism in Europe. They spoke continuously of the "objective revolutionary consequences" of Stalin's expansion over Europe. (Yes, yes, dear friends, Gutenberg's invention was a great and troublesome one, and we have before us what you wrote.)

We polemized against all this with all our vigor, receiving only abuse for our troubles. So, to use the colorful expression of Frank, we shrugged our shoulders. We remembered the humorous epigram of Sir Robert Walpole: "Today they are ringing the bells; tomorrow they will be wringing their hands."

Tomorrow came. Their whole policy of "unconditional defense" was a success, was it not? Their "Red" army won, with or without the aid of the "best soldiers" and those they urged to be best soldiers. Their "objective revolutionary consequences" had all the opportunity they needed to manifest themselves in Europe. So — they stopped ringing the bells and began wringing their hands. To conceal their disaster, they worked out the formula — so delicate, so tender, so refined, so euphemistic! — that the slogan of "defense" of Stalinist Russia has now "receded into the background." Why? In heaven's name, why? Surely not because the war is over, for we *know* now, do we not, that the war is not over? Surely not because of a shift in the military situation, for were not we of the (don't laugh!) "petty bourgeois opposition" learnedly instructed in 1939-40 that Marxists do not base their slogans on the shifts on the military map, but only on the map of the class struggle? Why, then, the "receding"?

And what has advanced to the foreground? Nothing less, it now appears, than the defense of the European revolution. Defense from what and whom, do you think? From "Trotsky's Red Army"? From the "socialism" being brought to Europe at the point of the guns of the GPU (excuse! — of the "Red" Army)? Defense from the "objective revolutionary consequences" of Stalin's progress? You may think so, but you are wrong. The European revolution must now be defended from the Stalinist counter-revolution, from the counter-revolutionary "Red" Army, that is, from the very forces whose victory "we" urged, in whose ranks "we" were to be the best soldiers, whose triumph over and subjugation of those peoples and countries who might now be contributing to the European Revolution "we" urged them to make possible. The European Revolution, that is, must now be defended from a threat which "our" policy helped (in its tiny way) to become big and serious.

One might be persuaded to write off the whole past, provided the present represented a step forward. But is the present position of the Cannonites a real advance? In the official resolution, reluctantly adopted under the pressure of the minority group, yes. But in the practice, no. One needs no more striking evidence of this than Cannon's anniversary speech, which means more than a dozen reluctantly adopted resolutions. In the speech, there is not a word about the "defense" slogan having "receded into the background," not even a hint at it. On the contrary, what with the empha- sis on the war still being on, the defense of Russia is presented as urgent- ly as ever. As for the defense of the European Revolution from Stalinist Russia, it is not in the foreground or in the background. Not a single thought, not one solitary word, is devoted to it in the entire speech. As for such demands as the independence of Poland, of the Baltic countries, or even the old traditional slogan of the independence of the Ukraine, not so much as a hint in the speech. There is good reason to believe that in the narrow factional interests of "deepening the split" with the Workers Party, and with the SWP minority group (Cannon's speech was directed at them primarily!), of justifying the indefensible opposition to unity in the United States, this line will be presented even more belligerently in the future — and more disastrously.

As for our political line on Stalinist Russia in the war (our opposition to defensism), let our critics speak up clearly and in detail. Let them show, if they can, where our line disoriented workers on Stalinism, where it result- ed in embellishing Stalinism and its counter-revolutionary army. Let them show if they can, where our line helped the *reactionary* enemies of Stalinism, or where it contributed to aligning the working class with these enemies. Let them show, if they can, how our opposition to defense of Stalinist Russia, adopted, we were told, under the pressure of the... bour- geoisie, led to the weakening, by so much as a hair's breadth, of our class opposition to our own bourgeoisie and its imperialist war, to the weaken- ing of our struggle against the labor lieutenants of the bourgeoisie. In other words, let our critics judge *the political consequences* of our line no less severely than their own. Naturally, if the correctness of the Cannonite line is to be proved, as Frank actually writes, black on white, by the fact that the SWP has recruited some new members — then the debate is over before it began. But neither we nor the Cannonites have yet won the debate on *that* ground. By this criterion, it is the Stalinists who have won (for the time being); it is their policy that has been "proved" correct.

11. TROTSKY'S INTERNATIONAL AT THE NADIR

As the Stalinists stamped on workers' struggles both east and west after the end of World War 2, the "orthodox" Trotskyists lurched, incoherently, towards a position approximating that taken by the "other Trotskyists" in 1939. In June 1946 they called for the withdrawal of Russian troops from Eastern Europe; at their congress in March 1948 they dropped "defend the Soviet Union" in favour of "defending what remains of the conquests of October". They explained that "by defending the remnants of the conquests of October we do not in any way consider the USSR as a whole". In the USA in 1947 the "official" and "unofficial" Trotskyists agreed to reunify. But there was no clear accounting. The unity agreement collapsed. And in July 1948, responding to the open conflict between Stalin and the new Stalinist ruler of Yugoslavia, Josip Broz Tito, the "orthodox" Trotskyists lurched back — definitively, as it would turn out, for the next forty-odd years — towards being democratic and left-wing critics of Stalinism. The Cold War, a decline of working-class combativity, a general shift of politics to the Right, a new pseudo-left phase of Stalinist policy and numerical decline and isolation for anti-Stalinist Marxism, made redressment difficult and, in the event, impossible.

Max Shachtman

USA: *THE TWO TROTSKYIST TRADITIONS*

MIDWAY IN ITS EXISTENCE the Trotskyist movement underwent its severest crisis. It did not survive it intact. Every organization, even the most radical, develops its own conservatism — in program, in thought, in mode of existence. Within limits, this is as it should be, for without the element of conservatism (strictly understood as conserving what has been confidently acquired) political continuity is rendered impossible and the organization loses its distinctiveness, integrity and therefore its power of attraction because its views are changed every other Sunday. But if the organization is lacking in the element of resiliency, if its steering gear is frozen fast in the accumulated ice of dogma, then, especially in times of abrupt turns and changes such as ours, it runs the risk of driving off unscheduled curves to disaster.

Faced with the outbreak of the Second World War and the outbreak — this one unforeseen — of Stalinist imperialism in the war, the Trotskyist movement, after its bitterest internal struggle, split in two. To this day the split has not only been healed but has widened, in the United States and almost everywhere else in the world. In the United States it resulted in the formation of our Workers Party. The separation between party comrades of yesterday and especially our break with so deeply respected a teacher as Trotsky was even more painful than is usual in such cases. Evil intentions were not enough to cause the split; good intentions were not enough to prevent it. We had to hold to our revolutionary convictions as our opponents to theirs. It was impossible for us to reconcile the duties of socialist internationalism with the Trotskyist position of defense of Stalinist Russia in the war which the others maintained out of wooden traditionalism. It was likewise impossible for us to remain silent about our views out of purely formal considerations of discipline, especially when it was not always loyally imposed upon us. The issue in the dispute was too great in importance and in the responsibilities we had to discharge.

With the advantage now given us by hindsight, it is perfectly clear that the war-split of the Trotskyist movement marked a decisive turning point in its history. At this point, two basic tendencies emerged from it and have since moved in divergent directions. One of them is represented by the Socialist Workers Party and the groups like it which are part of the Fourth International, a name maintained as if to make up for an unimposing existence with an imposing title.

All they have done to discredit the good name of Trotskyism is part of the gloomy history of our time. Almost all of them are tiny sects, opportunistic to the core, as petrified in their political thinking as the most wooden De Leonist, helplessly bewildered in every new political situation, rigidly

Abridged from *Labor Action*, November 1, 1948, "Twenty years of American Trotskyism".

ecclesiastical in their worship of a Marx and a Trotsky that never existed, intolerant, vulgarly boastful and bureaucratic, and perfectly sterilized against the possibility of exerting the least political influence upon any movement that seeks a way out of the proletarian dilemma of our time — right-wing socialism or Stalinism.

All of them have this in common: their political course is determined for them, willy-nilly, by the political course of Stalinism. They are tied to it by their theory that reactionary, totalitarian Stalinist Russia is still some kind of workers' state, by their base-policy that this state must be defended in every struggle with a capitalist state, by their theory-policy that the totalitarian Stalinist parties everywhere are workers' parties on a par with other workers' parties. They have been unable to detach themselves from this organic and fatal tie with the new barbarism that Stalinism represents. Once the revolutionary socialist opposition to Stalinism, official Trotskyism is today reduced to a mere democratic critic of Stalinism.

The other tendency is most clearly represented, I think, by our Workers Party. In the more than eight years of its independent existence, it has assembled and trained a group of socialist militants on the basis of principles, a program and a perspective collectively elaborated and clarified in such a way that it is recognized everywhere in the labor and socialist movements of *all* countries as a distinctive revolutionary socialist current. We do not pretend to a strength which we know must first be conquered in struggle. We know only too well our weakness, and the weakness of the Marxian movement throughout the world. But we do lay claim to a program which, while not "finished," has yet to be successfully refuted by any opponent.

Our party, alone among all others, had made a systematic analysis of the social and historical significance of Stalinism — the society of bureaucratic collectivism in Russia, the parties of totalitarian collectivism in the capitalist countries. No other party has pointed out and followed a course of implacable struggle against Stalinism in strict independence of capitalism and capitalist politics. No other party but ours has proved able to combat the capitalist influence of reformism in the labor movement without giving aid and comfort to the Stalinist sappers. The sectarians have divorced socialism from democracy and the reformists have divorced democracy from socialism — with fatal results to both. Our party has distinguished itself, in the great tradition of Marx and Lenin, by the way in which it has restored, for our own times, the inseparable relationship of the struggle for democracy and the struggle for socialism.

Where official Trotskyism still seeks to play the role of a wing of Stalinism, we see the role of the present-day Marxists as that of the loyal left wing of the authentic labor movement, the labor movement as it is, with all its defects and shortcomings. Where the reformist sects and parties see socialism lying beyond the road of defending American imperialism in the monstrous conflagration now being prepared, and the Trotskyist sects see socialism lying beyond the road of defending the totalitarian Stalinist state in the next war as in the last one, our party works unremittingly to build a workers' movement that is fully independent of Washington and Moscow, of decaying capitalism and Stalinist barbarism, that raises the banner of democracy and socialism, and fights to victory beneath it.

The twentieth anniversary of the formation of the Trotskyist movement in the United States is a day for us to celebrate. We do it not simply by reiterating now what we said twenty years ago. We pay deserved respects to the militants who did not hold back when it was necessary to lay new foundation stones and launch a new movement, and thereby added their names to the host of other exemplars of socialist idealism, conviction and resolution. Where they erred, where they put forward ideas which did not withstand the severe tests of life, we have not followed them and we need not. But much of what we said, much of what we worked for and fought for in the early days of the Trotskyist movement, did prove to be durable or proved to be the necessary basis on which to build what is durable. It is ours today.

Workers Party

THE FOURTH INTERNATIONAL

THE FOURTH INTERNATIONAL was established to bring to an end the crisis in leadership which alone has stood in the way of the victory of the socialist proletariat in our epoch. During the war, the Fourth International ceased to exist as an effective, organized, centralized International. A number of objective reasons, including the greatest difficulties under which the revolutionary movement ever had to operate in all its long history, may be adduced to explain this collapse. These are reasons which were beyond the control of any one or any group in the International. However, insofar as the collapse was due to reasons which were under the control of the International, the responsibility for the failure of the International, marked at one and the same time by its silence on the most important political problems of the time and by its unofficial tolerance or encouragement of the grossest political mistakes, lies primarily upon the shoulders of the leadership of the Socialist Workers Party.

The sections of the International survived the great trial of the war, even without international guidance and leadership. They did not, like the Stalinists, social-democrats, anarchists, centrists and syndicalists, capitulate to the wave of chauvinism and social-patriotism, and in that respect they held up the banner of socialist internationalism in the great tradition of Marx, Engels, Liebknecht, Luxemburg, Lenin and Trotsky. They survived a terror, above all in Europe, which both the bourgeoisie and the Stalinists mercilessly directed against them and which martyrized the best of our cadres and our militants. However, in the main political analysis and line which distinguished the International's official leadership and made its imprint upon the course of virtually all the sections, the most cat-

From a resolution of the Workers Party convention, June 1946, published in *New International*, April 1947.

460

astrophic errors were made. By its insistent repetition of the slogan of "unconditional defense of the Soviet Union" the International capitulated objectively to Stalinist imperialism and contributed its share to the disorientation of the vanguard of the proletariat. The reconstruction and future of the International depend upon the firmest and most clearly-grasped repudiation of this slogan. They require also the abandonment of the now utterly reactionary theory that Russia is a "workers' state" because property is still nationalized. The Workers Party categorically rejects this theory. While propagating its own theory throughout the International and the working class, the theory that Russia represents a reactionary social order, bureaucratic collectivism, the Workers Party is prepared to cooperate most closely with those groups and sections of the International which, while not sharing the full views of the Workers Party, have nevertheless abandoned the reactionary theory of the "workers' state" and the equally reactionary slogan of "unconditional defense." Therefore, without relinquishing its theoretical position or abandoning the theoretical discussion, the Workers Party will make a political bloc with all groups who now reject the theory of the "workers' state" and the slogan of "unconditional defense."

By its position on the national revolutionary movements in Europe, which was tantamount to sectarian abstentionism at worst and inconsistency and failure to understand the revolutionary tasks of the time, the leadership of the International failed to help the European sections seize the exceptional opportunity to emerge from their isolation and into the leadership of wide sections of the revolutionary peoples.

By its tacit support of and failure to condemn the opportunism and the bureaucratism in the SWP, and by its adoption of similar bureaucratic practises against minorities in the International, the present leadership has promoted the evil of monolithism in the movement and placed in danger the entire future of the International. It has failed to intervene firmly, and fraternally, against the bureaucratic opposition of the SWP leadership to the unification of the movement in the United States, and failed correspondingly to give support to the wholly progressive struggle for unity conducted by the SWP Minority. It has permitted the most disloyal and ignorant campaign to be directed against the German section of the International, whose revolutionary and political integrity is beyond question, and has now itself climaxed this campaign by the most bureaucratic act in the history of the Trotskyist movement, namely, reading the German section out of the International because of its theoretical position without previous notification to the German section, without previous discussion of its position in the International, and without affording the German section the elementary opportunity to defend itself before its accusers.

Nothing less than a complete reorganization of the leadership of the International can give the slightest assurance of a progressive and fruitful future. Nothing less than a loyally prepared and democratically conducted discussion throughout the International of all the questions in controversy, with full opportunity for every member to study the documents available, is required to put the International back on revolutionary rails. This means a discussion, in particular, of the theories and views put forward by the Workers Party, the German section and the Minorities in the SWP and the French party.

Max Shachtman

THE 1948 CONGRESS OF THE FOURTH
INTERNATIONAL

THE SECOND CONGRESS of the Fourth International held in Europe
earlier this year did not receive a good "press." The congress was held
under unwarranted pseudo-conspiratorial conditions, so that its delibera-
tions were known to the delegates and to the police authorities of the
United States, Britain and France, at the least (as we had occasion to
establish from different sources), but could not be observed by the interested public.

An official statement on the congress was prepared with the maximum
of care in order to give the minimum of information on what occurred at
the congress. Although months have passed since the congress ended, no
report of its sessions is available. There is not even a summary account of
the actual proceedings of the representatives, of the motions and counter-
motions, or of the voting record of the delegates. There is, to be sure, the
text of the resolutions adopted at the congress. But the text of the resolutions which were defeated, which contain the views of various oppositional tendencies in the Fourth International on questions of central importance, are not available and, so far as I know, their publication is not con-
templated. A strange congress!

The ingenious innovators who are responsible for all that has been published about the congress do not even refer to the existence of oppositional groups or opinions at the meeting, or to the kind of resolutions they presented — not even to the fact that there were any such resolutions. It is
hard to believe this, but the lamentable proof is available throughout the
"official" press (see, for example, the *Fourth International* of July 1948). It
should be added that the Fourth International is on record as being
against all the obfuscatory and disloyal methods employed against oppositionists by the Stalinists. Let us try in the course of this review to make
up for the oversight.

The congress was undoubtedly the most numerously attended and representative of all the international meetings of the Trotskyist movement.
Bourgeois or Stalinist repression and meagerness of financial resources
prevented many sections from sending their representatives. Yet, as never
before, delegates came to the meeting not only from Europe, but from
Asia, South Africa and several countries of the Western Hemisphere.
Their presence was an earnest of the devotion of the Trotskyist movement
to that socialist internationalism which has been abandoned by so many
backsliders, cynics and tired men. [The Congress opened toward the end
of March 1948 and its sessions ran into the following month].

The political preparation of the congress was, however, so inadequate,

Slightly abridged from *New International*, October 1948, "The Congress of the Fourth
International. An analysis of the bankruptcy of 'orthodox Trotskyism'". Johnson is C L R
James.

not to say factionally manipulated, as to call its authority into question from the very outset. It should be borne in mind that this was the first meeting of its kind to take place since the founding congress of the International in 1938.

Not a few problems accumulated for the International in the intervening ten years. Events of the greatest historical and political magnitude crowded into the decade. There were the Second World War, the Hitler-Stalin Pact, the tremendous national-revolutionary resistance movements, the crushing military and moral defeat of fascism, the radical change in the relation of political forces in the Orient and in Eastern Europe, the victory of Stalinist Russia in the war and its imperialist expansion in the East and the West, the resurgence of both the Social-Democratic and Stalinist parties. To these should be added the fact that practically every important pre-war prediction of the Fourth International proved to be wrong, that the International came out of the war weaker than it was even before the war, and that open splits exist in more than a dozen of its sections, including practically every important one.

A real congress would have the obligation of dealing with all the created problems. To deal with them, it would have to be a real congress. Such a congress would absolutely have to be preceded by a free, democratic and thoroughgoing discussion of the main questions, all of which are in dispute, and therefore a discussion of all the documents setting forth the disputed positions. Less than that would mean a congress without real authority or validity.

It was only on the basis of the formal and solemn assurance that there would be such a preliminary discussion that our Workers Party agreed to participate in the congress with the commitment, stupidly demanded of it by the International leadership, that it would thereupon abide by the democratic decisions of the congress. (To which our party clearly and firmly added the stipulation: *if* the unity of the WP and the Socialist Workers Party were achieved, that is, if the Workers Party no longer existed as an independent organization but only as an integral part of the united party.)

The formal and solemn assurance, given not only to our party but to all oppositional tendencies, was not worth the ink it was written in. There was hardly a pretense of a pre-congress discussion. The delegates came prepared to vote for positions they were more or less acquainted with, and to vote against positions with which they were partially or totally unfamiliar and which, in most cases, their organizations had never had the opportunity to examine in original form. To call an assembly convened under such conditions an authoritative congress is less than serious.

Therefore, a number of the delegates, at the opening session of the congress, joined in a resolution which declared that the meeting could not sit as a congress with full authority and that it should deliberate instead as an international conference. The principal sections of the resolution read:

"This world congress can absolutely not be considered as having been prepared at the present time.

(A) From the standpoint of the documents placed in discussion: in spite of the publication of a number of documents, the most important positions of the main oppositions are unknown in almost all the sections:

1. In the German language, only the official positions have been published, except for a very short article by Armstrong. The positions of the other tendencies are unknown in Germany, Austria and Czechoslovakia.

2. In the Spanish language, only the documents of the leadership have been published and that quite recently.

3. No section of the International (save the English-speaking ones) knows either the policy of the SWP during the war or the document of the Spanish Group of Mexico against this policy.

4. The Internal Bulletin of the International Secretariat on the Russian question has been translated only into English, and only half of it.

5. The documents of the Workers Party and of the Johnson-Forest tendency are unknown in all the non-English-speaking sections of the International — except for an article by Shachtman published in the IVe Internationale and an article by R. Stone recently published in the Internal Bulletin of the International Secretariat.

6. There is not a single section of the International which knows the differences that have led to the split in China or that determine the existence of two separate groups in Indo-China. Yet the Chinese documents were sent in March 1947. Neither does anyone know the documents of the Indian section on this same Chinese question which have existed since 1942.

7. Nobody — not even the International leadership — knows the political differences which separate the Trotskyist groups that abound in Latin America.

8. Nobody knows the documents of the Spanish Group on the national question.

9. Nobody knows the new English documents on the Russian question.

10. The 'definitive' documents of the International Secretariat were not published until February 1948; it was thus impossible not only to reply to these documents but even simply to discuss them in the sections. These same documents are characterized by the Swiss section — which is by and large in political agreement with the International Secretariat — as 'so compromising for the Fourth International and for the revolutionary cause in general that there is no other way for the International Secretariat to act except to withdraw formally its draft theses.'

(B) From the standpoint of the discussion in the sections: Even the published documents have served for nothing in practice, for it was not possible to organize a political discussion in the sections. In almost all the sections, no discussion has taken place up to the present on the political and organizational problems of the world congress — except on the Russian question, partly discussed in some sections. Even the documents of the International Secretariat have not been discussed, because of their extremely tardy publication.

To cite only two examples: the Viet-Namese section in France has never discussed the problems of the world congress. As for the French section, which passes for one of the most politicalized sections and for which the discussion is objectively easiest, since all the documents are first published in French, it has not been discussed either: at its national conference of March 28-29, only 20 per cent of the party was represented; the delegates who came from the few provincial regions that were represented all declared that the problems of the world congress had not been discussed in their regions; the Paris Region elected its delegates after three hours of discussion in all and for all the problems put together.

In the other sections the situation is worse, if possible. The conception according to which 'the discussion for the world congress is nothing new but the continuation of the discussion that took place up to now in the sections,' is absolutely erroneous, above all given the exclusively national character of the problems which were discussed up to now in the sections.

(C) From the standpoint of representation: Practically none of the delegates comes from a national congress or conference representing a political discussion in the ranks of the sections. The basis of representation recommended by the International Secretariat, with the division of countries into three categories, the arbitrary classification of countries into one category or another, the prohibition of the transfer of mandates [proxy voting] — a prohibition without precedent in the history of the communist movement — has as its only result the manufacturing of an a priori majority in this 'Congress.'

Consequently, this assembly can sit only as an international conference with the aim:

(a) from the political standpoint, of opening up the discussions which are on the agenda of the international discussion in order to prepare the convocation of a genuine *world congress resulting from a thoroughgoing political discussion;*

(b) from the organizational standpoint, of designating an Organizational Committee for the preparation of the world congress, with adequate representation of the oppositional tendencies, charged with the publication of the documents and with the organizing of the discussion in all the sections.

Any attempt to transform this assembly into a world congress would only give proof of an absolute lightmindedness and irresponsibility in the face of the extremely grave problems to which the revolutionary movement must respond today."

The resolution was signed and submitted by Munis, of the Spanish Group of Mexico; Chaulieu, of the left-wing group in the French section which bears his name; Gallienne, of another left-wing group in the French section; Antonin, of the "October" Trotskyist group in Indo-China; Armstrong, of the Irish section; and Shachtman, of the Workers Party. After a brief discussion, the resolution was defeated, the majority deciding that the congress which was not and could not be a congress would nevertheless be called a congress.

The signatories to the resolution thereupon submitted a statement, drafted in anticipation of the vote, declaring that they could not and would not accept the self-constitution of the assembly as a congress with authority to adopt conclusive decisions having disciplinary validity; that they would not commit themselves in advance to accept the decisions to be adopted by the assembly or to abide by its discipline; that they would remain bound only by the discipline of their respective organizations, but would nevertheless continue to attend the sessions in order to put forward their point of view on all the questions on the agenda. Confronted by this firm and unexpected declaration, the authors of the absurd "conditions" for attending the congress simply collapsed along with their conditions. Without daring to move for the ouster of the oppositionists, the leadership proposed to proceed with the agenda.

The first point of importance on the agenda of the congress (as we will now call it) was the report of the Executive Committee. One might think that such a report would form one of the central axes for an international meeting of the Trotskyist movement.

It would have to deal with the most important events of the ten stirring years since the preceding congress; with the analyses and the forecasts that had been made; with the policy pursued by the international leadership and the national sections; with the outstanding controversial questions which have divided the Fourth International into numerous pairs of politically irreconcilable viewpoints. It would have to serve as the necessary introduction to a broad discussion and a decision on the questions that have been in dispute especially since the outbreak of the war in 1939.

That is what it should have been. Actually, it was nothing of the kind. The only claim to distinction the report could make is that it was one of the most lamentable performances in the history of the movement. For carefully scraped-out emptiness it remained unexcelled by any of its rivals at other sessions.

To be sure, the reporter took care to refer to the reactionary character of the Stalinist and reformist parties; he noted with pride that the centrist organizations had not become mass movements, whereas the Fourth International, in the face of great difficulties, had not disappeared; he did not forget to dwell loudly upon his unshattered faith in the working class, his confidence in socialism and his conviction that the Fourth

International would overcome all obstacles — including, presumably, such reports as he was delivering.

It is debatable if the speech, sodden with cheerless commonplaces, would have been appropriate even at some anniversary celebration in a mountain village. Its suitability as a report of the Executive Committee to a congress was not debatable. Consequently, it was not debated — not at all, not by anyone, and not for a single moment.

This sounds like malicious exaggeration, but it is the literal truth. The chairman of the session positively pleaded with the delegates to take the floor in the discussion scheduled to follow the report. Understandably, nobody budged. What was there in the report to discuss? Perhaps the socialist aim, to which the reporter rededicated himself with the stertorous passion of a nineteenth-century French deputy? Or his confidence in the working class which he asseverated with a belligerency that failed to provoke, or even to awaken, the delegates?

Whereupon the report, so to speak, was adopted, so to speak, without a word of discussion and by a vote which matched it in dullness. It is still hard to believe, but the minutes of the congress would confirm it to the letter, which is not the smallest of the reasons why the minutes remain unpublished. As far as can be remembered, this is the first instance in the history of the movement where a congress failed to devote a single word to a discussion of the report of its Executive Committee, and a report of ten years at that!

The kilometric articles that the same delegates would write if such a thing were to happen at a Stalinist congress are not hard to imagine. The Stalinists at least pretend to discuss the congress reports of their executives. Here there was not even the pretense. Result: the congress met and adjourned without discussing or taking a position on —

The "proletarian military policy," particularly as pursued by the SWP during the war, which was condemned not only by our party but also by many French, English, Spanish, Mexican and other comrades;

The policy, the absence of a policy or the conflicting policies pursued by the various sections of the International (the International itself had *no* policy at all) toward the most significant revolutionary mass movements during the war, the underground national-resistance movements;

The policy of supporting China during the world war, rejected not only by our party but also by many if not most of the comrades of the Chinese, Indian, Spanish and other sections;

The way in which the International, as a functioning, *articulate*, central organism, was sabotaged to death during the world war, so that, with the exception of a "manifesto on India," which it would have been better not to write at all, there is nowhere a record of what the Fourth International — not this or that section but the International itself — had to say on any one of a score of vitally important political questions that arose during the greatest crisis of our generation.

The discussion on the question of Stalinist Russia and Stalinism in general fared somewhat better. But only in the sense that in this question the bankruptcy of the leadership of the International was revealed positively, by direct discussion, whereas it was revealed negatively, as it were, in the question of its political course for the past ten years by the complete absence of discussion.

The traditional theory of the Trotskyist movement on Russia was completely shipwrecked during the war. Nothing worthwhile is left of it now.

The Stalinist bureaucracy did *not* disintegrate during the war. On the contrary, while it is not one whit freer from contradictions and internal antagonisms than any other ruling class, it consolidated its *bureaucratic* (as against a genuinely popular) hold on the country to a greater degree than in the pre-war period when it was shaken by successive purges. In any case, it emerged from the war far more intact than the ruling class of any other country in the world.

The bureaucracy did *not* prove incapable of defending its country (and that is what Russia is today: *its* country), its rule, its social system and its economy from enemy attack. On the contrary, it not only defended it aggressively, unwaveringly and uncompromisingly, but much more effectively than the ruling class of most if not all the other belligerents. The fact that it did not carry on this defense in the interests of the working class, of democracy, of internationalism, of socialism or in conformity with their principles, is entirely beside the point. It did not carry on that kind of defense and, being what it is, it could not; we did not expect it to because there was not the slightest reason to expect it. It defended itself and its rule as reactionary classes have always done in wartime: in a reactionary way, by a demagogic exploitation of the noble sentiments of the people, by poisoning their minds and recklessly expending their bodies, by trampling coldly and brutally upon their interests and their rights, all in order to preserve and extend its own power and the bases of its power.

The bureaucracy did *not* capitulate to capitalism or its capitalist allies. On the contrary, while it made compromises and concessions to its capitalist allies of no greater number or significance than those that any ruling class is often compelled to make in a given relationship of forces, it succeeded, by a combination of physical and political strength and cunning and maneuvers, in weakening the capitalist world and, correspondingly, in strengthening its own international position, to an extent that exceeded *everybody's* expectations. The bureaucracy did *not* restore capitalism or abandon or undermine state ownership of the means of production and exchange, or develop the oft-predicted "bourgeois wing," nor did it show the slightest tendency in that direction. On the contrary, it not only fought and fights tenaciously for the maintenance of nationalized property, which is the property of *its* state and the indispensable economic foundation of *its* rule, but it managed to destroy the economic foundation of the bourgeoisie in a number of other countries and to replace it with nationalized property.

At the same time, this victorious "defense of the Soviet Union" resulted nowhere in the advancement of the cause of the working class, brought no benefit to the working class and revolutionary movements. Where Stalinist Russia and its agents did win or did extend their influence, the working class, the masses in general, suffered the heaviest blows. They were disoriented, demoralized, degraded. Where Stalinism took power, the revolutionary movement was relentlessly crushed, as in Russia, and the people reduced to the cruelest slavery.

There is no other way of judging the correctness of a political program or a slogan in the socialist movement than by the consequences which its

467

partial or complete fulfilment entail for the working class and the struggle for socialism. By this only valid criterion, the slogan of "unconditional defense of the Soviet Union" in the war was and remains criminal and reactionary. Whoever refuses to see this today should be conveyed with kindly speed to an institution for the blind or be given treatment for arrested mental development.

In the face of these facts, the resolution presented to the congress by the leadership was nothing less than a disaster. If someone had deliberately planned to confuse people about a problem which is certainly not simple to begin with, and to bewilder them hopelessly about his own views on the problem, the result could hardly have been different.

The resolution reiterates the position that Russia is still a workers' state because the means of production are still nationalized. Then, by a simple stroke of the obedient pen, it takes it for granted that because nationalized property exists in the Stalinist state just as it existed in the workers' state (this time without quotation marks) of the Lenin period, therefore the production relations that exist today are the same as those which existed before the conquest of power by the bureaucracy. Indeed, the resolution uses the terms "nationalized property" and "production relations" interchangeably, as if they were one and the same thing. It writes without blinking an eyelash and as though it were an incontrovertible commonplace that the production relations established by the Bolshevik revolution "have not yet collapsed," that they have been "bequeathed by the October revolution" on the bureaucracy, that the "sum total [!] of the production relations" in Russia today have been "inherited from the October revolution." Naturally, with this identification of the two concepts, the contradictions and downright gibberish which follow are inevitable. The authors have simply refused to let their skulls absorb the idea that the two *cannot* be identified in Russia.

Production relations are social relations; they are the relations between classes in the process of production. Under capitalism, the production relations are simply and clearly established. One class owns the means of production (the capital is owned by the capitalists) and the other class owns nothing but its labor power. It is on this fundamental basis that the two classes are obliged to enter into relations in the process of production. The capitalist state exists to maintain the fundamental basis and the fundamental social relations, and that is why it is, regardless of the political character of the régime, a capitalist state. For this reason it is not only convenient but correct to identify capitalist property relations with capitalist production relations.

The same identification is obviously not possible under conditions where property (that is, the means of production and exchange) is nationalized, is owned and controlled by the state and not by any class. Under such conditions, I cannot determine the character of the existing production relations by answering the question: "What class owns the property, the means of production?" for the good reason that it is not owned by any class, but by the state which is only the political instrument of a class. It can be determined *only* by asking and answering the question: "What class 'owns', i.e., controls, the state-which-owns-the-property?" In other words, in a state which owns the means of production, the production relations are more or less consciously determined by the class which has the

468

state power. *Nothing* else is or can be decisive in determining the production relations under such conditions.

After the October revolution, it was not the mere fact that private property was nationalized which determined a fundamental change in the production relations, but the fact that it was nationalized by the workers in political power, by the workers' state. The relations into which men entered with each other in the process of production — in the factories, the mines, on the railroads and the land, etc. — were consciously decided, established and maintained by the state power which, however bureaucratically distorted, was in the hands of the working class. The relations of production thus established made the working class the principal economic and social beneficiary of the results of the production process. With the triumph of the Stalinist counter-revolution, the working class was expropriated politically and a new state power established which maintained and even extended the form and predominance of collective, or nationalized or statified property. *Consequently,* it established new and fundamentally different relations in the process of production — again, in the factories, the mines, on the railroads and the land. The worker, as an individual or as a class, has absolutely nothing to do with determining the production relations, with determining the relations of his class to the process or the conditions of production or the relations to it of those who, as a social group, control and decide the conditions of production. Like *all* ruling classes, the latter thereby control and decide the distribution of the surplus product extracted from the producers.

Anyone who does not *know* the *fundamental* change that has taken place in the production relations since the Stalinist counter-revolution, does not know anything about the concrete social relations existing in Russia today and thereby disqualifies himself from a discussion of the question on the ground of gross ignorance. Anyone who *does* know the facts, and who can write down on patient paper that the "sum total [no less!] of the production relations" existing after the proletarian revolution in Russia still exists under Stalinism today, thereby writes himself down as a Stalinist or, at the very, very best, as a high-minded and well-intentioned apologist for Stalinism who has, moreover, laid down the theoretical foundation for capitulating to it.

Since the logical consequences of this position are too palpable and, to any Trotskyist, disturbing, the authors of the resolution felt impelled to twist and squirm away from them. They must find out what is, after all, so bad about the Stalinist bureaucracy. So we learn, in the first place, that "the bureaucracy defends the essence [yes, nothing less than the essence!] of the production relations inherited from October only as a basis for its privileges, and not as a basis for socialist development." This is both interesting and enlightening, even if not thought out. If it means anything, it is saying that the same "production relations" can be and are the basis for a socialist development or the basis for its opposite — an anti-socialist, counter-revolutionary, bureaucratic despotism. If the authors really mean production relations, they have made a unique contribution to Marxism! It is as if you were to say: A given bourgeois bureaucracy defends the essence of the production relations that underlie capitalism *only* as a basis for its own privileges, which are non-capitalist or anti-capitalist, and not as a basis for maintaining and developing capitalism. In other words, that production relations can simply be manipulated by a ruling bureaucratic clique against the social order for which these relations are indispensable and in the interests of the clique which is *inherently* alien and antagonistic to that social order.

It is a crying absurdity, but not the only one. Although it defends the "essence" because the relations are the very basis of its power and privileges, we learn, in the second place, that the same bureaucratic dictatorship "undermines more and more the production relations on the basis of which it keeps alive." How in the world is it doing this? If, as the authors say, the production relations simply mean the nationalized property, then undermining them could only mean that nationalized property is being abandoned progressively and replaced by private property. As is known, that is the *only* fundamental and serious sense in which the Trotskyist movement has always referred to the role of the bureaucracy in "undermining" nationalized property. But there is not only no sign whatsoever of the bureaucracy restoring private property, but the authors themselves announce, a couple of pages further on, that "the bureaucracy has been incapable of setting up conscious political tendencies, of orienting itself toward the restoration of the private ownership of the means of production for its own benefit." There is nothing monotonous about this resolution: on each page, a bright new thought; each thought in bellicose opposition to the one before it.

Since there is no evidence presented to show that the bureaucracy is abandoning nationalized property, and plenty of evidence to show that its power and privileges are based upon it, you would therefore conclude that the two are necessarily interlinked. Not so fast! The authors, on still another page, and in the third place, firmly reject "any attempt at simplification which tries to confuse the economic basis on which Stalinist Russia is built, with the monstrous degeneracy of its social superstructure." We are therefore back to the standpoint that the rule of the bureaucracy is in some fundamental way opposed to the maintenance of nationalized property. But only for one page. We learn, on the next page, in the fourth place, and with no little stupefaction, that "the production relations and bureaucratic management are more and more inextricably bound up. Consequently, the progressive character of the Russian *economy,* which is determined by its capacity to develop the productive forces, tends to become eliminated by the bureaucracy." Then, to make absolutely certain that the maximum of muddle is hammered into the resolution, we read on still other pages that "the policy and the very existence of the Stalinist bureaucracy constitute a permanent threat to all that is, in our opinion, still worth defending," that is, the "production relations," that is, nationalized property, "the maintenance of which imperiously demands the restoration of *workers' control,* the progressive introduction of *workers' management* of production."

The genius of the authors lies exclusively in their insistence that all this gibberish makes sense. The *only* reason Russia is still a workers' state and that it must be defended unconditionally, is that nationalized property still exists. The bureaucracy is reactionary and counter-revolutionary because it undermines the nationalized property. At the same time, it not only defends the essence of this property, and has produced no tendency to restore private property, but nationalized property is the very basis of

470

its life and privileges. However, its existence is in conflict with the maintenance of this property, to which it offers a permanent threat. Nevertheless, nationalized property and the bureaucracy are becoming so much intertwined that the progressive character of this economy is being eliminated. Still, to maintain this property demands — and imperiously! — the overthrow of the bureaucracy which bases itself on the property, which is kept alive by it, and which defends its very essence. Notwithstanding our defense of "what remains of the conquests of October," namely, nationalized property, which is progressive and makes Russia a workers' state, we say in the next breath that it "is more and more losing its value as a motive force for socialist development" even though its value lies in its existence which the bureaucracy maintains, undermines, defends, threatens, sustains, destroys, etc., etc. It takes real genius, and of no human variety.

The resolution was subjected to annihilating criticism during and before the Congress. The Swiss section, rigidly "Trotskyist," called for the immediate withdrawal of the resolution as too compromising for the International. R Johnson of the Workers Party of South Africa wrote a furious denunciation of it, wholly justified from the standpoint of the traditional position on the question, charging that the leadership has simply "capitulated to the petty-bourgeois tendencies which it had been resisting" up to now; that its "hatred of Stalinism, instead of being political, has become pathological" (this charge has a very familiar ring!); and that "not only are we taking over the language and vocabulary of Shachtman and Co., but of imperialism itself and are even attempting to surpass it."

A more thought-out criticism came from the British section, the Revolutionary Communist Party, and its delegation. Its position was probably the most significant feature not only of the Congress but of the development of the Trotskyist movement as a whole. It was put forward in the form of a few modest "amendments" to the resolution. If these were mere amendments then we do not know the meaning of a categorical counter-resolution.

The British, who flirted for a while with the comical theory that Russia is a capitalist state and then quietly reinterred it, now start again with the premise that Russia is a workers' state because it is based upon nationalized property. Once started, they shift with hydramatic smoothness into second gear. If that is the reason and the only reason for calling Russia a workers' state, then, for the same reason, it is now necessary to consider all the "buffer" countries (Poland, Yugoslavia, Rumania, Bulgaria, Hungary and Czechoslovakia) as workers' states as well, since in all these states the Stalinist régimes have either already nationalized the decisive sectors of the economy or are clearly on the road of all-out nationalization. On this basis, the British Trotskyist paper hailed the February coup in Prague, which installed the totalitarian dictatorship of Stalinism in Czechoslovakia, as a "victory" for the working class! It is hard to believe, but there it was, black on white, in the British *Socialist Appeal,* under the signature of the RCP leader. For this article, the RCP received a bitter letter from the Czech Trotskyists charging it simply with stabbing its Czech comrades in the back, a characterization which suffers from restraint but not from inaccuracy. While the British hailed the coup as a victory for the working class, the rest of the official Trotskyist press hailed it as a victory for the bourgeoisie which, with inexcusable perversity, was celebrating its triumph by jumping or being thrown out of high windows onto the pavement below.

If the premise is correct, the conclusion of the British is inescapable. Their argumentation is without a flaw. Only, they have obviously come to an abrupt halt half-way along the line. Yesterday, the buffer countries were capitalist states. Today, they are workers' states, degenerated or degenerating or qualified in any other sense. That means: state power has been transferred from the hands of one class into the hands of another. In all the languages of the earth, such a change is known as a social revolution (or counter-revolution). In the given cases, the British can only be saying that what has taken place is a *socialist revolution in its class type.* The socialist revolution is nothing but the transfer of power from the capitalist class to the working class, the overthrow of the capitalist state and the establishment of the workers' state. Who organized and led this socialist revolution? The Stalinist bureaucracy and nobody else! But in that case, why is it counter-revolutionary? Perhaps because of its suppression and oppression of the workers? Very well, let us grant that. But the fact remains (still according to the British Trotskyists, of course) that the capitalist states were transformed into workers' states under the leadership and hegemony of the Stalinists. From this, the conclusion is absolutely unavoidable: we must introduce into Marxian politics the category of the counter-revolutionary socialist revolution or a counter-revolutionary bureaucracy that carries through the socialist revolution.

Unfortunately, that is not all. If it has already been proved in life that the counter-revolutionary Stalinist bureaucracy can and does carry through the socialist revolution (bureaucratically, trickily, or however else you want to describe it, but carries it through nevertheless) in a number of countries, there is no serious or fundamental reason to believe that it *cannot* carry it through in the other capitalist countries. From this, some ineluctable conclusions:

The working class is a good thing to have around; so is a revolutionary Marxian party. One or both may even be necessary to develop a workers' state, once it is established, into a harmonious socialist society. But a self-acting, conscious, democratically-organized, revolutionary working class is not *indispensable* for the carrying through of the socialist revolution. The counter-revolutionary Stalinist bureaucracy can do that job just as fundamentally (even if not as pleasantly, democratically, etc., etc.). It can establish a workers' state not only without the support of the working class but in opposition to the working class.

If it can do this, then all grounds for the separate existence of an independent revolutionary party or International immediately disappear. The Stalinist parties and International may not then be everything that is desirable or required for the establishment of socialism, but they suffice for the socialist revolution, that is, for the establishment of a workers' state. The only justification for the separate existence of a Trotskyist movement is if it confines itself essentially to the role of a *democratic,* anti-bureaucratic, opposition to Stalinism and ceases to consider itself an opposition to Stalinism on fundamental principle. It can oppose Stalinism on the ground of its false theories or its bad methods, but not on the grounds that it is for preserving capitalism and against a socialist revolution.

This is what the British position, when thought out to the end, really means. If they hesitate to pursue their views to the logical conclusion, it is for the same reason that many hesitate to shift from second gear into high speed while racing down a hill with a dead end at the bottom. But downhill they are going, and they cannot remain for long in second gear without burning up the whole motor.

The leadership of the congress was uneasily aware of the significance of the British position. The question of the buffer countries is a decisive test of any position on the Russian question as a whole, and the views of the RCP confirmed only too clearly what we have been writing for years about the Russian position of the Fourth International. Caught between the pressure of the RCP position on the one side and the position of the Workers Party on the other, the International leadership presented a positively gloomy picture. The gloomy picture was paired with a ludicrous position. Against our views, they insisted (with what arguments, we have already seen) that Russia remains a workers' state. Against us and the British, they insisted that Yugoslavia, Poland and the other buffer countries are capitalist states. What, capitalist states? Yes, capitalist states!

Every political person in the world who is in the least degree informed *knows* that this is the sheerest fantasmagoria. Everyone knows that in the countries where the Stalinists have taken power they have proceeded, at one or another rate of speed, to establish exactly the same economic, political, social régime as exists in Russia. Everyone knows that the bourgeoisie has been or is rapidly being expropriated, deprived of all its economic power, and in many cases deprived of mortal existence; that industry has been or is being nationalized, in some cases faster than it was nationalized after the Bolshevik revolution. There is not a single capitalist, capitalist theoretician or capitalist spokesman in these countries (or anywhere in the world) who considers the Stalinist states as capitalist. Everyone knows that what remnants of capitalism remain in these countries will not even be remnants tomorrow, that the *whole tendency* is to establish a social system identical with that of Stalinist Russia.

Everyone knows this, even the British Trotskyist leadership knows this — but not the leadership of the Fourth International! Its ears muffed, its eyes blinkered, its mouth stuffed with cotton, its head in a blackened, soundproofed, waterproofed, uninflammable and airtight belljar, its hands lightly fixed on a ouija board, it communicates to the remoter planets the following intelligence: *"The capitalist nature of the economy of the 'buffer zone' countries is apparent... In the 'buffer' countries the state remains bourgeois... the state of the 'buffer' countries defends property which, despite its diverse and hybrid forms, remains fundamentally bourgeois in character... while maintaining bourgeois function and structure, the state of the 'buffer' countries represents at the same time an* extreme form of Bonapartism." (If only they could have read these consoling thoughts in time, King Peter would be asking to return to Yugoslavia, King Michael would never have left Rumania or Mickolajczyk Poland, and Masaryk would have died, if not a fully contented then at least a happier man!)

A state with a capitalist economy, with a state organization of the economy, and with a régime of police dictatorship which represents an "extreme form" of Bonapartism, is commonly known as a fascist state. The British delegates did not quite agree with this analysis. Instead of fascist states, they proposed to designate the Stalinist buffer countries as workers' states in the same sense as Russia, and therefore states which must be unconditionally defended from capitalist attack. The resolution of the majority declared that the "capitalist nature of these countries imposes the necessity of the strictest revolutionary defeatism in war time." This difference of opinion was settled by the vote. The British amendments were overwhelmingly defeated. However, being religiously for sacred discipline, which they voted into the statutes along with the others, the British committed themselves to abide by the decisions and line of the congress. So, if their press henceforth puts forward the line of the International that the buffer countries are fascist states (more or less), and capitalist in any case, which must not be defended in wartime, even though they themselves strongly believe that these countries are workers' states that should be defended, there will be no ground for astonishment. After all, is the difference really so great or important, especially in face of the infinitely greater importance of — of what? Oh yes, of discipline! The resolution of the leadership carried by a pretty lamentable majority. Those of us who supported the position of the Workers Party — that Russia and the buffer countries are bureaucratic-collectivist states — voted for the resolution of the French Chaulieu group which, while not identical with our position, was sufficiently close to it for purposes of the record vote. This resolution was supported by the delegates from the Chaulieu group, the German section, the Irish section, the Indo-Chinese October group and the Workers Party.

(The theory that Russia is a capitalist state was not really presented or defended at the congress. Munis, who holds to one version of this theory, spoke only briefly and in the most general way. The representative of the Gallienne group, which holds to another version, did not speak on the subject at all. There remained the delegate who supported the J R Johnson version, that Russia is a fascist capitalist state. He did not present Johnson's view at all and submitted no resolution for his specific position. Instead, he joined in a common resolution with Chaulieu, who had, in addition, a resolution of his own defending the theory of bureaucratic collectivism for which we voted. The joint resolution, which the highly principled Johnsonite signed with a sponsor of the theory of bureaucratic collectivism, for which the former professed such a detestation, mentioned neither that theory nor the theory of state capitalism. After the congress, the so-called convention of the SWP in this country voted unanimously to endorse the line of the congress, the Johnsonites supporting the vote. One side says Russia is a workers' state that must be unconditionally defended; the other side says it is a fascist state which must be unconditionally overthrown. Bah! a trifling difference among men of high revolutionary principle. Divide a vote over such a nuance? It would be preposterous. By avoiding the preposterous, the Johnsonites bravely committed hara-kiri. It was not unforeseeable or unforeseen. As Yeats wrote on the fallen Irish airman: "In balance with this life, this death.")

In the congress discussion, I said that while the majority could defeat the British amendment by a mere vote, so long as they preserved the basic premise from which the British started, they would have to take a double dose of the amendments tomorrow. Tomorrow came much sooner than anyone expected. My easy prediction was wrong in only one respect: the

474

leadership of the International hastily swallowed not just a double but a quadruple dose of the British position.

The hapless resolution, pointing out that "a more direct control by the Kremlin over the leadership of the various 'national' Stalinist parties has become necessary," added cautiously, "Nevertheless, one should not expect large cracks in the apparatus in the eventuality of war, because all the leading strata of the Communist parties are entirely aware that only their link with the USSR allows them to play a political role 'independent' of other reformist currents inside the labor movement." No sooner written than confirmed. Right after the congress adjourned, the Tito-Stalin conflict flared violently into the open, revealing spectacularly not only a "large crack in the apparatus," which "one should not expect," but the largest and most significant break in the history of the Stalinist movement. We, who had already analyzed the inexorable forces working to produce such and even greater cracks in world Stalinism, were therefore not caught off guard and found no need to improvise a position in twenty-four hours. What was the reaction of those whose main happiness comes from calling us petty bourgeois and themselves Marxists — perspicacious Marxists? They stumbled and fumbled and cleared their throats and then plunged into what is probably the most disgraceful position in the history of the Trotskyist movement.

The resolution of the congress said over and over again that while Russia is a workers' state, Yugoslavia is a capitalist state; and that while Russia must be unconditionally defended in any conflict with a capitalist state, its defenders must adopt a defeatist position toward a country like Yugoslavia — not just plain ordinary defeatism, but "the strictest revolutionary defeatism." But, after all, where was that said? In a resolution. And what, after all, is a resolution? It's a combination of the genius of an author, tolerant paper and flowing ink. Don't we still have ink that flows, paper that's tolerant, and the same author with his genius unimpaired? Of course! Then what's to prevent us from writing another document? Protests from the membership? Nonsense! All discussion is strictly prohibited after the congress. The next congress perhaps? More nonsense! Our congress does not even discuss the report of the line followed by the outgoing Executive. So the three basic ingredients were whipped together and new documents produced.

The new documents, over the signature of the Secretariat of the Fourth International, are a series of "open letters." To whom are they addressed? To the régime of Stalin, which heads a workers' state which we defend? No, to the régime of Tito, which represents "an extreme form of Bonapartism" and heads a capitalist state toward which we pursue a policy of the "strictest revolutionary defeatism." Do the letters to the Stalinist bureaucracy of Yugoslavia express a sympathetic attitude toward the Russian workers' state which we defend unconditionally? No, they express the most cordial and sympathetic attitude toward the Yugoslav capitalist state which must be defeated in any conflict with the Russian workers' state.

As political documents, these "open letters" are among the most revolting and shameless of our time. The line adopted by the just-concluded congress of the International is not even mentioned, which shows how much respect the leadership has for it, the same leadership which insists on everybody else complying with its official line. Nowhere do the letters say that the International considers Yugoslavia a capitalist state; nowhere do they hint that the International applies to it "the strictest revolutionary defeatism in wartime."

In the congress resolution, it says clearly enough: "Likewise, from the Russian occupation forces or from pro-Stalinist governments, which are completely reactionary, we do not demand the expropriation of the bourgeoisie, the setting up of a real foreign trade monopoly, an effective struggle against speculation and the black market." The minute the Tito-Stalin conflict broke out, all this was completely forgotten; more exactly, it was completely ignored.

The "open letters" are addressed to the congress, the Central Committee and the members of the Yugoslav Stalinist party. The letters are one long appeal to the counter-revolutionary Stalinist bureaucrats to become socialists — in their own interests. What the congress resolution said "we do not demand" of the Stalinist régimes, the "open letters" do demand, and in a sickeningly ingratiating tone. The July 13 letter goes into painstaking detail on what the Stalinist régime should do. It should adopt the road of the class struggle; it should establish full workers' democracy; it should nationalize the land; it should organize a Balkan Socialist Federation; it should adopt all the principles of Leninism; it should start a "vast campaign of re-education"; there should be a "real *mass mobilization,* to be brought about by your party."

Who is to perform these modest chores? Tito and Company, the counter-revolutionary Bonapartist bureaucracy which, said the congress, "has introduced special forms of exploitation" and has established "a Stalinist police dictatorship" in Yugoslavia! And what will happen to the Stalinist gang (because that is what they are in Yugoslavia too) in the course of all this? The "open letter" is most reassuring on this score. Dear police dictators, there is nothing to worry about: *"Your party has nothing to fear from such a development. The confidence of the masses in it will grow enormously and it will become the effective collective expression of the interests and desires of the proletariat of its country."* (My emphasis — MS.)

In the letter of September, the Secretariat admonishes the Yugoslav bureaucracy against party monolithism: *"If you cling to this conception you will head inexorably toward the foundering of your revolution and of your own party."* Tito and Company have not yet headed toward it, but if they "cling" they "will" head toward it! Toward what? *"The foundering of your revolution."* What revolution? When did it take place and what class did it bring to power? Weren't we (and the British) impatiently given to understand at the congress that there has been no revolution in Yugoslavia and that it is still a capitalist, not to say a fascist, country? *"It is your duty as well as in your own self-interest to raise the clarification of your conflict to the plane of the true ideological reasons, which pertain to the nature of Stalinism. Only in this way will you be able to arm your party and the Yugoslav masses... "*

The "new line," which makes the British amendments look like a bagatelle, justifies the Secretariat of the Fourth International in taking on an additional title: "Comradely Advisers to Stalinist Police Dictators on How to Transform Totalitarianism Into Democracy, Capitalism Into Socialism, Counter-revolutionary Parties Into Revolutionary Parties,

Oppressors of the People Into Progressive Leaders of the People, Rulers Into Ruled and Ruled into Rulers, in the Best Interests of the Dictators, Oppressors and Counter-revolutionists Themselves." Admittedly, this title is long and ignoble, but it is not inaccurate.

The Fourth International has proved incapable of abandoning its role of an utterly ineffectual left wing of Stalinist totalitarianism and counter-revolution. It has a powerful impulsion to follow in the wake of Stalinism and this is caused organically by its reactionary theory that Stalinist Russia is a workers' state. It is thereby compelled to have its political course and its future determined at every stage by the interests of the Stalinist bureaucracy. This dooms it as an independent revolutionary proletarian movement, dooms it to bankruptcy and impotence at every important political juncture, dooms it to disorient and demoralize the few thousand militants who follow it and to paralyze their revolutionary will.

Workers Party

STARTING ANEW

1. The Workers Party recognizes as one of its prime tasks to help in the reassembling and political clarification of the scattered and decimated forces of revolutionary socialism in the world.

2. It does not, however, view the realization of this task through the artificial creation of international organizations which, in presuming to speak for and to the world working class, serve only to discredit the very idea of a socialist international. Thus, the Workers Party rejects completely and in advance any effort to erect a new socialist International, while the forces for that International represent no more than a few isolated sects. A new socialist International must be capable, organizationally and politically, of speaking for a significant section of the working class.

3. The Fourth Internationalist movement has declared its own doom as an international center of revolutionary regroupment by its demonstrated inability to assess the major issues of our day, notably with respect to Stalinism, the national struggle and the struggle for democracy. Politically it has tended to degenerate increasingly into the left-wing of Stalinism. It has become a futile alignment of grouplets without any semblance of mass influence. The leadership of the Fourth International has, by its pretentious claims to world authority, merely underscored the sectarian sterility of the Fourth. Bureaucratically dominated, politically discredited, it can in no way serve as a center of revolutionary attraction today.

4. All recent experience with the Fourth International requires that the Workers Party abandon any attempt to seek membership in it. To do so would, in its opinion, require an intolerable violence to its program, given the bureaucratic decisions and régimes of the Fourth leadership; it would as well undermine the seriousness with which a socialist international must be approached in concept and achievement. However, the Workers Party remains, as it always has been, ready to collaborate in closest fraternal association and discussion with the comrades and groups of the Fourth International. The Workers Party holds that to become part of the organization of the Fourth would, in actuality, block the discharge of its international responsibilities.

"Resolution on the reconstruction of the socialist international", December 1948.

6. The pattern of international development to the point where the working class can once again look upon a specific body as its international spokesman, as with the great Internationals of the past, cannot now be foreordained. It cannot be "legislated" into existence by a handful of revolutionists. Maintaining the closest association with the various socialist elements, revolutionary Marxist and centrist, who are prepared to discuss principles and program with us, to work with us toward common objectives, we can contribute significantly in elaborating an international program and laying that organizational groundwork which will eventually bear fruit in a world-wide organization of socialist labor. Such an organization cannot be conceived or established exclusively by "Trotskyist" groups or on the basis of ultimatistic demands that the "Trotskyist" program be adopted. The socialist International will be reconstructed by a mutual clarification and fusion of various revolutionary currents. Towards that end the Workers Party stands ready to collaborate actively in all efforts designed by promote such programmatic clarification (as, for example, a periodical for international socialist discussion) and the growth of revolutionary forces. Towards that end the Workers Party is prepared to work in intimate collaboration with such groups as the ASR and RDR in France, the POUM in Spain and similar tendencies in other lands. In this collaboration, the Workers Party will continue to put forward the principles and policies which it has worked out in the past eight years and seek, in comradely discussion with all others, to have its views incorporated into the foundation of the new International.

Max Shachtman

THE SOCIALIST BANNER WILL WAVE IN VICTORY!

WE DETEST STALINISM for all that it has done to the working class, to the cause of socialist freedom, and even to the good name of socialism. But we are by no means ready to succumb to it in any way or in any sense. Those who see in Stalinism the wave of the future — as people used to say about Hitlerism — do not understand either Stalinism or the working class which it seeks to traduce.

Like capitalism, Stalinism is incapable of solving the burning problems of society. It brings not freedom but tyranny, not order but chaos, not security but starvation, not peace but war. The further it spreads, the more clearly it discloses its true countenance and true role.

The new barbarism can no more gain the support or even the toleration of the masses than the old capitalist barbarism. A dictatorship of police and assassins is in its very nature a dictatorship of instability, and any crisis may mean its end.

Trotsky — and in this respect we are entirely like him — derived his confidence in the ultimate victory of socialism from a true reading and a deep understanding of the proletariat and of the record of all the oppressed classes in history.

Jean Jaurès, the most prominent figure of the old socialist movement of

Excerpts from a speech delivered by Max Shachtman at the Trotsky memorial meeting in New York City on September 5, 1947.

Europe, used to describe this history with a matchless eloquence of gesture, of the eye and of the spoken word.

Back in antiquity, captive peoples, kept in the brutish ignorance of their times, isolated from each other into tiny handfuls, nevertheless succeeded in breaking the chains of chattel slavery and the apparently unbreakable power of the omnipotent slave-owners with their bare fists, with stones, with clubs and knives. In the days of feudalism, the serfs, scattered over the domains of Europe, were able to level the strongest fortresses and prisons of the nobility, again with their bare fists, their scythes and short swords, their bows and arrows.

Today we have a modern proletariat, infinitely more advanced and enlightened than its unbelievably backward predecessors, a proletariat that is the foundation of all society, a proletariat that can be destroyed only if class rule itself is destroyed. We have a proletariat which, come what may, is numerous and bound together in large compact masses by the very economic life of every country. Against it we have arrayed great forces, but forces of a ruling class whose days are numbered because it cannot restore order to society, because it bears within it a virus to wipe out society, because it is itself disintegrating and unsure of its power.

Is it possible, is it reasonable, for the intelligent mind to assume that where the tens of thousands were able in the past to overturn and free themselves from the ruling powers, the millions and tens of millions today will prove to be unable to accomplish their historic task?

Is it possible for the intelligent mind to believe that with all the setbacks and defeats that have been suffered, the masses of today will prove incapable of finally consummating the evolution toward which the whole of social history points so clearly? That the centuries-long struggle of the oppressed for freedom, which, in spite of everything, in spite of sufferings and sacrifices and setbacks nevertheless did succeed in bringing modern civilization to the world — that this struggle will come to a tragic halt in our time — that the modern working class will be unable to perform even greater (far greater) exploits in lifting the world to freedom than were performed by the ancient slaves, by the serfs and artisans and even the young bourgeois of only a few centuries ago?

That is how to look at the matter scientifically and historically. It is not sensible to act as have so many who abandoned the fight for socialism, and to conclude that because we have suffered such heavy defeats — and they have been heavy and grim — it follows that the proletariat is incapable of achieving, under capitalism and against capitalism, that historic task which far more backward, far more disorganized, far less numerous classes were able to achieve for humanity in their time. Such a conclusion seems to us ridiculous, and it is worthy of the soldier who does not understand the difference between a battle and a war.

It is these views that give us our unabated confidence in the working class and our determination to continue our freely chosen task of shaping and sharpening the revolutionary socialist vanguard movement to which Trotsky made such imperishable contributions.

We do not believe the world is doomed to fall into the barbarism of capitalism or the barbarism of Stalinism.

We do not believe that the masses will stand by impassively while the yoke is fastened firmly over their necks, while the wheels grind remorselessly to the war that threatens the extinction of civilization.

We see already the rising antagonism to American imperialism all over Europe, the preparation of the rebellion against it.

We see already the rising antagonism to Stalinist imperialism all over Russian-occupied Europe — in Poland, in Rumania, now in Hungary — and the preparation of the rebellion against it.

We see the rising tide of horror even among the American people, the American workers, against the threat of war, the rising feeling that it is necessary for the workingmen and women to enter the political field as a distinctive force in order to guide if not to determine the fate of the land. What else is the meaning, for example, of the huge audiences of workingmen that even a muddlehead like Wallace can command — a Wallace in whom the workers find at least some sort of expression of their will for peace and security?

We have seen in our own time how the "wave of the future" — the thousand-year Reich of Hitlerism — was broken, not in a thousand years, or a hundred, but in a mere dozen years — broken against the irrepressible resistance which all the peoples of Europe successfully offered to the mightiest empire the Old World had ever known and the one which finally collapsed most ignominiously.

The day of durable empires, of vast slave-camps of imperialism, of realms from which the rulers draw power and plunder from the people for generations and even centuries — that day is gone and there is no sign that it will return.

The dream of a new world empire is nothing but a dream, and those who dream it, be it in Washington or in Moscow, are duping themselves.

We remain therefore the confident party of international socialist freedom. We have no links to the dead and dying past. We are the party — not of Washington and not of Moscow — but of socialist independence.

Those ideas are our most precious capital. When they become the ideas of the masses they will be irresistible arms in the sacred struggle.

Neither Stalinism and the reform of Stalinism, nor capitalism and the reform of capitalism! Neither Moscow nor Washington. All efforts for restoring the independence of the working class, for restoring the socialist consciousness and program of the working class, for the socialist victory of the working class the world over!

That is the spirit, the essence, the meaning, the very heart of Trotskyism today. That is the meaning, and at the same time the vindication, of the fight for socialism today.

Like the great thinker and great warrior whom we honor tonight, as his name honored us, that is our banner. In heart and mind lies our certainty that it will wave in victory.

12. THE NEW RUSSIAN EMPIRE

In the 1940s the USSR emerged as the world's second super-power, and
— if we measure by direct political control in Eastern Europe and Asia,
rather than by economic clout — the world's greatest empire-holder.
Stalinist states with some autonomy from Moscow also emerged in
Yugoslavia and China. The provisional hypothesis advanced by Max
Shachtman and others in the Workers Party debates of 1940-41, that the
Stalinist bureaucracy was not a new predatory ruling class, but a
freakish and anomalous one, unlikely to be replicated outside the USSR,
had to be revised. The texts in this chapter present a pioneering analysis
of Stalinism as a substantial, though by no means stable and invincible,
force in world history.

RUSSIAN IMPERIALISM AND STALINISM

AT THE VERY OUTSET of the war, the founders of the Workers Party, in opposing the war as imperialist on both sides, set forth the position that Russia's role in the war was imperialist too, and that in two senses: one, that she was participating as an integral part of the imperialist war, and two, that she was pursuing imperialist aims of her own. Hence, the slogan of "unconditional defense of the Soviet Union" was outlived, had become reactionary, and could only serve the ends of Stalinist imperialism. If this question could be seriously debated among Marxists in 1939-1940, it is no longer possible to do so today. The position of our party has been confirmed to the very hilt. The proponents of support of Russia in the war, prompted though they were by revolutionary proletarian considerations, nevertheless capitulated objectively to Stalinist imperialism and helped to cover its deception and enslavement of other nations and peoples with radical arguments. Stalinist Russia today is a full-grown imperialist power. The sway of the reactionary ruling class in Russia extends over a dozen other lands and over tens of millions of other peoples. These peoples have been deprived of their elementary democratic right to national independence and self-government and reduced to the slavery imposed by bureaucratic-collectivism. Along with this right have disappeared all their other rights, for the first victim of the victory of Stalinism is the working class, its democratic organizations and rights (more accurately, the *very* first victim of Stalinism is the revolutionary vanguard of the working class). Revolutionary socialism does not recognize the right of any nation or people or class to deprive any other nation, people or class of these elementary rights except in the higher interests of democracy (as in the period of the great bourgeois revolutions) or in the higher interests of socialism (as in the period of the proletarian revolutions). In the case of bureaucratic-collectivist Russia, the peoples of the Baltic and the Balkans, of Rumania and Yugoslavia and Bulgaria, of Poland and East Prussia, of sections of Asia and the Middle East, have been thus disfranchised in the interests of Stalinist slavery and of the consolidation of the Stalinist bureaucracy. They have been enslaved as loot and booty of the struggle for the imperialist domination of the world. The revolutionist loses title to his name who does not protest and fight against this enslavement.

The claim that this "expansion" (i.e., imperialist aggression and annexation) is required "merely" for the "security" of Russia is a classical imperialist sophism. The defense of the frontiers of a nation (whether by purely defensive measures or by offensive measures is actually of no importance) is warranted only if it is fighting to acquire or maintain or extend democracy or socialism. "Security" by annexation to a nation which is itself ruled by a reactionary class which tramples democracy and socialism under foot

From *New International*, April 1947. From a resolution adopted by the Workers Party at its June 1946 convention.

more ruthlessly than anywhere else in the world, and enslaves every other people over whom it extends its dominion, is nothing but a euphemism and justification of imperialist oppression and exploitation. Every nation has the right to be ruled by its own people, even if they choose a reactionary régime, without unwarranted interference by another nation. On the other hand, every nation has the right to come to the aid of another people which is fighting to overturn its own tyrannical régime, provided this assistance is not aimed at replacing the old tyranny with another and thereby strengthening reaction as a whole. This basic socialist principle, observed by the revolutionary workers' state of Lenin and Trotsky, and proclaimed by it, is applicable in judging the policy not only of the imperialism of capitalist states, but as well to the imperialism of the Stalinist state.

The social sources of Stalinist imperialism have already been examined scientifically by the revolutionary Marxists. It is necessary to continue this examination with the greatest scientific objectivity, without prejudices, and through to the very end. It is not necessary, however, to wait until the last word has been uttered on this question in the scientific sphere before arriving at a judgment of Stalinist imperialism as it has already, and sufficiently, manifested itself, or before adopting a political position toward it.

If bureaucratic collectivism survives in Russia until the next war, the Stalinist state will enter the war on the same basis as its principal rival: for the purpose of defending its imperialist conquests and its reactionary rule at home, for the purpose of extending these imperialist conquests and this rule, for the purpose of winning the struggle for the domination of the globe. Whatever the abstract or historically remote possibilities may be, *all* the present indications, the *whole* present trend, show that the Third World War, if it is allowed to come, will be a struggle between the two monster imperialisms for world mastery, and consequently, a struggle that would decide the fate of the world for an indefinite period of time. Under such circumstances, it is impossible for the revolutionary Marxists to speak in any way of "defense of the Soviet Union." The resolution on the Russian question adopted by our party in 1941 deliberately "left the door open" with regard to the possibility of again raising the slogan of defense of Russia (not in the Second World War but in a conceivable later war). The party took the view that in examining a new social phenomenon that was still in the early process of formation, namely, bureaucratic collectivism, and without positive foreknowledge of the political face of the world in the post-war period, it did not have the right as a scientific Marxian organization to set forth its position categorically on all aspects of the question of Stalinism and for all time. Indeed, even now, the party does not lay claim to a position which applies forever and under all conceivable circumstances. But "all conceivable circumstances" is an abstraction which has its "rights" on the plane of abstraction. What is before us concretely is the development of Stalinist Russia as a full-fledged reactionary empire, oppressing and exploiting not only the Russian people, but a dozen other peoples and nations — and that in the most cruel and barbarous way. What is before us concretely is the overwhelming probability of the next world war being fought between two reactionary imperialist powers for the preservation and extension of their empires. In face of this reality, the Workers Party declares flatly that all talk of defense of Russian imperialism (or of American imperialism) in that war, or in the period of preparation for that war which we are now living through, is reactionary talk and signifies an abandonment of the principles and interests of the proletariat and of socialism.

The concretization of our party's position on the slogan of "defense of the Soviet Union" must be accompanied by an important correction in its resolution on Russia. The resolution, which has otherwise been confirmed so emphatically, contains an error. It declares that in the absence of a proletarian revolution, Stalinist Russia, after the war, "cannot, in all likelihood, escape integration into the capitalist system as a colony or a series of colonies of imperialism." It adds that the stages of development that will be passed "before bureaucratic collectivism in Russia is destroyed either by the proletarian revolution or capitalist counterrevolution, cannot be established categorically in advance." The end of the war has shown, however, that although capitalism has not been destroyed by the proletariat, bureaucratic collectivism in Russia has not only *not* been integrated into the capitalist system, has not only *not* been overturned, but has survived and expanded. This provisional forecast of the party's resolution was in error exactly to the extent to which it represented a hangover of the theory rejected by the party, namely, the theory that Russia is a "degenerated workers' state" which could not survive the war. Fortunately, this error was not seriously reflected in the current analyses of the party during the war, nor did it affect the political line of the party — its struggles against the war, against Stalinism, and Stalinist imperialism, for socialism, or its struggle on the theoretical and political planes against the theoreticians of the "workers' state."

Stalinist imperialism is unique in that, among other things, it has at its disposal a "native" mass movement in all other countries, the "Communist parties" and their affiliates. If one major section of the labor movement— the social democracy — is more and more an agency of American imperialist democracy, the other major section — the Communist parties — is outrightly the agency of Stalinist imperialism. The theory that the Stalinist parties (like the traditional reformist organizations) are agents of the capitalist class, that they "capitulate to the bourgeoisie," is fundamentally false. They are the agencies of Russian bureaucratic collectivism. To the extent that they serve the bourgeoisie of the capitalist countries, it is *only* as agents of the Kremlin who are temporarily hired out for service to the bourgeoisie of this or that country but only in the given interests of the Stalinist state, of its diplomatic maneuvers, of its imperialist objectives. The old Communist parties in the days of the opportunist leadership of the Comintern did tend to conciliate the bourgeoisie and to capitulate to it under stress. The present Stalinist movement has nothing but the name in common with these old parties. It serves, today, a strong imperialist master. In the interests of this master, it is capable of the most irreconcilable opposition to its "own" capitalist class and to its rule. It is imperative to understand this, for otherwise the whole struggle against Stalinism is falsified or nullified. If this is not understood, Stalinism stands to gain by being subjected only to attacks which are aimed at what Stalinism *is not*, instead of attacks aimed at what it is and at those points where it is really vulnerable. Stalinism is not, however, merely the servant of Russian imperialism. If this were the only role it played, the tenacity and "durability" of the Stalinist bureaucracy in the capitalist countries could not be adequately explained. This bureaucracy is not prompted exclusively or even primarily by such "idealistic" consideration as the preservation and consolidation of the Russian state bureaucracy. It has a material base of its own and its own social ambitions in every country. The Stalinist parties are fundamentally different from all the traditional working class parties, not only from those that are revolutionary socialist in character but also from those that are reformist, centrist or anarchist. The Stalinist parties are the parties of bureaucratic collectivism. As Trotsky set it forth in his ultimate judgment of the Stalinist bureaucracy, it seeks to establish in every capitalist country in which it functions the same social and political régime as prevails in Russia today.

The material basis of the Stalinist bureaucracies is provided by the deepening disintegration and decay of capitalism. The social democrat, the reformist, the old trade union bureaucracy rose and developed on the basis of the upswing of capitalist economy. In that period, a pro-capitalist labor bureaucracy was created. This reformist sector of the labor movement became tied to capitalist democracy. It was nurtured economically by the concessions which capitalism could still afford to give, and it received a satisfying political status from the prosperous bourgeoisie and its democracy. However, as capitalism decays and is wracked by agonizing crises, it can less and less afford economic or political concessions to the working class in general or to the reformist bureaucracy in particular. The material basis of reformism is narrowed both in the economic and the political spheres. Reformism does not break its ties with capitalist democracy; but decaying capitalism breaks its ties with reformism.

As capitalism decays and narrows the basis for existence of reformism, the bonds linking whole strata of the population to the foundations of capitalism — private property — are loosened. To maintain private property, which means nowadays to preserve the increasingly centralized and concentrated power of monopoly capitalism, requires the economic and political disfranchisement, the economic and political degradation not only of the proletariat but also of the middle and intermediate classes and social strata — peasants, small producers and manufacturers, small traders, professionals, civil servants, scientists, labor bureaucracies, industrial managers and supervisors, etc., etc. Fascism appeals to all these strata with a socially-demagogical program of "anti-capitalism" but with the social aim of maintaining precisely that form of capitalist ownership which is disfranchising, degrading and declassing the social strata to which fascism appeals. Stalinism, on the other hand, while appealing to the same strata, with a no less demagogical program of "socialism," nevertheless aims at removing from power that class — the monopoly capitalists — which stands in the way of the acquisition of social power by the Stalinist bureaucracy. In this sense, too, fascism and Stalinism, while not identical, are "symmetrical phenomena". Stalinism has a grip on the minds of the working class not only by virtue of its usurpation of the socialist traditions of the Bolshevik Revolution. It seeks, and often gains, support of the working classes because, while its anti-proletarian and anti-socialist nature is not immediately clear, its anti-capitalist nature *is* apparent. It cannot be considered an accident that the Stalinist bureaucracy attracts to its ranks, especially in countries where the decay of capitalism has reached an advanced stage, many of the former reformist bureaucrats whom capitalism no longer offers economic or political security. The expropriation of the bourgeoisie by the democratic proletariat means the beginning of the end of all bureaucratism and bureaucratic privilege. But the seizure of all social power by Stalinism means the legal and police sanctification of bureaucratic privilege and power. It is likewise no accident that Stalinism attracts to itself also such elements as the declassed worker, the disoriented and demoralized petty-bourgeois intellectuals and professionals whom capitalism allows an ever narrowing base for existence but whom the triumph of Stalinism offers exceptional privileges and social status.

The growth and triumph of the Stalinist bureaucracy means neither the victory nor the advancement of socialism and the proletariat. It means the establishment of the totalitarian tyranny known as bureaucratic collectivism. Such a tyranny is possible only in the absence of a socialist perspective. Inasmuch as the socialist perspective depends, in our period, on the ability of the revolutionary Marxists to establish a party able to place itself at the head of the working class and all other little people, the triumph of Stalinism is possible only under the condition of the absence of such a party. Conversely, it is impossible in the presence of such a party, since *all* the other conditions for the victory of the socialist proletariat have matured to the highest degree under capitalism.

The question of the perspective of Stalinism cannot, therefore, be resolved in a purely theoretical way. It can be resolved only in struggle. Every advance of Stalinism is not only a defeat for democracy but also a defeat for the proletariat and for socialism. Unlike reformism, Stalinism does not aim at the preservation of bourgeois democracy, let alone at the conquest of proletarian democracy. Stalinism is neither a democratic nor a socialist movement, but a bureaucratic totalitarian collectivist movement, which must be resisted by the organized proletariat at every turn.

The traditional policy of the revolutionary vanguard toward the labor-reformist movements (or bureaucracies) does not, therefore, apply to the Stalinist movements. Given its inability to lead the proletariat directly and in its own name, the revolutionary vanguard is prepared, as always, to give critical support to the reformist bureaucracies in their conflicts with the capitalist class. This makes possible, at least to some extent, the defense of the economic and political integrity of the working class and its movement, or even the defense of bourgeois democracy against fascism, i.e., the defense of the political conditions that are more favorable to the existence and development of the working class. The same policy cannot be applied to Stalinism, since it is neither a democratic nor a socialist movement and has neither democratic nor socialist aims. The revolutionary Marxists, therefore, maintain the general rule of no support of Stalinism of any kind and of irreconcilable opposition to any move calculated to strengthen its position.

Whether or not Stalinism can triumph in the capitalist world cannot be decided absolutely in advance. To repeat, it is a question of struggle. Up to now, it is established that Stalinism was able to triumph by overturning the rule of the proletariat (Russia). It was able to triumph in the Baltic countries annexed to Russia, but only by virtue of the military force of

Russian imperialism. In Poland and Yugoslavia, the Stalinist bureaucracy has taken power. In clear refutation of the analysis that it represents a "capitalist" force, the bureaucracy has not only disfranchised and enslaved the proletariat and peasantry, but has systematically expropriated the bourgeoisie and the landlords and converted their property into state property. This phenomenon gives the final blow to the theory that Russia is a "workers' state" because property is nationalized. But it does not establish the conclusion that Stalinist collectivism is guaranteed to replace capitalism in the world. Both in Poland and Yugoslavia, Stalinism came to power under exceptional circumstances, namely, in the absence of any organized bourgeoisie to speak of and by means of the direct and decisive aid of the armed forces of Russian imperialism. Nowhere has Stalinism shown its social ability to crush a free working class or, more important, its ability to overthrow the rule of the capitalist class. The countries in which it has triumphed are lands where the bourgeoisie was weak to begin with and where feudal remnants were thickly intertwined with capitalist relationships. Nowhere has Stalinism shown its social ability to overturn the rule of the capitalist class in a modern, advanced capitalist country. Hence, our denial and rejection of the theory of the "Stalinist epoch," our reaffirmation of the theory that Stalinist bureaucratic collectivism represents a mongrel social formation, and our reaffirmation of the concept that this is the epoch of the proletarian socialist revolution which will sweep away capitalism and bureaucratic collectivism alike.

GERMANY AND EASTERN EUROPE

NOWHERE DID THE PRE-WAR perspectives of the Fourth International stand in sharper contrast to the political reality produced by the war than in Germany. If there was still reason to assign to the German proletariat a pivotal role in the strategy of the European revolution up to Hitler's triumph in 1933, the successful mobilization of the German nation in 1939 without internal disturbances, the paralysis of the German proletariat during the Nazi conquest and subjugation of the Continent, and the absence of any repercussions within Germany to the military set-backs beginning at Stalingrad in the winter of 1942-1943, proved the need to re-examine the analysis that designated Germany the "'key to the international situation". A refusal to do the latter was only possible on the part of those who, as with the leadership of the SWP, stubbornly denied that the fascist conquest of Europe had hurled back the proletariat in terms of consciousness and organization. Those who insisted that fascism had taught the proletariat the lessons of revolutionary politics and that, consequently, it would emerge from the fascist oppression at a higher political level than before, could not but assign to the German proletariat the vanguard role in the European revolution. The colossal blunder of continuing to view the German proletariat in terms of 1918-1933 was an inseparable part of the totally false position which rejected the slogan of national liberation, which led to abstention from participation in the resistance movements, which foresaw the overthrow of Hitler as the proletarian revolution and which posed as the main slogan "the United Socialist States of

Europe." Basing themselves upon this completely unreal analysis, its authors momentarily expected, with amazing credulity and increasing desperation, the outbreak of the proletarian revolution as an automatic result of Germany's growing military catastrophes in 1944-1945. This gross misreading of the situation in Germany revealed that its perpetrators sadly lacked even an understanding of the mechanics of the proletarian revolution and conceived of it in terms of the sheerest automatism and spontaneity.

The defeat in 1933, the twelve-year long rule of Nazi terror, the devastation of six years of war, the conquest and occupation by the victorious powers and the infamous partition of Germany by the four powers for purposes of scientifically bleeding it of its economic potency and political viability as a nation makes it necessary to begin the task of again collecting in class organizations the shattered and dispersed forces of the German proletariat at the most primitive level. Of all the obstacles this task must overcome, the first and the greatest is the military occupation of Germany. Until this condition is ended, the scene will be dominated by the national struggle for liberation. The main slogan around which the German Marxists must orient the struggle in the coming period is "For a unified and independent Germany!" This struggle begins as a struggle for democratic rights against the military authorities of the occupying powers and their quisling supporters. Freedom of speech, of press, of assembly, of movement, of organization, of communication and the right to vote and the demand for a free national assembly will constitute the issues around which the political struggles will revolve and the masses will rally. Unless the German proletarian organizations take upon themselves the lead in this struggle and conduct it in the spirit of socialism and internationalism, this task will fall to the reactionary nationalists. They will utilize it for the reconstruction of the Nazi movement, regardless of the guise or the name under which it will appear. Neither the Social Democrats nor the Stalinists can give the proletariat a lead on this struggle. The former plays the role of adjutant to the Anglo-American authorities and the latter is the creature of the Russian oppressors. This struggle requires the speediest organization of a revolutionary Marxist party and, in turn, affords our German comrades a clear issue upon which to struggle for such a party.

The Marxists of the "victorious" nations have the special task of defending the democratic rights of the German people, by helping, in the first place, to free the land of the imperialist invaders. The reunification and liberation of Germany remains the first step toward the restoration of the truncated economy of the Continent. In this *historical* sense, Germany remains the key to Europe. The Marxists of Western Europe must link the struggle against American domination of their own countries with the struggle against the oppression of Germany by their own ruling classes. Such an international proletarian struggle in the defense of the German people will be one of the surest barriers to the reappearance of a Nazi movement in Germany. It will restore to the German proletariat the self-confidence and morale which has been its greatest deficiency since 1933. It will pose before the Stalinist-led workers of Western Europe the "German question" as a question of international proletarian solidarity and, thereby, pose before them the "Russian question" from the point of view of imperialist oppression. In this respect the effect of the struggle by the workers of the victorious powers upon the German proletariat is only an aspect of the whole mechanism by which the revolutionary impetus will be given to the German scene, i.e., via the revolutionary struggles of the international proletariat, above all those of Western Europe.

The conquest of virtually all of Eastern Europe by Stalinist imperialism has, as in the case of Hitler's conquests, burdened the masses with a combination of class exploitation and national oppression. In these countries especially the slogan of the "defense of the Soviet Union" can be nothing but a cover for the rapacity of Stalinist imperialism. The revolutionary Marxists are no less firmly committed to support of the demand for national liberation from the yoke of Stalinism than from the yoke of Hitlerism or any other form of imperialist subjugation and violation of the right of self-determination and self-rule. The Fourth International must adopt and propagate the slogan of national liberation for the peoples and nations oppressed by Stalinist Russia as an elementary internationalist duty and as an indispensable part of the internationalist education of the whole working class. As in the case of the movements which arose against German imperialism, the Workers Party will support every socialist or genuinely popular democratic movement of resistance against the imperialist oppressor in Eastern Europe, without giving any aid or support to reactionary landlord or capitalist-fascist elements who seek to exploit the progressive national sentiments of the masses. However, we do not take the Stalinists' word for it that all the partisans and partisan bands in Poland, for example, who are fighting against the invading oppressor or against the totalitarian "native" régime, are "Fascists." We are only too well aware of the Stalinist practice of labelling all its opponents as "Fascists." The struggle for national liberation is inseparably bound up in these countries with the fight for all democratic rights and liberties, including the right to free universal suffrage and a free Constituent Assembly. To attempt to substitute for this slogan the slogan of "Soviets" is false and preposterous. In countries like Poland, etc., there is no tradition whatsoever of the revolutionary Soviets established by the Bolshevik Revolution. What has appeared to these peoples in the name of "Sovietism" is the Stalinist reaction which they abhor and against which they are already striving with all their force. As in the case of Western Europe under the Nazi occupation, *our* support of the struggle for national freedom is not support for the return or restoration to power of the landlords and capitalists. Our demand for the Constituent Assembly is closely linked with the demand for the preservation of nationalized economy under democratic control, with the demand for the land to the peasants, but free from the police rule of the GPU satrapy.

The attempts of the Stalinist imperialists to consolidate their power and control in Eastern Europe cannot but lead to increased resistance of the masses. This resistance must inevitably take the form of struggle for ousting the invader and establishing the national sovereignty of the occupied lands. The masses of the conquered countries show, as they did during the war, both the organic need and organic capacity to oust the invader. Wherever the masses have had any opportunity to express themselves, they have manifested their hostility to the Stalinists: Austrian and Hungarian elections, mass demonstrations in Rumania, semi-civil war in Poland.

489

Failure to give staunch support to the movement for national freedom from Stalinist rule (both in the newly occupied countries as well as in those countries of the "Soviet Union" long ago usurped by the Kremlin autocracy) can only serve, moreover, to delay the inevitable crisis of Stalinism in Russia itself. To preserve itself, to enhance its power and privilege, to maintain its exploitation and oppression of peoples and nations annexed to the Russian empire, the bureaucracy is compelled to saddle the Russian masses with an even vaster bureaucratic monster, with an even vaster police and spy force, with a huge standing army, all of which are directed against the Russian people as well. The bureaucracy is compelled, like the ruling class of the capitalist empires, to deprive the masses of homes and a decent standard of living by concentrating upon preparation for imperialist war and upon production of the means of destruction. The returning soldiers who have seen other lands under circumstances which puts the Stalinist régime in a truer, that is, a less advantageous light, can only add to the restlessness and dissatisfaction which Stalinism generates among the people. The rise of the most brutal chauvinism in the upper ranks of the bureaucracy, especially the military bureaucracy, must clash with the war-weariness and yearning for peace and security of the people. The crisis of Stalinism cannot be too long postponed. It can weather this crisis if the Russian people feel themselves isolated. Their true ally in the struggle for emancipation is not the Stalinist bureaucracy but the peoples of the oppressed nations who are fighting for national freedom against this bureaucracy. The overturn of the Stalinist ruling class in Russia is now the common *direct* task of the Russian masses and the nations under the Russian heel.

Hal Draper

THE NEW RUSSIAN EMPIRE

DURING THE PERIOD since the end of the [2nd World] war, Russia has emerged not only as a major imperialist power but as one of the Big Two of the earth. Its imperialism has matured and expanded with a rapidity characteristic of change in our epoch. Beginning the war as Hitler's junior partner in the Stalin-Nazi Pact, it is today capitalist America's only rival for world domination — a rivalry not only between different imperialisms but also between two different systems of class exploitation, which meet each other with different political, social and economic weapons in the struggle for the "right" to oppress the peoples. Russia has not merely "expanded"; it has set out to build and has already acquired in part a far-flung empire on every side of its borders, consisting of states which are not

From *New International*, April 1949, "Stalinism and the Rise of the New Russian Empire", a Workers Party document written by Hal Draper.

merely "satellites" but subject nations held in chains by the same totalitarian terror that operates within Russia itself. The euphemism of Russian "expansionism" as a substitute for "imperialism" can be used only if all reality is ignored.

During the past two years the unfolding of Stalinist policy, in the satellite states especially, has helped to confirm and clarify the nature of Russia and Stalinism. First and foremost among these developments has been the clear fact that the Stalinist régimes have without exception pursued a policy of bureaucratic nationalization of the economy and destruction of the capitalist class. In all of the satellite states, the major part of industry has been nationalized; whatever sector of the economy still remains in private hands is almost exclusively made up of small enterprises, and even these are rapidly on the way to complete nationalization or state control.

The socio-economic system, as well as the political system, has been made identical with that of Russia itself in every important respect. The bourgeoisie has been expropriated not only politically but economically. The event which marked this development most dramatically was the CP coup in Czechoslovakia in February 1948, this being the last country in the Russian empire in which the bourgeoisie had retained any vestige of political control.

With this demonstration the last props have been knocked from under the two theories on the "Russian question" heretofore posed in the Marxist movement as alternatives to our own. The "orthodox" Fourth International theory that Russia is still a (degenerated) workers' state, since "nationalized property equals workers' state", now requires the conclusion that the East European satellites are likewise "workers' states". But this means that Stalinism — by no matter what unexpected or unpleasant means — has shown its ability to make the social revolution and overthrow capitalism in favor of a form of workers' power. It means further, that while the working class and a revolutionary-socialist workers' party is a good thing and perhaps even necessary for a further healthy development of the "revolution", they are not necessary for the making of the socialist revolution. It means further that the only role to be played by the revolutionary party is as a democratic opposition in, or wing of, the Stalinist movement. While formally only the British section of the Fourth International has actually openly acknowledged the conclusion that the satellite countries are workers' states, the reaction of the Fourth International to the Tito-Stalin break demonstrates that it is actually tending to assume this character and role of a "left wing" or "democratic wing" of Stalinism. While tradition and pressure from within may slow up or zigzag this trend, it is unquestionably demanded by the theory to which they still cling.

If the "workers' state" position has been well-nigh taken out of the realm of theoretical dispute by its refutation in life, the same is even more true of the theory that Russia is essentially capitalist — whether capitalism heavily overladen by statification, or capitalism at its "highest" peak of development — or the theory that Russia is developing in the direction of capitalism. The destruction of capitalism and of the capitalist class, the refusal of the Stalinist rulers to compromise with it, politically or economically, in the satellite zones, leave no more room for doubt that we

491

have here a social system different from and antagonistic to the capitalist system in any form. Meanwhile, on the negative side, in Russia itself all predictions of internal Russian development based on either the "workers' state" or "state capitalist" theory have utterly failed to show the slightest sign of being realized.

In noting the confirmation of our analysis of Russia and Stalinism by the events of the past two years, it must not be concluded that the Russian state and social system, or the international Stalinist movement, is already a finished social formation, about which a final set of formulas can be drawn up. Stalinism itself is still meeting new problems as a result of its new role in the world and its characteristics are emerging — even to itself — only step by step as it grapples with *its* new problems. It is only in this sense that we can and do claim that the theory of bureaucratic collectivism has shown itself to be the indispensable key to understanding the Stalinist phenomena.

The sweeping character of Stalinist nationalization in Eastern Europe also reinforces another conclusion. It has been traditional in the Marxist analysis of *capitalist* phenomena to make or allow a distinction between the "progressive form" and "reactionary social content" of certain capitalist developments (like the growth of monopoly out of large-scale production). The sense in which the term "progressive in form" was applied to monopoly was contained in the thought that the concentration and centralization of large-scale industrial enterprise in the hands of a few capitalists prepared the way technologically for socialist collectivization, provided in fact the prerequisites for the latter. This was and is correct.

It is impossible, however, to apply the same distinction to the bureaucratic nationalization of industry under Stalinism. Stalinist nationalization is in no sense at all a prerequisite for the socialization of the means of production; nor does it "prepare the way" for the latter. Industrialization and centralization in the past represented the impact of what Engels metaphorically called "the invading socialist society" upon capitalism, developing capitalism to the point where socialism first became *possible*; Stalinist nationalization and industrialization represents not a necessary preparation for socialism but an abortion of this pre-socialist evolution, resulting in a social system which is the deadly enemy of socialism. The form of nationalized economy *per se* as opposed to capitalist property forms can be characterized only as "potentially more efficient" — an abstraction which permits a social characterization of actual phenomena only given a live historical context.

Stalinist nationalization, therefore, is in no sense progressive, occurring as it does at a time when the problem before society on a world scale is no longer that of abolishing the domination of man by nature (sufficient at least for the realization of socialism) but when the problem is that of abolishing the domination of man by man. This is the only basic criterion for the category of "progressiveness" in today's world; that is "progressive" which is a prerequisite for, or does in fact lead to, the establishment of *socialist democracy*.

THE STALINIST ROAD TO POWER in the satellites: The events of the past period have provided also the historical spectacle of *new* Stalinist states and bureaucracies in the process of formation. Up to the end of the war, bureaucratic collectivism, which was analyzed as a new social formation different from both capitalism and socialism (as well as from all pre-capitalist societies) was still a Russian phenomenon, limited to one country. An analysis of this new society through this one case was complicated by the fact that in this single specimen bureaucratic collectivism had arisen through the degeneration of a nationally-confined socialist revolution. In the early years of the war, this bureaucratic-collectivism-in-one-country already had expanded its own borders through purely military conquests, but had not yet spawned.

The bureaucratic-collectivist states set up by Stalinism in East Europe did *not* arise through the degeneration of a socialist revolution in power. Nor did they all arise in exactly the same way. In the case of Poland, Rumania and Bulgaria, for example, the Stalinist régimes were set up, from the beginning of the "liberation" (from the Nazis), on the bayonets of the Russian army as pure-and-simple quisling régimes, put into power by military *ukase* and maintained in power by terrorism. If any other road to power was possible in these cases, the Russians at any rate did not experiment with it, although individual bourgeois captives were temporarily utilized as figureheads to ease the transition. These satellites were and are nothing but formally independent satrapies of the Russian power.

In Czechoslovakia, however, after five months of military occupation, the Russians left behind a mixed government, in which the Communist Party was handed control over the central institutions of state power (army, police) and of propaganda; but at the same time a certain measure of political power was shared with representatives of the shattered and weakened bourgeoisie who engaged themselves in return to follow the pro-Russian line in international relations. The difference between Czechoslovakia and the first type of satellite was determined essentially not by any greater power enjoyed by the Czech bourgeoisie as against the Polish, etc., but by the existence of a proletariat which was the most numerous and the best organized in Eastern Europe. The Czech CP did not dare to move for complete control until in the intervening period it had succeeded in insuring its rear by subjugating and breaking possible resistance by the working class to complete totalitarianization through a régime of constantly stepped-up terror. In the end the Stalinist drive to gather all power into their hands achieved success by counting on the passivity of the working class in the face of a coup from above by picked terror squads recruited *from* the proletariat and used *against* the proletariat.

The passive reaction by the Czech proletariat to the coup was based on the following conditions: (a) The essence of state power was already in the hands of the Stalinists as a result of the Russian conquest; the Stalinists were not overthrowing the state power but merely utilizing it to complete the totalitarianization of the country. (b) Czechoslovakia's geographical position and common border with Russia as well as its original military occupation by Russia had already put it in Moscow's orbit from the beginning; and this objective fact was recognized by all. The coup represented no change in this respect but only blasted the illusions of the bourgeois politicians and their followers that their country could revolve in Russia's orbit as a maverick planet. (c) There was no alternative visible to the workers which did not involve dependence on the totally discredited bourgeoisie, which was clinging to its own economic power by a thread and to its political power by sufferance. Like the majority of European workers, the Czech proletariat in the mass looked with hope only to socialism, nor was there left a viable bourgeoisie which could appear even as a practical lesser evil to Stalinism. In such an impasse, the immediate alternatives were only support of the Stalinist dictatorship for venal or illusory reasons, or passive toleration and immobilization.

The fact, however, that the Stalinist road to total power in Czechoslovakia did not take place completely under Russian guns but was at least consummated after a semi-public struggle of political forces permits an insight into another aspect of the nature of Stalinism. The CP apparatus, which came riding in on the Russian army's gun-carriages, sought to establish social roots of its own within the country. In the West (e.g., France and Italy) where the Stalinists place their anti-capitalist face out in front, it is well known that the Stalinist movement has displayed great attractive power for corralling militant and revolutionary elements in the working class who see no other mass party fighting the enemy in power, the capitalist class.

In most of Eastern Europe, where the CP leadership was plucked out of Moscow's Hotel Metropole and placed on top, the consequences are different. Insofar and as long as the Czech CP was still able to use the remnants of the bourgeoisie as a bogyman, it exercised a gravitational pull on socialist workers. With the tightening of its own reins and the progressive enfeeblement of bourgeois control in the government, its influence over the illusions of the workers and its possession of their active support waned (e.g., victory of the anti-Stalinist wing of the SDP over Fierlinger before the coup). Throughout, in any case, the Stalinists sought, and found, points of support outside the circle of pro-Stalinist workers with revolutionary illusions, knowing that the latter were unreliable props.

The Stalinist bureaucracy-in-formation seeks to recruit not merely to the ranks of the party but also specifically to the bureaucracy. In the conditions of the satellite zone, the first recruiting group is the labor and social-democracy bureaucracy itself. Already noted is the extent of the ideological kinship between the bureaucracies of reformism and of Stalinism, and, as the counterweight in the capitalist countries, the different social basis of the reformists and Stalinists. Where, however, capitalism has been well-nigh destroyed or at least seriously enfeebled, and on the way out, as in Czechoslovakia, the reformist labor bureaucracy is left rootless and its habitual ways of thought and life push sections of it to absorption into the Stalinist bureaucracy.

Hence the common phenomenon in Eastern Europe today of an influx of social-democrat turncoats into the Stalinist apparatus, in some case providing the tops with their only really native elements. A second fertile source of recruitment to the Stalinist bureaucracy under Eastern European conditions is the middle-class intellectual, socially rootless even under declining capitalism, repelled by the anarchy and inefficiency of capitalist society and its inability and unwillingness to give rein to his special talents even in its own behalf. The type is common, for example, in the leadership of the Yugoslav CP. Given the plethora of bureaucratic jobs opened up by Stalinist nationalization, to which must be added a large number of jobs not directly paid by the government but controlled by it, such elements — plus workers raised into an aristocracy of management — are absorbed into the new Stalinist régimes.

To them, in the case of Czechoslovakia, must be added the adaptable elements of the old bureaucracy. Far from requiring a clean sweep of the entire old bureaucracy when they take power, the Stalinists have a real need to try to integrate into their own régime as many of the old political *figures* and officeholders as possible.

The Czech coup showed that the Stalinists' aim is to *avoid* unleashing the mass action and revolutionary initiative of the workers in their road to power. While, as long as remnants of the bourgeoisie remain, they are willing to use gingerly the club of working-class action against them, the Stalinists do not themselves wish to arouse the masses to revolutionary self-activity even to make their own Stalinist coup. It would be a mistake to consider that this is due in any concrete situation only to a calculated fear that the masses may get completely out of hand, though this operates as a strong deterrent where the CP itself has no independent power. In Czechoslovakia, where the CP was already in complete control of the state apparatus of coercion, the awakening of mass revolutionary activity was neither necessary nor desirable for them. In France and Italy, where the CP has several times now led the proletariat to the verge of insurrectionary action in battering-ram action against the capitalist government, it has each time drawn back before the danger of revolution could spill over.

The Stalinist bureaucracy tends to develop the same mental cast toward action-from-below that is developed by every reactionary and anti-popular force which is interested in defending its own privileges above all. Just as even in the most democratic capitalist countries, this inherent fear of the masses takes forms not strictly demanded by the actual relationship of forces but flowing from the nature of the class (e.g., the widespread fear of revolution in the American bourgeoisie in the depression years of the '30s), so the Stalinists' fear of the masses flows from their anti-working-class character. Like the bourgeoisie itself at times, they *may* be compelled to call on working-class action to take the stage to a greater or lesser extent, while seeking to keep it within limits. They can moreover do this all the more freely in proportion as there is no organized working-class opposition to crystallize the anti-Stalinist democratic revolutionary forces. In this they follow a course analogous to the bourgeoisie's utilization of proletarian class struggle against feudal power in their time.

The Stalinists do not seek their road to power through working-class revolution or revolutionary action. They seek to utilize class struggle only to support the foreign policy of the Russian state or hasten the process of the breakdown and disintegration of the capitalist framework, to create a chaotic vacuum into which they can step from above. Their adventuristic sabotage strikes in France and Italy play the short-term game of pressure for a pro-Russian appeasement policy and serve the longer-range aim of creating the conditions under which Stalinism wishes to take power *without* the revolutionary intervention of the masses.

In France and Italy these conditions are not near; and neither, therefore, is Stalinist power on the Atlantic. The victory of Stalinism in Western Europe — which would mean the longest step toward world Stalinist domination — is abstractly a possibility; but it can be posed as a possibility only given an extreme stage of disintegration of Western capitalism such as was true in the East as a result of the Second World War and such as creates a near-vacuum of political and social power. But this abstract possibility has already been sufficiently expressed in the very enunciation of the historic alternatives of socialism or barbarism. Not abstractly but in terms of the real world situation, long before such a stage can be expected, war between Russia and the Western capitalist world and the revival of the movement for proletarian revolution will first have settled the question of the fate of capitalism. The last word is still to be said by the working class. The outcome is not to be deduced from abstract analyses but will be determined by the struggle itself.

THE LINE OF STRUGGLE AGAINST STALINISM: The first steps required are the beginnings of mass struggle for the simplest economic demands — on wages, vacations, working day, police régime in the factories, etc. The flowering of Russian imperialism and the consequent necessity of shaping the whole economy toward a permanent war footing, added to the enormous waste inherent in a bureaucratic collectivist economy, makes it impossible for the régime to allow an improvement in the standard of living of the masses. But under bureaucratic collectivism, there are not and cannot be any purely economic struggles. The struggle for the simplest economic demand is by definition from the beginning a struggle against the totalitarian state — a political struggle. Similarly, every struggle against the "excesses" of the police régime is a struggle for workers' democracy, for control of the nationalized economy by the people. But under bureaucratic collectivism the struggle for control of the nationalized economy by the people, the struggle for workers' democracy, is necessarily the struggle for socialism. Where the state already owns and controls the economy, every struggle over the state power becomes a struggle for the democratic rule of the working class as against the bureaucracy.

In the Stalinist states, the ruling class — and therefore the main enemy — is the bureaucracy. There is no big bourgeoisie at all, this class having been completely destroyed in all of the Russian satellites. There are remnants of the small and middle bourgeoisie in some sectors of the economy, shorn of all political power, and tightly controlled by the Stalinist state; even those socially powerless remnants are progressively being cut down by advancing statification and control. All responsibility for both economic and political life is centered in the hands of the Stalinist state, which necessarily is the focal point on which all movements of discontent and opposition converge. The aim of all opposition in such a state inevitably centers around the demands of *democracy*. Not only is this demand the essence of the *socialist* struggle under the bureaucratic-collectivist régime, it is at the same time the program around which the widest strata of the population can be effectively mobilized. Even in the case of the peasants — the only important social force remaining in the Stalinist satellites still based on private property — the socialist program, which advocates truly voluntary collectivization founded on education, supports the struggle of the small peasants against the despotism that deprives them of the land on the basis of a "collectivization" which scarcely conceals the fact that the peasants are reduced to state serfs of the land, exploited and lorded over by the government police. Such a program is a powerful

496

weapon capable of drawing the peasantry around the anti-Stalinist workers in opposition to the agrarian policies of a totalitarian state based on terrorism and enslavement to the state. The task of the Marxists, therefore, is to enter into battle against the main enemy alongside every genuinely popular movement of resistance to the despotism of the state. They will seek to organize the class forces of the working class independently in such a struggle, raise their own class banners and achieve working-class hegemony over this democratic struggle, along with whatever bourgeois elements are involved in the fight or are even temporarily at its head. The struggle of the Marxists and of the working class in such a popular democratic camp is in no sense a struggle for "bourgeois restoration" but on the contrary the only way in which bourgeois restoration can be fought as an alternative to Stalinism and the broad masses led in a socialist direction.

The threat of a bourgeois-restorationist movement in Eastern Europe looms, however, in proportion as disillusionment with the Stalinist régime finds no revolutionary alternative through which it can be channelized and in proportion to pressure by Western capitalism. Given the largely agrarian character of many of the Russian satellites and the presently atomized state of its working class, the revitalization of working-class revolt against Stalinism — the seeds of which revolt are sown by Stalinism itself — may require first a series of demonstrations in the West. Insofar as the Western proletariat shows that the power of Stalinism *can* be broken in their own countries; insofar as they prove that Stalinist power is not fated to roll over Europe's working class; insofar as they exhibit in struggle a *non-capitalist* alternative to Stalinist totalitarianism — to this extent the revolt of the East European peoples will be speeded, their self-confidence raised, and the situation created whereby they can take advantage of the cracks in the Stalinist structure and push through these fissures in a wave of assaults upon the Stalinist power. This demonstration, however, cannot be made as long as the working class of the West channelizes the fight against Stalinism through support of capitalism. The overthrow of Stalinism in the East requires the revolutionary struggle to overthrow capitalism in the West.

This basic political approach to the problem of fighting Stalinism is even more important in the West, where the Stalinist movements are still followed by large sections of the working class. During the past two years there has been a marked decline in Stalinist influence from the post-war high point in almost every country in Europe. This decline is due partly to the masses' experience with Stalinist policy both in the West and in the East, and partly to the Marshall Plan offensive of American capitalism. Neither the Marshall Plan nor the prospect of temporary economic improvement has, however, convinced the Western European workers that the restabilization of capitalism under American domination offers an alternative worth fighting for enthusiastically as against Stalinism. *The chief reason why the Stalinists still remain the strongest parties supported by the working class — in spite of their own crimes and progressive disillusionment with them — is the fact that they appear as fighters against capitalism and for peace.* Any movement which follows the policy of supporting capitalism as against Stalinism, or of supporting American imperialism as against Russian, deprives itself of the possibility of winning these masses away from the Stalinists and for a progressive movement. At the best, given sufficient self-exposure by the latter, the masses will be left without any alternative for which they are ready to fight devotedly and actively. The *sine qua non* for breaking the workers away from Stalinist leadership is the regroupment of the scattered forces with a revolutionary third-camp position and the making of a new beginning in forging a new instrument for the mobilization of the proletariat against both capitalism and Stalinism.

The *only* mass party of the working class in existence in Western Europe is the social-democracy, which bases itself on the "lesser-evil" policy. While it is the only movement which appears before militant workers as an alternative to following the Stalinists, the reformist pro-American and pro-bourgeois-democratic character of its line and leadership is an insuperable obstacle to its effectively playing the role of bulwark against Stalinism within the working class. Nevertheless, in most places, given the feeble state of the independent Marxist movement, the rise of a Marxist third-camp wing within the social-democratic movements offers the best opportunity for setting up a pole of attraction for the disillusioned Stalinist workers as well as for leftward-moving socialists; and thus contributing toward the regroupment of forces from the existing working-class movement.

Such a new beginning is the first task in Europe and America today. In most of the world, and above all in Europe, it is no longer enough for working-class revolutionists to chart the lines of class struggle against capitalism in the assurance that every blow struck against capitalism is a blow for the socialist future. They face two enemies: a capitalism which is anti-Stalinist and a Stalinism which is anti-capitalist. This three-cornered struggle for power was implicit in the Czech events; and it is this utterly new constellation of social forces which disorients and confuses the working-class movement. It is the recognition of this new stage which is the basis of the politics of the third camp. Without the working-class struggle, no socialism; this is truer than ever before. What is not true is that *mere* anti-capitalist struggle automatically equals socialist struggle. The conscious planned intervention and leadership of a revolutionary Marxist vanguard, anti-capitalist and anti-Stalinist, which has not been poisoned at its source by a false conception of the relation between socialism and workers' democracy, is more than ever the key to a socialist victory.

13. TROTSKY OR DEUTSCHER?

The Shachtmanites in the early 1940s were the dissidents, in the general school of thought defined by Trotsky. By the late 40s, however, there had developed, at the other pole of that school of thought, a New Trotskyism, or neo-Trotskyism, revising the classical Marxist framework much more radically than Shachtman had. Its most influential writer was Isaac Deutscher, author of justly famous books on Stalin and Trotsky. Effectively, Deutscher grafted into neo-Trotskyism the politics that in Trotsky's lifetime had been known in their "Communist" variant as "Brandlerism" and in their social-democratic version as "Bauerism".

Max Shachtman

TROTSKY'S STALIN

THE EMERGENCE OF RUSSIA as a power of first magnitude is indisso-
ciable from the name of Stalin. Now that Mussolini is gone, there is
nowhere a government chief that has ruled his country for so long a continuous period as Stalin, or ruled it so completely. His mark upon the destiny of Russia and for that matter of the rest of the world has certainly
been deeper than that of any other man alive today. Few other lives in a
century rampant with storm and strife have been as stormy as his or have
aroused as much controversy. In the face of this, the paucity of serious biographical literature about Stalin — as compared, let us say, with the
available literature on the life and work of Lenin or Hitler or even
Roosevelt — is astonishing.

This paucity is not so astonishing upon reflection, however. Like all other
outstanding personages, Stalin has both a personal history, linked with
his character, and a social history; he is at once an individual and a social
phenomenon. To treat of the individual "alone" offers virtually no difficulties in the case of a Hitler or a Roosevelt. Their lives are pretty much an
open book and what they have to conceal can be laid bare with a good
sneeze. As social figures the problem is no more difficult: each in his own
way was a child of a social order whose anatomy has long been familiar to
modern science. Not so in the case of Stalin. His true personal history is
not only obscure in large part, but it has been covered up, nailed down and
overlaid with a history manufactured and disseminated on a scale that is
utterly unprecedented, stupefying and, for its purpose, effective. His true
social history is, if anything, far more baffling, for here we are faced not
with a familiar but with a new, unfamiliar, unpredicted, unanalyzed social
order, of which Stalin is both the child and the parent.

The biographer thus faces a dual handicap without equal in history.
Superficiality, glibness, gullibility, impatience, carelessness, sensational-
ism, lack of a sympathetic understanding of the movement which nursed
Stalin and out of which he rose, personal animus, lack of scientific
method, lack of scrupulous objectivity — all or many of these characterize
the authors of the biographical attempts made up to now. Hence, even the
best of them only come abreast of the handicap but do not surmount it. No
man of our time had the qualifications for coping successfully with the
dual obstacle that Trotsky had. We know that he had to drive himself
physically, so to speak, to write his study of Stalin, for the subject is not
very attractive. But he was able to bring to the work an archaeological
patience and thoroughness in digging past layer upon layer of falsification
to reveal the bare bones of truth; a direct personal knowledge of the

From *New International*, October 1946. This is the full text, restoring small changes made
by Shachtman when he republished the article in 1962.

Bolshevik movement in its rise and decline, of its protagonists big and small, of the country and the conditions in which they lived and worked; a personal objectivity which is all the more striking in a man whom Stalin rightly considered his greatest and most dangerous adversary; and such a unifying and illuminating grasp of the riches of the Marxist method of analysis and synthesis as the philistines of Marxism, let alone the philistines in general, cannot possibly comprehend. (For them Marxism says: only classes exist, there are no individuals; man is made by history but history is not made by man; politics is a passive, automatic reflex of economics; man's actions are determined by the amount of cash in his purse; and more of the pitiful same.) As for Trotsky's universally-acknowledged literary qualifications, they need to be mentioned at all only because they help sustain interest in the narration and analysis of a life — Stalin's whole early period — which would otherwise be unbearably tedious.

Trotsky was not permitted by his subject to complete the work. He was murdered by a Stalinist gangster in the very midst of the biography. Only parts of the book can be considered Trotsky's finished product. To give greater coherence to the work, the translator has interpolated sections of his own, carefully set off between brackets, which, while based in large measure on notes and rough outlines by the author, are nevertheless so written as to conflict (in some places violently) with the thinking and the purpose of the author himself. The reader will do well to be on guard against this.[1]

Bearing all this in mind, the net result is an outstanding and durable triumph over the difficulties whose nature and dimensions we have indicated. It is a first-rate success. If, in our view, a qualification must be added to this, it is for reasons we shall venture to set forth as we go along.

Russian Czarism left its serious opponents no parliamentary alternative to the organization of a conspiratorial revolutionary movement. The historical peculiarities of Russia's backwardness left consistent democracy no alternative to the struggle for proletarian power and socialism. Bolshevism — with all that was singular about it as well as all that identified it with the international Marxian movement — can be understood only against the background of these two circumstances.

To overturn Czarism and lay the democratic foundations for socialism, argued Lenin, to overturn this centralized, autocratic monster which sprawled over vast and variegated lands and peoples, over such economic, political and cultural backwardness, which combined the refinements of contemporary imperialism with semi-feudal anachronisms — required a trained fighting force having at its command all the science and skill of modern class warfare. Lenin's appeal was answered by the most advanced workers of the country, and also by brilliant intellectual forces of the kind which, a century or two earlier, had made up the vanguard of the revolutionary bourgeois democracy of the Western countries.

---

1. Between brackets, to be sure, and on his own responsibility, the translator permits himself such phrases as "the vaunted democracy of the Soviets" and "centralization, that sure precursor of totalitarianism" and "the 'rule or ruin' attitude of the Bolsheviks," to cite a few. Trotsky never used and never could use such phraseology, with all it implies, and would never have authorized their use by his translator, even as bracketed-off interpolations. They are an offense both to the author and the readers, and mar a felicitous translation.

In the Bolshevik Party Lenin fused these two elements by unremitting efforts to raise the workers to the theoretical level of the intellectuals who, by mastering Marxism, placed themselves at its service, in order that they could unitedly raise the entire people to the level of a thoroughgoing revolutionary struggle against Czarism. In one of the first of his writings that revealed him as standing high above all his socialist contemporaries (*What Is To Be Done*), Lenin inveighed against the prevailing looseness, dilettantism and amateurishness of the Russian social-democratic movement and developed (far more broadly, profoundly, consciously and systematically than anyone before him) the concept of the "professional revolutionist."

Among the young students who had joined the Social Democracy was Stalin (in Georgia, at the age of 18). In 1904, a year after the split of the party into the Bolshevik and Menshevik factions, and after some five years of revolutionary underground activity behind him, Stalin associated himself with the Bolsheviks. He became one of Lenin's professional revolutionists, always at the disposal of the party, working illegally from one town to another to spread revolutionary ideas, to build up units of the party among the workers, to edit party periodicals and popular literature, to organize unions and strikes and demonstrations — even "expropriations" of Czarist funds with which to finance the underground activity — and to serve more than the usual number of years in Czarist prison and exile for his work.

For all that, we do not recognize the young Stalin in the Stalin of today; there does not even seem to be a strong resemblance. Trotsky demonstrates with meticulous attention to detail and overwhelming conclusiveness the facts that have been no secret for a long time:

Stalin was not particularly distinguished in that large group of intellectuals and workers turned Bolshevik professional revolutionists, with respect to grasp of theory, outstanding political ability and independence, or even success in organization — hundreds equalled him at his best and scores were his superior. Stalin was not always an unwavering Bolshevik, if by that is meant a consistent supporter of Lenin's views. Stalin, when he took a position "independent" of Lenin, only disclosed his own provincialism, theoretical backwardness and political mediocrity. Stalin, even after years of direct contact with Lenin and the party leadership, never contributed a positive original idea, never fully grasped the theories and spirit of Bolshevism, was indeed organically alien to them.

Stalin was never really a leader of masses, feared and shunned them in fact, and felt most at home in "committee meetings," in intrigue, in cunning combinations and mean maneuvers. Stalin was always devoid of idealism, nobility and a socialist passion for freedom, but he is characterized by rudeness, trickiness, brutality, lack of principle, vindictiveness and similar dark traits. More than that: the last year or more of the life of Lenin, founder of Bolshevism, the most authoritative and popular voice in the party as a whole, in the party leadership and the country as a whole, was devoted to increasingly stiff blows at Stalin, culminating in the rupture of all personal relations between them and Lenin's recommendation that Stalin be removed from his most prominent position, general-secretaryship of the ruling party.

Near the high point of Stalin's power, Trotsky insisted that he was only the "outstanding mediocrity" in the party, and this opinion is reiterated in the biography. But to this must be added facts such as these: the comparatively young Stalin was coöpted, under Czarism, to Lenin's Central Committee; remained a member of that Committee throughout Lenin's lifetime; was entrusted by Lenin and the leadership with highly responsible tasks; was linked with Trotsky by Lenin in his testament as one of the "two most able leaders in the present Central Committee"; was nevertheless crushingly assailed by Lenin at the same time in the proposal that he be removed from his post for rudeness, disloyalty and inclination to abuse power; was opposed and combatted at one time or another by virtually every well-known leader of the Bolshevik Party, yet emerged victor over them and in possession of such power and authority as probably no single individual has ever enjoyed in all history.

We seem to be in the realm of irresolvable contradictions. Trotsky did not set himself the mere pedantic task of tabulating the record of a man. Among the aims of the biography is the resolution, by analysis and explanation, of the contradictions, real and apparent.

Against a backdrop of the times — the country, the people, their social relations — Trotsky depicts for us, trait by trait, the personal character of Stalin. More truly, he patiently scrapes away and washes off the encrustation of false strokes and false colors with which Stalin's court painters have concealed his original portrait. That so much time and space should be devoted by a Marxist to personal characteristics in the writing of a political history (Trotsky's biography is nothing but a *political history*) must appear strange and out of place to those whose "concepts" about Marxism are vastly greater than their knowledge of it. Yet Trotsky is *entirely* in the Marxian tradition and a master-hand with the Marxian method. It was the old teacher Marx himself who once wrote in a letter to his friend Kugelmann that world history would indeed be of a "very mystical nature if 'accidents' played no rôle in it... But the acceleration or slowing-down [of the general course of development] are very much dependent upon such 'accidents,' among which also figures the 'accident' of the character of those people who at first stand at the head of the movement."

In restoring the portrait, Trotsky gives us the anatomy of its character. If we abstract each of its features and classify them (rather arbitrarily, as we will see) into "the good" and "the bad" we find, under one heading, firmness, courage, perseverance, will-power, and under the other, rudeness, low cunning, vengefulness, theoretical and political mediocrity, narrowness of horizon and lack of intellectual profundity or breadth, and so forth. The trouble is precisely the fact that these features of character simply cannot be abstracted. In fact, once they are "abstracted," that is the end of all sense in the study of Stalin.

Lenin valued Stalin for his characteristics — for most of them, at any rate — and was able to utilize them in the interests of the movement. And in this he was right. To appreciate this judgment, it is necessary to understand something about the class struggle in general and about working-class politics, and it is of course necessary to live in this world and not in an imaginary one. Before Lenin got to know Stalin personally — in 1913, during Stalin's first really important trip abroad in Cracow and Vienna where he came into intimate contact with the Bolshevik leader — he knew about him from reports, correspondence or through the opinions of other party men. Even if the views which Stalin ventured now and then to express in opposition to Lenin's had impinged on the latter's consciousness, they could not possibly have made a very deep impression. Lenin undoubtedly made allowances for that. He held no malice toward comrades who differed with him (after all, comrades much more prominent than Stalin and much closer to Lenin differed with him on countless questions of theory and policy without losing his esteem), and then Stalin was still a pretty young comrade and only of local importance in the organization. Yet Lenin, before really knowing him, successfully proposed his coöptation into the Bolshevik Central Committee, in 1912, only a month after the candidacy had been rejected at the party conference in Prague. How could this happen?

The revolution of 1905 was followed by a deep and widespread reaction. It was not long after its defeat that the whole social-democratic movement, the Bolshevik faction included, began to disintegrate. Those around Lenin who remained steadfast felt the vise of isolation tightening around them year after year, with no let-up until the resurgence began seven years later, in 1912. It should not be too hard for our own generation, which has also seen the consequences of defeats in the form of desertions, disorientation, skepticism, to understand what the movement must have gone through in Russia between 1906 and 1912. It does not, alas, sound altogether unfamiliar when we read Trotsky's description of the times:

"Desertion assumed a mass character. Intellectuals abandoned politics for science, art, religion, and erotic mysticism. The finishing touch on this picture was the epidemic of suicides. The transvaluation of values was first of all directed against the revolutionary parties and their leaders... News dispatches from local organizations to the party's central organ, which was again transferred abroad, were no less eloquent in recording the revolution's disintegration. Even in the hard-labor prisons, the heroes and heroines of uprisings and of terrorist acts turned their backs in enmity upon their own yesterdays and used such words as 'party,' 'comrade,' 'socialism' in no other than the ironic sense. Desertions took place not only among the intellectuals, not only among those who were here today and gone tomorrow and to whom the movement was but a half-way house, but even among the advanced workers, who had been part and parcel of the party for years... In 1909 Russia still had five or six active organizations; but even they soon sank into desuetude. Membership in the Moscow district organization, which was as high as 500 toward the end of 1908, dropped to 250 in the middle of the following year and half a year later to 150; in 1910 the organization ceased to exist".

Bolshevik leaders were no absolute exception to the trend. Some turned Menshevik; some turned "God-Seekers"; more than a few dropped out of the movement altogether, and if even the official biographies of many of those who became prominent again after the Bolshevik revolution say nothing about their activities from 1906 to 1912 (and sometimes to 1914 and even to 1916), it is because there were no activities to record.

In such times, Stalin's characteristics were of positive value — especially if the reader maintains simple historical balance and remembers that the Stalin of 1946 is not the Stalin of 35-40 years ago. Stalin was one of the not-too-many who did not flinch and did not quit. His tenacity stood out. He continued without perturbation to risk his life and freedom. If it

504

is said that there were others like him even in those hard days, it is no less true that there were far more unlike him. Lenin could but see in him perhaps not an inspired but a stubborn organizer, perhaps not a distinguished but a persevering party man, taking prison life or exile in his stride, returning to his party work without a breathing spell. It is not necessary to idealize the pre-war Stalin to understand this.

"Such attributes of character as slyness, faithlessness, the ability to exploit the lowest instincts of human nature [writes Trotsky] are developed to an extraordinary degree in Stalin and, considering his strong character, represent mighty weapons in a struggle. Not, of course, any struggle. The struggle to liberate the masses requires other attributes. But in selecting men for privileged positions, in welding them together in the spirit of the caste, in weakening and disciplining the masses, Stalin's attributes were truly invaluable and rightfully made him a leader of the bureaucratic reaction. [Nevertheless] Stalin remains a mediocrity. His mind is not only devoid of range but is even incapable of logical thinking. Every phrase of his speech has some immediate practical aim. But his speech as a whole never rises to a logical structure".

And again, in dealing with the reaction of the July days between the February and October revolutions, Trotsky writes:

"The mass movement had in the meantime weakened considerably. Half of the party had gone underground. The preponderance of the machine had grown correspondingly. Inside of the machine, the rôle of Stalin grew automatically. That law operates unalterably throughout his entire political biography and forms, as it were, his mainspring".

It is hard to contest a single word in the sentences quoted. They describe qualities which explain Stalin's rise not only in the post-Lenin reaction, but his slower and much more modest rise during Lenin's lifetime. The incapacity for logical thinking prevented him from developing as an independent political thinker, but he had a quality which enabled him to repeat day in and day out, in his own peculiar style, the simple, hammer-logical ideas of Lenin, and that made him a sufficiently reliable party organizer. His quality of vindictiveness was directed, in the pre-revolutionary days, primarily against backsliders and all other opponents of the party, so that he gave the impression, apart from isolated incidents and expressions of which few could have been aware, of political firmness. Even his quality of exploiting "the lowest instincts of human nature" must, in those days, have taken the form, so far as was generally known, of appealing to the popular hatred of Czarism and its social iniquities.

As for that law which Trotsky calls the mainspring of Stalin's rôle and evolution — rightly, we believe — its operation, too, was different at different times and under different controls. The period of post-1905 reaction was not the period of mass action. It was a period of trying to hold the party together, of preventing complete disintegration. The party was reduced to its local committees, important in general, exceptionally important in countries with an illegal movement, trebly important in the days of reaction. In the "committee" Stalin felt at home and probably discharged well the task of tasks — imbuing others with tenacity, with contempt for the deserters and liquidators, with contempt for bourgeois public opinion about Bolshevism and especially about its then prevalent "expropriations."

What held true before 1917 must have held true during and after 1917.

Stalin, *by himself*, was and certainly is incapable of logical thinking, let alone thinking in terms of revolutionary socialist internationalism and of the Marxian scientific method. He could repeat what Lenin said, not as well as some but better than many. But for that he had to know what Lenin said or thought. When Lenin's views were not yet known, during the first period after the overturn of Czarism, Stalin showed that he understood Bolshevism to mean that the proletariat, once the autocracy is destroyed, supports bourgeois democracy as a radical but more-or-less loyal opposition. The socialist perspective was only a perspective and a remote one. He supported the bourgeois Kerensky régime "in so far as it is not reactionary" — the same formula that some self-styled Trotskyists today use to support the Stalin régime.

But his rôle before Lenin's return to Russia did not and could not rule him out of the party leadership, in Lenin's eyes. Far more prominent leaders of the party took a position not one whit better than Stalin's and often worse. What's more, they maintained it more persistently than Stalin. Stalin had made disastrous mistakes from the standpoint of political leadership. But Lenin could not make lasting reproaches for that. He did not regard him as an outstanding political leader in his own right, and consequently did not apply to him the severe criteria to which others had to submit and to which they were, so to speak, entitled.

You might almost say that it was Stalin's very lack of political distinction, the fact that he laid no claim to independence of political and theoretical thought, his very characteristic of reiterating Lenin's thoughts (even if not very brilliantly), or of carefully reducing his disagreements to brief brushes followed by silent but prompt leaps on to the bandwagon — that made him valuable in the leadership. This is not to be construed in the least as an apology for political servility to the "party chief." It is simply that, politically speaking, Stalin was most useful when he faithfully repeated, as best he could, the ideas of Lenin. Not laying claim to being a politician in his own right, his errors could all the more easily be corrected.

So far — the negative. But positively, his usefulness in the days of preparing for the insurrection and in the days of the civil war that followed it assured him a place in the leadership, if not an eminent place then a solid place nevertheless. He had a "hand that did not tremble," and for those who are interested in the revolution getting off the paper to which it is normally confined, this is not a quality to sneeze at. By his very nature and bent, he was able, better than many others, to get the coöperation of all the lower ranks of the party machine — the committeemen of yesterday and today — and to protect the interests of the party, which he identified more and more with the party machine. Where a merciless hand was needed — as it so often is in revolutionary times, the critical observers to the contrary notwithstanding — his was always available, often used and sure to be merciless. In negotiations and such-like activities, he could more often than not be well trusted to represent the interests of the revolution: he had will-power; he could not easily be swayed by arguments of the adversary; his brutality could easily appear as imperious insistence; his cunning and slyness as effective ruse and guile in outwaiting and outwitting the enemy; his penchant for intrigue and forming a clique around himself as a sympathetic and tender ear for the woes and vicissitudes of the misunderstood comrade.

In the period of revolutionary rise and under the control of a revolutionary party, not all of Stalin's characteristics were negative. In the service of the revolution, many of them could be and were put to such uses as explain without too much difficulty his specific place in the leadership and Lenin's evaluation of him as a leader. A leadership, not on paper, but at the head of a real revolutionary party, cannot be made of men with uniformly high qualifications or with qualifications equally applicable in all fields.

A leadership composed only of Lenins and Trotskys is an alluring but utopian idea. *With all things properly arranged*, the Zinovievs and Stalins and all other first-class second-raters also find their place in the leadership and enrich its capacities. You cannot have an opera with only lyric sopranos in it, or a complex machine of fine steel without bronze or brass or baser alloys in it.

Calling Trotsky *and* Stalin the two most able men in the leadership was no mistake on Lenin's part. As we understand it, he meant that either of them, by virtue of the qualities each possessed, could hold the party together and lead it — each, that is, in his own way. Zinoviev, Kamenev, Pyatakov, Bukharin — the only other men Lenin mentions in his testament — were all leaders of the highest caliber. All belonged incontestably in the leadership. But none had the qualifications to hold the party firmly together and *lead* it. But because Lenin was not concerned merely with holding it together but with *how* it would be held together and *by whom*, he ended his testament with the appeal to remove, not Trotsky, but Stalin from his post and from his power. The appeal proved unsuccessful.

To explain the rise of Stalin and the unsuccess of Lenin's appeal — which was at the same time an appeal for the restoration and burgeoning of workers' democracy — Trotsky wastes little more than a passing comment on the ludicrous and infantile assertion that "Bolshevism leads to Stalinism" which has been popularized in recent years by deserters from the socialist struggle who would like to cover their retreat behind the cloud of a "theory," and by some helpless and hopelessly disoriented victims of Stalinism who take the odd revenge of supporting Stalin's claim to Lenin's succession. One of these "anti-Stalinist" deserters, who, in quick succession, abjured Bolshevism, Trotskyism and socialism itself, and then remembered with such indignation that Marx could not make a respectable living for his family that he sped with unerring instinct to a job which keeps him in the style to which his poetry did not accustom him — now calls himself a "radical democrat."

Irony! If Lenin had not appeared in April, 1917, and if the Bolshevik Party had not re-armed itself to make the Bolshevik revolution; and if (what was most unlikely) bourgeois democracy had consolidated itself in Russia — it is more than likely that the "disintegration of Bolshevism" would have taken the form of conversion into the mere left-wing opposition of bourgeois democracy, into the party of "radical democrats," with Stalin most probably that party's boss. That was how many Bolshevik leaders, Stalin prominently included, practically conceived of Lenin's formula of the "democratic dictatorship of proletariat and peasantry" that was to be established on the ruins of Czardom.

But Stalin's transformation from revolutionist to reactionary — a not uncommon change, unfortunately, as Mussolini showed — did not take place under conditions of the maintenance of bourgeois society, or of its restoration. His transformation is unique. Hence the complications; hence the mystery. To this transformation, Trotsky devotes a long and, alas, the unfinished section of his book. Enough remains of the draft, however, to preclude ambiguity about Trotsky's views.

Trotsky seeks the cause of the change neither in the alleged inherence of Stalinism in Bolshevism nor in the all-determining power of Stalin's personal character. He looks instead for those social and political factors which lent themselves to the actual evolution of Stalin and Stalinism and which were, in turn, significantly influenced by this evolution. Risking misunderstanding and vulgarization, Trotsky nevertheless does not hesitate to trace the Stalinist type, in embryo, to the old pre-war Bolshevik militant, the "committeeman."

We have often heard the argument made in the small revolutionary group: "How can we have bureaucrats among us? Bureaucratism is a social phenomenon. There are bureaucrats in the trade unions, because they have an economic base and a stake in capitalism. But among us? Aren't our officials poorly paid — when they are paid at all? Be a Marxist — show me the economic base for our alleged bureaucratism! You cannot? Then be off with you, and let's hear no more about bureaucratism in our little revolutionary party!" This is sacred ritual in the SWP, for example.[2] You are puzzled to know if the argument is made out of village ignorance or know-better demagogy. In either case, Trotsky smothers it — for good, we hope — in a couple of paragraphs. He is speaking, understand, of Lenin's Bolshevik Party, which was small, revolutionary, self-sacrificing from top to bottom, and worse than poor.

"The habits peculiar to a political machine were already forming in the underground. The young revolutionary bureaucrat was already emerging as a type. The conditions of conspiracy, true enough, offered rather meager scope for such of the formalities of democracy as electiveness, accountability and control. Yet undoubtedly the committeemen narrowed these limitations and considerably more than necessity demanded and were far more intransigent and severe with the revolutionary workingmen than with themselves, preferring to domineer even on occasions that called imperatively for lending an attentive ear to the voice of the masses".

One of the keys, and not the least important one, to the mystery of Stalin's rise, is an understanding of the relationship between the bureaucratism and power of the "committeeman" — "the young revolutionary bureaucrat" — on the one side, and the activity of the masses, their capacities at any given stage for effecting social changes, on the other. It gives clearer meaning to what Trotsky calls the "law" governing the change in the rôle and evolution of Stalin.

"Even the Bolshevik Party cadres [Trotsky continues elsewhere], *who enjoyed the benefit of exceptional revolutionary training, were definitely*

---

2. This is no doubt one of the reasons why Trotsky's work received such curt and indifferent — even cool — treatment in the SWP press, especially when contrasted to the whole series of unrestrained eulogies written on the "work" of the SWP chief, which is a studied apology for bureaucratism.

inclined to disregard the masses and to identify their own special interests with the interests of the machine on the very day after the monarchy was overthrown. What, then, could be' expected of these cadres when they became an all-powerful state bureaucracy? It is unlikely that Stalin gave this matter any thought. He was flesh of the flesh of the machine and the toughest of its bones".

In the course of the decay of the Bolshevik revolution, these bones acquired such flesh and muscles and flesh and mind and *social purpose* as nobody expected or foresaw, not Lenin or Trotsky and not even Stalin (in making this last point, Trotsky is entirely correct).

The revolution will flower into socialism provided it is soon followed by successful revolution in the more advanced countries of the West. The very barbarism of Czarist Russia made it possible for the working class of that country to be the first to take socialist power. In this respect, Trotsky's brilliant theory of the "permanent revolution" was brilliantly confirmed in 1917. But the same barbarism, to mention no other considerations, will prevent the realization of socialism by national efforts alone. This, too, was confirmed, not only tragically but in a unique and unpredicted way. If the revolution in the West does not come, said *all* the Bolsheviks, our revolution will perish. "Perish" simply meant: capitalism will be restored in Russia; the outside capitalist world will lend its overwhelming forces to the remaining capitalistic elements inside of Russia and crush the workers' government and its ruling party — all of it.

This did not happen. But the revolution did perish. Given the continued failure of the proletarian revolution to win in the West, the power of the working class was doomed in Russia — nothing else could save it. But if the prospect of maintaining workers' power in Russia alone was hopeless, the prospect of restoring capitalism in Russia was not hopeful. Fifty years earlier, the failure of the Paris Commune meant its automatic replacement by capitalist rule. First, the revolution that established the Commune was purely spontaneous, unprepared and did not have the enormous advantage of the directing brain and spinal column of a modern revolutionary political party. Second and more important, capitalism everywhere was still on the powerful upswing.

The Russian revolution, on the other hand, was planned, prepared for and carried through by an increasingly powerful and integrated political machine, in the best sense of the word. It overthrew a putrescent régime and destroyed almost overnight a small and economically feeble capitalist class, so that whatever capitalistic element remained in the country, the peasantry primarily, had no important and strong *urban* counterpart and consequently, no national class capable of giving it leadership in the struggle to restore capitalism. Capitalism cannot be restored or established by the "blind workings" of economy in general, but only by the living classes that these "blind workings" create. The capitalist class of the rest of the world, however — what of it? For reasons we need not dwell on — the fact alone suffices for the moment — it proved incapable of crushing the revolution by armed force in the early years. In the second and, we think, more decisive place, the decay of the revolution — what Trotsky calls the "unwinding process" — took place simultaneously with the decay and agony of capitalist society itself — a most significant conjunction of processes. Trotsky is more correct than is explicit in his own views when

509

he writes: "The Russian Thermidor would have undoubtedly opened a new era of bourgeois rule, if that rule had not proved obsolete throughout the world."

In agony itself, capitalism could not overturn the workers' state. Yet the rule of the workers could not be saved. What could be saved, and what was saved, and what was extended and expanded and rooted as deeply as never before were the special privileges of a new bureaucracy. It is in the course of this process that Stalin's qualities took the form they did, for that is what they were best suited to. In the process he emerged as traitor to the proletarian revolution and socialism — but hero, and rightly so considered, to the beneficiaries of the new régime.

For reasons already mentioned — more and even more cogent reasons could be adduced without number — the counter-revolution could not take place in the name of capitalist property or in its interests. The reaction in Russia took the form of a vast weariness of the masses. But if they were worn out in the rigorous struggle to maintain socialist power, they were not so worn out as to tolerate, let alone welcome, a restoration of capitalist rule. They would not surrender power to the classes they had overthrown in 1917. In this determination, they were joined not only by the ruling party in general, but by the party bureaucracy in particular. The restoration of capitalism would mean the crushing not only of the working class, *but of the bureaucracy as well*, whether in its 1923 form or in its form today. Whatever else the bureaucracy is ready to endure, that is a fate that is too much like death; it in no way corresponds to its aspirations or its evolution.

The counter-revolution could be carried through successfully only in the name of the revolution and for its ostensible preservation. What was really involved was the preservation and extension of the privileges and power of the bureaucracy.

Here it is necessary to be most precise, to distinguish between bureaucracy and bureaucracy, to avoid the imprecision which undermined Trotsky's analysis after a certain point. What must be distinguished, and clearly, is the stratum composed of "the young revolutionary bureaucrat" of the revolutionary and early post-revolutionary period, and the *present-day* Stalinist bureaucracy. The former was a *working-class bureaucracy*, or if you please, a revolutionary working-class bureaucracy. Its fate was tied up, consciously and in fact, with the working class, its revolution and *its rule*. In its struggle against the proletarian socialist opposition (Trotskyism), it *reflected*, like every labor bureaucracy, the pressure of hostile classes, but it was animated by the conviction that the maintenance and consolidation of the power of the bureaucracy was the only way in which to save the achievement of the socialist revolution itself. In this case, Trotsky is quite right about Stalin when he says that he did not "think through to the social significance of this process in which he was playing the leading rôle."

But even in this conviction, the bureaucracy was profoundly mistaken. Quite unconsciously, in all probability, it identified its rôle, *mutatis mutandis*, with the rôle of the bureaucracy in bourgeois society. In the latter case, it is absolutely true that, especially as capitalist society decays, the *only* way the rule of capitalism can be maintained is by the bourgeoisie surrendering its *political* power to an all-pervading bureaucracy in order to preserve its social power which is based on the ownership of capital.

The contrary is true in the transitional workers' state. There the political power exercised democratically by the working class can be replaced by a ruling bureaucracy, however beneficient and well-meaning, only in the most exceptional circumstances and for the briefest of periods (civil war, for example), for the decisive reason that the *peculiarity* of the rule of the working class lies in the fact that if it does not have political power (if it is not the "proletariat raised to political supremacy"), it does not have any power whatsoever and is in no sense the ruling class.

For this fundamental mistake, the already not-so-very "young revolutionary bureaucrats" paid the heaviest toll. After the opening of the factional struggle in the Bolshevik Party, Trotsky repeatedly declared that the party bureaucracy is opening the road to capitalist restoration, is the channel through which capitalism was pouring. This was popularly understood to mean — and Trotsky unfortunately contributed to this misunderstanding by saying it explicitly on more than one occasion — that the bureaucracy *aimed* at restoring capitalism. Entirely wrong! It could be held to be true only in one specific and limited sense: the bureaucracy was so undermining the revolutionary resistance of the proletariat as to deprive it of the strength with which to fight off the encroaching capitalist restoration which would enslave it as it would crush the power of the bureaucracy itself. As is known, this is not what happened. The bureaucracy could not rule *for* the proletariat. Consequence? It could not rule for itself either!

By the bureaucracy here, we are referring primarily to the old Bolshevik bureaucracy and not to its successors — and exterminators. This cannot be overemphasized. For the proletariat *to hold Russia together* required the world revolution which would assure a socialist development for Russia. Without the world revolution, the bureaucracy which shouldered out the working class not only could not assure a socialist development for Russia but *could not hold it together*. That bureaucracy took several political forms: from the "trinity" of Zinoviev, Kamenev and Stalin which began the open struggle against "Trotskyism," *i.e.*, workers' rule — down to the "all-Leninist" bloc of Stalin-Bukharin-Tomsky. It continually weakened the proletariat, undermined its will and power, and brought such chaos into the country as threatened its very integrity. Again and again, "the revolutionary bureaucracy" as a substitute for the proletariat could not hold the country together, could not give it any kind of strength.

What was needed was a "new corps of slave-drivers" (as Trotsky calls it in another book) — what we call the new ruling class in Stalinist Russia, bureaucratic-collectivist Russia. The decaying "revolutionary bureaucracy" contributed not a few members to this new ruling class, but the two are by no means identical. That is why the achievement and consolidation of power by the new bureaucracy was preceded not only by the destruction of the working-class opposition (Trotskyism) but also by the political and physical destruction of all the Zinovievists, all the Bukharinists, all the "conciliators," all the capitulators and virtually all the *original* Stalinist cadres as well, that is, *all* the sections, wings, tendencies, strata of the Bolshevik Party. This important fact is obscured but not refuted by the accidental and purely personal phenomenon of the presence in the leadership of the new régime of a *handful* of the old revolutionists (that is, exrevolutionists) like Stalin, Molotov and a very few others, a phenomenon with little more significance than the accidental presence in the leadership of the fascist régime of ex-socialists like Mussolini and another handful of turncoats like him.

The fact is symbolically but inadequately represented in a significant passage in Trotsky:

"The bloc with Zinoviev and Kamenev restrained Stalin. Having undergone long periods of schooling under Lenin, they appreciated the value of ideas and programs. Although from time to time they indulged in monstrous deviations from the platform of Bolshevism and in violations of its ideological integrity, all under the guise of military subterfuge, they never transgressed certain limits. But when the triumvirate split, Stalin found himself released from all ideological restraints".

The passage would be adequate if put in other terms. The Zinovievs, and even the Bukharins (in another way), represented the "revolutionary bureaucracy" and only *deviated*, however monstrously, from Bolshevism, that is, from the concept of workers' power and socialism. The Stalin of today and the class he defends represent an irreconcilable *break* with Bolshevism, an *anti*-working class force in every respect, including the most fundamental.

To bring this new reactionary class to absolute power was a task which, however unconsciously performed, coincided with Stalin's personal ambitions and was enormously facilitated by his personal characteristics. For this task, he was eminently indicated and useful. Who could more easily lead in the destruction of Bolshevism and the Bolsheviks in the very name of Bolshevism — an old monarchist or Menshevik or an old Bolshevik? Who could more lightly undo the basic achievement of the revolution — the establishment of the working masses as the ruling class — than one who felt organically alien to the masses, who saw in them nothing more than an instrument for the revolutionary "committeemen" whom he regarded as the only safe repository of what he understood by socialism? To whom would socialist science and Marxian tradition be a more superfluous burden when sailing before the winds of social reaction than to a man who never fully grasped them at his best and who regarded them as the toys of intellectuals at his worst? His very incapacity for logical thinking was invaluable in the performance of his social task. The rising bourgeoisie was capable of logical thought, of logical presentation of its historic claims to the public and in the name of progress. The rising proletariat, in its socialist form, is even more capable of doing the same thing and under an even greater necessity to do so. The new ruling bureaucracy in Stalinist Russia need not present an "independent program" in its own name, or in the name of logic. In fact, it cannot, by its very nature, do so. Bastard of history, it can do nothing but falsify history and falsify thought. Given his character, it found in Stalin its eminently "logical" exponent. Will-power to destroy a revolution in its own name, nerveless brutality in the execution of as monstrous a task as history knows, craftiness of the highest (lowest?) order in the successive cutting down of one section of Bolshevism after another or in getting one section to cut down another until there was nothing left — these qualities were required in highly-developed form. Stalin had them.

By himself he accomplished nothing, nor could he. He had social winds in his sails. He was pushed — with what degree of consciousness on his part or theirs is hard to say — by a gathering and powerful social force, the new bureaucracy. It saw in him, all things considered, an ideal representative. It did not hesitate to use the more-or-less capitalistic peasantry to destroy the power of the proletariat and the revolutionists. But not, by Heaven! for the sake of the peasantry or any capitalistic claimant to power. Restore capitalism? Why? In his important appendix to the biography, Trotsky says, without any supporting argument (we do not think there is any) that "the Stalinist bureaucracy is nothing else than the first stage of bourgeois restoration." In the text, however, Trotsky writes differently and far, far more correctly. The struggle between the new bureaucracy and the petty bourgeoisie "was a direct struggle for power and for income. Obviously the bureaucracy did not rout the proletarian vanguard, pull free from the complications of the international revolution, and legitimize the philosophy of inequality in order to capitulate before the bourgeoisie, become the latter's servant, and be eventually itself pulled away from the state feed-bag." And further on: "To guard the nationalization of the means of production and of the land, is the bureaucracy's law of life and death, for these are the social sources of its dominant position."

A thousand times right! To understand it is to begin to introduce the necessary corrective in Trotsky's old position which is implicitly abandoned in the above passages. The "social sources" of the bureaucracy's dominance are assured them, however, *only* by virtue of their political power, their control of the state — just as the nationalized means of production were the social sources of the proletariat's dominance *only* when it was assured of political power. *Political power, and therefore all power, to the bureaucracy is what Stalin's triumph gave this new ruling class.* More — far more — than any other individual, he so organized the "new corps of slavedrivers" and its system of exploitation so as to build up the mightiest (we do not say "the most durable" but only "the mightiest") of Russian Empires and thus endowed the slave-drivers as a whole with the greatest power and privilege a ruling class ever enjoyed.

What does this achievement, which it would be foolish to deny, do for Stalin as an historical figure? The recent "controversy" over the question: "Is Stalin a great man?" seems to us academic and sterile, a semantic quarrel at best. Everything here depends on your criteria. The English aristocracy still looks upon the great Napoleon as nothing but a miserable monster; the French damn Robespierre as a perverse gnome and — the Stalinists now glorify Ivan the Terrible. It can be freely admitted that Stalin was "underestimated" in the past, but only because, in our view, the social capacities of the new bureaucracy (which should not now, in turn, be overestimated) on which he bases himself were underestimated.

Trotsky is right, we think, in arguing that even Stalin's rise to a super-Caesaro-Papist totalitarian dictatorship is not due to his "genius." He was pushed to power by the bureaucracy which has no small share in the enjoyment of it. Yet the fact is that as he moved toward his power, Stalin pulled the new bureaucracy along with him, assembled it, gave it what self-confidence it has, codified and assured its privileges and, in general, lifted it to power next to his own throne.

To imagine that the bureaucrats look upon him as a mediocrity is to imagine that they have greater intellectual and cultural capacities than he, greater devotion to ideals in general or socialism in particular. Nothing of the sort is true. The ruling bureaucracy idealizes and worships Stalin with a certain enthusiasm and conviction, to say nothing of gratitude. To them he is a great man, perhaps the greatest in history, and according to their lights they are not far from right. How many men can you find in history who have been so ruthless and thoroughgoing in establishing and protecting the power of a ruling class? Bukharin compared Stalin with Genghis Khan. There is a big difference — the difference between primitive Asiatic despotism riding on Mongol ponies, as it were, and modern totalitarian tyranny whose GPU rides tractors and tanks. From the standpoint of the Stalinist bureaucracy, its *Vozhd* is by far the greater of the two!

There is another standpoint. The great man is the one who by thought or deed or both, and under whatever circumstances, by whatever methods or for whatever class, helped lift mankind a few feet closer to the light, helped it to acquire greater knowledge of itself, greater mastery over nature and society so that it might more speedily free itself from subjection to nature and from all physical and intellectual fetters. From this standpoint, it is doubtful if Stalin qualifies even as the "outstanding mediocrity" of Bolshevism. In measuring Stalin, Trotsky could not but employ the criterion which is, in our times, if not the only one, then at least the overwhelmingly decisive one: What contribution has he made to advancing the cause of working-class emancipation? Hounded into obscure exile, isolated, writing in the shadow of an assassin in the hire of the all-powerful victor, Trotsky gave his answer: "To me, in mind and feeling, Stalin's unprecedented elevation represents the very deepest fall." We who continue to share the deepseated socialist convictions which sustained Trotsky to the very end, share this terribly just judgment and comprehend it to the full. No great man ever wore to his death, as Stalin will, the brand of Cain and the stigma of traitor.

Max Shachtman

DEUTSCHER'S STALIN

WE COME FINALLY to Isaac Deutscher's biography of Stalin. The author's credentials entitle him to a serious hearing for a serious work. He was a militant in the old Polish Communist movement, then in the Polish Trotskyist movement which he seems to have left either just before or after the outbreak of the second world war. He is obviously at home in the history of the Russian revolution and of the revolutionary movement in general. His book is free of those bald errors, grotesque misunderstandings and falsehoods which swarm over the pages of most of the current literature about the Bolshevik revolution. His appraisal of Stalinism does not aim, as do most others written nowadays, to discredit that revolution and with it the fight for socialism.

Because he refuses to regard the Bolshevik revolution as the Original Sin from which all the evils of our time flow, and because he endeavors to present an objective sociological, even Marxian, analysis of Stalinism, free of the primitive diabolism which is generally substituted for analyses, an assortment of Menshevik and turncoat-communist reviewers has treated his book as the work of a Stalinist agent, a characterization which is meant to be taken literally. The only "evidence" that can be adduced for this charge is the firmness of the author's defense of the Bolshevik revolution as the great socialist emancipation act of our century. This appears to be enough to warrant the label of Stalinist in the eyes of these reviewers. Apart from this the book offers no worthwhile evidence to sustain the charge, even if it offers it in abundance, as will be seen, for a charge of a distinctly different kind.

What is Stalinism? Deutscher finds the basis for understanding it in what he sets forth as the fundamental development that "has been common to all revolutions so far". This, essentially, is the development:

"Each great revolution begins with a phenomenal outburst of popular energy, impatience, anger, and hope. Each ends in the weariness, exhaustion, and disillusionment of the revolutionary people. In the first phase the party that gives the fullest expression to the popular mood outdoes its rivals, gains the confidence of the masses, and rises to power... Then comes the inevitable trial of civil war. The revolutionary party is still marching in step with the majority of the nation. It is acutely conscious of its unity with the people and of a profound harmony between its own objectives and the people's wishes and desires. It can call upon the mass of the nation for ever-growing efforts and sacrifices; and it is sure of the response. In this, the heroic phase, the revolutionary party is in a very real sense democratic, even though it treats its foes with dictatorial relentlessness and observes no strict constitutional precept. The leaders implicitly trust their vast

From *New International*, September-October 1950. A long passage in the original defending Deutscher from the charge of being a Stalinist agent has been abridged here. Other changes in Shachtman's 1962 republication of this article have been restored.

plebian following; and their policy rests on that trust. They are willing and even eager to submit their policies to open debate and to accept the popular verdict".

But this relationship hardly survives the civil war. The party emerges weary and the people wearier. "The anti-climax of the revolution is there". The fruits of the now secured revolution ripen too slowly to permit immediate fulfillment of the promises made to the people by the party.

"This is the real tragedy which overtakes the party of the revolution. If its action is to be dictated by the mood of the people, it will presently have to efface itself, or at least to relinquish power. But no revolutionary government can abdicate after a victorious civil war, because the only real pretenders to power are the still considerable remnants of the defeated counter-revolution... The party of the revolution knows no retreat. It has been driven to its present pass largely through obeying the will of that same people by which it is now deserted. It will go on doing what it considers to be its duty, without paying much heed to the voice of the people. In the end it will muzzle and stifle that voice".

The chasm between the rulers and the people widens, without the former having a full understanding of what is happening as they "acquire the habits of arbitrary government and themselves come to be governed by their own habits". The party divides in two.

"Some of its leaders point in alarm to the divorce between the revolution and the people. Others justify the conduct of the party on the ground that the divorce itself is irremediable. Still others, the actual rulers, deny the fact of the divorce itself: for to admit it would be to widen further the gap between the rulers and the ruled. Some cry in alarm that the revolution has been betrayed, for in their eyes government by the people is the very essence of revolution — without it there can be no government for the people. The rulers find justification for themselves in the conviction that whatever they do will ultimately serve the interests of the broad mass of the nation; and indeed they do, on the whole, use their power to consolidate most of the economic and social conquests of the revolution. Amid charges and counter-charges, the heads of the revolutionary leaders begin to roll and the power of the post-revolutionary state towers hugely over the society it governs... It is in this broad perspective that the metamorphosis of triumphant Bolshevism, and Stalin's own fortunes, can best be understood."

That, according to Deutscher, is the law of revolutions, it is the "general trend of events; and this has been common to all great revolutions so far". To make his analysis more specific and to round it out, we must go further with Deutscher. Although Stalinism represents a "metamorphosis of Bolshevism", it is not its negation. In Stalin, there is still the Bolshevik, but no longer in the more or less pure state, as it were. His puzzled opponents ask: "What is Stalin, after all? The architect of an imperial restoration, who sometimes exploits revolutionary pretexts for his ends, or the promoter of Communist revolution, camouflaging his purpose with the paraphernalia of the Russian imperial tradition?" Deutscher answers: *Both!* Stalinism is revolutionism *and* traditionalism, stranded in strange interplay; or as he puts it elsewhere, in Stalin there is the "conflict between his nationalism and his revolutionism". As a result of this duality (in Stalin or Stalinism), he carried out, five years after Lenin's death, Soviet Russia's "second revolution". It is true that "The ideas of the second

516

empires or both, with the old feudalists and their economic forms, intact or more or less capitalistically transformed.

But because social progress required the victory of the bourgeois revolution, it did not follow that the bourgeoisie was everywhere the organizer and leader of the revolution. In our Marxist literature, the bourgeoisie of the period in which feudalism was generally replaced by capitalism is often referred to as having been "a revolutionary class" or "the revolutionary class". This is true, but only in a very specific, distinctly limited sense. The capitalist mode of production, even in its incipiency under feudalism, to say nothing of its post-feudal days, was inherently of a kind that constantly revolutionized society, that constantly required expansion, and was therefore an intolerant rebel against the feudal fetters upon it. The bourgeoisie was revolutionary primarily and basically only in the sense that it was at once the agent, the organizer and the beneficiary of capital, in the sense that it was the bearer of the new mode of production which was irreconcilable with the supremacy of feudal backwardness and stagnancy. But never — more accurately, perhaps, only in the rarest of cases — was the bourgeoisie revolutionary in the sense of organizing and leading the political onslaught on feudal or aristocratic society. That would have required either a radical break with the feudalists for which it was not prepared, or the unleashing of "plebian mobs and passions" which it feared — or both.

The Great French Revolution was great — the greatest of all the bourgeois revolutions, the classic among bourgeois revolutions — precisely because it was not organized and led by the French bourgeoisie! It was the work of the Jacobins, of the lowly artisans and peasants and tradesfolk, the plebian masses. The Cromwellian revolution was far more the work of the small independent landlord, the artisan, the urban tradesman than the work of the then English bourgeoisie — in fact, Cromwell's Puritans had to fight bitterly against the Presbyterian bourgeoisie. Napoleon, who extended the bourgeois revolution to so many lands of feudal Europe, based himself not so much upon the bourgeoisie of France as upon the new class of allotment farmers. In Germany, it was not the bourgeoisie that unified the nation and leveled the feudal barriers to the expansion of capitalism, but the iron representative of the Prussian Junkers, Bismarck.

He carried out the bourgeois revolution in the interests of the feudal Junkers, and made his united Germany a powerful capitalist country, but without the bourgeoisie and against it. Much the same process developed in distant Japan. As for that late-comer, czarist Russia, the bourgeoisie remained a prop of the semi-feudal autocracy to the last, and the bourgeois revolution was carried out in passing by the proletariat and only as an episode in the socialist revolution.

Yet in all the countries (except of course in Russia) where the bourgeois revolution *was* carried out — always without the bourgeoisie, often against the bourgeoisie — it did not fail to achieve its main and primary aim: to assure the social rule of the bourgeoisie, to establish the economic supremacy of its mode of production. This was all that was needed to satisfy the fundamental requirement of bourgeois class domination.

It cannot be underlined too heavily: Once the fetters of feudalism were removed from the capitalist mode of production, the basic victory and the expansion of the bourgeoisie and its social system were absolutely guaranteed. Once the work of destruction was accomplished, the work of constructing bourgeois society could proceed automatically by the spontaneous expansion of capital as regulated automatically by the market. To the bourgeoisie, therefore, it could not make a *fundamental* difference whether the work of destruction was begun or carried out by the plebian Jacobin terror against the aristocracy, as in France, or by the aristocracy itself in promotion of its own interests, as in Germany.

Neither the revolutionary French plebians nor the Napoleonic empire builders could replace feudalism with a special economic system of their own, or create any social system other than bourgeois society. In Germany, no matter how exclusively Bismarck was preoccupied with maintaining the power of the Prussian king and the Junkers, with modernizing the nation so that it could defeat its foreign enemies, the only way the nation could be united and modernized was by stimulating, protecting and expanding the capitalist economic order. A prerequisite for this was of course the removal of all (or most) feudal and particularist obstacles in its path.

If Bonapartism and Bismarckism prevented the bourgeoisie from exercising the direct political influence that, ideally, it prefers, this was more than compensated by the fact that they suppressed or curbed an infinitely greater threat to the rule of the bourgeoisie — the plebian and later the proletarian masses. And if the bourgeoisie gives up or allows the curbing or even destruction of its own representative parliamentary institutions, under a Bonapartist or Bismarckian régime, or under its most decadent manifestation, fascism, it only admits, to quote the famous passage from Marx, "that in order to preserve its social power unhurt, its political power must be broken; that the private bourgeois can continue to exploit the other classes and rejoice in 'property', 'family', 'religion' and 'order' only under the condition that his own class be condemned to the same political nullity of the other classes". But its social power is preserved "unhurt" just the same, and the evidence of that is the prosperity that the bourgeoisie enjoyed under Napoleon, Bismarck and Hitler.

When, therefore, Deutscher stresses the fact that east of the Rhineland the "popular forces arrayed against it [moribund feudalism] were too weak to overthrow it 'from below'; and so it was swept away 'from above'," he is as wide of the mark as he can possibly be *if this fact is adduced to show the similarity between "the chief elements of both historical situations"*, namely, the spread of Bonapartism and of Stalinism.

The absurdity of the comparison is clear if we bear in mind the equally incontestable fact that whether feudalism was swept away "from above" or "from below", the difference in the result was, at the very most, secondary. In both cases the victory of capitalist society was secured and its growth guaranteed. Once the feudal fetters on capitalism were broken — whether by Cromwell's Ironsides or Napoleon's Grand Army, by Robespierre's Jacobins or Bismarck's Junkers — capitalism *and only capitalism* could be solidly established.

According to Deutscher, feudalism could be swept away and the rule of capitalism installed by a revolution carried out, from above or below, by the plebian masses, the petty bourgeois masses, the bourgeoisie itself, even by feudal lords themselves (and even by the modern imperialist big bourgeoisie, as we know from their work against feudalism in some of the colonies they penetrated). For the comparison to be less than ludicrous, it would have to be demonstrated that today "moribund capitalism" can also be swept away and the rule of socialism also installed by a revolution carried out by the petty bourgeoisie, the bourgeoisie, and any other class, in addition to the proletariat. It would also have to be demonstrated that, just as it made no essential difference to the bourgeoisie how its revolution was effected, so today it makes no decisive difference to the proletariat whether it makes its own socialist revolution or the revolution is made by a GPU which enslaves and terrorizes it. To demonstrate that would be difficult.

The socialist revolution does not even lend itself to the kind of comparison with the bourgeois revolution that Deutscher makes.

The emancipation of the working class, said Marx, is the task of the working class itself. To which we add explicitly what is there implicitly: "of the conscious working class". Is this mere rhetoric, or a phrase for ceremonial occasions? It has been put to such uses. But it remains the basic scientific concept of the socialist revolution, entirely free from sentimentality and spurious idealism.

The revolution which destroys the fetters of feudalism, we wrote above, assures, by that mere act, the automatic operation and expansion of the new system of capitalist production. (We stress the word "new" to distinguish capitalism in the period of its rise and bloom from capitalism in its decline and decay, when the automatic regulators of production break down more and more frequently and disastrously. But that period is another matter.) Conscious direction of the capitalist economy plays its part, but at most it is secondary or, better yet, auxiliary to what Marx calls the "self-expansion of capital".

It is *altogether* different with the socialist revolution. In this case we cannot say that regardless of what class or social group destroys the fetters of capitalism, the act itself assures the automatic operation and expression of socialist production. Socialist production and distribution will take place automatically, so to speak (each will give what he can and take what he needs), only decades (how many we do not know or need to know) after the revolution itself has taken place, only after civilized socialist thinking and behavior have become the normal habit of all the members of the community.

But immediately after the socialist revolution takes place, production and distribution must be organized and regulated. The bourgeoisie can no longer organize production, since it has just been or is about to be expropriated, and thereby deprived of the ownership and control of the means of production. The market can no longer regulate production automatically, for it has been or is being abolished along with the other conditions of capitalist production; in any case, it disappears to exactly the extent that socialist production advances.

Unlike capitalist production, socialist production (that is, production for use) demands *conscious* organization of the economy so that it will function harmoniously. It is that consideration and it alone that requires of the new revolutionary régime the nationalization, sooner or later, of all the means of production and exchange. And it is this centralization of the means of production that makes possible, to an ever-increasing degree, the harmonious planning of production and distribution.

Planning, in turn, implies the ability to determine what is produced, how much of each product is produced, and how it is distributed to the members of the community (limited only by the level of the available productive forces) — to determine these things consciously, in contrast to capitalism which produces according to the dictates of the blindly-operating market and distributes according to glaring class inequalities.

Now, what assurance is there that the masses, who have made the revolution in order to establish a socialist economy, will be the main beneficiaries of the planned decisions that are taken and executed? (We say, cautiously, "main" and not sole beneficiaries, for obviously, in the first stage of the new society the economy will necessarily be encumbered by "parasitic" specialists, military households and bureaucrats.) Only one assurance: that the decisions on what and how much is produced and how it is distributed are taken by the masses themselves, concretely, through their freely and easily elected — and just as freely and easily recallable — representatives. Otherwise, there is no assurance whatever that those who make the decisions on how the economy shall be organized will make them in conformity with the economic principles of socialism, or principles that are socialist in type, socialist in direction.

In other words, the economic structure that replaces capitalism can be socialist (socialistic) *only* if the new revolutionary régime (the state) is in the hands of the workers, only if the working class takes and retains political power. For, once capitalist ownership is destroyed, all economic decisions are necessarily political decisions — that is, decisions made by the state which now has *all* the economy and all the economic power in its hands. And if the working class then does not have political power, it has no power at all.

Here we come to another basic difference between the two social systems, and not their similarity, as Deutscher says. It relates to the question of *how* social power is exercised in each case.

The bourgeoisie's power over society rests fundamentally upon its ownership of property (the means of production and exchange). That ownership determines, in Marx's excellent phrase, its mastery over the conditions of production, and therefore over society as a whole. Any state, any political power, which preserves capitalist property, is a bourgeois state, is indeed the "guardian and trustee" of the social power of the bourgeoisie. This holds for the state of Napoleon, Bismarck, Roosevelt, Ramsay Macdonald or Hitler. Deutscher understands that well enough, for he writes that "when the Nazi façade was blown away, the structure that revealed itself to the eyes of the world was the same as it had been before Hitler, with its big industrialists, its Krupps and Thyssens, its Junkers, its middle classes, its *Grossbauers*, its farm laborers and its industrial workers". The social power of the bourgeoisie was and remains its property ownership, its economic power.

It is exactly the other way around with the proletariat! It is not a property-owning class and it cannot be — not under capitalism, not under the revolutionary régime that separates capitalism from socialism, and certainly not under socialism itself, which knows neither property nor proletariat. The revolution which expropriates the bourgeoisie does not turn its property over to the workers (this worker or group of workers now owns a steel mill; that one a railroad; the other a bank, etc.). That would indeed be a revolution-for-nothing, for it would merely create a new type of capitalist, property-owning class. No, the revolution nationalizes, immediately or gradually, all property, turns it over to the new régime, the revolutionary state power. That is what happened in Russia in 1917, when the revolution was carried out "from below" (the "old Bolshevik" method). Every politically-educated person knows that it was a socialist revolution, that it raised the proletariat to the position of ruling class, that it abolished capitalist property and established socialist (socialistic) property in its place.

In that case, wherein lies the *fundamental* difference between that revolution and those carried out "from above" by Stalin throughout the Balkans and the Baltic? The bourgeoisie was expropriated, politically as well as economically, its property was nationalized and turned over to the new state power.

According to Deutscher, there is no basic difference, no class difference, so to say. Just as Napoleon carried the bourgeois revolution to Poland, so Stalin carried the socialist revolution all the way to Germany. The "orthodox" (Oof!) Trotskyists are reluctantly but irresistibly drawing closer to the same monstrous conclusion. Their embarrassment over Deutscher is due entirely to the fact that he has anticipated them.

Yet there is a difference and it is fundamental. The *Communist Manifesto* stresses (and how much more emphatically should we stress it in our time?) "that the first step in the revolution by the working class, is to raise the proletariat to the position of ruling class, to win the battle of democracy". It is not just some new political power in general that will socialistically expropriate the bourgeoisie, but the new proletarian power. As if in anticipation of present controversies, Marx underscores the point, at the beginning and at the end: "The proletariat will use *its political supremacy*, to wrest, by degrees, all capital from the bourgeoisie, to centralize all instruments of production in the hands of the state" — what state? to make sure he is understood, Marx adds: "i.e., *of the proletariat organized as the ruling class*". The test of this "formula" for the socialist revolution (to say nothing of a dozen other tests) was passed precisely by the Bolshevik revolution.

Nothing of the sort happens in the case of the Stalinist "socialist revolution", the revolution "from above". The proletariat is never allowed to come within miles of "political supremacy". What the new state "wrests" first of all, and not very gradually, either, are all the political and economic rights *of the proletariat*, reducing it to economic and political slavery. The difference between the revolution "from below" and the revolution "from above" is not at all a mere matter of difference in "method" but one of social, class nature. It might be compared to the difference between cropping a dog "from the front" and "from behind". By one "method", the tail is cut off, and the dog, according to some fanciers, is healthier and handsomer; but if the other "method" were employed and his head were cut off, we would not have a "bureaucratically-degenerated dog" but a dead one. Like all comparisons, this one too has its limitations: Stalinism does not cut off the head of the socialist revolution only because it does not even allow that revolution to grow a head.

Yet Stalin, while depriving the proletariat of all political power, did maintain state property in Russia, did extend it vastly, and did convert capitalist property into state property in Poland, Rumania, Czechoslovakia and elsewhere. Because the Bolshevik revolution established state property, and Napoleon's extension of bourgeois property seems to lend itself to analogy, Stalin becomes, to Deutscher, the representative of those rulers who, "on the whole, use their power to consolidate most of the economic and social conquests of the revolution", and even to extend these revolutionary conquests at home and abroad. The formula, alas, is originally that of Trotsky, who wrote that the Russian workers "see in it [the Stalinist bureaucracy] the watchman for the time being of a certain part of their own conquests". If that is true, so much the worse for the Russian workers; but in any case it does not reduce the magnitude of the error.

By what it says and implies, this formula tells us that the state is socialistic (a proletarian state) because the economy is nationalized, statified. The nature of the state is determined by the property form. That is indubitably true in all societies where private property exists. But it is radically false when applied to a society where the state owns the property. The exact opposite is then true, that is, the nature of the economy is determined by the nature of the state! That it is necessary to *argue* this ABC of Marxism and of evident social reality today, is one of the indications of the sorry state of the movement.

The theory that the economy is socialistic simply because the state owns it was originated by Stalinism. It was needed by Stalinism to help achieve its counter-revolution. It constitutes to this day the quintessential theoretical basis for its worldwide mystification. As early as 1925, almost coincidental, significantly enough, with the launching of the theory of "socialism in one country", the Stalinists began to put forth, cautiously but unmistakably, the theory that Deutscher has so uncritically taken for granted. As cautiously as the one but not so uncritically as the other, the then Leningrad Opposition (Zinoviev and Kamenev) took issue with the theory and warned against it. Kamenev's speech on the question of the nature of the economy in Russia, delivered at the 14th party congress toward the end of 1925, is therefore of prime interest:

"Do we perhaps doubt that our factories are enterprises of a 'consistently-socialist type'? No! But we ask: Why did Lenin say that our enterprises are 'enterprises of a consistently-socialist type'? Why didn't he say directly that they are genuinely socialist *enterprises?*

What does this mean: enterprises of a consistently-socialist type? It means that these enterprises are essentially socialistic *enterprises. They are socialist in what are called* property-relations. *The factories belong to the proletarian state, that is, to the organized working class...*

The correct conception of our state industry consists in this, that our state enterprises are really enterprises of a consistently socialist type, inasmuch as they represent the property of the workers' state, but that they are far from being complete socialist enterprises because the mutual relations of the people engaged in them, the organization of labor, the form of the labor wage, the work for the market, represent no elements of an unfolded socialist economy".

At this point, it is worth noting, the congress minutes report an interruption from one of the hostile Stalinist delegates: *"You have discovered America!"* In those early days, the Stalinists did not dare challenge, directly and openly, the simple ABC ideas Kamenev was expounding. His ideas are clear. The property, the economy, can be considered socialist-in-type (not even socialist, but as yet only socialist-*in-type*) only because "they represent the property of the workers' state", only because "the factories belong to the proletarian state, that is, to the organized working class". The character of the economy is determined by the character of the political power, the state!

The Stalinists needed the very opposite theory in order to cover up and justify their destruction of the political power of the working class and *therewith* of the workers' state. Where Kamenev, *and all other Marxists*, declared that the property is socialist only because it is owned by a workers' state, "that is, the organized working class" in power — the Stalinists declared the state is socialist simply because it owns the property. This theory is now canonized as constitutional law in all Stalinist lands and all arguments against it are promptly and thoroughly refuted by the GPU.

The theory is a Stalinist invention from start to finish. The finest-toothed comb drawn through all the writings of every Bolshevik leader — Lenin, Trotsky, Bukharin, Zinoviev, Kamenev — will not find so much as a phrase to sustain it. Until Stalin turned the Marxian view upside-down, every one of the Marxists, without exception, repeated literally thousands of times that because the state is in the hands of the proletariat, *therefore* the economy is proletarian (socialist-in-type). They never argued that because the economy is in the hands of the state, *therefore* the state is proletarian — never!

How could they? The proletariat, not similar to the bourgeoisie but in contrast to it, establishes, asserts and maintains its social power only when it gets and holds political power. As the bourgeoisie is nothing without its economic power, its ownership of property, so the proletariat is nothing without its political power. Only political power can give it economic power, the power to determine the "conditions of production". This was always understood by Marxists, not only by Trotsky as well but by him first and foremost. In different ways he always repeated what he wrote, for example, in 1928: *"The socialist character of our state industry... is determined and secured in a decisive measure by the role of the party, the voluntary internal cohesion of the proletarian vanguard, the conscious discipline of the administrators, trade-union functionaries, members of the shop nuclei, etc. ... the question reduces itself to the conscious cohesiveness of the proletarian vanguard"*. In a word, the nature of the economy is determined by the nature of the political power. In the Thirties, however, it became plain that while the proletariat of Russia had lost all political power and even the possibility of reforming the Stalinist régime, the latter had not introduced capitalism (as Trotsky erroneously predicted it would). Only then did Trotsky find himself impelled to reverse himself completely. He then argued that the fact that the state continued to own the property determined its character as a workers' state. It was not to be found in *any* of his preceding writings, not so much as a hint of it. It was to be found in the doctrines of Stalinism. That's where it still is; that's where it belongs. For socialists to adopt it would be to capitulate theoretically to Stalinism, which consistency would demand be extended to a political capitulation. In this case, capitulation means guaranteeing the triumph of a new tyranny, the abandonment of the "battle of democracy" which is won when the proletariat is raised to political supremacy.

Deutscher's theory, or rather his adoption and adaptation of Stalin's, leads him to downright apologetics for the new tyranny — all very objectively put, to be sure, for there seems no doubt about his personal antipathy toward the abominations of the régime.

There is, first of all, the law of revolutions which Deutscher sets forth, as we have quoted it above. It is superficial; it is false and misleading. Certainly all the old revolutions and their leaders made promises to the masses that they did not fulfill. But that is a "law" of all *bourgeois* revolutions and is absolutely characteristic of them. Bourgeois revolutions are made under the sign of *ideologies*, using that term strictly in the sense in which the early Marx used it, namely as a synonym for *false consciousness* or as we would say after Freud, for *rationalization*. They *think* and say they are fighting for Freedom. "They" includes, as Marx wrote, not only men like Danton, Robespierre, St Just and Napoleon, "the heroes as well as the parties", but even "the masses of the old French Revolution". But no matter what they think or what they say or what they do, the revolution does not and *cannot* go beyond the "task of their time: the emancipation and the establishment of modern bourgeois society". At bottom, all that Freedom can mean in the bourgeois revolution is... freedom of trade.

That's why the bourgeois revolutions could not keep their promises to the masses, why they often had to establish the most dictatorial governments over and against the masses in the post-revolutionary period. But since Deutscher has tried the impossible task of formulating a law of all revolutions, when he might have known that every different social revolution develops according to different laws, the most important fact has escaped his attention: *the bourgeois revolutions did fulfill their promises to the bourgeoisie*. The plebian masses were crushed after such revolutions, but that was only in the nature of the revolution: while it may have been made by them, it was not and could not have been made for them. It was made for the bourgeoisie and the bourgeoisie prospered under it. Which is why it deserves the not-at-all dishonorable name, bourgeois revolution!

Deutscher, however, gives Stalin's overturns the distinctly honorable name, *socialist revolution*, and adds with a refined shrug, if the masses suffered all sorts of horrors, cruelties and oppressions after this revolution, if the promises made to them were not kept, why, "this has been common to all great revolutions so far".

Preposterous conclusion: while the bourgeois revolution keeps its promises to the bourgeoisie for whom it is made, the socialist revolution does not keep its promises to the masses for whom it is made.

Correct conclusion: the Stalinist revolution is not a socialist revolution in any sense and therefore is not intended to make good its promises to the masses; it is a revolution of the totalitarian bureaucracy and it most decidedly does keep its promises to this bureaucracy!

There is, in the second place, Deutscher's weird justification of the "follies and the cruelties" of Stalin's "second revolution", the industrialization of Russia. We have listened with sheer amazement, in recent times, to the same justification on the lips of British socialists who are not abashed at abusing the name of Trotsky by assuming it. Now we see it in print under Deutscher's signature. Stalin's "follies and cruelties" we read, "inevitably recall those of England's industrial revolution, as Karl Marx described them in *Das Kapital*". He continues:

"The analogies are as numerous as they are striking. In the closing chapters of the first volume of his work, Marx depicts the 'primitive accumulation' of capital (or the 'previous accumulation', as Adam Smith called it), the first violent processes by which one social class accumulated in its hands the means of production, while other classes were being deprived of their land and means of livelihood and reduced to the status of wage-earners. The process which, in the Thirties, took place in Russia might be called the 'primitive accumulation' of socialism in one country... In spite of its 'blood and dirt', the English industrial revolution — Marx did not dispute this — marked a tremendous progress in the history of mankind. It opened a new and not unhopeful epoch of civilization. Stalin's industrial revolution can claim the same merit".

The comparison is so microscopically close to being an outrage as to be indistinguishable from one, and it shows how Deutscher has literally lost his bearings.

The period of the old Industrial Revolution was a brutal one, but a harsh social task faced society and it had to be performed. By whom? The feudal aristocracy could not perform it; the foetus of a proletariat was not yet able to perform it. There was left only the young, lusty, callous bourgeoisie. It proceeded to concentrate property and capital in its hands in sufficient quantity to develop the forces of production on a vast scale and at a breath-taking pace.

Who suffered the hideous cruelties and horrors of this accumulation? The little people — small peasants, the yeomanry, tradesfolk, the artisans and their social kith and kin. Who were the beneficiaries of these horrors? The bourgeoisie. Moral indignation apart, the process unfolded as it had to unfold, given the times, given the class relationships. It was a question of the primitive *capitalist* accumulation.

Accumulation is a need of all societies, the socialist included. Indeed, fundamentally the problem of a socialist accumulation was the economic rock on which the ship of state of the Russian Revolution foundered (a subject that requires the special study that it merits). The problem was not unknown to the leaders of the revolution. They debated it often and warmly. In the early Twenties, Preobrazhensky devoted a special work to the subject, which soon evoked a violent controversy. He pointed out that in the past, every social order achieved its particular accumulation at the expense of ("by exploiting") earlier and inferior economic forms. Therefore, continued Preobrazhensky:

"The more economically backward, the more petty-bourgeois, the more agricultural is the country that is passing over to a socialist organization of production, the slighter the heritage that the proletariat receives for the fund of its socialist accumulation at the time of the social revolution — the more the socialist accumulation will have to base itself upon the exploitation of the pre-socialist economic forms and the lighter will be the specific gravity of the accumulation derived from its own basis of production, that is, the less will this accumulation be based upon the surplus product of the worker in socialist industry". (*The Basic Law of Socialist Accumulation*, in the *Herald of the Communist Academy*, 1924.)

Although the Trotskyist Opposition, of which Preobrazhensky was a prominent leader, did not endorse his views, the Stalinists let loose a hue and cry against Preobrazhensky that echoed for years. In his restrained way, Stalin denounced these views because they would "undermine the alliance between the proletariat and the peasantry" and shatter the dictatorship of the proletariat — no less — for Preobrazhensky's views so easily lent themselves to the interpretation that the peasantry as a whole had to be exploited to build up the fund for socialist accumulation.

But what if someone had merely hinted, in the most delicate way, that the *socialist* accumulation fund would have to be built up not only by exploiting the peasantry, which is not, properly speaking, a socialist class, but also the proletariat, which is *the* socialist class; and that the *socialist* accumulation would have to proceed along the same barbarous lines as the primitive capitalist accumulation in England? If he were not hooted out of sight as a crude defamer of socialism, it would only be because everybody else would have been stricken with dumbfounded silence.

That Stalin's "second revolution" did start a process "by which one social class accumulated in its hands the means of production", and along the lines of the primitive capitalist accumulation, is absolutely true. But his accumulation, like the English, was directed against and paid for by the popular masses. It had nothing in common with socialism or socialist accumulation. It was not the "second revolution"; it was the counter-revolution.

"Marx did not dispute this", Deutscher reminds us. He did not dispute that the industrial revolution "marked tremendous progress in the history of mankind", but only for the reason given above: there was no other class but the bourgeoisie to carry it out and it carried it out in the class way characteristic of it. To have looked for the proletariat to carry out the old industrial revolution, was *utopian*, because whatever proletariat existed then in England or Europe was utterly incapable of performing the mission which therefore fell to the bourgeoisie.

It only remains to ask: is it likewise utopian to expect the present proletariat to carry out the modern revolution for the socialist reconstruction of society? Or, since capitalism today is moribund and cannot be reinvigorated by man or god, must the work of dispatching it be left to a social force that puts in its place the most obscene mockery of socialism and social progress ever devised by man?

Deutscher gives no direct answer, to be sure. But implicit in his theory, in his whole analysis, is an answer in the affirmative, even if it is accompanied by shuddering resignation.

He writes movingly about those tragic figures, the great captains of the revolution, who were paraded through the prisoner's dock of the Moscow Trials by a new ruling class installed in the "second revolution". He explains — rightly, on the whole, we think — what brought these once indomitable revolutionists from recantation to capitulation and capitulation to recantation until they finally allowed themselves to be used for the nightmarish indignities of the Trials. Deutscher's appraisal of the revolutionary capitulators is noteworthy:

"Throughout they had been oppressed by the insoluble conflict between their horror of Stalin's methods of government and their basic solidarity with the social régime which had become identified with Stalin's rule".

Insoluble conflict! Right. But especially right if we understand that all of them had abandoned any belief in the possibility of a proletarian revolutionary movement independent of Stalinism. That only removed the last barrier to an already indicated capitulation. They believed that the Stalinist régime represented at bottom a socialist or proletarian state, and horror over its methods could not eliminate the feeling that it was the régime of their class and by that sign also their own. So long as they thought, as Trotsky also did for a long time, that Stalinism represented a return to capitalism, they fought it openly and vigorously. They were wrong in that analysis and Stalin was not long in proving them wrong. When it became perfectly clear that Stalin mercilessly crushed capitalism wherever he had the power to do so, that he preserved and extended the realm of statified property, they simply equated his anti-capitalism with the defense of socialism. Their "basic solidarity with the social régime which had become identified with Stalin's rule" decided, if it did not guarantee, their capitulation to Stalinism.

And really, from the standpoint of Deutscher's analysis, why not? The German bourgeoisie may not have been enthusiastic over all the methods of Bismarck, of Wilhelm II, and later of Hitler. But they were "in basic solidarity with the social régime which had become identified", successively, with those three names. They never fought these régimes; they never rebelled against them, except, perhaps, for an inconsequential handful of bourgeois and military plotters against Hitler. In their way, they were certainly right: "It is our régime, the régime of our class".

"In his exile", writes Deutscher, after the words we quoted above, "Trotsky, too, wrestled with the dilemma, without bending his knees". True. We do not believe that Trotsky would ever have capitulated to Stalinism, and that not only because of his unsurpassable personal qualities as a revolutionist. To the extent that he shared the fatal theory that Stalinist Russia is a workers' state and that the Stalinist bureaucracy is still a sort of watchman over some of the conquests of the revolution, the same must be said of him as is said of Deutscher: the course of most of his followers since his death bears witness to this.

But everything within limits. In the first place, Trotsky introduced a radically modifying "amendment" to his theory, in a small but increasingly invaluable section of his ten-years-ago polemic against us which has proved so much more durable than those remaining sections which should be mercifully consigned to the oblivion of archives. The amendment did neither less nor more than allow that events might prove that the Stalinist "workers' state" was only a new class system of totalitarian collectivist exploitation, the state of neo-barbarism. In the second place, he replied unhesitatingly and confidently in the affirmative to the key question he posed there: "Will objective historical necessity in the long run cut a path for itself in the consciousness of the vanguard of the working class?"

These views, despite his internally contradictory theory about Stalinist Russia, enabled Trotsky to remain the active and dreaded mortal enemy of Stalinism. Because he could write that the one and only decisive standpoint for the revolutionist was the enhancement of "the consciousness and organization of the world proletariat, the raising of their capacity for defending former conquests and accomplishing new ones", he remained the greatest contemporary champion of the proletarian socialist revolution, that "revolution from below" which alone is socialist. It is these views that mark the chasm between their upholders, on the one side, and those who, out of despair or panic or premature fatigue, have retired from the struggle for socialism or gone over to an enemy camp.

Let them go. But those still resolved to carry on the fight must rid themselves and all others of the last trace of the view that, in some way, in some degree, the Stalinist neo-barbarism represents a socialist society. The view is disseminated, for different reasons but with similar results, by both the bourgeois and the Stalinist enemies of socialism. It has become the curse of our time. Of that, Deutscher's book is only another and saddening proof. Its value in the fight against Stalinism can only be to startle some people into thinking and rethinking the problem of Stalinism and seeing it for what it is. For it is a problem about which we can say with Jean Paul: "*Wenn Ihr Eure Augen nicht braucht, um zu sehen, so werdet Ihr sie brauchen, um zu weinen*" — If you do not use your eyes to see with, you will need them to weep with.

14. STALINISM AND THE MARXIST TRADITION

Was the idea that the USSR and its replications were a new form of class exploitative society, neither capitalist nor socialist, a radical revision of the basic tenets of Marxism? In 1940 ("Again and once more ...") Trotsky had argued emphatically that it was not. Here Max Shachtman develops those arguments.

Max Shachtman

STALINISM AND THE MARXIST TRADITION

THE THEORY THAT RUSSIA is neither a capitalist nor a workers' state but rather a bureaucratic collectivist state meets an initial resistance from all Marxists, with some of whom it is prolonged more than with others. This is perfectly natural and understandable. We adopted this theory only after a long and thoroughgoing discussion. We have no right to complain when others move at an even slower pace, or even if they refuse to move in our direction at all.

Those who resist our theory base themselves upon their understanding of the teaching of Marx. In a well known passage in his *Critique of Political Economy*, Marx wrote:

The bourgeois relations of production are the last antagonistic form of the social process of production — antagonistic not in the sense of individual antagonism, but of one arising from conditions surrounding the life of individuals in society; at the same time the productive forces developing in the womb of bourgeois society create the material conditions for the solution of that antagonism. This social formation constitutes, therefore, the closing chapter of the prehistoric stage of human society.

If capitalist society is the *last* antagonistic form of the social process of production, and if it creates the material conditions for the solution of this antagonism by the socialist society which is to be established by the working class — it is legitimate to ask what part is played in this Marxian system by our theory of bureaucratic collectivism? According to our theory, bureaucratic collectivism not only is not socialism but does not represent a workers' state of any kind. At the same time, we hold, it is not a capitalist state. Finally, by characterizing bureaucratic collectivism as a reactionary, exploitative, and therefore also an antagonistic society, it is implied that capitalism may not be the last antagonistic social formation. Paraphrasing Trotsky, one critic declares that our theory "would signify that not the workers but a new bureaucratic class was destined to displace dying capitalism." He then charges that "Shachtman... intervened and interposed a new class between the capitalists and the proletariat, thus reducing Marxism to utopian levels."

The questions raised are serious and weighty. There is no doubt whatsoever that they involve an appraisal of the whole question of the collapse of capitalism and the future of socialism — and thus of the future of mankind itself. Such questions deserve thought and the most objective discussion, not on the low level of ignorance and demagogy to which the problem is so often depressed but on the heights to which Marxism necessarily raises it. On these heights, it is possible to examine carefully and then to re-establish clearly the theoretical tradition of Marxism. This requires patient and earnest study, scrupulous objectivity and the application of the Marxist method itself.

This 1947 article is taken from *The Bureaucratic Revolution*, 1962. The penultimate paragraph in Part I was omitted in 1962, but is restored here.

"In broad outlines," wrote Marx in the sentence immediately preceding the passage already quoted from the *Critique,* "we can designate the Asiatic, the ancient, the feudal, and the modern bourgeois methods of production as so many epochs in the progress of the economic formation of society." (My emphasis — MS.)

"In broad outlines," but only in broad outlines! Like many such statements by Marx, this must not be construed in the rigid, dogmatic, mechanical sense against which Marx himself found it necessary to admonish his followers time and time again. It must not be construed as an absolute truth. Marx indicates here the *"principal* epochs in the economic formation of society," listing them, as he writes elsewhere, "in the order in which they were determining factors in the course of history." Marx would be the first one to reject the idea that every people in the world passed and had to pass from primitive communism through all the stages he indicated, one following in inexorable succession after the other, and ending, after the collapse of capitalism, in the classless communist society of the future. Such a mechanical interpretation of Marx, although not uncommon among Marxists, has nothing in common with Marxism.

Like everyone else acquainted with the history of society, Marx knew that there were stages in the development of communities, peoples and nations which could not be fitted into any pattern of iron succession. Where, in such a pattern, would we fit those "highly developed but historically unripe forms of society in which the highest economic forms are to be found, such as cooperation, advanced division of labor, etc., and yet there is no money in existence, e.g. Peru," about which Marx wrote (*Critique of Political Economy,* p.296)? Where, in this iron pattern, would we fit the régime of Mehmet Ali, the viceroy of Egypt in the early nineteenth century who was the sole owner of the land and the sole "industrialist," from whom all had to buy — a régime referred to in one of the works of Karl Kautsky? Where in this iron pattern would we fit any one of a dozen of the antique Oriental régimes which Marx himself placed in a special, exceptional category? The list can be easily extended.

Marx found himself obliged on more than one occasion to protest against all the absolutist constructions placed upon his materialist conception of history both by uninformed friends and uninformed adversaries. It is not without interest that many of his protests referred not only to interpretations made by Russian writers but to the way they applied Marx's ideas (as they interpreted them) to Russia.

Now what application to Russia could any critic draw from my historical outline? Only this: if Russia tries to become a capitalist nation, in imitation of the nations of Western Europe, *and in recent years she has taken a great deal of pains in this respect,* she will not succeed without first having transformed a good part of her peasants into proletarians; and after that, once brought into the lap of the capitalist régime, she will be subject to its inexorable laws, like other profane nations. That is all. But this is too much for my critic. He absolutely must needs metamorphose my outline of the genesis of capitalism in Western Europe into a historico-philosophical theory of the general course, fatally imposed upon all peoples, regardless of the historical circumstances in which they find themselves placed, in order to arrive finally at that economic formation which insures with the greatest of productive power of social labor the most complete

533

development of man. But I beg his pardon. He does me too much honor and too much shame at the same time. Let us take one example. In different passages of *Capital,* I have made allusion to the fate which overtook the plebeians of ancient Rome.

Originally, they were free peasants tilling, every man for himself, their own piece of land. In the course of Roman history, they were expropriated. The same movement which separated them from their means of production and of subsistence, implied not only the formation of large landed properties but also the formation of large monetary capitals. Thus, one fine day, there were on the one hand free men stripped of everything save their labor power, and on the other, for exploiting this labor, the holders of all acquired wealth. What happened? The Roman proletariat became not wage-earning workers, but an indolent mob, more abject than the former "poor whites" in the southern lands of the United States; and by their side was unfolded not a capitalist but a slave mode of production. Hence, strikingly analogical events, occurring, however, in different historical environments, led to entirely dissimilar results.

By studying each of these evolutions separately, and then comparing them, one will easily find the key to these phenomena, but one will never succeed with the master-key of a historico-philosophical theory whose supreme virtue consists in being supra-historical. (*The New International,* November, 1934, p110*f.*)

Engels, writing to the same Danielson on February 24, 1893, added: "I subscribe completely to the letter of our author [Marx]..."

Like Marx himself, his great co-workers found more than one occasion to protest against the vulgarization of the materialist conception of history worked out by the two founders of scientific socialism. Mehring, reading from the Berlin *Vorwärts* (October 5, 1890), quotes from an article in which Engels found it necessary, not for the first time and not for the last time, to correct bourgeois misinterpreters of Marx's concept, in the hope that it would be better understood by Marx's followers:

The materialistic method is transformed into its opposite when it is employed not as a guide to the study of history, but as a finished stencil in accordance with which one accurately cuts the historical facts.

To this declaration of Engels, Mehring himself adds:

Historical materialism is no closed system crowned with an ultimate truth; it is a scientific method for the investigation of human development.

Is not the attempt to cut the *fact* of Stalinist society into "a finished stencil," in which there is room only for capitalist state or workers' state, a perfect example of the transformation of Marx's materialistic method into what it is not and cannot be?

The view that Marxism presents an absolute schema of an iron succession of social orders which holds good for all peoples and all times; which excludes any intermediate stages, any leaps over stages, any retrogression into previous stages or any bastard social formations distinguished from the "principal epochs in the economic formation of society"; and which by the same token also excludes — and that absolutely — any unique social formation interposed between capitalism and a workers' state or between a workers' state and socialism (as, for example, the social *reality* which we have in the formation of the Russian bureaucratic collectivist state) — that is a view that does Marx "too much honor and too much shame at the same time." Such a view necessarily converts Marx's "outline of the genesis of capitalism in western Europe into a historico-philosophical theory of the general course, fatally imposed upon all peoples, regardless of the historical circumstances in which they find themselves placed."

Marx's materialist conception of history *in no way* "rules out" in advance, by theoretical interdiction, as it were, our theory of bureaucratic collectivism. That theory was arrived at "by studying each of these evolutions separately, and then comparing them," in order to "find the key" to the *unique* phenomenon of Stalinist society. When Marx wrote that "one will never succeed" in understanding such a social phenomenon as faces us in Russia today by means of "the master-key of a historico-philosophical theory whose supreme virtue consists in being supra-historical," it was as if he foresaw the hopeless dilemma, the growing confusion and political impotence of those who seek to force-fit Stalinist Russia into an iron pattern for which Marx bears no responsibility. To those who charge us with a "revision of Marxism," we will not retort that it is they who are revising Marxism. It suffices to reply that only those who do not understand Marx's materialist conception of history and Marx's method can attribute to him such an absolutist theoretical absurdity.

Neither Marx nor Engels could foresee the actual course of the Russian proletarian revolution, or the historical circumstances under which it took place. They had no need and there were no grounds for speculative writing on the possibility of a degeneration of a proletarian revolution confined to a backward country or on the form that this degeneration might take. In our own century, the question of degeneration of the revolution and the forms of its degeneration has been posed more than once, even before 1917. Is a classless communist society even a possibility? Can the proletarian revolution produce anything more than a victory only for the revolutionists who lead it? Best known of those who contended that the *socialists* may be victorious, but *socialism* never, was Robert Michels. In face of the reality of the Stalinist degeneration, more than one "disillusioned" revolutionist and more than one turncoat have proclaimed that Michels' theory has been confirmed by history.

How have Marxists dealt with such theories as Michels'? By the simple pious assertion that an anti-capitalist but non-socialist state is an absolute impossibility, that it is ruled out theoretically by Marxism? Let us see how the problem is discussed by so authoritative a Marxist as the late N.I. Bukharin in one of his best-known works which was written in the earliest periods of the Bolshevik revolution and served as a textbook, so to speak, for a whole generation of Marxists.

Referring to Engels, Bukharin points out that in all past societies there were contending classes, and therefore a ruling class, because of the "insufficient evolution of the productive forces."

...But communist society is a society with highly developed, increased productive forces. Consequently, it can have no economic basis for the creation of its peculiar ruling class. For — even assuming the power of the administrators to be stable, as does Michels — this power will be the power of specialists over machines, not over men. How could they, in fact, realize this power with regard to men? Michels neglects the fundamental decisive fact that each administratively dominant position has hitherto been an

535

envelope for economic exploitation. This economic exploitation may not be subdivided. But there will not even exist a stable, close corporation, dominating the machines, for the fundamental basis for the formation of monopoly groups will disappear; what constitutes an eternal category in Michels' presentation, namely, the "incompetence of the masses" will disappear, for this incompetence is by no means a necessary attribute of every system; it likewise is a product of the economic and technical conditions, expressing themselves in the general cultural being and in the educational conditions. We may state that in the society of the future there will be a colossal over-production of organizers, which will nullify the stability of the ruling groups. (N.I. Bukharin, *Historical Materialism*, p.310.)

This holds, however, and in our view it holds unassailably, for the *communist society,* one in which the productive forces have indeed been so highly developed and increased, and are available in such abundance, as to make even the highest level of the development of the productive forces attained by capitalism appear as miserably inadequate as it really is. But does it also hold for the transitional period that necessarily intervenes between the end of capitalism and the full flowering of communism? Obviously not. On that score there is not and, of course, there cannot be any disagreement.

But the question of the transition period *from capitalism to socialism, i.e., the period of the proletarian dictatorship, is far more difficult [continues Bukharin]. The working class achieves victory, although it is not and cannot be a unified mass. It attains victory while the productive forces are going down and the great masses are materially insecure. There will inevitably result a* tendency to *"degeneration," i.e., the excretion of a leading stratum in the form of a class-germ. This tendency will be retarded by two opposing tendencies; first, by the* growth of the productive forces; *second, by the abolition of the* educational monopoly. *The increasing reproduction of technologists and organizers in general, out of the working class itself, will undermine this possible new class alignment. The outcome of the struggle will depend on which tendencies turn out to be the stronger.* (N.I. Bukharin, *Ibid.*, p.310f.)

Take note especially of the two very precise formulations of Bukharin. One: "there will *inevitably* result a *tendency* of 'degeneration,' i.e., the excretion of a leading stratum *in the form of a class-germ.*" So far as we know, it occurred to nobody to denounce Bukharin as a "revisionist" for writing this, even though he wrote it long before so much as the outlines of the present Stalinist state could be visible. Bukharin is, of course, not referring to a new capitalist class that would be excreted when he writes of "a class-germ." He is writing, let us remember, of Michels' theory of a new *bureaucratic* class that would triumph as a result of the socialist revolution, and Bukharin does not hesitate to acknowledge — this almost thirty years ago! — that this is theoretically possible. He acknowledges the tendency. He promptly adds two of the counteracting tendencies. And his conclusion? He does not even suggest that the triumph of socialism is guaranteed by some abstraction, by some absolute force. Not for a minute! He concludes — that is his second formulation of importance to us — "The outcome of the struggle will depend on which tendencies turn out to be stronger." Or if we may formulate it in the way which excited so much horror among some self-styled "monists." "The question of the perspective of

Stalinism cannot be resolved in a purely, theoretical way. It can be resolved only in struggle." The theoretical tradition of Marxism is represented in the manner in which Bukharin deals with the problem but not at all in the manner in which the "monists" reject the "pluralism" which they ascribe to us.

Marx wrote before the Russian Revolution, and Bukharin wrote before the Stalinist society appeared as an organized whole and even before Stalinism itself made its appearance. The Trotskyist opposition has been the eye-witness of the rise of Stalinism and has been the only one to make a serious analysis of it. Next to Trotsky, the late Christian Rakovsky was the outstanding leader of the Trotskyist movement. After expulsion from the party and exile, Rakovsky wrote many penetrating analyses of Russian society under Stalinism. Given the conditions of his existence in that period, many, if not most, of his studies are probably irretrievably lost. But we have sufficient indication of the trend taken by his analysis prior to his tragic capitulation. Writing about "The Life of the Exiled and Imprisoned Russian Opposition," N. Markin (Leon Sedoff) gave the following information:

Concerning the bureaucracy, Comrade Rakovsky writes: "Under our very eyes, there has been formed, and is still being formed, a large class of rulers which has its own interior groupings, multiplied by means of pre-meditated cooptation, direct or indirect (bureaucratic promotion, fictitious system of elections). The basic support of this original class is a sort, an original sort, of private property, namely, the possession of state power. The bureaucracy 'possesses the state as private property,' wrote Marx (Critique of Hegel's Philosophy of Law)." (The Militant, December 1, 1930.)

There is, furthermore, ample evidence to show that Rakovsky's view was supported by not a few of the Trotskyists exiled and imprisoned by Stalin. The whole of Rakovsky's analysis is not at hand, neither are the whole of his conclusions; and it may well be that we shall never see them. But the trend of his analysis is sufficiently clear; the Stalinist bureaucracy is a new class based upon "an original sort of private property." It is a ruling class that derives its power from its complete domination of the state which owns all the means of production and exchange. Whatever may have been the thoughts which preceded or succeeded the section from Rakovsky's manuscript which Markin quotes, it is plain enough that Rakovsky's point of view is, if not identical with our own, at least analogous to it. Yet the publication of Rakovsky's views as long ago as 1930 did not bring down upon his head any such puerile denunciations of "revisionism" as we hear today.

Finally, Trotsky himself. He held, of course, to the position that Stalinist Russia still represented a workers' state, even if in degenerated form. He denied that Stalinist Russia represented either a capitalist state or a new social formation like bureaucratic collectivism. But he *did not exclude* the theoretical possibility that a bureaucratic collectivist state could come into existence.

At the very beginning of the war, on September 25, 1939, he warned: "Might we not place ourselves in a ludicrous position if we affixed to the Bonapartist oligarchy the nomenclature of a new ruling class just a few years or a few months prior to its inglorious downfall?" Trotsky firmly expected the solution of the problem of Stalinism by means of the triumph of the revolutionary proletariat in *direct connection* with the crises of the world war. That is completely clear in his polemics against us in 1939-40.

If this war provokes, as we firmly believe, a proletarian revolution, it must inevitably lead to the overthrow of the bureaucracy in the USSR and regeneration of Soviet democracy on a far higher economic and cultural basis than in 1918. In that case, the question whether the Stalinist bureaucracy was "a class" or a growth on the workers' state will be automatically solved.

Further, he wrote, that "it is impossible to expect any other more favorable conditions" for the socialist revolution than the conditions offered by the experiences of our entire epoch and the current new war. But suppose the proletarian revolution does not triumph in connection with the war, and suppose the Stalinist bureaucracy maintains or even extends its power? Trotsky did not hesitate to pose this question too — and to give a tentative answer to it.

If, contrary to all probabilities, the October Revolution fails during the course of the present war, or immediately thereafter, to find its continuation in any of the advanced countries; and if, on the contrary, the proletariat is thrown back everywhere and on all fronts — then we should doubtless have to pose the question of revising our conception of the present epoch and its driving forces. In that case it would be a question not of slapping a copy-book label on the USSR or the Stalinist gang but of re-evaluating the world historical perspectives for the next decades if not centuries: have we entered the epoch of social revolution and socialist society, or, on the contrary, the epoch of the declining society of totalitarian bureaucracy?

Thus, while Trotsky rejected the theory that Russia is a bureaucratic collectivist state, he did not, and as a Marxist he could not, rule out the possibility of a bureaucratic collectivist society on the basis of an *a priori* theory, or a "monistic concept" which we are now asked to believe is Marxism.

"We may have socialism, we may have Stalinism — who knows? Only the 'concreteness of the events' will show. In the theoretical sphere this is the most serious break possible with Marxist ideology." That is how the SWP Statement presents our view and condemns it, all in the name of a muddle it calls monism. Why no equally derisive condemnation of Trotsky? He writes, so that anyone who reads may understand, that it, "contrary to all probabilities," but *not* contrary to all *possibilities*, this, that or the other thing does happen, or this, that, or the other thing does not happen ("the concreteness of the events will show!"). The Marxists, in undisciplined defiance of the interdiction by the Socialist Workers' Party, will indeed have to pose the question: is it the epoch of socialism or the epoch of Stalinism? Different answers may be given to this question. Different conclusions may be drawn from those drawn by Trotsky or by us or by the Socialist Workers Party or by anyone else. Those are matters subject to the most objective and sober discussion. But it should be obvious that the *way* in which Trotsky *approaches* the problem is thoroughly Marxist, whereas the way in which the SWP approaches the problem is mechanistic and mystical (these are not mutually exclusive!) and utterly non-Marxist. The authors of the Statement are simply not at home in the theoretical tradition of Marxism.

Stalinist Russia can be understood only "by studying each of these evolutions separately and then comparing them." To analyze it we need no "historico-philosophical theory whose supreme virtue consists in being

538

supra-historical." We need only the "master-key" of historical materialism, not in the sense of a "closed system crowned with an ultimate truth," but as a scientific method, as a guide to the study of the real history of the Stalinist state, as the method by which its social anatomy can be laid bare.

II

OUR THEORY OF the class character of the Stalinist state, we are admonished, represents a break with Marxism, because we hold that Russia is neither working class nor capitalist but bureaucratic-collectivist. But that is not the worst of our crimes. According to a Trotskyist critic, we continue to deepen our break with Marxism. In 1941 we wrote that "bureaucratic collectivism is a nationally-limited phenomenon, appearing in history in the course of a singular conjuncture of circumstances." What has been added to this that makes our break with Marxism "deeper"? An analysis of the events that have occurred since 1941. The events represent an unforeseen and hitherto unanalyzed phenomenon, so far as Stalinism is concerned. They are a refutation, and a thorough one, of the predictions made by Trotsky.

Up to the outbreak of the Second World War, Stalinism represented a state that grew out of the proletarian state established by the Bolshevik revolution. It was a successor not to capitalism but to a revolutionary workers' state. It represented a triumph not over a capitalist state but a triumph over the working class and its revolutionary state. We may disagree on a dozen different aspects of the problem of Stalinism, but there is no conceivable basis for a difference on this simple fact. We may disagree on the conclusions to draw from the fact that the Stalinist state replaced not a capitalist state but the state of Lenin and Trotsky, but on the fact itself there can be no disagreement.

What, however, is new in the development of Stalinism since the outbreak of the war? Some people prefer not to be troubled with or even reminded of the facts which the entire world, both bourgeois and proletarian, is thinking about and discussing. It upsets them. It is much more convenient and infinitely less disturbing to repeat over and over again what was said yesterday, mumbling the same ritualistic formulae like pious people saying their beads over and over again and always in the same order. The trouble is, whether we like it or not, there are new beads to account for. Stalinism has successfully extended its state control over new countries. The régime in such countries as Estonia, Latvia and Lithuania is now identical in every respect with the régime of pre-war and post-war Stalinist Russia. In Yugoslavia, the Stalinists are in the process of establishing fundamentally the same type of state as exists in Stalinist Russia. In Poland, substantially the same holds true. In other Balkan countries where the Stalinists have gained domination, they are also engaged in establishing social régimes identical with the one that exists in Russia.

The triumph of Stalinism in all these countries has not occurred in the same way and on the same basis as in Russia. In these countries Stalinism did not succeed a proletarian revolution. In these countries there was no revolutionary workers' state for Stalinism to crush. In these countries, Stalinism triumphed over a bourgeois state and over a subject, not a ruling, proletariat. It expropriated, both politically and economically, the bourgeoisie and the landowning classes, or it is in the process of expropriating them, and nationalized their property. The idea that the bourgeoisie rules in *any* sense, be it economically, politically, socially or in any other way, is a grotesque absurdity. This absurdity may be swallowed by some ignorant people in the radical movement, but there is not a bourgeois in the entire world, let alone a bourgeois in these countries themselves, whom you could begin to convince that his class is still in power in any sense.

We doubt if it will be asserted that in the countries conquered by Stalinism a classless socialist society exists. If the bourgeoisie is not in power in these countries, what class is in power? What class rules?

Let us lay aside for the moment the question of what class rules in these countries, so long as it is agreed that the bourgeoisie does not rule. The transference of social power from one class to another is the outstanding characteristic of a revolution (or a counter-revolution). Such a transfer of power has taken place in these countries. Now, if we agree, as we must, that the rule of the bourgeoisie has been overturned in these countries; and if we agree further, as we must indeed, that the state established in these countries is substantially identical or is, at the very least, becoming identical with that which exists in Russia; and finally if we accept the theory that Stalinist Russia represents a degenerated workers' state — then the conclusion is absolutely inescapable: a workers' state, partly degenerated or wholly degenerated in any other way, has been established by Stalinism in the conquered countries of eastern Europe.

The conclusion would not necessarily alter the view that Stalinism is bureaucratic. That is granted. But it would necessarily destroy fundamentally the theory that Stalinism is counter-revolutionary — *in the sense in which some Trotskyists apply that term to Stalinism.* For, in the narrow Trotskyist concept, the term counter-revolutionary must be and is applied only to those social or political forces that are not merely anti-socialist and anti-working class but — by that very token, as it were — also pro-capitalist; that is, those forces which work either subjectively or objectively for the preservation of bourgeois society and the rule of the bourgeoisie. How reconcile this with the fact that Stalinism has wiped out or is wiping out the class rule of the bourgeoisie? How reconcile it with the view — which follows relentlessly from the definition — that Stalinism has established a workers' state in bourgeois countries? If that altogether too much abused word "dialectics" were to be manipulated a thousand times more skilfully than it is, it could not extricate the manipulators from their dilemma.

Unlike the post-mortem Trotskyists, we have sought to analyze the reality by means of the materialist method and to introduce those corrections of supplements into our theory which the reality demands of us. The Stalinist state is no longer confined to Russia. Bureaucratic collectivism has been established in other countries as a result of a triumph over the capitalist class, over the capitalist state of these countries. The pseudo-Marxist who contents himself, as Lenin once remarked contemptuously, with "swearing by God," finds no need to concern himself with the problem because for him the problem simply does not exist. To the serious

Marxist the problem of yesterday is posed today in a new form: what is the future of the Stalinist state, what is the perspective of Stalinism, in relation, on the one side to the future of capitalism and, on the other side, to the perspective of socialism?

We will not at this point set forth the analysis of this problem made by us in 1946. For the moment, we will only repeat one of the conclusions which the Trotskyist critic quotes:

The question of the perspective of Stalinism cannot be resolved in a purely theoretical way. It can be resolved only in struggle.

And again:

Whether or not Stalinism can triumph in the capitalist world cannot be denied absolutely in advance. To repeat, it is a question of struggle.

These sentences, which are nothing but simple ABC, at first evoke that sarcasm which the critic expressed with such mastery. He writes: "It is clear that our slogan, 'Socialism or Barbarism,' should now be amended to read: 'Socialism, Bureaucratic Collectivism or Barbarism?'" This is a telling blow, and while we are reeling from it, stiffer blows are rained down upon us. Sarcasm is not his only strong point. Theory, philosophy — he is at home in these fields as well.

We read that:

In 1946, by adopting the above-quoted resolution, the Workers Party rejected the heart *of the Marxist system: its* monistic concept. *Marxism holds that we live in a world of law, not of pure chance. This is true not only of the natural world, but also of human society. Shachtman (as usual, in passing) substitutes for Marxism an idealistic philosophy of* pluralism: *We may have socialism, we may have Stalinism — who knows? Only the "concreteness of the events" will show. In the theoretical sphere this is the most serious break possible with Marxist ideology... The perspective of the Trotskyist movement, based on Marx's world outlook as embodied in the* Communist Manifesto, *is discarded by the Workers Party in favor of an idealistic "multiple factors" concept, which is far closer to "True Socialism" than to Marxism.*

There it is, word for word. The reader will just have to believe that it is not invented by us but simply quoted from the original. The cross of "True Socialists," who have been dead and decently buried for a good century now, we will bear without too much murmur because it exerts not an ounce of weight upon our shoulders. As any reader who *knows* something about "True Socialism" is aware, the only reason it was thrown in was to impress the easily impressionable with a display of erudition which an impolite smile could suffice to dispose of.

But what is said about "monism" in general and our "pluralism" in particular, that is a little too much. You avert your eyes in embarrassment at the spectacle that that section of the human race which is in the revolutionary movement can sometimes make of itself. Where does the author of the Trotskyist Statement get the courage for his pugnacious illiteracy? Does he really think that there is nobody left in the world to laugh his head off at this pompous jabberwocky, this cool mauling of Big Words and Big Thoughts? It is positively painful to have to deal with such nonsense, which cannot even be termed philosophical mumbo-jumbo because it is just plain, ordinary, uninspired and very puerile mumbo-jumbo. But we have no choice in the matter.

What is the heart of the Marxist system? Its monistic concept. What is our most serious possible break with Marxist "ideology"? An idealistic philosophy of pluralism, which we have substituted for Marxism and, as usual, in passing. And just how have we substituted pluralism for Marxism? By saying that capitalism exists as a social reality; that socialism exists, if not yet as a reality, then, in any case, as a perspective; and — here is our sin — that Stalinism and bureaucratic collectivism exist both as a reality and as a perspective. To this we have added the other sinful thought: the perspective of Stalinism cannot be resolved in a purely theoretical way — it can be resolved only in struggle; it is wrong to deny absolutely in advance the possibility of the triumph of Stalinism in the capitalist world because that question can be decided only in the course of struggle.

That, you see, is the idealistic philosophy of pluralism. What, then, is monism, the heart of the Marxist system?

The development of Marxian thought has known its share of the "monism" that our author is babbling about. Every real student of Marxism is acquainted with Frederick Engels' polemical destruction of Eugen Dühring who — the truth is the truth — although also given to pompous phrasemongering, nevertheless stood intellectually a cubit above all ordinary phraseurs.

All-embracing being is one [wrote Dühring]. *In its self-sufficiency it has nothing alongside of it or over it. To associate a second being with it would be to make it something that it is not, namely, a part or constituent of a more comprehensive whole. We extend, as it were, our* unified *thought like a framework, and nothing that should be comprised in this concept of* unity *can contain a duality within itself. Nor again can anything escape being subject to this concept of unity...*

To which Engels replied in a famous passage: "If I include a shoe brush in the unity of mammals, this does not help it to get lacteal glands. The unity of being, that is, the question of whether its conception as a unity is correct, is therefore precisely what was to be proved, and when Herr Dühring assures us that he conceives being as a unity and not as twofold, he tells us nothing more than his own unauthoritative opinion."

What *is* the monistic concept of Marxism? In the same *Anti-Dühring* Engels sets forth *all* there is to monism, in the fundamental sense, so far as Marxists are concerned:

The unity of the world does not consist in its being, although its being is a pre-condition of its unity, as it must certainly be, *before it can be one. Being, indeed, is always an open question beyond the point where our sphere of observation ends. The real unity of the world consists in its materiality, and this is proved not by a few juggling phrases, but by a long and tedious development of philosophy and natural science.*

It is not necessary to read this passage more than once to understand that what the critic has written is *pretentious gibberish,* and nothing more. This is not a harsh but a very restrained judgment.

Let us amend this judgment — but only to show how restrained it really is. Let us try to surmount the insurmountable in order to see if any sense can be made out of the nonsense. In other words, is our critic actually trying to say something and if so, what is it? By painstakingly piecing together some elements of the muddle, we may be able to find out what idea it is he is trying to convey.

Our "pluralism," our "idealistic multiple factors concept" consists in the opinion that "we may have our socialism, we may have Stalinism — who knows?" in addition to our opinion that what we actually have in most of the world is capitalism. As the critic puts it so devastatingly, we hold that the old "monism" should now be amended to read: "Socialism, Bureaucratic Collectivism or Barbarism." Whoever says that more than one of these three is actually or theoretically possible in the course of the development of society, sets himself down as a pluralist. So far, so good.

And the monist — what does he say? He says, true monist that he is, true defender of the heart of the Marxist system that he is, true partisan of the perspective of the Trotskyist movement that he is, he says that he holds, without amendment, to "our slogan" and that slogan is (hold your breath, the lights are about to be turned on): "Socialism or Barbarism!"

Blinding light! Pluralism equals three and probably more than three. Monism equals — two. Anyone who does not understand this is an idiot, probably a congenital one. Anyone who disagrees with it, let him beware.

In their first program, Marx and Engels declared that capitalism was a historical society, that it had no basis for permanent existence, that its doom was inevitable, that it would be succeeded by *barbarism or socialism*. They left us with very little of a detailed picture of what socialism would be or what barbarism would be, because they rejected the kind of utopian and unscientific thinking that would try to paint such a picture. As Engels said, "Being indeed, is always an open question beyond the point where our sphere of observation ends."

Our sphere of observation today is far more comprehensive than that it was in the days of Marx and Engels. It includes the living phenomenon of Stalinism. Stalinism is precisely one of the forms of barbarism which has manifested itself in the course of the decay of a society which the proletariat has not yet succeeded in lifting onto a rational plane. Marx and Engels did not and could not foresee the Stalinism barbarism. What they could not foresee, we have the duty to see and to analyze. What does this imposing babble about "monism" aim to convey? That Stalinism is not a social phenomenon? That Stalinism is not a reality? That Stalinism is not a material part of the world today? "The real unity of the world consists in its materiality," said Engels. Stalinism is not socialism and it is not capitalism, but it is nevertheless a material part of the real (and therefore contradictory) unity of the world.

Can barbarism triumph over socialism? Of course it can! Is that triumph *theoretically* possible? Of course it is! If you deny this, you convert the scientific formula, "Barbarism or Socialism," into mere soap-box agitation, and demagogical agitation at that. Can the question of the perspective (the prospects) of barbarism "be resolved in a purely theoretical way"? Can the question of the triumph of barbarism "be denied absolutely in advance"? Whoever tries to answer that question in a "purely theoretical way," whoever tries to deny it "absolutely in advance," reads himself out of the circles of scientific Marxist thought. He may well remain a socialist, he may well continue to favor the ideal of socialism, but he is no longer *fighting* for this ideal inasmuch as he has denied theoretically and absolutely and in advance the very possibility of any other development except socialism. By this denial, he no longer *needs* to fight for socialism. It will come of itself and its triumph is absolutely guaranteed.

In the same sense, is it theoretically possible that bureaucratic collectivism — the Stalinist barbarism — can triumph over capitalism? Of course it is. Can this triumph be denied absolutely in advance? Not by Marxists! But far, far more important than this is our conclusion that the perspective (again, the prospects) of capitalism and socialism and Stalinism *can be resolved only in struggle.* How else? Whoever believes that the perspective is automatically guaranteed (one way or another) by some sort of mysterious natural process which unfolds without the *decisive* and *determining* intervention of the living struggle of the classes — there is the man who has rejected the heart of Marxism and committed the most serious break possible with Marxism. He belongs among those philosophers for whom Marx had such scorn because they only contemplate or analyze the world, but do nothing — or find no need to do anything — to change it. If he nevertheless calls himself a Marxist, he would do well to reflect on the teachings of the old masters on this vital point.

The question if objective truth is possible to human thoughts [Marx wrote in his famous second thesis on Feuerbach] is not a theoretical but a practical question. In practice man must prove the truth, that is, the reality and force, the this-sidedness of his thought. The dispute as to the reality or unreality of a thought, which isolates itself from the praxis is a purely scholastic question. (Appendix to Engels, *Ludwig Feuerbach, etc.*, Vienna, 1927, pp.73f.)

The necessity or, if you like, the *inevitability,* of socialism is demonstrable only in "praxis," that is, it is a matter that can be resolved only [by/in] the course of the class struggle.

The empiricism of observation alone can never sufficiently prove necessity. Post hoc, *but not proctor hoc (Enz, I, 84). This is so very correct that it does not follow from the constant rise of the morning sun that it will rise again tomorrow, and in actuality we know now that a moment will come when the morning sun* does *not rise. But the proof of necessity lies in human activity, in experiment, in labor; if I can do* this *post hoc, it becomes identical with the* proctor hoc." (Engels, *Dialektik und Natur,* Marx-Engels Archiv, Vol. II, p.282.)

It would be instructive to learn from our author, who seems determined to make monism synonymous with mumbo-jumbo, just how, in his view, the perspective of Stalinism will be resolved. If it is not to be resolved, as we say, "only in struggle" (or, as the early Marxists would say, in praxis), then we must conclude that the fate of Stalinism will be resolved theoretically or by some other pure and simple thought process. Alas, if the doom of Stalinism depended only on the thought processes and in general upon the theoretical wisdom of the critic, a bright future might well be guaranteed for it.

APPENDICES

WHAT THE 1939-40 DISPUTE WAS ABOUT

THE CANNON GROUP insists that it is impossible to deduce a correct position on the defense of the Soviet Union without first deciding the question of the class character of the Soviet state. The Minority, it charges, is an unprincipled bloc because it is composed of comrades having different opinions on this question.

It is true that Comrade Burnham, several weeks before the Plenum of the National Committee, presented a resolution which proposed to revise the party position on the Soviet Union as a workers' state.

Why was this resolution withdrawn and was it correct to do so? Why did comrades having different evaluations of the sociological nature of the Soviet Union unite on one resolution on the disputed Russian question and was it correct to do so?

In his article, "The USSR in War," Comrade Trotsky writes:

"Our critics refuse to call the degenerated workers' state — a workers' state. They demand that the totalitarian bureaucracy be called a ruling class. The revolution against this bureaucracy they propose to consider not political but social. Were we to make them these terminological concessions, we would place our critics in a very difficult position, inasmuch as they themselves would not know what to do with their purely verbal victory.

It would therefore be a piece of monstrous nonsense to split with comrades who on the question of the sociological nature of the USSR have an opinion different from ours, in so far as they solidarize with us in regard to the political tasks. But on the other hand, it would be blindness on our part to ignore purely theoretical and even terminological differences, because in the course of further development they may acquire flesh and blood and lead to diametrically opposite conclusions."

The Minority is united on a position which deals with the political tasks of the Fourth International on the Russian question. Regardless of the divergent views held on the sociological nature of the Soviet Union, all members of the Minority believe that it would be monstrous nonsense to split among themselves on this point. The comrades of the Minority are united, not because they are unprincipled and wish to conceal or suppress differences on the class nature of the Soviet state, but because of their agreement on the political tasks.

Was it unprincipled to include in the United Opposition Bloc of the Russian Communist Party (1926-1927) comrades who held that Russia was a workers' state and also those who held that it had ceased to be a workers' state, but who were in agreement on the Platform of the Opposition, i.e., on the political conclusions and tasks?

Was it unprincipled to include in that Opposition comrades who held that the class nature of the Chinese Revolution was represented by the formula "democratic dictatorship of the proletariat and peasantry" (Zinoviev) and also comrades who held that its class nature was represented by the formula "proletarian dictatorship supported by the peasantry" (Trotsky), but who were in agreement on the political tasks ahead (independence of the C.P., Soviets, etc.)?

It is true that these "terminological" differences subsequently proved to have a greater importance. It is true in the present case also that, as Trotsky writes, "in the course of further development they *may* acquire flesh and blood and lead to diametrically opposite conclusions." But it is impossible to write resolutions on the immediate political tasks of the party, or in general to engage in political activities, on the basis of differences that *may* develop in the future.

Does this mean that the Minority attaches no importance to the question of the class nature of the Soviet state? It means nothing of the kind. This was in no way implied by Burnham's withdrawal of his original document, and the Minority's support of his action. Exactly the contrary was not merely implied, but explicitly stated. When the Burnham resolution was first presented for discussion to the Political Committee, the Cannon group was opposed to any discussion of it in the party. Comrade Cannon, in his letter to the National Committee, denounced a discussion of this resolution, or for that matter, any discussion of

---

Abridged from Martin Abern, Bern (Paul Bernick), James Burnham, and Max Shachtman: "What is at issue in the dispute on the Russian question? A statement of the position of the Minority", December 26, 1939. In this text "Crux" and "Lund" are pen-names for Trotsky.

the Russian question, as a "luxury we cannot afford." The supporters of the Cannon group voted solidly against all motions submitted by comrades in the party branches in New York asking the National Committee Plenum to permit the opening of a discussion on the Russian question. Before the Plenum, the Cannon group in the Political Committee voted against even a theoretical discussion of the question in the party's theoretical organ, the *New International*. It was only after this utterly bureaucratic attitude became untenable in the party that the Cannon group became the champion of a discussion on the "fundamental questions" and on those alone.

What did the Minority propose? First, that the *theoretical* discussion be opened in the pages of the *New International*. Far from evading a discussion of the sociological nature of the Soviet state, the Minority insisted on it, and insisted on its being conducted in the field and on the plane where it properly belongs. Then, when it became increasingly clear that the differences in the party were not confined to the "terminological" (or, rather, the general theoretical and scientific) question but involved the immediate political tasks and slogans of the party, the Minority proposed a general party discussion. At and following the Plenum, it was finally decided unanimously that the discussion should be divided into two parts, so to speak: one that could and would be conducted publicly in the *New International*, a discussion inaugurated by Trotsky's article on "The USSR in War," and which would be confined to the theoretical ("terminological") question of the class nature of the Soviet state; the other that would be conducted in the membership, and which would deal with the concrete political questions. In this separation, the proposal of the Minority was in accordance with the best tradition and practise of the Bolshevik movement. This proposal was unanimously adopted by the Political Committee. To date, it has been carried out only by the Minority.

But, it is argued, while the Minority may say that it does not propose a revision of the party's basic position on the Soviet state, what assurance can the party have that next month or next year the Minority or any of its spokesmen will not raise the question for reconsideration? On that score, no guarantees can be given by the Minority or by any of its members. Nor should any be asked for, because they would be meaningless. Such guarantees cannot be given by the Minority; they cannot be given by the Cannon group; or by anyone else.

In the period to come, there may be developments in the Soviet Union which, in the opinion of this or that comrade, or group, or of the entire International, have produced such a radical change in the situation as to demand a change in our programmatic position on the question of the class nature of the Soviet state. Such developments may be, for example, the supplementary proletarian revolution in Russia, or, in the contrary case, a bourgeois counter-revolution; or, looking retrospectively at the Soviet Union from a point many months or years removed from the present moment, the International may conclude that the present Stalinist bureaucracy was a new, independent ruling class, as outlined hypothetically in the recent article by Trotsky. The Minority does not propose a revision of the party's program on this question. It is not the question in dispute. If the Cannon group insists that it is the question, and that if no one else raises it for decision, it raises it in a motion to "reaffirm the fundamental position of the party on the class nature of the Soviet state," then all comrades will vote on this question as they have in the past, namely, according to their opinions and convictions, and there will still be left for discussion and decision the question that is really at issue.

In its Plenum resolution, the Minority proposed "a revision of our previous concept of 'the unconditional defense of the Soviet Union'."

What was meant in the past by the Fourth Internationalists when they advocated and spoke of the "unconditional defense of the Soviet Union"? By "unconditional" we simply meant that we do not demand, as a condition for our defense of the Soviet Union, the preliminary removal of the Stalinist bureaucracy, that is, we will defend the Soviet Union even if, or in spite of, its domination by the Stalin machine. In the same sense, revolutionists have always said that they defend trade unions in their struggles even when they are headed by conservatives or reactionaries. That did not mean that we defend it in Stalin's way. On the contrary, we have no faith in the bureaucracy, no confidence that it will lead the defense of the Soviet Union effectively, along a consistent class line, in a revolutionary manner. Yet, in our independent class way, with our revolutionary internationalist line, we defend the Soviet Union. "For the Stalinist régime? No! For the socialist fatherland? Yes!"

Did that policy mean that we would support ("defend") every act of Stalinist diplomacy, every act of the Red Army, or the GPU, or the other armed forces of Stalin? Of course not. Comrade Lund is entirely wrong when he assumes that the Minority represents the traditional policy of the Fourth International in any other way, thereby disorienting especially the young comrades in our movement as to what has been our conception in the past. Naturally we did not in the past and do not today support the actions of the Red Army (or the GPU) in shooting down revolutionists in Russia or in Spain. Naturally we would not support the actions of the Red Army if it were to suppress a proletarian revolution in the Soviet Union — the political revolution which we advocate. Naturally we would not support the actions of the Red Army if it were to suppress an uprising of Ukrainian workers and peasants fighting for an independent Soviet Ukraine. In other words, our slogan of "unconditional defense of the Soviet Union" did not mean (nor does it today) that we defend the Stalinist bureaucracy or its Red Army in any war they conduct against the proletariat or against the revolution. On this score, there is no one who proposes a revision of our conception of our policy for the good and simple reason that no revision is needed.

Our slogan did, however, mean that we are unconditionally for the defense of the Soviet Union in any war it conducts *against a capitalist power*.

What basic conception motivated this clear and categorical position? The view that in a conflict with any capitalist country, the war, on the part of the Red Army, could only be *progressive*, that is, even under Stalin it would be defending in its own (i.e., bureaucratic) way the conquests of the October Revolution. That is how we understood matters in any war — not, to be sure, a war against the Russian Bolshevik-Leninists or the proletarian revolutionists in Spain, but a war with "democratic" England, fascist Germany, or even semi-colonial China.

This is the position that the Minority now proposes to revise. Such a revision is necessary because it has been revealed that the Soviet Union (that is, the Stalinist bureaucracy and its Army) is capable of carrying on not only progressive wars but also reactionary wars. More to the point, in the present dispute, the Stalinist bureaucracy has proved that it is capable of conducting a reactionary war *even against bourgeois states*. From this does not of course follow that we are defensists in the bourgeois states in question (their war against the Soviet Union is not less reactionary and we remain revolutionary defeatists under the slogan: "the main enemy is at home"); but it *does* follow that we can no longer hold to our previous concept of "unconditional defense of the Soviet Union" in a war against a capitalist power or powers.

At this point, the Cannon group interjects: "Your division of wars into progressive and reactionary, however correct it may be, leaves out of consideration precisely that criterion which we consider fundamental, namely, the class character of the state which is conducting the war."

The argument of the Cannon faction boils down to the ridiculous and unhistorical view that a capitalist state, because of its class nature, cannot *ever* fight a progressive war, and that a workers' state — even a degenerated workers' state, because of its class nature — cannot *ever* fight a reactionary war. This is the view of the mechanical-minded economic fetishists and not of revolutionary Marxists, for it is based upon the conception that in a war between "nationalized economy" and "private economy" the former automatically assures its own progressivism. This mechanical conception is all the more (not less) erroneous with reference to the Soviet Union. Writing on the difference between capitalist society and the Soviet Union, Trotsky says: "*...in general the productive forces, upon a basis of private property and competition, have been working out their own destiny. In contrast to this, the property relations which issued from the socialist revolution are indivisibly bound up with the new state as their repository. The predominance of socialist over petty bourgeois tendencies is guaranteed* not by the automatism of economy — *we are still far from that* — but by political measures taken by the dictatorship. The character of the economy as a whole thus depends upon the character of the state power.*" (Our emphasis.)

This entirely correct view applies with equal validity to the question of the war. The character of any war engaged in now by the Stalinist régime "is guaranteed not by the automatism of economy" — as the Cannon group falsely contends — but "depends (at least in large measure) upon the character of the state power," that is, of the political régime of the ruling bureaucracy. It would, however, be just as erroneous to draw the mechanical conclusion that because this bureaucracy is reactionary and counter-revolutionary, it cannot *ever* conduct a progressive war, any more than the reactionary character of the Chiang Kai-shek régime pre-determines the reactionary character of *any* war in which it is engaged. The correct formula would be:

The character of the war is determined by the predominant political and social *aims* of each of the belligerents and their enemy, and their objective consequences, and very often by the character of the régime which is conducting the war. Furthermore, particularly in our epoch, our attitude towards a given war must be based upon the interests of the *international proletariat* and of the world socialist revolution.

From this basic standpoint we must approach the question: What is the character of Russia's role in the *present* war — not the war as it was foretold on this or that occasion, and not the war into which this one *may or will be converted*, but the present war?

Stalin is not conducting a war for the defense of nationalized property from an attack of imperialism which aims to convert the Soviet Union into its colony. On the other side, the imperialists, in *this* war, are not fighting to divide the Soviet Union among themselves, but, for a series of reasons largely beyond their own control, they are conducting an inter-imperialist war at each other's expense, with one camp seeking to keep the Soviet Union as its ally and the other seeking to win it as its ally.

In the present war, the Stalin régime plays the role of agent of imperialism, facilitating the victory of the fascist bandits over the "democratic" bandits; in addition, it pursues (as we shall see later on) imperialistic aims of its own; it does not liberate but rather enslaves and disfranchizes the peoples it conquers; it tramples cynically upon the democratic and socialist sentiments of the masses, and drives them into the arms of the reactionary bourgeoisie. It is pursuing predominantly reactionary aims; it is playing a predominantly reactionary role. In a word, it is conducting a reactionary war and therefore the socialist proletariat cannot be for its defense.

The urgent problems of the role played by the Soviet Union (read: Stalin and his army) in the *present* war, are systematically avoided and evaded by the Cannon group. To the question: Are you for the "unconditional defense of the Soviet Union" in the war it is carrying on now? — the Cannon group replies: We are for the unconditional defense of the Soviet Union in the war it will carry on tomorrow, the war into which the present war will inevitably be converted.

In his letter of October 18, 1939 ("Again and Once More on the Nature of the USSR"), Comrade Trotsky writes: *"In every case the Fourth International will know how to distinguish where and when the Red Army is acting solely as an instrument of the Bonapartist reaction and where it defends the social basis of the USSR."* (Our emphasis.) It is necessary to introduce into this sentence at least one amendment: In place of *"will* know how to distinguish" should be placed *"should* know how to distinguish."

If we make the most calculated effort to eliminate all factional and polemical sharpness, and look back upon the September weeks in the party leadership with the utmost possible objectivity, we come to the conclusion that the Pact and Stalin's invasion of Poland caught the party (the Cannon group particularly) unawares and left it tongue-tied during the whole crucial period, so that it presented no policy, gave no answers, and very obviously *stalled for time.*

The Minority has said a dozen times, in writing, in resolutions, in speeches, that it does not base its views on the mere fact that Stalin shifted from a "democratic" to a fascist ally.

The Soviet Union is not engaged in a progressive war or defense of the remaining conquests of the Russian Revolution from imperialist attack, but rather as an integral part of a reactionary imperialist war. It is the *real war* that followed that compels us to change our position. Let us see more concretely why this is so.

How did we conceive specifically of the role of the Soviet Union in case of a war breaking out during the period of the Franco-Soviet Pact and of our position towards it?

Hitler would be engaged in a war against the Soviet Union, and at the same time against bourgeois France. If the Soviet Union were thus allied with one imperialist power against the other, our International declared that we would defend the Soviet Union without for a moment becoming defensists in the land of its imperialist ally. Concretely: the war between France and Germany would be a reactionary, imperialist war on both sides; Hitler's war against the Soviet Union, however, would be aimed at conquering the Ukraine, dismembering the Union as a whole, restoring private property, etc., and the Stalin régime, willy-nilly, would be fighting a progressive war of defense from imperialist attack. We too would defend the Soviet Union (in our own way, of course); we would be its foremost and best soldiers and defenders.

But the war presented us with a different picture when it finally broke out! And it is that war we must consider, unless, as Lenin once said, we are to be the kind of "Old Bolsheviks" who are "meaninglessly repeating a formula learned by rote instead of studying the unique living reality."

Instead of an attack upon the Soviet Union by imperialism, we had the outbreak of the inter-imperialist war between England-France and Germany. Instead of Stalin "helping" Poland resist Hitler (as he had earlier urged England and France to allow him to do, or at least pretended to urge this), Stalin and Hitler divided Poland between them, after crushing it by preliminary agreement and in military and political collaboration.

Now, in a general way, we predicted the possibility of a Hitler-Stalin pact. But we did not predict, as Trotsky pointed out in the *Socialist Appeal* of September 11, 1939, a *military alliance* with Hitler.

Naturally, it is not a matter here of "reproaching" our movement in general, or Comrade Trotsky in particular, for having failed to "forecast" or to "predict" every single event in all details. What is involved is the question of the character of the war that actually broke out and in which the Soviet Union is participating. Regardless of what *this* war will or may *become*, of what it will or may be *converted into*, Stalin is not defending the Soviet Union from imperialist attack; he is carrying on a *reactionary war of annexation* in alliance with Hitler. (We leave aside for the moment the question of Stalinist imperialism, which is dealt with below.)

It is only in light of this reality that the conduct of the Cannon faction can be understood. The actual war caught it unawares because it was not expected! The majority could not reconcile itself to the fact that the invasion was being conducted jointly by Hitler and Stalin. It clung to the old prognosis that Hitler was marching to attack Stalin, instead of meeting him half-way through Poland to divide the spoils.

Goldman thought Stalin invaded Poland without Hitler's support; therefore he endorsed the invasion. Goldman learned (what should have been clear to all from the beginning) that Stalin invaded Poland *with* Hitler's support; therefore he withdraws his endorsement. And the majority, the Cannon faction? It did not vote for Goldman's motion to endorse the invasion, and it refused to condemn the invasion for the simple reason, as Cannon put it at that time, that it cannot yet be known whether Stalin's invasion occurred with or without Hitler's agreement. To put it differently, the Cannon group could not decide whether Stalin entered the war to defend the Soviet Union from imperialist attack (Hitler) or entered the war with annexationist aims in collaboration with imperialism. It did *not* "know how to distinguish where and when the Red Army is acting solely as an instrument of the Bonapartist reaction and where it defends the social basis of the USSR".

Had Stalin invaded Poland without Hitler's blessing, Goldman (and presumably the Cannon faction as a whole) would approve the invasion. But in that case, what happens to the slogan in Trotsky's main article, voted for so firmly by the Cannon group at the Plenum, namely: "We were and remain against seizures of new territories by the Kremlin"? What does this slogan mean?

Now, there cannot be any doubt that Stalin's invasion of Poland, like his subsequent invasion of Estonia, Latvia, Lithuania and Finland, has as its purpose the *annexation* of these countries (or their transformation into military "protectorates," which is tantamount to the same thing, in the three Baltic countries). The Stalinists may claim that these invasions merely anticipate an imperialist attack on Russia, that they are undertaken for the defense of the Soviet Union from imperialism. Whatever position the Cannon group may take on this claim, they are nevertheless on record in opposition to the "seizures of new territories by the Kremlin," to "annexations." How then can Goldman, or the Cannon faction in general, "approve" the invasion (provided it is "not as a result of an agreement with Hitler") and at the same time oppose the annexation? Evidently, on the basis of opposing the annexation only *after* it has been accomplished. *After* Stalin has annexed the "new territories", we call upon the masses to fight against the annexation, for the right of self-determination, for separation; presumably also, we call upon the Russian masses to help the people of the new territories in this fight. But *before* the annexation of the new territories (according to the Cannon group), we call upon their population to fight for the defense of the Soviet Union, we support the invasion (which aims at annexing the new territories!), and we call upon the Soviet workers to give Stalin's army moral and material assistance in the invasion! We shall see where this preposterous line leads us in the case of Finland.

In less than two weeks, the Cannon faction, which prides itself on the firmness of its basic position, has presented the party with no less than two documented positions on the invasion of Finland — with two and a half positions if one adds the latest contribution to the discussion by Goldman.

The first position was contained in the *Appeal* editorial on December 1, 1939. In no sense was this editorial the product of Comrade Morrow alone; it was edited and approved jointly by a number of leaders of the Cannon faction. This editorial's characterization of Stalin's invasion of Finland leaves nothing to be desired: *"That the Kremlin's military intervention serves only the interests of the Kremlin and its imperialist ally (Hitler in Poland); that it is carried out without consideration of the will and feelings of the workers of the Soviet Union or the occupied territories or the international proletariat; that it compromises the Soviet Union and disorients the world working class — these are our criticisms..."* (Our emphasis.)

If these words are not meant as a literary flourish but as a political analysis of the war, they are equivalent to the declaration: the invasion is reactionary in every respect (it serves *"only"* the interests of the counter-revolutionary bureaucracy and of Hitler — *only* those interests!). That is the analysis. And the logical conclusion? "If a struggle breaks out between bourgeois Finland and the Soviet Union, it is the duty of the Finnish workers to be Soviet partisans in that struggle." In the war between Finland and the Soviet Union, Stalin and the Red Army pursue *only* reactionary aims and serve *only* reactionary interests; *therefore*, the Finnish workers must support the Red Army and the invasion!

This is the mumbo-jumbo to which we have been brought by the slogan of "unconditional defense" and it is sanctified in the eyes of its authors by the fact that they make the sign of the cross before the formula: Russia is a workers' state. It is with such a position that the Cannon faction believes that it will be able to combat the wave of chauvinist hysteria which the imperialists and democrats and social democrats are cleverly creating among the masses over "poor little Finland." It is a policy capable only of repelling workers — not the worst but the best — and of driving them closer into the arms of bourgeois patriotism.

How thoroughly untenable this position was (to say nothing of the reaction of the party membership), may be judged from the fact that even the Cannon group found it necessary to beat a retreat — a retreat conducted in its own characteristic way. The statement of policy of the PC (*Appeal*, December 9, 1939) was first presented to the meeting of the Committee without a word of explanation or justification. Not one word was said about the relation of this statement to the line of the editorial of December 1 — whether the lines coincided or conflicted. It was only on the insistent and formally recorded questioning of the Minority that 3 out of 4 Cannonite spokesmen replied: "This editorial, while the general line of it is more or less correct, is too loosely written to be considered a party position. The section which speaks of the Finnish workers as Soviet partisans is incorrect in its formulation. The statement which we have just adopted corrects the editorial and is to be considered the party line on the question."

But how is the average party or YPSL member, who does not see the minutes of the PC, to know that the first editorial on the not unimportant question of Finland was "loosely written," that the much-commented-on and much-disputed phrase about the Finnish workers being Soviet partisans "is incorrect" and does not correspond to the official party line? So far as he knows, he must still defend the policy of the first editorial as the party position; and moreover, he must defend it as in harmony with the second editorial which "is to be considered the party line on the question". Considered such by whom? Who knows about it? What party member or YPSL member? What reader of the *Appeal*? How are they to know about it? The party leadership does not deign to inform the membership or the *Appeal* readers that the slogan to the Finnish workers — "Be Soviet partisans in this invasion" — is "incorrect" now. It refuses to give any indication that it is "incorrect" in the party press. Such an indication might reflect somewhat on the carefully guarded prestige of the party leadership, that is, the Cannon faction. To all intents and purposes, therefore, and particularly so far as the readers of the *Appeal* are concerned (the facts will be learned by the membership only by reading the present statement), the Socialist Workers Party position on the Finnish invasion is represented by the December 1st statement (which is "incorrect") and also by the December 9th statement (which is "correct"). As for the fact that our enemies cunningly exploit the first editorial for their own reactionary ends, that is only another trifle compared with the considerations of bureaucratic prestige-politics.

Just what, however, and how much does the second position correct in the first position? The December 9th statement characterizes the Stalinist policy in Finland as follows: *"the protection of the interests and privileges of the bureaucracy in utter disregard of the sentiments and interests of the world proletariat"*. The characterization of the December 1st editorial is more exact and ample by far, but let us for the moment accept the second version. What follows from it? *"In the present military struggle a victory of the Red Army is a 'lesser evil' than the victory of the army of the Finnish puppet government of Wall Street and London."*

What is the concrete meaning of this conception of the "lesser evil" in Finland? In the first place, it means that there is no other choice facing the Finnish proletariat but these: *Either* the victory of the Finnish bourgeoisie and its army, *or* the victory of the Red Army. Since the revolutionary proletariat of Finland is too weak, unorganized, demoralized to fight for its independent Soviet power now, and since it is inadmissible in principle for it to support the Finnish bourgeoisie, "a victory of the Red Army is a 'lesser evil'". In that case, the slogan of the December 1st editorial — "Finnish workers to be Soviet partisans" — far from being "loosely written," is absolutely exact, far from being "incorrect" is absolutely correct. Why then does the Cannon group now repudiate the slogan? If "a victory of the Red Army is a 'lesser evil'" then the Finnish workers must be Soviet partisans. What species of political cowardice dictated the omission of this slogan from the December 9th editorial?

Paragraph "c", dealing with the tasks of the Fourth Internationalists in the Soviet Union, calls for "unceasing criticism and exposure of the Stalinist methods of starting and conducting the war, but not the slightest relaxation of material and military support". Good. Stalin's invasion of Finland is reactionary, it serves *only* the interests of the counter-revolutionary Bonapartist clique and of Hitler; its aim is the "protection of the interests and privileges of the bureaucracy" — and for those reasons the Russian workers and revolutionists must not relax in the slightest their material and military support to it. But why only the Russian workers? Why aren't the Finns (and for that matter the Americans) called upon to give the same material and military support to the Red Army?

In the Spanish Civil War, we rightly regarded the victory of the People's Front régime (bourgeois democracy) as the "lesser evil" compared with the victory of Franco (fascism). "Everywhere and always, where and when revolutionary workers are not powerful enough immediately to overthrow the bourgeois régime, they defend from fascism even the rotten bourgeois democracy and especially do they defend from fascism their own positions inside bourgeois democracy." (Crux.) Bourgeois democracy was conducting a progressive war against fascism; we were open, unashamed defensists in the former camp and defeatists in the latter. We said openly: For the victory of the Loyalist army; for the defeat of Franco's army. Moreover, we were *military defeatists* in the Franco camp. We called upon the workers and peasants and soldiers in the Franco camp to sabotage his war, to desert to the Loyalist side, *to facilitate the victory of the Loyalist army* (what else can be seriously meant by "defensism"?). In *both* camps, we called for material and military aid to *one* camp, namely, the Loyalists. Why doesn't the Cannon group say the same thing plainly about Finland? There was nothing mealy-mouthed about our position on Spain. The same cannot be said for the position of the Cannon group today. It is *shame-faced defensism*.

The December 16th editorial in the *Appeal* seeks to "popularize" the Cannon line. This is attempted by means of the much-abused comparison between the Stalinized Soviet Union and a bureaucratized trade union.

The Cannon faction, which is "principled", which is under no democratic or patriotic pressure, and which stuffs the minds of the party members with the "simple" trade union analogy in place of a concrete political analysis, ought to speak out flatly: The Finnish workers must facilitate the victory of the Red Army; it is the "lesser evil"; they must give it material and military aid; they must be Soviet (Red Army) partisans. As such, they must make a *united front* with the Kuusinen régime and the Finnish CP in order to speed the victory of the "lesser evil". They — especially the Finnish revolutionary vanguard — must retain their organizational and political independence, to be sure, but as an independent force they must make a united front with the Stalinists of Russia and Finland in the same way as we made a united front with Stalinists, social democrats and anarchists in Spain in order to speed the victory of the Loyalist army. That would not be the present shamefaced defensism of the Cannonites, but genuine defensism as we preached and practised it in Spain.

The final twist to the Cannon line is given, as usual without authorization or responsibility, by Goldman. He advocates now nothing more and nothing less than the slogan of the withdrawal of all Soviet troops from Finnish soil!

On what conceivable basis can the Cannon group or any of its spokesmen, given *their* political line, put forward the slogan of peace and the withdrawal of Soviet troops from Finnish soil? What then happens to the "lesser evil"?

Again: When Lenin advanced the slogan of peace in 1918, he was part of the government of Soviet Russia. He was not seeking to arouse the masses against that government. What would the Goldman slogan of peace, of withdrawal of troops from Finland, mean now in the Soviet Union? Presumably, the slogan is put forward as one to be raised by our comrades in the Soviet Union. But they are an *anti-government* party. They would have to raise that slogan *against* the government (the Stalin régime), against its policies, against its conduct of the war and those who support it. "*We are not a government party; we are the party of irreconcilable opposition, not only in capitalist countries but also in the USSR. Our tasks, among them the 'defense of the USSR,' we realize not through the medium of bourgeois governments and not even through the government of the USSR but exclusively through the education of the masses through agitation, through explaining to the workers what they should defend and what they should overthrow.*" (Trotsky: "The USSR in War".) In that case, the slogan of peace in the Soviet Union is the concrete slogan of *revolutionary defensism*. "*The experience of the years 1914-1918,*" say our theses on The War and the Fourth International (p.26), "*demon-*

554

strates at the same time that the slogan of peace *is in no way contradictory to the strategic formula of 'defeatism', on the contrary, it develops a tremendous revolutionary force, especially in case of a protracted war."*

That is why the Minority can and does advocate that slogan. That is why the Cannonites voted down the slogan Goldman said was "implicit" in their position (which did not prevent Morrow, another Cannonite, from advocating it publicly at a party mass meeting — anything goes once you swear by the "fundamentals"!). The slogan could not be adopted by the Cannon faction for the simple reason that its line boils down politically to trailing behind Stalinism in the best case and capitulation to it in the worst.

The line of the Cannon group as a whole, and of its individual spokesmen singly, demonstrates *in practise* that once you consent to swear solemnly and regularly that Russia is a workers' state, you are thenceforward permitted the most liberal experimentation with slogans and policies of the day and, at the same time, you acquire the right to accuse the Minority of "improvization".

The position of the Minority on the invasion of Finland can be stated very simply.

To the Finnish worker we must say: Your main fight is against your own bourgeoisie and the imperialists whose pawn it is. You are not fighting for the independence of Finland, for its sovereign integrity, but for the bankers and bandits of London, Paris and Washington. We know why you are fighting with such vehemence against the Stalinist forces. We understand fully your sentiments, for we know only too well what a victory of Stalinism would mean to you — the same slavery and oppression that your Russian brothers now endure. But do not react to the threat of Stalinist enslavement with such unthinking bitterness that you become blind cannon fodder of your main enemy, your class enemy. We know that Stalin aims to annex Finland for his own power, prestige and privilege. You must resist that; you must crack every dirty Stalinist finger that is outstretched now to enslave you. You have a right to a free and independent Finland. But you cannot conduct much less win that fight as tools of Mannerheim, under the domination of your bourgeoisie. First things come first. And your first job is to crush your ruling class, win over the army or create your own, establish your own power which will not be a tool of imperialism or the bankers and landlords but in which you can have full confidence. Then you will be able to resist the Stalinist invader. We cannot tell you, we Fourth Internationalists, to give material and military aid to the Red Army, now fighting a reactionary war, for its victory means annexation of Finland by Stalin, and its subjugation to the counter-revolutionary Kremlin. The day after that happened, we would have to tell you again to fight for your freedom, against annexation, against the Red Army which maintains it. On with the class struggle regardless of the results on the military front! Perhaps you will not win this time, but in the course of the war the Finnish bourgeois régime will collapse, as did the Polish régime, and your chance will come then. Then be doubly careful, for the Red Army will act as agents of the counter-revolution in the Kremlin, trying to cheat you of the fruits of your struggle. Seek also, therefore, to win over the Russian worker and peasant in uniform; fraternize with them; help establish mutual and comradely understanding. And when the day comes that you have the strength, strike against your oppressors.

To the Russian worker we must say: Stalin is conducting a reactionary war, which discredits and disgraces the Soviet Union and the working class movement. That war is conducted *only* in the interests of the bureaucracy; it serves *only* the Kremlin gang and Hitler. It is not your war. Stalin wants to annex Finland and deprive its people of the right of self-determination. What interest can you have in that? You want peace, you want an end to the rule of the bureaucratic assassins who abuse and degrade you in the name of "socialism". If Stalin were really defending the Soviet Union from imperialist attack, we would have to clench our teeth and help him all we could, settling accounts with him later. But this war is reactionary and we should not give him an ounce of political or material or military support. Does that mean you must shoot your officer tomorrow? Does that mean you refuse to fight? Does that mean you take Mannerheim's help against the Stalinists? Nothing of the kind. A thinking worker is not a putschist, an adventurist, or an individualist. Although we are too weak for anything like that now, let us use this occasion to educate our comrades in the Army and back home; to tell them the truth; to organize secret cells; prudently to promote every movement of mass discontentment against the perfidious régime; prudently to advocate fraternization with our Finnish brothers and the speediest calling off of this rotten war. We had nothing to do with the calling of this war, secretly planned by the bureaucracy in cahoots with Hitler. We must continue and expand our struggle against the Stalinist bureaucracy regardless of the results on the military front.

With such a policy, no tremendous successes will be achieved overnight on either side of the front. It "cannot give immediate miraculous results" — it is entirely in place to quote Trotsky here. "But we do not even pretend to be miracle workers. As things stand, we are a revolutionary minority. Our work must be directed so that the workers on whom we have influence" — even should they at first number no more than two or three — "should correctly appraise events, not permit themselves to be caught unawares, and prepare the general sentiment of their own class for the revolutionary solution of the tasks confronting us." ("The USSR in War".)

But what if the Red Army should win before the Finnish workers can make their own revolution, as is the more likely variant? And what if the Stalinists, for reasons of their own, should nationalize industry, or the land, or establish "Soviets"? We would still follow substantially the same policy towards the Stalinists. We would say to the Finnish workers: We must start now from the new situation. The old capitalists have been driven out, but the nationalization of industry and land can become really progressive only if you have workers' control and management of the plants; only if you drive the Kremlin commissars out of the factories and the land; only if you drive them out of the fake Soviets or rather set up genuinely democratic Soviets in their place; only if you fight for separation from the Soviet Union, for the right of self-determination. No aid to Stalinism while it fastens the yoke on your necks; no aid to Stalinism while you are unfastening that yoke.

But, we are asked finally, suppose the imperialists, using the Finnish invasion as a pretext, launch a real attack upon the Soviet Union, with the aim of carving it up among themselves, of restoring capitalism, of smashing not only Stalinism but everything that remains of what we fought for 22 years to maintain — will you then be for the defense of the Soviet Union? To which we answer simply: yes, if the character of the war really changes into a war of imperialist attack upon the Soviet Union, we shall take a clear-cut position of defensism — not the shamefaced defensism of the Cannonites in the present war, but unconditional defense of the Soviet Union. So we acted in Spain; so we would act in the Soviet Union. Our slogan is: Defense of the Soviet Union in any progressive war!

The Cannon group would like to dismiss such questions as the invasion of Finland with the epithet: "an incident" or "an episode" in the preparations for the imperialist war against Russia which is coming. How many more such "episodes" are required before they cease being mere "episodes"? First Poland, then Estonia, Latvia and Lithuania, now Finland, tomorrow and the day after somewhere else.

Then the Minority stands for the position of defeatism — cries the Cannon group. One is either a defensist, at least a half-hearted one as we are, or one is a defeatist. To which we reply: In the present war we have made it quite clear that we are not defensists; rather, we adopt a form of defeatism.

In the present conflict, the Stalinist bureaucracy and its army are conducting a reactionary war. They do not represent the interests of the world proletariat, or the socialist revolution, or the Soviet Union. They represent the interests, on the one hand, of German imperialism, and on the other of the counter-revolutionary anti-Soviet bureaucracy. In the present war, these interests are reactionary. "The economic transformations in the occupied provinces," writes Trotsky, and quite rightly, "do not compensate for this by even a tenth part!" We do not support this war, any more than we would "support such a shameful strike" as one organized "against the admission of Negro workers into a certain branch of industry" (Trotsky). If we do not support it, we oppose it.

What form does our opposition take? Revolutionary defeatism. That means: the continuation and intensification of the revolutionary struggle against the Stalinist régime and for its overthrow, regardless of the effects on the military front. Does this mean an alliance with the Finnish bourgeoisie? Does this mean the victory of the Finnish army? Nothing of the sort! In a war that is reactionary on both sides, our slogans are not national but international. The Finnish proletariat must overthrow (defeat) its own bourgeoisie and its army. The Soviet proletariat must overthrow the Stalinist bureaucracy and its army.

"But the war is on now. Which way shall the workers in the Red Army shoot?" The Cannonites ask this question of us with an air of triumph.

We are not putschists or anarchists. We do not believe that the armed uprising can be called into existence by mere will of the small vanguard. We do not believe that the actions of individuals can be substituted for the actions of the vanguard, or those of the vanguard for those of the class as a whole. It is not at all a question of what this or that worker or little group of workers should "do with his rifle." Until the vanguard has been brought together in an ideologically and organizationally distinct and powerful force, until it has acquired mass support, the question of a decisive action remains a perspective; that is, the *propaganda* slogan has not yet developed into a *slogan of action*. The whole question, however, is how to realize this perspective, what steps to take, what line to follow, in order to facilitate the progress of the vanguard. The argument: *If* there were an independent revolutionary movement already in existence we would support it; but since there is not we support the Stalinist invasion as the "lesser evil" — is essentially reactionary. The point is precisely this: The independent revolutionary movement cannot be brought into existence and advance if we support the Stalinist invasion. The forces of the *third camp* are already at hand — scattered, demoralized, without program or perspective. The problem is to bring them together, to infuse them with morale, to supply them with a program and perspective. To argue that these forces are small and insignificant, has no political meaning, for the argument could apply both ways (if they are insignificant, they can no more "defend" than they can "defeat"). Political meaning is contained only in the *line* upon which we expect the vanguard to come together and along which we urge them to act.

That is the meaning of the section of the Minority resolution on the war in Finland which declares that we must take into account "the military situation, the moods of the masses and also the differing economic relations in Finland and Russia". The concrete moment when a propaganda slogan can be turned effectively into a slogan of action, often depends upon the shifts in the military fronts. This has been observed in virtually every country where a revolutionary situation has developed, notably in the Russian revolution of 1917 and the German and Austrian revolutions a year later. (An army that records nothing but crushing victories is rarely inclined to listen to slogans calling for the overthrow of the régime that commands it!) Again, the concrete tactical forms of the slogans aimed at reaching a given strategical goal will always differ with the change in the moods of the masses, which are in turn affected by a whole series of objective factors. To have a strategical objective is decisively important, but not enough; it is necessary also to be able to translate this objective into specific slogans suitable for every conjuncture. From this alone follows the absurdity of the question — "What should they do now with their rifles?" "They" *will do* what the soldiers in every army must do, namely, obey the orders of their all-powerful officer-command *until such a time* when the officer-command is not all-powerful, that is, when the masses are strong and conscious enough to refuse to obey their officers. Again, the whole problem is: What political line shall we adopt in order most speedily to reach that time in the struggle?

Finally, our resolution pointed out the need of taking into account the different economic relations in the two countries. In other words, while the proletarian revolution in Finland will have the task of nationalizing industry by expropriating the bourgeoisie, the revolution in the Soviet Union will merely free the already nationalized property from the reactionary stranglehold of the parasitic bureaucracy.

The line of the Cannon group means that the third camp, however embryonic, must resign itself "for the present" to the victory of the Stalinist reaction. This is equivalent to a political capitulation to the Kremlin bureaucracy. The line of the Minority means that the third camp, however embryonic or weak, must orient itself at the very outset towards a decisive struggle not only against world imperialism, but also against the Stalinist reaction. An indispensable part of the preparations for this decisive struggle is the struggle against the Stalinist clique in the present war — for the peace slogan, for fraternization on the war front, for re-establishing the genuine Soviets in which the workers and peasants themselves can decide the questions of war and peace, for the conquest of the Red Army, for the overturn of the counter-revolutionary bureaucracy, etc.

"We often seek salvation from unfamiliar phenomena in familiar terms," Trotsky once wrote. And naturally so. Our epoch is so rich in new phenomena and the social-political lexicon is so limited, that we frequently characterize the new phenomena in terms of similar, even if not identical, phenomena of the past. Terminological "experimentation", while often risky and at times pointless, is sometimes the only way of illuminating, by analogy, a new phenomenon or an old phenomenon in new forms and of relating it, with the necessary changes, to phenomena with which we are already familiar. Let us see if, in this sense, it is permissible to speak of Stalinist imperialism.

The fact that all varieties of Menshevik, liberal and bourgeois politicians speak, and have spoken for twenty years, of "red imperialism" is not in itself an argument against the employment of the term "imperialism" to describe the present foreign policy of the Stalinist bureaucracy. Almost from the beginning of the Russian Revolution, the Mensheviks declared that what had triumphed in November 1917 was not the proletarian revolution but the Thermidorean counter-revolution. With the increasing restrictions on Soviet democracy and the growth, during the civil war, of the Red Army, the Mensheviks and Social Revolutionists even spoke of the triumph of Bonapartism in Russia, giving very learned and very stupid comparisons between the evolution of the Russian proletarian and the French bourgeois revolutions.

In one of his very first polemics against the ruling faction in Russia (*The New Course*), Trotsky argued that the attempt to make a comparison between the French and Russian revolutions was untenable. "The historical analogies with the Great French Revolution (the fall of the Jacobins) which liberalism and Menshevism establish and with which they console themselves," he wrote in 1923, "are superficial and inconsistent." And so they were and remain in our opinion.

But that did not for one moment prevent our own movement several years later from making legitimate comparisons, from which legitimate conclusions were drawn. Allowing for the necessary changes, we threw considerable light on the evolution of the Soviet régime by the analogy with the French Thermidor of more than a century ago. Polemicizing against our use of the term "imperialism" Trotsky now writes that in 1920 "the Mensheviks at that time already spoke of Bolshevik imperialism as borrowed from the traditions of Czarist diplomacy. The petty bourgeois democracy willingly resorts to this argument even now. We have no reason, I repeat, for imitating them in this." There is no doubt that the same argument was made, in its time, to the use of the term "Soviet Thermidor"; in fact, the official polemics against the Left Opposition in Russia of 10-12 years ago contained precisely this objection.

Again, on the employment of the term "Bonapartism" to characterize the Stalinist régime. The fact that all varieties of anti-Marxists had (and still do) used this term did not deter us from using it with the necessary qualifications to indicate the *limits of the analogy*, even though there was no lack of objection in our own ranks when Trotsky first formulated the characterization.

"The matter is complicated," he wrote early in 1935, *"when we apply the term* Bonapartism *to the Stalin régime and speak of 'Soviet Bonapartism'. 'No,' exclaim our critics, 'your Bonapartisms are too many; the term is becoming impermissibly extensive...' etc. Such abstract, formal, verbal objections are usually made when there is nothing to say about the essential. Incontestably, neither Marx, Engels nor Lenin applied the term Bonapartism to the workers' state; no wonder: they had no occasion to (that Lenin did not hesitate to apply terms of the bourgeois régime to the workers' state, with the necessary limitations, is proved, for example, by his expression 'Soviet state capitalism'). What is to be done, however, in those cases where the good old books do not give the necessary indications? In such cases you have to rely on your own common sense."* Trotsky's conclusion: Bonapartism is the "scientific-sociological definition" of the Stalin régime.

Again, although confusionists of all sorts speak glibly of the similarity between Russia and Germany, Trotsky, in *The Revolution Betrayed*, declares: *"Stalinism and fascism, in spite of a deep difference in social foundations, are symmetrical phenomena."*

It will be argued that in all these comparisons and analogies, the essential differences are also indicated. Quite right. This only means that if we speak of Stalinist imperialism it is necessary to point out wherein it differs from British or French or American or German imperialism, that is, from modern capitalist imperialism.

For some time now, the Fourth International has characterized the Stalin régime as an "agent of imperialism." That is correct. Up to yesterday, it was an agency of French imperialism; with its new alliance, it is an agency of German imperialism. And in general, the Stalinist bureaucracy is the agency through which world imperialism oppresses the Soviet proletariat and peasantry. In this respect, the Minority has no different appreciation of the position of Stalinism than does Comrade Trotsky. Furthermore, we reject the view that it is impermissible for a workers' state to maneuver among the imperialist powers, and even to make a bloc with one against another. But there is a fundamental difference between the "blocs" made by Lenin and the "blocs" made by Stalin.

In utilizing the contradictions in the imperialist camp, Lenin did not thereby become a *tool of imperialism.* Stalin, representing a counter-revolutionary government, does act as an agent of imperialism. But this "agent of imperialism" is not at all like such an agent of imperialism as, let us say, the compradore national bourgeoisie of China. It not only rests on a different economic foundation, with contradictions and problems peculiar to it, but it also has different ambitions, appetites, national and international aims. It is not *merely* an agent of imperialism; it follows, or tries to follow, an imperialist policy of its own.

In discussion with a Chinese comrade, the following statements occur:

"Crux: A *military alliance against Japan would be in any case preferable for China even with the (Soviet) bureaucracy as it is. But then we must say that we demand that the Soviet Union delivers munitions, arms for the workers and peasants; special committees must be created in Shanghai in workers' centers; the treaty must be elaborated with the participation not only of the Kuomintang but also with the workers' and peasants' organizations. We ask for an open proclamation from the Soviet bureaucracy that at the end of the war no part of China would be occupied without the consent of the Chinese people, etc.*

"Li: *Do you then think that the Soviet Union could be capable of conducting an imperialistic policy?*

"Crux: *If it is capable of organizing frame-ups, killing the revolutionaries, it is capable of all possible crimes.*" (Internal Bulletin, Dec. 1937, p.38.)

The Stalinist bureaucracy is capable of conducting an imperialistic policy! This concept and expression was first used in the Fourth International not by the Minority which is "imitating the petty bourgeois democracy", but by Comrade Crux.

Does this mean that Stalinist imperialism stands on the same level with French or German imperialism? Not at all! Does the use of such a characterization for the Stalinist régime violate the conceptions of Marxism? Not at all! It is quite true that we have generally used the term "imperialism" to describe *modern* imperialism, that is, the expansionist policy of capitalism in its last stage, of monopolistic finance capital. But Marxists have pointed out time and again that imperialist policy has characterized régimes and societies other than that of finance capitalism, and that each was distinguished from the others by properties peculiar to it. There is no doctrine of Marxism that prevents us from speaking of a "counter-revolutionary workers' state" or of "Soviet Bonapartism"; there is no doctrine of Marxism that prevents us from speaking of an imperialist policy peculiar to the Stalinist régime which has reached an unprecedented depth of degeneration, unforeseen by Marx or by Lenin. Trotsky himself writes: *"The driving force behind the Moscow bureaucracy is indubitably the tendency to expand its power, its prestige, its revenue. This is the element of 'imperialism' in the widest sense of the word which was a property in the past of all monarchies, oligarchies, ruling castes, medieval estates and classes. However, in contemporary literature, at least Marxist literature, imperialism is understood to mean the expansionist policy of finance capital which has a very sharply defined economic content."* (Internal Bulletin, Vol.II, No.2, p.2.)

The first two sentences of this quotation allow, theoretically, for the employment of the term "imperialism" — "in the widest sense of the word" — to the Stalinist bureaucracy. As for the last sentence quoted, one can only reply that in contemporary Marxist literature, Bonapartism, for example, *was* limited to the scientific-sociological definition of the rule of the bourgeoisie at a certain stage in its development. Its extension to cover the Stalinist régime, with the necessary qualifications, was in no way an offense against Marxism.

Similarly in the case of the term "imperialism." But what is the nature of Stalinist imperialism? What are the necessary qualifications that must be borne in mind in employing this terminology? And above all — this question is the most justified — what is the economic basis of this imperialism?

It would of course be absurd to *identify* it with the imperialism that prevails in the modern capitalist world. Monopolistic finance capital does not dominate the Soviet Union; the Soviet Union exports very little in commodities and even less in capital. The concept of Stalinist imperialism cannot be based on these familiar phenomena of modern capitalist imperialism. Nor can the concept be based upon what Trotsky calls the "historical-geographical argument" which he groundlessly attributes to the Minority, namely, the fact that Stalinist expansion is following more or less the same geographical lines followed by the old Czarist empire. We are not among those who readily cry "imperialism" the minute the troops of one country cross the frontiers into another...

The nature of Stalinist imperialism must be sought in the contradictions of the transitional economy of the Soviet Union and the relations of the "bourgeois bureaucracy"[1] to this economy.

Our fundamental objection to the theory of "socialism in a single country" has been that the contradictions inherent in its economy cannot be solved within the borders of one state. To the national-limitedness and Utopianism of the Stalinists, we counterposed the international socialist revolution. By that we meant: the Russian revolution must expand — or die! Without "state aid" from the working class in power in the economically and technologically more advanced countries of the world, the Russian revolution could not maintain itself. Although this prognosis did not materialize in exactly the form it originally had, it nevertheless remained fundamentally correct. If the Russian revolution did not collapse under the direct blows of the (internal or external) bourgeois counter-revolution, it has experienced a terrible degeneration.

Stalin has not been able to establish socialism in the Soviet Union, that is, a harmo-

---

1 This is a reference to Trotsky's argument in *Revolution Betrayed* that the Stalinist bureaucrats in the USSR embody "bourgeois right" in an underdeveloped workers' state.

niously balanced, planned, crisis-free economic order. All the contradictory successes of the first Five Year Plans are turning into their opposite under stress of economic and social forces beyond the control even of the all-powerful bureaucracy. The bureaucracy which first stimulated the development of the productive forces is now the principal brake on their development. The fixed capital of the early plans is reaching exhaustion. "The tendency toward primitive accumulation created by want breaks out through innumerable pores of the planned economy" (Trotsky); the thirst for "primitive accumulation", for more privileges, for more wealth, for an increase in the national wealth, for an increase in the national income and for a greater share of this income for itself, burns in the throats of the bureaucracy. The growth of Soviet industry has not brought the country closer to the Stalinist Utopia of autarchy, of economic self-sufficiency, but into greater dependence upon world economy.

Under Lenin and Trotsky, the inherent contradictions of Soviet economy were to be solved on the international arena by revolutionary means. In those days, the dilemma — "Expand or die" — was to be solved by extending the Russian revolution throughout the world. That "policy of expansion" was in complete harmony with the interests of the world proletariat. It was directed consciously against world imperialism, and not as an agency of imperialism; it meant the liberation of workers in other countries and not their enslavement. That is why the "invasion" of Poland in 1920 and the "invasion" of Georgia in the same period were of a fundamentally different character from Stalin's invasion of Poland hand in hand with German imperialism.

Under the Stalinist régime, the inherent contradictions of Soviet economy have increased and could not be resolved by the purely military-bureaucratic measures of the apparatus "in one country". Nowadays, too, and in a sense, far more acutely, the dilemma is still — "Expand or die!" But the Stalinist policy of expansion differs fundamentally from that of the revolutionary workers' state years ago precisely in that it is reactionary and counter-revolutionary. This policy is not based *solely* on the desire of the bureaucracy to assure itself *militarily* from attack by the imperialist powers. One of the main driving forces behind the policy of the bureaucracy is "the tendency to expand its power, its prestige, its revenues". We call this policy *Stalinist imperialism.*

To be sure, the Bonapartist bureaucracy cannot yet even hope of realizing the power or the dreams of the old capitalist imperialisms. To be sure, its own (comparatively) feeble economic base at home does not make possible the acquisition or domination of an empire in any way comparable to the British or French. But — "to each his proportionate share." The agent, or rather the minor partner, of imperialism must be content with a smaller share. The bureaucracy does not scoff at even such trifles as the oil wells of Western Ukraine, the timber and nickel of Finland, the modest wealth of Vilna, every factory and store of which was sacked by the Stalinists before they turned over the city to Lithuania, the commercially important ports of the Baltic and the North of Finland, to say nothing of the thousands of workers of Lvov shipped under guard to work in the Donetz coal mines, etc., etc.

Marxists have analyzed and spoken of "social-imperialism" as the policy of one section of the working class (the labor aristocracy and the bureaucracy) corrupted by imperialism and enjoying a small share of the fruits of imperialist expansion. With even greater reason it is possible to speak of Stalinist-imperialism as the policy of the counter-revolutionary bureaucracy in the Soviet Union.

How can a workers' state follow an imperialist policy? Or, as some comrades put it, how can a nationalized economy follow (!!) an imperialist policy? The "secret" lies in the fact that the nationalized economy does not "follow" any policy; the automatism of Soviet economy is not at all guaranteed; its character as a whole "depends upon the character of the state power". The state power is in the hands of a gluttonous, counter-revolutionary bureaucracy which, for a series of objective reasons, has acquired an enormous (relative) independence from its economic base.

Stalinist Bonapartism, in order to preserve itself, does not "sweep away everywhere the establishments" of world capitalism. On the contrary, it helps maintain capitalism; it rightly fears the proletarian revolution abroad like the devil fears holy water, for the international revolution means the finish of its power; it proudly proclaims itself, and with justice, as the guardian of private property — in Spain, in Estonia, in Lithuania, in Latvia, in Finland; and if it did not maintain private ownership in the Western Ukraine and Western White Russia it is essentially because the private owners (capitalists and landlords), who were ninety per-cent Polish in nationality, had either fled to safer regions or had already been driven out by the insurrectionary peasants who rose on the land even before the arrival of the Red Army.[2]

Here too it has been shown that there is no mechanical relationship between the nationalized property existing in the Soviet Union and the policies — even the economic policies — of the Stalinist régime. There is not the slightest doubt that if the Polish bourgeoisie and landlords had consented to collaborate with the Stalinists, their private property would have been preserved intact by the Kremlin and its army — exactly as was the case in Spain, and as is the case in Estonia, Latvia and Lithuania. The program of the Kuusinen "government" in Terioki, with its explicit opposition to expropriating the bourgeoisie, represents an assurance from the Stalinists that they will protect the social interests of the Finnish bourgeoisie if the latter will act like the bourgeoisie of the three Baltic countries.

The peculiar relationship of the Stalinist bureaucracy, of the political régime which has acquired such an enormous degree of independence, to the contradictions of the Soviet economy, enables it and to a growing extent compels it to pursue an imperialist policy, *not only* as an agent of capitalist imperialism, but an imperialist policy of its own.

Is this not a mere matter of terminology — a desire to avenge ourselves for Stalinist crimes by the employment of "strong" language? No. Without an understanding of this new phenomenon, a clear political line is impossible; and that for several reasons.

1. The majority has, for example, shown a complete inability to analyze and understand the "new turn" of the Communist International. The official analysis made of the "turn" by the representative of the Cannon group in the *Socialist Appeal* was woefully superficial — that is the best that can be said of it.

Although Stalin capitulated to Hitler, he is no mere tool of Germany. The "agent" plays an independent role in the "axis." Not only does the Comintern allow itself a few guarded but nonetheless significant remarks about the need of a "revolution" in Germany (something it spoke and acted against in the most violent manner in France, during the "fourth period"), but it is also carrying on a "revolutionary" agitation in those countries into which the Stalinist bureaucracy hopes next to direct its expansion.

Does this mean that the Stalinists have turned revolutionary? Not for a minute! The Stalinist bureaucracy, its régime, its policies, its Comintern, remain fundamentally counter-revolutionary. Its "rousing of the people" in such countries as Rumania, Yugoslavia, Iran, Irak, India and elsewhere has essentially the same significance as Hitler's or Mussolini's "rousing of the people" ("support" of the nationalist movement) in Great Britain's Arabian empire. (In passing, it does not follow that the independent revolutionary movements in these countries should refuse to accept and use Stalinist aid for their own purposes, just as the Irish in 1916 accepted and used German aid; but in return they need not facilitate the victory of Stalinism and the Red Army!) Whatever revolutionary struggle is developed by the masses in these countries will be crushed by the Stalinist counter-revolution, if it intervenes, and the peoples will be brought under the oppressive domination of the reactionary bureaucracy and its imperialist ambitions. The service which the "new turn" of the Communist International is doing to the Berlin-Moscow axis as a whole (more specifically, to German imperialism), is not the main objective of the "new turn". It is calculated to serve the expansionist interests of the independent (i.e., semi-independent) Stalinist bureaucracy. It is in this light that the "turn" must be explained to the masses so that their revolutionary interests may be properly safeguarded.

2. "We were and remain against the seizures of new territories by the Kremlin." As already mentioned above, one of the theorists of the Cannon group has explained that "Trotsky is merely restating here the classic Marxist position on self-determination". In other words, the seizure of new territories (Western Galicia, Estonia, Finland, etc.) is a violation of the right of self-determination and that is why "we were and remain against" such seizures.

In the past, however, we did not object to the violation of this right *provided it was in the interests of the defense of the Soviet Union.* "No Marxist who does not break with the fundamentals of Marxism and socialism," wrote Lenin in 1918, "will be able to deny that the interests of socialism stand higher than the interests of the self-determination of a people." Quite correct. Self-determination is a *bourgeois-democratic* right. We defend this right with the utmost intransigence against reactionary bourgeois or imperialist interests and "rights", and in the interests of democracy and socialism. But in those cases where this bourgeois-democratic right conflicts with proletarian-internationalist rights (with socialist interests), and

---

2 Trotsky commented on this in *In Defense of Marxism.* Shachtman evidently still thinks in terms of the restoration of capitalism. Trotsky, though he mislabels it, has a more realistic grasp of things as they are, of the independence and solidity of the USSR system. Shachtman, following Trotsky, will understand.

only in those cases, we subordinate the former to the latter and are even prepared to reject the former in the interests of the latter.

According to this entirely correct Marxian point of view, the formula of Trotsky should read: "We are against the seizure of new territories by the Kremlin because it violates the right of self-determination. But we are for the violation even of this (democratic) right if it serves the (socialist) right of the defense of the Soviet Union." But in that case, it would be necessary to say one of two things, and not both: (a) What is involved in the present case is the defense of the Soviet Union, and the violation of the right of self-determination in Poland, Estonia and Finland is either of secondary or no importance; consequently, the formula — "We are against the seizure of new territories by the Kremlin" — has no concrete meaning or purpose now; or (b) What is involved in the present case is *not* the defense of the Soviet Union; consequently, we are for the right of self-determination in Poland, Estonia and Finland and against Stalin's seizure of these territories, and Trotsky's formula does have concrete meaning and purpose. In the first case, we would have to say that despite the violation of the right of self-determination, it is necessary to give material and military aid to those who are violating the right; in the second case, we would have to say that because we are for this right, we do not give material and military aid to those who are violating it. In other words, in the concrete case, it is impossible to maintain and support *both*.

If we do *not* subordinate the (basically democratic) right of self-determination (if we do not support the seizure of new territories by Stalin) to support of the Red Army in the present war, it can only be because it is not a (basically socialist) war for the defense of the Soviet Union. It is, as the Minority has emphasized, a reactionary war for the realization of the Stalinist bureaucracy's aims at imperialist expansion. To the interests of that war, of those aims — we cannot and must not subordinate the right of self-determination.

It need hardly be added that the Finnish bourgeoisie, which is conducting the war against the Soviet army, is *not* fighting to maintain Finland's right to national independence, any more than the Servian bourgeoisie was fighting Austro-Hungary in 1914 for Servia's right to national independence. In both cases, the national independence of the country is a myth; in the latter the country was a vassal of Russian imperialism and in the former the country and its bourgeoisie are vassals of Anglo-French imperialism. The struggle for the genuine national independence of Finland can be conducted only by the independent Finnish proletarian *struggle for power*, since the struggle for national independence in that country is inseparably bound up with the working class struggle for a socialist Finland. Hence, the main enemy of the Finnish masses remains at home — the Finnish bourgeoisie.

The problem of the Ukraine may be understood and posed more clearly in the light of our standpoint. The Fourth International favors the right of self-determination for the masses of the present Soviet Ukraine, for their separation from the Soviet Union, and their unification with other Ukrainian peoples into a United Independent Soviet Ukraine. Why? Because the Stalinist régime oppresses the Ukrainian masses. But it oppresses the Russian (Great Russian) masses too. That is true, our opponents will reply, and that is why we raise the slogan of the political revolution against the Kremlin bureaucracy, a slogan applying to the whole of the Soviet Union. But the point is that for the Ukraine we have *added* to the slogan of political revolution the slogan of separation, precisely because in the Ukraine Stalinist oppression is also *national oppression*. What is the character of this national oppression? Is it sufficient to say that it is "bureaucratic"? But that would not distinguish it from Stalinist oppression in the rest of the Soviet Union which is — like oppression in general — also bureaucratic. For the *distinguishing* slogan in the Ukraine a *distinguishing* reason must be found. It lies in the fact that the Stalinist Muscovite bureaucracy, with its Great Russian nationalist outlook (detected by Lenin in Stalin years ago!) and ideology, with its contempt for and repression of Ukrainian national culture, with its exploitation of the resources of the country mainly in the interests of the Kremlin parasites, oppresses the Ukraine in an *imperialist* manner. It is not accidental that the Fourth International has raised for the Soviet Ukrainian masses the same slogan that it raises for the Ukrainian masses who are imperialistically oppressed in countries like Hungary, Rumania, Poland and Czechoslovakia.

3. The analysis of Stalinist imperialism makes it possible for the revolutionary vanguard more easily and clearly *"to distinguish where and when the Red Army is acting solely as an instrument of the Bonapartist reaction and where it defends the social basis of the USSR".* (Trotsky.)

But your position, it may be said, completely excludes any defense of the Soviet Union under Stalinist domination, for how can we defend imperialists? Not at all.

In the case of the Soviet Union, when the social-imperialist bureaucracy is conducting a reactionary war of expansion, we are not defensists; we subordinate the defense of the Soviet

Union to the intensification of the revolutionary struggle to overthrow the Stalinist régime, we are revolutionary defeatists. When the same bureaucracy is compelled to conduct a war to defend the Soviet Union from imperialism, and therefore to deal (willy-nilly) a blow at the latter's hope to restore itself to new vigor by dismembering the Soviet Union, it is playing an objectively progressive role and we are for the defense of the Soviet Union; that is, retaining our full political independence, we give material and military aid to the Soviets' armed forces in spite of their domination by the bureaucracy.

The slogan of "unconditional defense of the Soviet Union" as understood and interpreted by the Fourth International up to now, as still understood and interpreted by the Cannon group, makes it impossible for us to adopt officially the position which has been elaborated in this document. Our past slogan must be revised.

Defense of the Soviet Union when it is conducting a reactionary war, a war solely or predominantly in the interests of the bureaucracy and its imperialist expansionism, a war against the interests of the world revolution? No!

Defense of the Soviet Union when it is conducting a progressive war against imperialism, in the interests of the world revolution? Yes!

SHACHTMAN'S REPLY TO TROTSKY

Dear Comrade Trotsky: Your article of December 15, 1939 ("A Petty-Bourgeois Opposition in the Socialist Workers Party") raises a number of questions which enable me, in reply, to present and elaborate the standpoint of the Minority, in general, and of myself personally. The nature of the questions raised, and the manner in which you deal with them, impose a polemical form upon the present reply, not so much because your article was directly addressed to the party but primarily because I am compelled to disagree radically and uncompromisingly with the attacks you make upon the Minority and its political position, and with the solution you advance for resolving the party crisis.

This reply, supplementing the main documents already published by the Minority, will speak with the same welcome candour and even bluntness which you employ in your article, and will try to deal with all the essential points you raise, answering all and evading none.

You have discovered the class struggle, or rather its reflection, in the ranks of the party. The Cannon faction represents the proletarian wing of the party; the Minority is "incapable of giving the party Marxian leadership" because it is "leading a typical petty-bourgeois tendency". As to whether it is permissible to speak of class tendencies and class struggle in the party, and the extent to which it is permissible — these questions will be dealt with further on in this document. Here let us examine the basis for your characterization of the Minority faction.

What is involved, of course, is not the pride or prestige or subjective feelings of this or that comrade in the Minority, or of the group as a whole, but the objective validity of the characterization.

At the beginning of the crisis in the party, the Cannonites characterized the Minority in various ways. Of them all, however, as we pointed out in our document on "War and Bureaucratic Conservatism", only one even pretended to be a *political* characterization, namely, the Minority is yielding to the pressure of bourgeois patriotism, or, as you now put it, the Minority represents a petty-bourgeois tendency.

To which we replied: Political tendencies, either inside or outside the party, do not arise overnight, nor are they the spontaneously full-fledged product of the whims or aberrations of a group of individuals. Here and there we find an individual who, unexpectedly and suddenly, "accidentally", turns into his political opposite. A man with a long record of radicalism may suddenly turn patriot at the outbreak of war; a man with a long record of opportunism may suddenly turn radical at the same time. But these are individual cases and do not represent tendencies. We speak of political *tendencies* precisely because it is possible to say of a group of people that over an appreciable period of time, as revealed in the record of its political words and deeds, it has *tended* in a certain political direction and has finally crystallized into a distinct political group, or faction, or party. An isolated instance or two does not establish a tendency (much less a "petty-bourgeois tendency" and one that is "typical", at that), but at most a mistake or a deviation. Even on this small scale, one can apply the dialectical method and inquire into whether or not a quantitative change has been transformed into a qualitative change!

Therefore — continued our reply to the Cannon faction — to maintain your characterization, it is incumbent upon you to indicate in our political record, which is available to you, wherein this tendency has manifested itself in the last year or two among the representative spokesmen of the Minority. That is, in attacking us, in characterizing us politically, please do no less than all of us together have done with reference to bourgeois political groups, to the Stalinists, to the Thomasites, to the Lovestoneites, and even to such grouplets as Oehler, etc.; or, in our own movement, than we did, for example, with the Sneevliet tendency — characterizing it politically on the basis of its established record over a period of years.

But that is just what the Cannonites did not do and have not done. Moreover, they did not even attempt to do it, for everybody knows that the attempt would be fruitless and doomed

---

Max Shachtman: "The Crisis in the American Party: An Open Letter in reply to Comrade Leon Trotsky", from *New International*, March 1940.

in advance to failure. Not because the leading comrades of the Minority have no record to look into. Quite the contrary. They have one and, as said above, it is easily available. There are the records of the Political Committee, containing the views of all the comrades on every question; there are our articles in the press; there are our programs and manifestoes; there are our brochures and speeches. Let them be cited. There has been no lack of bourgeois-patriotic, anti-Soviet, reformist pressure upon our party in the past. Show us from the record when and where any of our leading comrades yielded to this pressure! I say confidently: It cannot be done. What the record *will* reveal is that we were not among the last — so far as Burnham and Shachtman in particular are concerned, I say without false modesty, that we were the first — of those who constantly defended the revolutionary-internationalist position on war against all species of reformists, patriots, People's Fronters, Stalinists, centrists, left-centrists, ultra-leftists, and who constantly sought to make the party more alert to the need of combatting the war danger and all it involved in the ranks of the working class.

By what political right, then, on the basis of what facts in our record, are we charged with being a petty-bourgeois tendency?

The Cannon faction never answered this question. Its silence implied that the only "right" it exercised was the right of necessity; it *needed* to give this political characterization of us, whether grounded in fact or not.

You ask in your article: *"Why did Burnham and Shachtman themselves so unexpectedly* (the word "unexpectedly", Comrade Trotsky, is itself a sufficient comment upon the unassailability of our political record) *shift to the position of the 'League of Abandoned Hopes'?"* (that is, of the petty-bourgeois intellectuals-in-retreat). And you answer: *"It is not difficult to find an explanation. The Kremlin's participation in the Republican camp in Spain was supported by the bourgeois democrats all over the world. Stalin's work in Poland and Finland is met with frantic condemnation from the same democrats. In spite of all its noisy formulas the opposition appears to be a reflection inside the SWP of the mind of the 'left' petty-bourgeoisie. This fact unfortunately is incontrovertible".*

In face of what "appears to be" an "incontrovertible fact", how are we to account for the fact that the pressure of the bourgeois-democrats throughout the Spanish civil war was not reflected among us in a tendency to yield to People's Frontism and the imperialist patriotism with which it was imbued? It is true that some ultra-leftists in the party at that time accused us and Cannon and Trotsky of precisely such a tendency; but the "fact" was just as "incontrovertible" then as now.

Although the Cannonites never even sought to find in our political record a justification for their characterization of our group, you have, it is true, presented *one* article out of that record calculated to establish a connection between our present position and our past, and thereby to warrant your political justification. It is the article "Intellectuals in Retreat" by Burnham and Shachtman, about which we exchanged some correspondence earlier in 1939. Quoting sections of what the two authors wrote about dialectical materialism, you declare that my allegedly unprincipled bloc with Burnham in the sphere of sociology (the question of the class nature of the Soviet state) and then in the sphere of politics ("unconditional defense of the Soviet Union") followed logically from and paralleled my unprincipled "bloc with Burnham in the sphere of philosophy" — all of which adds up, in your view, to the characteristics of a typical petty-bourgeois tendency.

Comrade Trotsky, I am, as I wrote to you many months ago in reply to your letter of January 20, 1939, only a student in the field of philosophy. The exigencies of party work do not always permit one to extend his knowledge and understanding of dialectical materialism to the degree really demanded of a revolutionary Marxist. I have always been greatly impressed by the fact that a generation ago Lenin took time out from the daily political struggle, so to speak, in order to devote himself to special studies and a separate volume in defense of Marxian philosophy from its bourgeois and revisionist critics. Lack of time, and a more extensive knowledge which it would make possible, have prevented me and others from venturing, however modestly, into a systematic, rounded-out and thoroughgoing defense of dialectical materialism from its modern (above all, American) critics in the public press. Whenever I can read and study what you and our great teachers have written on the subject, I do so with the greatest attention. Yet I must say:

Your accusations are entirely unwarranted and baseless. They form an arbitrary construction calculated to buttress a political conclusion which cannot be buttressed objectively. Let me indicate the grounds for this statement.

You quote from our article (*New International*, Jan. 1939) a section which explains how the authors, having different opinions on dialectical materialism, nevertheless write a joint article against the petty-bourgeois opponents of Bolshevism. You conclude that in the opinion of the two authors, "the method is not of great importance, we shall meditate upon methods sometime when we have more leisure, but now we have other things to do".

Excuse me! Nowhere in the article is there a word that could justify such a conclusion. In your article, you quote one paragraph of our explanation for the joint authorship. You omit from the paragraph a key sentence which I underline here. We wrote:

"The two authors of the present article differ thoroughly on their estimate of the general theory of dialectical materialism, one of them accepting it and the other rejecting it. *This has not prevented them from working for years within a single political organization toward mutually accepted objectives, nor has this required on the part of either of them any suppression of his theoretical opinions, in private or public*".

But that is not all. The following paragraphs from our article are not less important.

"*During 1907-08, Lenin was, as is well known, carrying on a philosophical dispute with the Machists and also a sharp political fight against the Mensheviks. Gorky inclined, on the philosophical questions, towards the Machists, and apparently considered that this might prevent him from making common political cause with Lenin against the Mensheviks on the concrete questions then at issue. On February 25, 1908, Lenin wrote to Gorky as follows:*

'I believe I must tell you my view quite openly. A certain scrap among the Bolsheviks in the question of philosophy I now consider quite unavoidable. But to split up on that account would be stupid, in my opinion. We have formed a bloc for the carrying through of a certain tactic in the Social Democratic Labor party. This tactic we have been and are continuing to carry through without *differences of opinion (the only difference of opinion occurred in connection with the boycott of the Third Duma), but firstly it never reached such a sharp point among us even to hint at a split; secondly, it did not correspond to the difference of opinion of the materialists and the Machists, for the Machist Bazarov, for example, was, like myself, against the boycott and wrote about it (a large feuilleton in the* Proletarii *[the journal then under Bolshevik direction]).*

'To obstruct the cause of the carrying through of the tactic of the revolutionary social democracy in the Labor party because of disputes over materialism or Machism, would be, in my opinion, an inexcusable stupidity. We must be at loggerheads over philosophy in such a way that the Proletarii *and the Bolsheviks, as a faction of the party, are not affected by it. And that is entirely possible'.*

These wise, responsible and humane words are those, of course, of the real Lenin, not the sanctimonious Pope of the Stalinist fairy tales nor the one-party tyrant who is now being imaginatively constructed by Eastman, Hook and Harrison.

Shortly after the time of the above letter, interestingly enough, one of the Mensheviks declared in the Neue Zeit *that the philosophical dispute was identical with the political dispute.* Proletarii *made the following editorial statement:*

'In this connection, the editorial board of Proletarii, *as the ideological representative of the Bolshevik tendency, deems it necessary to present the following declaration: 'In reality this philosophical dispute is not a factional dispute and, in the opinion of the editorial board, it should not be one; any attempt to represent these differences of opinion as factional is thoroughly erroneous. Among the members of both factions there are supporters of both philosophical tendencies'.*"

In the light of these remarks and quotations from Lenin, I still fail to see, as I wrote you months ago, wherein I was wrong in writing the joint article with Burnham and in taking, with him, the position on the dialectic quoted above. Quite the contrary. Under the same circumstances, I would do it again and again tomorrow.

You speak of my "bloc with Burnham in the sphere of philosophy". But that is precisely the sphere in which we did *not* make a bloc! The sub-title of our article was: "A *Political* Analysis of Some of the Recent Critics of Bolshevism: Sidney Hook, Max Eastman, Eugene Lyons, Ben Stolberg, and Others". The article pursued exclusively political aims: the defense of Bolshevism, the Russian Revolution, the Fourth International, from the petty-bourgeois intellectual critics, and an attack upon their political program. I still consider that defense and that attack good — at least no one in our ranks has yet disagreed with it, not even Cannon (then or now).[1]

---

1. Immediately upon reading the article, Comrade Dunne sent the authors an air-mailed letter declaring that he was proud to be a member of the party that had them in it. Neither he nor any other member of the present Majority faction noticed the unprincipled bloc in the sphere of philosophy at that time. In fact, it was generally understood that this long article was not just a literary exercise against intellectuals of no account, but, through them, an exposition and defense of the Bolshevik program on the main political questions of the day.

You say: "By allying himself in this question with the anti-dialectician Burnham, Shachtman deprived himself of the possibility of showing why Eastman, Hook, and many others began with a philosophical struggle against dialectics but finished with a political struggle against the socialist revolution". I can agree with this, more or less. On my part, it was a conscious and deliberate "self-deprivation". But it was more than compensated for, in my opinion, by the fact that I was able to defend our fundamental political principles and program from revisionist attack, and to defend it jointly with a comrade whose views on philosophy differ from mine in such a way that Eastman, Hook and Co. might be able to exploit it *politically* (should I attack Burnham at the same time). Burnham's opposition to dialectics is not consistent, in my view (as mine is not in his view), with his support of the revolutionary program of the Fourth International. I say about his philosophical views (as he does about mine) that, *in the long run*, they will or may have fatal effects upon his political position. Meanwhile, to the greatest possible extent, let us unite to defend that political position, which we hold in common with the rest of the Fourth International, against all its critics. If, in that connection, we have occasion to speak of philosophical questions, let us make it perfectly clear that on that subject we do not agree.

You consider that an unprincipled bloc. If it is a bloc at all, I think it is a good one. If Burnham and Shachtman were to write a joint article on *philosophy*, or specifically on Marxian dialectics, that would be unprincipled. To declare a *temporary* truce on philosophy, while the revolutionary political position is put forward — that is not unprincipled, rather it is a service to the party[2].

Rosa Luxemburg may have been able to write more thorough criticisms of Kautsky and Bernstein during the war if she had also attacked their revisionism in the sphere of philosophy. But in that case, Liebknecht would not have written or signed these criticisms with her, because of his well-known opposition to dialectical materialism. The philosophical front had to wait under the press of more urgent problems and disputes. My dispute with Burnham on the philosophical front will also have to wait — not because I believe, as you so unjustly write, that the dialectic does not matter, but because there are more urgent problems to settle and because Burnham is not making the dissemination of his philosophical views his main preoccupation in the party or even one of his preoccupations[2] and because — like virtually all the other leading members of the party who accept dialectical materialism — I do not yet feel sufficiently equipped to write the kind of defense of dialectical materialism which it deserves. Meanwhile, I repeat, I am ready to make a "bloc" with Burnham on the defense of the revolutionary program of the Fourth International, and to make it a hundred times over.

In the same letter to Gorky (Feb. 25, 1908), Lenin writes: "Plekhanov considered Bogdanov at that time as an ally in the struggle against revisionism, but as an ally who was wrong in so far as he went along with Ostwald and further with Mach". (That is, Bogdanov was a non-Marxist, a Machist, in the sphere of philosophy.) "*In the spring and summer of 1904, Bogdanov and I finally joined together as Bolsheviks and constituted that tacit bloc,* the bloc which tacitly excluded philosophy as a neutral field, *which lasted throughout the whole period of the revolution and gave us the possibility of carrying through jointly in the revolution that tactic of the revolutionary social democracy which, in my deepest conviction, was the only correct one*". (My emphasis — MS).

Wherein does what you call my "bloc with Burnham in the sphere of philosophy" differ from

---

2. If Burnham will forgive me for the comparison, let me quote what Lenin wrote about priests in the party: "*If a priest comes to cooperate with us in our work — if he consistently performs party work, and does not oppose the party program — we can accept him into the ranks of Social Democracy, for the contradictions between the spirit and principles of our program and the religious convictions of the priest could, in these circumstances, be regarded as a matter in which he contradicts himself, as one which concerns him alone. A political party cannot examine its members to see if there are any contradictions between their philosophy and their party program. Of course, such a case would be a rare exception even in Western Europe; it is hardly possible in Russia. But if, for example, a priest joined the Social Democratic party, and made it his chief and almost exclusive business to propagate religious views, then, of course, the party would have to expel him*" (May 26, 1909). Lenin would not write a joint article with a priest on religion; but he would not hesitate, I am sure, to write one with a priest-party-member in defense of the party's political position, explaining therein that he finds "the religious convictions of the priest... a matter in which he contradicts himself". With due respect for the difference in proportions, and in the person involved, the same applies in the case I am discussing.

Lenin's bloc with Bogdanov? Why was the latter principled and ours unprincipled? I should be very much interested to know the answer to this question.

How is it possible, some comrades ask, for Burnham, whose views on philosophy are not Marxian, to come to political conclusions which are Marxian? It would be quite sufficient to answer: It is possible, as may be demonstrated by *facts*. Burnham's position on the dialectics of nature, for example, did not prevent him from arriving at the political conclusions embodied in the program of the Fourth International, any more than the complete ignorance of dialectics on the part of some comrades prevents them from arriving at the same political conclusions.

Does this mean that the materialistic dialectic, the dialectical method, "are not important"? It means nothing of the kind. It does mean, however, that there is a contradiction, an inconsistency, in Burnham's position. This has not prevented the party as a whole from collaborating with Burnham on innumerable political questions, from presenting him as an authorized party spokesman, from appointing him an editor of its theoretical journal. By the same token, it does not and will not prevent me from collaborating with him on all those political questions wherein we agree.

The connection between a philosophical and a programmatic position, a philosophical and a political position, holds only "in the last analysis". The connection is not always direct and immediate. Political positions are not directly deduced from philosophical positions by means of concrete and scientific analysis. Lenin could speak of "our comrades in politics and opponents in philosophy" without revealing an inconsistency anywhere except in the comrades referred to. Both Engels and Lenin, furthermore, pointed out that the modern scientist, for all his "opposition" to dialectical materialism, is compelled to one degree or another to employ the dialectical-materialist method in his concrete scientific work. The materialist theory of knowledge, Lenin wrote, is one "which natural science instinctively holds". That is often true of the science of politics, too; and I have observed it more than once not only in the case of Comrade Burnham but of others as well.

These are, briefly, some of the reasons why I must reject not only your argument about the "unprincipled bloc" in philosophy, but also your reference to the Burnham-Shachtman article as a justification for characterizing our group as a petty-bourgeois tendency. As for the Cannon faction and the question of dialectical materialism, the less said on the subject the better for the faction. Following your article, its spokesmen may try their utmost to parade as the intransigent champions of Marxian philosophy, but the indifference to theoretical questions — to say nothing of philosophical questions — and even the contempt towards such questions which most of its representative leaders have fostered, is too notorious in the ranks of the party to require elaboration here.

The Burnham position on this, the second, question is bad enough, you write, but *"even worse and more dangerous, unfortunately, are those eclectics who express the idea that the class character of the Soviet state 'does not matter', since the direction of our policy is determined by 'the character of the war'. As if the war were an independent super-social substance; as if the character of the war were not determined by the character of the ruling class, that is, by the same social factor that also determines the character of the state. Astonishing how easily some comrades forget the ABCs of Marxism under the blows of events!"*

Who are the "eclectics who express the idea that the class character of the Soviet state 'does not matter'"? Who has said it? written it? and when and where? I know of no such comrade and no such document.

What then is our position? Simply this: It is impossible to deduce directly our policy towards a specific war from an abstract characterization of the class character of the state involved in the war, more particularly, from the property forms prevailing in that state. Our policy must flow from a concrete examination of the character of the war in relation to the interests of the international socialist revolution. Our fundamental position on this question has already been stated in the document on the Russian question presented by the Minority of the Political Committee. Let me elaborate some aspects of it here so that we may see how the different viewpoints are manifested in theory and in practice.

What is the position of the Cannon group, boiled down to its essentials? The nationalized property determines the class character of the Soviet Union as a workers' state. The Stalinist régime is based upon the forms of property created by the October Revolution, which are progressive and must be defended from imperialist attack. Consequently, in a war between the Soviet Union and a capitalist state, we are for the unconditional defense of the Soviet Union, for the victory of the Red Army and therefore for material and military support of the Red Army.

You add, Comrade Trotsky, that war is not "an independent super-social substance" and its character is determined by the character of the ruling class, "that is, by the same social factor that also determines the character of the state" — the property forms, in this case, the nationalized property.

In spite of my recently-acquired bad philosophical reputation, I cannot accept the clear implication of this position because I do not consider it a *dialectical view of the problem*. That is, it is based upon abstractions and not upon material realities considered in their dialectical inter-relationships.

According to this standpoint, private property is the social factor that determines the character of the capitalist state, the same factor also determining the character of the capitalist ruling class, which in turn determines the character of the wars carried on by it. And what holds true of the capitalist state, holds true, with the necessary changes, of the workers' state.

In the first place, to speak of "capitalist state" and "workers' state" is to speak in terms of abstractions which do *not*, by themselves, answer the question of the character of a given war.

The Germany of 1870 was not a feudal but a capitalist state, in which private property relations were predominant; this capitalist state conducted an historically *progressive* war (even under Bismarck and Wilhelm I) against Bonapartist France, its oppressor. The Germany of 1914, also a capitalist state in which private property relations were predominant, conducted a *reactionary* (imperialist) war against France. The same social class, based on the same property relations, was in power in the two countries both in 1870 and in 1914. If these factors alone, considered abstractly, determined the character of the war, it would be impossible for us to distinguish the progressive from the reactionary war.

The Italy of 1859 conducted a war against Austria and the Italy of 1915 conducted a war against Austria. The first war of these two wars has always been characterized as progressive by the Marxists; the second, as reactionary. What determined the characters of these wars? In the case of both countries, in both epochs, the ruling class was the same and was based on the same property relations.

The difference between the two epochs (and the two wars) lay in this: the *young* bourgeoisie was progressive because it fought for the establishment of national boundaries, for the establishment of the great national states of Europe, against feudal decay, particularism and atomization. The establishment of the great national (capitalist) states was progressive in its time not only because it broke down the feudal barriers to the development of the productive forces, but because it created the most favorable arena for the final struggle of an independent proletariat against the last exploiting class. With the development of imperialist decay of capitalism, the same social order with the same ruling class is capable of fighting only reactionary wars. Where it was once permissible for the Italian proletariat to support even King Victor-Emmanuel of the House of Savoy and the Italian bourgeoisie in their war for the national state (for freedom from Austrian oppression), it became impermissible for the proletariat to support the House of Savoy and the Italian bourgeoisie in their war "for the national state" against Austria in 1914. Moreover, it is impermissible for the proletariat to support the Italian ruling class today *even in a war against a feudal state* — Ethiopia.

If we go by abstractions alone, we cannot explain why the war of a capitalist state like Italy against a feudal (semi-feudal) monarchy like Austria was progressive in 1859 and a war of a capitalist state like Italy against a feudal monarchy like Ethiopia was reactionary in 1935.

The ultra-leftists, you will remember, also proceeded from such abstract deductions — "capitalist state — capitalist war" — in the case of the Spanish civil war, and therefore denied the admissibility of defending the Loyalist forces against the Fascist forces.

The character of the war fought by Bismarck in 1870 could not be determined *exclusively* or *immanently* from the character of the ruling class and its property basis, but from the social and political aims of the ruling class *at that time*, i.e. from its concrete historic role. From above, by bureaucratic-military (as against Jacobin-plebeian) means, it is true, Bismarck and the Junkers had as their aim the national liberation and unification of Germany from French and Russian oppression. That was historically progressive. When, at the end of the war, they aimed at expansion and annexation (the seizure of Alsace and Lorraine), the war was transformed into a reactionary war which was mercilessly condemned by Marx and Engels. But war is not an "independent, super-social substance", you say; war and the aims of war are not divorced from the social (social-economic) basis on which it is fought. That is true, of course. But the connection is not *automatic*, not mechanical or one-directional; it is a dialectical connection in which, very often, the *political régime* is the *primary* or immediate determining force, and the economic "régime" determines only *"in the last analysis"*.

A most instructive (and timely) exposition of the inter-relationship between the economic base and the political superstructure is contained in Lenin's famous polemical speech on the trade union question on December 30, 1920:

"Comrade Trotsky speaks of the 'workers' state'. Permit me, that is an abstraction. When we wrote on the workers' state in 1917, that was understandable; but when one says today: 'Why defend the working class, defend it against whom, there is no longer a bourgeoisie, we have a workers' state', one commits an obvious mistake. The joke of it is precisely this, that it is not quite a workers' state. Therein lies one of the basic mistakes of Comrade Trotsky!... Our state is in reality not a workers' state, but a workers' and peasants' state. From that follows a great deal... But still more. From our party program the following comes out — a document which is quite familiar to the author of the ABC of Communism — from this program it comes out that our state is a workers' state with bureaucratic deformations. We had to paste this — how shall we put it? — sorry label on it. That is the result of the transition. And now, do the trade unions have nothing to defend in such a practically-arisen state, can we even do without them for the protection of the material and spiritual interests of the universally organized proletariat? That is theoretically a perfectly false consideration. That leads us into the realm of abstraction or of the ideal which we shall have attained in 15-20 years, but I am not even convinced that we shall attain it in such a short period... Our present state is such that the inclusively-organized proletariat must defend itself and we must utilize these labor organizations for the protection of the workers against their state and for the protection of our state by the workers".

And later, on the same subject (Jan. 25, 1921), in speaking of "Politics and Economics, Dialectics and Eclecticism", Lenin emphasized: *"Politics is the concentrated expression of economics — I repeated in my speech, for I had already heard earlier the absurd reproach, inadmissible on the lips of a Marxist, that I treat the thing 'politically'. The primacy of politics over economics must serve as the unconditional rule. To argue otherwise means to forget the ABC of Marxism... The question stands only thus (and, Marxistically, cannot stand otherwise): without the correct political attitude towards the thing, the class in question cannot maintain its rule and consequently cannot fulfill its productive tasks either".*

I permit myself one further quotation, from Engels' letter to Conrad Schmidt (Oct. 27, 1890): *"The new independent (political) power must, of course, submit to the movement of production as a whole. But it also reacts, by virtue of the strength of its immanent, i.e. its once borrowed but gradually developed relative independence, upon the conditions and course of production. There is a reciprocity between the two unequal forces; on the one side, the economic movement; on the other, the new political power which strives for the greatest possible independence and which having once arisen is endowed with its own movement".*

Engels wrote the above with reference to a capitalist state. It applies with a hundred-fold multiplied force to the Soviet Union, where the political super-structure (the Stalinist state apparatus) has acquired a degree and type of independence from its social basis without parallel, at least in modern times.

Now, what importance have these quotations from Lenin and Engels in our present dispute? The Cannonites deduce their policy in the following simple, undialectical way: The economy is progressive, consequently the wars fought against capitalist states by the Stalinist régime, which bases itself on this economy, are also progressive. The quotation from your article, cited above, to the effect that the character of the war is determined by the character of the economy, follows the same line of thought.

It may be replied that this charge is groundless and a distortion of the position held by you and by the Cannon group. It may be pointed out that we have all spoken for years of a *degenerated* workers' state; that we have advocated for some time a *political* revolution, basing ourselves on that very contradiction between the social basis and the political régime; and that in your latest article you write directly that "in our struggle for the overthrow of the bureaucracy we base ourselves on this contradiction".

This reply is obviously based on fact. I do not for a moment intend to create a different impression. All I contend, in this connection, is that this all-important contradiction is not consistently considered and applied in the case of the wars conducted by the Stalinist régime.

Just as it was possible 20 years ago to speak of the term "workers' state" as an abstraction, so it is possible today to speak of the term "degenerated workers' state" as an abstraction. Just as it was once necessary, in connection with the trade union problem, to speak concretely of what *kind* of workers' state existed in the Soviet Union, so it is necessary to establish, in connection with the present war, the *degree* of the degeneration of the Soviet state. The dialectical method of treating such questions makes this mandatory upon us. And the *degree* of the degeneration cannot be established by abstract reference to the existence of nationalized property, but only by observing the realities of living events.

The Fourth International established, years ago, the fact that the Stalinist régime (even though based upon nationalized property) had degenerated to the point where it was not only capable of conducting reactionary wars against the proletariat and its revolutionary vanguard, and even against colonial peoples, but did in fact conduct such wars. Now, in our opinion, on the basis of the actual course of Stalinist policy (again, even though based upon nationalized property), the Fourth International must establish the fact that the Soviet Union (i.e., the ruling bureaucracy and the armed forces serving it) has degenerated to the point where it is capable of conducting reactionary wars even against capitalist states (Poland, Estonia, Lithuania, Latvia, now Finland, and tomorrow Rumania and elsewhere). This is the point which forms the nub of our difference with you and with the Cannon faction.

It is necessary to emphasize that there is a tremendous difference between the (relative) independence of the political régime in any given capitalist state and in the present Soviet state. Be it the democratic United States, constitutional-monarchical England, republican France or Fascist Germany, the political régime in each instance is the one best suited to preserve private property; in any case, that is its essential role. Even in Fascist Germany, where the bourgeoisie has been politically expropriated, we have said that the fascist régime is the *only* one under which capitalist private property can be preserved. In the Soviet Union, on the contrary, our program and theses point out that the political régime (the Stalinist bureaucracy) does not preserve but constantly *undermines* the social-economic basis of the Russian Revolution. It is not only, as Engels put it, "endowed with its *own movement*", and that to an exceptionally high degree, but this movement conflicts violently with "the movement of production as a whole". Put in more plainly political terms, the interests of the bureaucracy conflict with the interests of maintaining nationalized economy as the basis for the transition to socialism — the nationalized economy which is all we can defend in the Soviet Union.

Now, it is not the nationalized economy that goes to war; it is not the economy that decides when the war should be declared or started, or against whom it should be directed, or how it should be conducted. Nor does the working class make these decisions — either directly or indirectly — for it is gagged and fettered and straitjacketed. The decisions and direction of the war are *entirely* in the hands of the bureaucracy, which "is endowed with its *own movement*", that is, with its own social, economic and political interests, which are reactionary through and through.

Here we need not confine ourselves to theoretical speculation and argument. The invasion of Poland, the conquest of the three other Baltic states, the invasion of Finland — these make up in fact the reactionary war of the Stalinist bureaucracy. They are reactionary from a number of standpoints. They are reactionary because they drive the proletariat and the peasantry into the arms of imperialist patriotism, that is, they do not accentuate the class struggle but facilitate the submission of the proletariat to its class enemy. They are reactionary because they are not conducted for the defense of the Soviet Union (i.e. the preservation of nationalized property from imperialist conquest and colonization), but are conducted in agreement with Hitlerite imperialism. They are reactionary because they are not conducted for the defense of the Soviet Union, but are conducted for the greater glory, prestige, power, and revenue of the counter-revolutionary bureaucracy. They are reactionary because they are not defensive wars (I speak not in the military-technical or diplomatic sense, but in the historical-political sense), but wars of annexation — wars of what we call Stalinist-imperialism.

We *advocated* and urged support of a war to defend the Soviet Union from imperialist attack. In that case, we did not insist upon democratic formalities or even democratic realities as a condition for our defense. We said — the Minority continues to say it — that if the imperialists assail the Soviet Union with the aim of crushing the last conquest of the October Revolution and reducing Russia to a bunch of colonies, we will support the Soviet Union unconditionally. That would be a progressive war, even under Stalin's command and despite Stalin's command. We would fight for a democratic All-Soviet Congress to take over the helm, but we would not demand it as a preliminary condition for our support.

We did *not* advocate the invasion of Poland or the Baltic countries or Finland. We did not consider such actions necessary for the defense of the Soviet Union, conceived in a revolutionary-internationalist sense. On the contrary, we condemned the invasions; you even called the invasion of Poland "criminal and shameful". To this day, I do not understand by what right of formal or dialectical logic we should, in the light of this, call upon the workers to give material and military support to the invasion, which has as its clear-cut objective that very annexation which we condemn and oppose.

The Fourth International is now fettered by a dogmatic interpretation of the formula "Unconditional defense of the Soviet Union" — which means in practise (see the resolutions of the Cannon group! see our party press!) that our policies are determined for us by the reactionary interests (and the secret treaties, no doubt!) of the Stalinist bureaucracy. When it decides to launch a war, we say, in effect: We do not agree with the timing of the war, with the aims it pursues; but now that Stalin has launched it, we must give it unconditional support, material and military aid. You will say that this is a distortion of the views of the Fourth International? Let us see.

In your article, you write: *"In order to give at least an ounce of sense to their new formula, the opposition attempts to represent the matter as if up to now we had unconditionally defended the international policy of the Kremlin government with its Red Army and GPU. Everything is turned upside down! In reality for a long time we have not defended the Kremlin's international policy, not even conditionally, particularly since the time that we openly proclaimed the necessity of crushing the Kremlin oligarchy through insurrection! A wrong policy not only mutilates the current tasks but also compels one to represent his own past in a false light".*

And in your letter to me, dated Nov. 6, 1939, you write: *"You interpret our past policy as unconditional support of the diplomatic and military activities of Stalin! Permit me to say that this is a horrible deformation of our whole position not only since the creation of the Fourth International but since the very beginning of the Left Opposition. Unconditional defense of the USSR signifies, namely, that our policy is not determined by the deeds, maneuvers or crimes of the Kremlin bureaucracy but only by our conception of the interests of the Soviet state and world revolution".*

I pass over my "horrible deformation" and my "representation of our own past in a false light", for I am conscious of no such crime. I have never said that our position was unconditional or any other kind of support of Stalin's international policy, and I must therefore set down this charge too as gratuitous and polemical.

Let me accept, then, your characterization of our traditional position. We have never defended, not even conditionally, Stalin's international policy; we give no unconditional support to the Kremlin's diplomatic and military activities. Our policy is not determined by the Kremlin's deeds and crimes. Good!

We have never supported the Kremlin's international policy, I repeat with you. Concretely, for example, we did not support the Kremlin's policy toward bourgeois Finland (or Poland, etc.) But what is war? War is the continuation of politics by other means. Then why should we support the war which is the continuation of the international policy which we *did not* and *do not* support? The Fourth International also told the Russian proletariat not to support the Kremlin's foreign policy. Then why should we now tell the Soviet workers to support a war which is the continuation of that policy? According to the resolution on Finland of the Cannon faction (which you support), the Fourth International tells the Russian workers not only to be Soviet patriots in general, but to give material and military support to Stalin's army in Stalin's war (what attitude the Finnish proletariat should take toward the Red Army — our fearless "unconditional defensists" do not indicate by a single syllable). On what conceivable basis can we advocate such a policy to the Russian working class? How can we defend it before the American working class, or even its vanguard elements?

Perhaps the Red Army should be supported on the grounds that in Poland, for example, "the new authorities invited the population to expropriate the landowners and capitalists", as you put it in your new article. I have heard the Cannon group spokesmen, following your line, argue that this demonstrates the essentially progressive character of Stalin's war and that it is a significant reflection of the fundamental fact that the Kremlin is based on state property, which determines the character of its wars. This argument, in my opinion, is wrong on two counts.

In so far as it is calculated to prove that the wars of the bureaucracy are automatically determined by the existence of state property in the Soviet Union, the calculation runs directly counter to our previous political analysis, yours in particular, and to the recently established facts.

1. Two years ago you wrote in a polemic against Burnham and Carter: *"Hitler defends the bourgeois forms of property. Stalin adapts the interests of the bureaucracy to the proletarian forms of property. The same Stalin in Spain, i.e., on the soil of a bourgeois régime, executes the function of Hitler (in their political methods they generally differ little from one another). The juxtaposition of the different social roles of one and the same Stalin in the USSR and in*

Spain equally well demonstrate that the bureaucracy is not an independent class but the tool of classes..." (*Internal Bulletin*, Dec. 1937, p.5). In other words, there is no automatism of state property in the Soviet Union that forces the Kremlin bureaucracy to establish or even to seek to establish similar property forms outside the Soviet Union. Quite the contrary, outside the Soviet Union, it follows in most cases the policy of preserving private property and massacring those who seek to abolish it (Spain!).

2. How account for the fact that in Estonia, Latvia and Lithuania capitalist private property has remained intact under the rule of Red Army. If the automatism of state property is so direct that it not only determines the character of Stalin's wars but also its own extension to the capitalist countries invaded by Stalin (i.e. "social-revolutionary measures, carried out via bureaucratic-military means", as you call it), why hasn't this been the case in the three Baltic countries? Also, why does the program of the Kuusinen "government" insist so explicitly not only on its non-Soviet, bourgeois-democratic political character, but on the fact that it does *not* propose to expropriate and nationalize property? You wrote in "USSR in War" the following words: *"Let us for a moment conceive that in accordance with the treaty with Hitler, the Moscow government leaves untouched the rights of private property in the occupied areas and limits itself to 'control' after the fascist pattern. Such a concession would have a deep-going principled character and could become the starting point for a new chapter in the Soviet régime and consequently for a new evaluation on our part of the nature of the Soviet state".* The Kuusinen program, I repeat, proposes only such a "control" over the banks and industries of Finland. Would you consider this "new chapter in the Soviet régime" a basis for revising our slogan of unconditional defense?

The second count deals with the "progressive aspect" of the Stalinist invasion. In the article "USSR in War" you said: *"The primary political criterion for us is not the transformation of property relations in this or another section of the territory, no matter how important these may be by themselves, but rather the change in the consciousness and the organization of the world proletariat, the raising of its capacity for defending the old conquests and accomplishing new ones. From this,* the only decisive standpoint, *the politics of Moscow, taken as a whole,* preserve completely their reactionary character *and remain the chief obstacle on the road to the world revolution".* (My emphasis — MS).

War is a continuation of politics, and if Stalinist policy, even in the occupied territory where property has been statified, preserves completely its reactionary character, then the war it is conducting is reactionary. In that case, the revolutionary proletariat must refuse to give the Kremlin and its army material and military aid. It must concentrate all efforts on overturning the Stalinist régime. That is not our war! Our war is against the counter-revolutionary bureaucracy at the present time!

In other words, I propose, in the present war, a policy of revolutionary defeatism in the Soviet Union, as explained in the statement of the Minority on the Russian question — and in making this proposal I do not feel myself one whit less a *revolutionary class patriot* than I have always been.

You find our resolution on Finland ridiculous because it says that in applying the strategy of revolutionary defeatism on both sides, *"the Fourth International will, of course, take into account concrete circumstances — the military situation, the moods of the masses and also the differing economic relations in Finland and Russia".* Your comment is: "Definitely, nothing of this is comprehensible". Let me try to make it somewhat more comprehensible and less ridiculous.

In any country, whether we are defeatists or defensists, the *application* in the concrete of our strategical perspectives or slogans must take many things into consideration. For example, even under Kerensky, Lenin stood for the slogan of "transforming the imperialist war into a civil war". At one time, in the middle of 1917, he proposed the withdrawal of the slogan *in that form.* Why? Because of the military situation in the country and because of the moods of the masses. Moreover, taking into account precisely these moods — the fact that the masses were tried of the war and of fighting "in general" — the Bolsheviks *concretized* their perspective of civil war in the slogan of "peace". Again, taking into account the "military situation" during the Kornilov attack, the Bolsheviks again adapted their "civil war" perspective to the concrete situation. The sentence in our resolution which you ridicule so much was included mainly for the purpose of guarding against the vulgar misinterpretation of our position to mean that from now on, day in and day out, all we propose to do in Finland and in the Soviet Union is to repeat the phrase "revolutionary defeatism". As for taking into account the "differing economic relations" — this really speaks for itself. In Russia we tell the workers that they must establish their control over nationalized property. In Finland we tell the workers that they must first nationalize property after seizing power. When I write a resolution not about war but about the world *socialist* revolution, I shall take care, there too, to point out that in China and in the United States the Fourth International must take into account the differing economic relations, even though it is for the proletarian-socialist revolution in both lands. By the same token I will agitate for a political revolution throughout the Soviet Union, but in the Ukraine I will take into account the differing national element and there I will advocate, particularly, separation from the Kremlin. The whole point seems to me quite self-evident.

I cannot leave unmentioned your references to the "revolutionary" role of Stalinism in its recent invasions. *"In the first case (Spain), the bureaucracy through hangman's methods strangled a socialist revolution. In the second case (Poland) it gave an impulse to the socialist revolution through bureaucratic methods"*.

Here again, I find myself compelled to disagree with you. The bureaucratic bourgeois revolution — that I know of. I know of Napoleon's "revolution from above" in Poland over a hundred years ago. I know of Alexander's emancipation of the serfs "from above" — out of fear of peasant uprisings. I know of Bismarck's "revolution from above". I know that Hitler and Mussolini play with the idea of an Arab "national revolution" in Palestine out of purely imperialist and military reasons — directed against their rival, England. But the bureaucratic *proletarian* revolution — that I do not know of and I do not believe in it. I do not believe that it took place in Poland even for a day — or that it is taking place or is about to take place in Finland.

If Stalin "established" state property in the conquered territories in Poland, it was not at all because, as you imply elsewhere, he was "compelled" to do so on account of the irresistible force of state property in the Soviet Union. Stalin was perfectly willing to "share the power" with the Polish bourgeoisie, as he is doing it with the bourgeoisie of Lithuania, Latvia and Estonia, and on this basis: I will preserve intact your private property and you will turn over to me your political power, which I will assure with my army. This is what the Kremlin proposed during the negotiations with Anglo-French imperialism. The Polish bourgeoisie and landlords refused this "generous" offer for a division of power. The three Baltic countries had the offer imposed on them by force.

When the régime of the Polish Colonels collapsed under the blows of the German army, the bourgeoisie fled in every direction. In the Polish Ukraine and White Russia, where class exploitation was intensified by national oppression (the bourgeoisie of those territories was predominantly *Polish*), the peasants began to take over the land themselves, to drive off the landlords which were already half-in-flight. Even the garbled and censored reports of those days permit us to see that the workers were beginning to act similarly. In Vilna, a spontaneously formed "Soviet" was reported. The Red Army, entering Poland, encountered no resistance from the Polish bourgeoisie and its Army because there wasn't any to speak of. The Red Army came in as a *counter-revolutionary* force. Far from "giving an impulse to the socialist revolution" it strangled it (the Vilna "Soviet" was of course violently suppressed). Just what has since then been "nationalized", how it has been "nationalized" — I do not know and no one has yet been able to say exactly. In any case, I repeat with you that the nationalization, real or alleged, cannot be the *decisive criterion* for us. The Stalinist bureaucracy is capable only of strangling revolutions, not making them or giving an impulsion to them. To prove the contrary, some evidence must be produced, and I find none in your article.

I find even less for your — how shall I put it? — astonishing remarks about Finland. You say that we do not "mention by so much as a word that the Red Army in Finland expropriates large landowners and introduces workers' control while preparing for the expropriation of the capitalists".

True, not by so much as a word. Why? Because the first anyone has heard in our party — *anyone!* — of the expropriation of the large landowners and the introduction of workers' control in Finland by the Red Army, is in your article. Where is this taking place? On what reports do you base yourself? There is no trace of workers' control in the Soviet Union itself; there is even less than that in Finland. That at least so far as my knowledge goes, and on this point I have questioned unavailingly many Cannonites.

You continue: *"Tomorrow the Stalinists will strangle the Finnish workers. But now they are giving — they are compelled to give* (why? why in Finland and not in Spain or Estonia?) — *a tremendous impulse to the class struggle in its sharpest form. The leaders of the opposition construct their policy not upon the 'concrete' process that is taking place in Finland, but upon democratic abstractions and noble sentiments"*.

Where is this "tremendous impulse to the class struggle" in Finland — and "in its sharpest form", to boot? We base our policy on "abstractions"? Let us grant that. On what do you base your statement about the tremendous impulse to the class struggle? No one — *no one*, I repeat — in our party has seen the slightest sign of it as yet. Perhaps you have seen credible reports about it; in which case such important news should appear in our press.

Again, you write: *"The Soviet-Finnish war is evidently (?!) already beginning to be completed with a civil war in which the Red Army finds itself at the given stage in the same camp as the Finnish petty peasants and the workers'.* You write a little further that the Stalinist policy is "the policy of exterminating finance-capital". And finally, you write: *"As for the Kremlin it is at the present time forced — and this is not a hypothetical but a real situation — to provoke a social revolutionary movement in Finland (in order to attempt to strangle it politically tomorrow)".*

Where is the civil war in Finland which is "evidently already beginning"? Unless you refer to the government of the idiotic scoundrel Kuusinen, we have not yet seen the first traces of that civil war — regardless of how much we should like to see it, no matter how anxious we are to develop a policy that will promote it, no matter how firmly we count upon its eventual materialization. Do you deduce this "civil war" from an abstract and false theoretical estimation of the rôle of the Kremlin bureaucracy, or is there some objective evidence that this "'concrete' process is taking place in Finland"?

Where is the "social revolutionary movement in Finland" that the Kremlin is "forced to provoke"? Is it perhaps the program of the Kuusinen "Democratic People's" government that is provoking it? That program is, formally, the program of a bourgeois "democracy". Since the beginning of the war, one of the reasons why we condemned the Finnish invasion as reactionary was precisely the fact that by it Stalin was driving the Finnish workers and peasants into a bourgeois-patriotic frenzy, into the arms of the Mannerheims, into the "sacred union" and "national unity". What evidence is there that this has changed? We repeat: we know of none, not a scintilla! It is possible and even likely that, as the Finnish bourgeois régime begins to crumble, the workers and peasants will separate from it and take the first steps on the road to independent class action. But there is every reason to believe that they will not take the road to the Stalinist camp, that they will not, as Cannon tells the Russian workers to do, give "material and military support" to the annexationist invaders. If they did, their tragedy would be no less than that which they are suffering today as the pawns of bourgeois-patriotism.

You speak of the Stalinists representing "the policy of exterminating finance-capital". I find it difficult to believe that you mean this literally. No, the role the Stalinists have played, above all outside the borders of the Soviet Union, has been that of conservative prop of the rule of finance-capital. The Kremlin's agency of finance-capital has not become overnight the latter's exterminator. It does not play a revolutionary role — any more than the Chinese national bourgeoisie played a revolutionary role, any more than Gutchkov played a revolutionary role in March, 1917 in Russia; the role of the Stalinist bureaucracy is counter-revolutionary.

Would I tell the Finnish workers to accept arms and ammunition from Stalin? Would I tell the Hindu workers and peasants to accept arms and ammunition from Hitler? That is how you pose the question. My answer is: Of course I would! I would take arms for the revolution from Hitler, or Mussolini, or Stalin, or Daladier, or a Caucasian mountain bandit! If I get them free of charge, so much the better. But it would not follow for me that just because I welcome arms smuggled to me in Palestine by Hitler, that I would welcome Hitler if he sent *his army* to Palestine, or that I would urge *anybody* to give that army "material and moral support". The "character" of Hitler's intervention in Palestine would have changed. By the same token, when Stalin is conducting a reactionary, annexationist war in Finland, I would readily accept arms from him if I were a revolutionist in Finland (although, in that case, nine chances out of ten I would receive his "armed aid" in the form of a bullet in the heart or a bayonet in the throat); and under certain conditions, *given a favorable relation of forces* between his army and the Finnish revolutionary movement, I would even seek a practical military working agreement with him; but it does not follow from this that I call upon anyone now to give him "material and military support" in his reactionary war.

I repeat, I do not believe in the bureaucratic proletarian (socialist) revolution. I do not mean by this merely that I "have no faith" in it — no one in our movement has. I mean that I do not consider it possible. I reject the concept not out of "sentimental" reasons or a Tolstoyan "faith in the people" but because I believe it to be scientifically correct to repeat with Marx that the emancipation of the working class is the task of the working class itself. The bourgeois revolution, for a series of historical and social reasons, could be made and was made by other classes and social strata; the bourgeoisie could be liberated from feudal rule and establish its social dictatorship under the aegis of other social groups. But the proletarian revolution cannot be made by others than the proletariat acting as a mass; therein, among other things, it is distinguished from all preceding revolutions. No one else can free it — not even for a day.

You support the Cannon faction as the proletarian, Marxist group; you condemn the Minority as the petty-bourgeois group, and propose that it be disposed of accordingly. Reading your arguments, I involuntarily ask myself: How can the theoretical, political and practical leader of the struggle against the "troika" and then against Stalinism, come to such conclusions?

Comrade Trotsky, I have always been as close a student of the history of the revolutionary movement as possible. I have never considered such a study to be a substitute for active participation in the making of revolutionary history, but rather as a guide for such participation. My interest in this history is not so much for its own sake, but above all in order to learn how to avoid mistakes of the past and to emulate that which was worthy. In my own way, I have tried to keep unforgotten and to live up to the *best traditions* of a hundred years of revolutionary Marxism. So little do I ignore the traditions of our movement that I am sometimes perhaps rightly accused of "archivistic" extremes. In extenuation for this sin I have always pleaded the need of keeping alive in this generation of revolutionists — my generation — the best traditions of the past generations, to establish the idea and spirit of revolutionary continuity. If my comrades sometimes jokingly chide me for my predilection for "precedents" — they have some reason for it. In *good and tested* precedents, I often seek and find a "short-cut" in revolutionary politics. A "short-cut" in this sense, that I do not believe every single problem must be approach from the very beginning, as something brand new, as something which past experience of the movement cannot guide us in solving.

If, therefore, I refer in this section of my letter to experiences of the past, you will understand that it is not done in a brittle polemical sense, but rather in the sense of helping myself and the movement find the right road with the help of illumination from that past.

Burnham says it is not a workers' state; Abern says it is; Shachtman represents, as Hansen so tellingly puts it, the Doubtist faction. Their bloc on the question of "defense" and on the "organizational" question is therefore unprincipled, and typically petty-bourgeois. Let us grant for the moment that the "bloc" is as described. How many times have you been attacked by the Stalinists on the same grounds?

You made a bloc with the Zinovievist (Leningrad) Opposition in 1926. The Platform of the Opposition Bloc "evaded" the fundamental question of the theory of the permanent revolution. Why? The Stalinists insisted that the basic principled differences between Leninism (their "Leninism"!) and "Trotskyism" (revolutionary Marxism) revolved around the theory of the permanent revolution. The Zinovievists, who agreed basically with the Stalinist conception of the theory, agreed with you (that is, the Moscow, 1923, Opposition) to say that the theory was not at issue, and this was written into the documents of the Bloc. Was it unprincipled? I do not think so. The Bloc was united on the main political tasks before the Soviet Union and the International.

In the Bloc, at least for a considerable period of time, were not only you and the Zinovievists, who of course considered the Soviet Union a workers' state, but also the Democratic Centralists, who considered that it was not a workers' state. Yet, though you were formally closer to the Stalin-Bukharin group on that question, the Democratic Centralists supported the Opposition platform. Was that unprincipled? Again, I do not think so. In reply to one of the DC group comrades, Borodai, who asked you why steps should not be taken to reconsolidate the "forces of the Bolshevik guard", you wrote in 1928: *"Unfortunately the question is not rightly posed by you. It was not I who separated myself from the DC, but the DC group, which belonged to the general Opposition, separated itself from us... The initiative for the unification (into the Bloc) came from the DC. The first conferences with the Zinoviev people took place under the chairmanship of Comrade Sapronov (DC leader). I say this absolutely not as a reproach. For the Bloc was necessary and was a step forward".*

You made a bloc — rather, you were in one faction — with Radek, who characterized the famous Canton bourgeois government as a "peasants' and workers' government". The Zinovievists were for the "democratic dictatorship of the proletariat and peasantry" in China; you were for the proletarian revolution supported by the peasantry. The United Opposition, by the way, adopted the essential Zinovievist formula. The Stalinists sought to exploit these differences to the full. Yet the Bloc there too, except for mistakes that cannot be characterized as fundamental in my opinion, was principled: all its members agreed (more or less) on the basic and immediate political tasks in China. Suppose one were to say: on the fundamental principled question of the class nature of the Chinese revolution, Zinoviev had the Stalinist (i.e., petty-bourgeois) position (democratic dictatorship), while Trotsky said "it does

576

not matter". Wherein would such a reproach differ from the one you direct at us today?

We say in our resolution that we, the Minority, are united on the basic and immediate tasks of the Fourth International in the Soviet Union and the other belligerents. To the extent that we differ among ourselves on the "terminological" or "sociological" question — the class nature of the Soviet state — each comrade will vote on this question, if it is put, as he has voted in the past, according to conviction. Do you find that unprincipled? You wrote me on December 10, 1930 (the letter is to be found in my introduction to your book, *Problems of the Chinese Revolution*) that though Radek was always with Zinoviev on the question of the Chinese Communist Party withdrawing from the Kuomintang, *"up to 1926, I always voted independently in the Political Bureau on this question, against all the others"*. When the Bloc was formed, the majority was against you on this point. *"But since it was a question of splitting with the Zinovievists, it was the general decision that I must submit publicly and acquaint the Opposition in writing with my standpoint... Now I can say with certainty that I made a mistake by submitting formally in this question"*. Let me then ask if that made the Opposition Bloc unprincipled or that an error was merely made.

You made a number of additional and minor points against us which are hardly meritorious. You say our resolution "could be signed, perhaps with slight changes, by the Bordigists, Vereecken, Sneevliet, Fenner Brockway, Marceau Pivert and the like..." I assure you that also "perhaps with slight changes", Cannon's resolution would be signed by Oehler, Stamm, Marlen, and to the best of my knowledge, Molinier. You say our criticisms, our "terminology" in particular, is copied from the bourgeois press. With as much reason, I could reply that such terms as "Thermidor", "Bonapartism" and "totalitarian", applied by us to the Stalinist régime, were used much earlier by the bourgeois and Menshevik press. With different connotations? Different aims? Yes, but that is true in both cases.

You raise the question of Comrade Abern. It would have been preferable if that were dealt with by Cannon. You write: *"Abern, and only he, has his own traditional group which grew out of the old Communist Party and became bound together during the first period of the independent existence of the Left Opposition"*. On what do you base this — permit me to say it — fantastic charge? Of the comrades in our party today who "grew out of the old Communist Party" and who have been associated more or less consistently on the same side as Comrade Abern, and are with the Minority today, I can think of only *one* name. I would be interested in hearing at least a couple of more names! What is the basis of your information, Comrade Trotsky?

I have no intention of evading the famous "Abern question". I have had in the past many sharp disputes with the old Weber-Abern group in general, and with Comrade Abern in particular. Indeed, I once wrote a very harsh and bitter polemical document against that group which Cannon flatteringly calls a "Marxist classic". If a historical study-circle were to be formed tomorrow to consider that period in our party history, there is much in that document I would repeat, much I would moderate, much I would discard. Abern, I suppose, would act in kind. But we are *not* discussing that period, and I find it impossible to shape my politics on the basis of outlived disputes.

You know that before the fight against the Weber-Abern faction, there had been a sharp dispute between Cannon's faction and one led by me, a dispute lasting several years. One of the reasons I broke with many of the members of my then faction was because I insisted against them that the issues in the fight against Cannon had either lost their urgency or had the possibility of becoming moderated. Consequently, it was necessary to collaborate fraternally with the Cannon group on a new basis, and not continue a die-hard struggle on outlived or vague issues, or reminiscences.

I am against political feuds which go on endlessly like Kentucky feuds. I was against them when directed against Cannon. I am against them when directed at Abern.

Cannon knows how spurious it is to inject into the present discussion the "Abern question". He knows what every informed party leader, and many members, know, namely, that for the past several years at least there has been no such thing as an "Abern group". So true is this that at the Chicago convention of the party, two years ago, the slate for the Political Committee presented by Cannon and me had on it *four ex-"Abernites"* out of a total of *seven* members, i.e., a majority! So true is this that since that time Comrade Abern has been entrusted with some of the most responsible and even confidential tasks that the Political Committee could assign to him (a party-public document prevents me from going into detail on this point). At the last convention, in July, 1939, when the dispute arose over the "organization document" and later over the composition of the National Committee, Comrade Abern was in neither of the two contending groups, for which Cannon, in the debate, went out of his way to praise the "objectivity" and "organizational intelligence" of Abern!

577

I know what the Cannonites mean with their campaign against Abern. Abern is all right so long as he "comes along". However, the minute Abern expresses a different view from the Cannon leadership on an important question, then the campaign is launched against him not on the basis of any views he now defends but on the basis of a fight which is I-don't-know-how-many-years old. Here, too, I must remind you that you too joined with groups or "remnants" of groups against which you had fought vigorously in earlier years, which you and Lenin had even severely condemned — Workers' Oppositionists, Democratic Centralists, to say nothing of the Zinovievists. You will surely recall how the bureaucracy sought to concentrate the discussion not on the platform of the Opposition Bloc, but on what Zinoviev had written about Trotsky at one time, and vice versa, and about the "unprincipled mutual amnesty" they had extended each other.

You say that you and the Cannon group give a *class* characterization of the Minority, whereas "the opposition, on the contrary, precisely because of its petty-bourgeois character does not even attempt to look for the social roots of the hostile camp". I could answer this, in the first place, by emphasizing part of the preceding sentence: "Any serious factional fight in a party is always *in the final* analysis a reflection of the class struggle". Yes, generally and in the final analysis, but not at every given moment or with every factional grouping. I have no doubt of my ability to give many examples from the history of the Russian party after the revolution in which sharp factional fights took place; I think that it is doubtful if a clear class characterization could be given of all the factions involved. I could say, in the second and more important place, it is first necessary to prove (a) that the Minority represents a deviation from the proletarian Marxist line, (b) that this deviation is typically petty-bourgeois, and (c) that it is more than an isolated deviation — it is a tendency. That is precisely what has not been proved.

But is it true that the Minority has given no political characterization of the Cannon faction? It is somewhat surprising to read your article, to see in it reference to the allegedly long-lived Abern group, and to see not a single word about *the only permanent faction* in the party — the Cannon clique, the group of comrades you refer to euphemistically as "Cannon and his collaborators". When we speak of it as a permanent faction we do not confine ourselves to mere assertion. We are able to *prove* it from the records of the party, and we do prove it in our document on "The War and Bureaucratic Conservatism". How do you explain the existence of this faction-in-permanence, in season and out, during political disputes and during peace-times in the party?

We characterize this faction with the political designation: *"bureaucratic conservatism"*. Your comment on this is that we "see only 'conservatism', 'errors', 'bad methods' and similar psychological, intellectual and technical deficiencies". You consider our characterization of the Cannon faction to be "psychological". Excuse me, but I fail to understand. Let me quote from your polemic against the bureaucracy in the Russian party in 1923: *"The heterogeneous political ideology that now rises against bureaucratism can be controlled all the better, and it can be cleansed of all alien and harmful elements, if we take more seriously the road of the 'new course'. But that is impossible without a serious turn-about in the mentality and the intentions of the party apparatus. But on the contrary, we are now witnessing a new offensive of the latter, which eliminates all criticism of the 'old course', formally condemned but not yet liquidated, by treating it as a manifestation of factional spirit. If factions are dangerous — and they are — it is criminal to close one's eyes to the danger represented by the* bureaucratic conservative faction". (*The New Course*, p.43). Was that characterization of the then leadership of the party "psychological", "technical", "intellectual", and devoid of political or class significance? No more so than our present characterization of the Cannon faction!

You ask us to support this faction, or at least to subordinate ourselves to it. You declare that this is necessary because we are the petty-bourgeois revisionist tendency — Cannon the proletarian Marxist tendency. If your class characterizations of the two groups were correct, your proposed solution of the party crisis might have validity. In that case, and in accordance with our class doctrine, the petty-bourgeoisie must *follow* the proletariat, and not lead it or even be joint leader of the party with it. The petty-bourgeoisie, if it is admitted into the party *as an organized group*, should properly be given a "second-class" status. If it threatens to take over the leadership of the party, the proletarian wing has no other choice before it save to declare its organizational independence immediately, or in any case to have a split perspective precisely in view of the war situation. That is the political meaning I get from the concluding paragraphs of your article.

This solution we cannot and will not accept, Comrade Trotsky. We do not believe Cannon represents the proletarian, Marxist tendency — he represents the tendency of bureaucratic conservatism. And against this tendency, and particularly against its position on the Russian

578

question (which represents an increasingly clear political capitulation to Stalinism), we must continue our struggle until our views triumph.

Your support of the Cannon faction is very firm, Comrade Trotsky; but it is very wrong. This time, I am unable to support your standpoint, a fact I establish with regret and even reluctance. I can only hope that the divergences narrow down in the period to come. But to expect me or my associates to support the Cannon faction and its position, is to expect what we cannot and will not give. Several years ago, you stood insistently, even against widespread opposition, in support of the Molinier group in France. It, too, you represented as the revolutionary proletarian Marxist tendency. I do not hold that the opponents of Molinier represented — all of them, or on all questions — the best elements in the French or European movement. But in the end you declared openly that Molinier had nothing in common with the Fourth International or with the working class movement.

It goes without saying that Cannon is not Molinier, and it would be useless to try to make me appear to say so. But I believe that just as you were mistaken in your judgment of Molinier, so you are mistaken in our present dispute in your judgment of Cannon and his clique. Just as you later acknowledged your wrong estimate of Molinier, I am firmly convinced that you will be obliged to make a similar acknowledgement about the Cannon faction in time to come. Some six years ago, if my memory serves me rightly, you wrote a comment on the factional fight in the American section between the Cannon and Shachtman groups. In it you said that the party leadership (Cannon faction) represented a tendency toward Stalinist bureaucratism. You will be obliged, I am convinced, to reiterate that characterization in more elaborate, up-to-date form in the future.

In your personal letter to me, dated Dec. 20, 1939, which I permit myself to quote from, you write: "I believe that you are on the wrong side of the barricade, my dear friend". I should like to believe that this is a polemical metaphor. You add: "I don't hope to convince you with these lines, but I do express the prognosis that if you refuse now to find a way towards collaboration with the Marxist wing against the petty-bourgeois revisionists, you will inevitably deplore for years and years the greatest error of your life".

From all that I have said in this document you will understand why I find it impossible to accept your recommendation. For my part, I can only hope that your prognosis is wrong. In return, I can only say in a spirit which I believe you will understand to be animated by the objective interests of the cause and with a due sense of proportion: The support you are now giving to the Cannon faction leadership and its political position, you will have occasion in the not distant future to consider as one of the most serious mistakes in the history of the Bolshevik-Leninist movement.

January 1, 1940.

BURNHAM'S REPLY TO TROTSKY

Burnham says that despite his opposition to dialectics he has written many of the key policy documents of the SWP over the last few years, including the party's Declaration of Principles, and even the last conference resolution analyzing events in the USSR, apart from one or two paragraphs designating the USSR a degenerated workers' state: "... dialectics contributed to the resolution the 'fixed' category ('workers' state') of 'vulgar' and 'Aristotelian' thinking".

I DO NOT TAKE DIALECTICS SERIOUSLY as a scientific doctrine, but I take very seriously indeed the uses to which dialectics is put in some political disputes, and by Trotsky in the current dispute. I object, and very strongly, to the substitution of theological disputation in the manner of the Council of Nicaea (which split Europe over the question of whether the Son of God was of "one substance" or "similar substance" with the Father), of loose metaphors and platitudes about science and pseudo-science in the style of the 19th century popularizers of Darwin, for – clear discussion of the genuine issues of the politics of 1939 and 1940.

Consider: the opposition raises questions with references to the war, the Nazi-Soviet Pact, the actions of the Soviet Union, the invasion of Finland. The reply is: the problem is whether or not Russia is a workers' state. The opposition demonstrates convincingly that a decision on the definition of the class character of the Soviet Union cannot answer the strategic and tactical issues posed to the movement. The reply is: the problem is the law of dialectics. (There is a fourth stage which does not appear in written documents: the abominable personal gossip with which the Cannon clique corrupts its followers.) In an analogous manner, the opposition makes and proves concrete criticisms of the conservative and bureaucratic Cannon régime. The reply is: the problem is the alien petty-bourgeois social roots of the opposition.

Why is dialectics brought into the dispute? In the first instance, as an obvious and mechanical maneuver, which deceives no-one, of "trying to drive a wedge into the ranks of the opponents." But more generally: to evade issues that cannot be and have not been answered on their own legitimate plane, to escape from an inconvenient reality to a verbal jousting ground, to confuse and turn inside the attention of the membership from the actual problems that face them, to – in the century sanctioned way of all "authority", all "dogma", all bureaucracy – brand the critic as *heretic* so that his criticism will not be heard. The textbooks ("the school bench") give a name to this device: *Ignoratio Elenchi* or Irrelevant Conclusion. The remarks on it of Whately – a contemporary of Darwin, by the way – are not, however, themselves irrelevant: "Various kinds of propositions are, according to the occasion, substituted for the one of which proof is required;... and various are the contrivances employed to effect and conceal this substitution, and to make the conclusion which the sophist has drawn answer, practically, the same purpose as the one he ought to have established. I say 'practically the same purpose', because it will very often happen that some *emotion* will be excited – some sentiment impressed on the mind – (by a dextrous employment of this fallacy) such as shall bring men into the *disposition* requisite for your purpose, though they may not have assented to, or even stated distinctly in their own minds, the *proposition* which it was your business to establish."

Let us suppose, however, that I accept the entire first half of Trotsky's article, that I grant my errors on dialectics, and accept dialectics as the key to truth and socialism. What has changed with reference to the political issues in dispute, the problems discussed in the second half of his article? Nothing has been changed a centimeter. Everything remains just as it was when dialectics had never been mentioned. For Trotsky does not in any respect whatever establish any *connection* between what he says about dialectics in the first half of his article, and what he says about the defense of Russia, the Soviet-Finnish war, and the "orga-

James Burnham: "The politics of Desperation. Some notes on the article, 'A petty-bourgeois opposition in the Socialist Workers Party'", dated January 1940, and published in *New International*, April 1940. Abridged.

nizational question" in the second half. Does anyone doubt this? Let him re-read the article, and see for himself. It follows therefore that the entire discussion of dialectics is totally irrelevant – as Trotsky himself presents the discussion – to the political questions. "Consciousness grew out of the unconscious, psychology out of physiology, the organic world out of the inorganic, the solar system out of nebulae..." Very well; let it be so. Now show us how from generalizations of that type it follows – even by the most dialectical of logics – that... the Red Army is introducing workers' control in Finland and we ought to defend it.

The fact that Trotsky *thinks* and *says* there is a necessary connection between his dialectics and his politics has nothing to do with the question of whether there actually is such a connection. All through history, men have thought and said that there were connections between their scientific investigations or practical decisions on the one hand and their theologies or metaphysics on the other. Pasteur said that there was such a connection between his bacteriology and his Catholic faith; Einstein today between his field physics and his pantheistic idealism; Millikan finds God proved in his cosmic rays.

Either the dialectics is relevant or irrelevant to the empirical and practical questions in dispute. If it is irrelevant, to drag it in is scientifically useless. If it is relevant, the empirical and practical questions can in any case be settled on their own merits on the basis of the available evidence and our goals. In neither case is a decision as to dialectics required.

Trotsky writes: "To demand that every party member occupy himself with the philosophy of dialectics would be lifeless pedantry." I want to enquire: if it is true, as Trotsky claims, that dialectics is "the foundation of scientific socialism", if rejecting does, as he declares, define the one who rejects as an *alien class influence*, if dialectics is indeed the method whereby we can solve correctly political problems, then by what conceivable principle does Trotsky conclude that it would be "lifeless pedantry" for more than a few Party members to occupy themselves with it? Rather would we have to say that dialectics must be the first and last study of *all* party members if they wish to be consistent and clear-headed revolutionary socialists.

Or must we seek another kind of explanation for Trotsky's dictum: There is one doctrine – the "secret doctrine" – for the elite, the leaders, the inner circle; and another – the vulgar doctrine – for the mass, the ranks, the followers. What is the relation of the followers to the secret doctrine? They are not to know it, to study it, to test it in their own conscious and deliberate experience: that is excluded as "lifeless pedantry." But may they then consider it unimportant, or reject it? Not on your life: then they are alien class elements. No: they must *believe*, they must have *faith*. As for the doctrine itself, it is safe in the hands of the elite; *they* will bring it out on appropriate occasions (a sharp factional fight, for example) to smite and confound the enemy. For my own part, I do not believe in Faith.

My friend and colleague Max Shachtman (may he forgive me for the reference, as I must, perforce, forgive him for what he has recently written about me) says: I do not really understand much about dialectics; I am only a humble student of the subject; of course I believe in it as all good Marxists must. This attitude is not unique in Shachtman. Whenever I have talked to any pro-dialectics party comrade about dialectics – or tried to talk about it – I have been given the same response (except, to be complete, in the case of Wright, who seems to think he understands dialectics because its words so well express the conflicts and shifts and confusions in his own attitudes and actions.) We do not really understand it; we believe of course; we cannot formulate its laws; we cannot tell you how you can test them; some day we hope to get around to studying it. This response is as characteristic of pro-dialecticians in the Cannon clique as in the opposition. Few even pretend to "understand", for example, the first part of the Trotsky article which I am now discussing.

Now I ask Shachtman and all those comrades of the party; if you don't understand it, if you can't explain or prove it, why then do you "believe" it? Whence springs your faith?

Throughout the centuries, it has been characteristic of religious groups to have two doctrines: the "esoteric" doctrine of the "inner circle", the monopoly and carefully guarded secret of the high priests; and the "exoteric" doctrine of the "outer circle," for the followers. Is this not *exactly* the situation with dialectics – whether or not you "believe" in dialectics? And the existence of an esoteric doctrine is always potentially reactionary, anti-democratic. It is so because the esoteric doctrine is by the nature of the case irresponsible, not subject to control by the humble followers, a weapon in the hands only of the priests.

For the method which I advocate – the method of science – there is only one doctrine, available to all. And what it says is subject always to tests that can be made by any normal man. There is no revelation, and no short cut, and no prophet.

I conclude on dialectics with a challenge:

In the letter dated January 3rd it is clearly implied that my attitude toward dialectics is incompatible with my being editor of the theoretical journal of the party. In the article it is stated explicitly that my rejection of dialectics represents the influence of another class.

First I want to ask: Where in the program of the Socialist Workers Party or the Fourth International is a belief in dialectics made part of the programmatic basis of our movement, the acceptance of which defines the conditions of membership? And if it is not, by what right does Trotsky or any one else attack me politically or object to my editorship of an organ of the International *on the grounds of my attitude toward dialectics*?

Is not our movement founded on its program, decided by conventions representing the membership? Or – do we communists hide our views, and is our real program something different from our public and adopted program?

But if Trotsky is justified in what he says about dialectics, and the conclusions he draws in connection with dialectics, I say further:

Let him propose to the forthcoming convention that this lack of our program be filled, that the convention adopt a specific clause, to be added to the Declaration of Principles, affirming acceptance of the philosophy of dialectical materialism.

If he does not make such a proposal, then only one of two conclusions is possible: either what he is now writing about dialectics is not meant seriously, is mere polemical rhetoric for the faction fight of the moment; or dialectics is indeed an esoteric doctrine, not suited for the public opinion of the party to pass upon, but a private monopoly of the priests.

If he does make the proposal, it is true that he will have only one precedent in the history of labor politics: Stalin's program adopted at the Sixth Congress of the Comintern, in which the abandonment of Marxism was consummated. I confess that I should not like to feel that our movement is ready to regard such a precedent as appropriate.

If by a "workers' state" we mean that form of society transitional from capitalism to socialism, then Russia today can be considered a workers' state only on the basis of its nationalized economy. Of those various major features of the "transitional society" described in advance (in *State and Revolution*, for example) no one, absolutely no one in any political camp except that of the Stalinists themselves, maintains that any *other* socialist factor remains in Russia today except the nationalized economy. Nationalized economy must, therefore, in the view of those who hold that Russia is a workers' state, be a sufficient condition for so characterizing it, and by a workers' state Marxists have always meant, from Marx on, that form of society which is transitional from capitalism to socialism.

The assumption therein involved I, of course, reject. I hold that *at least* one other major condition is necessary for that form of society which is transitional to socialism – namely, workers' democracy; and that therefore Russia today is incorrectly characterized as a workers' state. This was Marx's opinion; and his opinion has been entirely confirmed by the experiences of the last fifteen years of Soviet history.

Nevertheless, even if the assumption is granted, if it is thus further granted that Russia today is a workers' state, this will not at all suffice to motivate a tactic of defense of the Soviet State and the Red Army in the present war (just as, conversely, if the assumption is denied and it is thus denied that Russia is a workers' state, this will not by itself suffice to motivate a tactic of defeatism). We cannot *deduce* a tactic of defense from our definition of the Soviet State any more than we could deduce it from the "law of the negation of the negation." Nor are we aided further in determining our tactic by the assumption that nationalized economy, in and by itself, divorced from the concrete social and political and historical relations which form the context of the nationalized economy, is "progressive" (an assumption which is involved in the initial assumption of our "dialectical" defenders of the workers' state doctrine – an assumption which effectively *eliminates* all the changing actual reality which they say dialectics teaches us to take into account, and substitutes: a static, abstract category.)

The general strategic aim of our movement is the world proletarian revolution (and socialism). We all hold (in words, at any rate) that this aim is now a goal not for the indefinitely remote future, but for the present period, that is, for the war and the post-war period. We concretize our goal in the statement of our "war aims" – united socialist states of Europe, the Americas, a free Asia and Africa, a world federation of socialist republics. Presumably we mean these seriously.

Any tactic we propose, therefore, can be justified only by *proof* that, directly or indirectly, it is in fact the best available means for reaching our general strategic goal.

Even granted, then, Trotsky's assumptions, granted that Russia is a workers' state, the tactic of defense can be justified only *if certain additional propositions are, in fact, true.*

These would have to include: (a) *Defense of the Red Army is in fact the best available means of defending the nationalized economy* (which for the purpose of discussion, let us assume to be in and of itself progressive); (b) *Defense of the Russian nationalized economy as a prima-*

ry task is the best available means, for promoting the world revolution.

But everyone grants (in words, at least) that the defense of Russia is not the *only* major necessary means for achieving our general strategic aim; other necessary means include, certainly: the overthrow of Stalinism; colonial revolts; the lifting of the revolutionary consciousness of the masses; the deepening of the class struggle throughout the world, in at least several major nations to the point of successful proletarian revolution. In and of itself, defense of the present (i.e. Stalinist) Russian state and the Red Army, even if 100 percent successful, would be of not the slightest value in achieving our goal; on the contrary, would make our goal impossible, since it would mean only the continuation in power and the extension of Stalinism.

Two propositions required by Trotsky to justify the tactic of defense therefore involve a third: (c) *Defense of Russia in the present war does, in fact, serve as the best available means, or as an integral part of the best available means, for promoting colonial revolts, the lifting of the revolutionary consciousness of the masses, the overthrow of Stalinism, the deepening of the class struggle throughout the world (including, naturally, Russia itself and those countries against which Russian military action is conducted), and the completion of this struggle in successful revolutions.*

Unless these three propositions are true, then the tactic of defense is not justified – no matter what may be the truth about dialectics and the definition of the Russian state. Their truth can be established in one way and one way only: not by changing quantity into quality or uniting opposites, but by relating them to the relevant evidence that can be brought to bear from modern historical experience – including prominently the evidence presented by the first months of the war itself.

Burnham presents an account of Trotsky's initial reaction to events in Poland and Finland, which had been shown to be seriously mistaken. He took expectations from theory for fact and saw events in Poland and Finland not as they were but through a distorting haze of theoretical preconceptions.

Knowing the Red Army fought against their interests and seeing no *third alternative*, the Finnish workers drew what seemed to them the only possible conclusion under the circumstances: to fight desperately for the bourgeois "fatherland"; with the third alternative (an independent struggle for freedom and power against the main enemy, at home, and the invading enemy) excluded, they chose what appeared to them as the "lesser evil." Those responsible for this reactionary conclusion are the imperialists on the one hand and the Stalinists on the other (and all others!) who, ruling out the third camp, posed the choice exclusively as either Mannerheim's army or Stalin's.

On the other side, according to our theses (War and the Fourth International), the Russian soldiers and workers *should* have been reacting as follows: "Within the USSR war against imperialist intervention will undoubtedly provoke a veritable outburst of genuine fighting enthusiasm. All the contradictions and antagonisms will seem overcome or at any rate relegated to the background. The young generations of workers and peasants that emerged from the revolution will reveal on the field of battle colossal dynamic power." But (to paraphrase a remark of Trotsky's), "events did not recognize our theses." In the Finnish war, the Russian soldiers and workers have shown – just the opposite, as everyone knows. There is no mystery here. The soldiers fight so poorly, so unenthusiastically, because – though without benefit of dialectics – they understand clearly that in this war the Red Army fights not for but *against* their interests and the interests of workers everywhere, and of socialism.

Who is it who is closest to *socialist* consciousness; those Soviet soldiers and workers who recognize the reactionary character of the war, are resentful and distrustful of it, and show no enthusiasm for it; or those (notably including the GPU) who are whipped up into a frenzy of Stalino-patriotism for it? We, the opposition, say: the former. Trotsky is compelled by his doctrine to say: the latter.

But, in the further course of the Finnish war, will not the class-struggle reassert itself in Finland? Certainly, as we have declared from the beginning. When the Finnish defense and the Finnish government begin to crack, just as in Poland the overt class struggle will reappear; workers and peasants will take social revolutionary steps, will, perforce, begin moves toward independent power and sovereignty. Above all will they do so if there are revolutionists and militants among them who have not, meanwhile, been functioning as spies of the counter-revolutionary Red Army, but have made clear to them that their struggle, in the first instance directed against the main enemy at home, finds an also implacable enemy

583

in the Kremlin and all its institutions, that the Red Army marches in not to aid them but to crush them; and if internationalists within the ranks of the Red Army have guided in a parallel manner the ranks of the Red soldiers, urging them to throw off the yoke of the Kremlin-GPU and to join in common struggle against their oppressors with the Finnish workers and peasants – not to obey the orders of the Kremlin to reduce the workers and peasants of Finland to a new type of slavery.

Does the policy of the Kremlin (through "compulsion" or voluntary will, it does not matter) in reality stimulate the class struggle, the social revolution? If so, then Marxism has been wrong *from the beginning*, for then the struggle for socialism can be carried on by bureaucratic-military means *as a substitute* (good and bad) for the popular, conscious and deliberate mass struggle of the workers and peasants. To accept Trotsky's interpretation of the events of the present war is to accept the theory of *the bureaucratic road to socialism*. I refer the reader to Max Shachtman's excellent discussion of this point in his recent reply to this same article of Trotsky's.

But is not the Kremlin stimulating the social revolution by its new policy, both directly through its own state agencies, and by the new line of the Comintern? If this is true – as Trotsky now holds – we cannot possibly explain intelligibly to the workers the meaning of the new line of the Communist International (and we have not done so up to now – everyone recognizes that from reading our press), we have no sufficient reason for not re-applying for admission as a faction of the Communist International

No. The present policy of the Kremlin stimulates the class struggle and is "socialist" only in the same general sense as Wilson's policy with reference to "defeatism" in Germany in 1917-18, or Chamberlain's policy in his broadcasts to and leaflet-droppings on Germany today, or Hitler's similar appeals. These "revolutionary" policies – with respect to the enemy country – are all simply supplementary military-strategic devices. As a matter of fact, in this sense the most "radical" of *all* of them at the present time is Hitler's, not Stalin's: Hitler's New Year speech was far more "socialist" than the proclamation of the Kuusinen government. True enough the nation employing this device is always playing with social dynamite – above all in *this* war. Even Chamberlain's propaganda is *capable* of "stimulating the class struggle" within Germany under appropriate circumstances – but we hardly support it, for that reason (though we *do* support the class struggle, no matter how stimulated). But the more usual effect is for it to aid in stifling the class struggle in the enemy nation, (precisely because it is not internationalist in character, and because the workers understand it as merely a maneuver of a rival oppressor). This is just what happened in Finland, just as in Germany after the Chamberlain leaflet raids.

Cannon and Trotsky tell us: But then you want the imperialists to take over the Soviet Union. This is nothing but the standard slander which has always been directed against those who uphold the internationalist position of revolutionary defeatism. We are for the defeat of *all* the belligerent armies and the overthrow of *all* the belligerent governments; but for defeat and overthrow *not* by the opposing armies in the field, but by the *third camp*, by the workers of each respective country.

But Cannon and Trotsky say nothing of the meaning of *their* alternative in relation to the general strategic aim, to the world proletarian revolution. *How,* just how, will a defensive tactic with respect to the Red Army serve the development of the revolution, how in *this war* – not the war of our theses – where the Red Army fights, in alliance with the Reichswehr, for the defense, preservation and extension solely and simply of the power, privileges and revenues of the counter-revolutionary bureaucracy? Trotsky and Cannon do not tell us, cannot tell us. And yet their position could rest only upon a clear, convincing and reasonable answer to this question.

Trotsky and Cannon *desperately* clinging to a doctrine no longer adequate to meet the test of events, have abandoned the strategy of the third camp. How revealing that even the phrase (used so effectively – after being mistakenly borrowed from the opposition – in putting forward the revolutionary position in the American Labor Party controversy between Rose and the Stalinists) has dropped out of the party press and agitation! They have joined one of the belligerent camps, one of the war camps. In this can be seen the basic *defeatism* of their perspective (they, who accuse us of being defeatist!), defeatism toward the possibility of successful proletarian revolution in the course of the war. They are compelled, more and more, to argue for Stalinism as the "lesser evil" (their description): this lesser evil is the goal they place before the workers – a fine goal indeed to inspire revolutionary struggle! They must reason in terms of the *maintenance* of existing governments (what if, Cannon asks in debate, Finland takes over Northern Russia?). Everything is turned upside down. The strategic aim of world revolution issuing out of the war is *subordinated* to defense of Russia.

Their whole policy becomes oriented around the tactic of defensism with respect to the Red Army – on the very best account, the part usurping the place of the whole. For the sake of a hand the head and heart are sacrificed.

Trotsky has permitted a frantic clinging to a false doctrine to drive him, in short, to *a policy of defeat and desperation.*

In the article, "The War and Bureaucratic Conservatism," we analysed the character of the Cannon group, its régime, and its present policy. We showed that it is not a principled tendency, but a permanent clique; that its only real policy is self maintenance; that it on all occasions subordinates political to organizational question; that in actuality it has no genuine program, but only the *substitute* for a program – the substitute being usually borrowed from Trotsky.

In the present dispute, Trotsky puts forward the program which the Cannon clique appropriates and Trotsky supports – unconditionally – the Cannon clique. Trotsky not merely supports the Cannon régime, but whitewashes it 100% – an attitude which even its most ardent follower in the party could not even pretend to justify by objective reference. Trotsky not merely condemns the opposition, but slanders it, mis-states and distorts not merely its views but its very words. Trotsky (for example, in the sheaf of letters of the first days of January) indulges in absurd exaggerations.

Now Trotsky has amply proved by his entire career that he above all takes ideas, doctrine, principles seriously, that he bases himself upon and operates from principles. When we keep this in mind, the picture of these months [*Trotsky's confused politics on Poland and Finland*] falls into a classic and often-repeated pattern; the pattern of one who proceeds from a theory, who is motivated in his actions by that theory, but where the theory itself is *false*. Clinging to the theory becomes under these circumstances an act of *desperation*; and the desperation communicates itself to the actions, even to the very style.

The theory, the doctrine, *at all costs*. But the doctrine is not in accord with events. Then, refusing to abandon the doctrine, there are only two solutions: to *evade* events (by treating, say, of very general theoretic questions or of dialectics), and to *falsify* events to bring them into accord with the (false) doctrine. No intent to deceive is involved in this: it follows almost automatically when one clings *desperately* to a *false* doctrine.

Therefore also the opposition must be smashed *at any cost*. The only vehicle for the doctrine is Cannon (who will accept any doctrine that suits his clique purpose). Therefore *complete* support for Cannon. But here, too, just as in treating international events, Trotsky must pay a heavy price – and the price, alas, is assessed not merely against Trotsky but against the International and indeed in the last analysis against the workers everywhere – for his false doctrine. To implement his (false) doctrine he finds he can utilize only a rotten bureaucratic clique; but by supporting this clique he becomes an accomplice in and defender of its crimes against the movement.

If we realize that Trotsky proceeds seriously and firmly from theory, and that his theory with relation to the war is false, his present political position, and the manner of his political and organizational intervention in the party dispute – so puzzling and often shocking to many comrades – become at once intelligible. (This of course is not that "class analysis" which Trotsky demands from all Marxists. All that such analysis could mean in this case would be: what social group is aided by the *effects* of Trotsky's present policy? The answer is perfectly evident: the Russian bureaucracy. His present policy is a deviation from the direction of the international proletarian struggle for socialism, toward Stalinism.)

The party and the International face in the immediate future the most serious decision of many years. We will either be dragged by a false doctrine, a distorted perspective, and a bankrupt régime into a blind gulf where the waves of the war will leave us floundering and finally drown us; or we will, with however painful a wrench, break out onto the high road, the best soldiers in the one army to which we can give our loyalty; the army of the third camp.

AT THE TURNING POINT OF THE TWENTIETH CENTURY: GERMANY 1933

I

PRESIDENT VON HINDENBURG, the victorious candidate of the socialist "Iron Front", the "bulwark of the Republic against fascism", has finally appointed Hitler to the Chancellorship of the Reich. The fact that Hindenburg, who was undoubtedly hostile to Hitler, even if not in a fundamentally class sense, finally called upon the Fascist leader to take over the government, is eloquent testimony to the desperation of the German bourgeoisie. Capitalism, in its "normal" state, never does more than keep its Fascist hordes in reserve. The German ruling class knows that the seizure of power by the Brown-shirted bandits, especially in a country with a well-organized and socialistically schooled working class, means civil war and the consequent disruption of the economic and political life of the country, at least until the issue of the struggle is decided. The German bourgeoisie has gone to all conceivable lengths to avoid the heavy expenses of a civil war: It has turned over the government to social democrats; it has drawn them into bourgeois coalitions; it has sought to preserve an equilibrium with the aid of the Bruening party of ultramontanism; it has resorted to the Bonapartist régimes of Papen and von Schleicher. But none of these expedients has enabled it to emerge from the profound crisis undermining its domination, the crisis which has driven hundreds of thousands of workers to the support of the party of social revolution. For just as the bourgeoisie finds it impossible to rule in the old way, the masses refusing to live in the old way.

That is why the bourgeoisie has been forced to resort to the desperate expedient of Fascism! Hitler in power means the commencement of the civil war in Germany. It is entirely unthinkable that the German working class, millions strong, trained in the school of the class struggle for years, having at its head the most powerful Communist party in the world outside of the Soviet Union, will permit the Nazi assassins to remain in power without a violent struggle. It is entirely unthinkable that Hitler will be able to accomplish his principal task without a bitter fight. His role is to crush every semblance of organized strength and militancy in the German working class, beginning with the Communist Party, the spearhead of the proletariat, following with the social democracy and the big trade union movement, and ending with the extermination of every other class conscious proletarian organization. It is already clear from the first news dispatches that the German proletariat, alarmed by the recent events and aroused out of the lethargy and the imaginary security into which they were lulled for the past year, has begun to resist with all the means at its disposal.

When we speak of Hitler's ascension to power, it does not yet mean that the power of Fascism has been established in Germany. Before this is definitely accomplished, blood will flow and many sanguinary battles will be fought. But only a blind man could fail to see that Hitler today is in a better position than the Hitler of several months ago. Hitler out of office has only his own forces at his disposal, the "illegal" detachments of black reaction. Hitler in office has the opportunity of strengthening the inchoate mass of demoralized petty bourgeoisie, students, and duped proletarians, who compose his forces. Hitler in office has the opportunity of really creating a powerful military force. It is not yet too late to smash Hitler and Fascism — only renegades and scoundrels will speak that way to the still undefeated working class of Germany. The decisive battle is still ahead. But it is now clear beyond dispute that the warnings of the International Left Opposition, the demand it made that Hitlerism be smashed before it reached the seats of power — were justified a thousand times over. Had the slogan of the Left Opposition for a genuine united front of the Communists, socialists and the trade unions, been realized in life at the right time, many many months ago, the Fascist monster would have been crushed like an eggshell and the revolutionary movement of the proletariat would have been far ahead on the road to victory.

Who bears the responsibility for the rise to power of Fascism? It is high time to draw the balance sheet and draw it completely.

By Max Shachtman. From *The Militant*, February and March 1933. The Reichsbanner was the Social Democratic Party's defense militia.

Above all in the first place, the leadership of the yellow social democracy. The course embarked upon in August 1914 has been crowned with the triumph of Hitlerism. It is the social democracy which first turned the masses into the slaughter house of the world war in the name of the imperialist fatherland. It is in the name of the social democracy that Noske the Bloodhound martyred the Berlin working class during the heroic days of the Spartacan uprising in 1919. It is the social democracy which sent Hoersing to slaughter the workers of Central Germany in 1921. It is the social democracy which joined with the reaction in 1923 to strangle the rising revolutionary movement in Saxony and Thuringia.

It is the social democracy which dragged its followers down to the lowest depths of degradation, giving active or "tolerant" support to one reactionary régime after another. It is the social democracy which made possible Bruening of the Emergency Decrees. It is the social democracy which dragged the workers into the shameful policy of the "lesser evil", during which it seated in the presidential chair the present patron of Hitler — Paul von Hindenburg, generalissimo of the Kaiser's Imperial armies during the war, and candidate of the social democratic "Iron Front", "bulwark of the Republic against Fascism" in 1931.

At every stage of its development in the past years, the social democracy paved the road for the march to power of Fascism, by dividing the ranks of the working class, by tying it to the chariot of the bourgeoisie, by bringing demoralization and confusion into the proletariat, by weakening it physically and morally so that its power of resistance to Fascism was appreciably lessened. Hitler will reward it for its services with the same contemptuous kick which its Italian colleagues received from Mussolini for their equally invaluable services to Fascism.

But the social democracy has not been the only force in the ranks of the proletariat that has served the interests of Fascism. Without the criminal blundering of the Stalinist leadership of the Communist International and of the German Communist Party, the Fascist hordes would not today be in the favorable position they actually occupy. The party had the matchless opportunity of mobilizing the masses of the German proletariat around the militant banner of the class struggle. It stubbornly refused to seize the opportunity. The Left Opposition was the very first to sound the alarm signal that Fascism threatened, that it had to be crushed by the united front of all the workers' organizations. We demanded that the Communist party initiate the movement for a real united front of all the workers to smash the Brown Shirts. Our demands fell on the deaf ears of the Stalinist bureaucracy. The latter operated on the theory of the "third period" and "social Fascism". No better assistance could have been offered to the Fascists on the one hand, and the Social Democratic leaders on the other. Instead of building a solid front, with their class brothers in the social democracy, the Communists were forced by the Stalinist leadership to enter into an indecent nationalistic competition with the Nazis.

The party reconstructed its program to read a "program of national and social emancipation." It allowed itself to be poisoned by the "national-Bolshevism" and anti-Semitism of the Lieutenant Scheringers. It alienated itself from the socialist masses by its criminal support of the Fascist referendum in Prussia. While the Fascists were gaining victory after victory, the party confined itself to the sterile ultimatist policy of demanding that the socialist workers concede in advance the leadership of the Communist party or else there would be no united front. The minds of the class conscious militants were hopelessly befuddled by the irresponsible Stalinist declarations that the Bruening régime was already the victory of Fascism, then, that the von Papen régime and finally the von Schleicher régime, were all the rule of Fascism. In this manner, the vigilance of the proletariat was relaxed, its attention was diverted from the real danger, its strength was not mobilized and consolidated. Unless a genuine united front of the Communist party, the social democracy, the socialist trade unions, the Reichsbanner and the Communist Red Front Fighters, is *immediately* formed, unless the Communists *immediately* take the initiative in calling for this united front and compel the social democratic leaders to enter into it — the results will be catastrophic not only for the German working class, but for the working class movement of the whole world, for the Communist International, and the Soviet Union!

A crushing defeat for the working class of Germany means a crushing defeat of the Communist Party, for it is the first organization against which the attack of the brigands of Hitler's shock troop detachments — assisted by the armed forces of the state — will be directed. A mortal blow at the German Communist Party means the breaking of the backbone of the Communist International and for this calamity we declare that the Stalinist leadership of the International will have been primarily responsible. A lasting triumph of Fascism in Germany, furthermore, is inconceivable without an armed attack upon the Soviet Union. Fascism in Germany can maintain itself in the face of chauvinist France only if it

587

becomes the vanguard of the imperialist intervention against the arch-enemy of imperialism — the Soviet Union. The consequences of a Fascist triumph are thus, it is easy to see, of far-reaching historical import for the whole ensuing period.

That is why the Left Opposition cries out today more loudly than ever: The Communist International must speak out in the language of Lenin, in defense of the international proletarian revolution, in defense of the German working class. It must speak out for the mobilization of the world proletariat to crush the monster of Fascism in Germany. It must speak out to say how this is to be done, for it can be done successfully in only one way: by the establishment of a Leninist united front of the whole German proletariat.

To smash Fascism is an obligation and task of the workers everywhere. Upon the class conscious militants and the Communist workers in this country devolves the solemn duty of joining with the Left Opposition to force that turn in party policy which is now so absolutely imperative, without which the worst calamities are ahead. Our call to the party to form the united front to smash Fascism before it took the governmental helm was not heeded, and the proletariat in Germany and the rest of the world has been set back accordingly. Today again we repeat: It is not too late! But the time to act is now!

The fate of the German working class of the Communist International, of the Soviet Union, of the world revolution hangs in the balance.

"Opposition's demand for United Front is need of the hour in Germany. Responsibility for rise of fascism must be established". February 4, 1933

II

AND THE COMMUNIST PARTY? A position of more hopeless confusion, irresolution and hopelessness in the midst of a situation that cries out for clarity, determination and audacity, can hardly be imagined. The parliamentary elections as the axis of the struggle constitute an enormous and treacherous swindle. What is the party doing to counteract it? There is only one thing that it can and must do: organize the genuine united front of all workers' organizations to launch the general strike, to mobilize the concerted strength of the German proletariat to crush Fascism. Is the party doing this? It has not even begun, for to begin it is imperative to throw overboard all the disastrous policies of yesterday which have rendered the party so impotent in the struggle. In the face of everything that has happened, the party still continues with its pernicious chatter about the "proletarian united front under the leadership of the Communist Party of Germany" (*Inprecorr*, No. 4), which is the old ultimatist policy: Socialist workers, recognize our leadership in advance or else there will be no united front! The Fascists are already in power, but they have far from consolidated it. They have not yet even taken over the whole power. And this circumstance still gives the German proletariat time enough to act decisively enough to destroy the brown-shirted monster. The attainment of this end lies through the united front of the Communist party, the trade unions, the Social Democratic party, the Reichsbanner and the Red Front Fighters, which the former must immediately initiate.

"Hitler lays new trap for workers." February 13, 1933

III

HITLER HAS TAKEN ANOTHER BIG STEP in the consolidation of exclusive Fascist domination of Germany. The social democrats whose policy of toleration to Bruening and von Schleicher and outright support for Hindenburg paved the way to the triumph of Hitler are being repaid by the latter with a brutal kick in the face. The social democrats now have not a single supreme government president or police chief in any part of Prussia. The Berlin correspondent of the New York *Sun* (2-14-1933) points out with an acumen which the Stalinists would do well to emulate that "Just as the Fascist party in Italy gradually took over the civil service and became undistinguishable from the Government itself, so the Nazis here hope slowly to undermine and eventually take over the entire government structure... The Nazi move is especially notable in police circles."

A two-year old child should be able to understand Hitler's tactics. Contrary to the infinitely stupid assertions of the Stalinists concerning the Fascist essence of social-democracy — which do not improve by repetition in the face of obvious facts — there is a sharp antagonism between the social democracy and Fascism. Hitler is trying every single day to prove to the Stalinist blockheads that while the social democrats are the principal prop of the "democratic" form of bourgeois rule, it becomes not merely superfluous but a direct hin-

588

drance to the bourgeoisie when it seeks to abolish all democratic forms and institutions and to rule by naked force, by the sword and the torch, in a word, by Fascist dictatorship.

This is why the Fascists attack not only the revolutionary wing of the labor movement, the Communists, but also seek to annihilate the points of support of the social democracy. If the eloquent experiences of Italian Fascism were not sufficient to make this clear, the first couple of weeks of Hitler as Chancellor should serve to enlighten even the most backward. But the Stalinist leaders of the Communist party continue with incredible obstinacy to prattle about "social Fascism" and the "united front from below". The crucial hour demands the extra-parliamentary mobilization of the whole German proletariat to crush Fascism before it entrenches itself too solidly. And this is just where the impotence of the official party and its leadership shows itself so strikingly. Where is the movement for the assembling of the factory councils and the unemployed on a national scale to prepare for the general strike of all the workers? Where is the organized movement of the workers to defend themselves against the growing encroachments of the brown-shirted bandits?

The only road for the German working class at the present moment is the united front of all the working class organizations. The party bureaucracy stands in the way of the united front. It is sacrificing the interests of the German working class, of the world revolution, of the Communist International for the sake of preserving the theory of infallibility of the Stalinist leadership, of preserving the bureaucratic, ultimatist formula of the "united front from below" which divides socialist from Communist workers instead of uniting them.

We say openly: The refusal to mobilize the genuine united front of all the workers' organizations *immediately,* is downright treason to the German proletariat! Now is the time! The Stalinists are playing with the situation! Tomorrow the individual workers who have been cut down by the Fascist thugs will be multiplied a thousand times, and under conditions not half so favorable to the workers of Germany as are the conditions of struggle at the present time.

The failure to organize the united front is only another way of capitulating to Fascism without a serious struggle. Hitler is well aware of this. Hitler knows his road and he follows it relentlessly. The working class must understand its own position and act resolutely too. It is all-powerful and invincible if it only unites its arms and strikes with determination. Those who stand in the way of this unity will bear a horrible responsibility for the impending catastrophe!

Let the Communist workers reflect — and act speedily. Let them demand an immediate reckoning from the self-satisfied bureaucrats who remain passive while the enemy prepares its death-blow!

"Hitler is consolidating the power of fascism in Germany! Whoever blocks the workers' united front is a traitor!" February 15, 1933

IV

BERLIN IS AN ARMED CAMP, with armored cars and 18,000 rifle-armed police concentrated heavily in the working class quarters. A new decree has been issued providing for heavy penalties against those "who give false information for foreign publications", as well as against those who print such "false" information in the German press. The *Rote Fahne*, central organ of the German Communist Party, which appeared for one day after its previous suspension, has had its printing plant confiscated and, in addition, has been suspended by the government until April 15. An edition of the paper printed in Leipzig was confiscated, together with the truck that carried the copies to Berlin. All the socialist papers in East Prussia have been suppressed. Even liberal journals have been ordered suspended. A mass meeting of the social democratic party to commemorate the fiftieth anniversary of the death of Karl Marx was dispersed by the police.

All these measures are part of a monstrous frame-up concocted by the Fascist butchers in control of the government. A fire of incendiary origin in the Reichstag building is being used as the pretext for delivering a mortal blow to the Communist party. Anybody who is even superficially acquainted with the theories and practises of the Communist party is sufficiently aware that arson is not in its program. That is a method of fighting practised almost exclusively by the Fascists. In the present instance, the frame-up is so flagrant that even the American correspondents in Berlin have not failed to comment adversely upon Hitler's crude attempt to crush the Communist party as a result of it.

Will the Communist party take up the challenge? It would be criminal to conceal the fact

589

that with its present policy, the party has proved impotent in the face of Hitler's murderous advance. The working class has not been mobilized either directly under its banner or under the banner of a united front movement initiated by the Communists. It is a fact, which we repeat here: In his march to power in Italy, Mussolini encountered a far more energetic, militant, sanguinary resistance on the part of the proletariat — than Hitler has thus far encountered in Germany, where the working class movement is far stronger than it ever was in Italy, where the working class does not play its role on the background of a defeat, as in Italy, and where the Communist party is ten times as strong as it was in Italy in 1922.

The twilight hour has been reached. The next stroke of the clock can still be controlled by the masses: Either it will strike the doom of the working class for a decade or more to come or it will strike the beginning of the end of Fascism!

The whole world situation hinges around the outcome of the terrible drama now being enacted before our eyes. The fate of the German proletariat hangs in the balance. With it is involved the fate of the whole Communist International. With it is also involved the fate of the workers' fatherland, the Soviet Union.

And in face of this, *the "leader of the world's proletariat", the Communist International, is as silent as a tombstone!* In face of the situation, *the "best disciple of Lenin", Joseph Stalin, is as silent as a tombstone!* In face of the dreadful catastrophe which threatens, the party leaders continue to babble philosophically about the "progress of the united front from below" as if they had months and years at their disposal in which to mobilize the German proletariat for the decisive battle which is impending.

Fascism has put the noose around the neck of the Communist party. It has aimed its knife at the heart of the German working class. Whoever is silent at a time like this, whoever relegates the decisive German situation to the background of second and third rate consequence, is drugging the proletariat and helping to prepare it for the slaughter! Whoever stands in the way of the genuine united front, from organization to organization — Communist party, social democracy, trade unions, Reichsbanner, Red Front — is betraying the working class!

Communist workers, militants everywhere! It is not yet too late. The masses await only the signal for action. The Communist party must give this signal. It must be aroused out of its awful lethargy and impotence. It must put a stop to the self-deceptive jabbering about the "united front from below" which "unites" only the Communists and their supporters, and set in motion the Leninist united front of all the workers to decimate the Fascist hydra.

Tomorrow? Tomorrow may see the materialization of Hitler's demand that "heads roll in the dirt". Then the miserable "self-criticism" practised by Stalinism after each defeat, will be of little avail. It is today, today, today that the party must change its disastrous course. It is now that it must strike for the united front which, in turn, will strike the dagger from the hands of Fascism and Fascism from the seats of power.

"Fascists frame-up the Communist Party. The life and death question: Leninist united front in Germany or disaster!" March 1, 1933

V

EVERY DAY BRINGS THE REPORT of a new blow dealt the German working class movement by the Hitler régime. The *Times* reports that "Communist arrests included the entire executive committee of the party in Berlin and Reichstag deputies and party executives elsewhere". In Berlin alone there are more than 300 Communists held. Raids for the apprehension of Communist militants and officials are now the order of the day. The Communist and socialist press — more than one hundred papers in all — remains suppressed and the Fascist swastika still waves from the Karl Liebknecht House. New decrees signed by "comrade" von Hindenburg, erstwhile presidential candidate of the Social Democracy, provide for the most rigorous penalties against revolutionary or militant working class activity. The silence of the Communist International on the German situation, its criminal failure to speak out plainly, has become a notorious international scandal of dreadful significance. The world movement of the proletariat is at stake in Germany; the fate of the Soviet Union is involved. Between Fascism in Germany and the workers' state there can exist only an irreconcilable antagonism which, in the long run, will be settled only by force of arms. This antagonism must not only not be concealed — it must be openly proclaimed to the workers of the world so that they may know how the situation stands and what the attitude of the Soviet Union really is. Instead of such a clear proclamation, we see disquieting signs of the contrary. Walter Duranty, the Moscow correspondent of the New York

Times now in Berlin, cables his paper as follows (3-2-1933):

"While it doubtless would be an exaggeration to say as some of Chancellor Hitler's close asso-
ciates do, that 'the Soviet Union wants a Hitlerite Germany because the Soviet Union knows
that would be a strong Germany, which the Soviet Union wants,' it is beyond question that
Moscow would welcome even a 100 per cent Hitler régime on the grounds that it would con-
jure away the nightmare that has harassed the sleep of Soviet statesmen for the past five years
— namely, an anti-Bolshevist European coalition or a 'holy war against the Red peril'.
Moscow already has reason to be gratified over the effect of Herr Hitler's rise to power on
France and Poland. But that is only one aspect of the case. Of greater practical interest is the
recent agreement concluded by the Deutsche Bank and Disconto-Gesellschaft and the
Dresdner Bank to provide $50,000,000 in new credits to the Soviet Union..."

The continuation of "normal business relations" with Germany under Hitler, right at the
moment when the decisive battle is imminent — a battle on whose outcome depends the next
decade or more of the world's development — as if nothing unusual was happening, as if the
Soviet Union were not concerned with what government was established in Germany —
means little short of leaving the German proletariat to fend for itself, leaving it in the lurch,
without the moral — and when necessary — the material assistance of the workers' state. To
this moment, the world remains unaware of the program of the Communist party. We put
the question, again: Does the Communist party and its leadership really intend to organize
the resistance of the proletariat to Fascism, or does it intend to capitulate without a struggle, on the half-formed or fully conscious theory that it is hopeless to fight, or that Fascism
will soon collapse and give way to Bolshevism? Are the party leaders preparing for the final
struggle or giving up the situation as hopeless? The Left Opposition does not consider the
situation hopeless. It knows very well — and the newspaper reports, to the humiliation of
the Communist movement, confirm it — that the Austrian and Scandinavian borders are
being passed by an increasing number of Communist officials and leaders from Germany.
For such capitulators, who are saving their hides, a revolutionist can have nothing but contempt and hatred. Of them, Trotsky wrote more than a year ago: " *'Without a victory over the*
social democracy, we cannot battle against Fascism' say such terrible revolutionists, and for
this reason... they get their passports ready. Worker-Communists, you are hundreds of thou-
sands, millions; you cannot leave for any place; there are not enough passports for you.
Should Fascism come to power, it will ride over your skulls and spines like a terrific tank.
Your salvation lies in merciless struggle. And only a fighting unity with the social democrat-
ic workers can bring victory. Make haste, worker-Communists, you have very little time left!"

Very little time left! Every hour counts! The socialist leaders, the traitors to the proletariat, will not act of their own accord. The Communist leaders must be forced out of their criminal passivity. They must be forced to put an end to this lightminded juggling with the fate
of the German proletariat.

There is no retreat: All that is left is mortal combat — or annihilation!

"No retreat! Struggle or annihilation!" March 3, 1933

Editor's note: In fact, the Communist Party did not attempt to fight the fascists in Germany.
Like the Social Democratic Party, it slunk into a needless grave. Stalin had as early as 1931
put it to his German lieutenant Heinz Neumann — who would be shot in 1937 — "If Hitler
comes to power in Germany, won't he keep them busy in the West, while we get on with
building socialism in Russia?"

THE FOURTH INTERNATIONAL IS FOUNDED

THE DRAMATIC AND TRAGIC political events of the last month in Europe were characteristic of the situation which dictated to the thirty delegates who came from eleven countries to attend the world conference of the revolutionary Marxists in Switzerland on September 3 the decision to found and organize the Fourth International — World Party of the Socialist Revolution. These events served to underscore heavily the fact that the working class, the toiling masses in general, have at their head a leadership in the form of the two old Internationals which is not only incapable of organizing their resistance to the most monstrous of all the products of capitalism — totalitarian war — but is actually the most vigorous force at work in the ranks of labor itself mobilizing the masses for enthusiastic support of the war. The period in which we live is preëminently the period of world economy and world politics, in which any form of self-enclosed existence — be it autarky, isolationism, or socialism-in-one-country — is either an illusion or dupery. The last quarter of a century has strikingly emphasized the indispensability of international organization, leadership and strategy for the proletarian movement. The working class can no more do without them than individual army corps can dispense with a directing general staff. When the old general staffs of the working class, the traditional Internationals, have proved themselves to be not merely bankrupt but a direct obstacle to the further progress of the labor movement, it is imperative that no time be lost in restoring the world revolutionary organization.

How blind one would have to be not to see the reactionary rôle played by the Second and Third Internationals during the critical September month when Europe see-sawed over the brink of war, a rôle neither unexpected nor accidental, but analyzed and forecast by us years in advance! What a contrast they presented even to the Second International on the eve of the war of 1914-1918. As is known, all the important parties of the International turned patriotic and chauvinistic, and formed a "civil peace" with their respective capitalist class once the war actually broke out. But in the terror-filled weeks before the beginning of August 1914, they at least made an effort to appear before the masses as opponents of the imminent holocaust. The International Socialist Bureau met in Brussels to discuss — very despondently and without much conviction, it is true — what could be done to mobilize the workers against the war-mongers. The rafters of Brussels' largest hall rang with the voices of thousands of workers echoing Jaurès' eloquent denunciation of the ruling class of all Europe. Similar scenes were repeated in most of the other European capitals and important population centers.

Even these impressive, if ineffectual, gestures were, however, everywhere absent in the crisis moments of 1938, when, a bare twenty years after the end of the last War to End All Wars, the world seemed to be catapulting to a new and infinitely more horrible disaster.

What passes for the leadership of the Second International — its world Bureau — did not even consider it necessary to hold a meeting for the purpose of appraising the situation and issuing a declaration that would guide the workers of all the countries who are affiliated to it. How could it meet? What could it say? Its policy is determined in each country not by proletarian internationalist considerations, but by the policy of its respective national bourgeoisie, or, as in the case of the exiled German social democracy, the bourgeoisie of another nation which has given it asylum, and which it considers at least for the time being as its very own — the French. With what felicity the social democracy followed the methods of its national ruling classes down to the minutest detail! Just as Chamberlain consulted with Daladier, without bothering to ask for the opinions of the Czech bourgeoisie, so did a delegation of the British Labour Party, headed by Sir Walter Citrine, consult in September with the leaders of the French Socialist Party without bothering to ask for the opinions of their "comrades-of-the-International" of the German and Czech social democracies. When Chamberlain, just before leaving for Munich, finally condescended to inform the great and democratic British Parliament of his policy and decisions, the leader of the British Labour Party, Major Attlee,

Abridged from, *New International*, November 1938, Max Shachtman: "The Fourth International is launched". Max Shachtman and James P Cannon represented the SWP USA at the founding conference of the Fourth International. Max Shachtman chaired the conference.

could say no more than his colleagues on the other benches: he too wished the Prime Minister Godspeed! It was too solemn a moment for His Majesty's Loyal Opposition to put forward its own independent position on the war question, which is symbolized by its attacks on the Tory government for failure to speed up the production of military airplanes. That the parties of the Second International have been voting with religious monotony for the war budget in every country where they are still allowed to vote, is too well known to need comment.

The parties of the Third International differed from the Second only in their more rabid patriotic zeal, in their unrestrained agitation for an immediate holy war of the Democracies against the Dictatorships. Daladier, in his statement to the Chamber's military commission defending the abrogation of the 40-hour week in the interests of "national defense", was able to refer good-humoredly to the antics of his Stalinist friends who demanded of him that he play the part of Don Quixote riding to the defense of imperilled civilization. Throughout the period of the Chamberlain-Hitler negotiations, the Stalinist press in England, France, Belgium and Czechoslovakia carried on an unbridled campaign of chauvinism which put even the outright reactionaries to shame. Shifting away from Daladier in France, the Kremlin hirelings frantically applauded the saber-rattling speeches of Henri de Kerillis, spokesman for the fascists in the Chamber. In England, the only demonstrations organized by the Stalinists were those that condemned Chamberlain for not immediately launching a war against Hitler; "British honor" and "England's interests" — these were the mouth-filling shibboleths of the Stalinist manifestations. Unbelievable as it sounds — yet, what is unbelievable about Stalinism nowadays? — the "communists" in Dublin, where the writer happened to be on the eve of the Munich agreement, ran up and down the city calling upon all good Irishmen and true to rally to the defense of that institution so deeply beloved by Erin — British Democracy.

It is this complete absence of a revolutionary international leadership that compelled the conference of the Bolshevik-Leninists not only to reaffirm their view that the two existing Internationals had become counter-revolutionary, but to found the new International. Properly speaking, the struggle for the new International dates back to the seizure of power by Hitler in 1933 and the lamentable capitulation of the communist and social-democratic parties, which retired from the field of battle without even firing a shot. It was then that the world movement that had developed around the struggle of the so-called "Trotskyist Opposition" in the Communist International, announced the abandonment of its ten-year-old position of concentration upon reforming this International. It issued the call for a new communist International and new communist parties to replace those that had collapsed so ingloriously. In the period of intense discussion and ferment that followed in the radical movement after the German events, the movement for the Fourth International gained strength in one country after another. In 1934, the famous Pact of Four in favor of the new International was signed by the International Communist League, the Independent Socialist Party of Holland and the Revolutionary Socialist Party of Holland (the last two-named organizations were soon to fuse into one), and the Socialist Workers Party of Germany. If the new International was not actually founded until four years later, it was only in order to allow for the elapse of a necessary period in which the fundamental discussions and the clarification and taking up of positions could occur. This was necessary, even if to a much smaller measure, for the International Communist League as well as for the numerous groups which were breaking or had already broken away from the old Internationals.

In this respect, the last four-five years have been among the most instructive and fruitful in our century. To the superficial observer, they appear to have constituted a period of chaos, of endless unifications and an even greater number of splits, of pointless academic disputes and meretricious personal recrimination — all largely incomprehensible and leading to nothing more positive than the constant churning up of stagnant water. The more careful observer, however, could discern both meaning and purpose in the developments of this period. Out of chaos comes the star, said the philosopher; and what appears to many to have been the chaos of these last five years was in reality the all-important period of gestation of the new international revolutionary movement.

Every movement that seeks to adapt itself intelligently to an important turn in history, finds almost invariably that there are elements in its ranks who, either because of forces and ideas latent in them or because of the conservatizing influence of yesterday's tactic, are unable to adjust themselves to the requirements of the new situation and, consequently, fly off at a tangent. In the past half-decade of the International Communist League's evolution, this phenomenon took the form of various ultra-leftist groups which in substance resisted the determination of our movement to become the effective leadership of the revolutionary vanguard. The struggle against these groups had only had a profound educational effect upon our movement, helping to inoculate it more deeply against infantile radicalism in its senile stage, but served to dissipate the legend injudiciously disseminated by our adversaries that there was something "innately sectarian" about the "Trotskyist movement". In the course of the struggle, which was often sharp and almost as often led to splits in our movement, the contending currents were subjected to decisive tests. Everywhere, and without exception, the ultra-leftists, who soon revealed that they were really imbued with a deep-rooted conservatism, stagnated and then began to decompose to the point where many of them disappeared into the political void. No less telling is the fact that in this whole period those that succeeded in maintaining a vegetable existence never managed to establish any serious international relationships among themselves; that is, none of them succeeded in rising above the level of a purely national existence. While our movement continued to move forward to deeper solidity and influence, Weisbord, Field, Oehler, Bauer, Eiffel, Vitte, Lasterade, Vereecken, Ridley, *etc., etc.,* have nothing left but wind-blown débris to show that at one time they were living groups.

As for those who scoffed disdainfully at our allegedly permanent process of schism, and who travelled light under the banner of "Unity", they have not a very encouraging balance-sheet to show. They not only did not succeed in averting splits — they have had little else but splits to record in the past period — but they did not learn anything from their splits and subsequent disintegration. The world is strewn with once large organizations which, under the slogan of unity with everybody in an "all-inclusive" party, ended up reduced to the smallest and least effectual of sects. The Italian Maximalist party of Balabanova, which tried to hold together the incompatible extremes of communism and social democracy in one party, which continues to bewail to the present day the "arbitrary splitting of the united Italian party by Lenin and Trotsky" some two decades ago, has become the tiniest of all Italian groups, a hazy myth around the head of its traditional spokesman. The tens of thousands of members of Britain's Independent Labour Party, whose leaders talked all the more about the virtues of "unity" in order to talk all the less about revolutionary principle, have been reduced to less than two thousand effective members — outnumbered today in the decisive London area by the despised "sectarians" of the unified British Bolshevik-Leninist organization. An even crueler fate overtook the German Socialist Workers Party (SAP). What happened to the "all-inclusiveness" of the Norman Thomas party in this country should be no less instructive to those still capable of learning from life.

Of all the currents and movements in the international working class, only the Fourth International can boldly and honestly claim the heritage of the great principles and traditions of revolutionary Marxism and its past protagonists. The movement for which it speaks has demonstrated the consistency, virility and lifeworthiness, determination and capacity, to mobilize the masses once again for the conclusive victory over exploitation and class rule. The two old Internationals have long ceased to pretend that they are our revolutionary rivals; they are only reactionary obstacles to the working class which it will sweep aside in its forward march. The groups outside the two Internationals still inimical to our movement — the disintegrating London Bureau and the disintegrated Brandler-Lovestone International (what, by the way, has happened to it? It would be interesting to read an official accounting!) — find that their revolutionary pretenses have become quite transparent. The road is left free to the Fourth International! The future belongs to it!

Beside constituting the Fourth International, and adopting the statutes that correspond to a serious, centralized world party, the main job of the international conference was the adoption of the revolutionary Transitional Program of the International — the program of immediate demands for the period in which we are fighting. The importance of this program cannot be overrated. Not only and not so much because of the thoroughgoing analysis it makes of the present period, for that analysis has been made before, but because of the rounded and concrete program it presents to the working class, the peasantry and the colonial peoples of the world for immediate action on all the pressing problems of life and struggle that now confront them. The program corresponds magnificently to the requirements for such a document laid down by Rosa Luxemburg some two generations ago: *"In actuality our whole program would be a miserable scrap of paper if it were not capable of serving us for all eventualities and in every moment of the struggle, and to serve us by virtue of its being practised and not by its being shelved. If our program is the formulation of the historical development of society from capitalism to socialism, then obviously it must formulate also all the transitional phases of this development, it must contain them in their fundamental features, and therefore also be able to indicate to the proletariat the corresponding attitude in the sense of approaching closer to socialism in every given moment. From this it follows that for the proletariat there cannot, in general, be a single moment when it would be compelled to leave its program in the lurch, or in which it could be left in the lurch by this program."*

Our international program of action, which will be read and re-read as one of the classic documents of Marxism, does not confine itself to the demand for the socialist republic, nor to general and abstract denunciations of the danger of war and fascism and the offensive of capitalist reaction. On the contrary, it is a document that indicates the line of action that must and can be taken by the proletariat today, now, in light of the contradiction between the objectively revolutionary situation and the ideological backwardness of the working class itself. It is a powerful weapon for cutting the bonds of political enslavement which fetter the international labor movement and at the same time a means of leading it into battle with slogans and demands that correspond to its aspirations and interests and to objective reality. Throughout it is permeated with the determination — repressed or suppressed by all other sections of the labor movement — to restore the *class independence of the workers*, that indispensable prerequisite to effective struggle; and it indicates the concrete practical steps by means of which this will be accomplished.

It will indeed be accomplished! The Fourth International is inspired by an irrepressible confidence in the resourcefulness, the initiative, the powers of recuperation, the invincibility and final triumph of the proletariat. If we are curt and contemptuous towards whimperers, people who have retired from the class struggle with despondent sighs, short-sighted people who identify a period of reaction, however black, with the conclusive defeat of the revolution, people who ascribe their own weakness, indecision and blundering to the proletariat — it is only because we have no patience with anyone who stands to any extent in the way of the serious movement that is resolved to continue the work of mobilizing the masses for the decisive assaults upon the enemy. Better that all these gentlemen stand aside and do their wailing and contemplating in private, before they are moved aside in a less polite way. We go ahead under the banner of the Fourth International, with our old convictions, our tested principles, and with no doubts as to the final outcome.

INDEX

471, 491, 493-495, 498, 524, 562, 592, 593.

Czar Alexander: 215, 326, 517, 574.

Democracy: 12-14, 24, 26, 32-37, 40-41, 43, 45-46, 51, 74, 78-79, 95-96, 99, 105-106, 118-119, 126, 137, 142, 146, 152, 160-161, 163, 165, 167, 169-182, 185-188, 190-191, 193, 195-199, 201-209, 213, 215, 218-220, 223-225, 227-229, 240, 246-248, 256, 264, 269, 274, 277, 283, 285, 293, 297, 300, 324, 345, 347, 350, 353, 373, 381-384, 395, 397-399, 401, 403, 405, 412, 415-416, 438, 440, 454, 459, 467, 476-477, 482, 484-486, 492, 496, 498, 501-502, 506-508, 523, 538, 554, 557-559, 561, 566-567, 575, 582.
and revolution: 174, 179, 199, 201, 212, 518, 582.
and socialism: 16, 40, 49, 57, 79, 87, 116, 139, 164, 179-180, 216, 262, 289, 299, 316-318, 453, 459, 482, 493, 501, 507, 510, 512, 534, 544, 561, 580, 582.
Paris Commune: 13-14, 20, 131, 164, 166, 176-178, 186, 198, 204, 283, 289, 509.

DC (Democratic Centralist Group): 576.
Sapronov, Timofey V: 300-301, 308, 576.

Deutscher, Isaac: 12, 499, 515-518, 520-524, 526-530.

Dialectics: 31, 68, 91, 93, 99, 424, 540, 567-568, 570, 580-583, 585.

Dictatorship of the proletariat: 12-14, 19, 32, 48, 51, 60-61, 65, 70-71, 81, 142, 174-177, 189, 194, 196, 198-199, 205-206, 212, 250, 304, 306-307, 309, 318, 528, 548, 576.

Draper, Hal: 145-146, 354, 490.

Eastern Europe: 31, 58, 70, 90, 122-123, 128-129, 131-132, 259, 267, 336, 364, 429, 457, 463, 481, 487, 489, 492-494, 497, 517, 540.

Economism: 69, 110, 113-114, 123, 130, 149.

Engels, Frederick: 11, 16, 18, 32, 34-35, 37, 40, 46, 49, 87, 110, 141-142, 175-

177, 191, 194, 196-197, 203, 206, 276, 278, 280, 319, 322, 352, 379, 451, 460, 492, 534-535, 542-544, 558, 568-571.
Erber, Ernest: 164-165, 175-183, 185, 188-198, 201-205, 266, 270, 440.

Estonia: 82, 249, 251, 257, 336, 357-359, 539, 552, 556, 560-562, 571, 573-574.

Fascism: 29-30, 36, 43, 45, 51, 65, 108, 122, 126, 129, 131, 137, 145, 168, 172, 180, 188, 196, 225, 245-246, 248-249, 256, 269, 273, 284-287, 289, 293, 296, 299, 318, 322, 324, 347, 350, 353, 358, 381, 390, 403, 415-416, 418-419, 438, 463, 485-487, 520, 554, 558, 586-91, 595.

Finland: 21, 45, 59, 66, 80, 82, 89, 91-95, 97-100, 102-103, 117, 124, 141, 163, 169, 237, 249, 251-252, 254-255, 257, 289-290, 328, 336-337, 342, 348-349, 354-355, 357, 414, 418-419, 441, 455, 552-557, 560-562, 565, 571-575, 580-581, 583-585.

Fourth International: 51, 66, 71, 73-75, 78, 83-84, 86, 88, 91, 95-96, 99, 103-106, 114, 120, 126-128, 131, 133, 136-138, 140, 229, 238, 240, 246, 248-249, 253-254, 261-262, 266, 268-270, 295, 315, 319, 328, 342, 347, 352-353, 378-379, 384, 402-404, 406, 411, 418, 426, 437, 439-441, 445, 448-450, 454, 458, 460, 462-466, 473, 475-477, 487, 489, 491, 548-549, 551, 554, 558-559, 562-563, 566-568, 571-574, 577, 579, 582-583, 592-595.

French Revolution: 32, 34-35, 41, 73, 169, 175, 177, 279, 326, 517, 519, 526, 558.

Gates, Albert: 342, 345, 394.

Georgia: 23, 224, 255, 334, 502, 560.

Germany: 17-19, 21, 29-31, 33, 36, 38, 40, 43-45, 49, 56, 79-80, 82, 92, 100-102, 121-122, 125, 128-129, 145, 176, 181, 183, 186, 196-199, 201, 213, 215, 225-226, 229, 240-242, 244-245, 248, 250-253, 256, 259, 266, 286-289, 291-293, 316-318, 321-323, 326, 333-337, 339, 342, 349-350, 352-353, 355-358, 362-365, 382, 389, 397-398, 402-404,

412, 415, 417, 419-420, 424, 430, 436, 438, 442, 453, 463, 487-488, 519-520, 523, 550-551, 558, 561, 569, 571, 584, 586-591, 593.
1918-92: 43, 95.
1923: 23-25, 27, 70, 135, 212, 225, 243, 300, 308-309, 388-389, 510, 558, 576, 578.

Glotzer, Al: 387-388, 394, 407.

Goldman, Albert: 89-90, 126-128, 237, 266, 350, 355-357, 361-362, 420, 440, 552, 554-555.
Morrison (pen name): 440, 446-447, 420-425.

GPU: 21, 38, 73, 98, 102-103, 154, 190, 204, 223-225, 228, 238, 243, 267, 297, 300, 310-314, 329-330, 338, 349, 355, 431, 437-438, 441-442, 445, 454, 456, 489, 514, 521, 525, 549-550, 572, 583.

Hitler, Adolf: 18, 27, 30, 37-38, 43-44, 56, 58, 60, 82-83, 85, 90, 92, 97, 99, 101, 117, 229, 237-242, 245-248, 250-252, 254, 256, 265-266, 268-269, 286-287, 289, 291, 310, 317-318, 320, 322, 328, 332, 334, 337, 342-351, 353-358, 360, 389, 392, 395, 402-405, 429, 434-435, 444, 446, 487, 489-490, 500, 520, 522, 529, 551-555, 561, 572-575, 584, 586-591, 593.

Hitler-Stalin Pact: 30, 59, 85, 118, 239-243, 247, 249-250, 264, 267-269, 318, 355-356, 359, 463, 552.

Imperialism, imperialist: 31, 56, 58-59, 64, 72-73, 77, 79-80, 82, 85-86, 89-92, 94-97, 100-101, 111-113, 116, 125, 127, 133, 135, 138-139, 141, 145-147, 160, 162-163, 169-170, 180-181, 185-186, 193, 205-207, 210-211, 225-226, 229, 237, 239, 241, 244-247, 250-260, 264-270, 276-277, 279, 284, 289-293, 298-299, 314, 316-317, 319-320, 322-323, 325, 327-328, 331-332, 334-336, 344, 348-354, 356-364, 379, 388-391, 402, 404-406, 414-416, 419, 421, 428, 430, 432, 434, 436-437, 440, 441, 443-444, 448-450, 456, 458-459, 461, 463, 471, 480, 482-485, 487, 488-491, 496-497, 501, 520, 551-552, 555-563, 568-569, 571, 573-574, 583, 588.

Imperialism, Stalinist: 91, 127, 237,

253-254, 290, 322, 331, 335, 458, 461, 480, 482-484, 489, 552, 557-560, 562.

Iran: 290, 337-338, 350, 357, 360-362, 455, 561.

Italy: 32, 73, 126, 213, 229, 245, 252, 256, 286, 316-318, 326, 333, 336, 352-353, 398, 436-438, 494-495, 517, 569, 588, 590.

Jacobs, Louis: 440, 310.

James, C L R: 62, 77, 80, 88-89, 93, 100, 117, 120, 122, 125, 128, 136, 140, 144, 146, 149, 155, 238, 264, 266-267, 270-271, 315, 319, 352, 355, 371, 383, 385, 387-388, 390-93, 462, 474, 548, 580.

Johnson, J R (see C L R James).

Kadets: 185, 189-191.

Kautsky, Karl: 47, 62, 137, 147, 149, 175, 179, 194, 199-200, 533, 567.

Kerensky: 112, 160-162, 169-170, 179-180, 183-184, 186, 189, 202-203, 215-216, 324, 345, 354, 372, 424, 506, 573.

Kornilov: 112, 162, 169, 184, 191-192, 196, 573.

Kronstadt: 167, 220, 229.

Kuomintang (see China).

Latvia: 82, 249, 251, 257, 287, 336, 357-359, 539, 552, 556, 560-561, 571, 573-574.

Left Opposition: 24-25, 46, 56, 71, 84, 99, 103, 112, 116, 119, 174, 214, 294, 558, 572, 577, 586-588, 591.

Lenin, V I: 11-12, 14-15, 17-19, 21-24, 27-28, 32, 34-35, 37, 40, 43, 49, 64, 67, 69, 81, 85, 99, 101, 110-112, 115, 121, 123, 125, 141-142, 145, 147, 165-167, 169, 171, 173-181, 183-186, 188-189, 193-199, 201-202, 204-207, 209-212, 215-216, 218-224, 227, 230-233, 243-244, 247, 250, 253-257, 261, 272, 278-279, 281-283, 286, 288-291, 294, 297, 300, 303, 306, 318-319, 321-323, 334, 345-347, 351-352, 362, 372, 374-379, 382, 384-385, 388-389, 391, 395-397,

399-401, 411, 418, 424, 451, 459-460, 468, 483, 500-509, 512, 516, 524-525, 539-540, 551, 554, 558-562, 565-568, 570, 573, 578.
on democracy: 171, 178, 179, 185-6.
State and revolution: 174, 179, 199, 582.

Lenin Levy: 24, 233.

Lithuania: 82, 249, 251, 257, 333, 336, 357-359, 539, 552, 556, 560-561, 571, 573-574.

"Locum" for working class: 21, 64-67, 70-71, 86-87, 110-114, 137, 142, 149.

Luxemburg, Rosa: 12, 18-19, 35, 43, 45, 166-167, 175, 178, 194-195, 198-201, 204-205, 207, 382, 384, 460, 567, 594.

Mandel, Ernest: 121-122, 132, 136-137.

Martov, Julius: 22, 206, 222.

Marx, Karl: 11, 13-18, 22, 31-32, 34-35, 37, 42, 49-50, 55-56, 58, 63, 83, 87, 107-108, 121, 141-142, 145, 151, 165-166, 176-177, 179, 181-183, 196-198, 202, 204-205, 208, 247, 261, 278, 281, 283, 318-324, 347, 350, 352, 374, 379, 382, 433, 451-452, 459-460, 503, 507, 520-523, 526-528, 532-535, 537, 541, 543-544, 558-559, 569, 575, 582, 589.

Mensheviks: 33, 41, 46, 66, 162, 169-170, 172, 178, 180, 183-186, 189-190, 193-196, 199, 201-202, 206, 211, 219, 225, 229, 310, 324, 557-558, 566.

Millenarianism: 114, 124, 126-127, 130, 133, 140, 142, 387, 409.

Morris, William: 41.

Morrow, Felix: 126-128, 270, 356-357, 402-406, 414-416, 426, 440, 446, 552, 555.

National Assembly: 199-201, 488.

Nationalisation: 28, 41, 57, 62, 69, 76, 87, 96, 107.
nationalised economy: 55, 62-64, 76-79, 81, 86-87, 98, 104, 110-113, 121, 124, 134, 316, 489, 492, 496, 550, 560, 571, 582.

nationalised property: 21, 41, 56-59, 62-63, 65-69, 74, 76-77, 79, 81, 86, 90, 94, 97-98, 101, 104, 112-113, 120, 123-125, 130, 132-134, 256-257, 273-276, 291-293, 301-305, 314, 316, 328, 348-350, 352, 354, 357-358, 417, 419-421, 424, 428, 433, 436, 449, 467-468, 470-471, 491, 551, 557, 561, 568-569, 571, 573.
state ownership: 51, 62, 120, 130, 276, 294, 359, 433, 467.
state property: 49-50, 57, 66, 76, 104, 135, 274, 276, 280, 293, 295-297, 302, 319, 323, 328, 330, 359, 417, 423, 487, 523-524, 572-574.
fetish, of nationalised property, planned economy etc: 84, 86, 94, 113, 142

Nationalities: 27, 84, 86, 160, 162-163, 210-211, 215, 241, 264-265, 322, 435.

National question: 82, 84, 92, 199, 388, 390-391, 397, 402, 455, 464.

Nazis: 43, 82, 85, 90, 128, 245, 268, 285, 287, 310, 312, 341, 363, 403, 412, 432, 444, 493, 587-588.

New Economic Policy (NEP): 21-26, 110, 119, 221, 331.

Noske, Gustav: 189, 199, 241, 225, 587.

Paris Commune (see Democracy).

Parliament: 35-36, 162, 177-178, 184-187, 203, 205, 592.

Permanent revolution: 121, 153, 182, 195-196, 296, 389, 400, 509, 576.

Poland: 30, 31, 80, 82, 84-85, 89-90, 92, 96-101, 103, 117, 124-126, 128-129, 169, 237, 240-242, 246-249, 251-252, 254-255, 259, 266-269, 289-290, 310-311, 313, 326, 328, 334, 336-338, 348-349, 354-355, 357, 360-361, 365, 416, 419, 429-436, 438, 441-442, 455-456, 471, 473, 480, 482, 487, 489, 493, 517, 523-524, 539, 551-552, 555, 556, 560-561, 562, 565, 571-572, 574, 583, 585, 591.

Political revolution: 58-59, 70, 72, 74, 83-84, 92, 104, 112-113, 115, 117, 123, 136, 142, 229, 254, 276, 288, 303, 396, 442, 550, 562, 570, 574.

78-79, 83, 86-89, 92, 96, 99-100, 103, 108-109, 111, 113-114, 116-123, 126-128, 131-135, 137-142, 145-147, 149-152, 155, 165, 167-168, 172-173, 196, 205, 207-208, 215, 226, 231, 238-239, 242, 244, 246, 248, 266, 270, 276, 283-284, 287-288, 292, 298, 310-311, 314, 324, 327, 329, 341, 346-347, 351, 358, 361-364, 379, 381, 387, 392, 395, 399, 409, 411-416, 421, 423, 429, 431-432, 438-442, 444, 447, 450, 456-457, 459, 466-467, 469, 471-472, 475-487, 489-498, 507-508, 515-518, 520, 523-525, 529-532, 537-544, 555-556, 558, 561, 574, 576, 579, 583-585, 587-89, 593.
Stalinist revolutions: 124, 137, 582.

Thermidor: 65, 67, 74, 301, 306, 308-309, 510, 558, 577.

Third Camp: 89, 97, 99-100, 114, 144, 146-147, 258, 260, 384, 434, 440, 498, 557, 583-585.

Third International: 44, 115, 257, 294, 303, 323, 395, 399, 437.

Third Period: 24, 126, 155, 369.

Tito, Josip Broz: 128, 132-135, 457, 475-476.

Tomsky, Mikhail: 47, 173, 219.

Transitional Programme: 64, 111, 383, 390, 594.

Trotsky, Leon: 11-12, 14-15, 17, 19, 21, 24-29, 31-34, 37, 39-41, 43-128, 130-131, 133-138, 140-142, 144-150, 153-155, 162, 166-169, 173, 183, 194-197, 204-207, 210, 212, 215, 219, 222, 231-234, 237, 240, 243, 250-251, 254-257, 260-262, 270-276, 278-281, 283-285, 288-289, 291-297, 300-305, 309, 315-319, 322, 327-330, 334, 338, 341, 343, 345, 347-349, 352, 355, 360-361, 363-364, 366-367, 369, 377-379, 382, 384, 388, 390-391, 393, 399, 401, 407, 409-410, 415-418, 420-421, 423-424, 428-429, 433-434, 436, 438-443, 445, 447-453, 455-460, 478-479, 483, 485, 499-505, 507-514, 518, 524-526, 529, 531-532, 537-539, 548-552, 554-562, 564-565, 568, 570, 576-585, 591, 594.
struggle against Stalin: 27, 102
on nature of Stalinist USSR: 301-304, 329-330.

Revolution Betrayed: 15, 48, 51, 57, 63, 66, 68, 74-75, 77, 79, 114, 118, 274-275, 278, 281, 283, 288, 290, 292, 417, 558-55.
The USSR in War: 57, 64, 104, 108, 114-115, 117-118, 122, 254, 270, 275, 548-549, 554, 556.

In Defence of Marxism: 93, 117-118, 122.

Trotskyist movement: 53, 56, 90, 97, 116, 121-122, 133, 240, 259, 274, 282, 386, 428, 438-439, 458, 460-462, 465, 467, 470-472, 475, 515, 537, 541, 543, 594.

Ukraine: 21, 27, 82-85, 90, 92, 94, 97-98, 163, 169, 224, 246, 254-255, 257, 265, 267-269, 336, 351, 456, 550-551, 560, 562, 574.

USSR
as workers' state: 86.
as bureaucratic collectivism: 330, 486.
as state capitalist: 492, 569.
defence of: 33, 46, 48, 56, 58, 72-73, 79-80, 83, 86, 89-90, 93-95, 101-102, 105, 110, 113, 115-119, 122, 124-125, 133, 141, 237, 271, 341, 363, 366.
foreign policy: 46, 74, 90-91, 96, 98, 101-102, 267, 332, 335, 446, 495, 557, 572.
reform of: 23, 26, 70-72, 111-112, 274, 276, 279, 302-304, 306-307, 309.

Utopian socialism: 16, 29, 33, 39.

War communism: 20-22, 32, 262, 278.

World War (Second): 31, 58, 138, 249, 255, 259, 264, 273, 289, 332, 341-342, 356, 384, 392, 394-395, 450-452, 458, 463, 483, 496, 515, 517, 539.

World War (Third): 114, 137-138, 449, 483.

World War: 18, 31, 52, 58, 63, 73, 80, 85, 106, 113-114, 116, 118, 122, 124-126, 137-138, 149, 155, 169, 206-207, 219, 232, 237, 241, 246, 249, 252-253, 255-256, 258-259, 264, 268, 273, 289, 291, 317, 325, 328, 332, 341-342, 349, 352, 356, 359, 362, 365, 384, 387, 392, 394-395, 402, 409, 449-452, 457-458, 463, 466, 483, 490, 496, 515, 517, 538-539.

Weber, Jack: 10, 310.

Whites: 19, 110, 534.

Yugoslavia: 19, 79, 84, 123, 133-134, 333, 337-338, 471, 473, 475-476, 481-482, 487, 539, 561.

Zinoviev, Gregory: 23-24, 26, 31, 174, 219, 225, 231-232, 308, 384,507, 511-512, 524-525, 548, 576-578.